Handbook of
Multicultural Measures

To the three people who have taught me the most about culture:
Christina Martinez Gamst (my wife), Richard H. Dana (mentor and friend),
and Frederick C. Gamst (my oldest brother).
—Glenn C. Gamst

To Alison Embow (my wife) and Nathaniel Liang (my son) and
my family (Shao Hay Liang, Lucy Ho, Maria, Cecilia, and Elsie), friends,
and teachers (faculty, colleagues, students, and community members):
Thank you for your guidance, patience, understanding, and support.
—Christopher T. H. Liang

To Vahan Hamamjian (my wife's (Armine) grandfather) and
Hagop Der-Garabedian (my grandfather), who not only survived
the Armenian genocide but also modeled for me how to thrive in
multilingual and multicultural environments.
—Aghop Der-Karabetian

Handbook of
Multicultural Measures

Glenn C. Gamst
Christopher T. H. Liang
Aghop Der-Karabetian
University of La Verne

Los Angeles | London | New Delhi
Singapore | Washington DC

For information:

SAGE Publications, Inc.
2455 Teller Road
Thousand Oaks, California 91320
E-mail: order@sagepub.com

SAGE Publications Ltd.
1 Oliver's Yard
55 City Road
London EC1Y 1SP
United Kingdom

SAGE Publications India Pvt. Ltd.
B 1/I 1 Mohan Cooperative Industrial Area
Mathura Road, New Delhi 110 044
India

SAGE Publications Asia-Pacific Pte. Ltd.
33 Pekin Street #02-01
Far East Square
Singapore 048763

Printed in the United States of America

Library of Congress Cataloging-in-Publication Data

Gamst, Glenn.
Handbook of multicultural measures / Glenn C. Gamst, Christopher T. H. Liang, Aghop Der-Karabetian.
       p. cm.
Includes bibliographical references and index.
ISBN 978-1-4129-7883-5 (cloth : acid-free paper)
   1. Multiculturalism—Research. 2. Multiculturalism—Psychological aspects. 3. Minorities—Research. I. Liang, Christopher. II. Der-Karabetian, Aghop. III. Title.

HM1271.G36 2011
305.8001'5118—dc22   2010026773

This book is printed on acid-free paper.

10   11   12   13   14   10   9   8   7   6   5   4   3   2   1

Acquisitions Editor:	Kassie Graves
Editorial Assistant:	Courtney Munz
Production Editor:	Brittany Bauhaus
Permissions Editor:	Adele Hutchinson
Copy Editor:	Kim Husband
Typesetter:	C&M Digitals (P) Ltd.
Proofreader:	Theresa Kay
Indexer:	Sheila Bodell
Cover Designer:	Candice Harman
Marketing Manager:	Dory Schrader

Brief Contents

Detailed Contents

Preface

The present handbook provides a summary of some of the best multicultural instrumentation, theorizing, and research in the social, behavioral, and health-related fields. Based on our inclusion criteria, summarized in Chapter 1, this text offers a fairly comprehensive compendium of empirically supported multicultural instrumentation that spans the following measurement subject areas: psychometrics, cultural competence, racial identity and ethnic identity, acculturation, racism and prejudice, gender, sexual orientation, and disability.

Our pedagogical goal was to place as many multicultural instrument summaries as we could create within one text. Of course, such "one-stop shopping" can often yield a double-edged sword; convenience must be tempered by the realization that any multicultural measurement compendium is but the beginning of a serious and thorough literature review. Therefore, we encourage readers to examine the citations covered in the instrument summaries and chapters found throughout this handbook. It should also be noted that we are not providing the actual multicultural instrument items. The interested investigator can find them in the instruments' primary references or by contacting the primary authors themselves.

We believe this handbook is suitable for a number of audiences. First, at the undergraduate level, students conducting their own original research or senior thesis should find this text a valuable resource. Second, graduate student master's thesis or doctoral dissertation research could also be informed by the multicultural

overviews and instrument summaries provided herein. Third, multicultural researchers may find this text to be an authoritative and convenient means of quickly differentiating among a variety of psychometrically sound and culturally valid measurement instruments. This handbook should also provide clinical practitioners with a useful starting point in their search for multicultural assessment devices they can use with diverse clients to inform clinical treatment. We also offer practitioners a multicultural framework and case illustration (the Multicultural Assessment-Intervention Process Model) to assist in the implementation of multicultural assessment in training and service delivery in counseling centers, community mental health centers, hospitals, and so forth.

TO THE READER

This handbook assumes that you, the reader, have had at least one multicultural course at either the undergraduate or graduate level. Typically, these courses cover multicultural concepts such as racism, discrimination, acculturation, ethnic and racial identity, sexual identity, sex roles, and so on. What is typically not covered in any great detail is a review of multicultural concepts integrated within a measurement context. This handbook provides such an integration by offering the reader a psychometric overview; a conceptual framework (Multicultural Assessment-Intervention Process) that helps the reader maneuver through this complex literature; a review of key concepts and major findings for each multicultural measurement domain covered;

as well as detailed summary information about each instrument included in this handbook.

As with any set of measurement instruments, caution should always be exercised in the use of these instruments to assist in clinical practice or to further our understanding of multicultural phenomena. Assessment clarity can be maximized when the practitioner or researcher is able to triangulate multiple multicultural measurement instruments during the assessment process.

Multicultural measures were included based on our inclusion criteria that we summarize in Chapter 1. Measures that were included in our summaries should not necessarily be viewed as an endorsement or promotion of the measure. We encourage readers to use the concepts addressed in Chapter 2 as a foundation for making informed decisions in selecting measures summarized in this handbook. Conversely, measures that were excluded simply did not meet our inclusion criteria, were developed by means of rational or theoretical bases, or were inadvertently omitted and do not necessarily indicate a lack of suitability for multicultural assessment.

—Glenn C. Gamst
—Christopher T. H. Liang
—Aghop Der-Karabetian
University of La Verne

Acknowledgments

We thank the many students each of us has had at the University of La Verne (in La Verne, CA). Your thoughtful questions, advice, experiences, and feedback have been absolutely invaluable. Special thanks go to four intrepid doctoral students in the Clinical-Community Psychology program at the University of La Verne: Michelle Alfaro, Rhona Harrison, Suzannia Holden, and Samantha Sharac, who devoted many hours capturing the articles, books, and measures that we subsequently summarized. Their collective positive spirit enabled us to finish this handbook.

We thank Drs. Alvin Alvarez (San Francisco State University), Bryan Kim (University of Hawaii at Hilo), Katie McDonald (Portland State University), Andrew Smiler (Wake Forest University), Dawn Syzmanski (University of Tennessee), Rebecca Toporek (San Francisco State University), Shawn Utsey (Virginia Commonwealth University), and Susanna Gallor (University of New Hampshire) for taking the time to provide us with feedback and suggestions for the inclusion and/or exclusion of measures.

We offer very special thanks for constructive feedback on several of the chapters by Joseph Ponterotto (Fordham University), Larry Meyers (California State University, Sacramento) and Rocio Rosales Meza (University of La Verne). Your diligence was most appreciated.

We would also like to thank our friend and confidant, Kassie Graves, Acquisitions Editor at Sage Publications. Her support throughout all phases of this project is much appreciated.

Lastly, we thank Angie Castillo, Administrative Assistant, Psychology Department, University of La Verne. Your patience, computer savvy, and gentle style have made us all much more productive, and we are sincerely in your debt.

The authors and SAGE also gratefully acknowledge the contributions of the following reviewers: James W. Bartee (West Virginia University), Linda G. Castillo (Texas A&M University), Catherine Y. Chang (Georgia State University), Kyle K. Colling (Montana State University Billings), James M. Croteau (Western Michigan University), Paul Pedersen (Syracuse University), John E. Queener (The University of Akron), Carla J. Reyes (*A Child's Place*), Delores D. Walcott (Western Michigan University).

List of Measures

1

Introduction

The terms *cultural, cross-cultural* and *multicultural* have sometimes been used interchangeably in the field of psychology. In order to understand the constructs, it is first useful to consider the definition of culture. Following the lead of cultural anthropology, we prefer to distinguish our working definition of culture as "a learned, socially transmitted, symbolically based mechanism for survival, which, like other phenomena of our universe, has order or pattern. . . . a system of learned and socially transmitted ideas, sentiments, social arrangements, and objects" (Gamst & Norbeck, 1976, p. 6). Whereas the term cultural has been used to refer to specific racial groups, the use of cross-cultural in mental health and psychology research typically refer to the study of similarities and differences across different cultural groups in the world. The term *multicultural*, in psychology, counseling, and other health-related fields, has been used more broadly to describe the diversity of social identities within a given population. Although some scholars may take a more narrow perspective on the term, including discussions relevant only to racial minority groups (i.e., racism, racial identity), we define *multicultural* as inclusive of issues and topics that address the socio-cultural-political experiences of people from different ethnic groups, genders, sexual identities, social classes, and disability backgrounds.

Multicultural psychology and multicultural counseling are fields of study and practice with considerable overlap. Both recognize the importance of the social, cultural, and political influences on an individual's beliefs, attitudes, thoughts, and psychosocial functioning. *Multicultural health* is a related field that addresses disparities in the treatment of or prevalence of behavioral or physical health problems experienced by underserved and underrepresented populations. Multicultural-oriented psychologists, counselors, and health practitioners come from many disciplines (e.g., clinical psychology, college student personnel, community psychology, counseling psychology, marriage and family therapy, nursing, psychiatry, social psychology, and social work). This book is oriented to provide enough breadth to satisfy scholars and practitioners in each of these disciplines. Given our training as psychologists, however, it is inevitable that our discussions focus more on the history and development of psychology.

With our more inclusive definition of *multicultural*, we include in this handbook issues and topics of concern for sexual minorities and persons with disabilities, as well as gender (including men's issues), with the more commonly addressed groups (e.g., racial minorities) covered in the fields of multicultural psychology, counseling, and health. We also move beyond issues more commonly addressed in the multicultural counseling literature (e.g., acculturation, multicultural competence) to address measures of prejudice, gender role conflict, sexual prejudice, attitudes toward persons with disabilities, etc. Hence, we define *multicultural measures* as survey instruments that facilitate the study of multicultural issues and that result in the promotion of the study of the sociopolitical and cultural experiences of individuals from a wide array of social identity groups as well as the contexts in which they may occur.

1.1 HISTORICAL PERSPECTIVE

The history of the psychological study of people from marginalized backgrounds (e.g., women, sexual minorities, racial minorities) is, for a majority of the early 20th century, replete with examples of how research was used to further oppression and to maintain the status quo. Several landmark studies (e.g., Clark & Clark, 1939; Hooker, 1957) notwithstanding, most research painted ethnic minorities, women, and persons with disabilities as inferior beings and sexual

minorities as deviant and psychologically sick. At this same time, heterosexual White American men's behaviors, emotions, and cognitions were established as normative. However, the study of the role of gender in the lives of men was absent until the late 1970s.

Influenced by the civil rights movement and feminists of the 1950s and 1960s, psychology has become a more inclusive field of study. Research now addresses a multitude of social and cultural issues. In fact, since the 1970s, the amount of research and theoretical papers published in peer-reviewed journals has increased substantially (see Table 1.0). In order to demonstrate the increase, we conducted a cursory search on PsycInfo, an electronic database of peer-reviewed journal, articles published between 1975 and 2009 using the following keywords: *acculturation, culture, disability, ethnic identity, gay, gender, homophobia, lesbian, masculinity, multicultural, prejudice, racial identity,*

Table 1.0   Frequency of Keyword Matches in Research Database Between 1975–2009

Keyword	1975–1979	1980–1984	1985–1989	1990–1994	1995–1999	2000–2004	2005–2009
gender	147	336	715	702	2468	8377	9872
women	773	369	272	297	1959	6408	9409
disability	330	539	1173	1934	3855	5388	6926
culture	191	227	427	587	1143	2617	3623
gay	17	33	107	402	552	1136	1302
lesbian	30	72	142	295	457	912	991
masculinity	89	94	104	126	161	449	781
acculturation	31	32	27	181	266	448	772
racism	19	28	43	103	140	401	644
prejudice	74	44	79	94	170	374	608
multicultural	11	28	35	142	268	493	534
ethnic identity	12	15	27	53	123	279	386
racial identity	4	2	27	51	85	164	181
homophobia	2	9	27	50	65	148	161
sexism	32	20	27	38	43	110	159

racism, *sexism*, and *women*. The keywords are listed by order of most published articles to least published articles for the most recent 5-year period (i.e., 2005–2009). Over the course of these 35 years, we noted an increase in nearly every multicultural-related topic of study, particularly between the 1990s and the first decade of the 2000s. Dramatic increases were observed for gender-, women-, disability-, and culture-related articles published. There are several limitations of this analysis, however. First, since it was not our intent to analyze the contents or methodology of the articles, we cannot make any claims regarding specific topics of interest within a field of study. Individuals interested in the contents of these articles for specific groups should see Cokley, Caldwell, Miller, and Muhammad (2001); Edwards and Pedrotti (2008); Huang, Brewster, Moradi, Goodman, Wiseman, and Martin (2010); Liang, Salcedo, Rivera, and Lopez (2009); or Phillips, Ingram, Smith, and Mindes (2003). The multicultural contents of specific journals also have been studied, and interested readers may wish to review Arredondo, Rosen, Rice, Perez, and Tovar-Gamero (2005) or Pope-Davis, Ligiero, Liang, and Codrington (2001). In recent years, the methods and contents of specific topics (e.g., coping with racism) within an area of study also have been presented. Some examples of these review articles are Brondolo, ver Halen, Pencille, Beatty, and Contrada (2009); Miller and Kerlow-Myers (2009); and Worthington, Soth-McNett, and Moreno (2007). Second, a number of articles may have multiple keywords and, as such, been counted twice. However, the fact that there has been an increase in the number of articles published in these areas still is clear. Third, we performed our search on only one database. Hence, the number of articles published in journals not cataloged in PsycInfo was not counted in our search. Finally, because of the wide diversity of ethnic groups in the United States (e.g., more than 40 Asian ethnic groups alone), the frequency of published articles addressing specific groups is not presented in this analysis. It is important to note that some authors have found that the proportion of articles published for ethnic groups relative to the total number of articles

published does not reflect the general ethnic makeup of our culture (e.g., Delgado-Romero, Galván, Maschino, & Rowland, 2005). Hence, research on some marginalized groups remains underrepresented relative to the proportion of individuals that make up the group. We argue that greater attention to the development of psychometrically sound instrumentation will not only allow for more culturally sensitive treatment (see Chapter 2) but also encourage more research.

1.2 PURPOSE AND STRUCTURE

As researchers and trainers of doctoral- and master's-level clinicians, we saw the need to organize the growing body of multicultural-related measures for our own projects as well as to facilitate the research and clinical endeavors of our students. With that said, we are aware of other books (e.g., Fisher, Davis, Yarber, & Davis, 2010; Nelson, 2009), book chapters (e.g., Smiler & Epstein, 2010), and manuscripts (e.g., Bastos, Celeste, Faerstein, & Barros, 2010) produced to meet some of those needs. Authors of previous works, however, have tended to offer reviews or critiques of measures on a narrow range of multicultural topics (e.g., prejudice) or based on a specific population (e.g., lesbian, gay, bisexual, and transgendered individuals). While these reviews and books are informative and help to shape that specific field of inquiry, their focus on one issue makes it more challenging for clinicians and researchers to identify measures addressing multiple social identities or experiences (e.g., prejudice and perceived racism; gender role conflict and disabilities). As such, the purpose of this book is to summarize and promote the use of multicultural-oriented measures across a wider range of populations and issues in (1) the training of students and staff, (2) culturally responsive service delivery of agencies, (3) clinical practice, as well as (4) research.

To meet our objectives for this handbook, readers will be presented with a review of important terms and concepts related to the process of developing a reliable and valid instrument in Chapter 2. This psychometric discussion is coupled with a multicultural augmentation that provides a multicultural measurement context.

In our effort to promote multicultural-responsive practice, we provide an overview of several multicultural assessment models in Chapter 3. We offer the Multicultural Assessment-Intervention Process (MAIP) Model as a framework to guide practitioners', agency directors', and educators' efforts for including the use of multicultural-oriented measures in clinical practice, service delivery, and training. In the remaining chapters, the development and psychometric properties of 236 measures are summarized. In Chapter 4, we provide a summary of 26 measures that address some aspect of multicultural competence in clinical, education, and training settings. In Chapter 5, we offer readers a summary of 27 measures of racial identity and ethnic identity. Although the two constructs represent distinct concepts (see Helms, 2007), we present these measures of race- or ethnic-based identity together. Measures summarized in Chapter 5 are developed for specific ethnic groups as well as for multiple ethnic groups. In Chapter 6, we summarize 48 measures addressing the multidimensional and bidirectional aspects of acculturation. Measures of enculturation, culturally based family conflict, cultural values orientations, as well as behavioral measures of acculturation are reported and summarized in this chapter. In Chapter 7, a summary of measures addressing the diverse literature regarding race-based prejudice, perceived discrimination, and stress is presented. In total, 37 racism- and prejudice-related measures are summarized in this chapter. The psychometric properties of instruments developed to assess for prejudicial attitudes as well as perceptions of race-based discrimination are presented. Several measures addressing multiple forms of discrimination or prejudice are summarized in this chapter as well. In Chapter 8, we summarize the development and properties of 41 measures addressing gender roles, gender identity, and perceived discrimination or attitudes. In this chapter, measures of masculine ideology and feminine ideology as well as their accompanying strain, stress, and conflict are summarized. Furthermore, summaries of measures of perceived sexism, attitudes, identity development, and gender invariance are provided. In Chapter 9, we offer the summaries of 21 measures addressing aspects of prejudice, sexual discrimination, identity development, and environmental stressors facing sexual minorities. We noted that most measures address lesbian and gay individuals with considerably less attention to issues and experiences of bisexual individuals. In Chapter 10, we provide a summary of 36 measures addressing the psychosocial experiences of persons with disabilities. The measures in this chapter do not address neurological assessments but will assist practitioners and researchers to in developing a greater understanding of stigma-related experiences of persons with disabilities.

Because our main focus is to provide readers with summaries of the development and properties of measures, the structure of each chapter will vary little from one to the next. In each chapter, we begin by providing a broad overview of the general terms used in the field of study. We follow that discussion with a summary of the historical development of the construct(s) of interest in each chapter, offer a general review of the theoretical or empirical literature guiding the development of instruments in the field, and provide some suggestions for continued research. We felt that a general overview was necessary to give readers the context and language through which to have a basic understanding of the nature of the field of study. Given the broad range of topics addressed, a specific research review of each area of study within a field (e.g., coping with racism in Chapter 7) was beyond the scope of each chapter. As such, we do not provide an in-depth review of research in both perceived discrimination and prejudice. Reviews of research on specific topics can be found elsewhere. As an example, individuals interested in the empirical coping with racism literature should read Brondolo, ver Halen, Pencille, Beatty, and Contrada's (2009) review. Finally, although the items of measures are not presented, readers are given the references to the primary journal sources and the contact information of the person for the instrument of interest.

1.3 METHOD FOR INCLUSION

In our review of the literature, we identified more than 300 measures addressing the topics and populations covered in this book. Measures summarized in this book were included if they met the following criteria: (1) was published in a peer-reviewed journal; (2) demonstrated evidence for factorial validity; (3) was developed for use or heavily used in the United States or Canada, and (4) had discernible scoring instructions. A preliminary list of measures was then sent to experts in their respective fields of study for review. These experts provided feedback to ensure that we did not erroneously exclude any measure of which they were aware.

1.4 MOVING FORWARD

To our knowledge, this handbook, which summarizes measures across many multicultural topics, represents the first of its kind. We are encouraged by the quantity of and rigor by which many of the measures have been developed. In engaging in this review, we observed that researchers are using increasingly more sophisticated methods by which to develop psychometrically sound instruments for use in addressing multicultural topics with diverse populations. Having said this, we also acknowledge that some measures summarized in this handbook do not evidence strong validity or reliability. We leave it for you, the reader, with your knowledge of issues of validity and reliability (see Chapter 2), to discern which instruments may be useful for you in your practice or research endeavors. Finally, we wish to acknowledge that although we are confident that we identified many of the strongest measures developed to date, we are aware that some may not have been captured through our search methods. Further, we also recognize that there are some dimensions of multiculturalism not addressed in this text. From our vantage point, important issues related to classism and social class cultures are not addressed in this handbook. Lack of inclusion of this topic was a result of our inability to identity a critical mass of such measures that met our criteria. Limitations notwithstanding, we believe this handbook is a comprehensive text that may serve to guide researcher and practitioner alike. We hope this compendium inspires (1) further research using well-known as well as lesser-known psychometrically sound measures; (2) researchers to engage in further tests of validity of current measures; and (3) researchers to develop measures for areas in which there appear to be none. We also hope that this handbook facilitates greater use of these measures among practitioners in the delivery of mental health services. On a more idealistic note, we hope that this book can foster greater awareness and understanding of multicultural issues.

2

Testing, Measurement, and Culture

This chapter provides a brief overview of testing and psychometric measurement issues needed to evaluate the scores of many multicultural instruments we will be summarizing. Excellent and more detailed presentations of this topic can be found in other sources (e.g., Kline, 2005; Kurpius & Stafford, 2006; McIntire & Miller, 2007; Nunnally & Bernstein, 1994). We begin with basic statistical concepts such as scales of measurement, qualitative versus quantitative scales, measures of central tendency and variability, standardization, and norms. These statistical concepts are important to us at this juncture of the book because they provide a mathematical foundation for the measurement concepts we will cover and also because these concepts will be mentioned on occasion throughout the multicultural measurement summaries beginning in Chapter 4. Following this statistical journey, we will consider types of reliability estimates as well as various sources of validity evidence. We conclude this chapter with a multicultural augmentation.

2.1 SCALES OF MEASUREMENT

When we measure something, we follow a set of rules that guides our practice in assigning values to objects or events. Stevens (1946, 1951) articulated *four scales of measurement* (nominal, ordinal, interval, ratio) to which Gamst, Meyers, and Guarino (2008) and Meyers, Gamst, and Guarino (2006) have offered a fifth scale, *summative response scaling*, to be inserted between ordinal and interval scales.

2.1.1 Nominal Scales

A nominal scale of measurement (also called categorical or qualitative) operates under one rule: Different entities receive different values. This rule asserts no quantitative dimension at all; thus, no one has more or less of a particular property. Examples of nominal scales include most demographic variables such as gender or ethnicity. Numerical coding of these nominal variables (e.g., 1 = female, 2 = male) is arbitrary and is not intended to carry any special meaning or relative value.

2.1.2 Ordinal Scales

Ordinal scales of measurement use numerical values to convey "less than" and "more than" information based on some quantitative dimension. However, these scales do not provide information on how far apart individuals are on the underlying dimension. Thus, if three individuals run a race, we can indicate who finished first, second, and third. We cannot determine how close the first- and second-place individuals were to one another.

2.1.3 Summative Response Scales

Summative response scales require respondents to assign values based on an underlying continuum such as four-point, five-point, and seven-point scales that represent attitudes or judgments. This type of measurement was developed by Rensis Likert (1932). Scale values depict an underlying continuum defined by scale anchors (e.g., 1 = Strongly Agree, 4 = Strongly Disagree) with no meaningful absolute zero. It is a summative scale because we can add (summate) the respondent's rating on multiple items to obtain a composite total score or an average total score. Summative scales address the inferential nonparametric dilemma of whether Likert-type scales can be analyzed with traditional statistical techniques (i.e., interval-like) even though they appear to be more ordinal than interval-like.

2.1.4 Interval Scales

Interval scales of measurement contain all of the properties of nominal, ordinal, and summative response scales but also include a fixed interval between the scale values. Fahrenheit and Celsius temperature scales are commonly used to illustrate an interval level of measurement. Hence, equal intervals of temperature result in the difference in temperature between 20° and 30° F and 70° and 80° F is comparable. Interval scales also contain an arbitrary zero point. Thus, 0°C does not mean the absence of temperature, but rather, the temperature at which water freezes. Like summative response scales, interval scales can be summed and averaged.

2.1.5 Ratio Scales

Ratio scales of measurement have all of the properties of nominal, ordinal, summative response, and interval scales and contain an absolute zero point that designates the absence of the property. As the name implies, meaningful ratios can be formed and statements can be made such as, "John has been married twice as many times as Betty."

2.1.6 Qualitative Versus Quantitative Scales

Investigators sometimes dichotomize measurement scales into *qualitative* and *quantitative* measurement. Qualitative measures are derived from nominal scales. These qualitative measures are often variously referred to as categorical variables, nonmetric variables, dichotomous variables (when there are only two values), and classification variables. It should also be noted here that "qualitative" as used here is not to be confused with the increasingly popular body of diverse qualitative procedures witnessing ascendance in some multicultural research.

Quantitative measures include ordinal, summative response, interval, and ratio measurement scales. Quantitative measures are often referred to as continuous variables or metric variables. While the ordinal scale has an underlying quantitative dimensionality to it, many researchers restrict the term to scales that can legitimately compute a mean (i.e., summative response, interval, and ratio). This capacity to compute means and form ratios opens the statistical technique cornucopia up to the investigator.

2.2 CENTRAL TENDENCY AND VARIABILITY

Measures of central tendency provide a single-value summary of the most typical score in a distribution of scores. Three measures of central tendency will be considered briefly: the *mean, median,* and *mode.* Conversely, measures of variability address how scores within a scale, subscale, or variable vary or deviate from the mean. Three measures of variability will be examined: the *range, variance,* and *standard deviation.*

2.2.1 Central Tendency: The Mean

The mean, or arithmetic mean, is the most common measure of central tendency used in psychometric research and practice. The mean is often referred to as an average in our daily vernacular.

The mean is computed by adding a set of scores and dividing the total by the number of scores in the set. The formula for the mean is as follows:

$$\bar{Y} = \frac{\Sigma Y}{n}.$$

These notational symbols indicate that $\bar{Y}$ (read Y bar) the mean is equal to ΣY (read sigma Y, the sum of the scores) divided by n, the total numbers of scores. Thus, if we had a subscale of five items on a 4-point Likert-type response scale of 4, 3, 3, 2, 1, then

$$\bar{Y} = \frac{\Sigma Y}{n} = \frac{13}{5} = 2.6.$$

2.2.2 Central Tendency: The Median

A second type of measure of central tendency is the *median*. The median is the midpoint or middle score when the scores are arranged from lowest to highest. Because the median is relatively impervious to extreme scores or *outliers* (often found with age and income variables), researchers will often report both the mean and the median of a distribution of scores.

To calculate the median, you simply arrange the scores in ascending order, and if there is an odd number of scores, the one in the middle is the median. If an even number of scores exists, you have two middle scores, and the median is the average of these two scores.

Thus, if we had the following set of ages: 25, 27, 30, 35, 40, then the median is 30. However, if we had the following distribution of ages: 25, 27, 30, 35, 40, 42, then the median is 30 + 35 = 65/2 = 32.5.

2.2.3 Central Tendency: The Mode

A third measure of central tendency is the mode. The mode is defined as the most common or frequent value in a distribution of scores. No special computation is needed to determine the mode, only an inspection of the frequency of occurrence of each data value in a distribution of scores. The mode is particularly useful in describing nominal data such us who was the modal mental health provider for a group of mental health clients (e.g., psychologist, psychiatrist, social worker, case manager, etc.).

Thus, if we have a set of scores: 8, 7, 5, 5, 1, then the mode is 5, the median is also 5, and the mean is 5.2.

2.2.4 Variability: The Range

As we noted previously, measures of variability are designed to describe how scores are dispersed on or about the mean. The simplest measure of variability is the range. The range, a single value, is computed as the highest score (the maximum score) minus the lowest score (the minimum score). Thus, from our previous example of the mode, the range is 7 (8 − 1). Because the range is a fairly crude measure of variability, it is used infrequently in the behavioral sciences.

2.2.5 Variability: The Variance

The variance (symbolized s^2) is a useful index of dispersion among scores within a distribution. The larger the variance, the greater the variability or spread of scores about the mean. Statistically, the variance is defined as an average of the squared deviation from the mean. The formula for the variance is as follows:

$$s^2 = \frac{\Sigma(Y_i - \bar{Y})^2}{n-1}.$$

From this formula we note that the variance is a function of the sum of the squared deviations from the mean divided by the sample size minus one. Thus, if we use the distribution of five scores from our previous example of the mode, we note that when we subtract the mean ($\bar{Y} = 5.2$) from each individual score (Y_i), we obtain the following set of "deviations from the mean": 2.8, 1.8, −0.2, −0.2, −4.2. When we sum these deviations ($\Sigma Y_i - \bar{Y}$), they will always sum to zero because the negative and positive values balance each other out. This zero sum can be eliminated by squaring all of the deviation scores (i.e., multiplying each deviation by itself), which, in turn, eliminates the negative valences on the deviation scores, and then summing them. For example, $(2.8)^2 = 7.84$, $(1.8)^2 = 3.24$, $(−0.2)^2 = 0.04$, $(−0.2)^2 = 0.04$, $(−4.2)^2 = 17.64$, and these squared deviations from the mean $\Sigma(Y_i - \bar{Y})^2$ sum to 28.8. By dividing this value by

$n - 1$, (28.8/4) = 7.2 we obtain the variance. In practice, the variance tells us that on average, the scores in this distribution deviate from the mean by plus or minus 7.2 "squared units" of deviation.

2.2.6 Variability: The Standard Deviation

Recall that to overcome the zero sum problem encountered in computing the variance, we squared each deviation score from the mean. This necessary procedure resulted in a variance of 7.2. As we noted previously, this value represents squared units of deviation and is thus difficult for researchers to interpret.

Therefore, most investigators compute an additional measure of variability called the standard deviation. The standard deviation (symbolized as *s* or *SD*) is defined as the square root of the variance:

$$SD = \sqrt{Variance}.$$

Thus, in the present example, $\sqrt{7.2} = SD = 2.68$.

By computing the square root of the variance, we in effect "unsquare" the variance. This allows us to interpret the dispersion of scores in the original units of measurement. For example, if our original scores measured hourly wages, we can say that on average the five individuals made $5.20 per hour ($\bar{Y} = 5.2$) and that on average these wages deviated above or below the mean by $2.68. This standard deviation value is more intuitive than a statement indicating the wages deviated by 7.2 squared dollars and cents.

2.2.7 Variability: Other Measures

We will briefly discuss several other measures commonly used to discuss the variability or dispersion of scores in a scale or variable. These measures include the *standard error of the mean*, *skewness*, and *kurtosis*.

2.2.8 Standard Error of the Mean

The standard error of the mean provides a confidence interval or range around the sample mean, where the population mean may be located. It is expressed as the standard deviation divided by the square root of *N*.

Often, researchers calculate either a 95% or 99% confidence interval around the sample mean by multiplying the standard error of the mean by the value of the Student's *t* distribution (with appropriate degrees of freedom). A 95% or 99% interval can be used to declare with a 95% or 99% confidence that the population mean lies within the interval range (Meyers, Gamst, & Guarino, 2009; Rosenthal & Rosnow, 2008).

2.2.9 Skewness

Skewness depicts how symmetrical a distribution of scores is. Values close to 0 represent a close approximation to the normal curve and symmetry. Negative skewness indicates the "tail" of the distribution points toward the left or low end, while positive skewness indicates the "tail" of the distribution of scores is pointing to the right side or high end. Many investigators endorse a stance that values in excess of +/– 1.00 are indicative of substantial departures from symmetry (Meyers et al., 2006).

2.2.10 Kurtosis

Kurtosis represents the degree to which a distribution of scores is peaked or flattened in comparison to the normal curve. Values closer to 0 represent a distribution approximating the normal curve. Negative kurtosis represents a relatively flat (or *platykurtic*) distribution of scores, whereas positive kurtosis indicates a relatively peaked (or *leptokurtic*) distribution. Values greater than +/– 1.00 represent substantial kurtosis (Meyers et al., 2006).

2.3 STANDARDIZATION

Standardizing a scale or variable transforms the obtained values and enables the investigator to determine the following two aspects of any score: (1) its position (above or below) with respect to the mean; and (2) the distance of a score from its mean (in standard deviation units; Meyers et al., 2009). This information is often not readily apparent when examining raw scores. The direction of a standard score is established because the value of the mean is transformed to a fixed and arbitrary point.

Figure 2.1	Area Under Normal Curve With Transformations

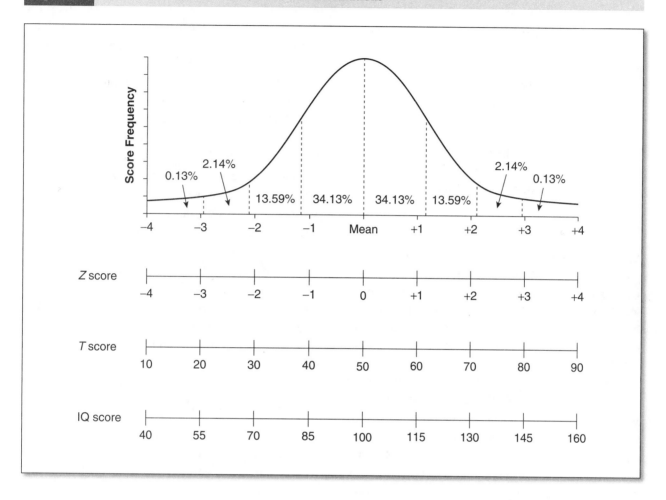

Examples of commonly used standardized scores are *z* scores, linear *T* scores, and intelligence test scores.

Z scores are deviation scores from the mean and are expressed in standard deviation units (Kurpius & Stafford, 2006). *Z* scores have a mean of 0 and a standard deviation of 1. The formula for a *z* score is

$$z = \frac{Y - \bar{Y}}{SD}$$

where *Y* is an individual score, $\bar{Y}$ is the sample means of the distribution, and *SD* is the standard deviation of the distribution.

As can be seen in Figure 2.1, negative *z* scores are below the mean and positive *z* scores are above it. Since the mean of a *z* score is fixed at zero, a *z* score of 1.00 falls exactly 1 standard deviation above the mean.

Linear *T* scores are computed such that they have a mean of 50 and a standard deviation of 10. *T* scores lower than 50 are below the distribution mean, and *T* scores higher than 50 are above the mean. Since linear *T* scores have a mean fixed at 50, a *T* score of 60 would be one standard deviation above the mean.

T scores are computed by multiplying the *z* score by 10 and adding 50. The formula for a *T* score is

$$T = 10(z) + 50.$$

Intelligence test or IQ scores typically have a mean of 100 (Wechsler Intelligence Test for Children, WISC) and a standard deviation of 15 (WISC) or 16 (the Binet IV). IQ scores lower than 100 are below the mean and scores above 100 are above the mean. For the WISC, since the mean is fixed at 100, a score of 115 is one standard deviation above the mean.

The formula for the WISC is

$$IQ = 15(z) + 100.$$

And the formula for the Binet IV is

$$IQ = 16(z) + 100.$$

2.4 NORMS

Multicultural-related scales and constructs have no predetermined standards of acceptability. Instead, individual scores are evaluated by comparing them to other scores. Such a process is the establishment of norms. Norms typically indicate the average performance on a measure and the frequency of deviation above and below the average.

Individual scores on multicultural-related scales are often compared to the entire distribution of scores. Two such approaches to scale normativity are referred to as *criterion-referenced* and *norm-referenced* scales (American Educational Research Association, American Psychological Association, & National Council on Measurement in Education, 1999; Kurpius & Stafford, 2006). A criterion-referenced scale or test uses a cutoff score (or lower possible score) on a measurable behavior, knowledge, or attitude to assess proficiency or interpret scale scores. Conversely, interpretations that are norm referenced are based on how individual scores compare to a normal distribution of scores.

Raw scores on a test or multicultural scale typically reflect a *norm group* that consists of a representative group of individuals upon whom the test was standardized. Kurpius and Stafford (2006) note three common types of norm groups: *normative sample, fixed-reference groups,* and *specific group* or *local norms*.

All norms reflect the normative population from which they are derived. A normative sample represents

a group of individuals' test or scale performance on a multicultural-related measure. Some normative samples are based on large national random probability samples, while other normative samples reflect students in introductory college courses.

Fixed-reference groups are often subgroups of the normative sample. For example, some multicultural-related instruments such as the California Brief Multicultural Competence Scale (CBMCS; Gamst et al., 2004) provide norm tables for fixed-reference race/ethnicity and gender groups. These fixed-reference norms allow an investigator to make informative comparisons between subgroups and the normative sample average score.

Lastly, specific group norms are typically based on a local or narrowly defined population. For example, a multicultural mental health assessment instrument that was developed at a single community mental health center may not be generalizable to all mental health consumers even though it does provide an accurate snapshot at the local level.

2.5 RELIABILITY AND ERROR

To this point on our psychometric journey, we have considered statistical concepts of measurement scales, central tendency, variability, standardization, and norms. This cursory statistical overview will now enable us to examine perhaps the most important attributes of a multicultural-related measurement instrument, namely its reliability and validity.

Reliability, in a multicultural context, represents the extent to which a multicultural-related measurement instrument is free of measurement error (Meyers, 2009). Some measurement authors (e.g., Kurpius & Stafford, 2006) use adjectives such as *trustworthiness, accuracy, stability,* or *consistency* to describe the reliability of a respondent's scores on a multicultural-related measure.

Much of our current understanding of reliability stems from *classical test theory* (CTT). The CTT assumes that an individual respondent's raw score (X) is composed of a *true component* (T) and a *random* error component (E). This relationship is commonly expressed as follows:

$$X = T + E.$$

This equation can be "translated" from CTT language to the language of variance (Meyers, 2009) and its partition (Gamst, Meyers, & Guarino, 2008). Hence, an observed score (scale or subscale) contains a certain amount of variance, some of which is true score variance and some of which is unaccounted-for error variance. This can be expressed as follows:

$$V_o = V_T + V_E,$$

where V_o is the obtained scores variance, V_T is the variance of the true score, and V_E is the error variance.

In practice, these CTT-derived equations provide a foundation for a conceptual definition of reliability. For example, if we had a perfectly reliable multicultural measure, all of the observed variance would be a function of the true score variance. In other words, observed score variance would equal true score variance ($V_o = V_T$). This relationship can be expressed as a numeric value or *reliability coefficient* that can range from 0 to 1.00. Like a correlation coefficient, a reliability coefficient of 1.00 implies a perfect relationship between observed and true variance. In actuality, reliability is never perfect; *measurement error* (i.e., respondent mistakes and inconsistencies) will always accompany a multicultural measuring instrument. So, to obtain a value of less than 1.00, a ratio must be formed between true score variance and observed score variance (which contains both true score variance and error variance). Thus, we have the following definition of reliability:

$$\text{Reliability} = \frac{V_T}{V_o}.$$

Or, reliability is the proportion of true score variance contained in a set of observed scores (Meyers, 2009).

Reliability in test measurement is often operationalized in terms of the following four approaches, which we will briefly discuss: *repeatability*, rater *agreement*, internal *consistency*, and *precision* (McIntire & Miller, 2007; Meyers, 2009).

2.5.1 Repeatability

This type of reliability is typically accomplished by means of the test-*retest* method. This procedure involves having the same group of respondents complete the same multicultural instrument on two separate occasions. A Pearson correlation coefficient is computed between the two instrument administrations to estimate the instrument's stability or repeatability over time. This procedure rests on the assumption that the respondents have not changed between the first and second administration of the instrument on whatever characteristics are under study. *Practice effects,* respondents scoring differently on a scale after obtaining "practice" during the first administration, are a possible concern to investigators employing this procedure. Some practice effects can be attenuated by short time lapses between instrument administrations (McIntire & Miller, 2007).

2.5.2 Rater Agreement

This method requires two or more individuals to evaluate observed events (e.g., to determine if a series of written statements are examples of racist micro-aggressions) and is called *interrater reliability.* Reliability with this method can be assessed by examining percentage of rater agreement, by computing Pearson correlation coefficients of ratings between pairs of raters, or by computing an *intraclass correlation* that compares responses of a rating panel of more than two raters or more than two sets of scores (McIntire & Miller, 2007).

2.5.3 Internal Consistency

This method of assessing reliability is based on the assumption that individuals completing multicultural instrumentation will respond in a similar manner (i.e., consistently) to items that are associated with the construct being examined by the content domain. Thus, an acculturation instrument might have items dealing with several domains (e.g., food preference or language preferences). To the extent that an individual responds consistently to items in the domain, the investigator can infer reliability. Internal consistency is typically assessed by means of *internal consistency coefficients* including the following, which we will briefly review: the *split-half method, Kuder-Richardson procedure,* and *Cronbach's coefficient alpha.*

2.5.4 Split-Half (Reliability) Method

The split-half method developed historically as the first interval consistency measure (Kline, 2005). This method involves arbitrarily dividing a measure into two sets of items, and the correlation between the two sets of scores is interpreted as the reliability coefficient. One difficulty with this approach is how to split a measure. Various strategies such as splitting items on the basis of odd or even numbers or various randomization strategies may produce halves with different variances or different content. Another concern of the split-half method is related to instrument length. Longer instruments produce more stable correlations and, thus, higher reliability than do shorter instruments. Hence, splitting an instrument in half tends to underestimate the reliability of the total instrument. Spearman (1910) and Brown (1910) independently created a "correction" for computing split-half reliabilities, which has become known as the *Spearman-Brown prophesy formula* (see also Gulliksen, 1987). The formula is as follows:

$$r_{SB} = \frac{(p)\,(r_c)}{1 + [(p-1)\,(r_c)]}$$

where r_{SB} is the Spearman-Brown (corrected) reliability, P is the proportional change in the length of the measure (e.g., 2 if it is doubled in length, 0.5 if it is half as long, 0.25 if it is quartered), and r_c is the current or original reliability.

2.5.5 Kuder-Richardson Procedure

Kuder and Richardson (1937, 1939) published a series of equations that allowed investigators to compare respondents' scores on all possible ways of splitting an instrument in halves (McIntire & Miller, 2007). Kuder and Richardson focused on items that are scored dichotomously (e.g., yes–no, true–false, correct–incorrect, 0–1). In their 20th equation (subsequently referred to as *KR20*), they modeled what the average would be if all possible splits of an instrument were made. The *KR20* equation is as follows:

$$KR20 = \frac{(k/k - 1)}{(V_T - \Sigma pq)/V_T}$$

where k is the number of items on the instrument, V_T is the variance of the total scale scores, p is the proportion of instrument takers getting the item correct, and q is the variance (hence, Σpq is the sum of the item variances).

2.5.6 Cronbach's Coefficient Alpha

A limitation of the *KR20* was its focus on items that were dichotomously scored. Items scored on summative response, interval, and ratio scales could not be evaluated by the *KR20*. Cronbach (1951; see also Cronbach & Shavelson, 2004) solved this problem by creating a statistic, coefficient alpha (or Cronbach's alpha) that can be applied to any level of an item scoring system. Most computer statistical packages such as IBM SPSS and SAS provide Cronbach's alpha. The formula is as follows:

$$\text{alpha } (\alpha) = \frac{(k/k - 1)}{(V_T - \Sigma V_I)/V_T}$$

where k is the number of items on the test, V_T is the variance of the total scale scores, V_I is the item variance, and ΣV_I is the sum of the item variances.

Recently, Ponterotto and Ruckdeschel (2007) offered an overview of coefficient alpha, and we have reproduced their reliability matrix (in Table 2.1) that

| Table 2.1 | Matrix for Estimating Adequacy of Internal Consistency Coefficients With Research Measures |

Items Per Subscale	Rating	Sample Size		
≤ 6	Excellent	.75	.80	.85
	Good	.70	.75	.80
	Moderate	.65	.70	.75
	Fair	.60	.65	.70
7–11	Excellent	.80	.85	.90
	Good	.75	.80	.85
	Moderate	.70	.75	.75
	Fair	.65	.70	.90
≥ 12	Excellent	.85	.90	.90
	Good	.80	.85	
	Moderate	.75	.80	.85
	Fair	.70	.75	.80

NOTE: Table extracted directly from Ponterotto and Ruckdeschel (2007). Readers incorporating the matrix criteria in their own writing should cite the original source in addition to this text.

examines the "adequacy of magnitudes for coefficient alpha in light of item count and sample size" (p. 1002).

This matrix provides a useful heuristic device for determining the adequacy of alpha coefficients based on trichotomized items per subscale (≤ 6, 7–11, ≥ 12) and sample size ($N < 100$, $N = 100$–300, $N > 300$) across four qualitative ratings (excellent, good, moderate, fair).

2.5.7 Precision

Precision is the last method of operationalizing reliability that we will briefly examine. In practice, precision is the absence of error variance in an instrument's raw scores (Kline, 2005; Meyers, 2009). Precision is expressed in instrument score units rather than in terms of a reliability coefficient. Investigators typically express precision with the *standard error of measurement (SEM)*, which indexes how much an individual's instrument score (X) is estimated to differ from the individual's true or theoretical score (T) (McIntire & Miller, 2007). The formula for *SEM* is as follows:

$$SEM = SD_T \ (\sqrt{1 - \alpha_T})$$

where *SEM* is the standard error of measurement, SD_T is the standard deviation of one administration of the multicultural instrument scores, and α_T is the reliability coefficient associated with the instrument.

The primary use of the SEM is to help construct a confidence interval or range around a particular score in the distribution. This confidence interval designates a range of scores that include the true score, with a certain degree of confidence on the part of the investigator.

The computations for calculating confidence intervals are covered in most psychometric texts (e.g., Kline, 2005; Kurpius & Stafford, 2006; McIntire & Miller, 2007; Nunnally & Bernstein, 1994).

2.6 VALIDITY AND ITS SOURCES OF EVIDENCE

So far we have discussed the consistency or reliability of a multicultural measure. We next turn our attention to the level of confidence we have in our multicultural instrument measuring what it purports to measure. For example, does the cultural competence instrument measure self-perceived culturally competent attitudes and behaviors of a mental health practitioner, or is it measuring clinical competence? Historically, a measurement instrument's validity was explored by the classic trichotomy of *content, criterion,* and *construct validity.* With the latest publication of *Standards for Educational and Psychological Testing* (1999), five sources of evidence of validity are emphasized instead of the classic validity trichotomy. It is to these sources of evidence that we will now turn.

The *Standards* begin with an opening chapter on validity that begins with the following three sentences that provide the general stance to this topic:

> Validity refers to the degree to which evidence and theory support the interpretations of test scores entailed by proposed uses of tests. Validity is, therefore, the most fundamental consideration in developing and evaluating tests. The process of validation involves accumulating evidence to provide a sound scientific basis for the proposed score interpretations. (p. 9)

We will now briefly examine the five sources of evidence that enable investigators to accentuate different aspects of this unitary concept we refer to as *validity.*

2.6.1 Evidence Based on Test Content

Evidence of validity can be garnered through an analysis of an instrument's content (i.e., item wording and format, tasks, questions, and procedures) and the underlying construct (e.g., acculturation, racism, racial identity, etc.) the instrument intends to measure. Historically, this process was known as content validity.

The challenge here is to ensure that the content of the instrument is adequate to encompass or tap all of the most important aspects of the construct domain. Content validity evidence can be based on either logical or empirical demonstrations that the instrument content is both representative and relevant to the interpretation of the scale or subscale scores.

Thus, if an acculturation investigator discovers through extensive library research and focus group interviews with recent immigrants that certain lifestyle facets (e.g., language, habits, living arrangement, ethnic norms, relationships, political orientation, and spirituality) are central to understanding acculturation phenomena, then it is incumbent on the investigator to develop relevant questionnaire items that reflect these logically/empirically developed facets. Multicultural researchers also often employ panels of independent cultural experts to either help develop appropriate item content or review item adequacy in regard to the construct under study.

2.6.2 Evidence Based on Response Processes

This type of evidence focuses on the removal of confounding from individual responses and historically was considered a facet of construct validity. The question of interest is, To what extent do the responses required of respondents align with the construct under scrutiny? For example, determining the extent of an individual's multicultural knowledge may be reasonably assessed with written response formats (e.g., multiple choice or fill in the blank). However, many indigenous peoples (e.g., Native American) might find a more narrative or open-ended response format the best response modality to discuss multicultural knowledge (Mohatt & Thomas, 2006; Vasgird, 2007).

Evidence for this domain comes from individual response analyses. Qualitative (i.e., open-ended questions) assessments that probe respondents' reasons and strategies used to answer items on an instrument can provide new insights or confirm hypotheses regarding a construct under study.

Not only should the response process of the individual respondents be scrutinized, but so should those involved in evaluating an instrument's item content (judges, raters, cultural experts) and administration procedures. Valuable evidence of validation can be provided through the documentation of the minimization of rater errors or the substantiation of relevant expert credentials.

2.6.3 Evidence Based on Internal Structure

Analysis of internal structure focuses on the statistical relationship of the multicultural instrument's items to the construct under study. Historically, this type of evidence was also considered part of construct validity. Types of evidence involve *item characteristic curves (ICCs)* that provide information about the capability of individual items to distinguish instrument takers of different performance levels (e.g., acculturated vs. unacculturated clients); *inter-item correlations* that indicate the degree of shared variance or redundancy of instrument items; and *item-total correlations* that describe the relationship between individual items and the total scale score.

Internal structure can also be assessed by means of multivariate data reduction analyses such as *factor analysis* and *principal components analysis* (Kline, 2005; Meyers et al., 2006). As evidenced by this handbook's inclusion criteria, composite items that are formed to create scales or subscales should not be capriciously or rationally developed (Meyers, 2006). Instead, some form of empirical (statistical) evidence (such as factor analysis) should support a particular concatenation of items that share sufficient variance to warrant their grouping. *Confirmatory factor analysis* can also be used to confirm and provide further evidence (sometimes called factorial validity) of the factor (subscale) structure of an instrument (Meyers et al., 2006).

2.6.4 Evidence Based on Relations to Other Variables

According to the *Standards*, there are at least three ways to assess evidence based on how a multicultural instrument relates (correlates) to other variables. We will briefly examine each in turn.

2.6.4.1 Convergent and Divergent Evidence

Historically, these concepts were also part of construct validity and employed two strategies: *convergent validity* and *divergent (discriminant) validity*.

These evidentiary strategies postulate that scores on a particular multicultural measure should correlate with a related multicultural measure (convergent evidence) and not correlate with scores from an unrelated measure (divergent evidence). For example, Gamst et al. (2004) reported a low moderate average correlation ($r = .31$) between the subscale scores of the California Brief Multicultural Competence Scale (CBMCS) and the subscale scores of the Multicultural Counseling Inventory (MCI; Sodowsky, Taffe, Gutkin, & Wise, 1994), two self-report cultural competence measures. While the Gamst et al. (2004) study did not specifically examine divergent evidence, a high negative correlation between the scores of the CBMCS and an altruism measure might have provided such evidence.

2.6.4.2 Test–Criterion Correlations

Historically, this type of evidence was referred to as criterion-related validity. Two types of criterion-related evidence are used: *predictive* and *concurrent* methods. In a predictive method, data on the criterion or dependent variable are collected *after* the predictor or independent variables are measured. Conversely, concurrent method data are collected on the criterion variable at about the *same time* as the predictor variables.

An instrument has evidence of predictive validity if its scores are correlated to the criterion. For example, if a number of clinical psychology interns score high on a measure of self-report cultural competence and later client evaluations rate them high on cultural sensitivity, and interns who evaluated themselves low on cultural competence receive low client evaluations, then we have evidence of predictive validity for the cultural competence instrument.

Conversely, if, in a mental health agency that routinely collects self-report appraisals of intern cultural competence and client satisfaction at roughly the same time each year, client satisfaction is high for services rendered by interns reporting high cultural competence and low client satisfaction is related to low intern self-perceived cultural competence, then we have evidence of *concurrent validity*.

2.6.5 Validity Generalization

The issue here is one of external validity, that is, can we generalize the multicultural evidence collected in one setting to another setting (McIntire & Miller, 2007; Meyers, 2009)? We will briefly mention one popular approach: *meta-analysis*.

Meta-analysis involves the qualitative (literature review) or quantitative (statistical) analysis of related published research studies. Quantitative meta-analyses examine *significance levels* (i.e., reject or accept the null hypothesis) or *effect sizes* (i.e., the magnitude of a treatment effect). Quantitative meta-analyses are evaluated by means of Pearson correlations (r) or Cohen's d (or mean difference divided by the population standard deviation; see Cohen, 1977). Useful meta-analysis reviews and discussions can be found in Glass, McGaw, and Smith (1981); Hunter and Schmidt (1990); Rosenthal and Rosnow (1979); Rosenthal and Rubin (1982); Griner and Smith (2006); and Smith (2010).

2.6.6 Evidence Based on Consequences of Testing

This is a new evidence domain recognized by the *Standards*. This source of validity evidence suggests that investigators be cognizant of both the positive and negative consequences of a measure. Specifically, if consequences can be linked to "construct underrepresentation" or "construct-irrelevant components," a case can be made for evidence of invalidity of the measure. This last source of validity measurement underscores the necessity of investigator vigilance concerning possible confounds of measurement and group membership.

2.7 A Multicultural Augmentation

In 2003, the American Psychological Association (APA) published a comprehensive set of multicultural guidelines titled *Guidelines on Multicultural Education, Training, Research, Practice, and Organizational Change for Psychologists* (APA, 2003). The report consists of six guidelines that address (1) cultural awareness and self-knowledge, (2) multicultural sensitivity and responsiveness, (3) multicultural psychological education, (4) culture-centered and ethical psychological research, (5) culturally appropriate skills in clinical practice, and (6) culturally informed organizational practices.

Of particular relevance to our measurement discussion are Guideline 4 (Research) and part of Guideline 5 (Practice), which address assessment. As a means of underscoring the linkage between measurement issues and multiculturalism, we will quote both guidelines and then briefly discuss some of the multicultural considerations they encompass.

> Guideline 4: Culturally sensitive psychological researchers are encouraged to recognize the importance of conducting culture-centered and ethical psychological research among persons from ethnic, linguistic, and racial minority backgrounds (APA, 2003, p. 388).

> Guideline 5: Psychologists are encouraged to apply culturally appropriate skills in clinical and other applied psychological practices (p. 390).

The *Guidelines* reflect, in part, major demographic shifts occurring in the United States as we move into the second decade of the 21st century. Baby boomers are aging, younger Latino/a populations are growing, and immigrant populations from Mexico and Asia are also expanding (Dana & Allen, 2008; Judy & D'Amico, 1997). Linguistic diversity also is flourishing in the United States with nearly 30 million households speaking Spanish at home and another seven languages (other than English) spoken at home by at least

1 million persons per language (APA, 2003). Clearly, multicultural research and its attendant psychometric measurement procedures must acknowledge these important changes.

Historically, the field of psychology has moved through a progression of phases where cultural variables were completely ignored and treated as irrelevant (with notable exceptions such as W. Wundt; see Danzinger, 1980; Ponterotto, 2008). White males became the focus of study upon which all others were compared, and norms were derived. Due to concerted criticism from feminists and multicultural researchers (e.g., Grady, 1981; D.W. Sue & D. Sue, 1977b), research studies began incorporating gender and race/ethnicity into experimental designs, usually playing a prominent role in the study's error variance (Sue, 1999). More recently researchers (Atkinson & Hackett, 1995; Fowers & Richardson, 1996; Hall, 2001; Pedersen, 1999; Ponterotto, 1998; Ridley, Hill, & Li, 1998; Rogler, 1999; Sue, Bingham, Porche-Burke, & Vasquez, 1999) have argued persuasively and cogently, in a variety of contexts, for incorporating multicultural effects as central contextual variables. The failure of centralizing culture in research designs may lead to the misidentification or even the pathologization of behavior (APA, 2003; Hill, Pace, & Robbins, 2010).

One interesting commonality can be gleaned from an examination of the various historical phases of cultural investigation within psychology (i.e., ignore culture, culture is nuisance or error, embrace cultural diversity); in each phase, seldom if ever is the underlying economic system (*capitalism)* explicitly critiqued, examined, or even considered as a parameter in the shaping of multicultural attitudes, behaviors, and values. As Braginsky (1992) notes, "Because mainstream psychology is embedded in the dominant political, economic, and religious ideologies, professional psychologists have upheld these ideologies rather than examining their impact upon the lives of others" (p. 881). As a consequence of her assertion, Braginsky (1992) labels much of the field of psychology as "the handmaiden of the status quo and of society's prevailing values" (p. 880).

The *Guidelines* note at least four major "cultural limitations" to psychological research that merit mention here. First, psychological research tends to focus on individualistic aspects of behavior and has been less concerned with collectivistic and ecological determinants of behavior (e.g., Quintana, Troyano, & Taylor, 2001). Second, research participant samples are of convenience and typically reflect college student populations (S. Sue, 1999). Third, within-group differences among racial ethnic groups tend to be ignored. One size does not fit all; within-group heterogeneity is often reflected in participant social class, language preference, regional differences, tribal affiliation, and so forth (U.S. Department of Health and Human Services, 2001). Last, research should be designed explicitly to serve the communities it is studying (LaFromboise & Jackson, 1996). Collaboration between researchers, community participants, and cultural leaders should be established to engender trust and credibility. Exemplar models of such collaboration are found in multiple chapters in Trimble and Fisher (2006).

The *Guidelines* encourage researchers to use a variety of modalities of inquiry to examine diverse cultural populations. Of particular psychometric relevance are issues pertaining to how diverse research participants interpret and respond to questionnaire items and formal interviews (Clarke, 2000; Westermeyer & Janca, 1997).

The *Guidelines* encourage investigators to utilize a variety of assessment techniques that include standardized instruments and procedures with proven evidence of validity and reliability across diverse multicultural populations. In this regard, the *Guidelines* note,

> Psychological researchers are urged to consider culturally sensitive assessment techniques, data-generating procedures, and standardized instruments whose validity, reliability, and measurement equivalence have been tested across culturally diverse sample groups, particularly the target research group(s). They are encouraged to present reliability, validity, and cultural equivalence data for use of instruments across diverse populations. (p. 389)

Multicultural researchers should consider cultural hypotheses and test for the possibility of moderator effects when analyzing and interpreting their data (Quintana et al., 2001). Likewise, multicultural practitioners should be aware of the cultural limitations of various standardized assessment instruments, practices, and methods and how different client worldviews interact with these assessment processes to distort test score reliability and validity (Helms, 2002; Ridley, Hill, & Li, 1998).

A medley of multicultural discourse processing issues should also be considered when interfacing with diverse respondent populations. For example, monitoring the readability or reading level of an instrument may be essential (Anderson, 1983). Instruments normed on college student populations may not be appropriate for children or some members of disadvantaged social groups. Likewise, appropriate translation methods must be used when adapting instruments that have been normed or validated for other cultural groups. While no agreed-upon standardization procedures currently exist, many cross-cultural researchers suggest that adapted instruments must demonstrate evidence of content, experimental, and semantic equivalence (e.g., Brislin, 1986; de la Cruz, Padilla, & Augustin, 2000; Geisinger, 1994; Jones & Kay, 1992; Kwan, Gong, & Maestas, 2010) when extending instruments to new cultural groups. Language and linguistic structure modifications (e.g., rare vocabulary, passive verb forms, conditional clauses, etc.) for English language learners should also be considered when developing multicultural instrumentation (Abedi, 2002; Frisby, 2008). Use of appropriate translation methods (e.g., Brislin, 1986; Geisinger, 1994) to ensure existing measures are appropriate for linguistically diverse individuals (e.g., different Spanish dialects) is essential.

A statistical issue that multicultural researchers should consider is the potential need to conduct a confirmatory factor analysis of an instrument that has already established evidence of factorial validity, but on another population. Such a process may be necessary before a researcher can adequately test his or her hypotheses. Similarly, multicultural researchers should consider establishing evidence for validity based on relationships proposed by a culturally relevant theory. For example, it may be questionable to develop an ethnic coping measure if we are relying on a Western (European-based) theory of healthy active coping (Lazarus & Folkman, 1984) to establish evidence of concurrent validity (e.g., lower levels of distress) when some culture's forbearance or self-restraint (avoidance coping) may be a more culturally sanctioned method and therefore may be related to lower levels of distress.

In closing this chapter on testing, measurement, and culture, we encourage investigators to carefully explore all facets of culture when designing, conducting, and interpreting multicultural research. Measurement procedures are most appropriate when quantitative multicultural research provides evidence of *cultural validity*. While a number of definitions for this construct exist, we prefer the pithy definition of Quintana et al. (2001):

> The authentic *representation* of the cultural nature of the research in terms of how constructs are operationalized, participants are recruited, hypotheses are formulated, study procedures are adapted, responses are analyzed, and results are interpreted for a particular cultural group as well as the *usefulness* of the research for its instructional utility in educating readers about the cultural group being investigated, its practical utility in yielding practice as well as theoretical implications about the cultural group, and its service utility in "giving back" to the community in important ways. (p. 617)

3

The Utility of Measurement

Application of the Multicultural Assessment-Intervention Process (MAIP) Model

3.1 MULTICULTURAL ASSESSMENT

The role of assessment has become ubiquitous through-out the behavioral health field. Qualitative assemblage of intake and personal history information coupled with the use of various quantitative standardized tests has become the treatment norm for clients receiving services at many behavioral health agencies (Grieger & Ponterotto, 1995; Suzuki, Kugler, & Aguiar, 2005). With the growing ascendancy over the past several decades of cultural for-mulations and the incorporation of cultural and multi-cultural variables in behavioral health clinical and research practice (American Psychological Association, 2003; Dana, 2005; Dana & Allen, 2008), multicultural assessment has come of age. Helpful recent reviews of the multicultural assessment research and practice literature pertaining to adults (Pieterse & Miller, 2010), children (Park-Taylor, Ventura, & Ng, 2010), and adolescents (Yeh & Kwan, 2010) are available.

The incorporation of cultural factors into assess-ment practice is associated with a variety of benefi-cial clinical outcomes (e.g., Griner & Smith, 2006; Smith, 2010; Sue, Zane, Hall, & Berger, 2009). Further, multicultural assessment is now considered by many to be an ethical imperative (Dana, 2005; Pieterse & Miller, 2010; Ridley, Tracey, Pruitt-Stephens, Wimsatt, & Beard, 2008).

Recently, Pieterse and Miller (2010) reviewed four models or frameworks that explicitly incorporate mul-ticultural variables into their assessment procedures. These models include the Multicultural Assessment Procedure (MAP; Ridley, Li, & Hill, 1998), Cultural Assessment Framework and Interview Protocol (CAIP; Grieger, 2008), Multicultural Personality Assessment Guidelines (MPAG; Roysircar-Sodowsky & Kuo, 2001), and the Multicultural Assessment-Intervention Process model (MAIP; Dana, 1993, 2005). A brief review of each multicultural assessment framework follows.

3.1.1 Multicultural Assessment Procedure (MAP)

The MAP (Ridley et al., 1998) is a four-stage clini-cal assessment protocol that comprises cultural data collection, hypothesis formulation, hypothesis testing, and clinical formulation and assessment. The MAP clinical interview is designed to elicit information on cultural factors such as acculturation, language preferences, and experiences of perceived racism and discrimination. The MAP is conceived of as a dynamic and nonlinear assessment protocol that incorporates multicultural variables throughout the clinical assessment interview process.

3.1.2 Cultural Assessment Framework and Interview Protocol (CAIP)

Grieger (2008) has developed a conceptual framework and interview protocol for cultural assessment. The CAIP, an extension of previous work by Grieger and Ponterotto (1995), contains 11 categories of direct inquiry: problem conceptualization; cultural identity; acculturation level; family structure; racial/cultural identity; experiences with bias; immigration issues; existential/spiritual issues; counselor characteristics; counselor-client relationship; and implications of cultural factors for diagnosis, case conceptualization, and treatment. Grieger (2008) recommends that the CAIP be used as a part of the diagnostic assessment process, preceding a formal *DSM* diagnosis.

3.1.3 Multicultural Personality Assessment Guidelines (MPAG)

Roysircar-Sodowsky and Kuo (2001) have offered a set of guidelines to ensure cultural validity during personality assessment. These guidelines include use of familiar language; assessment of acculturation status; appropriate measurement selection; use of appropriately translated measures; use of observational assessment; use of multiple assessment methods; use of caution with computerized reports; and use of culturally diverse racial/ethnic consultants.

While these multicultural assessment frameworks share important commonalities (e.g., focus on acculturation and ethnic/racial identity) and provide unique points of emphasis, the present text will utilize a fourth assessment framework, the Multicultural Assessment-Intervention Process model, as our means of providing a systematic research and practice integration of the many multicultural measures summarized in the current text.

3.2 MAIP OVERVIEW

The present chapter offers the Multicultural Assessment-Intervention Process (MAIP) model as one possible organizing schema for relating the various multicultural measurement instruments (examined in the present handbook) to research, clinical practice, and culturally competent behavioral health services delivery. The MAIP model was originally developed by Richard Dana (Dana, 1993, 1998, 2000, 2005) to provide a multicultural context to assess personality and psychopathology. Following its initial theoretical development, facets of the MAIP model have been examined through a series of empirical community mental health studies (Gamst, 2008; Gamst, Dana, Der-Karabetian, Aragon, Arellano, & Kramer, 2002; Gamst, Dana, Der-Karabetian, Aragon, Arellano, Morrow, & Martenson, 2004; Gamst et al., 2003; Gamst, Dana, Der-Karabetian, & Kramer, 2004; Gamst, Dana, Meyers, Der-Karabetian, & Guarino, 2009; Gamst, Rogers, Der-Karabetian, & Dana, 2006).

Essentially, the MAIP model serves as a conceptual framework for routing diverse multicultural behavioral health clients to scarce agency human and material resources (e.g., Costantino, Dana, & Malgady, 2008). The MAIP model was one of several comprehensive multicultural models that received careful conceptual scrutiny (Pieterse & Miller, 2010; Ponterotto, Gretchen, & Chauhan, 2001). The present chapter sketches a line of march that can be traversed by behavioral health practitioners and researchers who desire to systematically incorporate (i.e., measure) multicultural variables into their clinical or research practice at a behavioral health setting. Concomitantly, a multicultural research and practice agenda as proposed here requires careful planning, coordination, training of staff, elicitation of feedback from clients and community, and meticulous tracking of all multicultural and clinical assessments, as well as any dispositional decisions made by the behavioral health staff.

The MAIP model elucidates at least seven possible steps involved in a client-agency multicultural assessment-intervention interface (see Figure 3.1). These MAIP facets include client intake assessment, client–provider match, multicultural status assessment, provider self-perceived

Figure 3.1 Schematic Flow Chart of MAIP Model Components (adapted from Gamst, Rogers, Der-Karabetian, & Dana, 2006)

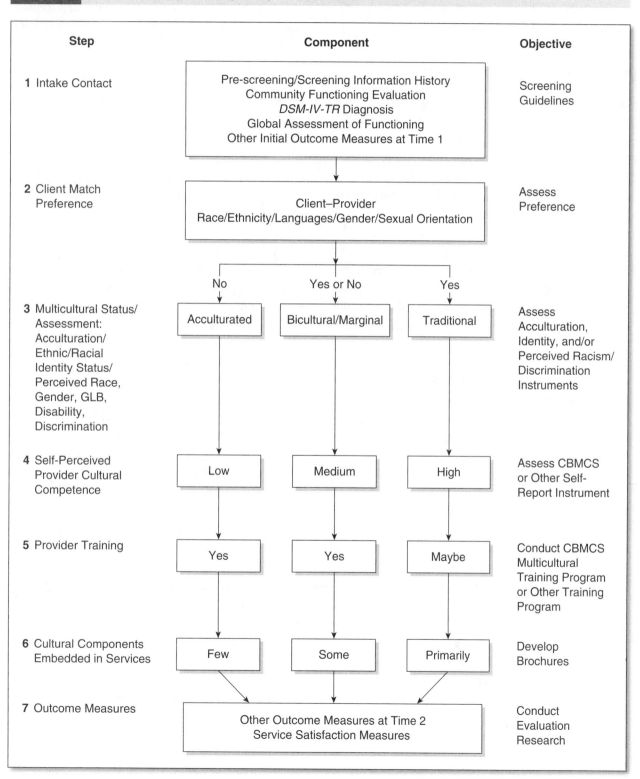

cultural competence, provider multicultural training, culturally sensitive service delivery, and outcome assessments, all of which will be briefly examined within the context of multicultural measurement.

3.3 CLIENT INTAKE ASSESSMENT

Clients of behavioral health services first interface with a counseling center, behavioral health center, or other health service delivery agency by a variety of means including telephone calls, personal visits, or other agency referrals. From this *initial contact* a decision is made by the client and/or the agency to schedule an *intake interview*. More empirical work needs to be conducted during this critical interval between first contact onset and the intake interview (e.g., Akutsu, Tsuru, & Chu, 2004, 2006). Critical questions that need to be addressed at this juncture of the therapeutic process include the following: What percent of clients fail to show up for their intake appointment? How long is the average delay interval? Are appropriate language services available to all potential clients? Is the behavioral health agency conducting effective and appropriate outreach for members of all racial/ethnic groups in the community or catchment area?

During the initial contact, basic demographic and other descriptive information is gathered including the client's name, age, gender, ethnicity, preferred language, income, telephone number, and names of nearest relatives. This information (sometimes referred to as a face sheet; see Appendix) provides the beginning of a client chart or medical record.

At the subsequent intake interview, the client and the practitioner (e.g., nurse, social worker, mental health counselor, marriage and family therapist, clinical or counseling psychologist, medical doctor, or psychiatrist) begin to forge a therapeutic relationship. This process has been variously referred to as "establishing the relationship" (Cormier & Hackney, 2008) or "opening" the interview (Scissions, 1993; Sommers-Flanagan & Sommers-Flanagan, 2004; 2009). During these sessions, providers glean additional identifying information, including pertinent case history data and presenting problems or issues, and also provide clarity and/or empathic support concerning fee structures and the range of available services and expectations provided by the agency, including an articulation of the personal goals of the client.

From a MAIP perspective, a crucial component of intake interviews, and sometimes the entire therapeutic process, that has been historically neglected (e.g., Dana, 1993, 2005; Groth-Marnet, 2009; Smith, 2004; Sundberg & Tyler, 1962) is attention to the practice of credible client service delivery styles for each racial/ethnic group (e.g., African American, Latino/a American, etc.).

Once behavioral health clients have been screened, their case history information and presenting problem(s) noted, and a cultural formulation and diagnosis rendered, a multicultural clinical assessment should be taken of each client at (or as close as possible to) the initial intake interview. The goal is to capture client functioning and multicultural information at the beginning of treatment. This information provides a useful benchmark for client functioning and also guides the practitioner in her or his selection of treatment strategies. This information is also necessary for the allocation of human resources by agency management. A profusion of clinical outcome measures, some of which are suitable for multicultural populations (American Psychiatric Association, 2000) and multicultural assessment instruments (see this volume), are available and suitable for either child or adult clients.

Current discourse and practice have taken a *levels-of-analysis* approach to the issue of clinical assessment of interventions with community mental health clients (Department of Mental Health, 2005). Such an orientation provides a useful schema to help evaluate and incorporate multicultural measurement into clinical and research practice.

For example, the California Department of Mental Health (DMH) "performance measurement design" initiatives (as well as other state agencies across the United States) embrace a levels-of-analysis perspective (Department of Mental Health, 2005). Performance is measured and tracked at three levels: (1) the individual client level, (2) the behavioral health program/system accountability level, and (3) the public/community impact level. While there are a variety of ways to operationalize objective indicators at each level, we believe the multicultural considerations within the MAIP model can inform this operationalization process. For example, at the individual client level, the DMH advocates for the collection of outcome/descriptive data on the following 15 indicators: housing, crime, employment, education, hospitalization, income, family preservation, symptoms, suicide, functioning, substance use, quality of life, illness self-management, individual goals, and physical health. While many of these indicators would provide behavioral health staff with useful client information, the MAIP formulation would also suggest, at this level, that client acculturation status, ethnic and racial identity levels, and perceptions of racism and discrimination should also be considered.

The second level of performance-measurement analysis that the DMH considers is the mental health system accountability level. Here the focus is on monitoring systems and programs, quality assurance, and multistakeholder coordination. DMH focuses at this level on client service satisfaction inventories such as the Mental Health Statistics Improvement Program (MHSIP) for adult clients (e.g., Jerrell, 2006) and the Youth Satisfaction Scale for Families (YSS-F) and Youth Satisfaction Scale (YSS), both of which are completed by parents/caregivers and children, respectively (Brunk, 2002; Brunk, Innes, & Koch, 2002). While client service satisfaction is a revealing and important indicator, the MAIP model would again refocus our attention upon cultural factors that may affect clinical outcomes at this program/system accountability level. For example, client–provider match (i.e., ethnic/racial, gender, language) preferences could be assessed at this level and tracked. Additionally, staff self-perceived cultural competence could also be assessed to determine future training needs and the assignment of clients to behavioral health providers (e.g., Gamst, Dana, Der-Karabetian, & Kramer, 2004).

The last level of performance measurement that DMH endorses deals with the public and community impact on behavioral health services. Issues relating to community outreach, education, prevention, and public relations are emphasized here. Again, the MAIP formulation would embrace these endeavors and encourage a multicultural focus for each one. For example, what are the most successful ways of conducting behavioral health outreach to Asian American, Latino/a American, African American, and Native American communities?

What special strategies need to be employed to overcome possible behavioral health service stigma for each ethnic/racial group? How do the various behavioral health practitioners tap the various ethnic community's strengths, resiliencies, and capacity for positive growth?

3.4 CLIENT–PROVIDER MATCH

Considerable research has been conducted on the effects of matching or not matching certain factors (e.g., race, ethnicity, gender, language) believed to be important in the therapeutic relationship between a behavioral health client and provider. Both earlier published work (e.g., Jerrell, 1995, 1998; Russell, Fujino, Sue, Cheung, & Snowden, 1996; Sue, Fujino, Hul, Takeuchi, & Zane, 1991) and more recent evaluations (Gamst et al., 2000, 2001, 2002, 2003, 2004; Lam & Sue, 2001; Maramba & Hall, 2002; Shin, Chow, Camacho-Gonsalves, Levy, Allen, & Leff, 2005) suggest conflicting effects of matching on clinical outcomes.

Some of these studies report the beneficial effect of client–provider ethnic/racial matching, particularly for Asian American and Latino/a American clients (e.g., Gamst et al., 2001, 2002, 2003; Zane et al., 2005). Other studies have failed to show a meaningful beneficial effect of matching for African American and White American clients (e.g., Gamst et al., 2000, 2004). Part of the variability found among studies that have reported statistically significant matching effects may be attributed to undocumented language matching and not specifically due to ethnic or racial matching, per se (e.g., Shin et al., 2005). Another possible factor contributing to the variability of the published literature on ethnic/racial matching is the racial/ethnic identity of the behavioral health provider who ultimately gets matched. In the public sector, behavioral health clients are seen by a variety of providers (e.g., psychiatrist, psychologist, marriage and family therapist, social worker, case manager, etc.) and thus, clarity on whom the match is based is crucial.

While the concept of client–provider matching is not pivotal to our discussion of multicultural measurement, determining and accommodating client matching preferences whenever possible is an important tenet of the MAIP model.

3.5 MULTICULTURAL STATUS ASSESSMENT

The MAIP model, as originally configured, advocated for the measurement of behavioral health client acculturation status and racial and ethnic identity (Dana, 1993; Gamst et al., 2006). Measurement of these constructs is essential because acculturation encompasses group and individual psychological adjustments that result from an interaction between a new and original culture (e.g., Aponte & Johnson, 2000; Dana, 1998; Chapter 6 of this book). Many acculturation researchers (e.g., Berry & Kim, 1988; Cuéllar, 2000) acknowledge the emergence of at least four acculturation strategies that behavioral healthcare clients can utilize: *assimilation, separation* (or traditional), *marginalization,* and *integration* (or bicultural; see Chapter 6 for a discussion of these strategies). Routine examination of the role of acculturation in assessment either by normative data, corrections for acculturation status (Dana, 1993), or direct evaluation (perhaps by means of some of the 48 acculturation or acculturation-related measurement instruments summarized in Chapter 6) is now feasible (Van de Vijver & Phalet, 2004). Client acculturation strategy assessment may also provide clinicians with helpful clues as to the most effective clinical intervention to take (e.g., solution-focused, directive, nondirective, etc.). Kohatsu, Concepcion, and Perez (2010) provide a useful framework for incorporating acculturation assessments into clinical practice.

Similarly, the measurement of client ethnic identity and/or racial identity also provides practitioners and researchers an equally important facet of the multicultural mosaic. As we will see in Chapter 5, racial and ethnic identity encapsulates the process whereby clients develop an awareness of themselves as ethnic, racial, or cultural beings. This awareness is assumed to be incorporated into a self-schema that can be augmented over time (Phinney, 1992; Trimble, Helms, & Root, 2003).

The MAIP model was originally predicated on the measurement of client acculturation and ethnic/racial identity to assist in the matching of client and mental health service provider and also to provide insight into

why a client is interacting with us in the manner that he or she is. For the purposes of this book, we have expanded the MAIP's Multicultural Status Assessment domain to also encompass measurement of perceived race-, gender-, sexual identity–, and disability-based discrimination and issues of gender role conflicts as well as other gender-based issues, sexual orientation, and disability. Such an expansion of client multicultural status concerns is appropriate and reflects the rich diversity of multicultural characteristics and experiences of behavioral healthcare clients today. It should be noted that the MAIP model does not necessarily advocate the complete measurement of all of these multicultural domains. Judicious appraisal of the client's presenting problems and needs coupled with limited agency or organizational resources will inevitably drive which multicultural measures are selected for a given client.

3.6 PROVIDER SELF-PERCEIVED CULTURAL COMPETENCE

The MAIP model encourages behavioral health agencies not only to incorporate and track client-provider matching preferences, client acculturation status, ethnic and racial identity, and perceptions of racism and discrimination but also to incorporate the providers' self-perceptions of their own cultural competence. Behavioral health staff vary in their training orientation, strategy for acculturation, racial and ethnic identity, personal values, social class, and so forth. These differences are also evident in the multicultural knowledge, skills, and abilities behavioral health staff members bring to the counseling session or clinical treatment activity (e.g., Sue, Zane, Hall, & Berger, 2009). Regularly evaluating providers' self-perceived cultural competence can offer a behavioral health agency an individualized multicultural training "roadmap" for each provider.

Currently, there is a plethora of cultural competency instruments from the research/practice literature (most of which are summarized in Chapter 4 of this book). These instruments all vary in length and the practitioner population they target, and most report adequate evidence of validity and reliability. While many different instruments could be utilized as a MAIP model fourth step or component (see Figure 3.1), the present authors have found good results with the California Brief Multicultural Competence Scale (CBMCS; Gamst et al., 2004).

The MAIP model is predicated on the assumption that all behavioral health staff who have contact with clients should have their self-reported cultural competence assessed so that a behavioral health agency (or training program) can identify the future multicultural training needs of each staff member. Such an assessment will also facilitate the "proper" MAIP model allocation of staff resources to meet diverse client needs.

3.7 PROVIDER MULTICULTURAL TRAINING

The MAIP model also affirms the necessity of behavioral health staff multicultural competency training. While there is an abundance of training programs in existence, few have had the benefit of empirical scrutiny. The MAIP model utilizes the *CBMCS Multicultural Training Program* (Dana, Gamst, & Der-Karabetian, 2008). This training program was developed from the 21-item CBMCS self-report instrument, whose items represent the multicultural competency training content universe with separate training modules derived from the four subscales. This 32-hour training program has received extensive practitioner scrutiny that has resulted in several complete revisions between 2002 and 2007. The training program is also accompanied by a *CBMCS Multicultural Training Program Participant Workbook* (Der-Karabetian, Dana, & Gamst, 2008) and a *CBMCS Multicultural Reader* (Gamst, Der-Karabetian, & Dana, 2008).

Regardless of what multicultural competence training program is used, it is a MAIP model imperative that staff self-report cultural competency be assessed both pre- and posttraining and that healthcare staff training needs are identified and addressed. It is only through assessment and subsequent training that limited behavioral healthcare resources can be appropriately allocated to meet diverse client needs (e.g., Mio, 2003).

3.8 CULTURAL COMPONENTS EMBEDDED IN SERVICE

Implementing the MAIP model at a behavioral health agency suggests a bifurcation in the client clinical treatment intervention strategy. Depending on the clients' matching preferences and their acculturation status, ethnic and racial identity orientation, or perceived race, gender, sexual orientation, and disability discrimination, ethnic-specific or -general interventions may be in order.

Briefly, an intervention strategy that is *ethnic-general* could be employed by many trained behavioral health practitioners. These interventions do not specifically incorporate cultural formulations but instead treat all behavioral health clients in a fairly similar manner. One such (ethnic-general) approach garnering considerable attention is the *recovery-oriented* service system proposed by Anthony (2000). This model emphasizes symptom relief, personal safety, client assessment, skills development, equal opportunity, basic survival support, empowerment, and healthy lifestyle promotion. For many White American clients and acculturated clients of color, such an approach offers many appealing possible outcomes. However, for unacculturated clients and/or clients with identity issues or traumatic discrimination experiences, ethnic-specific interventions from culturally competent providers may be in order (e.g., Tucker, Daly, & Herman, 2010). *Ethnic-specific* services have been advocated for many years and were available in culture-specific settings prior to managed care (see Dana, Behn, & Gonwa, 1992) and were examined in practice models for major ethnic/racial groups (Dana, 1998).

While a review of specific intervention strategies for each of the major ethnic/racial groups is beyond the scope of the present chapter, the interested reader is encouraged to consult the following sources:

- African Americans: Brooks, Haskins, & Kehe, 2004; Cook & Wiley, 2000; Dana, 1993, 2002; Helms & Cook, 1999; Livingston, 2006; Morris, 2001
- Latino/a Americans: Casas, Vasquez, & Ruiz de Esparga, 2002; Comas-Diaz, 1997, 2006; Gloria, Ruiz, & Castillo, 2004

- Asian Americans: Choi & Kim, 2003; Hall & Eap, 2007; Hsu, 1983; Zane, Morton, Chu, & Lin, 2004
- Native Americans: Gore, 2010; Jackson & Turner, 2004; Trimble & Thurman, 2004; Weaver, 2005

3.9 DISPOSITION COORDINATION

MAIP model steps 2 through 6 (i.e., match, consumer multicultural status assessment, provider self-perceived cultural competence, provider multicultural training, and ethnic-specific/general interventions) require not only assessment and interventions of one kind or another but also careful and informed disposition coordination.

The MAIP model formulation is predicated on the systematic allocation or routing of agency resources to meet the behavioral health and multicultural needs of each client. Hence, following the initial intake interview and clinical/multicultural assessment, clients are connected to appropriate modal behavioral health providers and culturally specific or generic programs on a case-by-case basis. This *disposition* process can occur on a weekly or more frequent basis with a team of mid-level clinical staff. The MAIP disposition process encourages a behavioral health agency to always try and accommodate client requests or preferences for a specific cultural, language, or gender match (see also Lam & Sue, 2001). Additionally, the MAIP model encourages the disposition team to funnel, whenever possible, unacculturated clients to culturally competent staff and programs that are better equipped to meet these clients' needs. Conversely, acculturated clients who indicate no specific matching preferences or other identified multicultural issues can be routed to (temporarily) less culturally sophisticated staff and/or ethnic-general treatment programs.

3.10 OUTCOME ASSESSMENTS AND COMPUTERIZED TRACKING

When clients terminate therapy of their own volition, are discharged by the behavioral health agency after successful completion of treatment, or reach annual (or 6-month) review for more serious/chronic disorders, these individuals should be given the same set of outcome measures and some of the multicultural measures that they received at intake with the exception of the acculturation, ethnic identity, and racial identity instruments. In addition to these posttest outcome measures, clients should also complete a service satisfaction instrument.

The MAIP model is predicated on the simultaneous coordination of multiple client and provider multicultural characteristics. Many of these measures can be administered in sessions after intake, as the case may arise, as a way for practitioners to (1) develop a better sense of the psychosocial experiences of the client; (2) to refine the treatment plan (e.g., restrictive emotionality in men as measured by the Gender Role Conflict Scale; O'Neil, Helms, Gable, David, & Wrightsman, 1986) or racism-related stress (as measured by the Index of Race-Related Stress; Utsey, Ponterotto, Reynolds, & Cancelli, 2000); (3) and/or to aid in the exploration of issues with a client (e.g., give an acculturation stress measure to not only get a sense of how a client is experiencing adjustment to the United States but also as a tool to use to discuss these issues, or give a male client a measure of masculine norms and then discuss those norms and the client's experiences of the norms as they relate to the problem at hand). Such a complex array of strategic variables requires a dedicated computerized tracking system, typically available at most behavioral health agencies (and other settings such as college counseling centers) to assist in billing and other business-side activities.

At a community mental health center in southern California, one of the authors developed a prototype tracking form called the *Consumer Outcome Profile (COP)* that was routinely generated after the initial intake processing and again at 6-month/annual review or discharge/termination (Gamst & Dana, 2005).

The COP provides pertinent demographic and descriptive information about the client along with any outcome data and a description of the modal therapist characteristics. Thus, an example of the COP presented in Table 3.1 indicates that the client was a Latina American, English-speaking mental

Table 3.1	Mental Health Center Consumer Outcome Profile

Staff Administering Outcome:	Visit Type:		Date: 05142003	
Consumer Information:				
Gender: F	Diagnosis Type: MOOD D/O		Cultural Preference: Doesn't Matter	
Ethnicity: Latino	Trauma Code:		Gender Preference: Doesn't Matter	
Language: English	Program: 160		Language Preference: English Only	
Education: 10th Grade	Referral: NONPSYCH PRIV HOSP		GAF T1: 50	
Living: LIVES ALONE HOME/APT			GAF T2: 75	
Modal Staff Information: 3 —	Gender: F	Last Activity Date: 4/10/03	Ethnicity: LATINO	Degree: N/A	Language: ENG

Outcomes:			
BPRS			
Anxious/Depression	5	(00–21)	Not Severe
Hostile/Suspiciousness	3	(00–21)	Not Severe
Thinking Disturbance	4	(00–21)	Not Severe
Withdrawal/Retardation	0	(00–14)	Not Severe
BPRS Total Score	18		Not Severe (18–77)
MHSIP			
Access	4.67	(00–05)	High
Appropriateness	5.00	(00–05)	High
Outcomes	5.00	(00–05)	High
Satisfaction	4.67	(00–05)	High
MHSIP Total Score	4.88		
QLSF-OBJECTIVE	0.92	(00–05)	Low
QLSF-SUBJECTIVE	5.22	(00–05)	High

health client with a mood disorder diagnosis. She was referred from a nonpsychiatric private hospital and indicated no particular cultural or language preferences. This client had a 10th-grade education and was living alone in a house or apartment. Her intake Global Assessment of Functioning (GAF) score was 50 and was evaluated at 75 at termination of treatment. Her modal therapist was also a Latina American; hence, both a gender and ethnic match occurred here, although no such match was requested by the client. This client's time-2 Brief Psychiatric Rating Scale (BPRS, a measure of clinical functioning; Overall & Gorham, 1988) total score (as well as her subscale scores) are well within the "not severe" range. Client service satisfaction, as measured by the Mental Health Statistics Improvement Program (MHSIP; Teague, Hornik, Ganju, et al., 1997), was also consistently high for the various MHSIP subscales. Apparently, at the end of treatment a contradiction emerged between this client's objective and subjective quality of life self-appraisals as measured by the Quality of Life—Short Form (QL-SF; Lehman, 1988, 1998). Objective quality of life (e.g., number of friends, family contacts, financial resources) was perceived to be low, while subjective quality of life (e.g., happiness with current situation) was relatively high.

3.11 CASE ILLUSTRATION: LISA

A case example is provided to illustrate the MAIP model steps outlined in Figure 3.1 and the information gleaned from the Consumer Outcome Profile (COP) of Table 3.1 captured at the end of treatment.

Lisa, a 28-year-old restaurant worker, has lived in southern California her entire life and is currently single. She has completed a 10th-grade education and lives alone in an apartment. Lisa considers herself to be Mexican American and speaks English only. Lisa (referred from a local hospital emergency room) presented at the local community mental health center with symptoms of depression and anxiety. Specifically, she reported feelings of restlessness, irritability, difficulty focusing, and an overall inability to enjoy life.

At her initial interview with an intake counselor, Lisa indicated no particular gender or cultural preference concerning her counselor but did indicate an English language preference. Lisa conveyed anxiety concerning the local job market and the high levels of unemployment in the fast-food industry. Lisa also reported a poor working relationship with her immediate supervisor (a White American female), whom she considered to be racist and abusive. Based on these presenting problems, the community mental center "Disposition Team" decided to match Lisa with a Latina American provider.

The Latina American provider that became Lisa's "modal" provider had a master's degree in counseling and had taken the self-report *California Brief Multicultural Competence Scale* (CBMCS; see Chapter 4) when she first began employment (one year previously) at the community mental health agency. Based in part on her CBMCS profile and the agency resources, this staff person was invited to participate in all four (8-hour) modules of the *CBMCS Multicultural Training Program*, which she successfully completed.

Several multicultural assessment and clinical outcome instruments were utilized during Lisa's initial intake to guide subsequent treatment planning. The *Multigroup Ethnic Identity Measure* (MEIM; see Chapter 5) indicated relatively high levels of the measured constructs of "Exploration" and "Commitment." Client acculturation status was probed with the *Acculturation Rating Scale for Mexican Americans-II* (ARSMA-II; see Chapter 6). Lisa's "Anglo Orientation Scale" (AOS) was relatively high and her "Mexican Orientation Scale" (MOS) was relatively low, indicating that Lisa was employing an "assimilated" acculturation strategy. As a consequence of Lisa attributing perceived racism as part of her work-related difficulties, the *General Ethnic Discrimination Scale* (GEDS; see Chapter 7) was administered. Lisa completed the measure before her next session as part of the homework assigned by her counselor.

In reviewing Lisa's responses to the General Ethnic Discrimination Scale, it was apparent to the counselor that Lisa's perceptions of racism were not isolated to her place of employment. Instead, results indicated that Lisa's experience of racism was chronic, perceived in work, social, and general settings, and appraised as somewhat stressful. Administering the GEDS allowed for the facilitation of a discussion of Lisa's reactions to the items on the measure and her own life experiences regarding racial discrimination. Lisa shared how she found it difficult to respond to the items and that reading them brought back memories of being teased and harassed for "no good reason." For instance, she reported how it would hurt her when peers at school "joked" about her and other Latino/a children being illegal immigrants. Even though those kids angered her, Lisa never confronted those individuals for their comments. In fact, she recalled how she just wanted to be White. She feels stupid now for wanting to be White but expresses how she always felt that things would just be easier for her if she were. The counselor showed empathy and maintained a nonjudgmental stance, which allowed for the development of a strong therapeutic relationship.

Through these discussions, Lisa was able to share her history of trying to fit in with her surroundings by "acting White" or by not bringing any attention to herself. Her counselor interpreted this discussion as an indication of Lisa's willingness to explore the role of racism in her life. The counselor offered that part of their work together could entail some time to understand racism and brainstorm strategies for coping with racist events. Lisa agreed that this may be helpful. In her treatment plan, the counselor sought to reduce levels of anxiety by increasing Lisa's knowledge and internal capacity to deal with events of discrimination in public settings, work settings, and social situations. Lisa also was encouraged to bolster her social supports and generalize these strategies to other stressful life events.

As a reflection of her knowledge of multicultural issues, particularly those salient for Latino/a individuals, the counselor supplemented traditional cognitive behavioral techniques aimed at increasing knowledge of anxiety and methods of stress reduction with multicultural-oriented interventions. Those included a focus on increasing Lisa's knowledge of racial oppression, developing additional racism-related coping strategies, and developing a new narrative. With the support of her supervisor, the counselor also worked to help Lisa develop a new narrative so that Lisa would be able to see herself in a more positive and empowered light. With a stance of empathic curiosity, the counselor helped Lisa develop alternate stories of her life experiences. Her old narrative, in which she saw herself as worthless and stupid for wanting to be accepted as White by others, was challenged and replaced with a new story in which she was able to honor her race-related trauma as well as this strategy (i.e., assimilating) for coping with an environment she perceived to be hostile. Through this re-storying, Lisa was also able to identify her own past and current agentic qualities, an ability to see herself as an individual who was reacting to an environment she did not quite understand. Instead of viewing herself as weak and stupid, she saw her behaviors, as well as those like her White American supervisor's, in the context of race and racism. In essence, Lisa developed a capacity to see behavior in the larger sociocultural context. Interestingly, Lisa developed greater empathy not only for herself but also for those who act on their prejudices. Lisa also was encouraged to understand that she could, if she wanted, take a more active role in changing oppressive systems.

At the end of treatment, as evidenced by the COP in Table 3.1, Lisa's clinical outcomes as measured by the *Brief Psychiatric Rating Scale* (BPRS) indicated all subscales (including "Anxious/Depression") to be in the "not severe" range. This instrument was also acknowledged by Lisa's modal provider, who increased her *Global Assessment of Functioning* (GAF) score from an initial 50 to 75 at termination. Lisa's evaluation of the mental health services she received, as evidenced by her *Mental Health Statistics Improvement Program* (MHSIP) subscale scores, was uniformly high, indicating satisfaction with treatment.

This case illustration was provided to assist the reader in her or his understanding of how the MAIP model may guide practice in a real-world context. In this case, Lisa was matched with a provider based on her stated preferences during the initial interview with an intake counselor. After the assignment, several measures were administered to develop a better understanding of her acculturation strategies and ethnic identity. Because of her stated problems with a supervisor she perceived to be racist, she also was given a measure of perceived racism to take home. This measure became the springboard for greater exploration of Lisa's experiences with race and racism as well as her coping strategies. The provider integrated cognitive behavioral interventions that have been established to be helpful for individuals experiencing anxiety and depression with a process that facilitated the re-authoring of her life. This experience contributed to alleviating symptoms associated with anxiety and depression, resulted in the development of more tools to cope with problems, and generated a greater understanding of the role of race in her life.

3.12 ASSESSMENT OF MULTICULTURAL VARIABILITY

In conclusion, the MAIP model offers researchers and practitioners one possible organizing framework for relating complex multicultural variables (dealing with the client and the practitioner) to client functioning and service satisfaction. The MAIP model should also provide a convenient frame of reference for determining the appropriateness of the myriad multicultural instruments in existence today.

4

Multicultural Competence Measures

4.1 MULTICULTURAL COMPETENCE DEFINED

An accurate portrayal of the multicultural competence (i.e., cultural competence) construct is inseparably bound up with its historical use. While the concepts of culture and race have been discussed within the field of psychology from its inception (e.g., Klineberg, 1935), the past four decades have witnessed an increasing convergence of multicultural interest as it pertains to the training of health and mental health practitioners and the delivery of health-related services to diverse clients.

Based on recommendations from the 1973 National Conference on Levels and Patterns of Professional Training (the Vail Conference; Korman, 1974), the American Psychological Association (APA) endorsed the ethical necessity of multicultural graduate training. Reinforcing this call to action were early notable publications of culturally sensitive counselor training texts (e.g., Atkinson, Morton, & Sue, 1979; Sue, 1981), mental health service disparities for African Americans (Sue, Mckinney, Allen, & Hall, 1974), Asian Americans (Sue & Mckinney, 1974), Latino/a Americans and Native Americans (Padilla & Ruiz, 1974; Sue, Allen, & Conaway, 1978), concerns ethnic minorities had about the counseling process (D.W. Sue & D. Sue, 1977a), and the academic research process (D.W. Sue & S. Sue, 1972).

Stemming from these and other early multicultural training and research initiatives, investigators began to explore frameworks for articulating multiculturally competent research and practice. Most influential was the development of the Cross-Cultural Counseling Competency Model (Sue et al., 1982) that identified 11 competencies across three broad cultural domains: beliefs/attitudes, knowledge, and skills. The model in this Division 17 (American Psychology Association) position paper was subsequently expanded to 31 competencies using the same three categories (Sue, Arredondo, & McDavis, 1992). In 1996, Arredondo et al. operationalized these competencies through 119 explanatory statements, and D. W. Sue et al. (1998) expanded the competencies to 34. These competencies became the driving force behind the guidelines for multicultural research, practice, and training adopted by the APA (APA, 2003). The original three competency domains required that the counselor (or service provider) be aware of her or his own personal biases, ethnic/racial identity, and sociopolitical outlook and how these considerations might influence the therapeutic alliance (*cultural beliefs/attitudes*); that the provider possesses *cultural knowledge* of the clients' ethnic/racial group, their social class, and possible institutional barriers to successful treatment; and lastly, culturally competent providers have the communication and intervention *cultural skills* to provide appropriate treatment for diverse clients.

The original D. W. Sue et al. (1982) conceptualization and its revisions have spawned a gallimaufry of definitions and operationalizations of cultural or multicultural competence. A recent review by Sue, Zane, Hall, and Berger (2009) noted the following definitions:

- to attend to cultural issues on therapy and counseling;
- to understand, appreciate, and respect cultural differences and similarities;
- to adapt interventions to meet culturally unique needs;
- to obtain positive clinical outcomes in multicultural interventions;
- to effectively communicate and intervene with diverse clients;
- to deliver effective culture-specific interventions;
- to coordinate a system of culturally congruent behaviors, attitudes, and policies within a system of care.

These conceptualizations and definitions have driven the development of a number of multicultural competence models that have attempted to elucidate the dynamics involved in the development of cultural competence by practitioners. These models provide clarity, descriptive and prescriptive modes of action, and the possibility of empirical validation (Mollen, Ridley, & Hill, 2003). A brief overview of some of the main multicultural competence models follows, based on the S. Sue et al. (2009) trichotomy: personal characteristics models, skills or tactics models, process-oriented models, and the Mollen et al. (2003) cultural competence model summary.

4.2 MULTICULTURAL MODELS

4.2.1 Personal Characteristics Models

Multicultural competence models that recognize and emphasize practitioner personal characteristics (e.g., knowledge, awareness, skills) have become ubiquitous in the counseling and clinical psychology literature.

- **Tripartite Model of Multicultural Counseling Competencies** (Sue et al., 1982; Sue et al., 1992). This model and its subsequent revision has had the most

impact on clinical/counseling practice of any model to date. The Tripartite model posits that multiculturally competent practice is a function of the knowledge, skills, beliefs, and attitudes of the mental health service provider.

- **Counselor Development Model** (Carney & Kahn, 1984). This model suggests that practitioners' cultural competence develops across five developmental stages that encourage three growth domains: cultural knowledge, cultural awareness and sensitivity, and cross-cultural skill. The five stages range from limited cultural knowledge and ethnocentric attitude (Stage 1) to embracing cultural pluralism and a social justice orientation (Stage 5).

- **Intercultural Sensitivity Model** (Bennett, 1993). This six-stage model suggests that providers move through three stages of ethnocentrism (denied, defense, and minimization) and three stages of ethnorelativism (acceptance, adoption, and integration).

- **Culturally Competent Model of Care** (Campenha-Bacote, 1994). This model argues that cultural responsiveness is a function of three cultural components: cultural awareness (e.g., understanding client worldviews), cultural knowledge (e.g., making cultural assessments), and cultural encounters (e.g., interacting with diverse clients).

- **Three-Factor Model** (Castro, 1998). This model is influenced by the early work of Cross, Bazron, Dennis, and Isaacs (1989). The three-factor model views cultural competence on a continuum from three levels of incompetence (cultural destructiveness, cultural incapacity, and cultural blindness) to three levels of competence (cultural sensitivity/openness, cultural competence, and cultural proficiency).

- **Cultural Competency Continuum** (Cross, 1988). The Cross Continuum was originally developed to describe six stages of organizational cultural competence. The stages range from cultural destructiveness (i.e., the superiority of one culture over another) to advanced cultural competency (i.e., organizations strive to serve the needs of diverse clientele).

4.2.2 Skills or Tactics Models

Authors of multicultural competence models that operate from a skills or tactics framework believe that cultural competence is a skill or strategy to be learned or employed by practitioners (Sue et al., 2009). Thus, multicultural competency can be considered one of many treatment tools in a practitioner's toolbox.

- **Three-Dimensional Model for Cross-Cultural Curricula** (Ridley, 1985). In this model, Ridley argues that practitioner cultural effectiveness can be enhanced by training psychologists to focus on three dimensions of graduate curricula: population target (e.g., major race/ethnic groups), intervention target (e.g., individual, group, community), and curriculum target (e.g., theory, research, and practice).

- **Cultural Adaptation** (Whaley & Davis, 2007). While not a formal model per se, Whaley and Davis's work emphasizes the imperative to develop and train for cultural adaptations (i.e., accommodations of diverse clients' cultural beliefs, attitudes, and behaviors) of empirically supported mental health treatments.

4.2.3 Process-Oriented Models

Multicultural competence process-oriented models emphasize the factors involved in client–provider interactions. The focus is on depicting the key cultural processes involved in acquiring and maintaining competency.

- **Multidimensional Process** (Sue, 1998). This model argues that provider cultural competence is a function of three dynamic cultural processes: (1) scientific mindedness (the ability to form and test cultural hypotheses about the client), (2) dynamic sizing (the ability to properly individualize or generalize client cultural issues), and (3) culture-specific resources (the knowledge and ability to appropriately apply culture-specific and culture-general interventions).

- **Process Model of Cultural Competence** (Lopez, 1997). Cultural competence for this model is determined by the provider's ability to shift between his or her own cultural framework and the client's cultural perspective. Four cultural process domains are emphasized: (1) engagement (where providers establish a meaningful therapeutic alliance), (2) assessment (where client functioning is assessed in a culturally informed manner), (3) theory provides an explanatory model (both the provider's and the client's) that addresses client functioning and potential treatment, and (4) methods (or clinical interventions) are developed to meet the diverse needs of each unique client.

- **Multicultural Assessment-Intervention Process (MAIP) Model** (Dana, 1993, 1998; Gamst, Dana, Meyers, Der-Karabetian, & Guarino, 2009). The MAIP model was designed to embed culturally competent care in mental health service delivery. Client variables (e.g., ethnic/racial match, ethnic identity, and acculturation) and provider variables (self-perceived cultural competence) are used to allocate agency resources to meet client needs and achieve better clinical outcomes.

- **Multidimensional Model for Developing Cultural Competence** (Sue, 2001). This three-dimensional model consists of (1) components of cultural competence (i.e., awareness, knowledge, skills), (2) foci of cultural competence (i.e., individual, professional, organizational, societal), (3) racial and culture-specific attributes of cultural competence (African American, Asian American, Latino American, Native American, White American). Cultural competence develops through the factorial combination or interaction of these three dimensions.

- **Multicultural Counseling Competence Assessment and Planning Model** (Toporek & Reza, 2001). This complex multidimensional model has the Sue et al. (1992) nine multicultural standards and competencies as its base. Three contexts (personal, professional, and institutional) orient a provider to a particular cultural milieu. Three modalities of change (cognitive, affective, behavioral) encompass all other model dimensions. The model also posits three assessment and planning components (assessment, needs, and activities/goals).

These multicultural models and other empirical cultural competence research have spawned a number of empirical self-report instruments. Beginning in the 1990s, partial reviews of these instruments have been realized (e.g., Constantine, Gloria, & Ladany, 2002; Dunn, Smith, & Montoya, 2006; Hays, 2008; Kocarek, Talbot, Batka, & Anderson, 2001; Kumas-Tan, Beagan, Loppie, MacLeod, & Frank, 2007; Ponterotto & Alexander, 1996; Ponterotto, Rieger, Barrett, & Sparks, 1994; Ponterotto, Utsey, & Pederson, 2006; Pope-Davis & Dings, 1995; Pope-Davis, Coleman, Liu, & Toporek, 2003; Pope-Davis, Liu, Toporek, & Brittan-Powell, 2001; Reynolds, 2001; Roysircar, 2006; Siegal, Haugland, & Chambers, 2003; Worthington, Soth-McNett, & Moreno, 2007).

4.3 CULTURAL COMPETENCE INSTRUMENTATION

The present review has identified 26 specific multicultural competence instruments that met our inclusion criteria. These instruments have been divided into the following eight multicultural competence domains: (1) Practitioner Self-Reports; (2) Counseling Supervisor Evaluations; (3) Self-Efficacy Measures; (4) Counseling Gay, Lesbian, Bisexual Individuals; (5) Counseling Women; (6) Consumer Perspective; (7) Teacher/Education Measures; and (8) Multicultural Personality.

4.3.1 Practitioner Self-Reports

These instruments attempt to capture mental health practitioner self-reports of their own cultural competence. The present review has identified the following seven instruments: (1) California Brief Multicultural Competence Scale (CBMCS; Gamst, Dana, Der-Karabetian, Aragon, Arellano, Morrow, & Martenson, 2004); (2) Multicultural Awareness, Knowledge, and Skills Survey-Counselor Edition-Revised (MAKSS-CE-R; Kim, Cartwright, Asay, & D'Andrea, 2003); (3) Multicultural Mental Health Awareness Scale (MMHAS; Khawaja, Gomez, & Turner, 2009); (4) Multicultural Counseling Competence and Training Survey-Revised (MCCTS-R; Holcomb-McCoy & Day-Vines, 2004); (5) Multicultural Counseling Knowledge and Awareness Scale (MCKAS; Ponterotto, Gretchen, Utsey, Reiger, & Austin, 2002); (6) the Multicultural Counseling Inventory (MCI; Sodowsky, Taffe, Gutkin, & Wise, 1994); and (7) Cultural Competence Assessment Instrument (CCA; Doorenbos, Schim, Benkert, & Borse, 2005).

4.3.2 Counseling Supervisor Evaluation

These measures evaluate cultural competence from a counseling supervisor perspective. The present review has identified three such instruments: (1) Cross-Cultural Counseling Inventory-Revised (CCCI-R; LaFromboise, Coleman, & Hernandez, 1991); (2) Multicultural Supervision Inventory (MSI; Pope-Davis, Toporek, & Ortega-Villalobos, 2003); and (3) Multicultural Environmental Inventory-Revised (MEI-R; Pope-Davis, Liu, & Toporek, 2000).

4.3.3 Self-Efficacy Measures

These measures are the "next of kin" to the Practitioner Self-Report instruments in that they attempt to assess a practitioner's confidence in providing culturally competent mental health care. The following three instruments were identified: (1) School Counselor Multicultural Self-Efficacy Scale (SCMES; Holcomb-McCoy, Harris, Hines, & Johnston, 2008); (2) Culturally Responsive Teaching Self-Efficacy Scale (CRTSE; Siwatu, 2007); and (3) Multicultural Counseling Self-Efficacy Scale—Racial Diversity Form (MCSE-RD; Sheu & Lent, 2007).

4.3.4 Counseling Gay, Lesbian, and Bisexual Individuals

The focus of these measures is on practitioner attitudes, skills, knowledge, beliefs, and behaviors concerning lesbian, gay, and bisexual individuals. This particular domain of cultural competence assessment has received limited attention (e.g., Sue et al., 2009) from both practitioner and client perspectives. The following four measures were identified: (1) Sexual Orientation Counselor Competency Scale (SOCCS; Bidell, 2005); (2) Lesbian, Gay, Bisexual Working Alliance Self-Efficacy Scales (LGB-WASES; Burkard, Pruitt, Medler, & Stark-Booth, 2009); (3) Gay Affirmative Practice Scale (GAP; Crisp, 2006); (4) Lesbian, Gay, and Bisexual Affirmative Counseling Self-Efficacy Inventory (LGB-CSI; Dillon & Worthington, 2003).

4.3.5 Counseling Women

One instrument focuses on self-perceived practitioner competency regarding practice with diverse female clients: Counseling Women Competencies Sale (CWCS; Ancis, Szymanski, & Ladany, 2008).

4.3.6 Consumer Perspective

One instrument examines mental health consumers' perceptions of their mental health provider's cultural competence: Consumer-Based Cultural Competency Inventory (C-BCCI; Cornelius, Booker, Arthur, Reeves, & Morgan, 2004).

4.3.7 Teacher/Education Measures

These instruments attempt to assess the multicultural competence of public school teachers and practitioners. Six instruments were identified: (1) Multicultural Awareness-Knowledge-Skills Survey—Teachers Form (MAKSS-FORM-T; D'Andrea, Daniels, & Noonan, 2003); (2) Multicultural Teaching Concerns Survey (MTCS; Marshall, 1996); (3) Teachers Multicultural Attitude Survey (TMAS; Ponterotto, Baluch, Grieg, & Rivera, 1998); (4) Multicultural Competence in Student Affairs-Preliminary 2 (MCSA-P2; Pope & Mueller, 2000); (5) Multicultural School Psychology Counseling Competency Scale (MSPCCS; Rogers & Ponterotto,

1997); and (6) Culturally Responsive Teaching Outcome Expectancy Scale (CRTOE; Siwatu, 2007).

4.3.8 Multicultural Personality

One instrument was identified that purports to measure personality dimensions that underlie multicultural effectiveness: Multicultural Personality Questionnaire (MPQ; Van der Zee & Van Oudenhoven, 2000).

4.4 FUTURE RESEARCH

In the three decades since the Sue et al. (1982) cultural competence guidelines were first published, a great deal of energy has been marshaled to examine the multicultural competence construct. This work has embodied conceptualizations, definitions, operationalizations, theoretical model building, lively discussions, and a modest amount of published empirical research regarding cultural competency implementation in practice. We will note a few of the many possible routes that future cultural competence research might take.

1. **Self-perceived cultural competence and clinical outcome.** Since most of the measures reviewed in this chapter are self-reports in nature, more empirical research linking these self-reports to actual measures of clinical outcome (i.e., client functioning and service satisfaction) and culturally competent practitioner behavior need to be conducted.

2. **Consumer perspective.** To what extent do providers' self-perceptions and consumer perceptions of provider cultural competence align?

3. **Individual, agency, and system levels.** How do we measure cultural competence at each level and integrate these domains into a unified and coherent line of march?

4. **Cultural competence: a global perspective.** As commerce, education, and recreation become increasingly global and transnational (see Dana & Allen, 2008), how will cultural competence training and measurement develop?

4.5 PRACTITIONER SELF-REPORT MEASURES

4.5.1 **Name of the Measure**	California Brief Multicultural Competence Scale CBMCS
Primary Reference	Gamst, G., Dana, R. H., Der-Karabetian, A., Aragon, M., Arellano, L., Morrow, G., & Martenson, L. (2004). Cultural competency revised: The California Brief Multicultural Competence Scale. *Measurement and Evaluation in Counseling and Development, 37*(3), 163–183.
Purpose	The CBMCS is a multidimensional self-report instrument that purports to measure the cultural competencies of mental health practitioners.
Description	The CBMCS contains 21 items. Each item is rated on the following 4-point Likert-type scale: 4 = Strongly Disagree, 3 = Disagree, 2 = Agree, 1 = Strongly Agree. The CBMCS is composed of a total scale score and four subscales: (1) Sociocultural Diversities (formerly Nonethnic Ability), (2) Awareness of Cultural Barriers, (3) Multicultural Knowledge, (4) Sensitivity to Consumers. The CBMCS initial item pool was developed through an amalgamation of four other previously published cultural competence scales, e.g., Cross-Cultural Counseling Inventory-Revised (CCCI-R; LaFromboise, Coleman, & Hernandez, 1991; Multicultural Awareness, Knowledge, Skills Survey (MAKSS; D'Andrea, Daniels, & Heck, 1991); Multicultural Counseling Awareness Scale-Form B (MCAS-B; Ponterotto & Alexander, 1996); Multicultural Competency and Training Survey (MCCTS; Holcomb-McCoy, 2000). A comprehensive questionnaire that included all four measures, demographic/personal characteristics questions, and the 33-item Social Desirability Scale (SDS; Crowne & Marlowe, 1960), and the Multicultural Counseling Inventory (MCI; Sodowsky, Kuo-Jackson, Richardson, & Corey, 1998; Sodowsky, Taffe, Gutkin, & Wise, 1994) was presented to a large number of California mental health practitioners. Through the process of social desirability checks, item review by a panel of multicultural experts and a panel of knowledgeable mental health consumers, and a series of principal components analyses (with varimax rotations), the initial item pool was reduced from 157 items to a final four-factor, 21-item simple structure that accounted for 59% of the total variance.
Samples	The normative sample was based on 1,244 (795 women, 397 men, 52 unknown) California mental health providers. The average age was 37.3 years ($SD = 16.8$). Self-reported race/ethnicity was White American (52%), Latino/a American (14%), African American (11%), Asian American/Pacific Islander (9%), and Native American (1%).

Scoring	The number of items in each of the four subscales is as follows:
	
	    Sociocultural Diversities (formerly Nonethnic Abilities): 7 items.
	
	    Awareness of Cultural Barriers: 6 items.
	
	    Multicultural Knowledge: 5 items.
	
	    Sensitivity and Responsiveness to Consumers: 3 items.
	
	    Total CBMCS: 21 items.
	
	Scoring the CBMCS consists of adding the participant's ratings on each item in the subscale to obtain subscale scores and dividing the score by the number of items in the subscale to obtain a subscale mean. A CBMCS scale mean is obtained by adding participant's ratings on all of the items and dividing by 21. No reverse coding or transformations are required.

Reliability	Cronbach's alpha for the scores were as follows:
	
	    Sociocultural Diversities: Alpha = .90
	
	    Awareness of Cultural Barriers: Alpha = .78
	
	    Multicultural Knowledge: Alpha = .80
	
	    Sensitivity to Consumers: Alpha = .75

Validity	Concurrent validity was established through the finding of low to moderate correlations between the scores of the CBMCS subscales and the scores of the MCI subscales. Confirmatory factor analyses with a separate sample ($N = 366$) supported the construct validity of a four-factor correlated model observed with the exploratory factor analysis. Social desirability contamination was minimal with the correlation of the scores of the CBMCS subscales, and the scores of the SDS were all close to zero.
Related References	Gamst, G., Dana, R. H., Meyers, L. S., Der-Karabetian, A., & Guarino, A. J. (2009). An analysis of the Multicultural Assessment Intervention Process model. *International Journal of Culture and Mental Health, 2*(1), 51–64.
Language Versions	English
Contact	Glenn Gamst Psychology Department University of La Verne 1950 3rd Street La Verne, CA 91750 (909) 593–3511, 4176 (W) (909) 392–2745 (fax) Email: ggamst@laverne.edu

4.5.2 Name of the Measure	Multicultural Awareness, Knowledge, and Skills Survey—Counselor Edition—Revised MAKSS-CE-R
Primary Reference	Kim, B. S. K., Cartwright, B. Y., Asay, P. A., & D'Andrea, M. J. (2003). A revision of the Multicultural Awareness, Knowledge, and Skills Survey—Counselor Edition. *Measurement and Evaluation in Counseling and Development, 36*, 161–180.
Purpose	The MAKSS-CE-R is a multidimensional, multicultural counseling competence measure that is based on Sue et al.'s model that focuses on multicultural awareness, knowledge, and skills.
Description	The MAKSS-CE-R contains 33 items. Each item is rated on one of the following 4-point Likert-type scales with the following response anchors: 1 = Very Limited, 4 = Very Aware, 1 = Very Limited, 4 = Very Good, 1 = Strongly Disagree, 4 = Strongly Agree. The MAKSS-CE-R is composed of a total score and three subscales: (1) Awareness-Revised, (2) Knowledge-Revised, (3) Skills-Revised. The MAKSS-CE-R is a revised and shortened version of the 60-item MAKSS-CE (D'Andrea, Daniels, & Heck, 1991). Subsequent principal factor analysis (with an oblique rotation) produced a three-factor simple structure that accounted for 29.8% of the total variance and reduced the scale to 33 items.
Samples	The normative sample consisted of 338 (272 women, 66 men) graduate counseling students. Ages ranged from 20 to 53 years ($M = 27.4$, $SD = 6.8$). Self-reported race/ethnicity was White American (44.1%), African American (31.4%), Asian American (10.1%), Latino/a American (3.0%), biracial American (2.1%), multiracial American (1.2%), Native American (0.3%), and no response (8.0%). About 41.1% of the participants had successfully completed at least one course in multicultural counseling. This sample was subsequently split in half to perform an exploratory and a confirmatory factor analysis.
Scoring	The number of items in each of the three subscales is as follows: Awareness-Revised: 10 items Knowledge-Revised: 13 items Skills-Revised: 10 items Total MAKSS-CE-R: 33 items Scoring the MAKSS-CE-R consists of adding the participant's ratings on each item in the subscale and dividing the subscale total by the number of subscale items to obtain a subscale mean. A composite scale mean can be obtained by adding the participant's scores on all 33 items and dividing that total by 33 to obtain a composite total score mean. Seven items are reverse scored.
Reliability	Cronbach's alpha for the scores were as follows: Awareness-R: Alpha = .71 Knowledge-R: Alpha = .85 Skilss-R: Alpha = .87 Total MAKS-CE-R: Alpha = .82

Validity	Construct validity was achieved by correlating the subscale scores of the MAKSS-CE-R with the subscale scores of the Multicultural Counseling Knowledge and Awareness Scale (MCKAS; Ponterotto, Gretchen, Utsey, Rieger, & Austin, 2002). Moderate to high positive correlations were found between same-named subscales of the two measures. Criterion-related validity was evidenced by means of multivariate analysis of variance with participants' multicultural counseling course experience as the independent variable (yes, no) and the three MAKSS-CE-R subscales serving as dependent variables. Results indicated that participants who completed at least one multicultural counseling course produced higher MAKSS-CE-R total scores and also Awareness-R and Knowledge-R subscale scores ($p < .01$).
Related References	Cartwright, B. Y., Daniels, J., & Zhang, S. (2008). Assessing multicultural competence: Perceived versus demonstrated performance. *Journal of Counseling & Development, 86*(3), 318–322.
Language Versions	English
Contact	Bryan S.K. Kim Department of Psychology University of Hawai'i at Hilo 200 W. Kawili St. Hilo, Hawai'i 96720-4091 (808) 974-7439 (W) (808) 974-7737 (Fax) Email: bryankim@hawaii.edu Website: www2.hawaii.edu/~bryankim/

4.5.3 Name of the Measure	Multicultural Mental Health Awareness Scale MMHAS
Primary Reference	Khawaja, N. G., Gomez, I., & Turner, G. (2009). Development of the Multicultural Mental Health Awareness Scale. *Australian Psychologist, 44*(2), 67–77.
Purpose	The MMHAS is a multidimensional instrument that purports to measure the multicultural competencies of mental health professionals in Australia.
Description	The MMHAS contains 35 items. Each item is rated on one of the following 5-point Likert-type scales: 1= Lacking, 2 = Limited, 3 = Good, 4 = Very Good, 5 = Excellent, or 1 = Not At All, 2 = A Little, 3 = Satisfactory, 4 = Fairly Well, 5 = Extremely Well. The MMHAS is composed of a total score and three subscales: (1) Multicultural Counselling Awareness, (2) Multicultural Counselling Knowledge, (3) Multicultural Counselling Skills. The initial 51-item pool was generated by the authors to reflect the cultural competencies enunciated in the Queensland Transcultural Mental Health (Khawaja, Gomez, & Turner, 2009) and the Sue et al. (1982) cultural competencies. Based on feedback from a panel of cultural experts, the item pool was refined and reduced to 44 items. Subsequently, a principal components analysis (with an oblique rotation) produced a 35-item three-factor simple structure that accounted for 70.3% of the total variance.
Samples	The normative sample consisted of 268 (190 women, 73 men, 5 no response) mental health professionals. Ages ranged from 18 to 65 years (*SD* = 12.4). Self-reported race/ethnicity was Anglo-Saxon (66%), Asian (12%), Latin (5%), Middle Eastern (2%), African (2%), European (7%), other (4%), no response (2%). Participant occupation was as follows: Clinical psychologist (18%), counselor (4%), social worker (2%), trainee psychologist (34%), other (39%), no response (3%).

Scoring	The number of items in each of the three subscales is as follows:
	
	    Multicultural Counselling Awareness: 15 items
	    Multicultural Counselling Knowledge: 9 items
	    Multicultural Counselling Skills: 11 items
	    Total MMHAS: 35 items
	
	Scoring the MMHAS consists of adding the participant's ratings on each item in the subscale to obtain subscale scores, or adding all of the participant's ratings on all of the 35 items to obtain a total scale score. No reverse coding or transformations are required.

Reliability	Cronbach's alpha for the scores were as follows:
	
	    Multicultural Counselling Awareness: Alpha = .89
	    Multicultural Counselling Knowledge: Alpha = .92
	    Multicultural Counselling Skills: Alpha = .90
	    Total MMHAS: Alpha = .91

Validity	Concurrent validity was achieved through the finding of moderate positive correlations between the MMHAS subscale scores and the subscale scores of the Multicultural Awareness-Knowledge-Skills Scale (MAKSS; D'Andrea, Daniels, & Heck, 1991). Discriminant validity was achieved in the finding that participants with previous multicultural training had statistically significantly higher total MMHAS scores ($M = 104.8$, $SD = 24.0$) as compared to professionals without such training ($M = 96.6$, $SD = 26.6$) ($p < .01$). The MMHAS subscale scores are positively correlated with correlations ranging from .75 to .81, among the three subscales.
Related References	
Language Versions	English
Contact	Nigar G. Khawaja Psychology and Counselling Queensland University of Technology Carseldine Campus Beams Road Brisbane, Qld 4034 Australia Email: n.khawaja@qut.edu.au

4.5.4 Name of the Measure	Multicultural Counseling Competence and Training Survey—Revised MCCTS-R
Primary Reference	Holcomb-McCoy, C. C., & Day-Vines, N. (2004). Exploring school counselor multicultural competence: A multidimensional concept. *Measurement and Evaluation in Counseling and Development, 37*(3), 154–162.
Purpose	The MCCTS-R is a self-report, multidimensional cultural competence instrument for school counselors.
Description	The MCCTS-R contains 32 items. Each item is rated on a 4-point Likert-type scale, with the following response options: 1 = Not Competent (Not Able to Perform at This Time), 2 = Somewhat Competent (More Training Needed), 3 = Competent (Able to Perform Competently), 4 = Extremely Competent (Able to Perform at a High Level). The MCCTS-R is composed of three subscales: (1) Multicultural Terminology, (2) Multicultural Knowledge, (3) Multicultural Awareness. The MCCTS-R is a revision of the MCCTS (Holcomb-McCoy & Myers, 1999). Items for the revised scale were reworded to better reflect the language used by school counselors. The revised item pool was reviewed by a panel of expert school counselors. A subsequent maximum likelihood factor analysis (with an oblique rotation) produced a three-factor, 32-item simple structure that accounted for 55.1% of the total variance.
Samples	The normative sample consisted of 209 (172 women, 37 men) school counselors randomly drawn from the membership list of the American School Counselor Association. Self-reported race/ethnicity was as follows: White American (89%), African American (3%), Latino/a American (1%), Asian American (2%), Native American (2%), and other (2%).

Scoring	The number of items in each of the three subscales is as follows:
	
	    Multicultural Terminology: 4 items
	
	    Multicultural Knowledge: 19 items
	
	    Multicultural Awareness: 9 items
	
	    Total MCCTS-R: 32 items
	
	Scoring the MCCTS-R consists of adding the participant's ratings on each item in the subscale to obtain a subscale score and dividing the score by the number of items within the subscale to obtain a subscale mean.

Reliability	Cronbach's alphas for the scores of the three MCCTS-R subscales were as follows:
	
	    Multicultural Terminology: Alpha = .97
	
	    Multicultural Knowledge: Alpha = .95
	
	    Multicultural Awareness: Alpha =.85

Reliability	Cronbach's alpha for the scores were as follows:
	Multicultural Counseling Skills: Alpha = .83
	Multicultural Counseling Awareness: Alpha = .83
	Multicultural Counseling Relationship: Alpha = .65
	Multicultural Counseling Knowledge: Alpha = .79
	Total MCI: Alpha = .88
Validity	A confirmatory factor analysis provided evidence of goodness-of-fit for the four-factor oblique model (RMSEA = .024).
Related References	Green, R. G., Kiernan-Stern, M., Bailey, K., Chambers, Claridge, R., Jones, G., et al. (2005). The Multicultural Counseling Inventory: A measure for evaluating social work student and practitioner self-perceptions of their multicultural competencies. *Journal of Social Work Education, 41*(2), 191–208.
	Sodowsky, G. R. (1996). The Multicultural Counseling Inventory: Validity and applications in training. In G. R. Sodowsky & J. Impara (Eds.), *Multicultural assessment in counseling and clinical psychology* (pp. 283–324). Lincoln, NE: Buros Institute of Mental Measurement.
	Sodowsky, G. R., Kuo-Jackson, P. Y., Richardson, M. F., & Corey, A. T. (1998). Correlates of self-reported multicultural competencies: Counselor multicultural social desirability, race social inadequacy, locus of control, racial ideology, and multicultural training. *Journal of Counseling Psychology, 45,* 256–264.
Language Versions	English
Contact	Gargi Roysircar-Sodowsky Department of Clinical Psychology Antioch University New England 40 Avon Street Keene, NH 03431–3516 (603) 283–2186 (W) Email: groysircar@antioch.edu

4.5.7 Name of the Measure	Cultural Competence Assessment Instrument CCA
Primary Reference	Doorenbos, A. Z., Schim, S. M., Benkert, R., & Borse, N. N. (2005). Psychometric evaluation of the cultural competence assessment instrument among healthcare providers. *Nursing Research, 54*(5), 324–331.
Purpose	The CCA is a self-report cultural competence instrument for healthcare providers.
Description	The CCA contains 27 items. Each item is rated on one of the following 5-point Likert-type rating scales: 1 = Strongly Agree, 2 = Agree, 3 = Disagree, 4 = Strongly Disagree 5 = No Opinion, or 1 = Always, 2 = Often, 3 = At Times, 4 = Never, 5 = Not Sure. The CCA is composed of a total score and two subscales: (1) Cultural Awareness and Sensitivity (CAS), (2) Cultural Competence Behaviors (CCB). The initial CCA 45-item pool was based on a literature review and the operationalization of four constructs: diversity experience, cultural awareness, cultural sensitivity, and cultural competence behaviors. Expert review reduced the item pool to 38 items. A subsequent principal axis factor analysis (with an oblique rotation) resulted in a 27-item, two-factor simple structure that accounted for 56% of the total variance.
Samples	The normative sample consisted of 405 healthcare workers conveniently sampled from nine healthcare agencies (gender was not noted). Sample mean age was 41 years ($SD = 11.7$). Sample self-reported race/ethnicity was as follows: White American (65%), African American (19%), Native American (4%), Latino/a American (2%), other (11%).

Scoring	The number of items in each of the two subscales is as follows:
	
	    Cultural Awareness and Sensitivity (CAS): 16 items
	    Cultural Competence Behaviors (CCB): 11 items
	    Total CCA: 27 items
	
	Scoring the CCA consists of summing the items from the CAS and CCB subscales. Higher scores indicate higher levels of cultural knowledge, more positive attitudes, and greater frequency of culturally competent behaviors. Four items are reverse coded.

Reliability	The Cronbach's alpha for the scores were as follows:
	
	    CCB: Alpha = .91
	    CAS: Alpha = .75
	    Total CCA: Alpha = .89
	
	Four-month test-retest reliability for the total CCA was $r = .85$.

Validity	Evidence of known-group validity was provided with the finding of statistically significantly higher CCA scores for healthcare workers reporting previous diversity training.
Related References	
Language Versions	English
Contact	Stephanie Myers Schim Wayne State University College of Nursing 240 Cohn 5557 Cass Ave. Detroit, MI 48202 (313) 577–4034 (W) (313) 577–4188 (Fax) Email: s.schim@wayne.edu

4.6 COUNSELING SUPERVISOR EVALUATION

4.6.1 Name of the Measure	Cross-Cultural Counseling Inventory—Revised CCCI-R
Primary Reference	LaFromboise, T. D., Coleman, H. L. K., & Hernandez, A. (1991). Development and factor structure of the Cross-Cultural Counseling Inventory—Revised. *Professional Psychology: Research and Practice, 22*(5), 380–388. Hernandez, A. G., & LaFromboise, T. D. (1985, August). *The development of the Cross-Cultural Counseling Inventory*. Paper presented at the meeting of the American Psychological Association, Los Angeles.
Purpose	The CCCI-R is a multidimensional measure of counselor trainees' cross-cultural competence (i.e., beliefs/attitudes, knowledge, skills) as assessed by counseling supervisors.
Description	The CCCI-R contains 20 items. Each item is rated on a 6-point Likert-type scale ranging from 1 = Strongly Disagree to 6 = Strongly Agree. The CCCI-R is composed of three subscales: (1) Cross-Cultural Counseling Skill, (2) Socio-Political Awareness, (3) Cultural Sensitivity. The CCCI-R was developed from its predecessor the 18-item Cross-Cultural Counseling Inventory (CCCI; Hernandez & LaFromboise, 1985). These 18 items were developed by the authors to address the recommendations of the American Psychological Association Division 17 Education and Training Committee on cross-cultural counseling competence (Sue et al., 1982). Two additional items were added, resulting in the 20-item CCCI-R. Subsequent principal components analysis (with varimax rotation) yielded a simple structure with three factors.
Samples	The normative sample upon which the principal components analysis was based consisted of 86 university students. Sample characteristics were not detailed, but the authors noted that "The raters were quite diverse with respect to age, ethnicity, socioeconomic status, and levels and fields of undergraduate, graduate, and postdoctoral training" (p. 384). All participants had completed at least one counseling course.

Scoring	The number of items per subscale are as follows:
	
	     Cross-Cultural Counseling Skill: 10 items
	
	     Socio-Political Awareness: 6 items
	
	     Cultural Sensitivity: 4 items
	
	     CCCI-R total scale: 20 items
	
	 Scoring the CCCI-R consists of adding the participant's ratings on each of the 20 items to obtain a total scale score that ranges from 20 to 120. Subscale scores can also be computed by summing participant's ratings on the items within each subscale. No reverse coding or transformations of items is required.

Reliability	Cronbach's alpha for the 20-item scale was .95.
Validity	Content validity was achieved through independent rating of item congruence with the Sue et al. (1982) cross-cultural counseling competencies.
Related References	Constantine, M. G. (2002). The relationship between general counseling self-efficacy and self-perceived multicultural counseling competence in supervisees. *The Clinical Supervisor, 20*(2), 81–90.
Language Versions	English
Contact	Teresa D. LaFromboise Native American Studies School of Education Stanford University (650) 723–1202 (W) (650) 725–7412 (Fax) Email: lafrom@stanford.edu

4.6.2 **Name of the Measure**	Multicultural Supervision Inventory MSI
Primary Reference	Pope-Davis, D. B., Toporek, R. L., & Ortega-Villalobos, L. (2003). Assessing supervisors' and supervisees' perceptions of multicultural competence in supervision using the Multicultural Supervision Inventory. In D. B. Pope-Davis, H. L. K. Coleman, W.M. Liu, & R.L. Toporek (Eds.), *Handbook of multicultural competencies in counseling & psychology* (pp. 211–224). Thousand Oaks, CA: Sage.
Purpose	The MSI purports to assess supervisees' and supervisors' perspectives of multicultural competence in supervision.
Description	The MSI contains 20 items. Two versions of the MSI are available. One version measures supervisor perceptions of their own self-perceived supervisory cultural competence. The second version measures supervisees' perceptions of the multicultural competence of their clinical or counseling supervisor's supervision practice. Each item is rated on a 5-point Likert-type scale with the following two anchors: 1 = Strongly Disagree to 5 = Strongly Agree. The MSI is composed of a total score and three subscales: (1) Supervisor's Competence, (2) Supervisor's Collaborative Relationships, (3) Supervisor's Support. The initial 43-item pool was developed through a previously unpublished scale development in the form of the Multicultural Supervision Competence Scale—Revised (MSC-R; later renamed the MSI; Pope-Davis, Toporek, & Ortega, 1999; Pope-Davis, Toporek, Ortega, Bashur, Liu, Brittan-Powell, et al., 2000). Subsequently, the 43 items were subjected to a principal components analysis (with a promax with Kaiser normalization rotation). This analysis resulted in a three-factor 20-item simple structure that accounted for 65% of the total variance.
Samples	The normative sample consisted of 208 (146 women, 57 men, 5 no response) graduate students ($n = 137$), faculty ($n = 64$), no response ($n = 7$). Supervisors' self-reported race/ethnicity was White American (72%), African American (12%), Asian American/Pacific Islander (9%), Jewish (4%), Latino/a American (3%). Supervisees' self-reported race/ethnicity was White American (69%), African American (11%), Jewish (8%), Latino/a American (2%), other (2%).

Scoring	The number of items in each of the three subscales is as follows:
	
	    Supervisor's Competence: 13 items
	    Supervisor's Collaborative Relationships: 3 items
	    Supervisor's Support: 4 items
	    Total MSI: 20 items
	
	Scoring the MSI consists of adding the participant's ratings on each item in the subscale to obtain subscale scores, or adding all of the participant's ratings on all items to obtain a total score. One item is reverse coded.

Reliability	Cronbach's alpha for the scores were as follows:
	Supervisor's Competence: Alpha = .96
	Supervisor's Collaborative Relationships: Alpha = .80
	Supervisor's Support: Alpha = .68
	Total MSI: Alpha = .92
Validity	For the most part, personal characteristics of the supervisors were not significantly related to perceived cultural competence. However, supervisees who had racially different supervisors rated their supervisors as more culturally competent than those who had racially similar supervisors.
Related References	
Language Versions	English
Contact	Donald B. Pope-Davis University of Notre Dame 502 Main Building Notre Dame, IN 46556 (574) 631–4694 Email: dpd@nd.edu

4.6.3 Name of the Measure	Multicultural Environmental Inventory—Revised MEI-R
Primary Reference	Pope-Davis, D. B., Liu, W. M., & Toporek, R. L. (2000). The development and initial validation of the Multicultural Environmental Inventory: A preliminary investigation. *Cultural Diversity and Ethnic Minority Psychology, 6*(1), 57–64.
Purpose	The MEI-R is a multidimensional instrument that purports to measure an individual's perceptions concerning graduate counseling programs' ability to address multicultural issues regarding curriculum, supervision, climate, and research.
Description	The MEI-R contains 27 items. Each item is rated on a 5-point Likert-type scale with the following three response anchors: 1 = Not At All, 3 = Moderately, 5 = A Lot. The MEI-R is composed of the following four subscales: (1) Curriculum and Supervision, (2) Climate and Comfort, (3) Honesty in Recruitment, (4) Multicultural Research. The initial 53-item pool of the MEI-R was developed from an earlier unpublished instrument, the Multicultural Environmental Inventory (MEI; Pope-Davis & Liu, 1997) that was based on an extensive literature review. Subsequently, the 53 items were subjected to a principal components analysis (with an oblique rotation) and yielded a 27-item, four-factor simple structure.
Samples	The normative sample consisted of 208 (146 women, 57 men, 10 no response) graduate students ($n = 137$) and faculty ($n = 64$). The mean age for students was 31 years ($SD = 9.0$), and for faculty 45 years ($SD = 10.2$). Self-reported race/ethnicity was as follows: White American (58%), African American (17%), Asian American and Pacific Islander American (7%), Latino/a American (7%), Native American (1%), no response (7%), and other (3%).

Scoring	The number of items in each of the four subscales is as follows:
	
	    Curriculum and Supervision: 11 items
	    Climate and Comfort: 11 items
	    Honesty and Recruitment: 3 items
	    Multicultural Research: 2 items
	    Total MEI-R: 27 items
	
	Scoring the MEI-R consists of adding the participant's ratings on each item in the subscale to obtain subscale scores. No reverse coding or transformations are required.

Reliability	Cronbach's alpha for the scores were as follows:
	
	    Curriculum and Supervision: Alpha = .92
	    Climate and Comfort: Alpha = .92
	    Honesty in Recruitment: Alpha = .85
	    Multicultural Research: Alpha = .83
	    Total MEI-R: Alpha = .94

	The original sample was split in half, and two independent principal components analyses yielded similar four-factor, 27-item simple structures.
Validity	A subsequent study (Toporek, Liu, & Pope-Davis, 2003) employing a confirmatory factor analysis ($N = 336$) suggested that the model and subscale structure of the MEI-R was an adequate fit of the data.
Related References	Toporek, R. L., Liu, W. M., & Pope-Davis, D. P. (2003). Assessing multicultural competence of the training environment: Further validation for the psychometric properties of the Multicultural Environment Inventory—Revised. In D. B. Pope-Davis, H. L. K. Coleman, W. M. Liu, & R. L. Toporek (Eds.), *Handbook of multicultural competencies in counseling & psychology* (pp. 183–190). Thousand Oaks, CA: Sage.
Language Versions	English
Contact	Donald B. Pope-Davis University of Notre Dame 502 Main Building Notre Dame, IN 46556 (574) 631–4694 Email: dpd@nd.edu

4.7 SELF-EFFICACY MEASURES

4.7.1 Name of the Measure	School Counselor Multicultural Self-Efficacy Scale SCMES
Primary Reference	Holcomb-McCoy, C., Harris, P., Hines, E. M., & Johnston, G. (2008). School counselors' multicultural self-efficacy: A preliminary investigation. *Professional School Counseling, 11*(3), 166–178.
Purpose	The SCMES is a multidimensional instrument that purports to measure the self-perceived cultural competence of professional school counselors.
Description	The SCMES contains 52 items. Each item is rated on a 7-point Likert-type scale with the following response anchors: 1 = Not Well At All to 7 = Very Well. The SCMES is composed of six subscales: (1) Knowledge of Multicultural Concepts, (2) Using Data and Understanding Systemic Change, (3) Developing Cross-Cultural Relationships, (4) Multicultural Counseling Awareness, (5) Multicultural Assessment, (6) Application of Racial and Cultural Knowledge to Practice. The initial item pool was developed by means of an interdisciplinary literature search and the input from a team of doctoral students in counselor education. Through this process, 90 items were generated. Subsequent principal axis factor analysis (with varimax rotation) yielded six orthogonal factors that accounted for 59.5% of the total variance, with 52 items.
Samples	The normative sample, 181 (127 women, 54 men), was based on a mail and electronic survey delivery of members of the American School Counselor Association. Self-reported race/ethnicity was as follows: White American (74.6%), African American (16%), Latino/a American (5.5%), Asian American/Pacific Islander (1.7%), Native American, multiracial, or other (2.2%).
Scoring	The number of items in each of the six subscales is as follows: Knowledge of Multicultural Concepts: 14 items Using Data and Understanding Systemic Change: 9 items Developing Cross-Cultural Relationships: 7 items Multicultural Counseling Awareness: 9 items Multicultural Assessment: 7 items Application of Racial and Cultural Knowledge to Practice: 6 items Total SCMES: 52 items Scoring the SCMES consists of adding the participant's ratings on each item in the subscale and dividing that total by the number of subscale items to obtain a subscale mean. No reverse coding or transformations are required.

Reliability	Cronbach's alpha for the scores were as follows:
	Knowledge of Multicultural Concepts: Alpha = .95
	Using Data and Understanding Systemic Change: Alpha = .91
	Developing Cross-Cultural Relationships: Alpha = .89
	Multicultural Counseling Awareness: Alpha = .93
	Multicultural Assessment: Alpha = .89
	Application of Racial and Cultural Knowledge to Practice: Alpha = .88
	Total SCMES: Alpha = .93
Validity	Concurrent validity was established by means of multivariate analyses of variance, demonstrating that ethnic minority participants had significantly higher self-perceived cultural capabilities than White American participants on five of the six subscales.
Related References	
Language Versions	English
Contact	Cheryl Holcomb-McCoy The Johns Hopkins University Department of Counseling and Human Services Rockville, MD 20850 (301) 294–7044 (W) Email: cholcom1jhu.edu

4.7.2 Name of the Measure	Culturally Responsive Teaching Self-Efficacy Scale CRTSE
Primary Reference	Siwatu, K. O. (2007). Preservice teachers' culturally responsive teaching self-efficacy and outcome expectancy beliefs. *Teaching and Teacher Education, 23*, 1086–1101.
Purpose	The CRTSE is a unidimensional measure that purports to assess teachers' beliefs in their ability to deliver specific teaching practices that are assumed to be associated with culturally responsive teachers.
Description	The CRTSE contains 40 items. Each item is rated on a 100-point Likert-type scale with the following two response anchors: 0 = No Confidence At All, 100 = Completely Confident. The CRTSE is a unidimensional instrument. The initial item development for the CRTSE (and its companion scale, the Culturally Responsive Teaching Outcome Expectancy Scale, CRTOE) was based on a literature review, and particularly the work of Bandura (1977a).
Samples	The normative sample consisted of 275 preservice teachers enrolled in two Midwestern U.S. teacher education programs (200 women, 75 men). Self-reported race/ethnicity was White American (92.7%) and non-White (i.e., Mexican American, Asian American, African American; 7.3%). Sample mean age was 21.9 years ($SD = 4.9$).
Scoring	Scoring the CRTSE consists of adding the participant's ratings on each item in the scale to obtain a total scale score. No reverse coding or transformations are required.
Reliability	Cronbach's alpha for the total scale was .96.
Validity	A positive correlation was found between the scores of the CRTSE and the companion CRTOE scale.
Related References	
Language Versions	English
Contact	Kamau Oginga Siwatu Department of Educational Psychology and Leadership College of Education Texas Tech University Box 41071 (806) 742–1998, 431 (W) (806) 742–2179 (Fax) Email: siwatu@ttu.edu

4.7.3 Name of the Measure	Multicultural Counseling Self-Efficacy Scale—Racial Diversity Form MCSE-RD
Primary Reference	Sheu, H.-B., & Lent, R. W. (2007). Development and initial validation of the Multicultural Counseling Self-Efficacy Scale—Racial Diversity Form. *Psychotherapy, Theory, Research, Practice, & Training, 44*(1), 30–45.
Purpose	The MCSE-RD is a multidimensional instrument designed to measure self-perceived capability to counsel racially diverse clients in the context of individual psychotherapy.
Description	The MCSE-RD contains 37 items. Each item is rated on a 10-point Likert-type scale with the following two anchors: 0 = No Confidence At All, 9 = Complete Confidence. The MCSE-RD is composed of a total score and three subscales: (1) Multicultural Intervention, (2) Multicultural Assessment, (3) Multicultural Session Management. The initial MCSE-RD item pool was based on Bandura's (1997a) dichotomized self-efficacy belief typology of content-specific self-efficacy (i.e., confidence in performing multiculturally informed counseling tasks) and coping efficacy (i.e., confidence handling difficult multicultural dialogue). From an extensive self-efficacy and multicultural psychology literature review, 120 items were developed and scrutinized by separate groups of doctoral students and multicultural experts. This process reduced the pool to 60 items that were subjected to a principal axis factor analysis (with an unspecified orthogonal rotation). A three-factor simple structure was achieved that accounted for 71% of the total variance, with 37 items.
Samples	The normative sample was based on 181 graduate students (149 females, 32 males). Self-reported race/ethnicity was as follows: White American (59%), African American (13%), Asian American/Pacific Islander (9%), Latino/a American (7%), multiethnic (6%), and international students (6%).
Scoring	The number of items in each of the three subscales is as follows: Multicultural Intervention: 24 items Multicultural Assessment: 6 items Multicultural Session Management: 7 items Total MCSE-RD: 37 items Scoring the MCSE-RD consists of adding the participant's ratings on each item in the subscale to obtain a subscale score and dividing that score by the number of items in the subscale to obtain a subscale mean. A total scale mean can be computed by adding all of the participant's ratings on all of the items and dividing that total by 37. No reverse coding or transformations are required.

(Continued)

(Continued)

Reliability	Cronbach's alpha for the scores were as follows:
	Multicultural Intervention: Alpha = .98
	Multicultural Assessment: Alpha = .92
	Multicultural Session Management: Alpha = .94
	Total MCSE-RD: Alpha = .98
	Two-week test-retest reliability were as follows:
	Multicultural Intervention: r = .73
	Multicultural Assessment: r = .88
	Multicultural Session Management: r = .69
	Total MCSE-RD: r = .77
	All three subscales were positively correlated.
Validity	Discriminant validity was demonstrated by statistically nonsignificant correlations between MCSE-RD scores and scores of the Multicultural Social Desirability Index (MCSD; Sodowsky, Kuo-Jackson, Richardson, & Corey, 1998). Convergent validity was evidenced by statistically significant positive correlations between MCSE-RD scores and scores of the Counselor Activity Self-Efficacy Scales (CASES; Lent, Hill, & Hoffman, 2003).
Related References	
Language Versions	English
Contact	Hung-Bin Sheu 302 Payne Hall, MC-0611 Division of Psychology in Education Arizona State University Tempe, AZ 85287–0611 (480) 965–2193 (W) (480) 965–2904 (Fax) Email: Hung-BinSheu@asu.edu

4.8 COUNSELING GAY, LESBIAN, AND BISEXUAL INDIVIDUALS

4.8.1 Name of the Measure	Sexual Orientation Counselor Competency Scale SOCCS
Primary Reference	Bidell, M. P. (2005). The Sexual Orientation Counselor Competency Scale: Assessing attitudes, skills, and knowledge of counselors working with lesbian, gay, and bisexual clients. *Counselor Education and Supervision, 44*(4), 267–279.
Purpose	The SOCCS is a multidimensional self-report instrument that purports to measure the attitudes, skills, and knowledge of counselors who work with lesbian, gay, and bisexual individuals.
Description	The SOCCS contains 29 items. Each item is rated on a 7-point Likert-type scale with the following two response anchors: 1 = Not At All True, 7 = Totally True. The SOCCS is composed of a total score and three subscales: (1) Skills, (2) Attitudes, (3) Knowledge. The initial SOCCS item pool was developed by means of a rationale-empirical approach (Dawis, 1987) and a comprehensive LGB and multicultural competence literature review that resulted in the creation of 100 items. Feedback from a panel of experts and a group of graduate students reduced the item pool to 42 items. A subsequent principal-axis factor analysis (with an oblique rotation) resulted in a 29-item, three-factor simple structure that accounted for 40% of the total variance.
Samples	The normative sample consisted of 312 (235 women, 77 men) students, counselor educators, and counselor supervisors. The mean age of the sample was 31.9 years. Self-reported race/ethnicity was White American (61.2%), Latino/a American (13.1%), Asian American (10.6%), African American (7.1%), biracial/mixed ethnicity (2.2%), Native American (1.3%), and other (4.5%). Self-reported sexual orientation was as follows: heterosexual (85.3%), lesbian, gay, bisexual (12.2%), and no response (2.5%).

Scoring	The number of items in each of the three subscales is as follows:
	
	    Skills: 11 items
	
	    Attitudes: 10 items
	
	    Knowledge: 8 items
	
	    Total SOCCS: 29 items
	
	Scoring the SOCCS consists of adding the participant's ratings on each item in the subscale to obtain subscale scores and dividing that score by the number of items in the subscale to obtain a subscale mean. A total scale mean can also be computed by adding all of the participant's ratings on all of the items and dividing by 29. Eleven items are reverse coded.

(Continued)

(Continued)

Reliability	Cronbach's alpha for the scores were as follows:
	Skills: Alpha = .91
	Attitudes: Alpha = .90
	Knowledge: Alpha = .76
	Total SOCCS: Alpha = .90
	One-week test-retest reliability coefficients were as follows:
	Skills: $r = .83$
	Attitudes: $r = .85$
	Knowledge: $r = .84$
	Total SOCCS: $r = .84$
Validity	Criterion validity was demonstrated by the finding that LGB respondents ($M = 5.33$, $SD = .96$) scored statistically significantly higher on the SOCCS total scale than did heterosexual respondents ($M = 4.53$, $SD = .82$, $p < .01$). Convergent validity was demonstrated by correlating the scores of the SOCCS-Knowledge subscale with the scores of the Multicultural Counseling Knowledge and Awareness Scale (MCKAS; Ponterotto, Gretchen, Utsey, Rieger, & Austin, 2002), which demonstrated moderate positive correlation.
Related References	
Language Versions	English
Contact	Marcus P. Bidell San Francisco State University Department of Counseling Burk Hall, Room 534 1600 Holloway Ave. San Francisco, CA 94132 (415) 338–1707 (W) (415) 338–0594 (Fax) Email: bidell@sfsu.edu

4.8.2 Name of the Measure	Lesbian, Gay, Bisexual Working Alliance Self-Efficacy Scales LGB-WASES
Primary Reference	Burkard, A. W., Pruitt, N. T., Medler, B. R., & Stark-Booth, A. M. (2009). Validity and reliability of the Lesbian, Gay, Bisexual Working Alliance Self-Efficacy Scales. *Training and Education in Professional Psychology, 3*(1), 37–46.
Purpose	The LGB-WASES is a multidimensional self-report, LGB-affirmative counselor self-efficacy instrument that purports to measure a counselor's perceived ability to develop a working alliance with a LGB client.
Description	The LGB-WASES contains 32 items. Each item is rated on an 11-point Likert-type scale with the following three response anchors: 0 = Cannot Do At All, 5 = Moderately Certain Can Do, 10 = Certain Can Do. The LGB-WASES is composed of a total score and three subscales: (1) Emotional Bond, (2) Establishing Tasks, (3) Setting Goals. Item development for the LGB-WASES was influenced by Bordin's (1979, 1994) working alliance theory and LGB-affirmative counseling principles (APA, 2000; Perez, Debord, & Bieschke, 2000), and a comprehensive literature review, which resulted in an initial item pool of 90 items. After a further review by a panel of LGB experts, this pool was reduced to 84 items. A subsequent principal-axis factor analysis (with promax rotation) produced a 32-item, three-factor simple structure that accounted for 73% of the total variance.
Samples	The normative sample consisted of 303 graduate students (249 women, 52 men). Ages ranged from 21 to 55 years (*M* = 28.3, *SD* = 7.2). Self-reported race/ethnicity was White American (83%), African American (6.3%), Asian American (2.0%), Latino/a American (2.3%), Native American (1.0%), international origin (2.0), biracial or multiracial (1.7%), no response (1.7%). Self-reported sexual orientation was heterosexual (93%), gay (1.0%), lesbian (1.3%), bisexual (1.3%), and no response (2.3%).
Scoring	The number of items in each of the three subscales is as follows: Emotional Bond: 13 items Establishing Tasks: 13 items Setting Goals: 6 items Total LGB-WASES: 32 items Scoring the LGB-WASES consists of adding the participant's ratings on each item in the subscale to obtain subscale scores and then dividing this score by the number of items in the subscale to obtain a subscale mean. A total scale mean can be computed by adding the participant's ratings on all of the items and dividing that total by 32. No reverse coding or transformations are required.

(Continued)

(Continued)

Reliability	Cronbach's alpha for the scores were as follows: Emotional Bond: Alpha = .97 Establishing Tasks: Alpha = .96 Setting Goals: Alpha = .94 Total LGB-WASES: Alpha = .98 Three-week test-reliability coefficients were reported to be moderate to high on the three subscales.
Validity	Convergent validity was established by correlating the total scale scores of the Counselor Activity Self-Efficacy Scales (CASES; Lent, Hill, & Hoffman, 2003) and the Multicultural Counseling Inventory (MCI; Sodowsky, Taffe, Gutkin, & Wise, 1994) with the total and subscale scores of the LGB-WASES. Low to moderate positive correlations were evidenced between the scores of the LGB-WASES and the CASES and MCI scores. Discriminant validity was achieved by demonstrating low positive and nonstatistically significant correlations between the scores of the LGB-WASES and the scores of the Marlowe-Crowne Social Desirability Scale (SDS; Crowne & Marlowe, 1960).
Related References	
Language Versions	English
Contact	Alan W. Burkard Department of Counselor Education and Counseling Psychology Marquette University Milwaukee, WI 53233 (414) 288–3434 (W) Email: alan.burkhard@marquette.edu

4.8.3 Name of the Measure	Gay Affirmative Practice Scale GAP
Primary Reference	Crisp, C. (2006). The Gay Affirmative Practice scale (GAP): A new measure for assessing cultural competence with gay and lesbian clients. *Social Work, 51*(1), 115–126.
Purpose	The GAP is a multidimensional, self-report cultural competence instrument that purports to measure practitioners' beliefs and behaviors in practice with gay and lesbian individuals.
Description	The GAP contains 30 items. Each item is rated on one of the following 5-point Likert-type scales: 1 = Strongly Disagree, 2 = Disagree, 3 = Neither Agree Nor Disagree, 4 = Agree, 5 = Strongly Agree, or 1 = Never, 2 = Rarely, 3 = Sometimes, 4 = Usually, 5 = Always.
	The GAP is composed of a total score and two subscales: (1) Behaviors in Practice and (2) Beliefs in Practice.
	The initial item pool of 372 items was developed through a comprehensive literature review. A panel of experts on gay affirmative practice evaluated the relevancy of these items and reduced the pool to 80 items. A subsequent confirmatory factor analysis (CFA) reduced the items to two 15-item domains labeled "belief" and "behavior." Details of the CFA were not provided (e.g., fit indexes, or structure coefficients).
Samples	The sample consisted of 488 (361 women, 127 men) randomly sampled National Association of Social Workers and American Psychological Association members, yielding a response rate of 16.3%. Self-reported sexual orientation was heterosexual (86.1%), bisexual (3.5%), and gay/lesbian (9.8%). Self-reported race/ethnicity was White American (92.0%), African American (2.5%), Asian American (1.0%), Latino/a American (2.0%), Native American (0.2%), other (0.6%).
Scoring	The number of items in each subscale are as follows:
	Beliefs About Practice With Gay and Lesbian Individuals: 15 items
	Behavior in Practice With Gay and Lesbian Individuals: 15 items
	Total GAP: 30 items
	Scoring the GAP consists of adding the participant's ratings on each item in the subscale to obtain subscale scores or adding all of the participant's ratings on all 30 items to obtain a total score. Higher scores reflect more affirmative practice with gay and lesbian clients. No reverse coding or transformations are required.
Reliability	Cronbach's alpha for the scores were as follows:
	Beliefs about Practice with Gay and Lesbian Individuals: Alpha = .93
	Behavior in Practice with Gay and Lesbian Individuals: Alpha = .94
	Total GAP: Alpha = .95

(Continued)

(Continued)

Validity	Construct validity was obtained by correlating the scores of the GAP Belief subscale with the Heterosexual Attitudes Toward Homosexuals Scale (HATH; Larsen, Reed, & Hoffman, 1980) and the scores of the GAP Behavior subscale and the scores of the Attitudes Toward Lesbians and Gay Men Scale (ATLG short form; Herek, 1988), both of which produced moderate positive correlations.
	Discriminant validity was evidenced by correlating the scores of the GAP total scale and the Marlowe-Crowne Social Desirability Scale (SDS; Crowne & Marlowe, 1960), which produced a correlation to zero.
Related References	Crisp, C., Wayland, S., & Gordon, T. (2008). Older gay, lesbian, and bisexual adults: Tools for age-competent and gay affirmative practice. *Journal of Gay and Lesbian Social Services, 20*(1/2), 5–29.
Language Versions	English
Contact	Catherine Lau Crisp Department of Social Work University of Arkansas at Little Rock 2801 S. University Ave. Little Rock, AR 72204 Email: clcrisp@ualr.edu

4.8.4 Name of the Measure	Lesbian, Gay, and Bisexual Affirmative Counseling Self-Efficacy Inventory LGB-CSI
Primary Reference	Dillon, F. R., & Worthington, R. L. (2003). The Lesbian, Gay, and Bisexual Affirmative Counseling Self-Efficacy Inventory (LGB-CSI): Development, validation, and training implications. *Journal of Counseling Psychology, 50*(2), 235–251.
Purpose	The LGB-CSI is a multidimensional self-report instrument that purports to measure various dimensions of LGB-affirmative counseling self-efficacy.
Description	The LGB-CSI contains 32 items. Each item is rated on a 6-point Likert-type scale with the following three response anchors: 1 = Not At All Confident, 3 = Moderately Confident, 6 = Highly Confident. The LGB-CSI is composed of a total score and five subscales: (1) Application of Knowledge, (2) Advocacy Skills, (3) Awareness, (4) Relationship, (5) Assessment. The initial LGB-CSI item pool of 101 items was developed through a comprehensive literature review of LGB counseling competencies. This item pool was then examined by a panel of experts for its appropriateness and reduced to 67 items. Based on graduate student feedback, the item pool was further reduced to 64 items. A subsequent principal-axis factor analysis (with an oblique rotation) resulted in a five-factor, 32-item simple structure.
Samples	The normative sample consisted of 336 graduate counselor trainees and mental health practitioners (240 women and 96 men). Ages ranged from 21 to 75 years (*M* = 34.7, *SD* = 10.4). Self-reported race/ethnicity was as follows: White American (79.8%), African American (8.9%), Latino/a American (4.5%), Asian American/Pacific Islander (4.1%), biracial/multiethnic (1.5%), Native American (0.6%), no response (0.6%).

Scoring	The number of items in each of the five subscales is as follows:
	
	    Application of Knowledge: 13 items
	    Advocacy Skills: 7 items
	    Awareness: 5 items
	    Relationship: 3 items
	    Assessment: 4 items
	    Total LGB-CSI: 32 items
	
	Scoring the LGB-CSI consists of adding the participant's ratings on each item in the subscale to obtain subscale scores and dividing the score by the number of items in the subscale to obtain a subscale mean. A total score mean can be computed by adding all of the participant's ratings on all of the items; total scores can range from 32 to 192. No reverse coding or transformations are required.

(Continued)

(Continued)

Reliability	Cronbach's alphas for the scores were as follows:
	Application of Knowledge: Alpha = .95
	Advocacy Skills: Alpha = .93
	Awareness: Alpha = .86
	Relationship: Alpha = .83
	Assessment: Alpha = .87
	Two-week test-retest reliabilities for the scores were as follows:
	Application of Knowledge: $r = .57$
	Advocacy Skills: $r = .48$
	Awareness: $r = .45$
	Relationship: $r = .37$
	Assessment: $r = .38$
	Total LGB-CSI: $r = .51$
Validity	Convergent validity was achieved by statistically significant positive correlations between the scores of the LGB-CSI total and the total and subscale scores of the Counseling Self-Estimate Inventory (COSE; Larson et al., 1992) correlations ranged from low to moderate positive. Discriminant validity was achieved by the lack of statistically significant correlation between the total scores of the LGB-CSI and the scores of the subscales of the Balanced Inventory of Desirable Responding (BIDR; Paulhus, 1991).
Related References	
Language Versions	English
Contact	Frank R. Dillon Fischler School of Education and Human Services Nova Southeastern University 1750 NE 167th Street, Room 321 North Miami, FL Email: fdillon@nova.edu

4.9 COUNSELING WOMEN

4.9.1 Name of the Measure	Counseling Women Competencies Scale CWCS
Primary Reference	Ancis, J. R., Szymanski, D. M., & Ladany, N. (2008). Development and psychometric evaluation of the Counseling Women Competencies Scale (CWCS). *The Counseling Psychologist, 36*(5), 719–744.
Purpose	The CWCS is a multidimensional self-report measure that purports to assess clinical and counseling psychology and other professional trainees' self-perceived competency regarding therapeutic practice with diverse female clients.
Description	The CWCS contains 20 items. Each item is rated on a 7-point Likert-type scale with the following two response anchors: 1 = Not At All True, 7 = Totally True. The CWCS is composed of a total score and two subscales: (1) Knowledge and Skills, (2) Self-Awareness. The initial 96-item pool development was based on a comprehensive literature review and reviewed by a panel of experts and 32 members of the Section for the Advancement of Women (Division 17, APA), which refined the items to 39. Subsequently, a principal-axis factor analysis (with an oblique rotation) produced a two-factor, 20-item simple structure that accounted for 45% of the total variance.
Samples	The normative sample consisted of 321 (250 women, 71 men) counseling (17%), psychology (43%), and other (40%) graduate students and professionals. Ages ranged from 21 to 89 years (*M* = 37.3, *SD* = 13.4). Self-reported race/ethnicity was White American (81%), African American (13%), Asian American (3%), Latino/a American (1%), and other (2%).

Scoring	The number of items in each of the two subscales is as follows:
	
	    Knowledge and Skills: 15 items
	
	    Self-Awareness: 5 items
	
	    Total CWCS: 20 items
	
	Scoring the CWCS consists of adding the participant's ratings on each item in the subscale and dividing that total by the number of items in the subscale to obtain a subscale mean. A total scale mean is obtained by adding the ratings on all of the scale items and dividing that total by 20. No reverse coding or transformations are required.

Reliability	Cronbach's alpha for the scores were as follows:
	
	    Knowledge/Skills: Alpha = .89
	
	    Self-Awareness: Alpha = .78
	
	    Total CWCS: Alpha = .90

(Continued)

(Continued)

Validity	Convergent validity was achieved with the finding of statistically significant positive correlations between the scores of the CWCS full scale and subscales and the various subscale scores of the Feminist Identity Development Scale (FIDS; Bargad & Hyde, 1991) and the Multicultural Counseling and Awareness Scale (MCKAS; Ponterotto, Gretchen, Utsey, Rieger, & Austin, 2002). The correlation between the two CWCS subscales was $r = .56$.
Related References	
Language Versions	English
Contact	Julie Ancis Department of Counseling and Psychological Services Georgia State University P.O. Box 3980 Atlanta, GA 30302–3980 (404) 413–8194 (W) Email: jancis@gsu.edu

4.10 CONSUMER PERSPECTIVE

4.10.1 **Name of the Measure**	Consumer-Based Cultural Competency Inventory C-BCCI
Primary Reference	Cornelius, L. J., Booker, N. C., Arthur, T. E., Reeves, I. G., & Morgan, O. (2004). The validity and reliability testing of a consumer-based cultural competency inventory. *Research on Social Work Practice, 14*(3), 201–209.
Purpose	The C-BCCI purports to measure community mental health consumers' perceptions of their mental health provider's perceived cultural competence.
Description	The C-BCCI contains 52 items. Each item is rated on a 6-point Likert-type scale with the following response options: 1 = Strongly Agree, 2 = Agree, 3 = Neither Agree or Disagree, 4 = Disagree, 5 = Strongly Disagree, 6 = Don't Know or Not Applicable. Initial items were developed by means of a comprehensive literature review, input from a panel of mental health practitioners, consumers, and researchers, and local and national cultural competence experts, along with feedback from multiple panels of consumers, therapists, and administrators. This process resulted in a 61-item scale that attempted to address the following eight concepts: (1) language fluency, (2) indigenous practices, (3) cultural differences, (4) patients' culture, (5) respectful behaviors, (6) patient–provider/organization interactions, (7) consumer involvement, and (8) consumer outreach. A subsequent principal components analysis (with varimax rotation) resulted in a 52-item, four-factor simple structure. However, the authors note that "the majority of the items from five of the eight [conceptual] subscales loaded on one of the four factors" (p. 206). The four factors were not labeled, thus rendering this scale functionally unidimensional.
Samples	The normative sample was 238 adult mental health consumers (ages 21 and older) from across the state of Maryland. Gender was not specified. Self-reported race/ethnicity was as follows: Latino/a American (16.8%), African American (51.7%), White American (14.5%), Native American (1.3%), Asian American and/or Pacific Islander (5.4%), and unknown (10%).
Scoring	Scoring the C-BCCI consists of adding the participant's ratings on all the items to obtain a total score sum. A total of 12 items are reverse coded.
Reliability	Cronbach's alpha for the total scale was .91.
Validity	No validity checks were reported.

(Continued)

(Continued)

Related References	Arthur, T. E., Reeves, I. G., Cornelius, L. J., Booker, N. C., Morgan, O., Brathwaite, J., Tufano, T., Allen, K., & Donato, I. (2005). A consumer assessment tool for cultural competency within Maryland's public mental health system. *Psychiatric Rehabilitation Journal, 28*(3), 243–250.
Language Versions	English, Spanish, Vietnamese
Contact	Llewellyn J. Cornelius University of Maryland School of Social Work 525 W. Redwood St. Baltimore, MD 21201 (410) 706–7610 (W) (410) 706–6046 (Fax) Email: lcorneli@ssw.umaryland.edu

4.11 TEACHER/EDUCATION MEASURES

4.11.1 **Name of the Measure**	Multicultural Awareness-Knowledge-Skills Survey—Teachers Form MAKSS-Form T
Primary Reference	D'Andrea, M., Daniels, J., & Noonan, M. J. (2003). New developments in the assessment of multicultural competence: The Multicultural Awareness-Knowledge-Skills Survey—Teachers Form. In D. B. Pope-Davis, H. L. K. Coleman, W. M. Liu, & R .L. Toporek (Eds.), *Handbook of multicultural competencies in counseling & psychology* (pp. 154–167). Thousand Oaks, CA: Sage.
Purpose	The MAKSS-Form T is a multidimensional instrument that purports to measure multicultural competence of public school teachers and undergraduate and graduate students in teacher education programs.
Description	The MAKSS-Form T contains 41 items. Each item is rated on a 4-point Likert-type scale with the following sets of response anchors: 1 = Very Limited, 4 = Very Aware, 1 = Very Limited, 4 = Very Good, 1 = Strongly Disagree, 4 = Strongly Agree. The MAKSS-Form T is composed of three subscales: (1) Multicultural Awareness, (2) Multicultural Knowledge, (3) Multicultural Skills. The MAKSS-Form T is an extension of previous work with the 60-item Multicultural Awareness-Knowledge-Skills Survey—Counselor Edition (MAKSS-CE; D'Andrea, Daniels, & Heck, 1991). This work resulted in a 60-item (unpublished) preliminary version of the MAKSS-Form T (D'Andrea, Daniels, & Noonan, 1994). Subsequent principal axis factor analysis (with varimax rotation) resulted in a 41-item three-factor simple structure that accounted for 62% of the total variance (D'Andrea, Daniels, & Noonan, 2003).
Samples	The normative sample was 171 (125 women, 46 men) undergraduate and graduate teacher education students. Participant self-reported race/ethnicity was Japanese American (46%), White American (19%), Filipino/a American (7%), Hawaiian American (7%), Chinese American (4%), Latino/a American (1%), biracial (7%), and other ethnic background (9%).
Scoring	The number of items in each of the three subscales is as follows: Multicultural Awareness: 8 items Multicultural Knowledge: 13 items Multicultural Skills: 20 items Total MAKSS Form T: 41 items Scoring the MAKSS-Form T consists of adding the participant's ratings on each item in the subscale to obtain a subscale score and dividing this score by the number of items that make up the subscale to obtain a subscale mean. No reverse coding or transformations are required.

(Continued)

(Continued)

Reliability	Cronbach's alpha for the scores were as follows:
	Multicultural Awareness: Alpha = .73
	Multicultural Knowledge: Alpha = .86
	Multicultural Skills: Alpha = .93
Validity	Subscale intercorrelations were all reported to be moderately positively correlated.
Related References	
Language Versions	English
Contact	Michael D'Andrea
	Department of Counselor Education
	University of Hawaii
	1776 University Ave.
	Honolulu, HI 96822
	(808) 956–4390 (W)
	Email: Michael@hawaii.edu

4.11.2 Name of the Measure	Multicultural Teaching Concerns Survey MTCS
Primary Reference	Marshall, P. L. (1996). Multicultural teaching concerns: New dimensions in the area of teacher concerns research. *The Journal of Educational Research, 89*(6), 371–379.
Purpose	The MTCS is a multidimensional self-report instrument that purports to assess the intensity of teachers' concerns about working with diverse student (K–12) populations.
Description	The MTCS contains 30 items. Each item is rated on a 5-point Likert-type scale with the following two response anchors: 1 = An Extremely Unimportant Concern For Me At This Time, 5 = An Extremely Important Concern For Me At This Time. The MTCS is composed of four subscales: (1) Cross-Cultural Competence, (2) Strategies and Techniques, (3) School Bureaucracy, (4) Familial/Group Knowledge. The MTCS initial item pool was developed from interviewing 206 teachers and student teachers with four open-ended questions concerning working with diverse students. This process generated more than 300 concerns and questions that were refined into 243 questions. Three independent judges further reviewed these items and reduced the total after three complete reviews to 64 items. These 64 items were subjected to a maximum likelihood factor analysis (with varimax rotation) that resulted in a 30-item, four-factor simple structure that accounted for 51% of the common variance.
Samples	The normative sample consisted of 146 (119 women, 27 men) preservice education majors (62%) and experienced teachers (38%). Ages ranged from 19 to 67 years. Self-reported race/ethnicity was White American (86.3%), African American (9.0%), Latino/a American (2.7%), Asian American (0.7%), and other (1.3%).

Scoring	The number of items in each of the four subscales is as follows:
	
	    Cross Cultural Competence: 10 items
	
	    Strategies and Techniques: 11 items
	
	    School Bureaucracy: 4 items
	
	    Familial/Group Knowledge: 5 items
	
	    Total MTCS: 30 items
	
	Scoring the MTCS consists of adding the participant's ratings on each item in the subscale to obtain subscale scores or computing subscale means by dividing each subscale score by the number of subscale items. No reverse coding or transformations are required.

(Continued)

(Continued)

Reliability	No measures of internal consistency were reported.
Validity	Face validity was achieved through independent expert (judge's) feedback during scale construction.
Related References	
Language Versions	English
Contact	Patricia L. Marshall North Carolina State University Department of Curriculum and Instruction College of Education and Psychology 602 H. Poe Hall Box No. 7801 Raleigh, NC 27695–7801 (919) 515–1780 (W)

4.11.3 Name of the Measure	Teacher Multicultural Attitude Survey TMAS
Primary Reference	Ponterotto, J. G., Baluch, S., Grieg, T., & Rivera, L. (1998). Development and initial score validation of the Teacher Multicultural Attitude Survey. *Educational and Psychological Measurement, 58*(6), 1002–1016.
Purpose	The TMAS is a unidimensional self-report measure of teacher (K–12) multicultural awareness and sensitivity.
Description	The TMAS contains 20 items. Each item is rated on a 5-point Likert-type scale with the following two response anchors: 1 = Strongly Disagree, 5 = Strongly Agree. The TMAS is composed of a single 20-item score with no subscale structure. The initial 50-item pool was developed by a diverse research team and informed by group discussion and a careful literature review. This process winnowed the items to a pool of 31 items that was further content validated by a panel of judges and two focus groups of teaching professionals. Subsequently, the 31 items were examined by means of a principal components analysis (with both varimax and oblique rotations) that yielded a 20-item, single-factor simple structure that produced the best fit of the data.
Samples	The initial normative sample consisted of 429 teacher education students (*n* = 220) and teachers (*n* = 201) (307 females and 116 males). Ages ranged from 19 to 73 years (*M* = 35.9, *SD* = 11.4). Self-reported race/ethnicity was White American (68%), Latino/a American (16%), African American (6%), Asian American (1%), and Native American (1%). A second sample of 227 teacher education graduate students (185 women, 35 men) was also used to study reliability and validity of the TMAS scores. Ages ranged from 19 to 52 years (*M* = 28.2, *SD* = 7.5). Self-reported race/ethnicity was White American (56%), Latino/a American (21%), African American (13%), Asian American (3%), and other or did not respond (7%).
Scoring	Scoring the TMAS consists of adding the participant's ratings on each item and dividing the total score by 20 to obtain a scale mean. Seven items are reverse coded.
Reliability	Cronbach's alpha for the scores of the total scale was .86. Three-week test-retest reliability with a separate sample of 16 students was .80.
Validity	Criterion-related validity was evidenced with low to moderate positive correlations with the Multiethnic Identity Measure (MEIM; Phinney, 1992) and the Quick Discrimination Index (QDI; Ponterotto et al., 1995). Further, the scores of the TMAS were not correlated with the Crowne and Marlowe (1960) Social Desirability Scale.

(Continued)

(Continued)

Related References	Cicchelli, T., & Cho, S.-J. (2007). Teacher multicultural attitudes. *Educational and Urban Society, 39*(3), 370–381.
Language Versions	English
Contact	Joseph G. Ponterotto Graduate School of Education Fordham University Division of Psychological and Educational Services 113 West 60th Street, Room 1016D New York, NY 10023 (212) 636–6480 (W) Email: Ponterotto@Fordham.edu

4.11.4 Name of the Measure	Multicultural Competence in Student Affairs—Preliminary 2 MCSA-P2
Primary Reference	Pope, R. L., & Mueller, J. A. (2000). Development and initial validation of the Multicultural Competence in Student Affairs-Preliminary 2 Scale. *Journal of College Student Development, 41*(6), 599–608.
Purpose	The MCSA-P2 is a unidimensional instrument that purports to measure multicultural competence in higher education, particularly among student affairs practitioners.
Description	The MCSA-P2 consists of 34 items. Each item is rated on a 7-point Likert-type scale ranging from 1 = Not At All Accurate to 7 = Very Accurate. The MCSA-P2 is a unidimensional scale due to the unreliability of its factor structure. Initial items (embodied in the MCSA-P1) were developed by a research team to reflect the Sue et al. (1982) tripartite multicultural competencies (awareness, knowledge, and skill). Fifty items resulted from this process and were further scrutinized by means of an independent card sort of the items, a focus group review, and a further review by a panel of multicultural experts, which reduced the item pool to 48. A subsequent principal components analysis (with varimax rotation) produced a one-factor simple structure that accounted for 26% of the total variance, with 34 items.
Samples	The normative sample consisted of 253 (156 women, 97 men) student affairs practitioners, faculty, and graduate students. About 84% of the participants were between 20 to 45 years old. Self-reported participant race/ethnicity was White American (63%), African American (23%), Latino/a American (6%), Asian American (4%), biracial (2%), and other (2%). Sample occupational status was as follows: assistant/associate directors/deans (36%), graduate students (23%), entry-level practitioners (21%), deans and vice presidents (14%), faculty (4%), and no response (2%).
Scoring	Scoring the MCSA-P2 consists of adding the participant's ratings on all of the scale items and dividing the scale total by 34 to obtain a composite scale mean. No reverse coding or transformations are required.
Reliability	Cronbach's alpha for the scores of the total scale was .91.
Validity	Criterion-related validity was demonstrated by the finding that "experts" had statistically significantly higher cultural competence scores ($M = 6.44$, $SD = .27$) as compared to graduate students ($M = 5.35$, $SD = .68$). In a second study, with an independent sample ($N = 190$), the MCSA-P2 total score was correlated with the total score of the Social Desirability Scale (SDS; Crowne & Marlowe, 1960), yielding a nonsignificant correlation.
Related References	King, P. M., & Howard-Hamilton, P. (2003). Assessment of multicultural competence. *NASPA Journal, 40*(2), 119–133.
Language Versions	English
Contact	Raechele L. Pope Department of Educational Leadership and Policy 482 Baldy Hall The University at Buffalo, SUNY Buffalo, NY 14260–1000 (716) 645–1098 (W) (716) 645–2481 (Fax) Email: rlpope@buffalo.edu

4.11.5 Name of the Measure	Multicultural School Psychology Counseling Competency Scale MSPCCS
Primary Reference	Rogers, M. R., & Ponterotto, J. G. (1997). Development of the Multicultural School Psychology Counseling Competency Scale. *Psychology in the Schools, 34(3)*, 211–217.
Purpose	The MSPCCS is a unidimensional scale that purports to measure trainers' perceptions of the multicultural school psychology counseling competencies of graduate student trainees.
Description	The MSPCCS contains 11 items. Each item is rated on a 4-point Likert-type scale with the following two response anchors: 1 = Not At All, 4 = Very Much. The MSPCSS has a unidimensional structure reflected by a mean total score. The 11 items of the MSPCSS were developed by the authors to reflect an operationalized version of the Sue et al. (1982) cross-cultural counseling competencies. The items were also reviewed by a panel of cultural experts. Subsequently, a principal components analysis suggested an 11-item, single-factor simple structure that accounted for 46.9% of the common variance.
Samples	The normative sample consisted of 121 directors of doctoral and nondoctoral school psychology training programs. A 57% response rate was achieved.
Scoring	Scoring the MSPCCS consists of adding the participant's ratings on each item in the scale to obtain a total score and dividing that score by 11 to obtain a scale mean. No reverse coding or transformations are required.
Reliability	Cronbach's alpha for the scores of the total scale was .88.
Validity	
Related References	Lopez, E. C., & Rogers, M. R. (2007). Multicultural competencies and training in school psychology: Issues, approaches, and future directions. In G. B. Esquivel, E. C. Lopez, & S. Nahari (Eds.), *Multicultural handbook of school psychology: An interdisciplinary perspective* (pp. 47–68). New York: Routledge.
Language Versions	English
Contact	Margaret Rogers Department of Psychology University of Rhode Island Chafee Building Kingston, RI 02881–0808 (401) 874–5082 (W) Email: mrogers@uri.edu

4.11.6 Name of the Measure	Culturally Responsive Teaching Outcome Expectancy Scale CRTOE
Primary Reference	Siwatu, K. O. (2007). Pre-service teachers' culturally responsive teaching self-efficacy and outcome expectancy beliefs. *Teaching and Teacher Education, 23*, 1086–1101.
Purpose	The CRTOE is a unidimensional measure that purports to assess teachers' beliefs that engaging in culturally responsive teaching practices will have beneficial effects on student outcomes.
Description	The CRTOE contains 26 items. Each item is rated on a 100-point Likert-type scale with the following two response anchors: 0 = No Confidence At All, 100 = Completely Confident. The CRTOE is a unidimensional instrument. The initial item development for the CRTOE (and its companion scale, the Culturally Responsive Teaching Self-Efficacy Scale, CRTSE) was based on a literature review, and particularly the work of Bandura (1977a).
Samples	The normative sample consisted of 275 preservice teachers enrolled in two Midwestern U.S. teacher education programs (200 women, 75 men). Self-reported race/ethnicity was White American (92.7%) and non-White (i.e., Mexican American, Asian American, African American) (7.3%). Sample mean age was 21.9 years (*SD* = 4.9).
Scoring	Scoring the CRTOE consists of adding the participant's ratings on each item in the scale to obtain a total scale score. No reverse coding or transformations are required.
Reliability	Cronbach's alpha for the total scale was .96.
Validity	A positive correlation was found between the scores of the CRTOE and the companion CRTSE scale.
Related References	
Language Versions	English
Contact	Kamau Oginga Siwatu Department of Educational Psychology and Leadership College of Education Texas Tech University Box 41071 Lubbock, TX 79409-1071 (806) 742–1998, 431 (W) (806) 742–2179 (Fax) Email: siwatu@ttu.edu

4.12 MULTICULTURAL PERSONALITY

4.12.1 Name of the Measure	Multicultural Personality Questionnaire MPQ
Primary References	Van der Zee, K. I., & Van Oudenhoven, J. P. (2000). The Multicultural Personality Questionnaire: A multidimensional instrument of multicultural effectiveness. *European Journal of Personality, 14,* 291–309. Van der Zee, K. I., & Van Oudenhoven, J. P. (2001). The Multicultural Personality Questionnaire: Reliability and validity of self- and other ratings of multicultural effectiveness. *Journal of Research in Personality, 35,* 278–288. Van der Zee, K. I., Zaal, J. N., & Piekstra, J. (2003). Validation of the Multicultural Personality Questionnaire in the context of personnel selection. *European Journal of Personality, 17,* S77–S100.
Purpose	The MPQ is a multidimensional instrument that purports to measure the dimensions that underlie multicultural effectiveness, particularly of expatriate populations.
Description	The MPQ contains 91 items. Each item is rated on a 5-point Likert-type scale with the following response options: 1 = Totally Not Applicable, 2 = Hardly Applicable, 3 = Moderately Applicable, 4 = Largely Applicable, 5 = Completely Applicable. The MPQ is composed of five subscales: (1) Cultural Empathy, (2) Open-mindedness, (3) Emotional Stability, (4) Social Initiative, (5) Flexibility. The initial item pool (of 138 items) for the MPQ was apparently derived from a literature review with the goal of measuring multicultural effectiveness. Early factor analytic versions of the MPQ yielded a 78-item, four-factor (Van der Zee & Oudenhoven, 2000) and five-factor versions (Van der Zee & Oudenhoven, 2001). Subsequent exploratory and confirmatory factor analyses, utilizing the original item pool, produced a 91-item, five-factor simple structure (Leone, Van der Zee, Oudenhoven, Perugini, Ercolani, 2005; Van der Zee & Brinkmann, 2004; Van der Zee, Zaal, & Piekstra, 2003).
Samples	The validation sample (Van der Zee et al., 2003) of the MPQ consisted of 264 job applicants from the Netherlands and Belgium (69 women, 195 men). Ages ranged from 20 to 56 years ($M = 35.4$, $SD = 7.9$).

Scoring	The number of items in each of the five subscales is as follows:
	
	    Cultural Empathy: 18 items
	    Open-Mindedness: 18 items
	    Social Initiative: 17 items
	    Emotional Stability: 20 items
	    Flexibility: 18 items
	    Total MPQ: 91 items
	
	Scoring the MPQ consists of adding the participant's ratings on each item in the subscale to obtain subscale scores and then dividing the score by the number of items within the subscale to obtain a subscale mean. Thirty-two items need to be recoded.

Reliability	Cronbach's alphas for the five MPQ subscales were as follows:
	Cultural Empathy: Alpha = .87
	Open-Mindedness: Alpha = .83
	Social Initiative: Alpha = .86
	Emotional Stability: Alpha = .83
	Flexibility: Alpha = .72
Validity	Construct validity was established (Van der Zee et al., 2003) by yielding statistically significant positive correlations between the scores of the MPQ Social Initiative and Emotional Stability subscales and Big Five (Digman, 1990) composite scores for Extraversion and Emotional Stability.
Related References	Leong, C.-H. (2007). Predictive validity of the Multicultural Personality Questionnaire: A longitudinal study on the socio-psychological adaptation of Asian undergraduates who took part in a study-abroad program. *International Journal of Intercultural Relations, 31,* 545–559.
	Ponterotto, J. G. (2010). Multicultural personality: An evolving theory of optimal functioning in culturally heterogeneous societies. *The Counseling Psychologist, 38*(5), 714–758.
	Ponterotto, J. G., Costa-Wooford, C. I., Brobst, K., Spelliscy, D., Mendelsohn-Kacanski, J., & Scheinholtz, J. (2007). Multicultural personality dispositions and psychological well-being. *Journal of Social Psychology, 147,* 119–135.
Language Versions	English, Dutch
Contact	Karen I. van Oudenhoven-van der Zee Department of Social and Organizational Psychology University of Groningen Grote Kruisstraat 2/1 9721 TS Groningen, The Netherlands Email: K.I.van.Oudenhoven-van.der.Zee@ppsw.rug.nl

5

Racial Identity and Ethnic Identity Measures

5.1 DEFINITIONS

Even though they are not synonymous, the terms *racial identity* and *ethnic identity* have often been used interchangeably in the literature (Helms, 2007; Trimble, 2007; Trimble, Helms, & Root, 2002). Whereas ethnic identity addresses sense of affiliation with one's ethnic group, racial identity refers to how racial minorities develop their self-concept in the context of racial oppression. Though distinct, racial identity development and ethnic identity development may be viewed as organizing constructs that share a common meaning. Both constructs (1) describe a sense of belonging to a social group through some perceived or attributed core of shared characteristics, (2) are associated with positive or negative attitudes toward one's social group as well as that of out-groups, and (3) vary in importance across time and context (Helms & Talleyrand, 1997; Phinney & Ong, 2007; Sellers, Smith, Shelton, Rowley, & Chavous, 1998; Trimble et al., 2002). In this chapter, we summarize measures of racial identity and ethnic identity as well as related constructs that address some dimension of race- or ethnicity-based social identity.

5.2 THEORETICAL FOUNDATIONS OF RACIAL IDENTITY AND ETHNIC IDENTITY MODELS

Erikson's (1968) developmental theory of ego identity and Tajfel's (1981) social identity theory have played a salient role in shaping the research, model building, theory development, and measurement strategies in the study of racial identity and ethnic identity. Erikson's (1968) theory presents identity formation as a process developed and achieved over time, particularly during adolescence and young adulthood, through reflection, exploration, and an eventual commitment to various domains of the broader self-concept, including racial and ethnic group membership. According to Tajfel (1981) and Tajfel and Turner (1986), ethnic identity is an aspect of social identity and the broader self-concept derived from one's knowledge of membership in a social group accompanied by values and emotions attached to that membership that foster and reinforce a sense of belonging. These theoretical perspectives imply the multidimensional nature of the constructs of racial identity and ethnic identity as well as the processes by which such identity is acquired or achieved.

Racial identity and ethnic identity development models have generally used some blended forms of Erikson's (1968) developmental theory of identity characterized by successive progression of stages or phases and Tajfel's (1981) social identity theory characterized by the dynamic interplay of intergroup relations associated with feeling toward one's own group. According to Erikson (1968), identity is at the core of the self, formed by the context of the communal culture that engenders a sense of affiliation and belonging. By extension, racial identity and ethnic identity are constructed or achieved through the context provided by the biological background and the sociopolitical circumstances surrounding the individual (Trimble et al., 2002). Moreover, racial identity and ethnic identity involve a level of commitment and attachment to a group (Marcia, 1980) and are dynamic constructs that change over time in response to contextual factors (Ethier & Deaux, 1994; Liebkind, 2006; Phinney, 2003; Trimble et al., 2002; Tsai, Ying, & Lee, 2000; Yip, 2005).

According to Liebkind (2006), contextual factors related to racial identity and ethnic identity include the following: (1) actual settings such as schools, workplaces, and neighborhoods; (2) historical and cultural circumstances; and (3) activities and tasks in which people engage. Some contexts may encourage and promote bicultural identity such as when adaptation to and interaction with a majority culture is possible and rewarding. In settings and societies where pluralism is encouraged and diversity is celebrated, racial identity and ethnic identity may be fostered and more easily achieved and manifested (Berry, 1997; Phinney, Horenczyk, Liebkind, & Vedder, 2001).

Social, economic, and political contexts, as well as the acculturative processes that accompany the relationships and interactions between a dominant culture and the cultures of minority ethnic and immigrant groups, are factors that impact the formation of racial identity and ethnic identity (Tajfel & Turner, 1986; White & Burke, 1987; Yaralian, Der-Karabetian, & Martinez, 2009; Yeh & Huang, 1996). The acculturation process, which entails contact at the boundaries of other ethnic and cultural groups, transforms the meaning and significance of the elements of one's own culture and impacts the sense of shared values and attitudes toward the cultural or racial group (Liebkind, 1992).

The terms *cultural identity* (Cortes, Rogler, & Malgady, 1994; Dana, 1998; Mezzich, Ruiperez, Yoon, Liu, & Zapata-Vega, 2009; Schwartz, Montgomery, & Briones, 2006), *ethnic consciousness* (Garcia, 1982), *Black self-consciousness* (Baldwin & Bell, 1985), *multicultural personality* (Ponterotto, Costa, & Werner-Lin, 2002), *collective identity* (Ashmore, Deaux, & McLaughlin-Volpe, 2004), and *self-construal* (Barry, Elliott, & Evans, 2000; Markus & Kitayama, 1991) also reflect the field's interest in identity development. While these concepts provide continuing developments in the study of racial identity and ethnic identity, their in-depth discussion is beyond the scope of this chapter. However, a brief overview of the theoretical and empirical models of racial identity and ethnic identity is provided in the following sections.

5.3 OVERVIEW OF RACIAL IDENTITY AND ETHNIC IDENTITY DEVELOPMENT MODELS

The Nigrescence theory of African American identity development (Cross, 1971) is the earliest model of racial identity development. This model served as the basis for subsequent racial or cultural identity models (e.g., Atkinson, Morten, & Sue, 1989; Cross & Vandiver, 2001; Helms, 1995; Horse, 2001; Kim, 2001; Parham, 1989). These theories are anchored in the idea that the identity development of minority groups occurs in the context of oppression and describes attitudes ranging from negative own-group appraisal to acceptance and positive valuing of one's racial group as well as of other groups. The development of White racial identity models (Helms, 1990a; McDermott & Samson, 2005), on the other hand, is based on the assumption that ego functioning develops in the context of power and privilege. Although some models address the development of increasingly more complex attitudes regarding race, scholars also have presented models that address centrality, salience, connectedness, or relationship (e.g., Baldwin, 1984; Ferdman & Gallegos, 2001; Rowe, Bennett, & Atkinson, 1994; Sellers, Shelton, Cooke, Chavous, Rowley, & Smith, 1998).

While studies of racial identity typically focus on the development of identity of African Americans (e.g., Helms, 1990a, 1996, 2007; Mandara, Gaylord-Harden, Richards, & Ragsdale, 2009; Seaton, 2009), scholars, recognizing that individuals from other ethnic and racial groups also experience racism, also have studied the construct of racial identity development on the psychological adjustment of Asian American (e.g., Alvarez & Helms, 2001; Alvarez, Juang, & Liang, 2006; Chen, LePhuoc, Guzmán, Rude, & Dodd, 2006; Iwamoto & Liu, 2010; Perry, Vance, & Helms, 2009) and Latino/a American groups (e.g., Altschul, Oyserman, & Bybee, 2008; Carter, Yeh, & Mazzula, 2008). Concomitant with this focus on racial identity, researchers also have been interested in the ethnic identity development of adolescents and adults.

Whereas models of racial identity address the development of identity in the context of racism and oppression (Helms, 2007), ethnic identity development frameworks address held knowledge of as well as emotional connection an individual attaches to his or her ethnic group of origin (Phinney, 2003) that is influenced by time, context, and behavior (Phinney & Ong, 2007). Given how the terms *race* and *ethnicity* are often used interchangeably or together (i.e., *race/ethnicity*) in the literature and general parlance, it is understandable that researchers and practitioners would assume that racial identity and ethnic identity are the same. However, measurement of these two constructs should be done with care and thought (Helms, 2007). Should a researcher or practitioner be interested in studying or developing a conceptualization of how a client's attitudes or psychological functioning have been impacted by racial dynamics, a measure of racial identity should be appropriate. On the other hand, a measure of ethnic identity would be more appropriate should the focus of research or treatment be related to learning more about a person's search, commitment, or affiliation to her or his ethnic group.

Ethnic identity also has been used interchangeably with acculturation. Although these two constructs are closely related (Laroche, Kim, & Tomiuk, 1998; Phinney, 1990; Schwartz et al., 2006), ethnic identity development may be conceptualized as addressing group affiliation, whereas acculturation (see Chapter 6) deals with the processes, behavioral practices, and values of an individual from a group (Cheryan & Tsai, 2007; Kim & Abreu, 2001). Thus, whereas measures of ethnic identity can aid in developing an understanding of an individual's emotional attachment to culture, acculturation instruments address the behaviors and values of that individual.

While much of the theoretical and empirical work has focused on articulating racial identity and ethnic identity among particular groups, there also have been efforts to address bicultural or multiple identities primarily involving identification with a minority ethnic group on the one hand and a dominant majority new culture on the other (Kazarian & Boyadjian, 2008; Phinney, 1992; Phinney & Ong, 2007). Authors of multigroup measures have viewed ethnic identity as a general phenomenon with features common across groups, but they have not addressed identity issues among individuals of mixed race or ethnicity.

Even though mixed-race or multiracial populations have received attention in the social science literature (e.g., Binning, Unzueta, Huo, & Molina, 2009; Bracey, Bamaca, & Umana-Taylor, 2004; Renn, 2004; Roccas & Brewer, 2002; Rockquemore & Brunsma, 2008; Shih & Sanchez, 2005, 2009), the study of racial identity and ethnic identity among individuals who are of mixed race and mixed ethnicity lacks valid measures (Choi-Misailidis, 2009). One recent attempt to develop a measure of multiracial identity is by Cheng and Lee (2009), who used the bicultural identity integration construct by Benet-Martinez and Haritatos (2005) as the basis for their measure, the Multiracial Identity Integration Scale (MII Scale). The bicultural identity integration construct comprises two distinct dimensions of distance and conflict. *Distance* refers to the degree to which the two identities are perceived and experienced as separate, and *conflict* refers to the perception of the norms and values reflected in the two identities as being contradictory.

5.4 SUMMARY

Theoretical models of racial identity and ethnic identity have evolved as the complexity and richness of the constructs have been revealed by research. The theoretical and empirical challenges in the operationalization and measurement of racial identity and ethnic identity have been described elsewhere (see Ponterotto, Casas, Suzuki, & Alexander, 2009; Ponterotto & Mallinckrodt, 2007; Ponterotto & Park-Taylor, 2007). Taken together, the existing models seem to suggest that the construct of racial identity and ethnic identity is multidimensional, has unique elements within groups, has common elements across groups, and is experienced as a dynamic process by individuals who might oscillate between various states, stages, and phases. As our understanding of each construct continues to be shaped by research and practice, certain issues that need clarity remain, such as the relationship among racial identity, ethnic identity, and acculturation.

5.5 MEASURES

Altogether 26 measures of racial identity and ethnic identity are presented in this chapter that fall into two major categories: (1) measures developed for specific racial and ethnic groups and (2) measures developed for use with multiple groups or across groups. Several measures of racial identity and ethnic identity were excluded primarily because of our inclusion criteria that required the use of data reduction methods, like factor analysis, in their developmental process, or our inability to find subsequent studies published in peer-reviewed journals applying such analyses.

5.6 AFRICAN AMERICAN RACIAL IDENTITY OR ETHNIC IDENTITY MEASURES

The following six African American racial identity measures are presented: African Self-Consciousness Scale (ASC; Baldwin & Bell, 1985), Multidimensional Inventory of Black Identity (MIBI; Sellers et al., 1997), Cross Racial Identity Scale (CRIS; Cross & Vandiver, 2001), Multidimensional Inventory of Black Identity—Teen (MIBI-T; Scottham, Sellers, & Nguyen, 2008), Racial Identity Attitude Scale (RAIS; Helms & Parham, 1996), and Racial Identity Scale for Low-Income African Americans (RISL; Resnicow & Ross-Gaddy, 1997).

5.7 LATINO/A AMERICAN ETHNIC IDENTITY MEASURES

The following four Latino/a American ethnic identity scales are presented: Cuban Behavioral Identity Questionnaire (CBIQ; Garcia & Lega, 1979), Ethnic Consciousness Among Mexican-Origin Populations (ECAMOP; Garcia, 1982), Multidimensional Measure of Cultural Identity Scale for Latinos (MMCISL; Felix-Ortiz, Newcomb, & Myers, 1994), and Strength of Ethnic Identity (SEI; Cislo, 2008).

5.8 ASIAN AMERICAN ETHNIC IDENTITY MEASURES

The following three Asian American ethnic identity scales are presented: East Asian Ethnic Identity Scale (EAEIS; Barry, 2002), Ethnocultural Identity Behavior Index (EIBI; Yamada, Marsella, & Hamada, 1998), and Internal-External Identity Measure (Int-Ext Id; Kwan, 2000).

5.9 WHITE AMERICAN RACIAL IDENTITY OR RACIAL CONSCIOUSNESS MEASURES

The following three White racial identity measures are presented: Oklahoma Racial Attitudes Scale—Preliminary (ORAS-P; Choney & Behrens, 1996), White Racial Consciousness Development Scale—Revised (WRCDS-R; Lee, Puig, Pasquarella-Denny, Rai, Dallape, & Parker, 2007), and White Racial Attitude Scale (WRAIS; Helms & Carter, 1990).

5.10 ITALIAN, JEWISH AMERICAN, ARAB, NATIVE AMERICAN, AND MULTIRACIAL IDENTITY MEASURES

The following five ethnic identity measures are presented for other groups, including Native American, Arab, Italian, and Jewish groups: Measure of Enculturation for Native American Youth (MENAY; Zimmerman, Ramirez-Valles, Washienko, Walter, & Dyer, 1996), Italian Canadian Ethnic Identity (ICEI; Laroche et al., 1998), Jewish-American Identity Scale (JAIS; Zak, 1973), Male Arabic Ethnic Identity measure (MAEIM; Barry, Elliott, & Evans, 2000), and Multiracial Identity Integration Scale (MII Scale; Cheng & Lee, 2009).

5.11 MULTIGROUP MEASURES OF ETHNIC IDENTITY

The following five measures of ethnic identity across racial and ethnic groups are presented: Ethnic Group Membership Questionnaire (EGMQ; Contrada et al., 2001), Ethnic Identity Scale (EIS; Umana-Taylor, Yazedjian, & Bamaca-Gomez, 2004), Collective Self-Esteem Scale (CSES; Luhtanen & Crocker, 1992), Self-Identity Inventory (SII; Sevig, Highlen, & Adams, 2000), and Multigroup Ethnic Identity Measure—Revised (MEIM-R; Phinney & Ong, 2007).

5.12 FUTURE RESEARCH

The study of the constructs of racial identity and ethnic identity has made significant strides in the last 40 years. The theory-building efforts have been group specific (Baldwin, 1981; Cross & Fhagen-Smith, 1996; Helms, 1995; Marcia, 1980; Padilla, 1980; Sabnani, Ponterotto, & Borodovsky, 1991), as well as across groups (Atkinson et al., 1989; Erikson, 1968; Phinney, 1990; Phinney & Ong, 2007; Tajfel, 1980). These advances have accompanied the development and refinement of measures that, in turn, has facilitated the exploration of the relationship of racial identity and ethnic identity to other constructs such as mental health, self-esteem, and acculturation. Because of the developmental nature of the construct, the populations that have been studied have involved mostly adolescents and young adults, especially in the development of measures.

Many questions and issues related to racial identity and ethnic identity remain to be explored (see Ponterotto & Park-Taylor, 2007). To continue to deepen the understanding of this rich and complex construct, we would like to affirm several areas of continuing research:

1. Studies establishing the evidence for validity and internal consistency across age groups of specific measures are needed.

2. Given how context shapes and influences the salience of a racial or ethnic identity as well as the need for affiliation from cultural group members, it seems necessary to establish the degree to which identity is situational or stable.

3. Measures and studies of racial identity and ethnic identity should include some assessment of the influence of both intergroup strain and intragroup pressure on social identity.

4. Researchers should continue to establish a theoretical rationale for expected relationships when establishing evidence for construct validity of racial identity and ethnic identity measures.

5. Measures of social desirability should be used to help establish evidence for the validity of racial identity and ethnic identity measures.

6. Researchers are encouraged to study how the development of bicultural identity involving monoracial individuals differs from the development of identity among individuals of mixed race or ethnic backgrounds (Choi-Misailidis, 2009). Given the increasing number of individuals with multiracial backgrounds and lack of utility of monoracial identity measures, it would be prudent to develop measures that can assess the racial identification of multiracial Americans.

7. We encourage researchers to develop measures that facilitate the examination of how racial identity or ethnic identity intersects with other aspects of an individual's social identity (e.g., disability, gender, sexual orientation).

5.13 AFRICAN AMERICAN RACIAL IDENTITY AND ETHNIC IDENTITY MEASURES

5.13.1 **Name of the Measure**	African Self-Consciousness Scale ASC
Primary Reference	Baldwin, J. A., & Bell, Y. R. (1985). The African Self-Consciousness Scale: An Africentric personality questionnaire. *The Western Journal of Black Studies, 9,* 61–68.
Purpose	The ASC Scale measures the self-consciousness of African Americans in terms of attitudes, beliefs, values, and interests regarding African American culture, history, self-knowledge, and philosophical positions.
Description	The ASC Scale is based on the Afrocentric theory of the interrelatedness of all things and is considered a unidimensional construct. The original Scale has 42 items. Each item is rated on an 8-point Likert-type scale with the anchors ranging from 1–2 = Strongly Disagree to 7–8 = Strongly Agree. A later study by Stokes, Murray, Peacock, and Kaiser (1994) factor analyzed the scale to retain 32 items where an oblique rotation was most satisfactory and identified the following four subscales: (1) Personal Identification With the Group; (2) Self-Reinforcement Against Racism; (3) Racial and Cultural Awareness; and (4) Value for African Culture.
Samples	The original scale was developed using exclusively samples of African American students in Southern colleges (Baldwin & Bell, 1985). Stokes et al. (1994) used a noncollege sample of 141 African Americans (82 women and 65 men) from southern California cities. The scale has also been used with community-based adults and college students from other parts of the United States.
Scoring	The subscales identified by Stokes et al. (1994) were formed by unit weighting of items with factor structure coefficients greater than .30. Odd-numbered items are negatively worded and should be reverse coded. Baldwin and Bell (1985) recommend the use of the ASC Scale total score.
Reliability	The Cronbach's alpha for the subscale scores reported by Stokes et al. (1994) were as follows: 　Personal Identification With the Group: Alpha = .77 　Self-Reinforcement Against Racism: Alpha = .62 　Racial and Cultural Awareness: Alpha = .62 　Value for African Culture: Alpha = .62 　Total ASC: Alpha = .78 Later studies by Pierre and Mahalik (2005) and Simmons, Worrell, and Berry (2008) reported Cronbach's alphas ranging .70–.80 for Personal Identification with the Group and .00–.60 for the other factors. Six-week test-retest reliability for the total score with a sample of African American college students was .90.

Validity	The structural or construct validity of the ASC Scale is not clear. Factor analytic studies with college and noncollege samples have yielded seven factors (Myers & Thompson, 1994), four factors (Stokes et al., 1994) and two factors (Simmons et al., 2008).
	There is evidence of the convergent validity of the total ASC Scale and the subscale of Personal Identification With the Group.
Related References	Pierre, M. R., & Mahalik, J. R. (2005). Examining African self-consciousness and Black racial identities as predictors of Black men's psychological well-being. *Cultural Diversity and Ethnic Minority Psychology, 11,* 28–40.
	Simmons, C., Worrell, F. C., & Berry, J. M. (2008). Psychometric properties of scores on three Black racial identity scales. *Assessment, 15,* 259–276.
Language Versions	English
Contact	Joseph A. Baldwin Department of Psychology Florida Agricultural and Mechanical University 501 Orr Drive, Room 302 C Gore Education Complex (GEC) Tallahassee, FL 32307 Tel: (805) 599–3014 Email: famuspsychology@famus.edu

5.13.2 Name of the Measure	Multidimensional Inventory of Black Identity MIBI
Primary Reference	Sellers, R. M., Rowley, S. A., Chavous, T. M., Shelton, J. N., & Smith, M. A. (1997). Multidimensional Inventory of Black Identity: A preliminary investigation of reliability and construct validity. *Journal of Personality and Social Psychology, 73*, 805–815.
Purpose	The purpose of MIBI is to measure African American racial identity as a multidimensional construct.
Description	The MIBI was based on the Multidimensional Model of Racial Identity (MMRI) theory described by Sellers, Smith, Shelton, Rowley, and Chavous (1998). The theory assumes a hierarchically ordered identity focused on beliefs regarding the significance of race and the qualitative meaning of belonging to the African American racial group. The MIBI is a 51-item scale with six subscales: (1) Centrality; (2) Private Regard; (3) Assimilation; (4) Humanist; (5) Minority; and (6) Nationalist. Items are rated on a 7-point Likert-type scale ranging from 1 = Strongly Disagree to 7 = Strongly Agree. An original list of 71 items was developed to cover three dimensions and seven subscales. The factor structure for each of the three dimensions was investigated separately using maximum extraction and promax rotation for a confirmatory factor analysis. The 71 items were reduced to 51. All items with factor structure coefficients below .30 were eliminated. Later studies have revised the factor structure and the number of items in the MIBI (See Related References section below).
Sample	The sample was composed of 474 (68% female, 32% male) African American students from the mid-Atlantic region enrolled in introductory psychology courses in one predominantly Black ($n = 185$) and one predominantly White university ($n = 289$).

Scoring	The three negatively keyed items are reversed; then item ratings in each subscale are added and then divided by the number of items in the subscale to produce subscale means.
	
	The number of items in the six subscales is as follows:
	
	    Centrality: 8 items
	    Private Regard: 7 items
	    Assimilation: 9 items
	    Humanist: 9 items
	    Minority: 9 items
	    Nationalist: 9 items
	    Total MIBI: 51 items

Reliability	The Cronbach's alpha for the six subscale scores are as follows: Centrality: Alpha = .77 Private Regard: Alpha = .60 Assimilation: Alpha = .73 Humanist: Alpha = .70 Minority: Alpha = .76 Nationalist: Alpha = .79
Validity	Predictive validity was established by examining the relationship of the MIBI subscales to race-related behaviors. Students who had an African American best friend, compared to those who did not, had higher scores on the Centrality and the Nationalist subscales and lower scores on the Assimilation, Humanist, and Minority subscales. There was no difference on the Private Regard subscales. Moreover, students who had taken at least one Black studies course scored higher on the Centrality and Nationalist subscales. Also, MIBI scales were correlated with scores on the Interracial Contact Scale (Wegner & Shelton, 1995). Greater contact with other African Americans was positively correlated with Centrality, Nationalist, and Private Regard. Greater contact with Whites was correlated negatively with Centrality and Nationalist subscales.
Related References	Cokley, K. O., & Helm, K. (2001). Testing the construct validity of scores on the Multidimensional Inventory of Black Identity. *Measurement and Evaluation in Counseling and Development, 34,* 80–95. Shelton, J. N., & Sellers, R. M. (2000). Situational stability and variability in African American racial identity. *Journal of Black Psychology, 26,* 27–50. Simmons, C., Worrell, F. C., & Berry, J. M. (2008). Psychometric properties of scores on three black racial identity scales. *Assessment, 15,* 259–276.
Language Versions	English
Contact	Robert M. Sellers Department of Psychology College of Literature, Science and the Arts University of Michigan Ann Arbor, MI 48109–1109 Tel.: (734) 763–0045 Email: rsellers@umich.edu http://www.lsa.umich.edu/psych/faculty-bio/?uniquename=rsellers

5.13.3 Name of the Measure	Cross Racial Identity Scale CRIS
Primary Reference	Cross, W. E., Jr., & Vandiver, B. J. (2001). Nigrescence theory and measurement: Introducing the Cross Racial Identity Scale (CRIS). In J. G. Ponterotto, J. M. Casas, L. A. Suzuki, & C. M. Alexander (Eds.), *Handbook of multicultural counseling* (2nd ed.), pp. 371–393. Thousand Oaks, CA: Sage. Worrell, F. C., Cross, W. E., Jr., & Vandiver, B. J. (2001). Nigrescence Theory: Current status and challenges of the future. *Journal of Multicultural Counseling and Development, 29,* 201–210.
Purpose	The purpose of the CRIS is to measure six of the nine Nigrescence identity attitudes proposed by the expanded Nigrescence model (Cross & Vandiver, 2001): Assimilation, Miseducation, Self-Hatred, Anti-White, Afrocenricity, and Multiculturalist Inclusive.
Description	The CRIS is composed of six subscales, five items in each subscale, with 10 unscored filler items, rated on a 7-point Likert-type scale, ranging from 1 = Strongly Disagree to 7 = Strongly Agree. The theoretical base of the CRIS is the Nigrescence theory first proposed by Cross (1971), later revised by Cross (1991, 1995), and then expanded by Cross and Vandiver (2001) and Worrell, Cross, and Vandiver (2001). The subscales assume different stages in identity development. The CRIS was developed in six phases over a 5-year period, resulting in six subscales: (1) Pre-encounter Assimilation, (2) Pre-encounter Miseducation, (3) Pre-encounter Self-Hatred, (4) Immersion-Emersion Anti-White, (5) Internalization Afrocentric, and (6) Internalization Multiculturalist Inclusive. A series of exploratory and confirmatory factor analyses across the six phases of scale development have affirmed the six-factor structure of the CRIS with college students (Cross & Vandiver, 2001), which was also supported later by Simmons, Worrell, and Berry (2008). The six-factor structure has also been supported with emerging adults (Vandiver, Cross, Worrell, & Fhagen-Smith, 2002), adults (Worrell, Vandiver, Cross, & Fhagen-Smith, 2004), and school-aged adolescents (Gardner-Kitt & Worrell, 2007).
Sample	During its development, African American college student samples were used from two predominantly White universities, one in the mid-Atlantic area and the other in the New England area. Participants' ages ranged from 17 to 59 with a mean age of 21 (*SD* = 3.66) across samples. There were typically twice as many women as men, and in general the demographics of the samples were comparable. The CRIS has been used with African American women and men, adolescents, and college students from historically Black and predominantly White schools, as well as with adults from different parts of the country.
Scoring	Subscale scores are obtained by adding the scores on the five items and dividing by five. The use of standard scores with a mean of 10 and a standard deviation of 3 is suggested by the authors. However, the use of mean subscale scores is more

	The number of items in each subscale is as follows:
	Pre-encounter Assimilation: 5 items
	Pre-encounter Miseducation: 5 items
	Pre-encounter Self-Hatred: 5 items
	Immersion-Emersion Anti-White: 5 items
	Internalization Afrocentric: 5 items
	Internalization Multiculturalist Inclusive: 5 items
	Total CRIS: 40 items
Reliability	Cronbach's alpha for the six subscale scores ranges from .59 to .90 across the six phases of the development. At phase six, all the Cronbach's alphas were above .80 except for Pre-encounter Miseducation, which had an alpha of .78. In an adult population, the alphas have ranged from .70 to .85 (Worrell et al., 2004)
Validity	Convergent validity was established by moderate correlations between the CRIS subscales and the subscales of the Multidimensional Inventory of Black Identity (MIBI) (Vandiver et al., 2002).
	Discriminant validity was established by showing lack of significant correlations of the CRIS subscales with the Marlowe-Crowne Social Desirability Scale (Crowne & Marlowe, 1960) and the Big Five personality factors (Vandiver et al., 2002).
Related References	Simmons, C., Worrell, F. C., & Berry, J. M. (2008). Psychometric properties of scores on three Black racial identity scales. *Assessment, 15,* 259–276.
	Vandiver, B. J., Cross, W. E., Jr., Worrell, F. C., & Fhagen-Smith, P. E. (2002). Validating the Cross Racial Identity Scale. *Journal of Counseling Psychology, 49,* 71–85.
	Vandiver, B. J., Fhagen-Smith, P. E., Cokley, K. O., Cross, W. E., Jr., & Worrell, F. C. (2001). Cross Nigrescence model: From theory to scale to theory. *Journal of Multicultural Counseling and Development, 29,* 174–200.
	Worrell, F. C., Vandiver, B. J., Cross, W. E., Jr., & Fhagen-Smith, P. E. (2004). Reliability and structural validity of Cross Racial Identity Scale scores in a sample of African American adults. *Journal of Black Psychology, 30,* 489–505.
Language Versions	English
Contact	Beverly J. Vandiver Counseling Psychology Program The Pennsylvania State University 327 CEDAR Building University Park, PA 16802 Email: bjv3@psu.edu

5.13.4 Name of the Measure	Multidimensional Inventory of Black Identity—Teen MIBI-T
Primary Reference	Scottham, K. M., Sellers, R. M., & Nguyen, H. X. (2008). A measure of racial identity in African American adolescents: The development of the Multidimensional Inventory of Black Identity—Teen. *Cultural Diversity and Ethnic Minority Psychology, 14*, 297–306.
Purpose	The purpose of MIBI-T is to measure Black identity among African American adolescents.
Description	The MIBI-T is a 21-item scale with the following seven subscales: (1) Centrality; (2) Private Regard; (3) Public Regard; (4) Nationalist; (5) Humanist; (6) Assimilationist; and (7) Minority. The items are rated on a 5-point Likert-type scale: 1 = Really Disagree; 2 = Kind of Disagree; 3 = Neutral; 4 = Kind of Agree; 5 = Really Agree. The MIBI-T was based on the conceptual framework of the Multidimensional Model of Racial Identity (MMRI) (Sellers, Smith, Shelton, Rowley, & Chavous, 1998). The MMRI acknowledges the heterogeneity of Black identity and allows individuals to express what it means for them to be Black. The MIBI-T is an extension of the Multidimensional Inventory of Black Identity (MIBI) developed to measure Black identity among African American adults (Sellers, Rowley, Chavous, Shelton, & Smith, 1997). The appropriateness and wording of the items were established through several focus groups of 7th- and 10th-grade African American boys and girls. An initial pool of 63 items was generated dealing with the seven sub-dimensions of the MMRI. Through factor analysis and structural equation modeling, 21 items were selected, with 3 items in each of the seven subscales. Seven exploratory factor analyses were conducted using the initial pool of 63 items with principal components as the method of extraction, discarding items correlating less than .30. The remaining items were included in a single confirmatory factor analysis with seven interrelated factors representing the seven subscales of the MIBI. The 21 items were selected to generate the most parsimonious model solution that could be identified in the structural equation model. The fit of the data across groups (middle school and high school) was tested using three increasingly restricted structural equation models. The underlying structural model of the MIBI-T was comparable for both the middle school and high school students in the sample. Also, the underlying structure of the MIBI-T was found to be invariant across gender in terms of the way items correlated on factors.
Samples	The sample consisted of 489 (289 girls, 200 boys) African American students who came from six middle schools and four high schools in a small Midwestern city in the United States. The mean age was 13.7 (*SD* = 1.20) ranging from 12–16. Grade level breakdown was 33% 7th grade, 33% 8th grade, 18% 9th grade, and 16% 10th grade.
Scoring	The scores are obtained by adding the ratings on each item of a subscale and dividing by the number of items in the subscale to produce a subscale mean. No reverse scoring or score transformations are needed.

	The number of items in the subscales are as follows:
	Centrality: 3 items
	Private Regard: 3 items
	Public Regard: 3 items
	Nationalist: 3 items
	Humanist: 3 items
	Assimilationist: 3 items
	Minority: 3 items
	Total MIBI-T: 21 items
Reliability	The Cronbach's alphas for the seven 3-item subscale scores were as follows:
	Centrality: Alpha = .55
	Private Regard: Alpha = .76
	Public Regard: Alpha = .66
	Nationalist: Alpha = .70
	Humanist: Alpha = .50
	Assimilationist: Alpha = .70
	Minority: Alpha = .57
Validity	Correlations with race-related phenomena were used to demonstrate concurrent validity. Greater African American contact was associated with higher scores on Centrality, Private Regard, and Nationalist. More frequent conversations about race were associated with higher scores on Centrality and Nationalist.
Related References	Chavous, T. M., Rivas-Drake, D., Smalls, C., Griffin, T., & Cogburn, C. (2008). Gender matters too: The influence of school racial discrimination and racial identity on academic engagement outcomes among African American adolescents. *Developmental Psychology, 44*, 637–654.
	Sellers, R. M., Rowley, S. A., Chavous, T. M., Shelton, J. N., & Smith, M. A. (1997). Multidimensional Inventory of Black Identity: A preliminary investigation of reliability and construct validity. *Journal of Personality and Social Psychology, 73*, 805–815.
	Sellers, R. M., Smith, M. A., Shelton, J. N., Rowley, S. A. J., & Chavous, T. M. (1998). Multicultural Model of Racial Identity: A re-conceptualization of African American racial identity. *Personality and Social Psychology Review, 2*, 18–39.
Language Versions	English
Contact	Krista Scottham Department of Psychology Pettingill Hall Bates College Lewinston, ME 04240 Email: kscottha@bates.edu

5.13.5 Name of the Measure	Racial Identity Attitude Scale RIAS-A (Short Form), RIAS-B (Short Form), RIAS-L (Long Form)
Primary Reference	Helms, J. E., & Parham, T. A. (1996). The Racial Identity Attitude Scale. In R. L. Jones (Ed.), *Handbook of tests and measurements for Black populations* (pp. 167–172). Oakland, CA: Cobb & Henry.
Purpose	The purpose of the RIAS is to measure racial identity development among African Americans.
Description	The RIAS and its derivatives were originally constructed rationally based on the four stages of Cross's (1971) Nigrescence model, a developmental process that African Americans are presumed to go through within an oppressive society. The four stages of development and accompanying attitudes are (1) Pre-encounter (Anti-Black, Pro-White); (2) Encounter (Challenge Pre-encounter Attitudes); (3) Immersion/Emersion (Reversal of Pre-encounter Attitudes); and (4) Internalization (Internalized Black/Accepting White) (Helms & Parham, 1996).
	There are three versions of the RIAS: RIAS-A, RIAS-B, and RIAS Long Form. The RIAS-A was developed by rewriting Cross's (1971) original 30 Q-sort items into attitude items within each developmental stage (Parham & Helms, 1981). The second short form (RIAS-B) was developed by factor analyzing RIAS-A items using principal axis and varimax rotation with two different samples, resulting in a 30-item, four-factor scale reflecting Cross's four-stage Nigrescence developmental model, with some items reassigned to different factors. The RIAS-L was developed by adding 20 items to the 30 in RIAS-B to increase the reliability of the various scales. The factor analysis (unspecified) of the long form resulted in 38 items.
	The rating format on all the forms is a 5-point Likert-type scale ranging from 1 = Strongly Disagree to 5 = Strongly Agree.
	Helms and Parham (1996) reported factor analytic support for the construct validity of the RIAS-B in two samples. However, other studies using exploratory and confirmatory factor analyses with the RIAS-B and the RIAS-L have reported support only for a three-factor structure that did not include the Encounter subscale (Ponterotto & Wise, 1987; Yanico, Swanson, & Tokar, 1994).
Samples	Samples used in the Helms and Parham (1996) study that developed RIAS-B were primarily African American college male and female students. However, later uses of the scales have involved noncollege African American community members (e.g., Fischer, Tokar, & Serna, 1998; Tokar & Fisher, 1998).
Scoring	Scores are obtained on each of the four scales by adding the ratings of each item within a subscale and dividing the sum by the number of items in the scale to produce a subscale mean.
	In the 30-item RIAS-B, the following is the number of items in each subscale:
	Pre-encounter: 9 items
	Encounter: 4 items
	Immersion/Emersion: 8 items
	Internalization: 9 items

	In the 38-item RIAS-L, the following is the number of items in each subscale:
	Pre-encounter: 14 items
	Encounter: 4 items
	Immersion/Emersion: 9 items
	Internalization: 12 items
	Note: Some items are used in multiple subscales.
Reliability	The Cronbach's alphas of the RIAS-B and the RIAS-L items have been reported as follows by Helms and Parham (1996) for African American college students ranging in age from 17 to 72, suggesting low reliability scores for Encounter subscale items.
	RIAS-B
	Pre-encounter: Alpha = .69
	Encounter: Alpha = .50
	Immersion/Emersion: Alpha = .67
	Internalization: Alpha = .79
	RIAS-L
	Pre-encounter: Alpha = .76
	Encounter: Alpha = .51
	Immersion/Emersion: Alpha = .69
	Internalization: Alpha = .80
	The internal consistency of the Encounter subscale items has also been found to be questionable in later studies by Fischer et al. (1998) and Tokar and Fischer (1998).
Validity	Helms and Parham (1996) refer to several studies that suggested convergent and discriminant validity of the subscales by showing conceptually predictable correlations of the subscales to Black or White counselor preference, self-esteem, anxiety, rational decision making, and anger or hostility. A later study by Fischer et al. (1998) using the RIAS-L with community members and students provided only limited support for the convergent and discriminant validity of the subscales, particularly for the Pre-encounter and Encounter subscales. Whatley, Allen, and Dana (2003) using the RIAS-B showed that the subscale scores predicted select MMPI scale scores.
	Helms (1990a) refers to an unpublished study by Grace (1984) that showed appropriate correlations of the RIAS-B subscales and the subscales of the Developmental Inventory of Black Consciousness (DIB-C; Milliones, 1980). Pierre and Mahalik (2005), also using college men and the RIAS-B, showed that those who reflected Pre-encounter and Immersion/Emersion attitudes and did not resist against anti-African/Black forces reported less self-esteem and more psychological distress. Those who reflected greater internalization attitudes and greater resistance to anti-African/Black forces reported greater self-esteem.

(Continued)

(Continued)

Related References	Perry, J. C., Vance, K. S., & Helms, J. E. (2009). Using the People of Color Racial Identity Attitude Scale among Asian American college students: An exploratory factor analysis. *American Journal of Orthopsychiatry, 79,* 252–260.
	Pierre, M. R., & Mahalik, J. R. (2005). Examining African self-consciousness and Black racial identity as predictors of Black men's psychological well-being. *Cultural Diversity and Ethnic Minority Psychology, 11,* 28–40.
	Whatley, P. R., Allen, J., & Dana, R. H. (2003). Racial identity and the MMPI in African American male college students. *Cultural Diversity and Ethnic Minority Psychology, 9,* 345–353.
Language Versions	English
Contact	Janet E. Helms Campion Hall, Room 318 Boston College 140 Commonwealth Ave. Chestnut Hills, MA 02467 Tel: (617) 552–4080

5.13.6 **Name of the Measure**	Racial Identity Scale for Low-Income African Americans RISL
Primary Reference	Resnicow, K., & Ross-Gaddy, D. (1997). Development of a racial identity scale for low-income African Americans. *Journal of Black Studies, 28,* 239–254.
Purpose	The purpose of the RISL is to assess racial identity among African Americans with low literacy skills.
Description	The RISL is composed of 20 items. About half the items were adopted from existing measures of African American racial identity and the others were developed by the authors. The wording of the adopted items was simplified. The readability of the items was fifth-grade level. These items generally dealt with recognition of racism (anti-White) and positive Afrocentric attitudes/behaviors (pro-Black). Exploratory factor analysis using varimax rotation yielded the five following factors: (1) Recognition of Racism, (2) Afrocentric Attitudes, (3) Afrocentric Involvement, (4) Integrationism, and (5) Interpersonal Trust. Eigenvalues ranged from 3.8 to 1.2. The nature of the factors appeared to have correspondence to some aspects of the four stages of the Nigrescence theory. Items 1 to 18 are rated on a Likert-type scale ranging from 1 = Agree a Lot to 4 = Disagree a Lot. The last two items are rated on a five-point scale ranging from 1 = Never to 5 = More Than Three Times. Seven of the first 18 items and the last two are keyed negatively where lower values indicate stronger racial identity.
Sample	The sample was composed of 261 African American women. Trained research assistants read the items along with the participants in their homes who were guardians or parents of children participating in an after-school health education project. The mean age was 35 (range 20–69), most were unmarried, earned less than $15,001 a year, and did not finish college.
Scoring	Negatively keyed items are reversed, then factor scores are obtained by multiplying each item rating with the regression coefficient of the rated factor structure coefficients. The subscales have the following number of items: Recognition of Racism: 7 items Afrocentric Attitudes: 3 items Afrocentric Involvement: 4 items Integrationism: 3 items Interpersonal Trust: 3 items Total RISL: 20 items

(Continued)

(Continued)

Reliability	The RISL had a 3- to 4-month test-retest reliability of .62 among a convenience sample of 40 individuals from the original sample. Cronbach's alpha of the scores for the 20 items was .70. No internal consistency measures were reported for the subscales.
Validity	For criterion validity, correlations were run between subscale factor scores and past experiences with racism, education, and income. Afrocentric Involvement factor scores were related with past experience with racism and education. Interpersonal Trust was correlated with education. Income was uncorrelated with any of the subscale factor scores. Criterion-related validity appears to be marginal.
Related References	Resnicow, K., Soler, R., Braithwaite, R. L., Ahluwalia, J. S., & Butler, J. C. (2000). Cultural sensitivity in substance use prevention. *Journal of Community Psychology, 28,* 271–290.
	Nollen, N., Ahluwalia, J. S., Mayo, M. S., Richter, K., Choi, W. S., Okuyemi, K. S., & Resnico, K. (2007). A randomized trial of targeted educational materials for smoking cessation in African Americans using transdermal nicotine. *Health Education and Behavior, 34,* 911–927.
Language Versions	English
Contact	Ken Resnicow University of Michigan 3867 SPT/I 109 South Observatory Ann Arbor, MI, 48109–2029 Email: kresnic@umich.edu

5.14 LATINO/A AMERICAN ETHNIC IDENTITY MEASURES

5.14.1 Name of the Measure	Cuban Behavioral Identity Questionnaire CBIQ
Primary Reference	Garcia, M., & Lega, L. I. (1979). Development of a Cuban ethnic identity questionnaire. *Hispanic Journal of Behavioral Sciences, 1,* 247–261.
Purpose	The purpose of the CBIQ is to measure the degree of Cuban ethnic identity among the general population of Cuban Americans.
Description	The CBIQ is an 8-item, single-factor measure that is composed of questions dealing with ethnic behaviors, familiarity with Cuban musicians and idiomatic expressions, Cuban food, friendships and Cuban media, and use of Spanish with children. Each item is rated on a 7-point Likert-type scale or a 7-point index of correct cultural responses.
	The CBIQ was intended for use independently to measure Cuban American identity or in conjunction with other measures of American identity to assess degree of bicultural identity.
	An initial pool of 38 items was developed through in-depth interviews of 12 Cuban Americans from Miami and New Jersey ranging in age from 15 to 64. Through several item reduction methods, eight items were retained, which were then subjected to principal components factor analysis with varimax rotation. A single factor emerged maintaining all eight items that explained 48.8% of the total variance. Item structure coefficients ranged from .24 to .81.
Samples	Two samples were used. One sample was used for item screening and reduction composed of 53 Cuban Americans from Miami, 53 Cuban Americans from New Jersey, and 24 non-Cuban Latino/a Americans from New Jersey. The second sample was used for scale validation composed of 56 Cuban Americans from Miami, 48 Cuban Americans from New Jersey, and 38 non-Cuban Latino/a Americans from New Jersey. No gender breakdown was provided. The two samples were comparable in terms of gender, length of residency in the United States, occupation, education, income, and marital status. In terms of age, the second sample was older (mean age = 37.3 years) than the first sample (mean age = 32.8 years).
Scoring	The two samples were combined to run a multiple regression using the eight items as predictors of a single-item, 10-point self-rated level of Cubanness. The eight items explained 67% of the variance and their standardized regression coefficients (beta values) were used to obtain the score in the following formula:
	CBIQ = .4342 x Question 1 + .0656 x Question 2 + .0203 x Question 3 + .0555 x Question 4 + .0800 x Question 5 + .3262 x Question 6 + .2862 x Question 7 + .2805 x Question 8 = .9333.
Reliability	The Cronbach's alpha of the scores was .84.

(Continued)

(Continued)

Validity	Criterion validity was demonstrated by running a multiple regression using demographic factors as predictors of the CBIQ score. As expected, the significant predictors were age at time of arrival, length of residency in the United States, and Cuban density of the neighborhood of residence.
	Furthermore, CBIQ was a strong predictor of nationality: Cuban versus non-Cuban. Discriminant analysis showed that 94% of all cases were correctly classified, with 97% of actual non-Cubans being classified as non-Cubans, and 93% of actual Cubans being classified as Cubans.
Related References	Jane, D. M., Hunter, G. L., & Lozzi, B. M. (1999). Do Cuban American women suffer from eating disorders: Effects of media exposure and acculturation. *Hispanic Journal of Behavioral Sciences, 21,* 212–218.
Language Version	English
Contact	Margarita Garcia-Estevez Psychology Department Dickson Hall Room 149 Montclair State University Montclair, NJ 07043 Tel: (973) 655–7395

5.14.2 Name of the Measure	Ethnic Consciousness Among Mexican-Origin Populations ECAMOP
Primary Reference	Garcia, J. A. (1982). Ethnicity and Chicanos: Measurement of ethnic identification, identity and consciousness. *Hispanic Journal of Behavioral Science, 4,* 295–314.
Purpose	The purpose of ECAMOP is to measure ethnic consciousness among people of Mexican origin (adults) as a multidimensional construct.
Description	The ECAMOP is a 12-item, four-factor measure composed of questions that deal with attitudinal aspects of cultural preferences and behavior tendencies. The four factors are (1) Preferred Associations, (2) Cultural Preferences, (3) Associational Behavior, and (4) Cultural Holidays. There was no one consistent rating format. The items were adopted from the National Chicano Pretest Survey conducted in Detroit, Michigan, during the first half of 1978. A rotated factor matrix (unspecified) yielded four factors with 12 items that explained 69.1% of the total variance. Factor one, Preferred Associations, accounted for 28.4% of the variance and represented associational preferences to interact with fellow Chicanos in work, neighborhoods, church, children's schoolmates, etc. Factor two, Cultural Preference, accounted for 20.9% of the variance and represented cultural preferences to watch Spanish television, entertainment or read about and visit Mexico. Factor three, Associational Behavior, explained 10.4% of the variance and represented behavioral aspects of associational preferences indicated in factor one. The fourth factor, Cultural Holidays, accounted for 9.4% of the variance and represented behavioral extensions of cultural preferences such as observation of cultural holidays.
Sample	The sample was composed of 111 adult participants who were interviewed for the National Chicano Pretest Survey. The women constituted 58.7% ($n = 65$), and the overall mean age was 41.2 years. Thirty-eight percent of the respondents were immigrants from Mexico.

Scoring	The measure has 12 items. The items in each subscale is as follows:
	
	    Preferred Association: 4 items
	
	    Cultural Preferences: 4 items
	
	    Association Behavior: 2 items
	
	    Cultural Holidays: 2 items
	
	The ethnic consciousness score was the product of respective factor scores with each respondent's summated z-score.

Reliability	No Cronbach's alphas or other reliability measures were reported.

(Continued)

(Continued)

Validity	There were several low positive associations among the four dimensions of ethnic consciousness. Cultural Preferences was associated with Preferred Associations, Cultural Holidays, and Associational Behaviors. Also, political consciousness, defined in terms of perceived systemic versus individual barriers to work and educational opportunities, was negatively associated with Cultural Preferences and Cultural Holidays, while none of the dimensions was associated with seeking coalitions with other ethnic groups. These findings leave the validity of the measure somewhat uncertain while suggesting the relative independence of the dimensions.
Related References	
Language Versions	English and Spanish
Contact	John A. Garcia University of Arizona Department of Political Science Tucson, AZ 85721

5.14.3 Name of the Measure	Multidimensional Measure of Cultural Identity Scale for Latinos MMCISL
Primary Reference	Felix-Ortiz, M., Newcomb, M. D., & Myers, H. (1994). A Multidimentional Measure of Cultural Identity for Latino and Latina Adolescents. *Hispanic Journal of Behavioral Science, 16,* 99–115.
Purpose	The purpose of MMCISL is to measure cultural identity as a multidimensional construct that assesses bicultural and monocultural orientation among Latino/a adolescents.
Description	The MMCISL is a 35-item scale composed of 10 subscales in three domain areas. The three subscales of the Language domain are (1) Spanish Proficiency (4 items), (2) Spanish Language Preference (4 items), and (3) English Proficiency. The four subscales of the Behavior/Familiarity domain are (4) Familiarity with American Culture (4 items), (5) Familiarity with Latino/a Culture (4 items), (6) Latino/a Activism (4 items), and (7) Preferred Latino/a Affiliation (3 items). The three subscales of the Values/Attitude domain are (8) Perceived Discrimination (3 items), (9) Respeto (3 items), (10) Feminism (3 items). A pool of an unspecified number of items was selected from several existing acculturation and cultural identity measures, and new items were added. Items were included because of their relevance, specificity of content, and clarity. The scales used to rate individual items were not specified. Separate exploratory maximum likelihood factor analyses with oblique rotations were conducted for each of the three domains of Language, Behavior/Familiarity, and Value/Attitude to identify the subscales under each domain. The factors were chosen based on high item structure coefficients, correlations on one factor, and interpretability of the eigenvalues. The factors under the Language Domain explained 63% of the total variance; the factors under the Behavior/Familiarity domain explained 41% of the total variance; and the factors under the Value/Attitude domain explained 28% of the total variance.
Samples	A convenience sample of 130 college students from a west-coast urban university was used in the study. Of the total sample, 68% were women and 32% men; 73% were of Mexican descent, 9% were Salvadorans, and the rest from other Latin American countries not including Honduras, Venezuela, Ecuador, Bolivia, Chile, Uruguay, and Paraguay; 62% were born in California and 37% were foreign-born; 40% were first generation and 50% were second generation; and 92% had lived most of their lives in California.
Scoring	The number of items in each of the subscales was as follows: Spanish Proficiency: 4 items Spanish Language Preference: 4 items English Proficiency: 3 items

(Continued)

(Continued)

	Familiarity with American Culture: 4 items
	Familiarity with Latino/a Culture: 4 items
	Latino/a Activism: 4 items
	Preferred Latino/a Affiliation: 3 items
	Perceived Discrimination: 3 items
	Respeto: 3 items
	Feminism: 3 items
	Total MMCISL: 35 items
	Although not specified, from the reported descriptive statistics, it can be inferred that the subscale scores were obtained by summing the responses to the items.
Reliability	The Cronbach's alphas of the subscale scores were as follows:
	Spanish proficiency: Alpha = .88
	Spanish Language Preference: Alpha = .87
	English Proficiency: Alpha = .91
	Familiarity with American Culture: Alpha = .69
	Familiarity with Latino/a Culture: Alpha = .77
	Latino/a Activism: Alpha = .79
	Preferred Latino/a Affiliation: Alpha = .89
	Perceived Discrimination: Alpha = .72
	Respeto: Alpha = .77
	Feminism: Alpha = .81
Validity	For criterion validity, the 10 subscales of the MMCISL were correlated with the four criterion measures of the Short Acculturation Scale (Marin, Sabagal, Marin, Otero-Sabagal, & Perez-Stable, 1987), generation status, length of residence in the United States, and number of years in school. All criterion variables were correlated with all three of the language scales: Spanish Language Proficiency, Spanish Language Preference, and English Proficiency.
	Familiarity with American Culture was correlated positively with residency in the United States, and with English Proficiency as measured by Marin et al.'s (1987) Short Acculturation Scale. U.S. residency was correlated positively with Latino/a Activism and negatively with Perceived Discrimination, and Respeto was correlated negatively with English Proficiency as measured by the Short Acculturation Scale.

Related References	Esparza, P., & Sanchez, B. (2008). The role of attitudinal familism in academic outcomes: A study of urban, Latino high school seniors. *Cultural Diversity and Ethnic Minority Psychology, 14,* 193–200.
	Yeh, M., McCabe, K., Hough, R. L., Dupuis, S., & Hazen, A. (2003). Racial/ethnic differences in parental endorsement of barriers to mental health services for youth. *Mental Health Services Research, 5,* 65–77.
Language Versions	English
Contact	Michael Newcomb Counseling Psychology Waite Phillips Hall 503 University of Southern California Los Angeles, CA 90089 Tel: 213–740–3259 Fax: 213–740–3262 Email: newcomb@mizar.usc.edu

5.14.4 Name of the Measure	Strength of Ethnic Identity SEI
Primary Reference	Cislo, A. M. (2008). Ethnic identity and self-esteem: Contrasting Cuban and Nicaraguan young adults. *Hispanic Journal of Behavioral Sciences, 30,* 230–250.
Purpose	The purpose of SEI is to assess the importance placed on ethnic labels among Cubans and Nicaraguan youth.
Description	The SEI measure is composed of 10 items related to feelings and attitudes about one's group. The items are rated on a 7-point scale ranging from 1 = Strongly Agree, 4 = Neither Agree or Disagree, to 7 = Strongly Disagree. Principal components factor analysis with varimax rotation yielded two factors: (1) Ethnic Identity and (2) In-group Social Preference. Because of the strong positive correlation between the factors, all 10 items are combined for the total score.
Sample	The sample was composed of 291 respondents to the first and second wave of interviews conducted in the Dade County public school system during 1998/2000 and 2000–2002, respectively, who self-reported being of Cuban ($n = 212$; 47% females) or Nicaraguan ($n = 79$; 39% females) background. At the time of the second wave of interviews, the respondents were mostly between the ages of 21 to 23 (Turner, Taylor, & Van Gundy, 2004). Sixty-seven percent of the Cubans and 4% of the Nicaraguans were born in the United States.
Scoring	The SEI score is obtained by reverse coding the ratings on all 10 items, summing the reversed scores and standardizing the summed values.
Reliability	The Cronbach's alpha of the total score for the whole sample was .83, .84 for the Cuban sample, and .78 for the Nicaraguan sample.
Validity	As predicted, SEI scores were lower for Nicaraguans compared to Cubans, who are the majority and possess higher socioeconomic power, suggesting known-group validity. Higher Spanish language preference was associated with stronger SEI scores for Cubans and Nicaraguans providing some support for criterion validity among Cubans. The relationship of SEI scores to self-esteem was positive for Cubans and negative for Nicaraguans, needing further exploration.
Related References	
Language Versions	English
Contact	Andrew M. Cislo Department of Sociology & Center for Population Health and Aging Duke University Durham, NC 27709–0088 Email: amc63@soc.duke.edu

5.15 ASIAN AMERICAN ETHNIC IDENTITY MEASURES

5.15.1 **Name of the Measure**	East Asian Ethnic Identity Scale EAEIS
Primary Reference	Barry, D. T. (2002). An ethnic identity scale for East Asian immigrants. *Journal of Immigrant Health, 4*, 87–94.
Purpose	The purpose of EAEIS is to measure ethnic identity of immigrants from East Asia (China, Japan, and Korea).
Description	The EAEIS contains 41 items and three subscales: (1) Family Values; (2) Ethnic Pride; and (3) Interpersonal Distance. Each item is rated on a 7-point Likert-type scale ranging from 1 = Strongly Disagree, 4 = Neutral, to 7 = Strongly Agree. An initial sample of 18 individuals composed of six Chinese, six Japanese, and six Koreans was interviewed in depth to generate a pool of items. The item pool included selected items from existing measures of ethnic identity: Ethnic Identity Scale (Meredith, 1967), Ethnic Identity Questionnaire (Connor, 1997), and Multigroup Ethnic Identity Measure (Phinney, 1992). The three subscales were derived by a principal components analysis using varimax rotation. Items with factor structure coefficients less than .40 or high correlations on two or more factors were dropped. Several items were also dropped because they did not conceptually fit the content of the factor. Percentage of explained variance was not reported.
Samples	A total of 150 participants were recruited from a university campus using networking and electronic and print announcements. The sample was composed of 50 Chinese, 50 Japanese, and 50 Korean students with an even number of women and men in each group. The ages ranged from 18 to 54 years (*M* = 27.91, *SD* = 6.1).
Scoring	The total score for each subscale is derived by summing the ratings of the reverse-scored and the positively scored items. All together, 7 items are reverse scored. The number of items in each subscale is as follows: Family Values: 14 items Ethnic Pride: 13 items Interpersonal Distance: 14 items Total EAEIS: 41 items
Reliability	The Cronbach's alphas for the scores of subscales were as follows: Family Values: Alpha = .81 Ethnic Pride: Alpha = .85 Interpersonal Distance: Alpha = .80 Total EAEIS: Alpha = .80

(Continued)

(Continued)

Validity	To show criterion validity, EAEIS scores were correlated with interdependent and independent Self-Construal (Singelis, 1994). As expected, interdependent Self-Construal was positively correlated with Family Values, Ethnic Pride, Interpersonal Distance, and the total scale score. Interpersonal Distance was also correlated with independent Self-Construal. Number of years in the United States was not correlated with any of the EAEIS scores. In another study (Barry & Grilo, 2002), the Interpersonal Distance subscale was negatively associated with personal willingness to seeking psychological help among East Asian adult immigrants.
Related References	Barry, D. T., & Grilo, C. M. (2002). Cultural, psychological, and demographic correlates of willingness to use psychological services among East Asian immigrants. *The Journal of Nervous and Mental Disease, 190,* 32–39.
Language Version	English
Contact	Declan T. Barry Department of Psychiatric Research at Congress Place Yale University School of Medicine P. O. Box 208098 301 Cedar Street New Haven, CT 06520–8098 Tel: 203–781–4650 Ext. 268 Email: barry@yale.edu

5.15.2 Name of the Measure	Ethnocultural Identity Behavioral Index EIBI
Primary Reference	Yamada, A. M., Marsella, A. J., & Yamada, S. Y. (1998). The development of the Ethnocultural Identity Behavioral Index: Psychometric properties and validation with Asian Americans and Pacific Islanders. *Asian American and Pacific Islander Journal of Health, 6,* 36–45.
Purpose	The purpose of EIBI is to measure ethnocultural identity in multiple ethnic groups, specifically among Asian and Pacific Islanders.
Description	EIBI is a 19-item scale composed of ethnic-focused behaviors relevant to multiple ethnocultural Asian and Pacific Islander groups. Items are rated on a 7-point scale indicating how often they engage in a particular behavior with 1 = Never, 4 = Half the Time, and 7 = Always. EIBI has three subscales: (1) Cultural Activity, (2) Social Interaction, and (3) Language Opportunity. An initial pool of 40 items was developed based on three focus groups with members from different ethnocultural traditions. Items were eliminated for duplication and overlap, leading to 27 items. The 27 items were subjected to a principal components analysis with oblique rotation. Items with structure coefficients of greater than .40 on a second factor were eliminated if they also correlated higher than .20 on another factor. All together, 19 items were retained. Four of the 19 items correlated with two or more factors and were retained in each factor. The three factors accounted for 60% of the variance. The Cultural Activity factor accounted for 40.7% of the variance, Social Interaction for 11.8%, and Language Opportunity for 7.3%.
Sample	The participants were 352 undergraduate students in social science courses at the University of Hawaii at Minoa. The gender breakdown was 221 (63%) women and 130 (37%) men. The ethnocultural groups comprised 14% Chinese, 11% Filipino, 34% Japanese, and 12% part-Hawaiian. The average age was 21.8 years ($SD=4.6$).

Scoring	The number of items in each subscale is as follows:
	
	    Cultural Activity: 9 items
	
	    Social Interaction: 6 items
	
	    Language Opportunity: 8 items
	
	    Total EIBI: 23 items
	
	The scores are obtained by averaging the ratings of the items in each subscale. The total EIBI score is computed as the average across all 19 items. No items are reverse-scored.

(Continued)

(Continued)

Reliability	The Cronbach's alphas of the subscale scores were as follows:
	Cultural Activity: Alpha = .88
	Social Interaction: Alpha = .83
	Language Opportunity: Alpha = .87
	Total EIBI: Alpha = .90
Validity	For criterion validity, the scores of the USA-born, not including part-Hawaiian ($n = 225$) and foreign-born ($n = 70$), were compared. The foreign-born scored significantly higher than the USA-born on the total EIBI scale, and the Cultural Activities and Language Opportunity subscales. Moreover, the total EIBI score was moderately and positively correlated with a single-item measure of Strength of Identity and with a single-item measure of Cultural Pride.
Related References	Acosta, J. (2003). The effects of cultural differences on peer group relationship. *Journal of Prevention and Intervention in the Community, 25,* 13–26.
Language Version	English
Contact	Ann-Marie Yamada School of Social Work University of Southern California Los Angeles, CA 90089–0411 Email: amyamada@usc.edu

5.15.3 Name of the Measure	Internal-External Identity Measure Int-Ext Id
Primary Reference	Kwan, K. -L. K. (2000). The Internal-External Identity Measure: Factor analytic structures based on a sample of Chinese Americans. *Educational and Psychological Measurement, 60,* 142–152.
Purpose	The Purpose of Int-Ext Id is to measure ethnic identity among Chinese Americans.
Description	The Int-Ext Id measure is composed of 24 items rated on a 6-point Likert-type scale with 6 = Agree Strongly, 5 = Agree, 4 = Tend to Agree, 3 = Tend to Disagree, 2 = Disagree, and 1 = Disagree Strongly. The items reflect the conceptual framework articulated by Breton, Isajiw, Kalbach, and Reitz (1990) and Phinney (1992). Internal items assess a sense of pride and belonging to one's racial ethnic group and attachment to cultural values. External items assess specific ethnic behaviors and practices. An initial pool of 47 items (21 Internal and 26 External) was constructed. Some of the items were adapted from Phinney's (1992) Multigroup Ethnic Identity Measure and from Sodowsky, Lai, and Plake's (1991) Majority-Minority Relations Scale. Through exploratory principal component factor analysis using varimax rotation, 9 Internal items and 15 External items were retained, yielding four factors that explained 46.26% of the variance: (a) Ethnic Friendship and Affiliation, (b) Ethno-Communal Expression, (c) Ethnic Food Orientation, and (d) Family-Collectivism.
Samples	The total sample of respondents was 224 (100 men and 124 women) who were children of Chinese immigrants or immigrants. The mean age of the women was 29.19 (*SD* = 12.02) and the mean age of the men was 32.67 (*SD* = 12.88). The respondents came from the West Coast (*n* = 94), the Midwest (*n* = 83), the East coast (*n* = 33), and the Southwest (14). Of the total sample, 45.1% were students.

Scoring	The number of items for each of the subscales is as follows:
	
	    Ethnic Friendship and Affiliation: 10 items
	
	    Ethno-Communal Expression: 5 items
	
	    Ethnic Food Orientation: 3 items
	
	    Family Collectivism: 6 items
	
	    Total Int-Ext: 24 items
	
	The four subscale scores are obtained by summing the rating of items in each of the subscale scores. Scores of the internal and external measures are obtained similarly.

(Continued)

(Continued)

Reliability	The Cronbach's internal-consistency alphas were as follows:
	Ethnic Friendship and Affiliation: Alpha = .88
	Ethno-Communal Expression: Alpha = .80
	Ethnic Food Orientation: Alpha = .97
	Family-Collectivism: Alpha = .72
	Total Int-Ext Id: Alpha = .90
Validity	The factor analysis that resulted in four factors suggests the construct validity of Int-Ext Id measure. No other validity indicators were reported using the four subscales of the total scale. Using an earlier 35-item version of the scale, Kwan and Sodowsky (1997) provided some evidence of the criterion validity of the Internal and External Identity measure; Internal ethnic identity predicted loss of face and External Identity predicted cultural stress. Also, Internal Identity, External Identity, and the full scale score correlated with reported salience of ethnicity.
Related References	Breton, R., Isajiew, W. W., Kalbach, W. E., & Reitz, J. G. (1990). *Ethnic identity and equality*. Toronto, Canada: University of Toronto Press.
	Kwan, K.-L. K., & Sodowsky, G. R. (1997). Internal and external ethnic identity and their correlations: A study of Chinese American immigrants. *Journal of Multicultural Counseling and Development, 25,* 51–67.
Language Versions	English
Contact	Kwong-Liem Karl Kwan Department of Counseling San Francisco State University 1600 Holloway Ave Burk Hall 527 San Francisco, CA 94132 Tel: 415-338-2005

5.15.4 **Name of the Measure**	Taiwanese Ethnic Identity Scale TEIS
Primary Reference	Tsai, G., & Curbow, B. (2001). The development and validation of the Taiwanese Ethnic Identity Scale (TSAI): A "derived etic" approach. *Journal of Immigrant Health, 3,* 199–212.
Purpose	The purpose of the TEIS is to measure ethnic identity among Taiwanese women.
Description	The TEIS is a 26-item measure rated on a 4-point Likert-type scale ranging from 1 = Strongly Disagree to 4 = Strongly Agree with higher scores indicating more traditional values. An initial pool of 131 items was developed and pared down to 50 items by a "derived etic" approach that included in-depth interviews, free listing, card sorting, and cognitive interviews of Taiwanese American women regarding values, behaviors, and attitudes related to Taiwanese and American cultures. Using principal components analysis with varimax rotation, 26 items were retained, yielding conceptually meaningful six factors that explained 55% of the total variance. The factors were as follows: (1) Rituals and Traditions, (2) Language, (3) Good Child, (4) Parental Opinion, (5) Individualism, and (6) Collectivism.
Samples	The sample was composed of 305 Taiwanese American women and 354 women from Taiwan ranging in age from 15 to 25. The Taiwanese American sample was recruited from various social and cultural organizations and student groups that had a mean age of 19.4 years. The Taiwanese sample was recruited from a high school and a university that had a mean age of 18.1 years. While 51.1% of the Taiwanese American sample was Christian, in the Taiwanese sample 37.3% were Buddhist and 32.8% had no religion.

Scoring	The number of items in each subscale is as follows:
	
	    Rituals and Traditions: 7 items
	    Language: 5 items
	    Good Child: 5 items
	    Parent Opinion: 3 items
	    Individualism: 3 items
	    Collectivism: 3 items
	    Total TEIS: 26 items
	
	The total score and the subscale scores are obtained by summing the item ratings.

Reliability	Cronbach's alphas of the subscale scores were as follows:
	
	    Religions and Traditions: Alpha = .85
	    Language: Alpha = .84

(Continued)

(Continued)

	Good Child: Alpha = .58
	Parental Opinion: Alpha = .56
	Individualism: Alpha = .58
	Collectivism: Alpha = .42
	Total TEIS: Alpha = .82
Validity	Criterion validity was established by correlating the total TEIS scores with indicators of acculturation. The total TEIS score for the Taiwanese American women was negatively correlated with length of residence in the United States and positively correlated with age of immigration to the United States.
Related References	Tsai, G., Curbow, B., & Heinberg, L. (2003). Sociocultural and developmental influences on body dissatisfaction and disordered eating attitudes and behaviors of Asian women. *The Journal of Nervous and Mental Disease, 191,* 309–318.
Language Versions	English and Chinese
Contact	Barbara Curbow College of Public Health and Health Professions University of Florida HPNP Bldg, Room 4157A P.O. Box 100175 Gainesville, FL 32610–0175 Tel: 352–273–6095 Fax: 352–273–6048 Email: bcurbow@phhp.ufl.edu

5.16 WHITE RACIAL IDENTITY MEASURES

5.16.1 Name of the Measure	Oklahoma Racial Attitudes Scale—Preliminary ORAS-P
Primary Reference	Choney, S., & Behrens, J. (1996). Development of the Oklahoma Racial Attitude Scale—Preliminary Form (ORAS-P). In G. R. Sodowsky & L. Impara (Eds.), *Multicultural assessment in counseling and clinical psychology* (pp. 225–240). Lincoln, NE: Buros Institute of Mental Measurements.
Purpose	The Purpose of ORAS-P is to measure White racial consciousness.
Description	The ORAS-P is a 42-item instrument scored on a 5-point Likert-type scale that ranges from 1 = Strongly Disagree to 5 = Strongly Agree. The items are composed to reflect attitudes about issues or ideas about racial minorities.
	The ORAS-P was based on the White racial consciousness model proposed by Rowe, Bennett, and Atkinson (1994) adopted from Phinney's (1989) stages of ethnic identity.
	The model comprises two statuses and seven types of social consciousness that define the subscales of the ORAS-P: Unachieved status: (1) Avoidant; (2) Dependent; and (3) Dissonant types; Achieved Status: (4) Dominative; (5) Reactive; (6) Conflictive; and (7) Integrative types.
	An initial pool of 70 items was generated by researchers in the field of multicultural counseling according to the theoretical model. The items then were revised over a 3-year period using six different administrations applying subject-centered scaling and exploratory and confirmatory factor analyses.
	A confirmatory factor analysis with 238 participants was conducted using a standardized phi matrix setting. The adjusted goodness of fit was .77 with a root mean square residual of .085.
Samples	The final administration provided the psychometric information reported here. The sample was composed of 249 (136 women and 113 men) White American undergraduate students in educational psychology or introductory psychology classes who received experimental credit for their participation. The mean age of the women was 20.4 years and the mean age of the men was 20.1 years.
Scoring	The scores are obtained by summing the ratings of the items in each subscale. No items are reverse scored. The number of items in each of the subscales is as follows: Unachieved status: Avoidant: 3 items Dependent: 3 items Dissonant: 4 items

(Continued)

(Continued)

	Achieved Status:
	
	    Dominative: 7 items
	
	    Reactive: 8 items
	
	    Conflictive: 8 items
	
	    Integrative: 8 items

Reliability	The Cronbach's alphas of the subscale scores were as follows:
	
	Unachieved status:
	
	    Avoidant: Alpha = .68
	
	    Dependent: Alpha = .82
	
	    Dissonant: Alpha = .75
	
	Achieved status:
	
	    Dominative: Alpha = .77
	
	    Reactive: Alpha = .80
	
	    Conflictive: Alpha = .72
	
	    Integrative: Alpha = .79
	
	The test-retest reliabilities for 49 participants with a 4-week interval were as follows:
	
	Unachieved status:
	
	    Avoidant: $r = .68$
	
	    Dependent: $r = .51$
	
	    Dissonant: $r = .46$
	
	Achieved status:
	
	    Dominative: $r = .67$
	
	    Reactive: $r = .76$
	
	    Conflictive: $r = .67$
	
	    Integrative: $r = .60$

Validity	Construct validity was demonstrated by the confirmatory factor analysis reported above. Convergent validity has been demonstrated by moderate correlations between the comparable subscales of the ORAS-P and the WRAIS (Pope-Davis, Vandiver, & Stone, 1999). Also, in a hierarchical regression analysis by Cumming-McCann & Accoridino (2005), ORAS-P subscales explained variability in the subscales of the Multicultural Counseling Inventory (MCI; Sodowsky, Taffe, Gutkins, & Wise, 1994) among White American practicing vocational rehabilitation

	counselors beyond demographic and educational variables. The Dissonant subscale of the ORAS-P was a predictor of all four of the MCI subscales (Awareness, Knowledge, Relationships, and Skills). The Reactive subscale predicted Awareness, and the Dependent subscale predicted Relationships and Skills.
Related References	Cumming-McCann, A., & Accordino, M. P. (2005). An investigation of rehabilitation counselor characteristics, White racial attitudes, and self-reported multicultural counseling competencies. *Rehabilitation Counseling Bulletin, 48,* 167–176. Pope-Davis, D. B., Vandiver, B. J., & Stone, L. G. (1999). White racial identity attitude development: A psychometric examination of two instruments. *Journal of Counseling Psychology, 46,* 70–79.
Language Versions	English
Contact	Mark Leach SSBox 5025 University of Mississippi Hattiesburg, MS 39406–5025

5.16.2 Name of the Measure	White Racial Consciousness Development—Revised WRCDS-R
Primary Reference	Lee, S. M., Puig, A., Pasquarella-Daley, L., Denny, G., Rai, A. A., Dallape, A., & Parker, W. M. (2007). Revising the White Racial Consciousness Development Scale. *Measurement and Evaluation in Counseling and Development, 39,* 194–208.
Purpose	The purpose of WRCDS-R is to measure White racial consciousness.
Description	The WRCDS-R is a 40-item measure rated on a 5-point Likert-type scale, ranging from 1 = Strongly Agree to 5 = Strongly Disagree.

It is composed of four factors: (1) Contact; (2) Reintegration; (3) Pseudo-Independence; and (4) Autonomy.

Claney and Parker (1989) initially developed the WRCDS based on Helms's (1984) five-stage theory of White racial consciousness: (1) Contact; (2) Disintegration; (3) Reintegration; (4) Pseudo-independence; and (5) Autonomy. It had 15 items, 3 items in each subscale, but showed low internal consistencies, with no attempt for item reduction or test of construct validity by factor analysis.

Lee et al. (2007) revised the WRCDS that generated the four-factor version. Using focus groups and personal interviews, they generated an original pool of 99 items that covered Helms's (1984) five stages. The number of items was further reduced to 65 as a result of independent ratings of items by the research team members for their correspondence to the racial identity statuses. The original 15 items were added to the 65 for the final pool of 80 items, which were then subjected to an exploratory factor analysis using varimax and promax rotations and excluding items with structure coefficients of less than .40. The promax rotation provided the most interpretable extraction where the items intended for the Disintegration status were collapsed into the Contact and Reintegration factors. The four factors accounted for 51.6% of the variance.

Confirmatory factor analysis with another sample of 148 participants composed of counselors and counselor educators showed satisfactory confirmation of the four-factor structure with a mean square residual of .069. |
| Samples | The participants were recruited from a state university in the southeastern United States. Of the total participants ($N = 544$), the responses of $n = 402$ White American students were used. Their mean age was 22.04 years (SD = 4.43), ranging from 17 to 66 years, and 69% were female; also, 8% were freshmen, 14% were sophomores, 27% were juniors, and 51% were seniors. |
| Scoring | The score for each subscale is obtained by summing the ratings of the items and then dividing by the number of items in the subscale. Higher mean subscale scores indicate higher levels of the particular stage. |

	The number of items in each subscale was as follows:
	
	    Contact: 8 items
	    Autonomy: 9 items
	    Reintegration: 14 items
	    Pseudo-independence: 9 items
	    Total WRCDS: 40 items

Reliability	The Cronbach's alphas of the subscale scores reported by Parker et al. (1998) were as follows:
	
	    Contact: Alpha = .83
	    Autonomy: Alpha = .84
	    Reintegration: Alpha = .89
	    Pseudo-independence: Alpha = .78

Validity	Contrasted group validity was demonstrated by comparing the student group with the counselor group using structural equation modeling. The counselor group scored significantly lower on the Reintegration subscale and significantly higher on the Contact, Autonomy, and Pseudo-independence subscales. Social desirability bias was not assessed.
Related References	Claney, D., & Parker, W. M. (1989). Assessing White racial consciousness and perceived comfort with Black individuals: A preliminary study. *Journal of Counseling & Development, 67,* 449–445. Parker, W. M., Moore, M. A., & Neimeyer, G. J. (1998). Altering White racial identity and interracial comfort through multicultural training. *Journal of Counseling and Development, 76,* 302–310.
Language Versions	English
Contact	San Min Lee 201, Department of Education College of Education Korea University 1, 5-ga, Anam-dong, Seongbuk-gu Seoul Korea Email: leesang@korea.ac.kr

5.16.3 Name of the Measure	White Racial Identity Attitude Scale WRAIS
Primary Reference	Helms, J. E., & Carter, R. T. (1990). Development of the White racial identity inventory. In J. E. Helms (Ed.), *Black and White racial identity: Theory, research, and practice* (pp. 67–80). Westport, CT: Greenwood Press.
Purpose	The purpose of WRAIS is to measure White racial identity.
Description	The WRAIS is a 50-item measure with items rated on a 5-point Likert-type scale ranging from 1 = Strongly Disagree to 5 = Strongly Agree. It is composed of five subscales with 10 items in each. The subscales reflect attitudes associated with the five stages of racial identity development theorized by Helms (1984): (1) Contact; (2) Disintegration; (3) Reintegration; (4) Pseudo-Independence; and (5) Autonomy. Each stage is characterized by attitudes regarding Whiteness and Blackness with increasing sensitivity to race and racism. A principal components analysis with varimax rotation was conducted with items correlating on multiple factors, suggesting that the subscales were factorially complex. Other studies have found different factorial structures with less than adequate psychometric properties, questioning the underlying construct being measured (Mercer & Cunningham, 2003; Pope-Davis, Vandiver, & Stone, 1999; Swanson, Tokar, & Davis, 1994). It has also been suggested that WRAIS may be more of a measure of racism and prejudice than racial identity (Behrens, 1997; Lowery, Unzueta, Knowles, & Geoff, 2006).
Samples	The sample was composed of 506 White American university students (women = 339, men = 167) from predominantly White American universities in the Eastern United States.

Scoring	The number of items for each of the subscales is as follows:
	
	    Contact: 10 items
	
	    Disintegration: 10 items
	
	    Reintegration: 10 items
	
	    Pseudo-Independence: 10 items
	
	    Autonomy: 10 items
	
	    Total WRAIS: 50 items
	
	The score for each subscale is obtained by adding the ratings of the 10 items. Higher scores on a subscale are more descriptive of the respondent at that stage of racial identity. Authors suggest using scores on all subscales to form a profile of respondents.

Reliability	Cronbach's alphas for subscale scores for the sample of 506 White American students were as follows:
	Contact: Alpha = .55
	Disintegration: Alpha = .77
	Reintegration: Alpha = .80
	Pseudo-Independence: Alpha = .71
	Autonomy: Alpha = .67
Validity	Criterion validity was shown by reporting correlations of the WRAIS subscales to other personality constructs. Higher Contact scores were correlated with lower anxiety and lower likelihood of initiating social contact with African Americans; higher Disintegration scores were correlated with symbolic racism and preference for White American counselors; Reintegration tended to be related to idealization of Whiteness and low desire to interact with African Americans; Pseudo-Independence was associated with more liberal attitudes about racial issues and intellectual explanations of racial discomfort; and Autonomy was associated with support of racial integration and lesser preference for White American counselors.
Related References	Lowery, B., Unzueta, M., Knowles, E., & Geoff, P. (2006). Concern for the in-group and opposition to affirmative action. *Journal of Personality and Social Psychology, 90,* 961–974.
	Mercer, S. H., & Cunningham, M. (2003). Racial identity in White American colleges students: Issues of conceptualization and measurement. *Journal of College Student Development, 44,* 217–229.
Language Versions	English
Contact	Janet E. Helms Campion Hall, Room 318 Boston College 140 Commonwealth Ave Chestnut Hills, MA 02467 Tel: (617) 552–4080

5.17 ITALIAN, JEWISH AMERICAN, ARAB, NATIVE AMERICAN, AND MULTIRACIAL IDENTITY MEASURES

5.17.1 Name of the Measure	Italian Canadian Ethnic Identity ICEI
Primary Reference	Laroche, M., Kim, C., & Tomiuk, M. A. (1998). Italian ethnic identity and its relative impact on the consumption of convenient and traditional foods. *Journal of Consumer Marketing, 15,* 125–151.
Purpose	The purpose of ICEI is to measure ethnic identity of Italians living in Montreal, Canada.
Description	The ICEI is an 11-item measure of ethnic identity with three subscales: (1) Italian Language Use With Family Members, (2) Italian Social Participation/Interaction, (3) and Catholicism. The Italian language use is rated on a percentage of time spent speaking Italian and English with spouse, children, and parents to add to 100% for each language. Italian social participation/interaction and Catholicism are rated on a 10-point Likert-type scale. Maximum likelihood factor analysis with an oblique rotation resulted in a three-factor solution that explained 46.7% of the total variance. The pattern of item structure coefficients captured the proposed structure of the ICEI. Confirmatory factor analysis showed good fit indexes greater than .90, confirming the three-factor structure. The correlations between factors were moderate, indicating that items should not be summed into a single score.
Samples	The sample was randomly collected using area sampling of Montreal census tracts. A total of 469 usable questionnaires were collected, 67.8% women. The age range varied widely with the largest percentage being 20–29 years (26.5%) and 40–49 years (26.1%). Of the total, 71.2% reported being first-generation Canadians.

Scoring	The number of items in the subscales is as follows:
	
	    Italian Language Use With Family Members: 3 items
	
	    Italian Social Participation/Interaction: 6 items
	
	    Catholicism: 2 items
	
	    Total ICEI: 11 items
	
	The three subscales are scored separately by averaging the ratings of items in each.

Reliability	Cronbach's alphas for the scores of the three subscale were as follows:
	
	    Italian Language Use With Family Members: Alpha = .78
	
	    Italian Social Participation/Interaction: Alpha = .70
	
	    Catholicism: Alpha = .80

Validity	Evidence for convergent validity of the ICEI was demonstrated by showing moderate correlations between ICEI and an acculturation measure specially developed for the study. The acculturation measure asked for the percentage of times participants used

	Italian and English in the contexts of watching television, listening to radio, reading newspapers, and reading magazines and books. For criterion validity all three subscales, as expected, were positively related to traditional food consumption and negatively with consumption of certain convenient food groups (i.e., frozen and canned foods, chips, etc).
Related References	Kim, C., Laroche, M., & Tomiuk, M. A. (2001). A measure of acculturation for Italian Canadians: Scale development and construct validity. *International Journal of Intercultural Relations, 25,* 607–637. Laroche, M., Kim, C., Tomiuk, M. A., & Belisle, D. (2005). Similarities in Italian and Greek multidimensional ethnic identity: Some implications for food consumption. *Canadian Journal of Administrative Science, 21,* 143–167.
Language Versions	English and Italian
Contact	Michel Laroche John Molson School of Business Concordia University 1455 de Maisonneve Blvd. West Montreal (Quebec), Canada, H3G 1M8. Tel: 514–848–2424, extension 2942 Email: laroche@msb.concordia.ca

5.17.2 Name of the Measure	Jewish-American Identity Scale JAIS
Primary Reference	Zak, I. (1973). Dimensions of Jewish-American identity. *Psychological Reports, 33,* 891–900.
Purpose	The Purpose of the JAIS is to measure the Jewish and American Identities of Jewish Americans.
Description	The JAIS is a 19-item measure rated on a 7-point Likert-type scale ranging from 1 = Disagree Strongly, 4 = Neutral, to 7 = Agree Strongly.

An initial pool of 80 items was developed that addressed sensitivity to Jewish issues, centrality of Jewishness, importance of Jewish belonging, and sense of interdependence of Jews in the world. Based on the content of the items and item-total correlations with a sample of 164 Jewish students, 10 items were selected to form the Jewish scale. The items that measured American identity addressed parallel domains of issues such as sensitivity to American issues, centrality of being American, American belonging, and sense of interdependence of Americans. The language of the items on the Jewish and American subscales was mostly identical with the word *Jewish* replaced by *American.*

Factor analysis using oblique and varimax rotations was conducted separately with four samples. Two factor solutions emerged in each of the samples that were very much alike in terms of common variance shared by each factor in each solution. Moreover, the correlations between the factors were low and the coefficients of parsimony were high in each sample. Given such similarity, the four samples were combined and responses factor analyzed. Orthogonal and oblique solutions were similar and each yielded two similar factors, accounting for 89% of the common variance, one Jewish and the other American. For the final version, 8 Jewish and 11 American items were retained. The correlations between the two subscales was $r = .07$.

The JAIS has been used with minor modifications with other ethnic groups such as Israeli Moslem Arabs (Zak, 1976), Armenian Americans (Der-Karabetian, 1980), Turkish Armenians (Der-Karabetian & Balian, 1992), and Mexican Americans (Der-Karabetian & Ruiz, 1997). Essentially, in these studies the words *Jewish* and *American* were replaced by corresponding ethnic or majority identities, and several of the original items were dropped. |
| **Samples** | The participants were 1,006 Jewish American college students between the ages of 17 and 25. They were recruited from four different settings: The Hebrew language department of Queens College, New York; non-Hebrew majors from other New York colleges; college students from the greater Boston area; and students who had visited Israel in organized tours. |

Scoring	The number of items in the two subscales is as follows:
	Jewish Identity: 8 items
	American Identity: 11 items
	Total JAIS: 19 items
	The scores on the subscales are obtained by averaging the ratings of the items in each subscale.
Reliability	The Cronbach's alpha for the scores were as follows:
	Jewish Identity: Alpha = .88
	American Identity: Alpha = .89
	The alphas in the four samples for the Jewish Identity subscale ranged from .72 to .88, and from .84 to .89 for the American Identity subscale.
Validity	The factor analytic support for the hypothesized orthogonal dimensions of the Jewish and American subscales suggests evidence of construct validity of the JAIS.
Related Reference	
Language Versions	Arabic and English
Contact	S. A. Isbell P. O. Box 9229 Missoula, MT 59807–9229

5.17.3 Name of the Measure	Male Arabic Ethnic Identity Measure MAEIM
Primary Reference	Barry, D., Elliott, R., & Evans, E. M. (2000). Foreigner in a strange land: Self-construal and ethnic identity in male Arabic immigrants. *Journal of Immigrant Health, 2,* 133–144.
Purpose	The Purpose of MAEIM is to measure ethnic identity among Arab men in the United States.
Description	The MAEIM is a 33-item self-report measure with four subscales: (1) Religious-Family Values, (2) Sense of Belonging/Ethnic Pride, (3) Friends, and (4) Ethnic Arabic Attitudes and Practices. Items are rated on a 7-point Likert-type scale ranging from 1 = Strongly Disagree, 4 = Don't Agree or Disagree, to 7 = Strongly Agree. Initial pool of items was derived through interviews with 10 Arab men from seven different Middle Eastern countries and incorporated items from Phinney's (1992) Multigroup Ethnic Identity Measure, and Zak's (1976) Ethnic Identity Scale. Principal components factor analysis with varimax rotation was conducted to identify the subscales. Items with structure coefficients of less than .30 were
Samples	The sample was composed of 115 Arab men ranging in age from 18 to 54 years. They had lived in the United States for an average of 6.4 years (*SD* = 5.5), and all had post–high school education. About 84% described themselves as Muslims. The participants were from 13 different Middle Eastern countries and were recruited from the University of Toledo and over the Internet. Participants recruited over the Internet were sent hard copies by regular mail. Of the 80 who supplied addresses, 70 were returned. No statistical differences on the measure were observed between the college and Internet groups.
Scoring	The number of items in the subscales is as follows: Religion-Family Values: 14 items Sense of Belonging/Ethnic Pride: 7 items Friends: 7 items Ethnic Arabic Attitudes and Practices: 5 items Total MAEIM: 33 items The scores are derived by summing the reverse-scored and positive-scored items in the four subscales. The total score of the MAEIM is similarly derived.
Reliability	The Cronbach's alphas of the subscale scores were as follows: Religious-Family Values: Alpha = .89 Sense of Belonging/Ethnic Pride: Alpha = .81 Friendship: Alpha = .69 Ethnic Arabic Attitudes and Practices: Alpha = .69 Total MAEIM: Alpha = .89

Validity	The total score of the MAEIM was negatively correlated with length of stay in the United States, suggesting criterion validity. Longer stay tended to be associated with lower scores on ethnic identity. Also, as predicted, Independent Self-Construal was uncorrelated with any of the MAEIM subscales, suggesting discriminant validity. And, as predicted, Interdependent Self-Construal was moderately and positively correlated with all of the subscales and the total score of the MAEIM, suggesting convergent validity. In another study by Barry (2005), MAEIM's total and subscale scores were moderately and positively correlated with the Separation/Assimilation scores on the Male Arab Acculturation measure in further support of criterion validity.
Related References	Barry, D. T. (2005). Measuring acculturation among male immigrants in the United States: An exploratory study. *Journal of Immigrant Health*, 7, 179–184.
Language Versions	English
Contact	Declan Barry Department of Psychiatry Yale University School of Medicine CMHC/SAC Room 200 34 Park Street New Haven, CT 06519–1187 Tel: 203–785–7200 Email: declan.barry@yale.edu

5.17.4 Name of the Measure	Measure of Enculturation for Native American Youth MENAY
Primary Reference	Zimmerman, M. A., Ramirez-Valles, J., Washienko, K. M., Walter, B., & Dyer, S. (1996). The development of a measure of enculturation for Native American Youth. *American Journal of Community Psychology, 24,* 295–310.
Purpose	The purpose of the MENAY is to measure enculturation of Native American youth into the Native American culture, including a measure of ethnic identity.
Description	The MENAY is a 15 item measure. It has three components that are combined to form a single enculturation score: (1) Cultural Affinity, which has five items rated on a 5-point scale ranging from 1 = Very Little, 3 = Some, to 5 = A Lot; (2) Native American Identity, which is a single item rated on a 4-point scale ranging from 0 = Not at All, 1 = Little, 2 = Some, to 3 = A Lot; and (3) Family Activities, which is composed of nine activities checked by the respondents with a score ranging from zero (No activity checked) to nine (All activities checked).
	A factor score for enculturation was created by summing the standardized scores on Cultural Affinity, Native American Identity, and Family Activity. Exploratory factor analysis yielded a single factor that explained 47% of the total variance with item structure coefficients ranging from .52 to .81. In a confirmatory factor analysis, the factor scores of the three components correlated consistently on a single factor in the expected direction in three separate samples, the reported fit index (CFI) values were .989, .940, and .999.
Samples	The first sample included 120 Native American youth from two Midwestern tribes, representing 40% of the tribal youth. The mean age was 11.5 ($SD = 2.8$), ranging from 7–18. The girls composed 50% of the sample, and 40 of the youth lived in the reservation. The second sample included 69 youth, 56% girls, with a mean age of 11.5 ($SD = 2.8$), same as the first sample. The third sample included 42 youth, 58% girls, again with the mean age of 11.5 ($SD = 2.8$).
Scoring	Enculturation factor scores were obtained by addition of the standardized scores of the three components. The number of items in the each of the three components is as follows: Cultural Affinity: 5 items Native American Identity: 1 Item Family Activities: 9 items Total MENAY: 15 items
Reliability	Cronbach's alpha of the scores in the first sample of 120 participants was .70. The one-year test-retest reliability of the factor scores for a sample of 69 participants was .50.

Validity	Criterion validity was demonstrated by positive correlations between the enculturation factor scores and number of Native American friends, mother's perceived Native American identity, father's perceived Native American identity, and self-esteem.
Related References	
Language Versions	English
Contact	Marc A. Zimmerman School of Education University of Michigan 610 E. University Ave. Ann Arbor, MI 48109–1259 Tel: 734–647–0224 Email: marcz@umich.edu

5.17.5 Name of the Measure	Multiracial Identity Integration Scale MII Scale
Primary Reference	Cheng, C.-Y., & Lee, F. (2009). Multiracial Identity Integration: Perceptions of conflict and distance among multiracial individuals. *Journal of Social Issues, 65,* 51–68.
Purpose	The purpose of the MII Scale is to measure compatibility between multiple racial identities.
Description	The MII Scale is an 8-item measure rated on a 5-point Likert-type scale ranging from 1 = Completely Disagree to 5 = Completely Agree.
	The MII Scale is based on the construct of bicultural identities proposed by Benet-Martinez and Haritatos (2005) that has been used to examine the relationship of multiple social identities such as cultures, genders, or professions (Cheng, Sanchez-Burks, & Lee, 2008; Shih & Sanchez, 2009). The identity integration construct has two components: Conflict and Distance. Conflict represents perceptions of contradicting norms and values in different social identities. Distance represents the perception of the degree of separation of the different identities. The eight items composing the conflict and distance subscales of Bicultural Identity Integration Scale (Benet-Martinez & Haritatos, 2005) were adapted to reflect racial identities without referring to any one particular identity. Participants also responded to a 4-item measure on multiracial pride (Cheng, 2005). Participants completed the measures before and after a task that asked them to recall positive or negative multiracial experiences.
	The scores were subjected to principal axis factor analysis using oblique and varimax rotations for the two separate administrations of the MII Scale to the same sample. The resulting two factors were identical to the two original subscale constructs of Conflict and Distance at both times. The percentage of variance accounted for was not reported. Items of the MII Scale may be found in the primary reference.
Samples	The participants were 57 graduate and undergraduate students at one Midwestern and one northeastern university who self-identified as multiracial. The sample was composed of 20 males and 37 females with a mean age of 21.84 years *(SD = 7.03)*. Of the total sample, 82.5% reported two racial backgrounds, 8.8% reported three racial backgrounds, and 8.8% reported four racial backgrounds.
Scoring	The number of items in the subscales is as follows:
	Distance: 4 Items
	Conflict: 4 Items
	Total MII: 8 items
	The scores on the subscales are obtained by averaging the subscale item ratings. Lower scores on the subscales indicate more multiracial identity integration.

Reliability	The Cronbach's alphas of the subscale scores at the two administrations were as follows:
	Before recall task:
	Distance: Alpha = .80
	Conflict: Alpha = .74
	After recall task:
	Distance: Alpha = .77
	Conflict: Alpha = .70
Validity	Criterion validity was examined by the correlation of the subscale scores with multiracial pride scores. Both before and after the recall task, lower Distance scores were significantly correlated with higher Multiracial Pride. Conflict scores were not significantly correlated with multiracial pride at either administration but tended to be in the expected direction.
	Predictive validity was demonstrated by comparing scale scores before and after a recall task of negative or positive multiracial experiences. As predicted, both Distance and Conflict scores increased for participants who were asked to recall negative experiences and decreased for those who recalled positive experiences, suggesting higher multiracial identity integration.
	Social desirability bias was not measured.
Related References	
Language Versions	English
Contact	Chi-Ying Cheng
	School of Social Sciences Management University
	Level 4
	90 Stamford Road
	Singapore 178903
	Email: cycheng@smu.edu.sg

5.18 MULTIGROUP ETHNIC IDENTITY MEASURES

5.18.1 Name of the Measure	Ethnic Group Membership Questionnaire EGMQ
Primary Reference	Contrada, R. J., Ashmore, R. D., Gary, M. L., Coups, E., Egeth, J. D., Sewell, A., Ewell, K., Goyal, T. M., & Chasse, V. (2001). Measures of ethnicity-related stress: Psychometric properties, ethnic group differences, and associations with wellbeing. *Journal of Applied Social Psychology, 31,* 1775–1820.
Purpose	The purpose of EGMQ is to measure ethnic identity across multiple ethnic groups.
Description	The EGMQ is a 11-item measure consisting of three factors that were based on items adopted from Luhtanen and Crocker's (1992) measure of collective self-identity: (1) Public Regard, (2) Private Feelings, and (3) Identity Centrality. The items are rated on a 7-point Likert-type scale ranging from 1 = Strongly Disagree, 3 = Neutral, to 7 = Strongly Agree. Prior to completing the EGMQ, participants are instructed to think about the ethnic label they would use to describe themselves. Factor analysis of the data with African American, Asian American, and Latino/a American participants using varimax rotation indicated three factors with eigenvalues greater than 1.0 that accounted for 65% of the variance. The factor analyses with White American participants and the full sample were comparable.
Samples	The sample was composed of 333 first-year Rutgers University students, 242 women and 91 men. The ethnic breakdown of the sample was as follows: 208 White American, 34 African American, 31 Latino/a American, and 60 Asian American/Pacific Islander. The average age of respondents was 17.9, ranging from 16–29.
Scoring	The number of items in each subscale is as follows: Public Regard: 4 items Private Feelings: 3 items Identity Centrality: 4 items Total EGMQ: 11 items Five of the items are worded negatively. The scores are obtained by averaging the ratings of items on each subscale after reversing the negatively stated items.
Reliability	For African American, Asian American, and Latino/a American participants collectively, the Cronbach's alphas of the scores were as follows: Public Regard: Alpha = .80 Private Feelings: Alpha = .77 Identity Centrality: Alpha = .77

	For White American, participants the Cronbach's alphas of the scores were as follows:
	Public Regard: Alpha = .71
	Private Feelings: Alpha = .73
	Identity Centrality: Alpha = .87
	For the whole sample, the Cronbach's alphas of the scores were as follows:
	Public Regard: Alpha = .78
	Private Feelings: Alpha = .74
	Identity Centrality: Alpha = .84
Validity	The subscales of EGMQ were weakly correlated with indicators of perceived discrimination, stereotype confirmation, and own-group conformity pressure (all three indicators were fashioned specifically for the study by the authors for this study based on a variety of sources), supporting discriminant validity. A hierarchical multiple regression analysis showed the Public Regard subscale as a significant predictor of negative mood (Usala & Hertzog, 1989) and life satisfaction (Diener, Emmons, Larsen, & Griffin, 1985), supporting criterion validity.
	Known-group validity was demonstrated, with predictable differences on the subscales between different ethnic groups. On the Public Regard subscale, African Americans scored significantly lower than each of the other ethnic groups, and White Americans scored higher than Latino/a Americans. On the Identity Centrality subscale, as expected, Asian Americans, Latino/a Americans, and African Americans did not differ from each other and scored higher than White Americans. Consistent with social identity theory, there were no differences between the ethnic groups on the Private Regard subscale.
Related References	
Language Versions	English
Contact	Richard J. Contrada Department of Psychology Rutgers University 53 Avenue E Piscataway, NJ 08854–8040. Tel: 732–445–3195 Email: contrada@rci.rutgers.edu

5.18.2 Name of the Measure	Ethnic Identity Scale EIS
Primary Reference	Umana-Taylor, A. J., Yazedjian, A., & Bamaca-Gomez, M. (2004). Developing the Ethnic Identity Scale using Eriksonian and social identity perspectives. *Identity: An International Journal of Theory and Research, 4,* 9–38.
Purpose	The purpose of EIS is to measure ethnic identity formation among any ethnic group.
Description	EIS is composed of 17 items and three independent subscales: (1) Exploration, (2) Resolution, and (3) Affirmation. These subscales represent the theoretical dimensions of Eriksonian identity development and social identity theory. Items are rated on a 4-point Likert-type scale: 1 = Does Not Describe Me At All, 2 = Describes Me A Little, 3 = Describes Me Well, and 4 = Describes Me Very Well. The primary reference includes the items.
	Two studies were conducted in the development of the scale. The first study examined and refined the factor structure of the EIS among college students. The second study examined if the EIS applied to high school students. An initial pool of 46 items was developed in consultation with four scholars that reflected the three theoretically defined identity development dimensions of Exploration, Resolution, and Affirmation. An exploratory factor analysis of the 46 items using maximum likelihood extraction with oblique rotation and retention of items with structure coefficients greater than .40 resulted in a 22-item, three-factor measure that explained 49% of the variance. Confirmatory factor analysis of the 22 items resulted in a poor fit. Five items were identified as having significantly larger residuals and were discarded. The 17-item model provided a better fit (GFI = .86, CFI = .91, RMSEA = .09).
Samples	The sample of the first study was composed of 615 four-year university students, 297 from the Midwest and 318 from the west coast. The total sample included 73% women. The ages ranged from 18 to 56 years ($M = 21.8$, $SD = 3.91$). In the total sample, 192 ethnic backgrounds were self-identified, which were grouped into six categories: White American (45%); Latino/a American (12%); Asian American (20%) including peoples from east, west, southwest, and south Asia, Pacific Islanders, and Middle East; African American (8%); Multi-ethnic/racial (7%); other (4%), and 5% did not report ethnic/racial background.
	The sample of the second study included 231 11th-grade high school students from the Midwest. Of the total sample, 54.5% were girls. The ages ranged from 15 to 18 years ($M = 16.6$, $SD = .59$). Participants self-reported 88 different ethnic backgrounds, which were grouped into six categories: White American (28%); Latino/a American (21%); Asian American (11%); African American (20%); Native American (1%); Multi-ethnic/racial (8%); other (3%); and 4% did not report ethnic/racial background.

Scoring	The number of the items in the subscales is as follows:
	Exploration: 7 items
	Resolution: 4 items
	Affirmation: 6 items
	Total EIS: 17 items
	Ten of the items are positively stated and seven of the items are negatively stated. The scores on each subscale are obtained by summing the ratings of the items in the subscale after reversing the negatively stated items. Higher scores indicate greater endorsement of the subscale dimension.
Reliability	The Cronbach's alphas of the scores of the three subscales were as follows for the university sample:
	Exploration: Alpha = .91
	Resolution: Alpha = .92
	Affirmation: Alpha = .86
	For the high school sample the Cronbach's alphas of the scores were as follows:
	Exploration: Alpha = .89
	Resolution: Alpha = .89
	Affirmation: Alpha = .84
Validity	In further support of the criterion validity, in the university sample, self-esteem (Rosenberg, 1979), as expected, was reported to be significantly correlated with the Exploration and Resolution subscales, and uncorrelated with the Affirmation subscale for ethnic minority participants as a group. Also, for the ethnic group participants, Familial Ethnic Socialization (Umana-Taylor, 2001) was significantly correlated with the Exploration and the Resolution subscales but not with the Affirmation subscale. Moreover, among White American participants, while self-esteem was uncorrelated with any of the subscales, Familial Ethnic Socialization was significantly correlated with the Exploration and the Resolution subscales. In the high school sample, correlations with Familial Ethnic Socialization mirrored the university sample. However, among the high school ethnic minorities as a group, self-esteem was correlated with three of the subscales, and for White Americans, self-esteem was correlated only with the Affirmation and the Resolution subscales.
	Furthermore, the authors demonstrated that subscale scores may be used to classify respondents into eight different group typologies with predictable relationships to self-esteem and Familial Ethnic Socialization.

(Continued)

(Continued)

Related References	Umana-Taylor, A. J. (2005). Ethnic Identity Scale. In K. A. Anderson Moore & L. H. Lippman, *What do children need to flourish* (pp.75–91). New York: Springer.
	Umana-Taylor, A. J., & Shin, N. (2007). An examination of ethnic identity and self-esteem with diverse populations: Exploring variation by ethnicity and geography. *Cultural Diversity and Ethnic Minority Psychology, 13,* 178–186.
	Umana-Taylor, A. J., & Updegraff, K. A. (2007). Latino adolescents' mental health: Exploring the interrelationships among discrimination, ethnic identity, cultural orientation, self-esteem, and depressive symptoms. *Journal of Adolescence, 30,* 549–567.
Language Versions	English
Contact	Adriana J. Umana-Taylor University of Illinois at Urbana-Champaign Department of Human and Community Development Urbana, IL 61801 Email: umana@uiuc.edu

5.18.3 Name of the Measure	Collective Self-Esteem Scale CSES
Primary Reference	Luhtanen, R., & Crocker, J. (1992). A collective self-esteem scale: Self-evaluation of one's social identity. *Personality and Social Psychology Bulletin, 18,* 302–318.
Purpose	The purpose of CSES is to assess social identity in reference to membership in a group such as ethnicity, gender, race, religion, or socioeconomic class.
Description	The CSES is a 16-item measure based on the social identity theory (Tajfel & Turner, 1986). It is composed of four subscales with four items each: (1) Membership Esteem, (2) Private Collective Self-Esteem, (3) Public Collective Self-Esteem, and (4) Importance of Identity. Items are rated on a 7-point Likert-type scale ranging from 1 = Strongly Disagree, 4 = Neutral, to 7 = Strongly Agree. Participants are instructed to choose a particular group they belong to, write it down on the form, and respond to the items in reference to that group.
	The CSES was developed over a series of three studies. A pool of 43 items was composed to reflect the four subscale domain areas. Using an initial principal components analysis with 83 participants and varimax rotation, four items were selected in each domain based on their highest structure coefficients, which were greater than .58, and all except two were greater than .70. Further principal components analysis with varimax rotation accounted for 72.3% of the variance, with items correlating on their appropriate factors.
	The first study reexamined, using a much larger sample of 887 college students, the factor structure of CSES with an exploratory and confirmatory factor analysis. The principal components analysis replicated the four-factor structure that explained 60.7% of the variance with item loadings ranging from .54 to .83 in their appropriate factors. The confirmatory factor analysis used the maximum likelihood method of estimation to test the fit of four models. The 4-factor uncorrelated and hierarchical models showed the best fit in study one as well as in the subsequent two validity studies. The fit indexes were all over .90 for both the correlated and the hierarchical models.
Samples	The sample in study one was composed of 887 college students from a northeastern university. The ethnic composition was 91.2% White American, 3.6% African American, and 5.2% Asian American; 51% were women.
Scoring	The number of items for each of the four subscales is as follows:
	Membership Esteem: 4 items
	Private Collective Self-Esteem: 4 items
	Public Collective Self-Esteem: 4 items
	Importance of Identity: 4 items
	Total CSES: 16 items
	The score on each subscale is the sum of the ratings after reversing the ratings on the eight negatively stated items. The total scale score is the sum of all 16 items after reversing the eight negatively stated items. The CSES may be modified to refer to a specific achieved group membership or have a general form referring to "my group."

(Continued)

(Continued)

Reliability	The Cronbach's alphas for the subscale scores in study one were as follows:
	Membership Esteem: Alpha = .73
	Private Collective Self-Esteem: Alpha = .74
	Public Collective Self-Esteem: Alpha = .80
	Importance of Identity: Alpha = .76
	Total CSES: Alpha = .85
	In study two, the 6-week test-retest coefficients of reliability were as follows:
	Membership Esteem: $r = .58$
	Private Collective Self-Esteem: $r = .62$
	Public Collective Self-Esteem: $r = .66$
	Importance of Identity: $r = .68$
	Total CSES: $r = .68$
Validity	In study one, Rosenberg Self-Esteem scale (Rosenberg, 1979) was correlated moderately with the CSES subscales and more strongly with the Membership Esteem subscale than others, supporting convergent validity. Also, belief in having been discriminated against was negatively correlated with the Public and Private Collective Self-Esteem subscales as expected, but not with the other subscales, providing support for criterion validity. Moreover, White American subjects, as expected, scored significantly higher than the other two ethnic groups on Public Collective Self-Esteem.
	Study two further examined convergent and discriminant validity by correlating CSES with other widely used self-esteem scales and the Marlowe-Crowne Social Desirability scale (Crowne & Marlowe, 1964). The total CSES scale and its three subscales, except the Importance of Identity subscale, were moderately correlated with the Rosenberg Self-Esteem Scale (Rosenberg, 1965), Coopersmith Self-Esteem Inventory (Coopersmith, 1967), and the Janis-Field Feelings of Inadequacy Scale (Janis & Field, 1959), supporting convergent validity. This finding was in line with predictions from social identity theory that collective and personal self-esteem are similar yet distinct. None of the subscale scores or the total score of the CSES was correlated with the Marlowe-Crowne Social Desirability scale, supporting discriminant validity.
	In study three, to further assess the convergent validity of the CSES, it was correlated with several collectivism and individualism related measures, such as the Hui's (1988) Individualism-Collectivism scale, the Wagner and Moch's (1986) Individualism-Collectivism in the Work Place scale, and the Maslach, Stapp, and Santee (1985) Individuation scale. As predicted, the total Hui Collectivism-Individualism Scale was correlated moderately with the total CSES and its subscales. Also, the CSES Importance of Identity subscale was most strongly related to the Individualism-Collectivism in the Work Place total score. Moreover, all the SCES subscales except Importance of Identity subscale showed significant correlations with the Individuation Scale.

Related References	Alvarez, A. N., & Helms, J. (2001). Racial identity and reflected appraisals as influences on Asian Americans' racial adjustment. *Cultural Diversity and Ethnic Minority Psychology, 7,* 217–231. Cassidy, C., O'Conner, R. C., Howe, E., & Warden, D. (2004). Perceived discrimination and psychological distress: The role of personal and ethnic self-esteem. *Journal of Counseling Psychology, 51,* 329–339. Contrada, R. J., Ashmore, R. D., Gary, M. L., Coups, E., Egeth, J. D., Sewell, A., Ewell, K., Goyal, T. M., & Chasse, V. (2001). *Journal of Applied Social Psychology, 31,* 1775–1820. Crocker, J., Luhtanen, R., Blaine, B., & Broadnax, S. (1994). Collective self-esteem and psychological well-being among White, Black and Asian college students. *Personality and Social Psychology Bulletin, 20,* 503–513.
Language Versions	English
Contact	Riia K. Luhtanen Myllymatintie 4 as 2 48400 Kotka, Finland Email: riia.luhtanen@gmail.com or riialuhtanen@yahoo.com GSM: + 358505604425

5.18.4 Name of the Measure	Self-Identity Inventory SII
Primary Reference	Sevig, T. D., Highlen, P. S., & Adams, E. M. (2000). Development and validation of the Self-Identity Inventory (SII): A multicultural identity development instrument. *Cultural Diversity and Ethnic Minority Psychology, 6,* 168–182.
Purpose	The purpose of the SII is to measure identity development across identities and cultural groups such as race, ethnicity, gender, sexual orientation, class, age, religion, or disability.
Description	The SII is based on the Optimal Theory Applied to Identity Development (OTAID; Myers, Speight, Highlen, Cox, Reynolds, Adams, & Hanley, 1991). The OTAID model is applied to diverse identities and cultural groups in the context of a Eurocentric dominant culture of the United States.
	The SII is a 71-item instrument designed to measure the six developmental phases stipulated by the OTAID model through its six subscales: (1) Individuation, (2) Dissonance, (3) Immersion, (4) Internalization, (5) Integration, and (6) Transformation. Each item is rated on a 6-point Likert-type rating scale ranging from 1 = Strongly Disagree to 6 = Strongly Agree. The items refer to "My group" as the target of identity. Participants are asked to describe their identity at the top of the survey form—for example, African American, poor person, Latino American, gay male, etc.—and then proceed to respond to the questions replacing "My group" with the identity they put down.
	An initial pool of 195 items was developed rationally based on the description of the OTAID's six phases by a team of researchers. Each item was rated by two judges independently for clarity and placement in a phase. Then items were pilot tested with six individuals of different social groups. After items were excluded by initial factor analysis because of poor fit and low factor structure coefficients, confirmatory factor analysis was conducted with six factors. The goodness of fit index, GFI, ranged between .91 and .93, and the adjusted GFI ranged from .86 to .90.
Samples	A convenient sample of 325 participants from the general population and universities was obtained from 24 states through 19 contacts. The sample comprised 74% women, and the overall age ranged from 18–82 ($M = 33.8$, $SD = 15.2$). Ethnically the sample was 10% African American, 2% biracial or multiracial, 83% White American, and 2% Latino/a American; Moreover, 6% were bisexual, 4% were gay males, 16% were lesbian, and 74% were heterosexual. The income level of participants ranged from under $15,000 to above $75,000, and the percentages with $10,000 increments ranged from 15% to 18%.
Scoring	The number of items in each of the subscales is as follows: Individual: 14 items Dissonance: 11 items Immersion: 10 items

	Internalization: 11 items
	Integration: 11 items
	Transformation: 15 items
	Total OTAID: 71 items
	Items from different phases are ordered randomly and all are scored in the positive direction. The score for each subscale is obtained by averaging the ratings of the items in the subscales.
Reliability	Of the total sample, 66 participants completed the survey a second time 6–10 weeks after the first time.
	Cronbach's alphas of the scores of the six subscales were as follows:
	Individuation: Alpha = .84
	Dissonance: Alpha = .90
	Immersion: Alpha = .84
	Internalization: Alpha = .72
	Integration: Alpha = .78
	Transformation: Alpha = .90
	The test-retest reliability coefficients of the six subscales ranged from .72 to .92.
Validity	Content validity was assessed by item-scale correlations for each of the subscales. Most of the item-scale correlations exceeded .30 with only four items in the Internalization scale between .25 and .30.
	Five of the six subscales were highly correlated with their adjoining scales. Also, as expected, Integration and Transformation scores were negatively correlated with Individuation. For convergent validity, the SII subscales were correlated with the Tolerance Scale of the California Psychological Inventory (Gough, 1987), and the Belief System Analysis scale (Montgomery, Fine, & Myers, 1990) that measure similar constructs. The Tolerance scale, as expected, was correlated negatively with Dissonance, Immersion, and Internalization and positively with Individuation, Integration, and Transformation. The Belief System Analysis scale was correlated positively with Individuation, Integration, and Transformation, negatively with Dissonance, and uncorrelated with Immersion and Internalization. A later study by Munley, Lidderale, Thiagarajan, and Null (2004) showed predictable correlations between the subscales of the SII and the Knowledge and Awareness subscales of the Multicultural Counseling Knowledge and Awareness scales (Ponterotto, Gretchen, Utsey, Rieger, & Austin, 2002).
	Discriminant validity was demonstrated by the absence of correlation between the subscales of the SII and the Social Desirability Scale of the Personality Research Form-Form E (Jackson, 1984).

(Continued)

(Continued)

Related References	Munley, P. H., Lidderdale, M. A., Thiagarajan, M., & Null, U. (2004). Identity development and multicultural competency. *Journal of Multicultural Counseling and Development, 32,* 283–295. Myers, L. J., Speight, S. L., Highlen, P. S., Cox, C. I., Reynolds, A. L., Adams, E. M., & Hanley, C. P. (1991). Identity development and worldview: Toward an optimal conceptualization. *Journal of Counseling and Development, 70,* 54–63.
Language Versions	English
Contact	Todd D. Sevig Counseling and Psychological Services University of Michigan 3100 Michigan Union Ann Arbor, MI 48109 Tel: 734–764–8312 Email: tdsevig@umich.edu Pamela S. Highlan Department of Psychology Ohio State University 1885 Neil Avenue Mall Columbus, OH 43210

5.18.5 Name of the Measure	Multigroup Ethnic Identity Measure—Revised MEIM-R
Primary Reference	Phinney, J. S., & Ong, A. D. (2007). Conceptualization and measurement of ethnic identity: Current status and future directions. *Journal of Counseling Psychology, 54,* 271–281.
Purpose	The purpose of the MEIM-R is to assess ethnic identity across diverse ethnic
Description	The MEIM-R is a six-item measure composed of two subscales: (1) Exploration and (2) Commitment. The Other Group identity subscale that was part of the original MEIM (Phinney, 1992) was not used in the development of the MEIM-R, since it is considered a measure independent and separate from ethnic identity. The items of the MEIM-R (this scale is a further modification of the MEIM proposed by Roberts, Phinney, Masse, Chin, Roberts, & Romero, 1999, that bears the same abbreviation) are rated on a 5-point Likert-type scale ranging from 1 = Strongly Disagree, 3 = Neutral, to 5 = Strongly Agree. The items precede with an open-ended self-label of ethnic identity. The items are worded such that they can be used with any ethnic group. At the end of the measure, respondents are asked to identify their ethnic background on a given list of appropriate ethnic groups. Two university samples were used to identify the factor structure of MEIM-R. In the first sample, using a 10-item version of the MEIM, an exploratory maximum likelihood factor analysis was conducted with an oblique rotation. The results suggested a two-factor structure. Four items were dropped with structure coefficients less than .40. The remaining list of six items was composed the two subscales: Exploration with three items, and Commitment with three items. Using an independent second sample of university students, a confirmatory factor analysis was conducted with maximum likelihood estimation. After testing for various factorial models, a correlated two-factor model was found to have the best fit: AGFI = .96, CFI = .98, and RMSEA = .04. For reference, the original MEIM (Phinney, 1992) was composed of 20 items, where 14 items measured three aspects of ethnic identity as a single factor: (1) Affirmation/Belonging, (2) Ethnic Identity Achievement, and (3) Ethnic Behavior, and six items measured Other-group identity separate from ethnic identity.
Samples	Two University samples were used in developing the MEIM-R. The first sample used for the exploratory factor analysis was composed of 192 ethnically diverse university students: 70% Latino/a American, 20% Asian American, 5% White American, 13% African American, and 2% of mixed ethnicity; 65% were women. The mean age was 17.9 years. The second university sample used for the confirmatory factor analysis was also ethnically diverse; 51% Latino/a American, 26% Asian American, 9% White American, 14% of mixed ethnicity; 78% were women, and 26.5% were foreign born. The mean age was 19.7 years.

(Continued)

(Continued)

Scoring	The number of items in the subscales is as follows: 　Exploration: 3 items 　Commitment: 3 items 　Total MEIM: 6 items The subscale scores are calculated as the mean ratings of the items in each subscale. The combined total MEIM-R score is the average rating of the 6 items.
Reliability	The Cronbach's alphas of the scores of the MEIM-R subscales were as follows: 　Exploration: Alpha = .76 　Commitment: Alpha = .78 　Total MEIM-R: Alpha = .81
Validity	No evidence for criterion, discriminant, or convergent validity was reported for the MEIM-R. However, the exploratory and confirmatory factor analyses point to strong construct validity. There is much evidence in the literature regarding various types of validity for the original MEIM because of its extensive use in research.
Related References	Phinney, J. S. (1992). The Multigroup Ethnic Identity Measure: A new scale for use with diverse groups. *Journal of Adolescent Research, 7,* 156–176. Roberts, R. E., Phinney, J. S., Masse, L. C., Chin, Y. R., Roberts, C. R., & Romero, A. (1999). The structure of ethnic identity of young adolescents from diverse ethnocultural groups. *Journal of Early Adolescence, 19,* 301–322.
Language Versions	English. However, the original MEIM has been used and translated to a number of languages.
Contact	Jean S. Phinney Department of Psychology California State University, Los Angeles Room KH C3061 Los Angeles, CA 90032–8227. Email: jphinney@calstatepa.edu

6

Acculturation Measures

6.1 ACCULTURATION DEFINED

Acculturation as a construct has received scrutiny within the social, behavioral, and health sciences over at least the past seven decades. Theoretical and empirical treatment of the construct often begins with a ubiquitous mention of early anthropological and sociological scholars' (e.g., Gordon, 1964; Redfield, Linton, & Herskovitz, 1936) views on acculturation. Redfield et al. (1936) considered acculturation to be a function of different cultural *groups* coming into regular first-hand intercultural contact. This perspective influenced and motivated a generation of acculturation scholarship such as Gordon's (1964, 1978) linear seven-stage process model of how immigrants *assimilated* to mainstream culture and Graves's (1967) notions of *psychological acculturation* on the *individual* level.

Since the publication of these and other early acculturation articles, a number of empirical acculturation research and concomitant comprehensive review articles, chapters, and books have been produced in subsequent decades (e.g., Adrados, 1993; Berry, 1980, 1990a, 1990b, 1997, 2003; Cabassa, 2003; Chun, Balls Organista, & Marin, 2003; Cuéllar, Siles, & Baracamontes, 2004; Dana, 1993; Flannery, Reise, & Yu, 2001; Kim & Abreu, 2001; Kohatsu, 2005; Koneru, Weisman de Manani, Flynn, & Betancourt, 2007; Lam, 1995; Liebkind, 2006; Matsudaria, 2006; Navas et al., 2005; Olmedo, 1979; Padilla, 1980; Rivera, 2008; Rogler, Cortes, & Malgady, 1991; Roysircar-Sodowsky & Maestas, 2000; Rudmin, 2003, 2009; Sam & Berry, 2006; Schwartz, Unger, Zamboanga, & Szapocznik, 2010; Skinner, 2001; Van de Vijver & Phalet, 2004; Zane & Mak, 2003).

Most recent scholarship in clinical and counseling psychology (e.g., Cuéllar, Arnold, & Maldonado, 1995; Kim & Abreu, 2001; Marin & Gamba, 2003; Rivera, 2008) views acculturation as a process of individual changes within the behavioral, cognitive, and affective domains that individuals experience due to intercultural contact.

6.2 CONTEXT OF ACCULTURATION

Ethnic/racial minorities, immigrants, refugees, and migrant laborers do not acculturate from their culture of origin to a new culture in a social vacuum. The present economic system that prevails in the United States, capitalism (a topic often neglected in the psychological literature), provides and regulates certain "antecedent conditions" that influence all acculturation phenomena (Berry, 1997; Cabassa, 2003; Lam, 1995; Rivera, 2008). Some of these contextual factors include the following:

- **Volitional intent** (e.g., travel/study abroad, military action);
- **Fluidity** (e.g., immigrate to new country, colonization);

- **Perpetuity** (e.g., long- or short-term duration);
- **Pecuniary aspects** (e.g., availability of financial and human resources);
- **Oppression** (e.g., personal experience of racism and discrimination);
- **Sociodemographics** (e.g., occupation, education); and
- **Similarity** (e.g., linguistic, cultural, geographic).

These contextual variables precede the acculturation experience and help create the conditions for the quality and intensity of contact (either positive or negative) individuals of all ethnicities experience with the new culture.

6.3 ACCULTURATION DIMENSIONALITY

Much of the acculturation measurement literature (e.g., Cuéllar et al., 1995; Kim & Abreu, 2001; Zane & Mak, 2003) has concerned itself with describing the dimensions of acculturation phenomena. One way to conceptualize this dimensionality is to posit an interaction between two domains of acculturation dimensions (lifestyle dimensions x psychological dimensions) for both the culture of origin and the new culture (e.g., Lam, 1995). Following the lead of Matsudaria (2006) and Rudmin and Ahmadzadeh (2001), the present chapter will use the term *culture of origin* instead of home, heritage, or ethnic culture. Likewise, we prefer the term *new culture* as opposed to host, dominant, or mainstream culture. We believe this terminology both conveys respect and avoids many unintended connotations.

Lam (1995) has identified at least seven sociocultural lifestyle facets or dimensions. During the process of acculturation (to the new culture) or enculturation (to the culture of origin), these lifestyle dimensions may undergo a variety of changes to reflect either the culture of origin and/or the individual's new culture. These lifestyle dimensions take the following form:

- **Language** (i.e., oral and written communication);
- **Daily habits** (e.g., food, music, media preferences, etc.);
- **Living arrangement** (e.g., housing, furniture, transportation, personal property);

- **Ethnic norms/heritage** (e.g., gender roles, child rearing, celebrations, work ethic, affect display, time orientation);
- **Social relationships** (e.g., interaction style, playmates, marriage partners);
- **Political affiliation** (e.g., involvement, orientation);
- **Religious affiliations** (e.g., orientation, involvement, ancestor views).

Lam (1995) posits that individual acculturative change can occur among the seven lifestyle facets along the following three psychological dimensions:

- **Attitudes or values;**
- **Knowledge or cognition; and**
- **Behavior or practice.**

Hence, in this dynamic acculturative framework, an individual could experience various attitudes or values (i.e., feelings, beliefs, preferences), hold or develop knowledge (i.e., insights, proficiencies, sophistication, awareness, etc.), and emit a variety of behaviors that influence his or her cultural practice, all of which can depart from or intersect with the culture of origin and new culture.

Historically, acculturation dimensionality has been examined by means of unidirectional and bidirectional models of acculturation (e.g., Flannery et al., 2001). Unidirectional models (e.g., Gordon, 1964) view the course of acculturation as a linear, one-way street, sometimes referred to as a zero-sum (Rogler et al., 1991), in which the individual surrenders the culture of origin in favor of a new culture. As Flannery et al. (2001) aptly note, this teeter-totter effect often conceals the multidimensionality of unidirectional models. In other words, unidirectional models can posit a variety of dimensions or facets (e.g., language, ethnic norms, etc.) all moving at various rates toward assimilation.

Most recent scholarship has acknowledged the severe limitations of a unidirectional perspective (e.g., Rivera, 2008; Ryder, Alden, & Paulhus, 2000), with some notable exceptions (e.g., Flannery et al., 2001; Rudmin, 2003). The alternative bidirectional conceptualization has currently gained ascendancy in the acculturation literature (e.g., Kim & Abreu, 2001; Rivera, 2008; Zane & Mak, 2003). Bidirectional theorists (Berry, 1980, 2003; Berry & Sam, 1997; Marin & Gamba, 1996) argue that the process of acculturation operates simultaneously and independently on two cultural orientations, the culture of origin and the new culture. Acculturating individuals are assumed to vary in the cultural relationship strategies they employ with the two cultures; they can embrace both, incorporate neither, or adhere to a combination of both.

Berry (1990, 2003) has articulated perhaps the most widely influential bidirectional model of acculturation. This model asserts that acculturating individuals adopt one of four acculturation *strategies*:

- **Separate (Traditional).** The individual maintains strong positive ties with the culture of origin and does not associate with the new culture.
- **Assimilation (Americanized).** The individual rejects the culture of origin and embraces the new culture.
- **Marginalization (Alienated).** The individual does not relate to either the culture of origin or the new culture.
- **Integration (Bicultural).** The individual relates well to both the culture of origin and the new culture.

Berry's bidirectional model has helped motivate a large amount of theoretical and empirical research (e.g., Berry, 2003; Rivera, 2008) and helped encourage the development of bidirectional acculturation instruments (e.g., Cuéllar et al., 1995). Berry's fourfold typology of acculturation strategies has also come under critical scrutiny (Rudmin, 2003, 2009) on both logical and empirical grounds. Further, researchers and practitioners have been encouraged (Rivera, 2008) to explore multidirectional instruments (Chung, Kim, & Abreu, 2004) and multidirectional (tridirectional) models (e.g., Flannery et al., 2001).

Before proceeding with our review of 48 specific acculturation-related instruments that met our inclusion criteria, a brief examination of cultural issues pertinent to each major ethnic/racial group will provide a contextual framework to better understand the plethora of acculturation instruments to be summarized.

6.4 AFRICAN AMERICAN ACCULTURATION ISSUES

The legacy of more than 300 years of brutal slavery (see Stampp, 1956) only to be supplanted with illusory emancipation and segregation still haunts African Americans' interconnection with White American "mainstream" culture (e.g., Loewen, 2005). A genuine paucity of African American acculturation instruments exists currently. Historically, this circumstance has been punctuated by viewing African Americans only as a racial group and not as both a racial *and* ethnic group with a unique culture (Landrine & Klonoff, 1994) and set of family values that emphasizes collective kinship and spirituality (Chun & Akutsu, 2003).

As empirical evidence was amassed in psychology, sociology, and anthropology for African American ethnic identity, with unique values, beliefs, and behaviors (e.g., Asante, 1987; Baldwin, 1984; Cross, 1978; Dana, 1993; Jones, 1991; McAdoo, 1981; Myers, 1987; Nobles, 1980; Parham, 1989; Thomas, 1971; White, 1984), several authors began to conceptualize and construct acculturation instruments for African Americans.

Currently, four instruments have been developed that meet the minimum criteria for inclusion in this volume. The first scale to measure African American acculturation was the 74-item African American Acculturation Scale (AAAS; Landrine & Klonoff, 1994), which was immediately condensed into a 33-item short form (AAAS- 33; Landerine & Klonoff, 1995), which was subsequently revised, due to critical feedback concerning some of the items, into its current 47-item unidirectional eight-dimension version (AAAS-R; Klonoff & Landerine, 2000).

Snowden and Hines (1999) developed a second unidirectional acculturation scale that was initially validated as a unidimensional instrument. Recent confirmatory factor analytic work with this 10-item instrument (AAAS; Reid, Brown, Peterson, Snowden, & Hines, 2009) has identified some dimensionality.

A recent addition to the African American acculturation literature is the development of the Two-Dimensional Black Acculturation Scale (T-DBAS;

Cole & Jacob Arriola, 2007). This bidirectional multidimensional instrument attempts to measure Black college students' adaptation to predominantly White American college campuses by tapping both Black cultural heritage and identity and major group relationships.

Lastly, Grills and Longshore (1996) have developed a 15-item self-report measure of Africentrism called the Africentrism Scale (AS). The AS attempts to measure the degree to which African Americans adhere to the *Nguzo Saba* (Seven Principles) in African and African American culture.

6.5 ASIAN AMERICAN ACCULTURATION ISSUES

Asians have been immigrating to the United States in waves beginning in the 1840s to labor in gold mining operations, the linking of the transcontinental railroad, and the Hawaiian sugar and pineapple plantations (Kim, Ahn, & Lam, 2009). Subsequent waves of Asian immigrants followed due to World War II, the Korean War, and the Vietnam War.

The concept of *Asian American* is somewhat of a convenient fiction for multicultural researchers due to the ethnic diversity of this racial group. In the United States, Asian Americans consist of more than 24 separate ethnic groups including Chinese Americans, Filipino/a Americans, Asian Indians, Vietnamese Americans, Korean Americans, Japanese Americans, and smaller subgroups (Kim & Hong, 2004; Zane, Morton, Chu, & Lin, 2004). Underscoring the heterogeneity of these groups is the variability found in identification with basic Asian cultural values such as collectivism, conformity, emotionality, achievement recognition, filial piety, and humility (Kim, Yang, Atkinson, Wolfe, & Hong, 2001).

Additional factors that affect the assessment of Asian American acculturation include internal family dynamics such as intergenerational conflict or "distancing" (Hwang, 2007), perceptions of racism and discrimination (Chan & Hune, 1995), overcoming racist stereotypes (Alvarez, Juang, & Liang, 2006), as well as differences between Asian immigrants and refugees (Salant & Lauderdale, 2003).

The present review identified 14 Asian American acculturation-related instruments that met our minimal inclusion criteria. Five measures focused on various aspects of Asian American acculturation: Asian American Multidimensional Acculturation Scale (AAMAS; Chung, Kim, & Abreu, 2004), Asian Values Scale—Revised (AVS-R; Kim & Hong, 2004), Asian American Values Scale—Multidimensional (AAVS-M; Kim, Li, & Ng, 2005), Suinn-Lew Asian Self-Identity Acculturation Scale (SL-ASIA; Suinn, Rickard-Figueroa, Lew, & Vigil, 1987), and European American Values Scale for Asian Americans–Revised (EAVS-AA-R; Hong, Kim, & Wolfe, 2005). Three additional scales focused on Southeast Asians: Acculturation Scale for Southeast Asians (ASSA; Anderson, Moeschberger, Chen, Kunn, Wewers, & Guthrie, 1993), Acculturation Scale for Vietnamese Adolescents (ASVA; Nguyen & von Eye, 2002), Khmer Acculturation Scale (KAS; Lim, Heiby, Brislin, & Griffin, 2002). Individual acculturation scales for an additional four ethnic groups were as follows: Cultural Values Conflict Scale for South Asian Women (CVCS; Inman, Ladany, Constantine, & Morano, 2001), A Short Acculturation Scale for Filipino Americans (ASASFA; de la Cruz, Padilla, & Butts, 1998), General Ethnicity Questionnaire (GEQ; Tsai, Ying, & Lee, 2000), and the Brief Acculturation Scale (BAS-J; Meredith, Wenger, Liu, Harada, & Kahn, 2000). Lastly, two additional measures explore Asian American acculturation-related issues of cultural adjustment with the Cultural Adjustment Difficulties Checklist (CADC; Sodowsky & Lai, 1997), and culturally based inter-generational family conflicts with the Asian American Family Conflicts Scale (FCS; Lee, Cho, Kim, & Ngo, 2000).

6.6 LATINO/A AMERICAN ACCULTURATION ISSUES

There are currently more than 35.3 million Hispanic or Latino/a Americans living in the United States accounting for 12.5% of the total population (U.S. Census Bureau, 2009). Latino/a Americans represent diverse ethnic sub-cultures that include individuals from Mexico, Central and South America, and Caribbean countries (Cuba, Dominican Republic, Puerto Rico). While the Spanish language and certain customs, beliefs, and values are shared among these different cultures, acculturation scales are tasked with capturing the underlying cultural commonality and the overarching cultural heterogeneity.

Early reviews of the Latino/a acculturation literature (Dana, 1993, 1996; Olmedo, 1979; Padilla, 1980) lamented the paucity of valid and reliable measures and their infrequent use in assessment practice. Some of the more recent reviews (e.g., Cuéllar, Siles, & Bracamontes, 2004; Hunt, Schneider, & Comer, 2004; Lara, Gamboa, Kahremanian, Morales, & Hayes Bautista, 2005; Siatkowski, 2007; Valencia & Johnson, 2008; Wallace, Pomery, Latimer, Martinez, & Salovey, 2009; Zemore, 2007) have been critical of the overreliance of these scales on language behaviors and preferences and U.S. residency length in assessing Latino/a American acculturation.

The present review identified 21 Latino/a American acculturation-related scales that met our minimum inclusion criteria. Eight scales were designed to measure adult Latino/a American acculturation facets: Short Acculturation Scale for Hispanics (SASH; Marin, Sabogal, Ortero-Sabogal, & Perez-Stable, 1987), Acculturation Rating Scale (ARS; Montgomery, 1992a), Acculturation and Structural Assimilation Scales (ASAS; Hazuda, Stern, & Haffner, 1988), Bidimensional Acculturation Scale for Hispanics (BAS; Marin & Gamba, 1996), Brief Acculturation Rating Scale for Mexican Americans-II (Brief ARSMA-II, or ARSMA-II-SF; Bauman, 2005; Cuéllar, Arnold, & Maldonado, 1995), Multidimensional Acculturation Scale (MAS II; Rodriguez, Bingham Mira, Paez, & Myers, 2007), Los Angeles Epidemiologic Catchment Area Acculturation Scale (LAECAAS; Burnam, Telles, Karno, Hough, & Escobar, 1987), and Padilla's Acculturation Scale (PAS; Padilla, 1980). Two scales focus on adult Puerto Rican acculturation issues: Psychological Acculturation Scale (PAS; Tropp, Erkut, García Coll, Alarcón, & Vásquez

García, 1999), and Puerto Rican Biculturality Scale (PRBS; Cortes, Rogler, & Malgady, 1994). Five scales focus on child/adolescent Latino/a American accultura-tion assessment: Children's Acculturation Scale (CAS; Franco, 1983), Short Acculturation Scale for Hispanic Youth (SASH-Y; Barona & Miller, 1994), Acculturative Stress Inventory for Children (ASIC; Suarez-Morales, Dillon, & Szapocznik, 2007), Measure of Acculturation for Chicano Adolescents (MACA; Olmedo, Martinez, & Martinez, 1978), and the Cultural Life Styles Inventory (CLSI; de Leon & Mendez, 1996; Mendoza, 1989). The last six scales address issues of Latino/a cul-tural socialization, family attitudes, and values: Cultural Socialization Scale (CSS; Romero, Cuéllar, & Roberts, 2000), Pan-Hispanic Familism Scale (P-HFS; Villarreal, Blozis, & Widaman, 2005), Attitudinal Familism Scale (AFS; Steidel & Contreras, 2003), Expectations of Filial Piety Scale-Spanish Version (EFPS-SV; Kao & Travis, 2005), Latino/a Values Scale (LVS; Kim, Soliz, Orellana, & Alamilla, 2009) and the Multiple Assessment of Cultural Constructs-Short Form (MACC-SF; Cuéllar, Arnold, & Gonzalez, 1995).

6.7 NATIVE AMERICAN ACCULTURATION ISSUES

Native Americans and Alaska Natives consist of about 2.5 million people dispersed among 560 separate tribal nations (Gone, 2007). Tribal identification over racial identification tends to predominate for this group, resulting in rich cultural heterogeneity among tribes (Choney, Berryhill-Paapke, & Robbins, 1995).

The concept of Native American acculturation and assimilation is inseparably bound up with the racist and genocidal legacy of oppression by European and later U.S. government policies imposed upon the indigenous native people of North America. Native Americans have endured and struggled against attempted slavery, reli-gious indoctrination and conversion, forced removal and relocation, extermination, forced assimilation through re-education, and native religious persecution (Duran & Duran, 1995; Jenkins, 2004; Snipp, 1989; Weaver & Yellow Horse Brave Heart, 1999).

Centuries of Native American acculturative trauma have resulted in the following:

- Reduction of the Native American population to 5% of its original size;
- More than 25% living in poverty;
- Five times more likely to die of alcohol-related issues than White Americans;
- Suicide rates that are 50% higher than the national average (U.S. Department of Health and Human Services, 2001).

For the purposes of the present review, we identified five published Native American acculturation scales: Navaho Family Acculturation Scale (NFAS; Boyce & Boyce, 1983), Navaho Community Acculturation Scale (NCAS; Boyce & Boyce, 1983), Native American Acculturation Scale (NAAS; Garrett & Pichette, 2000), Rosebud Personal Opinion Survey (RPOS; Hoffman, Dana, & Bolton, 1985), and the Traditional Behavior Scale (TBS; Arambula Solomon & Gottlieb, 1999). However, because none of these instruments met our stated psychometric inclusion criteria, we have reluctantly eliminated all of the Native American acculturation instruments from this review. Our review is basically in accord with a previous evaluation by Kim and Abreu (2001), who noted, "there appears to be a great need for more research that aims to improve or establish the psychometric properties of instruments designed to measure Native American acculturation" (pp. 415–416). We can only echo this sentiment and hope that this overview motivates future empirical research on Native American acculturation and its valid and reliable measurement.

6.8 MULTIGROUP ACCULTURATION ISSUES

Multicultural societies like the United States require that culturally competent practitioners and researchers are capable of providing cultural assessments of racially and ethnically diverse clientele. As a consequence, a growing number of investigators have begun developing multigroup acculturation instruments and exploring the role of acculturation in a multicultural context (Van de Vijver & Phalet, 2004).

The present review has identified nine such instruments: Orthogonal Cultural Identification Scale (OCIS; Oetting, Swaim, & Chiarella, 1998), Vancouver Index of Acculturation (VIA; Ryder, Alden, & Paulhus, 2000), Majority-Minority Relations Survey (MMRS; Sodowsky, Lai, & Plake, 1991), Acculturation, Habits, and Interests Multicultural Scale for Adolescents (AHIMSA; Unger, Gallaher, Shakib, Ritt-Olson, Palmer, & Anderson Johnson, 2002), Abbreviated Multidimensional Acculturation Scale (AMAS-ZABB; Zea, Asner-Self, Birman, & Buki, 2003), Stephenson Multigroup Acculturation Scale (SMAS; Stephenson, 2000), American-International Relations Scale (A-IRS; Sodowsky & Plake, 1991), Cortes, Rogler, and Malgady Bicultural Scale (CRM-BS; Mezzich, Ruiperes, Yoon, Liu, & Zapata-Vega, 2009), and Acculturative Stress Scale for International Students (ASSIS; Sandhu & Asrabadi, 1994).

6.9 FUTURE RESEARCH

Incredible progress has been made over the past seven decades since Redfield et al. (1936) was tasked to begin to define acculturation and outline an empirical line of march. Nevertheless, much work remains to be accomplished regarding the measurement of acculturation and its application to physical and mental health service delivery. We see the following as a brief list of acculturation topics that merit additional future empirical scrutiny.

1. **Proxy versus full measures of acculturation.** When if ever are proxy measures adequate for assessing acculturation status? Do proxy variables provide enough information to justify their pragmatic utility?

2. **Ethnic/racial-specific versus multigroup acculturation measures.** What is gained and lost from the use of a culture-general acculturation instrument?

3. **What are the important dimensions of future bidirectional and multidimensional acculturation instruments?** Lifestyle dimensions (e.g., language,

preferences, ethnic norms, etc.) and psychological dimensions (e.g., attitudes, cognition, and behavior) need further clarification.

4. **How can acculturation contextual issues be better incorporated into acculturation measurement?** To what extent do antecedent conditions (e.g., refugee status, poverty, personal resources, oppression) drive much of an individual's acculturative behavior and subsequent acculturative strategies under capitalism?

5. **Acculturation as a process versus an acculturative static snapshot.** Clearly, the process of acculturation and enculturation develops over time, yet most acculturation measures do not examine the acculturative time course.

6. **Acculturation measure for Native Americans.** There is a genuine paucity of psychometrically sound Native American acculturation measures. Valid and reliable measures could further empirical research and aid in the delivery of culturally competent mental health services.

7. **Latino/a American Acculturation Measures.** Future research would benefit from the development of a comprehensive Latino/a American acculturation scale that links mental and physical health issues with "prominent beliefs, values, and practices" of Latino/a Americans (Siatkowski, 2007).

6.10 AFRICAN AMERICAN ACCULTURATION MEASURES

6.10.1 Name of the Measure	African American Acculturation Scale—Revised AAAS-R
Primary Reference	Klonoff, E. A., & Landrine, H. (2000). Revising and improving the African American Acculturation Scale. *Journal of Black Psychology*, 26(2), 235–261.
Purpose	The AAAS-R is a unidirectional, multicultural acculturation scale that was derived from its predecessor, the 74-item African American Acculturation Scale (AAAS; Landrine & Klonoff, 1994, 1996). The AAAS-R purports to measure eight dimensions of African American culture. High scores reflect traditional cultural orientation or immersion in African American culture and low scores reflect an acculturated orientation or low immersion in African American culture.
Description	The AAAS-R contains 47 items. Each item is rated on a 7-point Likert-type scale with the following three anchors: 1 = I Totally Disagree, Not True At All, 4 = Sort of Agree, Sort of True, 7 = I Strongly Agree, Absolutely True. The AAAS-R is composed of a total score and eight subscales: (1) Religious Beliefs and Practices, (2) Preference for Things African American, (3) Interracial Attitudes, (4) Family Practices, (5) Health Beliefs and Practices, (6) Cultural Superstitions, (7) Racial Segregation, (8) Family Values. The AAAS-R is a revised and shortened version of the 74-item African American Acculturation Scale (AAAS) by Landrine and Klonoff (1994, 1996). The revised AAAS-R was based on a sample of 520 African American adults who completed the AAAS. Twenty-six items were eliminated prior to dissemination based on feedback from participants in prior studies. The subsequent 48 items were analyzed by means of a principal components analysis with an orthogonal rotation. One additional item was eliminated due to a lack of correlation with any of the subsequent eight subscales, resulting in a 47-item, eight-subscale instrument.
Samples	The sample consisted of 520 African American adults (277 women and 243 men). Ages ranged from 18 to 79 years ($M = 28.2$, $SD = 10.01$). Education levels were as follows: 57 (11.5%) had not completed high school, 140 (28.2%) had graduated from high school, 235 (47.3%) had some college course work, and 65 (12.5%) had undergraduate or graduate degrees. Employment status was as follows: 183 (37.3%) worked full time, 81 (16.5%) were full-time students, 73 (14.9%) were students who worked part time, 63 (12.9%) worked part time, 13 (2.7%) were full-time housewives, 68 (13.9%) received supplementary income, and 9 (1.8%) were retired.
Scoring	The number of items in each of the eight subscales is as follows: Religious Beliefs and Practices: 10 items Preferences for Things African American: 9 items Interracial Attitudes: 7 items Family Practices: 4 items Health Beliefs and Practices: 5 items Cultural Superstitions: 4 items

	Racial Segregation: 4 items
	Family Values: 4 items
	Total AAAS-R: 47 items
	Scoring the AAAS-R consists of adding the participant's ratings on each item in the subscale to obtain subscale scores or adding all of the participant's ratings on all items to obtain a total score.
	Item missing values may be imputed with the subscale mean. No reverse coding or transformations are required.
Reliability	Cronbach's alpha ranged from .67 to .89 across the eight subscales:
	Religious Beliefs and Practices: Alpha = .89
	Preferences for Things African American: Alpha = .89
	Interracial Attitudes: Alpha = .87
	Family Practices: Alpha = .79
	Health Beliefs and Practices: Alpha = .77
	Cultural Superstitions: Alpha = .76
	Racial Segregation: Alpha = .76
	Family Values: Alpha = .67
	Total AAAS-R: Alpha = .93
	Guttman split-half reliability: $r = .79$
	Correlation of total AAAS-R with total AAAS: $r = .97$
Validity	Concurrent (group differences) validity was established by dividing the sample into three "segregation groups" based on their Racial Segregation subscale scores. MANOVA results indicated that the segregation groups differed significantly in their scores on all seven AAAS-R subscales; high-segregated participants scored higher (more traditional) and low-segregated participants scored lower (more acculturated) on the AAAS-R subscales.
Related References	Landrine, H., & Klonoff, E. A. (1994). The African American Acculturation Scale: Development, reliability, and validity. *Journal of Black Psychology, 20*(2), 104–127.
	Landrine, H., & Klonoff, E. A. (1995). The African American Acculturation Scale II: Cross-validation and short form. *Journal of Black Psychology, 21*(2), 124–152.
	Landrine, H., & Klonoff, E. A. (1996). *African American Acculturation: Deconstructing race and reviving culture.* Thousand Oaks, CA: Sage.
Language Versions	English
Contact	Elizabeth A. Klonoff San Diego State University Psychology Department 5500 Campanile Dr. San Diego, CA 92182–4611 (619) 594–5358 (Office) (619) 594–1332 (Fax) Email: eklonoff@sunstroke.sdsu.edu

6.10.2 Name of the Measure	African American Acculturation Scale AAAS
Primary Reference	Reid, R., Brown, T., Peterson, N., Snowden, L., & Hines, A. (2009). Testing the factor structure of a scale to assess African American acculturation: A confirmatory factor analysis. *Journal of Community Psychology, 37,* 1–13.
Purpose	The AAAS (not to be confused with the AAAS-R by Klonoff & Landrine, 2000) is a unidirectional, multicultural acculturation scale that was originally developed by Snowden and Hines (1999) as a measure of African American acculturation. Subsequent research with this scale (Reid, Brown, Peterson, Snowden, & Hines, 2009) suggests that this scale represents three dimensions of African American acculturation.
Description	The AAAS contains 10 items. Each item is rated on 4-point Likert-type scale with the following anchors: 1 = Strongly Disagree, 4 = Strongly Agree. The AAAS is composed of three subscales: (1) Media Preference, (2) Social Interaction Patterns, and (3) Attitudes. This 10-item measure was originally construed as a single-factor or unidimensional construct (Snowden & Hines, 1999) and subsequently reconstrued as a unidirectional, multicultural acculturation construct by means of confirmatory factor analysis (Reid et al., 2009).
Samples	The original sample (Snowden & Hines, 1999) consisted of 923 African American adults (533 women and 390 men). Respondents were interviewed (between 1991–1992) by means of telephone interviews with a national multistage random probability sampling scheme. A second sample (Reid et al., 2009) consisted of 301 African American adults (214 women and 87 men). Respondents were interviewed by means of telephone interviews with a random-digit-dialing probability sampling scheme. This sample closely approximated a U.S. Census (2000) demographic profile for African Americans in this northeastern U.S. city.
Scoring	The number of items in each of the three subscales is as follows: Media Preference: 3 items Social Interaction Patterns: 4 items Attitudes: 3 items Total AAAS: 10 item Scoring the AAAS consists of adding the participant's ratings on each item in the subscale and dividing by the number of subscale items to obtain a subscale mean. A total AAAS mean score can be computed by adding participants' ratings on all 10 items and dividing that total by 10. No reverse coding or transformations are required. Lower subscale means represent higher levels of acculturation to the dominant culture.

Reliability	Cronbach's alphas were not reported for the AAAS total scale score or for the three subscale scores.
Validity	AAAS subscales were moderately intercorrelated. For the most part, age, gender, education, and income were not correlated with the total AAAS or its subscales.
Related References	Snowden, L. R., & Hines, A. M. (1999). A scale to assess African American acculturation. *Journal of Black Psychology, 25*(1), 36–47.
Language Versions	English
Contact	Robert Reid 1 Normal Ave. Montclair, NJ 07043 Email: reidr@mail.montclair.edu

6.10.3 Name of the Measure	Two-Dimensional Black Acculturation Scale T-DBAS
Primary Reference	Cole, E. R., & Jacob Arriola, K. R. (2007). Black students on White campuses: Toward a two-dimensional model of Black acculturation. *Journal of Black Psychology, 33*(4), 379–403.
Purpose	The T-DBAS is a bidirectional, multidirectional, Black college student acculturation scale. The T-DBAS purports to measure two dimensions of Black college students' adaptation to predominantly White institutions: (a) cultural and political experiences of Blacks, and (b) intergroup or out-group relations.
Description	The T-DBAS contains 42 items. Each item is rated on a 5-point Likert-type scale ranging from 1 = Strongly Disagree to 5 = Strongly Agree.
	The T-DBAS is composed of two subscale scores: (1) Culture, Heritage, and Identity (CHI) and (2) Out-Group Comfort (OC).
	The T-DBAS was constructed through an initial item pool of 81 items assumed to be related to the underlying acculturation constructs (i.e., Black culture and intergroup relations). Based on feedback from a panel of experts, social desirability analysis, and an unspecified exploratory factor analysis with a varimax rotation, a 42-item simple structure was achieved with two factors accounting for 25% of the total variance. Item structure coefficients ranged from .40 to .72 across the two factors.
Samples	The initial validating sample consisted of 216 African American college students (117 women and 99 men). Ages ranged from 17 to 30 years ($M = 21.2$, $SD = 2.5$). Sample education was as follows: first year (38%), second year (17%), third year (19%), and fourth year and beyond (26%).
Scoring	The number of items in each of the two subscales is as follows:
	Culture, Heritage, and Identity: 26 items
	Out-Group Comfort: 16 items
	Total T-DBAS: 42 items
	Scoring the T-DBAS consists of adding the participant's ratings on each item in the subscale to obtain a subscale total sum. Reverse coding is required for 19 items.
Reliability	Cronbach's alpha for the scores of the two subscales was as follows:
	Culture, Heritage, and Identity: Alpha = .89
	Out-Group Comfort: Alpha = .84
	Respondent ratings on the CHI and OC subscales produced a small negative correlation.
Validity	Construct and convergent validity was achieved with two separate samples ($N = 83$ and 143, respectively) by correlating the scores of the CHI and OC with the Collective Self-Esteem Scale (CSES; Luhtanen & Crocker, 1992), the Black Racial Identity Attitudes Scale (RAIS-B; Helms, 1990), and the Racelessness Scale (Arroyo & Zigler, 1995).

Related References	Cole, E. R., & Yip, T. (2008). Using outgroup comfort to predict Black students' college experiences. *Cultural Diversity and Ethnic Minority Psychology, 14*(1), 57–66.
Language Versions	English
Contact	Elizabeth R. Cole Women's Studies Program and Center for AfroAmerican and African Studies University of Michigan 204 S. State St. Ann Arbor, MI 48109–1290 Email: ecole@umich.edu

6.10.4 Name of the Measure	Africentrism Scale AS
Primary Reference	Grills, C., & Longshore, D. (1996). Africentrism: Psychometric analyses of a self-report measure. *Journal of Black Psychology, 22*(1), 86–106.
Purpose	The AS is a self-report measure of Africentrism operationalized as the degree to which a person adheres to the *Nguzo Saba* (Seven Principles) in African and African American culture.
Description	The AS contains 15 items. Each item is rated on the following 4-point Likert-type scale: 1 = Strongly Disagree, 2 = Disagree, 3 = Agree, 4 = Strongly Agree. The AS is a unidimensional measure. The initial 25-item pool was developed from statements derived from the seven principles of the *Nguzo Saba: Umoja* (Unity), *Kujichagulia* (Self-determination), *Ujima* (Collective work and responsibility), *Ujamaa* (Cooperative economics), *Nia* (Purpose), *Kuumba* (Creativity), and *Imani* (Faith). Three alternative forms were created from this pool of items. Form A includes 17 items that can be administered in dyadic interviews. Most of the items are worded to pertain to African Americans. The word "group" present in some items is replaced by the ethnic identity of the interviewees as stated by them prior to the administration (e.g., "African American" or "Black"). Form B includes 13 items intended for use across ethnic groups. Most of the items are somewhat reworded versions of Form A in race-neutral terms. Four of the items on Form A did not have race-neutral counterparts. Form C is identical to Form A except it has 15 items. Two items were removed because of low item total correlations. A subsequent principal components analysis (with an oblique rotation) indicated a one-factor, 15-item simple structure that accounted for 30% of the total variance and provided the best representation of the data. This final version of the AS was designated Form C.
Samples	Four different studies were conducted using six different samples. Four of the samples were African American and two were White American. In Study 1, 29 African Americans (gender unspecified) in a substance use recovery group in Los Angeles participated in dyadic interviews. In Study 2, 57 African American (20 women, 37 men) and 21 White American (8 women, 13 men) clients in a methadone maintenance clinic in Los Angeles self-administered Form B. In Study 3, 25 African Americans (gender unspecified) attending a community study group of African American history self-administered Form A.

	In Study 4, the normative sample was based on 78 African American (26 women and 52 men) and 93 White American (27 women and 65 men) arrestees serving sentences in Los Angeles city and county jails. Socioeconomic characteristics between African American and White American participants was deemed comparable by the authors.
Scoring	Scoring the AS consists of adding the participant's ratings on each of the 15 items to obtain a total composite score. Six items are reverse coded.
Reliability	Cronbach's alpha for the scores of African Americans using Form C (the 15-item version) was .79.
Validity	Evidence of construct validity was offered through demonstrating positive correlations between the AS score and the subscale scores of the Multigroup Ethnic Identity Measure (MEIM; Phinney, 1992). Known-group validity was evidenced by the finding of statistically significantly higher AS scores among African American as opposed to White American participants. Kwate (2003) found a similar factor structure to the original one reported by Grills and Longshore (1996), with a diverse sample of African Americans.
Related References	Cokley, K. (2005). Racial(ized) identity, ethnic identity, and Afrocentric values: Conceptual and methodological challenges in understanding African American identity. *Journal of Counseling Psychology, 52*(4), 517–526.
	Kwate, N. O. A. (2003). Cross-validation of the Africentrism Scale. *Journal of Black Psychology, 29*, 308–324.
	Neblett, E. W., Jr., Hammond, W. P., Seaton, E. K., & Townsend, T. G. (2010). Underlying mechanisms in the relationship between Africentric worldview and depressive symptoms. *Journal of Counseling Psychology, 57*, 105–113.
Language Versions	English
Contact	Cheryl Tawede Grills Psychology Department Loyola Marymount University 1 LMU Drive Los Angeles, CA 90045–2659 (310) 338–3016 (W) Email: cgrills@lmu.edu

6.11 ASIAN AMERICAN ACCULTURATION MEASURES

6.11.1 Name of the Measure	Asian American Multidimensional Acculturation Scale AAMAS
Primary Reference	Chung, R. H. G., Kim, B. S. K., & Abreu, J. M. (2004). Asian American Multidimensional Acculturation Scale: Development, factor analysis, reliability, and validity. *Cultural Diversity and Ethnic Minority Psychology, 10*(1), 66–80.
Purpose	The AAMAS is a tridirectional, pan-ethnic Asian American acculturation scale (adapted from the Suinn-Lew Asian Self-Identity Acculturation Scale; Suinn, Rickard-Figueroa, Lew, & Vigil, 1987). Respondents are asked to rate 15 items according to three reference groups: (a) their culture of origin, (b) other Asian Americans, and (c) European Americans.
Description	The AAMAS contains 45 items. Each item is rated on a 6-point Likert-type scale with the following two anchors: 1 = Not Very Much, 6 = Very Much. Fifteen items are rated for each of three referent groups (cultural dimensions) comprising three separate scales: (a) AAMAS-Culture of Origin (AAMAS-CO), (b) AAMAS-Asian American (AAMAS-AA), and (c) AAMAS-European American (AAMAS-EA). The AAMAS items capture information about four acculturation domains (subscales) for each of the four ethnic referent groups: (a) Cultural Identity, (b) Language, (c) Cultural Knowledge, and (d) Food Consumption. Factor analysis and confirmatory factor analysis provided evidence that within each cultural dimension (AAMAS-CO, AAMAS-AA, AAMAS-EA) exists four acculturation domains: Cultural Identity, Language, Cultural Knowledge, and Food. A confirmatory factor analysis (with a separate sample, $N = 138$) provided further evidence of the four-factor (subscale) structure within each scale.
Samples	Three separate studies (samples) were reported. Study 1 sample: (Initial Factor Structure) consisted of 342 (118 men and 223 women) Asian American undergraduates of a large West Coast university. Ages ranged from 17 to 31 years ($M = 20.8$, $SD = 1.7$). Sample ethnicity was 91 Chinese (27%), 47 Korean (14%), 42 Japanese (12%), 38 Filipino (11%), 38 Vietnamese (11%), and 86 "Other Asian American" (25%). Sample generational status in the United States was as follows: 194 First generation (foreign born) (57%), 96 second generation (28%), 9 third generation (3%), 28 fourth generation (8%), and 12 fifth generation or above (4%). Study 2 sample: (Further Replication) consisted of 138 (41 men and 97 women) Asian American undergraduates from a West Coast university. Ages ranged from 18 to 35 years ($M = 21.3$, $SD = 3.6$). Sample ethnicity was 42 Chinese (30%), 32 Korean (23%), 17 multiethnic Asian (12%), 13 Filipino (9%), 12 Asian Indian (9%), 12 Japanese (9%), 6 Taiwanese (4%), and 4 Vietnamese (3%). Sample generational status was as follows: 47 first generation (foreign born) (34%), 67 second generation (49%), 10 third generation (7%), 12 fourth generation (9%), and 2 fifth generation and above (1%).

	Study 3 sample: (Test-Retest Reliability) consisted of 44 (25 men and 19 women) Korean Americans residing in Southern California. Ages ranged from 21 to 32 years ($M = 26.8$, $SD = 3.0$).

Scoring	The AAMAS is composed of three separate 15-item scales that reflect three unique perspectives or referent groups: Culture of Origin (AAMAS-CO), Asian American (AAMAS-AA), and European American (AAMAS-EA).
	
	Within each referent group (or cultural dimension) are four subscales (or acculturation domains):
	
	    Cultural Identity: 6 items
	
	    Language: 4 items
	
	    Cultural Knowledge: 3 items
	
	    Food Consumption: 2 items
	
	Scoring the AAMAS consists of adding the participants' ratings on each subscale and dividing by the number of items that compose the particular subscale to compute a subscale mean. One item (in the Cultural Identity subscale) is reverse scored. Total scale means for each of the three AAMAS scales can also be computed.

Reliability	Cronbach's alpha (internal reliability) was consistently high for the three AAMAS scales across all three studies. Study 1: AAMAS-CO (.87), AAMAS-AA (.78), AAMAS-EA (.81) Study 2: AAMAS-CO (.89), AAMAS-AA (.83), AAMAS-EA (.81) Study 3: AAMAS-CO (.89 & .91), AAMAS-AA (.83 & .83), AAMAS-EA (.76 & .81) Test-retest reliability (after 2 weeks): AAMAS-CO (.89), AAMAS-AA (.75), and AAMAS-EA (.78)
Validity	Criterion-related validity was assessed by correlating each of the three AAMAS scale scores with participants' generational status. The correlation between AAMAS-CO and generational status was low negative, and the other scales were not statistically significant. Concurrent validity was established by correlating the three AAMAS scales with the scores from the SL-ASIA, where mostly moderate correlations were observed. Divergent validity was found by comparing AAMAS scores with the subscale scores of the Intergenerational Conflict Inventory (ICI; Chung, 2001). Low correlations were observed, indicating little overlap between the two constructs.

(Continued)

(Continued)

Related References	Kim, B. S. K., Ahn, A. J., & Lam, N. A. (2009). Theories and research on acculturation and enculturation experiences among Asian American families. In N.-A. Trinh, Y. C. Rho, F. G. Lu, & K. M. Sanders (Eds.), *Handbook of mental health and acculturation in Asian American families*. Humana Press: Totowa, NJ. Koneru, V. K., Weisman de Mamani, A. G., Flynn, P. M., & Betancourt, H. (2007). Acculturation and mental health: Current findings and recommendations for future research. *Applied and Preventive Psychology, 12*(2), 76–96.
Language Versions	English
Contact	Ruth H. Gim Chung Division of Counseling Psychology Rossier School of Education WPH 1003C University Park University of Southern California Los Angeles, CA 90089–0031 Email: rchung@usc.edu

6.11.2 Name of the Measure	Asian Values Scale—Revised AVS-R
Primary Reference	Kim, B. S. K., & Hong, S. (2004). A psychometric revision of the Asian Values Scale using the Rasch model. *Measurement and Evaluation in Counseling and Development, 37,* 15–27.
Purpose	The AVS-R is a unidirectional and unidimensional self-report scale that is designed to assess adherence to Asian cultural values.
Description	The AVS-R contains 25 items. Each item is rated on a 4-point Likert-type scale with the following response options: 1 = Strongly Disagree, 2 = Disagree, 3 = Agree, 4 = Strongly Agree. The AVS-R is a unidimensional assessment of Asian American adherence to Asian cultural values. The AVS-R is a revised and shortened version of the 36-item Asian Values Scale (AVS; Kim, Atkinson, & Yang, 1999). Based on a Rasch polytomous response model, 11 items were eliminated from the original AVS, along with the 7-point Likert-type response scale.
Samples	The sample consisted of 618 Asian American adult college students (315 women, 303 men). Ages ranged from 18 to 37 years ($M = 21.0$, $SD = 4.7$). Ethnic breakdown was as follows: 152 (24.6%) Chinese, 136 (22.0%) Koreans, 86 (13.9%) Filipino/as, 64 (10.4%) Japanese, 51 (8.3%) Asian Indians, 29 (4.7%) multiethnic Asians, 26 (4.2%) Vietnamese, 15 (2.4%) Taiwanese, 14 (2.3%) multiracial Asians, and 42 (6.8%) other Asian Americans; 3 (0.5%) did not report their ethnicity. Generational status was as follows: 277 (44.8%) were second generation, 239 (38.7%) were first generation, 40 (6.5%) were third generation, 33 (5.3%) were fourth generation, 20 (3.3%) were fifth generation or greater, and 9 (1.5%) did not respond to this item.
Scoring	Scoring the AVS-R consists of adding the participant's ratings on each of the 25 items and dividing this value by 25 to obtain a AVS-R total scale mean. Ten of the 25 items require reverse coding. The larger the mean, the stronger the participant's adherence to Asian cultural values is assumed.
Reliability	No Cronbach's alpha was reported for the AVS-R score.
Validity	Authors report a high positive correlation between the AVS and AVS-R scores, which demonstrates some concurrent validity.
Related References	Kim, B. S. K., Atkinson, D. R. & Yang, P. H. (1999). The Asian Values Scale: Development, factor analysis, validation, and reliability. *Journal of Counseling Psychology, 46,* 342–352.

(Continued)

(Continued)

	Kim, B. S. K., Li, L. C., & Liang, C. T. H. (2002). Effects of Asian American client adherence to Asian cultural values, session goal, and counselor emphasis of client expression on career counseling process. *Journal of Counseling Psychology, 49,* 342–354.
Language Versions	English
Contact	Bryan S. K. Kim Department of Psychology University of Hawai'i at Hilo 200 W. Kawili St. Hilo, Hawai'i 96720–4091 (808) 974–7439 (W) (808) 974–7737 (Fax) Email: bryankim@hawaii.edu Website: www2.hawaii.edu/~bryankim/

6.11.3 Name of the Measure	Asian American Values Scale—Multidimensional AAVS-M
Primary Reference	Kim, B. S. K., Li, L. C., & Ng, G. F. (2005). Asian American Values Scale—Multidimensional: Development, Reliability, and Validity. *Cultural Diversity and Ethnic Minority Psychology, 11*, 187–201.
Purpose	The AAVS-M is a bidirectional, multidimensional acculturation scale that was partially derived from its predecessor, the Asian Values Scale (AVS; Kim, Atkinson, & Yang, 1999). The original AVS yielded an unreliable six-factor structure (i.e., low coefficient alphas), necessitating the use of the participants' composite total scale score and not the scores of the six subscales. The AAVS-M attempts to provide a multidimensional assessment of cultural values that differentiate between Asian Americans and White Americans, thus reflecting values of acculturation.
Description	The AAVS-M contains 42 items. Each item is rated on a 7-point Likert-type scale: 1 = Strongly Disagree, 2 = Moderately Disagree, 3 = Mildly Disagree, 4 = Neither Agree or Disagree, 5 = Mildly Agree, 6 = Moderately Agree, 7 = Strongly Agree. The AAVS-M is composed of a total scale score and five subscales: (1) Collectivism, (2) Conformity to Norms, (3) Emotional Self-Control, (4) Family Recognition Through Achievement, (5) Humility. The AAVS-M item pool was developed by eliciting a pool of 180 items (30 items for each of the six original AVS factors) from a national sample of Asian American psychologists. These items were subjected to a principal components analysis (with a varimax rotation), resulting in a 42-item, five-factor solution. A separate sample, employing a confirmatory factor analysis, supported this solution.
Samples	The original validating sample consisted of 163 (82 women and 81 men) Asian American college students. Ages ranged from 18 to 28 years ($M = 19.2$, $SD = 2.0$). Ethnic backgrounds were as follows: 36 (22.1%) Koreans, 31 (19.0%) Asian Indians, 25 (15.3%) Chinese, 21 (12.9%) Filipino/as, 17 (10.4%) multiracial, 9 (5.5%) Taiwanese, 6 (3.7%) Vietnamese, 3 (1.8%) Japanese, 2 (1.2%) Cambodian, 1 (0.6%) Indonesian, 1 (0.6%) Laotian, 1 (0.6%) Pakistani, and 10 (6.1%) others. Generation status was: first 72 (44.2%), second 83 (50.9%), third 3 (1.8%), fourth 1 (0.6%), fifth 1 (0.6%), and 1.8% missing data.
Scoring	The number of items in each of the five subscales is as follows: Collectivism: 7 items Conformity to Norms: 7 items Emotional Self-Control: 8 items Family Recognition Through Achievement: 14 items Humility: 6 items Total AAVS-M: 42 items

(Continued)

(Continued)

	Scoring the AAVS-M consists of adding the participant's ratings on all 42 items and then dividing by 42 to obtain a total scale or mean. Subscale scores or means are obtained by adding participant's ratings on each item in the subscale and dividing by the number of subscale items. A total of 13 items need to be reverse coded across the five subscales.
Reliability	Cronbach's alpha (.89 total scale score) ranged from .79 to .90 across the five subscales: Collectivism: Alpha = .80 Conformity to Norms: Alpha = .79 Emotional Self-Control: Alpha = .80 Family Recognition Through Achievement: Alpha = .90 Humility: Alpha = .81 Test-retest reliability scores over a 2-week period (separate sample, $N = 38$ Asian American college students) was $r = .92$ for the total scale score and ranged from .73 to .92 across the scores of the five subscales.
Validity	Concurrent validity was achieved by demonstrating positive correlations between the AAVS-M scores and the AVS scores, and negative correlations between the AAVS-M scores and scores of the Attitudes Toward Seeking Professional Psychological Help-Short Form (ATSPPH-SF; Fischer & Farina, 1995). Discriminant validity was achieved by demonstrating a low correlation between the AAVS-M total and subscale scores and the Rosenberg Self-Esteem Scale (RSES; Rosenberg, 1965).
Related References	Kim, B. S. K. (2009). Acculturation and enculturation of Asian Americans: A primer. In N. Tewari & A. N. Alvarez (Eds.), *Asian American psychology: Current perspectives* (pp. 97–112). Mahwah, NJ: Lawrence Erlbaum Associates.
Language Versions	English
Contact	Bryan S.K. Kim Department of Psychology University of Hawaii at Hilo 200 W. Kawili St. Hilo, Hawai'i 96720–4091 (808) 974–7439 (W) (808) 974–7737 (Fax) Email: bryankim@hawaii.edu Website: www2.hawaii.edu/~bryankim/

6.11.4 Name of the Measure	Suinn-Lew Asian Self-Identity Acculturation Scale SL-ASIA
Primary Reference	Suinn, R. M., Rickard-Figueroa, K., Lew, S., & Vigil, P. (1987). The Suinn-Lew Asian Self-Identity Acculturation Scale: An initial report. *Educational and Psychological Measurement, 47,* 280–287.
	Suinn, R. M., Ahuna, C., & Khoo, G. (1992). The Suinn-Lew Asian Self-Identity Acculturation Scale: Concurrent and factorial validation. *Educational and Psychological Measurement, 52,* 1041–1046.
Purpose	The SL-ASIA is an essentially unidirectional and Asian acculturation scale that was modeled after the original Acculturation Rating Scale for Mexican Americans (ARSMA; Cuéllar, Harris, & Jasso, 1980). The SL-ASIA is typically depicted on an acculturation continuum from Asian-identified values, behaviors, and attitudes at the low end and Western-identified values, behaviors, and attitudes at the high end. Biculturalism is represented at the middle of the continuum.
Description	The original SL-ASIA contains 21 multiple-choice items that follow the ARSMA format with items that address behavior (5), language (4), identity (4), friendship choice (4), generation level/geographic history (3), and attitudes (1). Five additional "experimental" items have been offered that provide further coverage of values (2), social interactions (2), and a classification scheme (1).
	The initial SL-ASIA article (Suinn, Rickard-Figueroa, Lew, & Vigil, 1987) was not informed by any factor analytic validity checks. Subsequent work (e.g., Suinn, Ahuna, & Khoo, 1992; Suinn, Khoo, & Ahuna, 1995), using principal components analysis (with an oblique rotation), has produced five interpretable factors. None of this multivariate work has been developed to establish or validate this component structure as separate dimensions of Asian acculturation (see also Ponterotto, Baluch, & Carielli, 1998).
Scoring	Scoring the SL-ASIA consists of adding the participant's ratings on each of the 21 items (which range from 1 to 5) and dividing this total score by 21 to obtain a mean acculturation score. A mean score of 1 indicates low acculturation or Asian-identified, a mean score of 3 indicates a bicultural orientation, and a mean score of 5 indicates an assimilated or Western-identified orientation. The senior author encourages investigators to experiment with various combinations of his five new acculturation items (# 22–26) (see Psychosocial Measures for Asian Americans: Tools for Practice and Research, www.columbia.edu/cu/ssw/projects/pmap).
Reliability	Cronbach's alpha for the scores of the 21-item scale was .88. Alphas for any derived subscales were not computed.

(Continued)

(Continued)

Validity	Content validity was achieved by having the SL-ASIA format shadow the original ARSMA. Convergent validity has been observed by demonstrating relationships between SL-ASIA scores and years of U.S. schooling, self-rating of acculturation, generation level, etc. (Ponterotto et al., 1998).
Related References	Ponterotto, J. G., Baluch, S., & Carielli, D. (1998). The Suinn-Lew Asian Self-Identity Acculturation Scale (SL-ASIA): Critique and research recommendations. *Measurement and Evaluation in Counseling and Development, 31,* 109–124.
	Ryder, A. G., Alden, L. E., & Paulhus, D. L. (2000). Is acculturation unidimensional or bidimensional? A head-to-head comparison in the prediction of personality, self-identity, and adjustment. *Journal of Personality and Social Psychology, 79*(1), 49–65.
	Suinn, R. M., Khoo, G., & Ahuna, C. (1995). The Suinn-Lew Asian Self-Identity Acculturation Scale: Cross-cultural information. *Journal of Multicultural Counseling and Development, 23,* 139–148.
Language Versions	English
Contact	Richard M. Suinn Emeritus Professor Department of Psychology Colorado State University Fort Collins, CO 80523

6.11.5 Name of the Measure	European American Values Scale for Asian Americans—Revised EAVS-AA-R
Primary Reference	Hong, S., Kim, B. S. K., & Wolfe, M. M. (2005). A psychometric revision of the European American Values Scale for Asian Americans using the Rasch model. Measurement and Evaluation. *Counseling and Development, 37,* 194–207. Wolfe, M. M., Yang, P. H., Wong, E. C., & Atkinson, D. R. (2001). Design and development of the European American Values Scale for Asian Americans. *Cultural Diversity and Ethnic Minority Psychology, 7*(3), 274–283.
Purpose	The EAVS-AA-R purports to measure Asian American acculturation to European American values. The EAVS-AA-R was derived from an earlier version of the scale (the 18-item EAVS-AA; Wolfe, Yang, Wong, & Atkinson, 2001) on the basis of a psychometric analysis using the Rasch Model (Rasch, 1960). This led to a new unidirectional and unidimensional measure.
Description	The EAVS-AA-R contains 25 items. Each item is rated on a 4-point Likert-type scale with the following response options: 1 = Strongly Disagree, 2 = Disagree, 3 = Agree, 4 = Strongly Agree. The authors reexamined the initial item pool of 180 items that was developed by Wolfe et al. (2001) through a careful literature review, selection of potential items from the World Values Survey (WVS; Inglehart, Basanez, & Moreno, 1993), and the identification of 36 value domains that discriminated North Americans from Asians. Items were eliminated from the pool if European Americans scored significantly higher than first-generation Asian Americans. This process produced the original EAVS-AA 18-item scale. A reanalysis of the original 180-item pool, with a less stringent alpha level item-inclusion criteria, yielded a new reduced pool of 49 items, including the original 18 items. Subsequent Rasch item analyses reduced the original 7-point response anchor to a new 4-point anchor with 25 items, 5 of which were included from the original EAVS-AA.
Samples	The sample consisted of 257 Asian American college students (145 women and 112 men). Ages ranged from 18 to 64 years ($M = 21.6$, $SD = 4.5$). Ethnic breakdown for the Asian American sample was as follows: Chinese American (110), Korean American (37), Vietnamese American (29), Filipino/a American (26), Japanese American (22), Asian Indian American (4), Cambodian American (3), and 22 indicated "other." Sample generation status was first generation (57.6%), second generation (36.2%), third generation (1.2%), fourth generation (2.3%), fifth generation (1.2%), and 1.6% indicated "other" or did not respond.
Scoring	The EAVS-AA-R is a unidirectional and unidimensional 25-item scale. Scoring the EAVS-AA-R consists of adding the participant's ratings on the 25 items and then dividing the total score by 25 to obtain a mean score. Seventeen items are reverse scored.
Reliability	A Cronbach's alpha of .77 was reported for the scores on the 25-item scale. Person and item separation reliability was reported to be .78 and .98, respectively.

(Continued)

(Continued)

Validity	No validity checks were provided.
Related References	Kim, B. S. K. (2007). Adherence to Asian and European American cultural values and attitudes toward seeking professional psychological help among Asian American college students. *Journal of Counseling Psychology, 54,* 474–480. Omizo, M. M., Kim, B. S. K., & Abel, N. R. (2008). Asian and European American cultural values, bicultural competence, and attitudes toward seeking professional psychological help among Asian American adolescents. *Journal of Multicultural Counseling and Development, 36,* 15–28. Park, Y. S., & Kim, B. S. K. (2008). Asian and European American cultural values and communication styles among Asian American and European American college students. *Cultural Diversity and Ethnic Minority Psychology, 14,* 47–56.
Language Versions	English
Contact	Sehee Hong Department of Psychology Ewha Womans University 11–1 Daehyun-dong Seodaemun-gu, Seoul, 120–750 Republic of Korea Email: shong@ewha.ac.kr

6.11.6 **Name of the Measure**	Acculturation Scale for Southeast Asians ASSA
Primary Reference	Anderson, J., Moeschberger, M., Chen, M. S., Jr., Kunn, P., Wewers, M. E., & Guthrie, R. (1993). An acculturation scale for Southeast Asians. *Social Psychiatry and Psychiatric Epidemiology, 28,* 134–141.
Purpose	The ASSA is a bidirectional, multidimensional acculturation scale that focuses on Southeast Asia ethnic groups (i.e., Cambodians, Laotians, and Vietnamese). Two subscales were derived that focus on language, social, and food preferences.
Description	The ASSA contains 13 items. All items are measured on a variety of Likert-type scales. Language Proficiency (English and language of origin) items were measured on a 4-point scale: 1 = Not At All, 2 = Not Too Well, 3 = Pretty Well, 4 = Very Well. Language Usually Used items were measured on a 5-point scale: 1 = Only Origin, 2 = Mostly Origin, 3 = Origin and English Equally, 4 = Mostly English, 5 = Only English. People Seen Every Day items were measured on a 3-point scale: 1 = Mostly Origin, 2 = Equally Origin and American, 3 = Mostly American. The single Food Preference item was measured on a 5-point scale: 1 = Only Origin, 2 = Mostly Origin, 3 = Origin and American Equally, 4 = Mostly American, 5 = Only American.
Samples	The sample consisted of 1,126 Southeast Asian adults (330 women and 796 men). These participants were further identified by Southeast Asian ethnic group as follows: 381 Cambodian (115 women and 266 men), 350 Laotian (101 women and 249 men), and 395 Vietnamese (114 women and 281 men). Ages ranged from 18 to 89 years ($M = 37.0$, $SD = 14.3$). Average education level was 7.2 years ($SD = 4.1$). The average number of years participants had spent in the United States was 7.1 years ($SD = 4.9$).
Scoring	Two subscales were ultimately created with maximum likelihood factor analysis with varimax rotation. The number of items in each of the two subscale is as follows: English and Language of Origin Proficiency: 7 items Language, Social, and Food Preferences: 6 items Total ASSA: 13 items Authors scored the ASSA by creating two composite English Language Proficiency (4 items) and Language of Origin Proficiency (3 items) variables. Median splits on these variables (i.e., respondents were classified as high or low) were then classified into the following mutually exclusive acculturation groups: Low on both languages. Low on English but high on language of origin. High on both English and language of origin. High on English but low on language of origin. No reverse coding or transformations are required.

(Continued)

(Continued)

Reliability	Authors report in Abstract "Inter-item reliability of the scales was demonstrated for each of the three ethnic groups, with Cronbach's alpha coefficients of 0.76 or above" (p. 134). Actual alpha coefficients were not reported.
Validity	Concurrent validity was demonstrated through expected correlations of the two subscales with key demographic variables (e.g., age, years in the United States, and education).
Related References	Shelley, D., Fahs, M., Scheinmann, R., Swain, S., Qu, J., & Burton, D. (2004). Acculturation and tobacco use among Chinese Americans. *American Journal of Public Health*, 94(2), 300–307.
Language Versions	English
Contact	Melvin Moeschberger College of Public Health Ohio State University B-104 Star Loving 320 W. 10th Ave. Columbus, OH 43210 (614) 293–3713 (Office) Email: moeschberger.1@osu.edu

6.11.7 Name of the Measure	Acculturation Scale for Vietnamese Adolescents ASVA
Primary Reference	Nguyen, H. H., & von Eye, A. (2002). The Acculturation Scale for Vietnamese Adolescents (ASVA): A bidimensional perspective. *International Journal of Behavioral Development, 26*(3), 202–213.
Purpose	The ASVA is a bidirectional and multidirectional acculturation scale that assesses an adolescent's level of involvement in the Vietnamese and (mainstream) Anglo-American cultures. The ASVA attempts to depict contemporary attitudes, values, and behaviors of Vietnamese youth living in the United States.
Description	The ASVA contains 50 items. Each item is rated on a 5-point Likert-type scale, where participants are asked the extent to which they agree with each statement: 1 = Strongly Disagree, 2 = Disagree, 3 = Neutral, 4 = Agree, 5 = Strongly Agree; or engage in the behavior described: 1 = Never, 2 = Rarely, 3 = Sometimes, 4 = Often, 5 = Always. The ASVA is composed of two 25-item subscales: Involvement in Vietnamese culture (IVN) and Involvement in American culture (IUS). Each subscale contains items related to four *life-domains* (developed a priori to any multivariate analyses): Group interactions, Everyday lifestyles, Family orientation, and Global involvement. Two separate confirmatory factor analyses on the IVS and the IUS subscales validated the four life domains for each subscale.
Samples	The convenience sample consisted of 191 Vietnamese adolescents (84 female and 107 male). Ages ranged from 6 to 12 years (*M* = 15, *SD* = 2.5). Country of birth was Vietnam (80%), United States (19%), and Malaysia (1%). Over 95% of the participants parents were born in Vietnam.
Scoring	There are 25 items in each of the two ASVA subscales (IVN and IUS). Each subscale contains four life domains with the following number of items per domain. IVN subscale VN: Group Interactions: 7 items VN: Everyday Lifestyles: 8 items VN: Family Orientation: 7 items VN: Global Involvement: 3 items IUS subscale US: Group Interactions: 7 items US: Everyday Lifestyles: 8 items US: Family Orientation: 7 items US: Global Involvement: 3 items Scoring the ASVA consists of adding the participant's ratings on each item in the subscale (IVN or IUS) and dividing by 25 to obtain a subscale mean. The four life domains can also be computed by adding the participant's ratings on each item within the domain and dividing by the number of domain items to obtain life domain means. No reverse coding or transformations are required.

(Continued)

(Continued)

Reliability	Cronbach's alpha for the subscale scores were as follows: IVN: Alpha = .89 IUS: Alpha = .88 Five of the eight life domains also showed good reliability. The IVN and IUS subscales produced a negative correlation.
Validity	Concurrent validity was established by demonstrating that higher scores on the IVN were related to participants who were born in Vietnam, who came to the United States at a later age, and who spoke Vietnamese fluently. Conversely, higher scores on the IUS were related to participants who had lived longer in the United States, had more U.S. schooling, and who were younger when they first arrived in the United States.
Related References	Suinn, R. M. (2009). Acculturation: Measurements and review of findings. In N.-H. Trinh, Y. C. Rho, F. G. Lu, & K. M. Sanders (Eds.), *Handbook of mental health and acculturation in Asian American families*. Totowa, NJ: Humana Press.
Language Versions	English
Contact	Huong H. Nguyen Brandeis University Heller Graduate School Mailstop 035 Waltham, MA 02454–9110 (781) 736–2693 (W) Email: huong@brandeis.edu

6.11.8 Name of the Measure	Khmer Acculturation Scale KAS
Primary Reference	Lim, K. V., Heiby, E., Brislin, R., & Griffin, B. (2002). The development of the Khmer Acculturation Scale. *International Journal of Intercultural Relations, 26,* 653–678.
Purpose	The KAS is a 69-item multidimensional acculturation measure for use with Cambodians living in the United States. The KAS consists of two orthogonal subscales that measure Cambodian and Anglo-American orientation.
Description	The KAS contains 69 items. Each item is rated on a 4-point Likert-type scale: 1 = Strongly Disagree, 2 = Disagree, 3 = Agree, 4 = Strongly Agree. All items are presented in English and Khmer.
	The KAS is composed of two orthogonal subscales: the Khmer Orientation Scale (KOS) and the Anglo American Orientation Scale (AOS).
	The KAS was designed to reflect Berry's (1990) multidimensional acculturation model. Hence, the KOS assesses the degree of enculturation to Cambodian culture, and the AOS assesses the degree of acculturation to American culture.
	The initial item pool of 130 items was developed through literature review and from feedback from a panel of 22 cultural experts and judges. Two separate factor analyses (principle axis factoring with promax rotations) were performed on the KOS and AOS subscales. These analyses resulted in a final 69-item KAS, with 33 items on the KOS and 36 items on the AOS.
Samples	The sample consisted of 410 Cambodian adults (212 women and 196 men) living in nine U.S states. Ages ranged from 18 to 79 years (*M* = 34.7, *SD* = 12.4). Levels of education in the United States were as follows: 56 (13.7%) had no formal education, 51 (12.4%) had 6 years or less, 20 (4.9%) had 7–9 years, 63 (15.4%) had 11–12 years, and 184 (44.9%) had a college degree or higher. The majority of the sample, 380 (92.7%), was born in Cambodia.
Scoring	The number of items in the two KAS subscales is as follows:
	Khmer Orientation Scale: 33 items
	Anglo Orientation Scale: 36 items
	Total KAS: 69 items
	Scoring the KOS and AOS subscales consists of adding the participant's ratings on each item in the subscale to obtain a subscale score or sum. A higher score on the AOS indicates greater Anglo American acculturation, and a higher score on the KOS is indicative of greater Khmer enculturation. No reverse coding or transformations are required.

(Continued)

(Continued)

Reliability	Cronbach's alpha for the scores were as follows:
	KOS: Alpha = .92
	AOS: Alpha = .94
	Total KAS: Alpha = .82
	Test-retest reliability (over an approximately 2.4 month interval) was $r = .78$.
Validity	Criterion validity was achieved somewhat by demonstrating a modest positive correlation between the KAS and the Suinn-Lew Asian Self-Identity Acculturation Scale (SL-ASIA; Suinn, Rikard-Figueroa, Lew, & Vigil, 1987). Construct validity was achieved through multiple regression analyses indicating higher scores on the KOS subscale to be significantly related to older age, years of Cambodian education, fewer years living in the United States, and less annual income. Conversely, higher scores on the AOS subscale were significantly related to a younger age, years educated in the United States, years living in the United States, and higher income.
Related References	
Language Versions	English and Khmer
Contact	Elaine Heiby Department of Psychology University of Hawaii at Manoa 2430 Campus Rd. Honolulu, HI 96822 (808) 942–0738 (W) (808) 956–4700 (Fax) Email: heiby@hawaii.edu

6.11.9 Name of the Measure	Cultural Values Conflict Scale for South Asian Women CVCS
Primary Reference	Inman, A. G., Ladany, N., Constantine, M. G., & Morano, C. K. (2001). Development and preliminary validation of the Cultural Values Conflict Scale for South Asian women. *Journal of Counseling Psychology, 48*(1), 17–27.
Purpose	This self-report multidimensional measure examines one aspect of acculturation: Cultural value conflicts (e.g., family relations, dating-premarital sexual relations, marriage, and sex role expectations) experienced by some South Asian women who live in the United States.
Description	The CVCS contains 24 items. Each item is rated on a 6-point Likert-type scale: 1 = Strongly Disagree, 2 = Disagree, 3 = Neutral, 4 = Agree, 5 = Strongly Agree, 6 = Not Applicable.
	The CVCS is composed of a total scale mean and two subscales: (1) Intimate Relations (IR) and (2) Sex Role Expectations (SRE).
	A preliminary 40-item CVCS was mailed to 1,014 English-speaking South Asian women, contacted by means of a nonrandom snowball scheme, resulting in 319 usable questionnaires for a final response rate of 32%. Based on item analyses and a preliminary confirmatory factor analysis, the original 40 items were further reduced to 24. These 24 items were analyzed by means of a common factor analysis with a varimax rotation, resulting in a 24-item, two-subscale instrument that accounted for 35% of the total variance.
Samples	The validation sample consisted of $N = 319$ South Asian women (147 first-generation women and 172 second-generation women). Ages ranged from 20 to 44 years ($M = 27.2$, $SD = 5.54$). Marital status was as follows: single (55%), married (40%), divorced (2%), cohabiting (2%), and separated (1%). Birthplace was as follows: India (59%), Pakistan (2%), Sri Lanka (2%), Bangladesh (2%), United States (30%), other countries (5%). Religious breakdown was as follows: Christian (9%), Hindu (70%), Muslim (11%), Sikh (2%), Jain (3%), Buddhist (1%), other religion (4%).
Scoring	The number of items in each of the two subscales is as follows:
	Intimate Relations (IR): 11 items
	Sex Role Expectations (SER): 13 items
	Total CVCS: 24 items
	Scoring the CVCS consists of adding the participant's ratings on each item in the subscale and dividing by the number of items to obtain a subscale mean, or adding all of the participants' ratings on all of the 24 items and dividing by 24 to obtain a total score mean.

(Continued)

(Continued)

Reliability	Cronbach's alpha for the two subscales and the total score were as follows:
	Intimate Relations: Alpha = .87
	Sex Role Expectations: Alpha = .85
	Total CVCS: Alpha = .84
	Test-retest reliability (with a second sample and a 2 week interval $N = 91$): The scores for IR achieved $r = .63$, SRE $r = .82$, and total scale score $r = .81$.
Validity	Discriminant validity was established by demonstrating that the CVCS discriminated between first- and second-generation South Asian women. Some evidence of social desirability effects with both CVCS subscales was observed.
Related References	Inman, A. G. (2006). South Asian women: Identities and conflict. *Cultural Diversity and Ethnic Minority Psychology, 12*(2), 306–319.
Language Versions	English
Contact	Arpana G. Inman Counseling Psychology Lehigh University Iacocca Hall, Room A-231 111 Research Dr. Bethlehem, PA 18015 (610) 758–4443 (W) (610) 758–6223 (fax) Email: agi2@lehigh.edu

6.11.10 **Name of the Measure**	A Short Acculturation Scale for Filipino Americans ASASFA
Primary Reference	de la Cruz, F. A., Padilla, G. V., & Butts, E. (1998). Validating a short acculturation scale for Filipino Americans. *Journal of the American Academy of Nurse Practitioners, 10*(10), 453–460.
Purpose	The ASASFA is a unidirectional, multidimensional acculturation scale for Filipino/a Americans that was adapted from the A Short Acculturation Scale for Hispanics (ASASH; Marin, Sabogal, Marin, Otero-Sabogal, & Perez-Stable, 1987). The ASASFA measures three dimensions of Filipino/a acculturation. High scores reflect an acculturated orientation, and low scores reflect a more traditional Filipino/a cultural orientation.
Description	The ASASFA contains 12 items. Each item is rated on a 5-point Likert-type scale with one of the following two sets of response choices: 1 = Only Philippine Language(s), 2 = More Philippine Language(s) than English, 3 = Both equally, 4 = More English than Philippine Language(s), 5 = Only English; or 1 = All Filipinos, 2 = More Filipinos than Americans, 3 = About Half and Half, 4 = More Americans than Filipinos, 5 = All Americans.
	The ASASFA is composed of a mean total acculturation score and three subscales: (1) Language Use, (2) Ethnic Social Relations, (3) Media Language Preference. The ASASFA is a modified version of A Short Acculturation Scale for Hispanics (ASASH; Marin et al., 1987) that was adapted for use with Filipino/a Americans. Special diligence was taken to ensure linguistic and cross-cultural validity through content, technical, experiential, semantic, and conceptual equivalence. ASASFA factor structure was established by means of principal components analyses with varimax rotation. These analyses resulted in a three-factor, 12-item solution for both English and Tagalog versions.
Samples	A convenience sample of 295 outpatients of several southern California health maintenance organizations, who were prequalified as to their ability to speak and read English and Tagalog, were mailed questionnaires. A total of 165 (62.4% women) were returned, yielding a 56% return rate. Sample age range was not provided. Eighty percent of sample was married. All were first generation, who were born in the Philippines. Sample median income ranged from $30,000 to $50,000.
Scoring	The number of items in each of the three subscales is as follows: Language Use: 5 items Ethnic Social Relations: 3 items Media Language Preference: 4 items Total ASASFA: 12 items

(Continued)

(Continued)

	Scoring the ASASFA consists of adding the participant's ratings on each item in the subscale and then dividing by the number of subscale items to obtain a subscale mean. A total scale score mean is obtained by adding participants' ratings on all 12 items and then dividing by 12. No reverse coding or transformations are required.
Reliability	Respondents were asked to complete both an English and a Tagalog version of the ASASFA, providing a reliability test of equivalence of $r = .85$. Cronbach's alphas for the ASASFA total scale score (for both English and Tagalog versions) were .85.
Validity	Known-group validity was evidenced by asking respondents to self-report if they viewed themselves as (a) "very Filipino," (b) "more Filipino than American," and (c) "almost fifty-fifty Filipino and American." Analysis of variance results indicated that mean acculturation scores were lowest for the "very Filipino" group and highest for the "fifty-fifty" group.
Related References	de la Cruz, F. A., Padilla, G. V., & Agustin, E. O. (2000). Adapting a measure of acculturation for cross-cultural research. *Journal of Transcultural Nursing, 11*(3), 191–198.
Language Versions	Tagalog and English
Contact	Felicitas de la Cruz School of Nursing Azusa Pacific University P.O. Box 7000 Azusa, CA 91702–7000 (626) 815–5386 (W) Email: fdelacruz@apu.edu

6.11.11 Name of the Measure	General Ethnicity Questionnaire GEQ
Primary Reference	Tsai, J. L., Ying, Y.-W., & Lee, P. A. (2000). The meaning of "being Chinese" and "being American": Variation among Chinese American young adults. *Journal of Cross-Cultural Psychology, 31*(3), 302–332.
Purpose	The GEQ is a bidirectional and multidimensional acculturation instrument that was developed to test unidimensional and bidimensional aspects of Chinese and American acculturation.
Description	The GEQ consists of two 37-item scales that purport to measure Chinese (GEQC) and American (GEQA) cultural orientations independently. Each item is rated on a 5-point Likert-type scale with the following types of anchors: 1 = Strongly Disagree, 5 = Strongly Agree, or 1 = Very Much, 5 = Not at All. One additional item is asked on the GEQC (Are You Bilingual?) only. The initial study that validated the GEQ eliminated several items (1 or 5) from the GEQC and GEQA, respectively, due to small structure coefficients found for some of the items. This resulted in an "abridged" GEQC scale with 36 items and an "abridged" GEQA scale with 32 items. The subscale structure for each scale was as follows. General Ethnicity Questionnaire—Chinese (GEQC): (1) Chinese Language Use and Proficiency, (2) Affiliation with Chinese People, (3) Participation in Chinese Activities, (4) Pride in Chinese Culture, (5) Exposure to Chinese Culture, (6) Preference for Chinese Food. General Ethnicity Questionnaire—American (GEQA): (1) English Language Use and Proficiency, (2) Affiliation with American People, (3) Participation in American Activities, (4) Pride in American Culture, (5) Preference for Media in English, (6) Preference for American Food. The items that compose the GEQ were apparently developed from a review of other unidirectional and bidirectional acculturation inventories. Subsequent factor analyses (with varimax rotations) produced six reliable factors for both the GEQC and GEQA (see above).
Samples	The normative sample consisted of 353 Chinese American college students (179 female, 174 male). Ages ranged from 17 to 32 years ($M = 20.2$, $SD = 1.8$). The sample was divided into three mutually exclusive groups: (1) American-born Chinese (ABC) 122, (2) Immigrants who arrived at or before age 12 (Imm < 12) 119, and (3) those who arrived after age 12 (Imm > 12) 112. Among the ABC, over 89% were of second-generation status or higher.

(Continued)

(Continued)

Scoring	Scoring the GEQ consists of computing six subscale means for both the GEQC and GEQA, respectively. Participant's ratings are summed on each item in the subscale to obtain a subscale score, and then divided by the number of items in the subscale to obtain a subscale mean. Total scale means can also be computed. Fourteen items on each scale are reverse coded.
Reliability	Cronbach's alpha for the scores were as follows: GEQC: Alpha = .92 GEQA: Alpha = .92 One-month test-retest reliability coefficients were as follows: GEQC: $r = .62$ GEQA: $r = .57$
Validity	Concurrent validity was evidenced by means of correlations between the total scale means and various indices of acculturation (i.e., age of arrival, generational status, etc.), all of which were found to be in the predicted direction. Discriminant validity was achieved by demonstrating that the three Chinese American groups differed statistically significantly and predictably on the various subscales of each scale.
Related References	Tsai, J. L., Mortensen, H., Wong, Y., & Hess, D. (2002). What does "being American" mean? A comparison of Asian American and European American young adults. *Cultural Diversity and Ethnic Minority Psychology, 8*(3), 257–273. Tsai, J. L., Ying, Y.-W., & Lee, P. A. (2001). Cultural predictors of self-esteem: A study of Chinese American female and male young adults. *Cultural Diversity and Ethnic Minority Psychology, 7*(3), 284–297.
Language Versions	English
Contact	Jeanne L. Tsai Department of Psychology Stanford University Building 420 Jordan Hall Stanford, CA 94305 (650) 723–3102 (W) (650) 725–5699 (Fax) Email: jtsai@psych.stanford.edu

6.11.12 Name of the Measure	Brief Acculturation Scale BAS-J
Primary Reference	Meredith, L. S., Wenger, N., Harada, N., & Kahn, K. (2000). Development of a brief scale to measure acculturation among Japanese Americans. *Journal of Community Psychology, 28,* 103–113.
Purpose	The BAS-J is a brief unidirectional and unidimensional measure of Japanese American acculturation. The BAS-J was derived from the Suinn-Lew Asian Self-Identity Acculturation Scale (SL-ASIA; Suinn, Rikard-Figueroa, Lew, & Vigil, 1987) and is intended for English-speaking Japanese Americans. The BAS-J should not be confused with the Bidimensional Acculturation Scale for Hispanics.
Description	The BAS-J contains four items. Each item is dummy (binary) coded as 0 or 1, with 1 representing the base value of each variable. A questionnaire, containing the SL-ASIA, was mailed to several southern California Japanese American community samples ($N = 1,097$), which yielded 867 completed questionnaires for a 79% return rate. Feedback from focus group participants and unspecified factor analytic work reduced the SL-ASIA to four items.
Samples	The primary validating sample came from three Japanese American Community Centers and one Japanese retirement facility in the Los Angeles area. Sample characteristics were not provided.
Scoring	The four items that make up the BAS-J and their scoring criteria are as follows: "Which language do you prefer to speak?" Responses coded as 1 = "English" and 0 = "Japanese." "Where were you raised?" Responses coded as "In Japan only," "Mostly in Japan," "Mostly in the U.S.," "In the U.S. only," "Other (Specify)." This 4-category variable was reweighted from 0 to 1 (i.e., .20, .40, etc.) where a higher score indicates a greater tendency to be raised in the United States only (versus Japan or some other combination). (a) "Were you born in the United States?" Responses coded as "Yes" or "No." (b) "Were either or both of your parents born in the United States?" Responses coded as "None," "One parent," "Both parents," "Don't know." (c) "Were any of your grandparents born in the United States?" Responses coded as "None," "One grandparent," "Two grandparents," "Three grandparents," "Don't know." This 8-category variable (derived from items 3 a–c) was reweighted from 0 to 1 (i.e., .08, .16, etc.), where a higher score indicates that more individuals in a respondent's immediate family (self, parents, and grandparents) are born in the United States.

(Continued)

(Continued)

	"What is your racial or ethnic group?" Responses coded as 1 = "Japanese American," 0 = "Japanese or Other (Specify)."
	Scoring the BAS-J consists of creating a composite mean for the four items and rescaling them to range from 0 to 100 points. A higher BAS-J score reflects greater Japanese American acculturation.
Reliability	Cronbach's alpha for the total scores of the BAS-J (full sample) was .84.
Validity	Face validity was achieved by demonstrating incremental increases in acculturation from the earliest acculturation group (Issei) to the latest grouping (Yonsei).
Related References	
Language Versions	English
Contact	Lisa S. Meredith RAND Health P.O. Box 2138 1700 Main St. Santa Monica, CA 90407–2138 Email: lisa-meredith@rand.org

6.11.13 Name of the Measure	Asian American Family Conflicts Scale FCS
Primary Reference	Lee, R. M., Cho, J., Kim, G., & Ngo, V. (2000). Construction of the Asian American Family Conflicts Scale. *Journal of Counseling Psychology, 47*(2), 211–222.
Purpose	This multidimensional measure purports to assess typical Asian American generational family conflicts that reflect acculturation differences between parents and late-adolescent and young-adult children.
Description	The FCS consists of 20 items. Items are rated on one of two 5-point Likert-type scales with one of the following two sets of response anchors: 1 = Almost Never to 5 = Almost Always or 1 = Not At All to 5 = Extremely. The FCS is composed of two subscales: (1) FCS-Likelihood of Occurrence and (2) FCS-Seriousness of Conflict. The 20 items that compose the FCS subscales were developed through a literature review and three focus groups (composed of cultural and mental health experts). These items dealt with 10 typical conflict situations that might elicit parent–child differences in Asian American families. Two subsequent confirmatory factor analyses, on independent measurement models for the FCS-Likelihood and FCS-Seriousness subscales, yielded very good fits between the data and the models (e.g., Comparative Fit Index was .97 and .95, for the FCS-Likelihood and FCS-Seriousness models, respectively).
Samples	The normative sample (Study 1) consisted of 186 Asian American college students (85 women, 99 men, 2 unidentified) from a West Coast university. Respondents' ages ranged from 17 to 30 years ($M = 21.3$, $SD = 2.1$). Self-reported ethnicity was as follows: Chinese American (34.4%), Vietnamese American (32.8%), Filipino/a American (12.9%), Korean American (9.7%), other (10.2%).

Scoring	The number of items in each of the two subscales is as follows:
	
	    FCS-Likelihood of Occurrence: 10 items
	
	    FCS-Seriousness of Conflict: 10 items
	
	    Total FCS: 20 items
	
	Scoring the FCS consists of adding the participant's ratings on each item in the subscale to obtain subscale scores. Each subscale has a possible range of 10–50. No reverse coding or transformations are required.

Reliability	Cronbach's alpha for the scores were as follows:
	
	    FCS-Likelihood: Alpha = .89
	
	    FCS-Seriousness: Alpha = .91
	
	The two FCS subscales are highly intercorrelated.

(Continued)

(Continued)

	Three-week test-retest reliability for the scores were as follows:
	FCS-Likelihood: $r = .80$
	FCS-Seriousness: $r = .85$
Validity	Construct validity was achieved by demonstrating statistically significant correlations between the scores of both FCS subscales and the scores of the three family conflict items from the Social, Attitudinal, Familial, and Environmental Acculturation Stress Scale (SAFE; Mena, Padilla, & Maldonado, 1987). A second set of confirmatory factor analyses with an independent sample ($N = 153$) again provided strong initial fit between the data and the models (both Comparative Fit Indexes were .96).
Related References	Lee, R. M., Jung, K. R., Su, J. C., Tran, A. G. T. T., & Bahrassa, N. F. (2009). The family life and adjustment of Hmong American sons and daughters. *Sex Roles, 60*(7–8), 549–558.
	Su, J., Lee, R. M., & Vang, S. (2005). Intergenerational family conflict and coping among Hmong American college students. *Journal of Counseling Psychology, 52*(4), 482–489.
Language Versions	English
Contact	Richard M. Lee Counseling Psychology Program Department of Psychology University of Minnesota-Twin Cities Minneapolis, MN 55455 (612) 625–6357 (W) (612) 626–2079 (Fax) Email: richlee@umn.edu

6.11.14 Name of the Measure	Cultural Adjustment Difficulties Checklist CADC
Primary Reference	Sodowsky, G. R., & Lai, E. W. M. (1997). Asian immigrant variables and structural models of cross-cultural distress. In A. Booth, A. C. Crouter, & N. Landale (Eds.), *Immigration and the family: Research and policy on U.S. immigrants* (pp. 211–234). Mahwah, NJ: Lawrence Erlbaum Associates.
Purpose	The CADC is a bidirectional and multidimensional acculturation scale that purports to assess Asian American and Asian immigrant issues concerning acculturation, the family, immigrant sociocultural factors, and cultural adjustment difficulties.
Description	The CADC contains 48 items. Each item is rated on a 6-point Likert-type scale with the following response anchors: 1 = A Very Inaccurate Description of You to 6 = A Very Accurate Description of You. The CADC consists of two subscales: (1) Acculturative Stress and (2) Intercultural Competence Concerns. Item development for the 48-item CADC was a function of a comprehensive literature review that tapped the following Asian immigrant issues: interpersonal problems, alienation, self-efficacy, language preferences, social customs, age at time of immigration, years of U.S. residency, and ethnic friendship networks. A subsequent (unspecified) exploratory factor analysis (with an oblique rotation) produced a two-factor, 48-item simple structure that accounted for 29.4% of the total variance.
Samples	The normative sample consisted of 200 (96 women and 104 men) Asian immigrant students, faculty, and staff. Ages ranged from 20 to 60 years (Mdn = 27). Self-reported ethnicity was Chinese Americans (27.5%), Asian Indians (26.0%), Vietnamese (16.0%), Koreans (10.5%), Japanese Americans (9.0%), other Asian Americans (6.5%), and Filipinos (4.5%). Respondent generational status was as follows: first generation (73.0%), second generation (18.5%), third generation (16.0%), and fourth generation (0.5%).

Scoring	The number of items in each of the two subscales is as follows:
	
	    Acculturative Distress: 27 items
	    Intercultural Competence Concerns: 21 items
	    Total CADC: 48 items
	
	Scoring the CADC consists of adding the participant's ratings on each item in the subscale to obtain a subscale score and dividing by the number of items within the subscale to obtain a subscale mean. A total of 24 items are reverse coded.

(Continued)

(Continued)

Reliability	Cronbach's alphas for the scores were as follows:
	Acculturative Distress: Alpha = .89
	Intercultural Competence Concerns: Alpha = .88
	Total CADC: Alpha = .91
	The intersubscale correlation was low positive.
Validity	Convergent validity was achieved by comparing the two-factor structure with the Asian immigrant sample to a two-factor structure from a separate Asian sojourner sample, using a maximum likelihood confirmatory factor analysis. All fit indices indicated acceptable levels of fit between the two samples.
Related References	Yeh, C. J. (2003). Age, acculturation, cultural adjustment, and mental health symptoms of Chinese, Korean, and Japanese immigrant youths. *Cultural Diversity and Ethnic Minority Psychology, 9*(1), 34–48.
Language Versions	English and Spanish
Contact	Gargi Roysircar Sodowski Department of Clinical Psychology Antioch University New England 40 Avon Street Keene, NH 03431–3516 (603) 283–2186 (W) Email: groysircar@antioch.edu

6.12 LATINO/A AMERICAN ACCULTURATION MEASURES

6.12.1 Name of the Measure	Short Acculturation Scale for Hispanics SASH
Primary Reference	Marin, G., Sabogal, F., VanOss Marin, B., Ortero-Sabogal, R., Perez-Stable, E. J. (1987). Development of short acculturation scale for Hispanics. *Hispanic Journal of Behavioral Science, 9*(2), 183–205.
Purpose	The SASH is a brief unidirectional and multidimensional measure of acculturation for Latino/as.
Description	The SASH contains 12 items. Each item is rated on a 5-point Likert-type scale with the following types of response options: 1 = Only Spanish, 2 = More Spanish than English, 3 = Both Equally, 4 = More English than Spanish, 5 = Only English, or 1 = All Latinos/Hispanics, 2 = More Latinos than Americans, 3 = About Half & Half, 4 = More Americans than Latinos, 5 = All Americans. Based on previous research and literature reviews, participants were presented with 17 behavioral acculturation items, demographic questions, and cultural values items. Subsequent separate principal components analyses (with varimax rotation) for the Latino/a American and non-Hispanic White subsamples produced a common 12-item, three-factor simple structure.
Samples	The normative sample consisted of 591 adults primarily from the San Francisco Bay Area (Latino/a American $n = 363$, 225 women and 138 men and non-Hispanic Whites $n = 228$, 130 women and 98 men). The Latino/a American subsample consisted of 160 Mexican Americans, 21 Cuban Americans, 174 "Other Hispanics," 7 Puerto Ricans. Ages (of the Latino/a American respondents) ranged from 15 to 75 years ($SD = 11.6$).

Scoring	The number of items in each of the three subscales is as follows:
	
	    Language Use/Ethnic Loyalty: 5 items
	
	    Media: 3 items
	
	    Ethnic Social Relations: 4 items
	
	    Total SASH: 12 items
	
	Scoring the SASH consists of adding the participant's ratings on each item in the subscale and dividing the subscale score by the number of items in the subscale to obtain a subscale mean. A total scale mean can also be produced. No reverse coding or transformations are required.

(Continued)

(Continued)

Reliability	Cronbach's alpha for the scores were as follows:
	Language Use/Ethnic Loyalty: Alpha = .90
	Media: Alpha = .86
	Ethnic Social Relations: Alpha = .78
	Total SASH: .92
Validity	Concurrent validity was demonstrated by a high positive correlation between a participant's total SASH score and his/her generational status. Discriminant validity was evidenced by statistically significant differences between first- ($M = 2.37$) and second-generation ($M = 3.42$) Latino/a Americans on the SASH total score, indicating less assimilation of the first generation Latino/a Americans.
Related References	Marin, G., Perez-Stable, E. J., & Marin, B.V. (1989). Cigarette smoking among San Francisco Hispanics: The role of acculturation and gender. *American Journal of Public Health, 79*(2), 196–198.
	O'Malley, A. S., Kerner, J., Johnson, A. E., & Mandleblatt, J. (1999). Acculturation and breast cancer screening among Hispanic women in New York City. *American Journal of Public Health, 89*(2), 219–227.
Language Versions	Spanish and English
Contact	Gerardo Marin
	University of San Francisco
	2130 Fulton St.
	San Francisco, CA 94117
	(415) 422- 2199 (W)
	Email: marin@usfca.edu

6.12.2 Name of the Measure	Acculturation Rating Scale ARS
Primary Reference	Montgomery, G. T. (1992b). Comfort with acculturation status among students from south Texas. *Hispanic Journal of Behavioral Sciences, 14*(2), 201–223.
Purpose	The ARS is a bidirectional, multidimensional acculturation measure for Mexican Americans. This scale purports to measure how individuals vary in their Mexican and Anglo cultural orientation and their ethnic identity comfort.
Description	The ARS contains 28 items plus a question on generation status. Four items are evaluated with a 5-option multiple-choice format. The remaining 24 items are rated on the following 5-point Likert-type scales: 1 = Very Uncomfortable, 2 = A Little Uncomfortable, 3 = Comfortable, 4 = Mostly Comfortable, 5 = Very Comfortable, or 1 = Not at All, 2 = Very Little, 3 = A Little, 4 = A Lot, 5 = Very Much.
	The ARS is composed of a total score and five subscales: (1) Spanish Language, Media, and Traditions, (2) English Language, Media, and Anglo American Traditions, (3) Ethnic Identity Preference, (4) Self-Rated Ethnic Identity, (5) English Language Comfort.
	The ARS items were patterned after Cuéllar, Harris, and Jasso (1980) and Szapocznik, Scopetta, Kurtines, and Aranalde (1978) acculturation scales. Factor analysis (with varimax rotation) yielded a 5-factor simple structure.
Samples	The normative sample consisted of White American (*n* = 133) and Mexican American (*n* = 711) high school and college students from the Rio Grande Valley of Texas (*N* = 844, 468 women, and 376 men). The mean age for the total sample was 18.8 years.
Scoring	The number of items in each of the five subscales is as follows:
	Spanish Language, Media, and Traditions: 10 items
	English Language, Media, and Anglo American Traditions: 7 items
	Ethnic Identity Preference: 5 items
	Self-Rated Ethnic Identity: 3 items (if generation status is excluded)
	English Language Comfort: 3 items
	Total ARS: 28 items (29 items including generation status)
	Scoring the ARS consists of adding the participant's ratings on each of the 28 items and dividing this total score by 28 to obtain a total score mean. Subscale means are computed by adding participant's ratings on each item of the subscale and dividing by the number of subscale items. Ten items require reverse coding.

(Continued)

(Continued)

Reliability	Cronbach's alpha for the scores were as follows: Spanish Language, Media, and Traditions: Alpha = .92 English Language, Media, and Traditions: Alpha = .86 Ethnic Identity Preference: Alpha = .92 Self-Rated Ethnic Identity: Alpha = .90 English Language Comfort: Alpha = .92 Total ARS: Alpha = .94
Validity	Discriminant validity was achieved by demonstrating statistically significant differences among the means of the five ARS subscales for the White American versus Mexican American participants.
Related References	Montgomery, G. T. (1992). Acculturation, stressors, somatization patterns among students from extreme south Texas. *Hispanic Journal of Behavioral Sciences, 14*(4), 434–454.
Language Versions	English and Spanish
Contact	Gary T. Montgomery Department of Psychology and Anthropology The University of Texas-Pan American Edinburg, TX 78539 (956) 381–2572 (W) Email: gtm6b5e@utpa.edu

6.12.3 Name of the Measure	Acculturation and Structural Assimilation Scales ASAS
Primary Reference	Hazuda, H. P., Stern, M. P., & Haffner, S. M. (1988). Acculturation and assimilation among Mexican Americans: Scales and population-based data. *Social Science Quarterly, 69,* 687–706.
Purpose	The ASAS is a set of seven scales that purports to measure unidirectional and multidimensional Mexican American acculturation and structural assimilation.
Description	The ASAS consists of 31 items. Items are evaluated on either 1–3, 1–4, or 1–5, Likert-type or multiple-choice response frames. The ASAS consists of the following five acculturation scales and two structural assimilation scales. Acculturation: (1) Childhood experience with English vs. Spanish language, (2) Adult proficiency with English, (3) Pattern of English vs. Spanish usage, (4) Value placed on preserving Mexican culture, (5) Attitude toward traditional family structure and sex roles. Structural Assimilation: (1) Childhood interaction with mainstream society and (2) Adult interaction with mainstream society. The ASAS is an attempt to operationalize key concepts from Gordon's (1964, 1978) seven-dimension model of assimilation (i.e., cultural assimilation, structural assimilation, marital assimilation, identificational assimilation, attitude receptional assimilation, behavior receptional assimilation, and civic assimilation). Items were developed based on these broad dimensions and informed by literature review and community cultural experts. All items and scales met rigorous discrimination criteria, including cluster analysis to ensure homogeneity of scale items.
Samples	The normative sample consisted of a stratified random sample of 3,078 Mexican American (1,052 females and 809 males) and Non-Hispanic White (696 females and 521 males) adult respondents. Sample age ranged from 25 to 64 years. Sample generational status was 19.4% first generation, 42.3% second generation, and 38.4% third generation or higher.
Scoring	The number of items in the five acculturation scales and the two structural assimilation scales is as follows: Acculturation: Childhood experience with English vs. Spanish language: 2 items Adult proficiency with English: 3 items Pattern of English vs. Spanish usage: 10 items Value placed on preserving Mexican culture: 3 items Attitude toward traditional family structure and sex roles: 7 items

(Continued)

(Continued)

	Structural Assimilation: Childhood interaction with mainstream society: 3 items Adult interaction with mainstream society: 3 items Scoring the ASAS consists of adding the participant's ratings on each item in the scale to obtain a subscale score. Acculturation scales have the following score ranges: Scale 1 (2 items rated on a 1 to 3 metric) = a range of 2–6 points. Scale 2 (3 items rated on a 1 to 4 metric) = a range of 3–12 points. Scale 3 (10 items rated on a 1 to 5 metric) = a range of 10–50 points. Scale 4 (3 items rated on a 1 to 5 metric) = 3–15 points. Scale 5 (7 items rated on a 1 to 5 metric) = a range of 7–35 points. Structural assimilation scales have the following score ranges: Scale 1 (3 items rated on a 1 to 3 metric) = a range of 3–9 points. Scale 2 (3 items rated on a 1 to 3 metric) = a range of 3–9 points. A high scale score is indicative of a more Anglo orientation, and a low scale score is more indicative of a Mexican American orientation. A separate composite Functional Integration with Mainstream Society scale can be computed by standardizing and amalgamating the scores of Acculturation Scales 2 and 3 with Structural Assimilation Scale 2.
Reliability	All of the scores on the ASAS scales were reported to have achieved a Cronbach's alpha .80 or greater.
Validity	A consistent pattern of statistically significant ethnic differences (Mexican American vs. White) was found across all five acculturation dimensions, even after controlling for socioeconomic status.
Related References	Hazuda, H. P., Haffner, S. M., Stern, M. P., & Eifler, C. W. (1988). Effects of acculturation and socioeconomic status on obesity and diabetes in Mexican Americans. *American Journal of Epidemiology, 128*(6), 1289–1301. Suarez, L., & Pulley, L. (1995). Comparing acculturation scales and their relationship to cancer screening among older Mexican-American women. *Journal of the National Cancer Institute Monographs, No. 18*, 41–47.
Language Versions	English
Contact	Helen P. Hazuda School of Medicine The University of Texas Health Science Center at San Antonio San Antonio, TX 78264 (210) 567–6678 (W) Email: hazuda@uthscsa.edu

6.12.4 Name of the Measure	Bidimensional Acculturation Scale for Hispanics BAS
Primary Reference	Marin, G., & Gamba, R. J. (1996). A new measurement of acculturation for Hispanics: The Bidimensional Acculturation Scale for Hispanics (BAS). *Hispanic Journal of Behavioral Sciences, 18,* 297–316.
Purpose	The BAS is a bidirectional and multidimensional acculturation scale for Latino/a Americans that provides an acculturation score for each respondent on two cultural dimensions (Hispanic and non-Hispanic domains). (Not to be confused with the Brief Acculturation Scale for Japanese.)
Description	The BAS contains 24 items. Each item is rated on a 4-point Likert-type scale with response options taking the following form: 1 = Almost Never, 2 = Sometimes, 3 = Often, 4 = Almost Always or 1 = Very Poorly, 2 = Poorly, 3 = Well, 4 = Very Well.
	The BAS consists of two 12-item cultural domains (Hispanic and non-Hispanic). Each of the two domains is composed of the following three subscales: (1) Language Use, (2) Linguistic Proficiency, (3) Electronic Media.
	The BAS multidimensional scale development evolved from previous unidimensional acculturation scale design with the Short Acculturation Scale for Hispanics (SASH; Marin, Sabogal, Marin, Otero-Sabogal, & Perez-Stable, 1987). BAS items were developed by identifying 30 acculturative behaviors in the literature. Items were written that reflected these behaviors for both Hispanic and non-Hispanic cultural orientations, yielding 60 items. Principal component analyses with oblique rotations reduced the item pool to 24 items and produced three reliable factors.
Scoring	The BAS 24 items are divided equally into two 12-item Hispanic and non-Hispanic cultural domains. Each domain is composed of three language-related (English or Spanish) subscales with the following number of items:
	Language Use: 3 items
	Linguistic Proficiency: 6 items
	Electronic Media: 3 items
	Respondents should be allowed to respond to the BAS in either English or Spanish. Scoring the BAS consists of adding the participant's ratings on the 12 items in each cultural domain (Hispanic or non-Hispanic) and then dividing the total domain score by 12 to obtain a domain score mean (which can range from 1 to 4). Each participant produces two cultural domain means, which can be used to identify a respondent's bidirectional acculturation status. The authors note that respondents who score above 2.5 on both cultural domains can be considered bicultural.
Reliability	Cronbach's alpha for the combined subscales was .90 for the Hispanic domain and .96 for the non-Hispanic domain.

(Continued)

(Continued)

Validity	Concurrent validity was established by demonstrating strong correlations between the BAS subscale and domain scores and various acculturation-related variables (e.g., generation status, residence length in the United States, formal education, etc.), with the exception of the Electronic Media subscales.
Related References	Gonzalez, G. M., Carter, C., & Blanes, E. (2007). Bilingual computerized speech recognition screening for depression symptoms. *Hispanic Journal of Behavioral Sciences, 29*(2), 156–180.
Language Versions	English and Spanish
Contact	Gerardo Marin University of San Francisco 2130 Fulton St. San Francisco, CA 94117 (415) 422–2199 (W) Email: marin@usfca.edu

6.12.5 **Name of the Measure**	Acculturation Rating Scale for Mexican Americans—II Brief ARSMA-II (aka ARSMA-II-SF)
Primary Reference	Bauman, S. (2005). The reliability and validity of the Brief Acculturation Rating Scale for Mexican Americans—II for children and adolescents. *Hispanic Journal of Behavioral Sciences, 27*(4), 426–441. Cuéllar, I., Arnold, B., & Maldonado, R. (1995). Acculturation Rating Scale for Mexican Americans—II: A revision of the original ARSMA scale. *Hispanic Journal of Behavioral Sciences, 17*(3), 275–304. Lopez, F. A. (2009). Developmental considerations and acculturation of children. *Hispanic Journal of Behavioral Sciences, 31*(1), 57–72.
Purpose	The Brief ARSMA-II is a Mexican American acculturation scale that was derived from its predecessors, the Acculturation Rating Scale for Mexican Americans (ARSMA; Cuéllar, Harris, & Jasso, 1980), and the Acculturation Rating Scale for Mexican Americans-II (ARSMA-II; Cuéllar, Arnold, & Maldonado, 1995). The Brief ARSMA-II, like its predecessor the AMSMA-II, allows the investigator to assess Mexican American acculturation as either a linear (unidimensional) or orthogonal (bidirectional) construct.
Description	The Brief ARSMA-II contains 12 items. Each item is rated on a 5-point Likert-type scale with the following response options: 1 = Not at All, 2 = Very Little or Not Very Often, 3 = Moderately, 4 = Much or Very Often, 5 = Extremely often or almost always. Both English and Spanish versions of the scale appear on a single page. The ARSMA (Cuéllar et al., 1980) was originally developed as a unidirectional measure of Mexican American acculturation. Fifteen years later, Cuéllar et al. (1995) developed the ARSMA-II, which provided investigators the option of examining Mexican American acculturation bidirectionally by computing two separate measures of cultural orientation, the Anglo Oriented Scale (AOS) and the Mexican Oriented Scale (MOS). Cuéllar has suggested a simple alternative to the Cuéllar et al. (1995) cutoff score rubric for determining acculturation typologies. Instead, respondents can be classified into four mutually exclusive groups based on the sample means of the AOS and MOS scale scores. These groups are as follows: (1) Marginalized (below means on the AOS and MOS), (2) Integrated (above the means on the AOS and MOS), (3) Traditional (above the MOS mean and below the AOS mean), (4) Assimilated (above the AOS mean and below the MOS mean) (I. Cuéllar, personal communication, August 4, 2003). Additional items on the ARSMA-II focused on different types of marginality and are not included in the Brief ARSMA-II. Cuéllar et al. (1995) reported separate factor analytic work (varimax rotation) with the ARSMA-II MOS and AOS scales. Three interpretable factors were discovered for the MOS: language, ethnic identity, and ethnic interaction. Two factors emerged for the AOS scale: language and ethnic interaction. Recent published work with the Brief ARSMA-II has focused on Mexican American children and adolescents (e.g., Bauman, 2005; Lopez, 2009). No published norms with adults have been reported. All Brief ARSMA-II norms in this summary are based on Bauman (2005). Factor analytic work (principal components, varimax rotation) supports a two-factor solution, with structure coefficients representing either the AOS or MOS scales.

(Continued)

(Continued)

Samples	Bauman's (2005) total sample consisted of 408 middle school students (227 females and 181 males) from the southwestern United States. Grade level was 32 in third grade, 39 in fourth grade, 45 in fifth grade, 120 in sixth grade, 102 in seventh grade, and 70 in eighth grade. Ethnic breakdown was as follows: Latino/a American 335, White American 21, African American 6, Asian American 5, Native American 7, and 33 did not respond. A total of 65 respondents chose the Spanish version of the questionnaire.
Scoring	The Brief ARSMA-II consists of 12 items. Two scales can be formed, the AOS and the MOS, each with six items. Scoring the AOS or MOS consists of adding the participant's ratings on each item in the scale to obtain a scale total and then dividing the total score by 6 to obtain a scale mean. No reverse coding or transformations are required.
Reliability	Cronbach's alpha for the scores were as follows: MOS: Alpha = .91 AOS: Alpha = .73 Split-half reliability coefficients were as follows: MOS: r = .92 AOS: r = .81
Related References	Cuéllar, I., Siles, R. I., & Bracamontes, E. (2004). Acculturation: A psychological construct of continuing relevance for Chicana/o psychology. In R. S. Velasquez, L. M. Arellano, & B. W. McNeill (Eds.), *The handbook of Chicana/o psychology and mental health* (pp. 23–42). Mahwah, NJ: Lawrence Erlbaum. Gamst, G., Dana, R. H., Der-Karabetian, A., Aragon, M., Arellano, L. M., & Kramer, T. (2002). Effects of Latino acculturation and ethnic identity on mental health outcomes. *Hispanic Journal of Behavioral Sciences, 24*(4), 479–504. Gamst, G., Herdina, A., Mondragon, E., Munguia, F., Pleitez, A., Stephens, H., Vo, D., & Cuéllar, I. (2006). Relationship among respondent identity, acculturation, and homeless status on a homeless population's functional status. *Journal of Clinical Psychology, 62*(12), 1485–1501.
Language Versions	English and Spanish
Contact	Israel Cuéllar (deceased) C/O Danny Layne Julian Samora Research Institute Michigan State University 301 Nisbet Bldg., 1407 S. Harrison Rd. East Lansing, MI 48823–5286 (517) 432–1317 (W) (517) 432–2221 (Fax) Email: www.jsri.msu.edu

6.12.6 Name of the Measure	Multidimensional Acculturation Scale MAS II
Primary Reference	Rodriguez, N., Bingham Mira, C., Paez, N. D., & Myers, H.F. (2007). Exploring the complexities of familism and acculturation: Central constructs for people of Mexican origin. *American Journal of Community Psychology, 39,* 61–77.
Purpose	The MAS II is a bidirectional and multidimensional acculturation instrument that purports to measure a respondent's involvement in and identification with Mexican and American culture.
Description	The MAS II contains 22 items. Each item is rated on a 6-point Likert-type scale with the following response anchors: 0 = Does Not Apply, 5 = Very Well/ Very Much.
	The MAS II is composed of the following four subscales: (1) English Proficiency, (2) Spanish Proficiency, (3) Mexican Cultural Identity, (4) American Cultural Identity.
	The MAS II was developed from its predecessor, the Multidimensional Acculturation Scale (MAS; Rodriguez, Myers, Bingham Mira, Flores, & Garcia-Hernandez, 2002). A principal components analysis (with varimax rotation) yielded four reliable factors that accounted for 67.3% of the total variance.
Samples	The validating sample consisted of 248 adults of Mexican origin (124 women and 124 men). Ages ranged from 18 to 64 years (*M* = 36.4, *SD* = 11.9). Participants were recruited from the Los Angeles area, with average education level of 12.4 (*SD* = 3.6) years. Participant marital status was as follows: 150 married, 68 single, 26 divorced/separated, and 4 widowed. About 51% of the participants requested to be interviewed in Spanish.
Scoring	The number of items in each of the four subscales is as follows: English Proficiency: 6 items Spanish Proficiency: 5 items Mexican Cultural Identity: 6 items American Cultural Identity: 5 items Total MASII: 22 items Scoring the MAS II consists of adding the participant's ratings on each item in the subscale and dividing that total by the number of items in the subscale to obtain a subscale mean. No reverse coding or transformations are required.
Reliability	Cronbach's alpha for the scores of the four subscales was reported to range from .78 to .93.

(Continued)

(Continued)

Validity	Criterion-related validity was evidenced by statistically significant correlations between participant generation level and English Proficiency scores, Spanish Proficiency scores, and American Cultural Identity scores. Likewise, proportional length of U.S. residence was statistically significantly related to English Proficiency scores, Spanish Proficiency scores, and American Cultural Identity scores.
Related References	Rodriguez, N., Myers, H. F., Bingham Mira, C., Flores, T., & Garcia-Hernandez, L. (2002). Development of the Multidimensional Acculturative Stress Inventory for Adults of Mexican Origin. *Psychological Assessment, 14,* 451–461.
Language Versions	Spanish and English
Contact	Norma Rodriguez Department of Psychology Pitzer College 1050 N. Mills Claremont, CA 91711 Email: norma_rodriguez@pitzer.edu

6.12.7 Name of the Measure	Los Angeles Epidemiologic Catchment Area Acculturation Scale LAECAAS
Primary Reference	Burnam, M. A., Telles, C. A., Karno, M., Hough, R. L., & Escobar, J. I. (1987). Measurement of acculturation in a community population of Mexican Americans. *Hispanic Journal of Behavioral Sciences, 9*(2), 105–130.
Purpose	The LAECAAS is a unidirectional and unidimensional acculturation scale for Mexican American adults.
Description	The LAECAAS contains 26 items. Most items are rated on a 5-point forced-choice format (the higher the number, the more acculturated the respondent is assumed to be) with the following response options: 1 = Spanish Only, 2 = Mostly Spanish, 3 = About the Same, 4 = Mostly English, 5 = English Only, or 1 = All Hispanic, 2 = Most Hispanic, 3 = Half Hispanic, 4 = Few Hispanic, 5 = None Hispanic, or 1 = All of the Time, 2 = Most of the Time, 3 = Half of the Time, 4 = Sometimes, 5 = Never, or 1 = All Hispanic, 2 = Mostly Hispanic, 3 = Half Hispanic, 4 = Some Hispanic, 5 = None Hispanic, or 1 = Mexican, 2 = Chicano, 3 = Mexican American, 4 = Latin American, other Hispanic American, or Anglo American or other, or two items are rated with the following 2- or 4-point response choices: 2 = Other, 4 = U.S., and 2 = Mostly Hispanic, part U.S., 3 = Equal, 4 = Mostly U.S., part Hispanic, 5 = U.S. only. The LAECAAS items were derived from a literature review and the previous acculturation scale development of Cuéllar, Harris, and Jasso (1980) and Szapocznik, Scopetta, Aranalde, and Kurtines (1978). Principal components analysis (with an unspecified orthogonal rotation) on the subsequent 26 items included by the authors yielded three highly correlated factors. Hence, the authors recommend using a unidimensional scaling (composite) of all 26 items.
Samples	The sample was based on a random probability sample of 1,196 Mexican American adults residing in the Los Angeles area (628 females, 568 males). Participant educational level was eighth grade or less (*n* = 488), high school 9th–12th grade (*n* = 512), and college (*n* = 191). Participant language preference was English (*n* = 614) and Spanish (*n* = 581).
Scoring	Scoring the LAECAAS consists of adding the participant's ratings on each of the 26 items to obtain a scale total score and dividing that total by 26 to obtain a scale mean. No reverse coding or transformations are required.
Reliability	Cronbach's alpha for the scores of the total sample was .97.
Validity	Concurrent validity was evidenced by the finding that LAECAAS scores significantly increased from first-generation (*M* = 1.8) to second-generation (*M* = 3.3) to later-generation groups (*M* = 3.9) of participants.
Related References	Burnam, M. A., Hough, R. L., Karno, M., Escobar, J. I., & Telles, C. A. (1987). Acculturation and lifetime prevalence of psychiatric disorders among Mexican Americans. *Journal of Health and Social Behavior, 28,* 89–102.

(Continued)

(Continued)

Language Versions	Spanish and English
Contact	M. Audrey Burnam RAND 1776 Main Street P.O. Box 2138 Santa Monica, CA 90407–2138 (310) 393–0411, 6370 (W) (310) 260- 8152 (Fax) Email: aburnam@rand.org

6.12.8 Name of the Measure	Psychological Acculturation Scale PAS
Primary Reference	Tropp, L. R., Erkut, S., Garcia Coll, C. G., Alarcon, O., & Vazquez Garcia, H. A. (1999). Psychological acculturation: Development of a new measure for Puerto Ricans on the U.S. mainland. *Educational and Psychological Measurement, 59*(2), 351–367.
Purpose	The PAS is a unidirectional and unidimensional measure of Puerto Rican acculturation that purports to assess psychological components of acculturation (e.g., cultural loyalty, solidarity, identification, and comprehension) rather than behavioral or attitudinal dimensions.
Description	The PAS contains 10 items. Each item is rated on a 9-point Likert-type scale, with the following two anchors: 1 = Only Hispanic/Latino, 9 = Only Anglo/American. Items and item wording (in both English and Spanish) were developed through literature review, six focus groups, and rigorous cross-language equivalence procedures. Principal components analysis (rotation method not specified) yielded a single factor of psychological acculturation.
Samples	The validating sample (Study 2) consisted of 107 Puerto Ricans (64 females, 39 males, and 4 nonresponses). Ages ranged from 12 to 58 years ($M = 27.9$). Participants' place of birth was 85 born in Puerto Rico and 21 born in the United States. Average percent of participant lifetime spent in the United States was 92%.
Scoring	Scoring the PAS consists of adding the participant's ratings on each of the 10 items and dividing the total score by 10 to obtain a scale mean. No reverse coding or transformations are required.
Reliability	Cronbach's alpha for the scores of the Spanish and English versions of the scale was .90 and .83, respectively.
Validity	Discriminant validity was demonstrated by showing that participants who were born in Puerto Rico had statistically significantly lower PAS scores ($M = 3.3$) than did participants born on the U.S. mainland ($M = 4.2$) $p < .01$. Convergent validity was observed through a positive correlation between the PAS scores and percentage of lifetime spent in the United States.
Related References	Stevens, G. W. J. M., Pels, T. V. M., Vollebergh, W. A. M., & Crijnen, A. A. M. (2004). Patterns of psychological acculturation in adult and adolescent Moroccan immigrants living in the Netherlands. *Journal of Cross-Cultural Psychology, 35*(6), 689–704.
Language Versions	English and Spanish
Contact	Linda R. Tropp Department of Psychology Tobin Hall, 135 Hicks Way University of Massachusetts at Amherst Amherst, MA 01003 (413) 577–0934 (W) (413) 545–0996 (Fax) Email: tropp@psych.umass.edu

6.12.9 Name of the Measure	Puerto Rican Biculturality Scale PRBS
Primary Reference	Cortes, D. E., Rogler, L. H., & Malgady, R. G. (1994). Biculturality among Puerto Rican adults in the United States. *American Journal of Community Psychology, 22*(5), 707–721.
Purpose	The PRBS is a bidirectional and multidimensional acculturation scale for Puerto Rican adults that purports to assess involvement in both American and Puerto Rican culture.
Description	The PRBS contains 18 items. Each item is rated on a 4-point Likert-type scale with the following response anchors: 1 = Not At All to 4 = Very Much. The PRBS consists of two 9-item thematic categories (involvement in Puerto Rican or American culture). PRBS initial item development was realized through a series of focus groups with adult Puerto Rican residents of the South Bronx in New York City. From these groups, 10 items were constructed that reflected degree of involvement in Puerto Rican culture, and 10 parallel items were constructed reflecting American culture. A subsequent maximum likelihood factor analysis (with varimax rotation) yielded a 20-item, two-factor, simple structure that accounted for 46% of the total variance. Two items referring to children's friends were deleted due to low structure coefficients, resulting in two 9-item subscales.
Samples	A stratified random probability sample of 403 adult Puerto Ricans residing in the greater New York metropolitan area was interviewed in their homes. Sample consisted of 254 that were born in Puerto Rico (90% first generation) and 149 that were born in the United States (53% second generation). Sample mean age was 38.9 years ($SD = 15.8$), and average years of education was 9.8 ($SD = 3.6$).

Scoring	The number of items in each subscale is as follows:
	
	    Involvement in American Culture: 9 items
	
	    Involvement in Puerto Rican Culture: 9 items
	
	    Total PRBS: 18 items
	
	Scoring the PRBS consists of adding the participant's ratings on the 9 items in each involvement domain (Puerto Rican or American) to obtain a subscale sum or total (which can range from 9 to 36). No reverse coding or transformations are required.

Reliability	Cronbach's alpha for the scores were as follows:
	
	    Involvement in American Culture: Alpha = .78
	
	    Involvement in Puerto Rican Culture: Alpha = .73
	
	The correlation between the scores of the two subscales was low negative.

Validity	Criterion-related validity was established by correlating the PRBS subscale scores with the following variables: generational status, age at arrival in the United States, and number of years in the United States. Both PRBS subscales were statistically significantly related to these criterion variables in the expected directions.
Related References	Cortes, D. E., Deren, S., Andia, J., Colon, H., Robles, R., & Kang, S. Y. (2003). The use of the Puerto Rican Biculturality Scale with Puerto Rican drug users in New York and Puerto Rico. *Journal of Psychoactive Drugs, 35*(2), 197–207.
	Mezzich, J. E., Ruiperez, M. A., Yoon, G., Liu, J., & Zapata-Vega, M. I. (2009). Measuring cultural identity: Validation of a modified Cortes, Rogler, and Malgady Bicultural Scale in three ethnic groups in New York. *Culture, Medicine, and Psychiatry, 33*(3), 451–472.
Language Versions	English and Spanish
Contact	Dharma E. Cortes Harvard Medical School Cambridge Health Alliance The Cambridge Hospital 1493 Cambridge St. Cambridge, MA 02139 (617) 503–8469 (W) (617) 503–8470 (Fax) Email: dharma_cortes@hms.harvard.edu

6.12.10 Name of the Measure	Children's Acculturation Scale CAS
Primary Reference	Franco, J. N. (1983). An acculturation scale for Mexican-American children. *The Journal of General Psychology, 108,* 175–181.
Purpose	The CAS is a unidirectional and unidimensional acculturation scale for Mexican American children. The instrument is completed by a parent, teacher, or caregiver.
Description	The CAS contains 10 items. The 10 items are rated on a multiple-choice format with scores ranging from 1 to 5, with 1 indicating a very Mexican orientation and 5 indicating a very Anglo orientation.
	The item pool was developed through a literature review, expert evaluation, other acculturation scales, and interviews with a variety of Mexican Americans. The primary focus of this scale is to provide an assessment tool for very young children who do not have very well-developed reading skills.
	Factor analysis of the scores from the normative sample (with varimax rotation) yielded three interpretable factors dealing with language usage (5 items), parental occupations (4 items), child's music preference (1 item). This dimensionality should be considered descriptive only as no reliability or validity measures were reported on the three factors or subscales.
Samples	The normative sample consisted of 175 first, third, and sixth graders from New Mexico and Texas (females = 85 and males = 90). Sample ethnicity was 141 Mexican American and 34 White American children.
Scoring	Scoring the CAS consists of adding the participant's ratings on each of the 10 items and then dividing that total by 10 to obtain a total score mean. The higher the mean, the greater is the assumed acculturation (Anglo orientation) of the child. No reverse coding or transformations are required.
Reliability	Cronbach's alpha for the scores of the CAS were reported to be .77. Test-retest reliability over a 5-week period was .93.
Validity	Construct validity was obtained by correlating the CAS scores with the scores from the Acculturation Rating Scale for Mexican Americans (ARSMA; Cuéllar, Harris, & Jasso, 1980), resulting in a positive correlation.
Related References	
Language Versions	English
Contact	Juan N. Franco University of Nebraska–Lincoln 106 Canfield Administration Building P. O. Box 880423 Lincoln, NE 68588–0423 (402) 472–3755 (W) Email: jfranco2@unl.edu

6.12.11 Name of the Measure	Short Acculturation Scale for Hispanic Youth SASH-Y
Primary Reference	Barona, A., & Miller, J. A. (1994). Short Acculturation Scale for Hispanic Youth (SASH-Y): A preliminary report. *Hispanic Journal of Behavioral Sciences, 16*(2), 155–162.
Purpose	The SASH-Y is a unidirectional and unidimensional acculturation scale for Hispanic youth that was derived from the Short Acculturation Scale for Hispanics (Marin, Sabogal, VanOss Marin, Otero-Sabogal, & Perez-Stable, 1987). This short, self-report instrument purports to measure cultural behaviors in the context of both the family and social/media influences.
Description	The SASH-Y contains 12 items. Each item is rated on a 5-point Likert-type scale. The response options for item 1 were 1 = Only Spanish, 2 = Spanish Better than English, 3 = Both Equally, 4 = English Better than Spanish, and 5 = Only English. Response options for items 2 through 9 were 1 = Only Spanish, 2 = More Spanish than English, 3 = Both Equally, 4 = More English than Spanish, and 5 = Only English. Response options for items 10 through 12 were 1 = All Hispanic, 2 = More Hispanic than White, 3 = About Half and Half, 4 = More White than Hispanic, and 5 = All White. The SASH-Y is composed of a total score and three subscales: (1) Extrafamilial Language Use, (2) Familial Language Use, (3) Ethnic Social Relations. A maximum likelihood factor analysis with a promax rotation yielded three interpretable factors. However, due to the cross-loading of item 1 (i.e., high structure coefficients) with factors 1 and 2, the authors recommend using only the total score and not the subscale scores.
Samples	The sample consisted of 141 Latino/a American and 230 non-Hispanic White American children (*N* = 371) from an urban school district in the Southwest. Grade level was 22% fifth grade, 22% sixth grade, 22% seventh grade, and 35% eighth grade. Total sample consisted of 194 males, 10.5 to 16.1 years (*M* = 13.2, *SD* = 1.62) and 177 females, 10.7 to 15.5 years (*M* = 13.0, *SD* = 1.60).
Scoring	Scoring the SASH-Y consists of adding the participant's ratings on each of the 12 items to obtain a total scale score that ranges from 12 to 60, with higher scores indicating higher acculturation to mainstream U.S. culture.
Reliability	Cronbach's alpha for the total sample was .94, and for the Latino/a American and non-Hispanic samples it was .92 and .85, respectively. A split-half reliability measure was .96 for the total sample.
Validity	A statistically significant main effect of ethnicity demonstrated that the scale discriminated between Latino/a American and non-Hispanic White American youth. Some evidence of construct validity was achieved with the discovery of the three-factor simple structure.

(Continued)

(Continued)

Related References	Serrano, E., & Anderson, J. (2003). Assessment of a refined short acculturation scale for Latino preteens in rural Colorado. *Hispanic Journal of Behavioral Sciences, 25*(2), 240–253.
Language Versions	English
Contact	Andres Barona Division of Psychology in Education Arizona State University Tempe, AZ 85287–0611 (480) 965–2920 Email: barona@asu.edu

6.12.12 Name of the Measure	Acculturative Stress Inventory for Children ASIC
Primary Reference	Suarez-Morales, L., Dillon, F. R., & Szapocznik, J. (2007). Validation of the Acculturative Stress Inventory for Children. *Cultural Diversity and Ethnic Minority Psychology, 13*(3), 216–224.
Purpose	The ASIC is a unidirectional and multidimensional self-report instrument that purports to measure acculturative stress in Hispanic children.
Description	The ASIC contains 12 items. Each item is rated on a 6-point Likert-type scale with the following response anchors: 0 = Doesn't Apply to 5 = Bothers Me a Lot. The ASIC is composed of a total score and two subscales: (1) Perceived Discrimination and (2) Immigration-Related Stress. The ASIC is a revision of a 60-item scale developed by Padilla and colleagues (Padilla, Wagatsuma, & Lindholm, 1985; Padilla, Alvarez, & Lindholm, 1986) for adults (the Societal Attitudinal, Familial, and Environmental Acculturative Stress Scale, SAFE) that was further modified into a 24-item measure by Fuertes and Westbrook (1996), and then reconfigured as a 36-item acculturation stress scale for use with children by Chavez, Moran, Reid, and Lopez (1997) and renamed the Societal, Attitudinal, Familial, Environmental, Acculturative Stress Scale for Children (SAFE-C). Chavez et al. (1997) eliminated one 16-item subscale of the SAFE-C that dealt with general social stress, leaving a 20-item measure. A subsequent principal axis factor analysis (with varimax rotation) yielded a two-factor, 12-item simple structure. Five of the 12 items had communalities of less than .30.
Samples	The normative sample was based on 139 Latino/a American children, all of whom were in the fifth grade.

Scoring	The number of items in each of the two subscales is as follows:
	
	    Perceived Discrimination: 8 items
	    Immigration-Related Stress: 4 items
	    Total ASIC: 12 items
	
	Scoring the ASIC consists of adding the participant's ratings on each item in the subscale to obtain subscale scores or adding all of the participant's ratings on all 12 items to obtain a total score. No reverse coding or transformations are required.

(Continued)

(Continued)

Reliability	Cronbach's alpha for the scores were as follows:
	
	    Perceived Discrimination: Alpha = .79
	
	    Immigration-Related Stress: Alpha = .72
	
	    Total ASIC: Alpha = .82
	
	Two-week test-retest reliability estimates were as follows:
	
	    Perceived Discrimination: r = .93
	
	    Immigration-Related Stress: r = .77
	
	    Total ASIC: r = .84

Validity	Convergent validity was demonstrated by statistically significant moderate correlations between the ASIC total scale score and its two subscales and the total scores on the Daily Hassles Questionnaire (DHY; Rowlinson & Felner, 1988), and the Revised Children's Manifest Anxiety Scale (RCMAS; Reynolds & Richmond, 1978). Discriminant validity was evidenced by no statistically significant association among the ASIC total or subscale scores and the scores on the RCMAS Lie Scale.
Related References	
Language Versions	English
Contact	Lourdes Suarez-Morales Center for Family Studies 1425 NW 10th Ave., Suite 315 Miami, FL 33136 (305) 243–5505 (W) Email: LSuarez@med.miami.edu

6.12.13 Name of the Measure	Measure of Acculturation for Chicano Adolescents MACA
Primary Reference	Olmedo, E. L., Martinez, J. L. Jr., & Martinez, S. R. (1978). Measure of acculturation for Chicano adolescents. *Psychological Reports, 42*, 159–170.
Purpose	The MACA is a unidirectional and multidimensional measure of acculturation for Chicano/a Americans adolescents. Acculturation is defined as a linear combination of semantic and sociocultural variables.
Description	The MACA contains 20 items. Each item is rated on a 7-point scale. The 11 sociocultural items can be evaluated with the following anchors: 1 = Very True to 7 = Not At All True. The nine semantic variables (e.g., Father: Simple-Complex) are evaluated such that the left member of the pair is at the low end of the 1–7 continuum and the right member is at the high end. The MACA is composed of a total standardized score. The MACA was constructed through an initial item pool of 127 semantic and sociocultural items. Subsequent multivariate analyses of variance and multiple regression analyses winnowed the item pool to 20 items. A principal factor analysis (with oblique rotation) yielded three factors: (1) Nationality-Language, (2) Socioeconomic Status, and (3) Semantic. These three dimensions were not converted into separate subscales.
Samples	The normative sample consisted of 924 junior and senior high school students from Southern California (436 females and 488 males). The sample contained 254 Chicano/a Americans and 670 White Americans.
Scoring	Scoring the MACA consists of computing an individual acculturation score for each respondent. This score is defined "as the linear combination of semantic and sociocultural variables which provides the best least squares estimate of that individual's score on a dichotomous variable in which Chicano/a Americans are assigned a value of 0 and Anglos a value of 1" (p. 165).
Reliability	Test-retest reliability, over a 3-week period (with a separate sample, 129 Chicano/a American and White American junior college students), yielded reliability coefficients .84, .89, and .66, for the total sample, Chicano/a Americans, and White Americans, respectively.
Validity	A double cross-validation procedure suggested that the 20-variable regression equation showed stability across independent subsamples.
Related References	
Language Versions	English
Contact	Esteban L. Olmedo 1961 Calle Bogota Rowland Heights, CA 91748 (626) 810–4224 (H) Email: eolmedo@adelphia.net

6.12.14 Name of the Measure	Cultural Life Styles Inventory CLSI
Primary Reference	de Leon, B., & Mendez, S. (1996). Factorial structure of a measure of acculturation in a Puerto Rican population. *Educational and Psychological Measurement, 56*(1), 155–165. Mendoza, R. H. (1989). An empirical scale to measure type and degree of acculturation in Mexican-American adolescents and adults. *Journal of Cross-Cultural Psychology, 20*(4), 372–385.
Purpose	The CLSI measures bidirectional and multidimensional acculturation in Mexican American adolescents and adults. The CLSI measures acculturation on five orthogonal dimensions and can be used to identify four cultural lifestyle or acculturation orientations.
Description	The CLSI contains 29 items. Each item is rated on a 5-point multiple-choice format that corresponds with the following response codes: a or b = Mexican Oriented, c or d = U.S. Oriented, e = Multicultural Oriented, f or g = Not Applicable, Blank items = No Response. The items that are not applicable or left blank are not included in the subsequent computations. Item 26 is rated as: a or b = U.S. Oriented, c or d = Mexican Oriented, e = Multicultural Oriented, f or g = Not Applicable, Blank items = No Response. The CLSI is composed of the following four mutually exclusive, computed, acculturation orientations: (1) Mexican Oriented Acculturation (formerly called Cultural Resistance), (2) U.S. Oriented Acculturation (formerly called Cultural Shift), (3) Multicultural Oriented Acculturation (formerly called Cultural Incorporation), (4) Eclectic Oriented Acculturation (formerly called Cultural Eclecticism). The CLSI item pool was developed through a literature review and several panels of cultural (White American and Mexican American) experts who generated cultural practices that were subsequently developed into 83 items. An item pool was then developed that effectively discriminated the responses between a sample of Anglo Americans ($n = 82$) and a sample of Mexican Americans ($n = 97$). Five latent factors were discovered that best represented the 29 CLSI items: Intrafamilial Language Use, Extrafamilial Language Use, Social Affiliation, Cultural Familiarity, and Cultural Identification and Pride. The five-factor dimensional structure of the CLSI was purported to have been developed through principal components analysis, cluster analyses, and multidimensional scaling (Mendoza, 1989). Because the details of these data reduction analyses were not reported in Mendoza (1989), we will use in this summary, for validation evidence, a subsequent study with Puerto Rican college students (de Leon & Mendez, 1996). De Leon and Mendez (1996) report the results of factor analysis (with varimax rotation) that yielded a five-factor solution similar but not identical to Mendoza's (1989) five-factor solution with Mexican Americans. The de Leon and Mendez (1996) five-factor solution was as follows: Cultural Definition and Identity (10 items), Ethnicity in Social Interactions (four items), Language Use in Family and Personal Interactions (six items), Language for Cultural and Educational Exchange (five items), Language Spoken With Spouse and Children (two items).

Samples	The de Leon and Mendez (1996) validating sample consisted of 402 Puerto Rican college students with 203 from Puerto Rico (126 females and 77 males), and 199 Puerto Rican students from the United States (126 females and 73 males). Ages ranged from 18 to 52 years (*median* = 20.5). About 25% of the sample was Catholic.
Scoring	Scoring the CLSI consists of adding the participant's ratings on each item in the five acculturation subscales identified by either Mendoza (1989) or de Leon and Mendez (1996) and then dividing by the number of items within the subscale to obtain a subscale mean.
	Mendoza (1989, 2006) recommends using the CLSI scores to calculate four mutually exclusive cultural life style orientations: Mexican Oriented Acculturation, U.S. Oriented Acculturation, Multicultural Oriented Acculturation, and Eclectic Oriented Acculturation. This is accomplished in the following four steps.
	CLSI items are coded to determine if responses reflect Mexican Oriented, U.S. Oriented, or Multicultural Oriented acculturation tendencies. Coding is determined as indicated in the previous description section.
	Participant responses on the 29 items are partitioned into the number of items answered in a Mexican Oriented, U.S. Oriented, or Multicultural Oriented acculturation tendency.
	Proportions of the 29 items (or items not left blank or coded "f" or "g") are computed for each of the three acculturation types with the following formulas: Mexican Oriented Score = Total Mexican Oriented Responses/Total Mexican, U.S. and Multicultural Responses; U.S. Oriented Score = Total U.S. Oriented Responses/Total Mexican, U.S. and Multicultural Responses; Multicultural Oriented Score = Total Multicultural Oriented Responses/Total Mexican, U.S. and Multicultural Responses.
	The three proportions are compared statistically (with *z* scores) to determine if the participant has a **dominant** Mexican, U.S., or Multicultural Oriented acculturation typology, or a **nondominant** Eclectic Oriented acculturation. See Mendoza (2006) for additional details.
Reliability	De Leon and Mendez (1996) report Cronbach's alphas for the scores of their samples' subscales to range from .64 to .87. Mendoza (1989) reported Cronbach's alphas for the scores of his subscales to range from .84 to .91.
	Test-retest reliability (Mendoza, 1989) was *r* = .91 over a 2-week period.
Validity	Mendoza (1989) demonstrated construct validity by finding a statistically significant positive correlation between generational status and U.S. Oriented acculturation. Similarly, generational status and Mexican Oriented and Multicultural Oriented acculturation was negatively correlated.
Related References	Mendoza, R. H. (2006). Cultural Life Styles Inventory for Mexican-American Adolescents and Adults (Version 3.0). Unpublished manuscript, California School of Professional Psychology at Alliant International University, Los Angeles, Alhambra, CA.
Language Versions	English and Spanish
Contact	Richard H. Mendoza California School of Professional Psychology at Alliant International University, Los Angeles Alhambra, CA 91803–1360 Email: rmendoza@alliant.edu

6.12.15 Name of the Measure	Padilla's Acculturation Scale PAS
Primary Reference	Padilla, A. M. (1980a). The role of cultural awareness and ethnic loyalty in acculturation. In A. M. Padilla (Ed.), *Acculturation: Theory, models, and some new findings* (pp. 47–84). Boulder, CO: Westview.
Purpose	The PAS is a unidirectional and multidimensional Mexican American acculturation scale that purports to assess two important components (cultural awareness and ethnic loyalty) of Padilla's (1980a) acculturation model.
Description	The PAS consists of 155 items. All items were coded such that "a high score reflected awareness or loyalty to the Mexican culture" (p. 53). The PAS consists of two separate scales, each with four subscales. Cultural Awareness (CA) Scale: (1) Respondent's Cultural Heritage, (2) Spouse's Cultural Heritage and Pride, (3) Parent's Cultural Heritage and Pride, (4) Perceived Discrimination. Ethnic Loyalty (EL) Scale: (1) Language Preference and Use, (2) Cultural Pride and Affiliation, (3) Cultural Identification and Preference, (4) Social Behavior Orientation. Item development reflected the Padilla (1980a) acculturation model constructs of cultural awareness and ethnic loyalty. A total of 584 questions from the interview schedule were pooled into 108 items that reflected 18 CA concepts and another 77 items that reflected 15 EL concepts. Psychometric item analyses reduced these 185 items to 155 items in which 90 were grouped into 19 CA concepts and 65 into 11 EL concepts. Composite CA and EL concepts were created and became the constituents for two separate principal factor analyses (with oblique rotations) that resulted in separate four-factor simple structures.
Samples	The normative sample consisted of 381 (313 women, 68 men) Southern CA Mexican American adults. Ages ranged from 18 to 70 years ($M = 43.0$). Self-reported marital status was: married (83.7%), widowed (6.3%), divorced (5.8%), separated (2.6%), and single (1.6%). Respondent generational status was as follows: first generation (37.8%), second generation (22.3%), third generation (7.1%), and fourth generation (5.2%), mixed second generation (11.8%), no response (15.8%).
Scoring	The CA scale was composed of 90 items grouped into 19 concepts that were factor analyzed into the following four subscales: Respondent's Cultural Heritage Spouse's Cultural Heritage and Pride Parent's Cultural Heritage and Pride Perceived Discrimination

	The EL scale was composed of 77 items grouped into 11 concepts that were factor analyzed into the following four subscales: Language Preference and Use Cultural Pride and Affiliation Cultural Identification and Preference Social Behavior Orientation PAS Scoring details can be obtained from the author.
Reliability	All eight subscales were reported to be "highly reliable in terms of internal consistency with four of the scales . . . yielding coefficients equal to or greater than .90" (p. 63). A positive correlation was found between the scores of the CA and EL factors.
Validity	Discriminant validity was achieved by clustering respondents' scores according to the locus of their scores in respect to a two-dimensional space defined by their CA and EL responses.
Related References	Padilla, A. M., & Perez, W. (2003). Acculturation, social identity, and social cognition: A new perspective. *Hispanic Journal of Behavioral Sciences, 25*(1), 35–55.
Language Versions	English and Spanish
Contact	Amado M. Padilla Psychological Studies in Education Stanford University 485 Lasuen Mall Stanford, CA 94305–3096 (650) 723–9132 (W) Email: apadilla@stanford.edu

6.12.16 Name of the Measure	Cultural Socialization Scale CSS
Primary Reference	Romero, A. J., Cuéllar, I., & Roberts, R. E. (2000). Ethnocultural variables and attitudes toward cultural socialization of children. *Journal of Community Psychology, 28*(1), 79–89.
Purpose	The CSS is a bidirectional and multidimensional instrument that purports to assess parent attitudes toward cultural socialization to U.S American culture and to Latino/a American culture.
Description	The CSS contains 18 items. Each item is rated on a 5-point Likert-type scale with the following two response anchors: 1 = Not At All to 5 = A Lot. The CSS is composed of two subscales: (1) U.S. American Cultural Socialization (ACS), (2) Latino/a Cultural Socialization (LCS). CSS items were developed to reflect several lines of research including the social cognitive model of cultural socialization (Knight, Bernal, Cota, Garza, & Ocampo, 1993), notions of independence and interdependence (Markus & Kityama, 1991), and the work of Triandis (1989). Subsequent principal axis factor analyses (with varimax rotations) on the items of the ACS and LCS produced unstable factor structures and were treated as composite ACS and LCS subscales.
Samples	The normative sample was 244 (177 women, 91 men) students who were parents and who were of Mexican descent. Average age was 27 years and ranged from 17 to 63 years. Self-reported ethnicity was Mexican American (87%), Mexican (8%), White American (5%). Self-reported generational status was First generation (14%), second generation (40%), third generation (4%), fourth generation (24%), fifth generation (18%).

Scoring	The number of items in the two subscales is as follows:
	
	   U.S. American Cultural Socialization (ACS):8 items
	
	   Latino/a Cultural Socialization (LCS): 10 items
	
	   Total CSS: 18 items
	
	Scoring the CSS consists of adding the participant's ratings on each item in the subscale and dividing that total by the number of subscale items to obtain a subscale mean. No reverse coding or transformations are required.

Reliability	Cronbach's alpha for the scores were as follows:
	
	   ACS: Alpha = .78
	
	   LCS: Alpha = .73

Validity	Construct validity was demonstrated with the finding of a strong relationship between Mexican identity as measured by the Cultural Identification Scale (CIS; Oetting & Beauvis, 1990–1991), acculturation, as measured by the Acculturation Rating Scale for Mexican Americans-II (ARSMA-II; Cuéllar, Arnold, & Maldonado, 1995), and the scores of the LCS.

Related References	
Language Versions	English
Contact	Andrea J. Romero Mexican American Studies & Research Center University of Arizona Cesar E. Chavez Building #23 Room 203A-1 1110 E. James E. Rogers Way Tucson, AZ 85721 (520) 626–8137 (W) (520) 621- 7966 (Fax) Email: romeroa@u.arizona.edu

6.12.17 Name of the Measure	Pan-Hispanic Familism Scale P-HFS
Primary Reference	Villarreal, R., Blozis, S. A., & Widaman, K. F. (2005). Factorial invariance of a Pan-Hispanic Familism Scale. *Hispanic Journal of Behavioral Sciences, 27*(4), 409–425.
Purpose	The P-HFS is a unidimensional measure of Hispanic familism that purports to assess attitudinal familism (i.e., attitudes about the importance of family) among Hispanic adults.
Description	The P-HFS contains five items. Each item is rated on the following 5-point Likert-type scale: 1 = Strongly Disagree, 2 = Disagree, 3 = Neutral, 4 = Agree, 5 = Strongly Agree.
	The P-HFS is composed of a total scale score.
	The five items that compose the P-HFS were selected from two scales developed by Gaines, Marelich, Bledsoe, and Steers et al. (1997), and Gil, Wagner, and Vega (2000). A subsequent confirmatory factor analysis found the one-factor model to be a good fit to the data (RMSEA = .009).
Samples	The normative sample consisted of 762 Latino/a American adults, randomly sampled with a national telephone survey. Ages ranged from 18 to 65 years.
Scoring	Scoring the P-HFS consists of adding the participant's ratings on all items and dividing by five to obtain a total scale mean. No reverse coding or transformations are required.
Reliability	Cronbach's alpha for the total scale was .82.
Validity	Construct validity and factorial invariance of the P-HFS was demonstrated through confirmatory factor analysis, which suggested invariance of the measure across respondent country of origin groupings (United States, Mexico, and Latin America).
Related References	Villarreal, R., & Peterson, R. A. (2009). The concept and marketing implications of Hispanicness. *The Journal of Marketing Theory and Practice, 17*(4), 303–316.
Contact	Ricardo Villarreal De Silva University of San Francisco School of Business and Management 2130 Fulton Street, Malloy Hall 217 San Francisco, CA 94117–1045 (415) 422–4507 (W) (415) 422–2502 (Fax) Email: rvillarrealdesilva@usfca.edu

6.12.18 Name of the Measure	Attitudinal Familism Scale AFS
Primary Reference	Steidel, A. G. L., & Contreras, J. M. (2003). A new familism scale for use with Latino populations. *Hispanic Journal of Behavioral Sciences, 25*(3), 312–330.
Purpose	The AFS is a multidimensional measure of Latino/a familism (attitudes about the importance of family) that purports to target less acculturated Latino/a American adults.
Description	The AFS contains 18 items. Each item is rated on a 10-point Likert-type scale with the following two response anchors: 1 = Strongly Disagree and 10 = Strongly Agree.
	The AFS is composed of a total score and four subscales: (1) Familial Support, (2) Familial Interconnectedness, (3) Familial Honor, (4) Subjugation of Self for Family.
	The 18 items of the AFS were adapted from four previous studies (e.g., Bardis, 1959; Cuéllar, Arnold, & Gonzalez, 1995; Fuligini, Tseng, & Lam, 1999; Gaines et al., 1997), and some new items that reflected four components of familism proposed by the authors: family comes first, interconnectedness, familial reciprocity, and family honor. A subsequent principal components analysis (with an oblique rotation) yielded an 18-item, four-factor, simple structure that accounted for 51.2% of the total variance.
Samples	The normative sample consisted of 125 Latino/a American adults residing in Cleveland, Ohio. Participant average age was 42 years (*SD* = 18.5). Respondent self-reported ethnicity was Puerto Rican (86.7%), the remaining 13.3% belonged to Dominican, Colombian, and Salvadoran ethnic groups.
Scoring	The number of items in each of the four subscales was as follows:
	Familial Support: 6 items
	Familial Interconnectedness: 5 items
	Familial Honor: 4 items
	Subjugation of Self for Family: 3 items
	Total AFS: 18 items
	Scoring the AFS consists of adding the participant's ratings on each item in the subscale and dividing that score by the number of items within the subscale to obtain a subscale mean. A total scale mean can be obtained by adding all of the participant's ratings on all of the items and dividing by 18. No reverse coding or transformations are required.
Reliability	Cronbach's alpha for the scores were as follows:
	Familial Support: Alpha = .72
	Familial Interconnectednes: Alpha = .69
	Familial Honor: Alpha = .68
	Subjection of Self for Family: Alpha = .56
	Total AFS: Alpha = .83
	All of the subscales were moderately positively correlated.

(Continued)

(Continued)

Validity	Criterion validity was established by demonstrating a low positive correlation between the scores of the total AFS and the scores of the Acculturation Rating Scale for Mexican Americans-II Latino (Mexican) Orientation Scale (ARSMA-II; Cuéllar, Arnold, & Maldonado, 1995). Conversely, total AFS scores and ARSMA Anglo Orientation Scores were negatively correlated.
Related References	Rodriguez, N., Bingham Mira, C., Paez, N., & Myers, H. (2007). Exploring the complexities of familism and acculturation: Central constructs for people of Mexican origin. *American Journal of Community Psychology, 39*(1–2), 61–77. Schwartz, S. J. (2007). The applicability of familism to diverse ethnic groups: A preliminary study. *The Journal of Social Psychology, 147*(2), 101–118.
Language Versions	English and Spanish
Contact	Angel Lugo Steidel Clinical Psychologist 5110 12th Avenue Brooklyn, NY 11219

6.12.19 Name of the Measure	Expectations of Filial Piety Scale—Spanish Version EFPS-SV
Primary Reference	Kao, H.-F. S., & Travis, S. S. (2005b). Development of the Expectations of Filial Piety Scale-Spanish version. *Journal of Advanced Nursing, 52*(6), 682–688.
Purpose	The EFPS-SV is a multidimensional instrument that purports to measure Latino/a American parents' expectations of care and support from their adult children.
Description	The EFPS-SV contains 16 items. Each item is rated on the following 4-point Likert-type scale: 1 = No Need At All, 2 = Somewhat In Need, 3 = Pretty Much In Need, 4 = Very Much In Need.
	The EFPS-SV is composed of a total score and four subscales: (1) Respect for Parents, (2) Honoring Parents, (3) Supporting Parents, (4) Family Unity.
	The 31 Spanish translated items used in the initial item pool came from an unpublished dissertation (Dai, 1995). Subsequent principal components analysis (with a varimax rotation) resulted in a 16-item, four-factor simple structure that accounted for 59.7% of the total variance.
Samples	The normative sample consisted of 318 (192 women and 126 men) Latino/a American parents of adult children over the age of 18 years. Sample ages ranged from 34 to 88 years (*M* = 48.7, *SD* = 11.6). Half of the sample was U.S.-born Mexican Americans (49%), and the rest of the sample came from Central and South America.
Scoring	The number of items in each of the four subscales is as follows:
	Respect for Parents: 7 items
	Honoring Parents: 3 items
	Supporting Parents: 3 items
	Family Unity: 3 items
	Total EFPS-SV: 16 items
	Scoring the EFPS-SV consists of adding the participant's ratings on each item in the subscale to obtain subscale scores or adding all of the participant's ratings on all 16 items to obtain a total score. No reverse coding or transformations are required.
Reliability	Cronbach's alpha for the scores were as follows:
	Respect for Parents: Alpha = .84
	Honoring Parents: Alpha = .66
	Supporting Parents: Alpha = .66
	Family Unity: Alpha = .68
	Total EFPS-SV: Alpha = .82

(Continued)

(Continued)

Validity	Convergent validity was established by demonstrating higher EFPS-SV total scores for the foreign-born subsample as compared to the U.S.-born participants.
Related References	Kao, H.-F. S., & Travis, S. (2005a). Effects of acculturation and social exchange on the expectations of filial piety among Hispanic/Latino parents of adult children. *Nursing and Health Sciences, 7*(4), 226–234.
Language Versions	English, Spanish, Chinese
Contact	Hsueh-Fen Kao School of Nursing University of Texas at El Paso 1101 N. Campbell, Room 405 El Paso, TX 79902 (915) 747–7279 (W) Email: hkao@utep.edu

6.12.20 Name of the Measure	Latino/a Values Scale LVS
Primary Reference	Kim, B. S. K., Soliz, A., Orellana, B., & Alamilla, S. G. (2009). Latino/a Values Scale: Development, Reliability, and Validity. *Measurement and Evaluation in Counseling and Development, 42*(2), 71–91.
Purpose	The LVS is a multidimensional measure of enculturation that purports to assess various dimensions of Latino/a cultural values.
Description	The LVS contains 35 items. Each item is rated on a 4-point Likert-type scale with the following two response anchors: 1 = Strongly Disagree to 4 = Strongly Agree. The LVS is composed of a total score and four subscales: (1) LVS-Cultural Pride, (2) LVS-Simpatia, (3) LVS-Familismo, (4) LVS-Espiritismo. Note: the authors recommend against using the Simpatia and Espiritismo subscales for future research due to the finding of relatively low internal reliability (Cronbach's alpha) for the scores of these two scales. The initial LVS item pool was developed through a comprehensive literature review and focus group discussions. Eleven Latino/a value dimensions were developed. A group of 36 members of the National Latino/a Psychological Association generated 189 value statements from these dimensions that were independently winnowed down to a pool of 120 items. Two groups of participants, White American (*n* = 32) and first-generation Latino/a American (*n* = 29), were compared on the 120 items by means of a series of *t*-tests. A total of 35 items produced statistically significantly higher ratings for the Latino/a American sample, and these items were deemed the LVS. A subsequent principal components analysis (with varimax rotation) on the 35-item LVS resulted in a 24-item, four-component, simple structure that accounted for 40.6% of the total variance. Eleven of the original 35 LVS items did not load on any component.
Samples	The normative sample consisted of 181 West Coast university students (135 women and 46 men). Ages ranged from 18 to 29 years (*M* = 18.6, *SD* = 1.5). The sample included 147 Latino/a Americans and 34 White Americans. Latino/a American ethnicities included Mexican or Chicano (80.3%), Salvadoran (6.1%), Guatemalan (1.4%), Chilean (0.7%), Ecuadorian (0.7%), Honduran (0.7%), Peruvian (0.7%), Uruguayan (0.7%), other (1.4%), and no response (1.4%). Latino/a American generational status was as follows: first generation (19.7%), second generation (62.6%), third generation (6.1%), fourth generation (7.5%), fifth generation (2.7%), and other (1.4%).

Scoring	The number of items in each of the four subscales is as follows:
	
	    LVS-Cultural Pride: 10 items*
	
	    LVS-Simpatia: 6 items
	
	    LVS-Familismo: 5 items*
	
	    LVS-Espiritismo: 3 items

(Continued)

(Continued)

	Note: Eleven items did not correlate on any of the above components (subscales).
	Total LVS: 35 items
	Asterisk (*) indicates that the authors recommend the use of these subscales for future research.
	Scoring the LVS consists of adding the participant's ratings on each item in the subscale to obtain subscale scores and dividing the total by the number of items in the subscale to obtain a subscale mean. A total scale mean can be obtained by adding the participant's ratings on all of the items and dividing by 24. Fourteen items are reverse coded.
Reliability	Cronbach's alpha for the scores were as follows:
	Cultural Pride: Alpha = .89
	Simpatia: Alpha = .65
	Familismo: Alpha = .75
	Espiritismo: Alpha = .53
	Two-week test-retest reliability coefficients were as follows:
	Cultural Pride: $r = .75$
	Familismo: $r = .75$
	Total LVS: $r = .78$
Validity	Concurrent validity was demonstrated by the finding of a positive correlation between the scores of the LVS, LVS-Cultural Pride, and LVS-Familismo and the scores of the Latino/a subscale of the Cultural Identification Scale (CIS-Latino/a; Oetting & Beauvais, 1991). Discriminant validity was established by the lack of a statistically significant correlation between the scores of the LVS, LVS-Cultural Pride, and LVS-Familismo and the scores of the Social Desirability Scale (SDS; Crowne & Marlowe, 1960). Factorial validity was further established by means of a confirmatory factor analysis using four first-order latent variables, which composed the scores of the 24 indicators, and a second-order latent variable that represented the LVS score. Results indicated an acceptable fit of the data.
Related References	
Language Versions	English
Contact	Bryan S. K. Kim Department of Psychology University of Hawaii at Hilo 200 W. Kawili St. Hilo, Hawai'i 96720–4091 (808) 974–7439 (W) (808) 974–7737 (Fax) Email: bryankim@hawaii.edu Website: www2.hawaii.edu/~bryankim/

6.12.21 Name of the Measure	Multiphasic Assessment of Cultural Constructs—Short Form MACC-SF
Primary Reference	Cuéllar, I., Arnold, B., & Gonzalez, G. (1995). Cognitive referents of acculturation: Assessment of cultural constructs in Mexican Americans. *Journal of Community Psychology, 23,* 339–356.
Purpose	The MACC-SF purports to measure the following five separate dimensions of Latino/a American cultural attitudes, ideas, beliefs, and values associated with Latino/a American acculturation: familism, fatalism, machismo, personalismo, and folk beliefs.
Description	The MACC-SF contains 62 items. Each item is rated on a True/False scale. The MACC-SF consists of five separate subscales, each with its own subscale structure: (1) Familism (a) Dependence on Relatives, (b) Family Priority, (c) Respect for Parental Authority; (2) Fatalism (a) Inevitability, (b) Mastery; (3) Machismo (a) Male Superiority, (b) Male Gender Role, (c) Female Gender Role, (d) Male Strength; (4) Folk Beliefs (a) Experience, (b) Belief in Supernatural, (c) Folk Practice Ideologies; (5) Personalismo (a) Friendliness, (b) Sociability, (c) Social Influence. The initial item pool was developed from a longer (9-construct) unpublished version of the MACC. An unspecified number of items were eliminated due to negative or low item-total correlations, resulting in the present 62-item MACC-SF. Five subsequent factor analyses (with an unspecified extraction and varimax rotation) resulted in the previously stated factor structures. Total variance accounted for across the five analyses ranged between 41–48%.
Samples	The normative sample consisted of 379 university students (197 women and 182 men). Ages ranged from 17 to 64 years ($M = 25$, $SD = 6.7$). The sample consisted of 89% Mexican origin and 11% non-Latino/a.
Scoring	The number of items in each of the five (cultural constructs) subscales is as follows: Familism: 12 items Fatalism: 8 items Personalismo: 11 items Folk Illness Beliefs: 14 items Machismo: 17 items Total MACC-SF: 62 items Scoring the MACC-SF consists of adding participant's "true" subscale responses. High scores indicate close adherence to the cultural value and low scores indicate nonadherence. Other researchers (Ferrari, 2002; Ramos-Sanchez & Atkinson, 2009) recommend scoring individual subscales by means of 6-point Likert-type scales (0 = Strongly Disagree to 6 = Strongly Agree), or 5-point Likert-type scales (1 = Strongly Disagree to 5 = Strongly Agree). One item in the Folk Illness Beliefs subscale requires reverse coding.

(Continued)

(Continued)

Reliability	Cronbach's alphas for the subscale scores of the MACC-SF ranged from .47 to .78. Familism: Alpha = .65 Fatalism: Alpha = .63 Machismo: Alpha = .78 Folk Beliefs: Alpha = .75 Personalismo: Alpha = .47
Validity	Evidence of construct validity was demonstrated by statistically significant correlations between four of the five MACC-SF subscales (Familism, Fatalism, Machismo, and Folk Illness Beliefs) and generational status and acculturation as measured by the Acculturation Rating Scale for Mexican Americans-II (ARSMA-II; Cuéllar, Arnold, & Maldonado, 1995).
Related References	Ferrari, A. M. (2002). The impact of culture upon child rearing practices and definitions of maltreatment. *Child Abuse & Neglect, 26*(8), 793–813. Ramos-Sanchez, L., & Atkinson, D. R. (2009). The relationships between Mexican American acculturation, cultural values, gender, and help-seeking intentions. *Journal of Counseling and Development, 87*(1), 62–71.
Language Versions	English and Spanish
Contact	Israel Cuéllar (deceased) C/O Danny Layne Network and Publications Administrator Julian Samora Research Institute Michigan State University 301 Nisbet Bldg., 1407 S. Harrison Rd. East Lansing, MI 48823–5286 (517) 432–1317 (W) (517) 432–2221 (Fax) Email: www.jsri.msu.edu

6.13 MULTIGROUP ACCULTURATION MEASURES

6.13.1 Name of the Measure	Orthogonal Cultural Identification Scale OCIS
Primary Reference	Oetting, E. R., Swaim, R. C., & Chiarella, M. C. (1998). Factor structure and invariance of the Orthogonal Identification Scale among American Indian and Mexican American youth. *Hispanic Journal of Behavioral Sciences, 20*(2), 131–154.
Purpose	The OCIS is a bidirectional, multidimensional, and multigroup acculturation inventory that purports to measure an individual's level of identification with any or multiple cultures.
Description	The OCIS consists of six "root items" that assess (a) identification with a specific way of life or culture, (b) perceived or expected success in that culture, and (c) involvement in cultural activities and traditions. Each of the three queries is contextualized in terms of the respondent and his/her family. Each of the six items is independently rated on a 4-point Likert-type scale for each ethnic minority identification under study (e.g., "American Indian way of life," "American Indian culture," or "Mexican American way of life," or "Mexican American culture") and the majority culture (e.g., "White American or Anglo way of life," or "White American or Anglo culture"). The response options are 4 = A lot, 3 = Some, 2 = Not Much, 1 = Not at All. A subsequent confirmatory factor analysis (Oetting, Swaim, & Chiarella, 1998) tested four different models and found the best fit to be the Cultural Factors-Independence model. This model assumes that family and individual cultural identification are linked and that the three components of culture (traditions, success, and lifestyles) are correlated but independent measured variables of the latent factor, cultural identification.
Samples	The normative sample consisted of 2,048 Native American and Mexican American adolescents (1,122 females, 926 males). Self-reported ethnicity was Native American ($n = 1,144$) and Mexican American ($n = 904$). Participant education level was 7th through 9th grade ($n = 1,017$) and 10th through 12th grade ($n = 1,031$).
Scoring	Scoring the OCIS consists of adding participant's ratings on each of the two items dealing with minority traditions (family and individual traditions) and dividing by 2 to obtain a Minority Traditions subscale mean. Likewise, the two items dealing with success (family and individual) and the two items dealing with lifestyles (family and individual) can also be computed into Minority Success and Minority Lifestyles subscales. A composite mean of all six "minority" items will produce a Minority Identification scale. Conversely, Majority Traditions, Majority Success, Majority Lifestyles, and a Majority Identification composite can be obtained in a similar fashion.

(Continued)

(Continued)

Reliability	Internal consistency was not reported for this scale.
Validity	Factorial validity for the CF/I model (see above) was provided through a series of confirmatory factor analyses.
Related References	Oetting, E. R., & Beauvais, F. (1990–1991). Orthogonal cultural identification theory: The cultural identification of minority adolescents. *International Journal of the Addictions, 25,* 655–685.
Language Versions	English
Contact	E. R. Oetting Tri-Ethnic Center for Prevention Research Department of Psychology Colorado State University Fort Collins, CO 80523–1879

6.13.2 Name of the Measure	Vancouver Index of Acculturation VIA
Primary Reference	Ryder, A. G., Alden, L., & Paulhus, D. L. (2000). Is acculturation unidimensional or bidimensional? A head-to-head comparison in the prediction of personality, self-identity, and adjustment. *Journal of Personality and Social Psychology, 79*(1), 49–65.
Purpose	The VIA is a bidirectional and unidimensional measure of multigroup acculturation that purports to assess the heritage and mainstream dimensions of acculturation.
Description	The VIA contains 20 items. Each item is rated on a 9-point Likert-type scale with the following five anchors: 1 = Strongly Disagree, 3 = Disagree, 5 = Neutral/Depends, 7 = Agree, 9 = Strongly Agree. The VIA is composed of two orthogonal subscales: the Heritage dimension and the Mainstream dimension. The VIA items were developed through literature review, recommendations from an expert in the acculturation field, and item analyses with several different multicultural samples. Principal components analyses (with a promax rotation) yielded two orthogonal simple structures across four ethnic subsamples.
Samples	The final validating sample consisted of 414 Chinese, non-Chinese East Asian, and non-English-speaking adults (294 women, 120 men). Ages ranged from 17 to 37 years (*M* = 20.0, *SD* = 1.80). Generational status for the total sample was 183 first generation and 231 second generation.

Scoring	There are 10 items in each of the two VIA subscales.
	
	    Heritage Dimension: 10 items
	
	    Mainstream Dimension: 10 items
	
	    Total VIA: 20 items
	
	Scoring the VIA subscales consists of adding the participant's ratings on each item in the subscale to obtain subscale scores and then dividing the subscale total by 10 to obtain a subscale mean. The Heritage Dimension subscale mean is the mean of the odd-numbered items, and the Mainstream Dimension subscale mean is the mean of the even-numbered items. No reverse coding or transformations are required. Authors recommend that depending upon the mainstream context, researchers change "North American" to other descriptors such as "American" or "British," etc.

Reliability	Cronbach's alpha for the scores were as follows:
	
	    Heritage Dimension: Alpha = .91
	
	    Mainstream Dimension: Alpha = .87

(Continued)

(Continued)

Validity	Concurrent validity was demonstrated by statistically significant correlations between the VIA subscales and key demographic indicators (e.g., percentage of time lived in West, generational status, English first language, etc.).
Related References	Huynh, Q-L., Howell, R. T., & Benet-Martinez, V. (2009). Reliability of bidimensional acculturation scores. *Journal of Cross-Cultural Psychology, 40* (2), 256–274. Woo, J. S. T., & Brotto, L. A. (2008). Age of first sexual intercourse and acculturation: Effects on adult sexual responding. *The Journal of Sexual Medicine, 5*(3), 571–582.
Language Versions	English
Contact	Andrew G. Ryder Department of Psychology Concordia University 7141 rue Sherbrooke O. Montreal, Quebec H4B 1R6 Canada (514) 848–2424, 5379 (W) (514) 848–4523 (Fax) Email: andrew.ryder@concordia.ca

6.13.3 Name of the Measure	American–International Relations Scale AIRS
Primary Reference	Sodowsky, G. R., & Plake, B. S. (1991). Psychometric properties of the American-International Relations Scale. *Educational and Psychological Measurement, 51,* 207–216.
Purpose	The AIRS is a unidirectional and multidimensional instrument that purports to measure the acculturation of international students and academicians to White American culture.
Description	The AIRS contains 34 items. Each item (either multiple-choice or Likert-type) is rated on a 6-point scale with the following response anchors: 1 = Strong Affiliation with White U.S. Society to 6 = Strong Affiliation with One's Nationality Group.
	The AIRS is composed of three orthogonal subscales: (1) Perceived Prejudice, (2) Acculturation, (3) Language Usage.
	The initial 92-item AIRS was developed through a literature review based on international students and U.S. immigrants, a review of acculturation instruments, and a final review of items from a panel of multicultural/international experts. This process reduced the item pool to 40 items. A subsequent principal factor analysis (with varimax rotation) yielded a three-factor solution that accounted for 34.4% of the total variance.
Samples	The normative sample was based on a convenience mail sample of 481 international students, scholars, academicians, and permanent U.S. residents. Sample details were not provided other than, "There were approximately equal numbers of cases from Asia, Africa, Latin America, and the two genders. Europeans and Australians were less in number than the other culture groups" (p. 210).
Scoring	The number of items in each of the three subscales is as follows:
	Perceived Prejudice: 20 items
	Acculturation: 11 items
	Language Usage: 3 items
	Total AIRS: 34 items
	Scoring the AIRS consists of adding the participant's ratings on each item in the subscale to obtain subscale scores or sums. Reverse coding on some items is required.
Reliability	Cronbach's alpha for the scores were as follows:
	Perceived Prejudice: Alpha = .88
	Acculturation: Alpha = .79
	Language Usage: Alpha = .82

(Continued)

(Continued)

Validity	No validity data were provided with the normative sample publication. However, Sodowsky and Plake (1992), analyzing the same data set, provided evidence of concurrent and discriminant validity by examining various sociocultural independent variables with the three AIRS subscales as dependent variables in a series of multivariate analyses of variance. Results indicated higher levels of Perceived Prejudice for African, Asian, and South American international students as compared to European students. Likewise, higher levels of Acculturation were evidenced by the Africans, Asians, and South American students (indicating less acculturation) than the European students.
Related References	Sodowsky, G. R., & Plake, B. S. (1992). A study of acculturation differences among international people and suggestions for sensitivity to within-group differences. *Journal of Counseling & Development, 71,* 53–59.
Language Versions	English
Contact	Gargi Roysircar-Sodowsky Department of Clinical Psychology Antioch University New England 40 Avon Street Keene, NH 03431–3516 (603) 283–2186 (W) Email: groysircar@antioch.edu

6.13.4 **Name of the Measure**	Majority–Minority Relations Survey MMRS
Primary Reference	Sodowsky, G. R., Lai, E. W. M., & Plake, B. S. (1991). Moderating effects of sociocultural variables on acculturation attitudes of Hispanics and Asian Americans. *Journal of Counseling and Development, 70*(1), 194–204.
Purpose	The MMRS is a unidirectional and multidimensional acculturation scale for Asian Americans and Hispanics. The MMRS was derived from its predecessor, the American-International Relations Survey (AIRS; Sodowsky & Plake, 1991).
Description	The MMRS contains 43 items. The Likert-type attitudinal items and multiple-choice items are all rated on the following scale: 1 = Strong Affiliation with the Majority Group to 6 = Strong Affiliation with One's Minority Group. The MMRS is composed of three subscales: (1) Perceived Prejudice, (2) Acculturation, (3) Language Usage. The MMRS is a revised and longer version of the 34-item AIRS (Sodowsky & Plake, 1991). The nine new items that were added to the MMRS attempted to strengthen the measurement of attitudes dealing with ethnic food preferences, cultural pride and values, and the use of languages in dreaming, reading, and writing. Confirmatory factor analyses using the new MMRS confirmed the original factor structure found with the AIRS instrument.
Samples	A convenience sample of 282 (131 women and 151 men) Hispanic and Asian American students, faculty, and staff from a Midwestern university completed a mail survey. Median age of the sample was 24 years. Self-reported ethnicity for the Hispanic ($n = 132$) and Asian American ($n = 149$) respondents was Mexican Americans ($n = 87$), South and Central Americans ($n = 21$), Puerto Ricans ($n = 10$), Cubans ($n = 4$), other Latino/as ($n = 10$), Asian Indians ($n = 26$), Chinese Americans ($n = 24$), Japanese Americans ($n = 24$), Vietnamese ($n = 24$), Koreans ($n = 22$), Filipino/as ($n = 12$), Pacific Islanders ($n = 3$), and Middle Easterners ($n = 1$). Sample generational status was as follows: first generation ($n = 133$), second generation ($n = 65$), third generation ($n = 50$), and fourth generation ($n = 34$).

Scoring	The number of items in each of the three subscales is as follows:
	
	    Perceived Prejudice: 21 items
	
	    Acculturation: 16 items
	
	    Language Usage: 6 items
	
	    Total MMRS: 43 items
	
	Scoring the MMRS consists of adding the participant's ratings on each item in the subscale to obtain a subscale score and then dividing that score by the total items within the subscale to obtain a subscale mean. Some of the items on this scale require reverse coding.

(Continued)

(Continued)

Reliability	Cronbach's alpha for the scores were as follows: Perceived Prejudice: Alpha = .92 Acculturation: Alpha = .89 Language Usage: Alpha = .94
Validity	Concurrent validity was demonstrated by the finding that first-generation respondents perceived significantly more prejudice, were less acculturated, and used significantly less English than did second- or later-generation respondents. Correlation coefficients between the three MMRS subscales and the various demographic indicators were not reported.
Related References	Sodowsky, G. R., & Plake, B. S. (1991). Psychometric properties of the American-International Relations Scale. *Educational and Psychological Measurement, 51,* 207–216.
Language Versions	English
Contact	Gargi Roysircar-Sodowsky Department of Clinical Psychology Antioch University New England 40 Avon Street Keene, NH 03431–3516 (603) 283–2186 (W) Email: groysircar@antioch.edu

6.13.5 Name of the Measure	Acculturation, Habits, and Interests Multicultural Scale for Adolescents AHIMSA
Primary Reference	Unger, J. B., Gallaher, P., Shakib, S., Ritt-Olson, A., Palmer, P. H., & Anderson Johnson, C. (2002). The AHIMSA acculturation scale: A new measure of acculturation for adolescents in a multicultural Society. *Journal of Early Adolescence, 22*(3), 225–251.
Purpose	The AHIMSA is a brief, multigroup, unidirectional, unidimensional acculturation scale designed for diverse adolescent samples.
Description	The AHIMSA contains 8 items. Each item is evaluated on a 4-option forced-choice format: a = The United States, b = The Country My Family Is From, c = Both, d = Neither. The AHIMSA has a unidimensional structure that can be partitioned into four acculturation orientations or scores: (1) Assimilation, (2) Separation, (3) Integration, (4) Marginalization. Items for the AHIMSA scale were developed through a literature review, a multicultural research team evaluation process, and small adolescent focus groups, which reduced the initial item pool of 30 items to the final 8-item scale. An unspecified exploratory factor analysis (with a promax rotation) on the scores of the AHIMSA (which were recoded to 1 = United States and 0 = all other responses) yielded a single-factor solution that accounted for 41% of the total variance.
Samples	The normative sample consisted of 317 Los Angeles-area sixth-grade middle school students (161 females, 156 males). Ages ranged from 10 to 13 years (*M* = 11.5, *SD* = .54). Participant self-reported race/ethnicity was 53.0% Latino/a American, 19.2% Asian/Pacific Islander American, 14.2% Filipino/a American, 8.5% White American, 2.2% African American, 1.3% Other, and 1.6% no response.
Scoring	Each AHIMSA item is responded to with the letters *a*, *b*, *c*, or *d* (see above). Four AHIMSA acculturation orientation scores can be computed by participant responses to the 8-item scale. Assimilation = the total number of code "a" or "The United States" responses. Separation = the total number of code "b" or "The country my family is from" responses. Integration = the total number of code "c" or "Both" responses. Marginalization = the total number of code "d" or "Neither" responses. The acculturation orientation score can range from 0 to 8 for each of the four orientations. The scale authors note that all four orientations cannot be entered as independent variables in a single multiple regression model due to the linear dependence of these independent variables. No reverse coding or transformations are required.

(Continued)

(Continued)

Reliability	Cronbach's alpha for the 8-item AHIMSA was reported to be .79.
Validity	Convergent and discriminant validity was achieved by demonstrating a positive correlation between the scores of the AHIMSA Assimilation subscale and the scores of the ARSMA-II "U.S. Orientation" or AOS subscale (Cuéllar, Arnold, & Maldonado, 1995). Similarly, the scores of the AHIMSA Separation subscale and the ARSMA-II "Other Country" or MOS subscale achieved a moderate correlation.
Related References	Fosados, R. et al. (2007). The influence of acculturation on drug and alcohol use in a sample of adolescents. *Addictive Behaviors, 32,* 2990–3004.
Language Versions	English
Contact	Jennifer B. Unger School of Community and Global Health Claremont Graduate University Harper Hall 150 E. 10th Street Claremont, CA 91711 (909) 621–8000 (W) Email: Jennifer.unger@cgu.edu

6.13.6 Name of the Measure	Stephenson Multigroup Acculturation Scale SMAS
Primary Reference	Stephenson, M. (2000). Development and validation of the Stephenson Multigroup Acculturation Scale (SMAS). *Psychological Assessment, 12*(1), 77–88.
Purpose	The SMAS is a bidirectional, unidimensional, multigroup acculturation instrument that purports to measure the degree of immersion (i.e., behaviors related to language, interaction, food, and media) in new and original societies.
Description	The SMAS contains 32 items. Each item is rated on the following 4-point Likert-type scale: 1 = False, 2 = Partly False, 3 = Partly True, 4 = True. The SMAS is composed of two subscales: (1) Dominant Society Immersion (DSI) and (2) Ethnic Society Immersion (ESI). The SMAS initial item pool was developed through a comprehensive literature review and item generation from a diverse team of community professionals and consultants that resulted in a pool of 95 items. Subsequent principal components analysis (with varimax rotation) resulted in two orthogonal factors with a total of 32 items.
Samples	The normative sample consisted of 436 adults (304 women and 132 men) contacted by means of snowball sampling in New York City, Boston, and Springfield, MA. Participant ages ranged from 18 to 73 years ($M = 30.0$, $SD = 13.3$). Participant education ranged from seventh grade to graduate education ($M = 13.0$, $SD = 1.5$). Participant ethnicity was as follows: African American 35 (8%), Asian American 33 (8%), White American 125 (29%), Latino/a American 85 (19%), and African descent 158 (36%). Generational status was first generation 206 (47.3%), second generation 83 (19.0%), third generation 58 (13.3%), and fourth generation or more 89 (20.4%).

Scoring	The number of items in the two SMAS subscales is as follows:
	
	    Ethnic Society Immersion (ESI): 17 items
	
	    Dominant Society Immersion (DSI): 15 items
	
	    Total SMAS: 32 items
	
	Scoring the SMAS consists of adding the participant's ratings on each item in the subscale to obtain subscale scores and dividing the subscale score by the number of subscale items to obtain a subscale mean. No reverse coding or transformations are required.

Reliability	Cronbach's alpha for the scores were as follows:
	
	    ESI: Alpha = .97
	
	    DSI: Alpha = .90

(Continued)

(Continued)

Validity	Analysis of variance results indicated that mean DSI and ESI differed statistically significantly across generation levels. Correlational results (with a separate sample $N = 208$) between the SMAS subscales and the subscales of the ARSMA-II (Cuéllar, Arnold, & Maldonado, 1995) and the subscales of the BAS (Marin & Gamba, 1996) showed that the scores of the ESI were positively related to the scores of the ARSMA-II MOS and the Hispanic Domain of the BAS. Conversely, the scores of the DSI were found to be positively related to the scores of the ARSMA-II AOS and the non-Hispanic Domain of the BAS.
Related References	Gamst, G., Rogers, R., Der-Karabetian, A., & Dana, R. H. (2006). Addressing mental health disparities: A preliminary test of the Multicultural Assessment Intervention Process (MAIP) model. In E. V. Metrosa (Ed.), *Racial and ethnic disparities in health and healthcare*. Hauppauge, NY: Nova Science. Huynh, Q.-L., & Howell, R. T. (2009). Reliability of bidimensional acculturation scores. *Journal of Cross-Cultural Psychology, 40*(2), 256–274.
Language Versions	English
Contact	Margaret Stephenson 42 Wendell Ave., Suite 4 Pittsfield, MA 01201 (413) 442–4878 (W) Email: stephensonloiodice@yahoo.com

6.13.7 Name of the Measure	Abbreviated Multidimensional Acculturation Scale AMAS-ZABB
Primary Reference	Zea, M. C., Asner-Self, K. K., Birman, D., & Buki, L. P. (2003). The abbreviated multidimensional acculturation scale: Empirical validation with two Latino/Latina samples. *Cultural Diversity and Ethnic Minority Psychology, 9*(2), 107–126.
Purpose	The AMAS-ZABB is a bidirectional, multidimensional, multigroup acculturation measure.
Description	The AMAS-ZABB contains 42 items. Each item is rated on a 4-point Likert-type scale with the following response options: 1 = Strongly Disagree, 4 = Strongly Agree for the cultural identity subscales and 1 = Not at All, 4 = Extremely Well/Like a Native for the language and cultural competence subscales. The AMAS-ZABB is composed of a total score, two dimension scores (U.S.-American Dimension and Culture-of-Origin Dimension), and three subscale scores for each dimension. The subscales are (1) U.S.-American Cultural Identity, (2) U.S.-American English Language, (3) U.S.-American Cultural Competence, (4) Culture-of-Origin Cultural Identity, (5) Culture-of-Origin Language, (6) Culture-of-Origin Cultural Competence. An initial 80-item pool was apparently developed through literature review, previous unpublished empirical research, and a number of focus groups with immigrant participants. This process reduced the item pool to the final 42-item version. A subsequent maximum likelihood factor analysis (with varimax rotation) on two combined community and college samples ($N = 246$) yielded six orthogonal factors.
Samples	The validating sample was a combined sample of 246 community and college Latino/a adults (approximately 56% were women). Participant average age was 31.2 years ($SD = 10.8$). Sample place of birth was Central America (45.5%), United States (28.4%), South America (18.3%), Caribbean (4.1%), Mexico (2.8%), and Spain (0.9).
Scoring	The number of items in each of the six subscales is as follows: U.S.-American Cultural Identity: 6 items U.S.-American English Language: 9 items U.S.-American Cultural Competence: 6 items Culture-of-Origin Cultural Identity: 6 items Culture-of-Origin Language: 9 items Culture-of-Origin Cultural Competence: 6 items Total AMAS-ZABB: 42 items Scoring the AMAS-ZABB consists of adding the participant's ratings on each item in the subscale to obtain a subscale score and then dividing the subscale score by the number of subscale items to obtain a subscale mean. A "U.S.-American Dimension" and a "Culture-of-Origin Dimension" can also be computed by averaging the three subscales of each respective dimension. No reverse coding or transformations are required.

(Continued)

(Continued)

Reliability	Cronbach's alpha for the scores were as follows: Original Culture: Alpha = .88 Dominant U.S. Culture: Alpha = .80 Total CRM-BS: Alpha = .91 5-day test-retest reliability coefficients were as follows: Original Culture: $r = .78$ Dominant U.S. Culture: $r = .82$
Validity	Discriminant validity was achieved by demonstrating higher CRM-BS-Original Culture scores for the multiethnic sample ($M = 19.9$, $SD = 5.7$) than the White American sample ($M = 4.8$, $SD = 2.9$). Conversely, Dominant U.S. Culture scores were statistically significantly higher for the White American sample ($M = 22.0$ $SD = 5.8$) as compared to the multiethnic sample ($M = 15.1$, $SD = 6.1$). Construct validity was achieved by the finding of older generational subsamples had higher mean scores on the Original Culture subscale.
Related References	
Language Versions	English, Spanish, Chinese, Korean
Contact	Juan E. Messich Division of Psychiatric Epidemiology and the International Center for Mental Health Mount Sinai School of Medicine New York, NY 10029 Email: juanmezzich@aol.com

6.13.9 Name of the Measure	Acculturative Stress Scale for International Students ASSIS
Primary Reference	Sandhu, D. S., & Asrabadi, B. R. (1994). Development of an Acculturative Stress Scale for International Students: Preliminary findings. *Psychological Reports, 75,* 435–448.
Purpose	The ASSIS is a multidimensional instrument that purports to measure the acculturative stress of international students.
Description	The ASSIS contains 36 items. Each item is rated on a 5-point Likert-type scale with the following three response anchors: 1 = Strongly Disagree, 3 = Not Sure, 5 = Strongly Agree.
	The ASSIS is composed of a total score and six subscales: (1) Perceived Discrimination, (2) Homesickness, (3) Perceived Hate, (4) Fear, (5) Stress Due to Change/Culture Shock, (6) Guilt.
	The initial pool of 125 items was developed through focus group interviews with international students and a comprehensive literature review. From this process, 125 items that corresponded to 12 acculturative stress themes (e.g., discrimination, isolation, identity, inferiority, homesickness, fear, anger, mistrust, communication, shock, hatred, and guilt) were pilot tested and reduced to a 78-item scale. Subsequent principal components analysis (with varimax rotation) produced a 36-item, six-factor simple structure that accounted for 70.6% of the total variance. Ten of the 36 items produced low structure coefficients that correlated with multiple factors and contributed only to the unexplained variance.
Samples	The normative sample consisted of 128 (42 women, 86 men) international students from across the United States. Sample mean age was 23.2 years. Participant country/geographic location of origin was as follows: Asia (China, India, Japan, Korea, Taiwan) (43.8%), Latin America (26.6%), Middle East (17.2%), Europe and Africa (12.4%).
Scoring	The number of items in each of the six subscales is as follows:
	Perceived Discrimination: 8 items
	Homesickness: 4 items
	Perceived Hate: 5 items
	Fear: 4 items
	Stress Due to Change/Culture Shock: 3 items
	Guilt: 2 items
	10 items were not included in the above six subscales.
	Total ASSIS: 36 items

(Continued)

(Continued)

Reliability	Cronbach's alpha (reported in Sandhu & Asrabadi, 1998) was .95 for the total score. Guttman split-half reliability was .97.
Validity	
Related References	Sandhu, D. S., & Asrabadi, B. R. (1998). An Acculturative Stress Scale for International Students: A practical approach to stress management. In C. P. Zalaquette & R. J. Wood (Eds.), *Evaluating stress: A book of resources* (Vol. 2, pp. 1–33). Lanham, MD & London: The Scarecrow Press.
	Yeh, C. J., & Inose, M. (2003). International students' reported English fluency, social support satisfaction, and social connectedness as predictors of acculturation stress. *Counselling Psychology Quarterly, 16*(1), 15–28.
Language Versions	English
Contact	Daya Singh Sandhu Educational & Counseling Psychology University of Louisville Belknap Campus Louisville, KY 40292 (502) 852- 6646 (W) Email: daya.sandhu@loisville.edu

7

Racism- and Prejudice-Related Measures

7.1 AN OVERVIEW OF RACISM AND PREJUDICE

Although related, racism and prejudice reflect two different meanings. According to Allport (1954), *prejudice* is composed of generalized beliefs and attitudes that are inherently negative. While prejudice is formed through learned stereotypes, *racism* is a manifestation of prejudice. Specifically, racism is the differential treatment enacted by an individual, group, or organization on individuals based on assumptions of a group's phenotypic, linguistic, or cultural differences. Racism can occur at *institutional* (e.g., discriminatory laws and practices), *societal* (e.g., race hate groups), and *individual* (e.g., racial stereotyping by an individual) levels and be *overt* (i.e., old-fashioned) or *covert* (i.e., modern). Whereas overt racism reflects open hostility and acts of aggression toward a member or individuals from a minority group, covert racism is composed of the subtle behaviors that are influenced by prejudice. Covert racism also can be further understood as *intentional* and *unintentional* (Ridley, 1995). Intentional covert racism reflects subtle discriminatory behaviors that allow the perpetrator to act willfully and "hide" the intent of her or his behavior. Unintentional covert racism, also known as *aversive racism,* is unintentional acts that are discriminatory in nature.

Racism takes place in the context of power and thus reflects discriminatory behaviors that are supported by institutional or cultural practices. *Horizontal racism* denotes negative attitudes and prejudice minority group members might have toward one another (Wijeyesinghe, Griffin, & Love, 1997). The term acknowledges how individuals from minority groups may act on their prejudice toward other groups but do so without the power to institutionally influence the lives of others. *Internalized racism,* on the other hand, denotes how an individual from a marginalized group may incorporate into his or her own self-schema the dehumanizing messages of his or her own in-group made by others. This individual may, as an outcome of exposure to negative stereotypes, denigrate his or her own in-group and act to distance himself or herself from members of that group. In essence, regardless of the form, racism is the behavioral manifestation of held beliefs and attitudes of a group.

7.2 BRIEF HISTORY OF RACISM RESEARCH IN AMERICAN PSYCHOLOGY

According to Duckitt (1992), there are seven distinct stages in the psychological study of race evident from the early 1900s to the 1990s. Duckitt explained that the field emerged from studies in which the main focus of research was to examine racial differences. The findings

251

of these studies, interpreted within a widely held framework of White racial superiority, perpetuated held assumptions of the inferiority of other racial groups. The interpretation of empirical findings both reflected prejudice that was prevalent at that time and helped to support negative stereotypes of the intellectual ability and hypersexuality of African Americans. The focus of study during the 20th century was also analyzed by Dovidio (2001). In his analysis, Dovidio collapsed several of the periods identified by Duckitt into three "waves" of research.

According to Dovidio (2001), there are three overlapping waves of prejudice research. During the first wave, psychologists viewed prejudice as a form of individual psychopathology or as a result of a pathological personality or defense mechanism (e.g., displacement). For instance, theories implicating authoritarian personalities as more likely to hold prejudicial attitudes and beliefs emerged then (e.g., Adorno, Frenkel-Brunswick, Levinson, & Sanford, 1950). This focus on individual-level psychopathology and shift away from *race theories,* in which White superiority was promoted, likely stemmed from historical events. Namely, Americans during this period needed to resolve their own racial prejudices with the anti-Semitism that fueled attempts of genocide in Europe during World War II (Duckitt, 1992). The second period emerged toward the end of the 1950s and considered prejudice as a normative process. The shift in views also reflected a change from an individual-level focus to a macro-level influence on prejudicial attitudes and beliefs. Toward the end of this period, researchers noted the importance of measuring aversive racism (Gaertner & Dovidio, 1986), modern racism (McConahay, 1986), and symbolic racism (e.g., Kinder & Sears, 1981; McConahay & Hough, 1976). They argued that, as a result of the civil rights movement of the 1960s, White Americans became more hesitant to openly express their racial hostility. Scholars argued that many White Americans hold egalitarian attitudes but harbored racist ideology that manifested behaviorally in subtle forms. During the last period, which emerged in the 1990s, prejudice was studied as a multidimensional process in which both the holder and target of prejudice are examined. Specifically, whereas the focus of attention in the first two waves was to understand the personality of prejudiced individuals and the contents of their attitudes, research in the last wave examines the cognitive process involved in stereotype formation and management *and* the psychological responses of racism by targets. Researchers not only continued to study the old and modern forms of racial prejudice and the strategies used to control them (e.g., Dunton & Fazio, 1997; Plant & Devine, 1998), they also studied the psychological effects of perceived racism on the psychological and physiological functioning of African Americans (Bynum, Burton, & Best, 2007; Fang & Myers, 2001; Landrine & Klonoff, 1996; McNeilly et al., 1996; Utsey & Hook, 2007; Utsey, Ponterotto, Reynolds, & Cancelli, 2000).

More recently, researchers have begun to seek to understand the relationships among racism, coping strategies, and psychological functioning of other targeted groups (see Brondolo, ver Halen, Pencille, Beatty, & Contrada, 2009). For instance, there has been an incredible growth in the body of literature addressing the psychological sequelae of racism on Asian Americans (e.g., Alvarez, Juang, & Liang, 2006; Gee, Delva, & Takeuchi, 2006; Lee, 2003, 2005; Liang, Alvarez, Juang, & Liang, 2007; Liang & Fassinger, 2008; Noh & Kaspar, 2004; Yoo, Burrola, & Steger, 2010; Yoo & Lee, 2005). Researchers also have studied the racial experiences of Latino/a Americans (e.g., Alderete, Vega, Kolody, & Aguilar-Gaxiola, 1999; Cassidy, O'Conner, Howe, & Warden, 2004; Finch, Kolody, & Vega, 2000; Moradi & Risco, 2006) and have begun to explore discrimination encountered by Arab Americans (e.g., Moradi & Hasan, 2004). Shifting their attention from the formation of prejudicial attitudes among White Americans, researchers also have begun to understand the costs of racism to Whites (e.g., Spanierman & Heppner, 2004). Aiding the proliferation of these studies has been the increased attention to the development of race-related measures (see Bastos, Celeste, Faerstein, & Barros, 2010; Kressin, Raymond, & Manze, 2008).

7.3 THEORETICAL FOUNDATIONS

Racism and prejudice research has been guided by theory. Studies with a focus on prejudice initially relied on psychodynamic perspectives (e.g., Adorno et al., 1950), but these studies with their focus on individual-level differences were acontextual and could not address institutional racism (Duckitt, 1992). Gordon Allport's seminal book, *The Nature of Prejudice* (Allport, 1954), also was highly influential in the study of prejudice as it served as the foundation for subsequent conceptualizations (i.e., social-cognitive and social identity; Dovidio, 2001). The social-cognitive perspective (Hamilton, 1981) has led to studies of people's cognitions as they relate to people, groups, or social situations. Social identity theory (Tajfel & Turner, 1986) also has influenced studies of paths by which stigma influences a target's self-concept (e.g., Major & O'Brien, 2005; Steele & Aronson, 1995). Other studies of the effects of perceived racial discrimination on physical and psychological health (see Williams, Neighbors, & Jackson, 2003) have been influenced by transactional stress frameworks (Harrell, 2000; Lazarus & Folkman, 1984) and biopsychosocial models (see Brondolo, Gallo, & Myers, 2009; Myers, 2009).

In this review we identified four main categories of measures that cut across the last two waves identified by Dovidio (2001). The 37 measures summarized in this chapter fall into one of the following four categories: (1) Racial Attitudes and Prejudice; (2) Perceived Racial Discrimination; (3) Psychological Responses to Racism; and (4) Adolescent Experiences.

7.4 RACIAL ATTITUDES AND PREJUDICE

Racial attitudes and prejudice have been a major area of study in the psychology of race. Perhaps, as evidence of the importance and relevance of this field of study, Nelson (2009) recently published the *Handbook of Prejudice, Stereotyping, and Discrimination,* in which past research and theory are presented and synthesized. In this chapter, we identified 13 self-report measures of racial attitudes and prejudice to summarize. Within this category there were five subcategories. The Miville-Guzman

Universality-Diversity Scale (M-GUDS; Miville et al., 1999) and the Color-Blind Racial Attitudes Scale (CoBRAS; Neville, Lilly, Duran, Lee, & Browne, 2000) comprised the first subcategory. These two instruments were designed to measure general attitudes regarding racial issues. The second subcategory consisted of four measures focused on attitudes held of specific groups. For instance, the Attitude Toward Black Males Scale (ATBM; Bryson, 1998), the Symbolic Racism 2000 Scale (SR2K; Henry & Sears, 2002), and Modern and Old Fashioned Racism Scale (MOFRS; McConahay, 1986) measure attitudes held of African Americans. The Scale of Anti-Asian Stereotypes (SAAS; Lin, Kwan, Cheung, & Fiske, 2005) was one instrument within this subcategory designed to measure the attitudes held of a group other than African Americans. The third subcategory was composed of three instruments that were designed to measure multiple targets of prejudicial attitudes and beliefs (e.g., women, racial minorities, etc.). They were the Quick Discrimination Index (QDI; Ponterotto, Burkard, Rieger, Grieger, et al., 1995), the ISM scale (ISMS; Aosved, Long, & Voller, 2009), and the Modified Godfrey-Richman ISM Scale (M-GRISMS; Godfrey, Richman, & Withers, 2000). The fourth category is composed of the Internal Motivation to Respond Without Prejudice Scale and External Motivation to Respond Without Prejudice Scale (IMRPS/EMPRS; Plant & Devine, 1998) and Motivation to Control Prejudiced Reactions Scale (MCPRS; Dunton & Fazio, 1997), which reflects the recognition of the fact that prejudice is composed of automatic and controlled processes. The final two instruments reflect the need to also study privilege. The White Privilege Attitudes Scale (WPAS; Pinteritis, Poteat, & Spanierman, 2009) and the Privilege and Oppression Inventory (POI; Hays, Chang, & Decker, 2007) were developed to measure privilege attitudes.

7.5 PERCEIVED RACIAL DISCRIMINATION

Researchers have long proposed that there are psychological costs of racism to its targets (e.g., Allport, 1954). While some authors argued that individuals from stigmatized groups experienced lower levels of self-esteem, a review of the literature actually indicated mixed support for this contention (see Crocker & Major, 1989). One potential explanation is that self-esteem may actually have served as a protective factor against discrimination. Another possible explanation is that membership in a marginalized group does not in and of itself indicate racial experiences as a member of that group. In order to address this gap, researchers studied the relationship between perceived discrimination on a number of psychological outcomes (see Williams & Mohammed, 2009). There has been great variability in the measurement of perceived racial discrimination in these studies (Bastos et al., 2010; Kressin et al., 2008; Williams et al., 2003). Several self-report measures ($n = 9$), however, have been identified and are summarized in three subcategories. Three measures of perceived racial discrimination designed specifically for use to understand racism experiences of African Americans comprise the first subcategory. They are the Perceptions of Racism Scale (PRS; Green, 1995), Schedule of Racist Events (SRE; Landrine & Klonoff, 1996), and Perceived Racism Scale (PRS; McNeilly et al., 1996). As a way to extend the study of racism and its impact on other minority groups, the Perceived Ethnic Discrimination Questionnaire (PEDQ; Contrada et al., 2001), Experiences of Discrimination (EOD; Krieger, Smith, Naishadham, Hartman, & Barbeau, 2005), General Ethnic Discrimination Scale (GEDS; Landrine, Klonoff, Corral, Fernandez, & Roesch, 2006), and the Scale of Ethnic Experience (SEE; Malcarne, Chavira, Fernandez, & Liu, 2006) have been developed. Interestingly, the Intragroup Marginalization Inventory (IMI; Castillo, Conoley, Brossart, & Quiros, 2007) and Own-group Conformity Pressure Scale (OGCP; Contrada et al., 2001) have been developed to measure perceptions of within-group experiences of discrimination and acculturative stress.

7.6 PSYCHOLOGICAL RESPONSES TO RACISM

A natural extension to the study of perceptions of racism is to examine the psychological outcomes of those experiences. As noted earlier, researchers have found mixed but largely consistent support for the negative effects of perceived racism on health (see Carter, 2007; Williams et al., 2003). In this category of race-related instruments, we identified two subcategories. In the first subcategory, eight instruments measuring intrapersonal stress or coping are summarized. They are the Hispanic Stress Inventory (HIS; Cervantes, Padilla, & de Snyder, 1991), Stereotype Confirmation Concern Scale (SCCS; Contrada et al., 2001), Colonial Mentality Scale (CMS; David & Okazaki, 2006), Asian American Racism Related Stress Inventory (AARRSI; Liang, Li, & Kim, 2004), Race-Related Stressor Scale (RRSS; Loo et al., 2001), Africultural Coping Systems Inventory (ACSI; Utsey, Adams, & Bolden, 2000), Index of Race-Related Stress (IRRS; Utsey & Ponterotto, 1996), Internalization of the Model Minority Myth Measure (IM-4; Yoo, Burrola, & Steger, 2010). In the second subcategory, two instruments measuring interpersonal as well as intrapersonal outcomes of racism were summarized. These were the Psychosocial Costs of Racism for Whites (PCRW; Spanierman & Heppner, 2004) and the Cultural Mistrust Inventory (CMI; Terrell & Terrell, 1981).

7.7 ADOLESCENT EXPERIENCES

The final category of race-related instruments addresses race-related experiences of adolescents, including those measures that address perceived discrimination as well as racial socialization, the process by which a family and/or community imbues lessons about race relations and cultural pride to younger generations. Stevenson (1994) argued that racial socialization protects individuals from the negative effects of racial discrimination. There were five instruments included in our summary. They were the Everyday Discrimination Scale—Modified (EDS-M; Clark, Coleman, & Novak, 2004), Racial Bias Preparation Scale (Fisher, Wallace, & Fenton, 2000), Adolescent Discrimination Distress Index (Fisher et al., 2000), the Scale of Racial Socialization—Adolescents (SORS-A; Stevenson, 1994), and the Teenager Experience of Racial Socialization Scale (TERS; Stevenson, Cameron, Herrero-Taylor, & Davis, 2002).

7.8 FUTURE RESEARCH

The inception of the field of racism and prejudice research nearly 100 years ago has, over the past 25 years, grown considerably (Major & O'Brien, 2005). Aiding this development has been the building of theory and measurement. Physiological, neurological, and behavioral measures all serve to provide researchers with the tools necessary to understand different facets of prejudice and racism. The purpose of this chapter was to provide a summary of self-report measures that may be employed in research and which, because of their ease of use, have potential clinical utility. In the course of summarizing the process by which measures were developed, we noted several potential areas for instrument development.

1. All measures of perceived racism summarized here address the experiences of monoracial individuals. However, the growth of the multiracial population is significant enough to warrant the development of instruments to measure multiracial individuals' experiences of discrimination. These instruments should be grounded in existing theoretical or empirical literature.

2. The body of measures of perceived racism treats race as the primary (and only) dimension by which individuals experience discrimination. However, individuals are members of multiple targeted social identity groups and may experience discrimination for each. Members of multiple targeted groups also may experience discrimination based on their fused identities (Moradi & Subich, 2003). Heterosexual men of color, who are privileged with respect to their gender and sexual orientation, may experience discrimination based on their gender *and* race, e.g., "angry Black male," "effeminate Asian American male." Scholars have only recently begun to explore the intersectionality or fused nature of discrimination. Instruments developed to detect these experiences are needed to more fully understand how discrimination may influence psychological and physiological health.

3. More attention to within-group discrimination is needed. For instance, measures of *colorism,* the differential treatment among African Americans based on skin color, may be one direction for researchers to take.

4. While studies indicating a link between perceived discrimination and health indicate that there is great potential clinical utility of these measures, little work has been done to translate these instruments for use in clinical settings. For instance, some measures may be too long to administer or may require more advanced reading levels than may be found in community mental health settings. Thus, further work to reduce the cost (i.e., time) of administering instruments and greater attention to readability of racism measures is needed.

5. Since many of these measures are relatively new, more scrutiny of their psychometric properties is needed (see Chapter 2).

6. The study of attitudes and prejudice has a longer history than that of perceived discrimination. The field of study has made incredible advances from learning about the content of attitudes and the personality of prejudiced individuals to understanding the cognitive processes involved in developing beliefs and managing behaviors (Schneider, 2004). However, Stangor (2009) has argued that while much has been learned, psychologists have done little in real-world settings. He suggests greater efforts to link theory and research findings to social policy and educational practice. In line with the recommendations offered by Stangor, we call for the use of theory and measures of prejudice in real-world settings to help reduce intergroup conflict.

7.9 RACIAL ATTITUDES AND PREJUDICE

7.9.1 Name of the Measure	Intolerant Schema Measure ISM
Primary Reference	Aosved, A. C., Long, P. J., & Voller, E. K. (2009). Measuring sexism, racism, sexual prejudice, ageism, classism, and religious intolerance: The Intolerant Schema Measure. *Journal of Applied Social Psychology, 39,* 2321–2354.
Purpose	The ISM is designed to measure intolerance toward others based on gender, race, sexual orientation, age, social class, and religious affiliation.
Description	The ISM is a 54-item self-report inventory. Each item is rated on a 5-point Likert-type scale with the following anchors ranging from 1 = Strongly Disagree to 5 = Strongly Agree.
	The ISM is composed of six subscales: (1) Sexual Prejudice; (2) Classism; (3) Sexism; (4) Racism; (5) Ageism; and (6) Religious Intolerance.
	Finding a lack of a single instrument designed to measure intolerance of multiple dimensions of difference, the authors combined established measures with items they created to form a 146-item version of the Intolerant Schema Measure. The existing measures included the Attitudes Toward Women Scale (AWS; Spence, Helmreich, & Stapp, 1973), Neosexism Scale (NS; Tougas, Brown, Beaton, & Joly, 1995), the religious intolerance items from the Modified Godfrey-Richman ISM scale (M-GRISM; Godfrey, Richman, & Withers, 2000), Modern Homophobia Scale (MHS; Raja & Stokes, 1998), Modern and Old-Fashioned Racism Scale (MOFRS; McConahay, 1986), Economic Beliefs Scale (EBS; Stevenson & Medler, 1995), and the Frabroni Scale of Ageism (FSA; Frabroni, Saltstone, & Hughes, 1990). A principal components analysis with varimax rotation yielded a six-factor solution. Two separate confirmatory factor analyses indicated a similar factor structure. Goodness-of-fit indices were not reported.
Samples	The measure was established using three samples. The first sample, composed of 523 college students (325 females, 198 males) attending a university in the Midwest of the United States, ranged in age from 18–55 (M = 20.5 years, SD = 3.5). This sample was composed of White Americans (n = 432), African Americans (n = 16), Latino/a Americans (n = 9), Native Americans (n = 25), and Asian Americans (n = 28). Thirteen individuals reported "other." With respect to sexual orientation, 98% reported being heterosexual. A majority of the participants were Protestants (n = 358), Catholic (n = 71), Buddhist, Muslim, or Hindu (n = 15), Agnostic or Atheist (n = 17), Wiccan (n = 1), nonaffiliated (n = 43), and other (n = 17).
	A second independent sample was composed of 475 college students (181 females; 294 males), in the Midwest of the United States, who ranged in age from 18–54 (M = 19.8 years, SD = 2.9). The sample was composed of White Americans (n = 403), African Americans (n = 10), Latino/a Americans (n = 19), Asian Americans (n = 25), and "other" (n = 5). Ninety-eight percent reported being heterosexual. A majority of the participants were Protestants (n = 313), Catholic (n = 60), Buddhist, Muslim, or Hindu (n = 6), Agnostic or Atheist (n = 15), Wiccan (n = 1), Jewish (n = 1), nonaffiliated (n = 54), and other (n = 24).

	A third sample (N = 115) of college students (84 female, 30 male, 1 not reported) was recruited from undergraduate psychology and sociology courses at a small west coast university. These participants ranged in age from 18–55 (M = 22.0 year, SD = 6.2). This sample was composed of Latino/a Americans (n = 47), White Americans (n = 38), African Americans (n = 15), Native Americans (n = 2), Asian Americans (n = 3), biracial (n = 6), and "other" (n = 4). Ninety-six percent of the sample reported being heterosexual. A majority of the participants were Protestants (n = 37), Catholic (n = 45), Buddhist, Muslim, or Hindu (n = 4), Agnostic or Atheist (n = 10), Jewish (n = 1), nonaffiliated (n = 13), and other (n = 3).
Scoring	The number of items in each of the subscales of the ISM is as follows:
	Sexual Prejudice: 9 items
	Classism: 9 items
	Sexism: 9 items
	Racism: 9 items
	Ageism: 9 items
	Religious Intolerance: 9 items
	Total ISM: 54 items
	Scoring the ISM consists of summing subscale items and dividing by the number of items in the specific subscale. Higher scores indicate more intolerant belief systems. No transformations are required.
Reliability	The range in Cronbach's alpha for the scores on the total and subscales were as follows:
	Sexual Prejudice: Alpha = .89–.92
	Classism: Alpha = .80–.85
	Sexism: Alpha = .82–.84
	Racism: Alpha = .78–.83
	Ageism: Alpha = .78–.82
	Religious Intolerance: Alpha = .70–.80
	Total ISM: Alpha = .93
	Two week test-retest reliability coefficients were as follows:
	Sexual Prejudice: r = .91
	Classism: r = .84
	Sexism: r = .85
	Racism: r = .86
	Ageism: r = .78
	Religious Intolerance: r = .72
	Total ISM: r = .90

(Continued)

(Continued)

Validity	Criterion-related validity was established by examining the correlations between the ISM subscale scores and the full original score from which items were derived. Each subscale was correlated strongly and positively to the original score. All subscale scores (except for Sexual Prejudice) were inversely correlated with social desirability. Social dominance (Sidanius & Pratto, 1999) also was found to be significantly positively correlated with each subscale score.
	Known-groups validity also was established. Specifically, ethnic minorities reported greater racial tolerance than did White Americans. Men also reported higher levels of gender intolerance than did women. Gay, lesbian, and bisexual men and women reported less sexual prejudice than did heterosexual individuals.
Related References	
Language Versions	English
Contact	Allison Aosved Pacific Islands Health Care System 459 Patterson Road Honolulu, HI 96819

7.9.2 **Name of the Measure**	Attitudes Toward Black Males Scale ATBM
Primary Reference	Bryson, S. (1998). Relationship between race and attitudes toward black men. *Journal of Multicultural Counseling and Development, 26,* 282–293.
Purpose	The ATBM is intended to measure an individual's attitudes toward Black men.
Description	The ATBM is a 47-item self-report inventory. The measure utilizes a 6-point Likert-type scale with the following anchors: 1 = I Agree Very Much to 6 = I Disagree Very Much. The ATBM is composed of eight subscales: (1) Intellectual Ability; (2) Criminal Justice; (3) Expectations of Preferential Treatment; (4) Personality; (5) Sociability; (6) Employment; (7) Self-Confidence; (8) Global Characteristics. Along with other professionals, the author of the instrument examined the Attitudes Toward the Disabled Person Scale (ATDS; Yuker, Block, & Campbell, 1962) for appropriateness for use as a measure of attitudes toward Black males. Nearly all of the items of the ATDS were retained, with the word *Disabled* replaced with *Black males*. Additional items also were included based on a review of the professional literature. This process generated 80 items but was reduced to 68 after a review by a panel of three experts. A principal components analysis with varimax rotation and an examination of a scree plot yielded eight factors. Items were retained if they met the author's .30 criterion. A 55-item measure resulted from this process. Reliability analysis indicated an improved Cronbach reliability coefficient through the deletion of eight items. Thus, the final measure contains 47 items.
Samples	Initial validation of the measure was established using a sample of 694 graduate (19%) and undergraduate college (81%) students (59% women; 41% men) attending a large comprehensive research university in the Midwest. Data from 630 participants from this sample were used to compare differences between White American and African American students. Of these participants, 187 (30%) were African American and 442 (70%) are White American.

Scoring	The number of items in each of the subscales of the ATBM is as follows:
	
	    Intellectual Ability: 2 items
	    Criminal Justice: 3 items
	    Expectations of Preferential Treatment: 6 items
	    Personality: 11 items
	    Sociability: 6 items
	    Employment: 4 items

(Continued)

(Continued)

	Self-Confidence: 5 items
	Global Characteristics: 10 items
	Total ATBM = 47
	Some items, which are worded in the positive direction, required recoding. Scoring the ATBM consists of summing subscale items. Higher scores indicated more agreement with negative stereotypes. No transformations are required.
Reliability	Cronbach's alpha for the scores on the total scale and its subscales were as follows:
	Intellectual Ability: Alpha = .72
	Criminal Justice: Alpha = .62
	Expectations of Preferential Treatment: Alpha = .69
	Personality: Alpha = .81
	Sociability: Alpha = .65
	Employment: Alpha = .29
	Self-Confidence: Alpha = .76
	Global Characteristics: Alpha = .84
	Total ATBM: Alpha = .94
Validity	Convergent validity was determined through significant relationships in the expected direction with measures of Ambivalent Sexism (Glick & Fiske, 1996) and Subtle Prejudice (Pettigrew & Meertens, 1995).
	Concurrent validity was established through the use of t-tests and chi-square analysis. Results indicated significant differences between White and Black participants on 5 of the 8 subscales (i.e., intellectual ability, criminal justice, sociability, self-confidence, and global characteristics) and the total score, such that White participants held more negative attitudes toward Black men than did their Black counterparts.
Related References	
Language Versions	English
Contact	Seymour Bryson Southern Illinois University, Carbondale 110 Anthony Hall Carbondale, IL 62901–4341 (618) 453–2350 Email: Bryson@siu.edu

7.9.3 Name of the Measure	Motivation to Control Prejudiced Reactions Scale MCPRS
Primary Reference	Dunton, B. C., & Fazio, R. H. (1997). An individual difference measure of motivation to control prejudiced reactions. *Personality and Social Psychology Bulletin, 23*, 316–326.
Purpose	The MCPRS is designed to measure factors that contribute to controlling immediate negative racial attitudes toward Blacks.
Description	The MCPRS is a 17-item self-report inventory. Each item is rated on a 6-point Likert-type scale with the following anchors: −3 = Strongly Disagree and +3 = Strongly Agree. The MCPRS is composed of a two subscales: (1) Concern With Acting Prejudiced; (2) Restraint to Avoid Dispute. Based on a review of literature on prejudice, the authors developed 19 statements measuring participants' desire to control appearing prejudiced to others, distaste for negative reactions that they may have in their interactions with Blacks, and avoidance of conflict. Two of the initial 19 items were removed after reliability analysis demonstrated that they did not contribute to the internal consistency of the measure. This analysis resulted in a 17-item measure. A principal components analysis with varimax rotation yielded five factors. However, the authors indicated that these factors were not stable across their three samples. Instability also was evident when the authors attempted to force a four- and three-factor solution. A two-factor solution did yield a stable factor structure. The authors reported using Everett's (1983) factor comparability coefficient procedure to directly determine that two factors should be retained.
Samples	Validation of the measure was established using three pooled samples. The first sample was composed of 418 undergraduate students. The second sample was composed of 429 undergraduate students. The final sample was composed of 207 individuals who responded to an advertisement in local and campus newspapers. The demographic background of the participants was not reported.
Scoring	The number of items for each subscale was not reported. A number of items require reverse scoring. It appears that scoring the MCPRS consists of summing subscale items. Higher scores indicate more desire to control prejudiced reactions. Means were not reported. No transformations are required.
Reliability	Cronbach's alpha for the full scale score ranged from .75 to 77.

(Continued)

(Continued)

Validity	Criterion validity was established through significant inverse correlations with the Modern Racism Scale (McConahay, 1986) and self-reported prejudiced attitudes toward African Americans.
Related References	Glaser, J., & Knowles, E. D. (2008). Implicit motivation to control prejudice. *Journal of Experimental Social Psychology, 44*, 164–172. Muraven, M. (2008). Prejudice as self-control failure. *Journal of Applied Social Psychology, 38*, 314–333.
Language Versions	English
Contact	Russell H. Fazio Department of Psychology 1835 Neil Avenue Ohio State University Columbus, OH 43210–1287 (614) 688–5408 Email: fazio.11@osu.edu

7.9.4 Name of the Measure	Modified Godfrey-Richman ISM Scale M-GRISMS-M
Primary Reference	Godfrey, S., Richman, C. L., & Withers, T. N. (2000). Reliability and validity of a new scale to measure prejudice: The GRISMS. *Current Psychology, 19,* 3–20.
Purpose	The M-GRISMS-M was designed to measure cognitions, actions, and behaviors associated with racism, sexism, and heterosexism.
Description	The M-GRISMS-M is a 33-item self-report inventory that utilizes multiple response formats: yes/no, rankings, and Likert-type ratings. The authors describe the M-GRISMS-M as being composed of the following three or four subscales: Racism, Sexism, and Heterosexism. A religion subscale was found to not have strong internal consistency. Factor analysis, however, indicates that the M-GRISMS is composed of 10 factors: (1) Violations of Social Roles; (2) Anti-Jewish; (3) Religious Morality; (4) Social Morality; (5) True Male Behaviors; (6) Power Motive; (7) Self-Centered; (8) Stereotypical Character Flaws; (9) Male Aggression vs. Affection; and (10) Competence. An initial 90-item measure composed the original GRISMS. Fifty of those items were selected for further study. Based on interitem correlations and response scale, some items were deleted before data from the M-GRISMS were submitted for factor analysis. This deletion process yielded a 33-item M-GRISMS-M measure. With an oblimin extraction method, factor analysis with data from the Attitudes toward Women Scale (Spence, Helmreich, & Stapp, 1973) and the M-GRISMS-M yielded 10 factors.
Samples	Validation of this measure was established using a sample of 131 college students (71 women, 60 men) who ranged from 18 to 23 years of age. The sample was composed mostly of White American individuals (93%). African Americans (5%) and Asian and Native Americans (2%) also were represented in the sample. The sample primarily identified as Christian in faith (92%). The sample also was composed of Agnostic or Atheist (5%). All but 1% of the sample identified as heterosexual in sexual orientation.
Scoring	The number of items for each subscale of the M-GRISMS-M is as follows: Violations of Social Roles: 5 items Anti-Jewish: 3 items Religious Morality: 3 items Social Morality: 3 items True Male Behaviors: 4 items Power Motive: 4 items Self-Centered: 3 items Stereotypical Character Flaws: 3 items

(Continued)

(Continued)

	Male Aggression vs. Affection: 3 items Competence: 2 items Total M-GRISMS: 33 items A score on the M-GRISMS-M subscales or total scale may be computed by including a sum of all items of the subscale or by excluding items that are reflective of that group.
Reliability	Reliability coefficients were calculated for the proposed subscales and for the total scale but not for the factors that emerged from factor analysis. Racism Subscale: Alpha = .64 Sexism Subscale: Alpha = .52 Heterosexism Subscale: Alpha = .72 Religion Subscale: Alpha = .40 Total M-GRISMS-M: Alpha = .82 8-Week Test-retest reliability coefficients also were presented: Racism Subscale: $r = .80$ Sexism Subscale: $r = .77$ Heterosexism Subscale: $r = .81$ Religion Subscale: $r = .75$ Total M-GRISMS-M: $r = .89$
Validity	Construct validity was established through a significant relationship found between measures of racism (McConahay, Hardee, & Batts, 1981), heterosexism (Larsen, Reed, & Hoffman, 1980), and sexism (Spence et al., 1973).
Related References	
Language Versions	English
Contact	The full scale can be found in Godfrey et al. (2000).

7.9.5 Name of the Measure	Privilege and Oppression Inventory POI
Primary Reference	Hays, D. G., Chang, C. Y., & Decker, S. L. (2007). Initial development and psychometric data for the Privilege and Oppression Inventory. *Measurement and Evaluation in Counseling and Development, 40,* 66–79.
Purpose	The POI is designed to measure an individual's awareness of privilege and oppression around issues of race, gender, sexual orientation, socioeconomic status, and religion.
Description	The POI is a 16-item self-report inventory. Each of these items is rated on a 6-point Likert-type scale with the following anchors: 1 = Strongly Disagree to 6 = Strongly Agree.
	The POI is composed of 4 subscales: (1) White Privilege Awareness; (2) Heterosexism Awareness; (3) Christian Privilege Awareness; and (4) Sexism Awareness.
	The instrument was developed through several steps. An initial pool of 107 items was created based on data from two qualitative studies, a review of research literature regarding multicultural counseling competencies, multicultural assessment, social advocacy, and privilege and oppression in counseling. Six multicultural experts reviewed the items for clarity and appropriateness of content. This resulted in an 83-item instrument.
	Sampling adequacy was first established. Principal axis extraction with promax oblique rotation was then conducted and yielded nine factors of eigenvalues greater than 1.0. A four-factor solution was selected as most interpretable. Items with structure coefficients loadings of .30 or greater on only one factor were retained. All other items were deleted. This resulted in a 39-item POI. Confirmatory factor analysis, using AMOS (Arbuckle, 1999), was used to test for stability of the factor structure. Their data fit a four-factor solution best.
Samples	A sample of 428 diverse trainees (81.5% women) attending a counseling-related program with a median age of 27 years. A second sample of 206 trainees from eight counseling programs also was used. Their mean age was 31 years. The first sample was composed of 70% White Americans, 19% African Americans, 5% Multiracial/Biracial Americans, 3% Asian Americans, 2% Latino/a Americans, and 1% Native Americans. These two samples were combined for the study of the validity and structure of the POI. Data from a subsample (not used in the EFA) of the original sample were submitted to a confirmatory factor analysis.

(Continued)

(Continued)

Scoring	The number of items for each of the four subscales of the POI is as follows:
	White Privilege Awareness: 13 items
	Heterosexism Awareness: 10 items
	Christian Privilege Awareness: 8 items
	Sexism Awareness: 8 items
	Total POI: 39 items
	Two items require reverse scoring. Scoring the subscales consists of summing subscale items and dividing by the number of items of which it is composed. Higher scores indicate higher experience of the psychosocial costs of racism. No transformations are required.
Reliability	Cronbach's alpha for the subscale scores ranged from .63–.78.
	White Privilege Awareness: Alpha = .92
	Heterosexism Awareness: Alpha = .81
	Christian Privilege Awareness: Alpha = .86
	Sexism Awareness: Alpha = .79
	Two-week test-retest reliability coefficients were as follows:
	White Privilege: $r = .89$
	Heterosexism Awareness: $r = .86$
	Christian Privilege Awareness: $r = .84$
	Sexism Awareness: $r = .79$
Validity	Convergent validity of POI subscales was established through expected positive correlations with M-GUDS (Fuertes et al., 2000), and the QDI (Ponterotto, Potere, & Johansen, 2002) and a negative correlation with social desirability (Crowne & Marlowe, 1960).
Related References	
Language Versions	English
Contact	Danica Hays Educational Leadership and Counseling 110 Education Building Old Dominion University Norfolk, VA 23529 Email: dhays@odu.edu

7.9.6 **Name of the Measure**	The Symbolic Racism 2000 Scale SR2KS
Primary Reference	Henry, P. J., & Sears, D. O. (2002). The Symbolic Racism 2000 Scale. *Political Psychology, 23,* 253–283.
Purpose	The SR2KS is designed to measure the racial attitudes of White Americans and members of other racial groups toward African Americans.
Description	The SR2KS is an 8-item Likert-type self-report inventory. Most of these items are rated on a 4-point Likert-type scale with the following anchors: 1 = Strongly Agree to 4 = Strongly Disagree. One item included a 4-point scale with different anchors (i.e., "trying to push very much too fast," "going too slowly," and "moving at about the right speed"). Other items were measured on a 3-point scale that included options such as "A Lot," "Only Some," and "Not Much at All" or "All of It," "Most," "Some," "Not Much at All." The SR2KS is composed of two subscales: (1) Traditional Racial Attitudes and (2) Political Predisposition. The instrument was developed through several steps. Items were constructed based on a review of the symbolic, subtle, aversive, and modern racism literature and upon previous iterations of the Symbolic Racism Scale. The authors submitted data, gathered from three previous studies, to an exploratory factor analysis with oblique rotation. This analysis yielded a two-factor solution. The first factor, traditional racial attitude, included themes of "work ethic and responsibility for outcomes" and "excessive demands." The second factor, political predisposition, included "denial of continuing discrimination" and "underserved advantage." Data from other previous studies were submitted for confirmatory factor analysis. The authors reported using a principal axis method with oblique rotation.
Samples	Data from five studies involving 647, 694, 145, 142, and 702 college students were used to establish and test the psychometric properties of this measure. The sample included 887 White Americans, 512 Latino/a Americans, 496 Asian Americans, and 186 African Americans with 248 individuals reporting a multiracial background or who did not specify. Data presented below reflect analyses involving White American participants.
Scoring	The number of items in each of the two subscales is as follows: Traditional Racial Attitudes: 4 items Political Predisposition: 4 items Total SR2KS: 8 items Several items are reverse scored. Scoring the subscales consists of summing subscale items. Higher scores indicate higher levels of negative attitudes toward African Americans. No transformations are required.

(Continued)

(Continued)

Reliability	The Cronbach alpha coefficient for the total score ranged from .59 to .79 across the samples.
Validity	Predictive validity was established through significant correlations between conservative political predispositions and opposition to racial policy preferences. Known-groups validity also was demonstrated through one-way analysis of variance procedures, which indicated that African Americans scored lower on this measure than did other groups.
Related References	Green, E. G. T., Staerklé, C., & Sears, D. O. (2006). Symbolic racism and Whites' attitudes toward punitive and preventive crime policies. *Law and Human Behavior, 30*, 435–454.
Language Versions	English
Contact	http://condor.depaul.edu/~phenry1/SR2Kinstructions.htm

7.9.7 Name of the Measure	Scale of Anti-Asian American Stereotypes SAAAS
Primary Reference	Lin, M. H., Kwan, V. S. Y., Cheung, A., & Fiske, S. T. (2005). Stereotype content model explains prejudice for an envied outgroup: Scale of Anti-Asian American stereotypes. *Personality and Social Psychology Bulletin, 31,* 34–47.
Purpose	The SAAAS is intended to measure an individual's stereotypic attitudes toward Asian Americans.
Description	The SAAAS is a 25-item self-report inventory. The measure utilizes a 6-point Likert-type scale with the following anchors: 0 = Strongly Disagree to 5 = Strongly Agree. The SAAAS is composed of two related subscales: (1) Competence and (2) (Un)sociability. Seventy-six undergraduate students developed a list of stereotypes of Asian Americans. This list was content analyzed and revealed three major areas of stereotypes (i.e., [un]sociability, competence, and foreignness). This process lead to an initial 131-item measure. A principal components analysis with varimax rotation yielded three factors. Items were retained if they met the authors' .50 criterion. None of the items correlating with the third factor met this criterion. Items with a high structure coefficient on a second factor also were not retained. Through this process, the SAAAS was shortened to 25 items. An unweighted least-square factor analysis with oblique rotation determined the eventual two-factor structure of the SAAAS. Additional analyses using LISREL VIII (Joreskog & Sorbom, 1993) with two samples confirmed that data fit a two-factor solution better than a one-factor model.
Samples	Initial validation of the measure was established using three samples of undergraduate college students from the University of Massachusetts, Amherst. The first sample was composed of 296 individuals (237 women, 59 men) who received extra credit for their participation. This sample was composed of 231 White Americans, 32 non-Asian people of color, 27 Asian Americans, and 6 individuals who did not indicate their racial background. The remaining two samples involved White American students enrolled in lower-level undergraduate psychology courses. The first of these two samples was composed of 429 students (248 women, 178 men, and 3 unspecified).

Scoring	The number of items on the subscales are as follows:
	
	    Competence: 12 items
	
	    (Un)sociable: 13 items
	
	    Total SAAAS: 25 items

(Continued)

(Continued)

	Seven of the items are negatively worded. Scoring the SAAAS consists of summing subscale items. Higher scores indicated more prejudice. No transformations are required.
Reliability	Cronbach's alpha for the total and subscale scores were as follows: Sociability: Alpha = .91 Competence: Alpha = .92 Total SAAAS: Alpha = .94
Validity	Convergent validity was determined through significant relationships in the expected direction with measures of Ambivalent Sexism (Glick & Fiske, 1996) and Subtle Prejudice (Pettigrew & Meertens, 1995). Concurrent validity also was established through the use of one-way multivariate analysis of variance. Results indicated a significant effect of prejudice level on self-reported everyday interactions with Asian Americans. Specifically, individuals with high levels of prejudice reported less effort to socialize with Asian Americans, have less active exposure to Asian American culture, overestimate the percentage of Asian Americans on campus, and have fewer Asian American acquaintances than those with low levels of prejudice. Individuals with lower levels of prejudice against Asian Americans also were more likely to choose to have an Asian American roommate, have read literature with Asian American authors, and be more curious about Asian Americans than those with higher levels of prejudice. Correlation analyses in a separate study supported these findings. Further evidence of concurrent validity was established in another study. Individuals who held high levels of attitudes of Asian Americans as (un)sociable had negative impressions of an Asian American confederate. Individuals who held high levels of attitudes of Asian Americans as sociable did not perceive the Asian American confederate in a negative or positive manner. Individuals who viewed Asian Americans as less sociable also were found to make more mistakes on a recall task. Specifically, they made more mistakes recalling what the Asian American confederate announced.
Related References	
Language Versions	English
Contact	Susan T. Fiske Department of Psychology Princeton University Princeton, NY 08544–1010 Email: Sfiske@princeton.edu

7.9.8 Name of the Measure	Modern and Old Fashioned Racism Scale MOFRS
Primary Reference	McConahay, J. B. (1986). Modern racism, ambivalence, and the Modern Racism Scale. In J. F. Dovidio & S. L. Gaertner (Eds.), *Prejudice, discrimination, and racism* (pp. 91–125). New York: Academic Press. McConahay, J. B., Hardee, B. B., & Batts, V. (1981). Has racism declined in America? It depends on who is asking and what is asked. *Journal of Conflict Resolution, 25,* 563–579.
Purpose	The MOFRS is designed to measure the cognitive component of racial attitudes of White Americans toward African Americans.
Description	The MOFRS is a 12-item self-report inventory. Each of these items is rated on a 6-point Likert-type scale with the following anchors: 1 = Strongly Disagree to 5 = Strongly Agree. The MOFRS is composed of two subscales: (1) Modern Racism and (2) Old Fashioned Racism. The instrument was developed through several steps. First, items were constructed based on a review of the racism literature, the literary definition of symbolic racism, and the theory of modern racism. A series of factor analyses have been conducted to test the structure of the MOFRS. In these studies, maximum likelihood methods with oblique rotations were used to extract factors. Results indicated a two-factor solution, with Modern Racism and Old Fashioned Racism being distinct and correlated.
Samples	Three samples of White American adults or White American college students were used in one of three studies. In the first sample, 875 White American adults from Kentucky were used. The second study was composed of 709 White American adults, also from Kentucky. In the third sample, 167 White American college students from private university in the south were used. Gender was not reported.

Scoring	The number of items for the two subscales of the MOFRS is as follows:
	
	    Old Fashioned Racism (OFRS): 6 items
	
	    Modern Racism (MRS): 6 items
	
	    Total MOFRS: 12 items
	
	Scoring the subscales consists of summing subscale items and dividing by the number of items of which it is composed. Higher scores indicate higher levels of old fashioned and modern racism. No transformations are required.

Reliability	A Cronbach coefficient alpha of .82 was reported for the score of the Modern Racism Scale and .75 to .79 for score on the Old Fashioned Racism Scale.

(Continued)

(Continued)

Validity	Convergent validity of MOFRS subscales was established through expected findings of significant negative correlations with attitudes toward busing (McConahay, 1982), positive correlations with preference for a White American candidate in an election (Kinder & Sears, 1981; McConahay & Hough, 1976), and positive associations with sympathetic identification with the underdog (McConahay & Hough, 1976) and anti-Black feelings as measured by the Feeling Thermometer (Campbell, 1971).
	Construct validity was established through a series of experiments in which results indicated that individuals reported lower levels of Old Fashioned Racism when the test administrator was African American than in cases in which the test administrator was a White American. In this same experiment, as predicted, responses to Modern Racism were unaffected by the racial background of the test administrator. A second study employing similar research methodology found similar results. In another study, individuals with more positive attitudes toward African Americans also were more likely to have positive attitudes toward hiring them.
Related References	Goff, P. A., Steele, C. M., & Davies, P. G. (2008). The space between us: Stereotype threat and distance in interracial contexts. *Journal of Personality and Social Psychology, 94*, 91–107.
	Lun, J., Sinclair, S., Whitchurch, E. R., & Glenn, C. (2007). (Why) Do I think what you think? Epistemic social tuning and implicit prejudice. *Journal of Personality and Social Psychology, 93*, 957–972.
	Sabnani, H., & Ponterotto, J. (1992). Racial/ethnic minority-specific instrumentation in counseling research: A review, critique, and recommendations. *Measurement and Evaluation in Counseling and Development, 24*, 161–187.
Language Versions	English
Contact	The items of the MOFRS may be found in McConahay (1986).

7.9.9 Name of the Measure	Miville-Guzman Universality-Diversity Scale M-GUDS
Primary Reference	Miville, M. L., Gelso, C. J., Pannu, R., Liu, W., Touradji, P., Holloway, P., & Fuertes, J. (1999). Appreciating similarities and valuing differences: The Miville-Guzman Universality-Diversity Scale. *Journal of Counseling Psychology, 46,* 291–307.
Purpose	The M-GUDS is designed to measure an individual's awareness and acceptance of similarities and differences in others.
Description	The M-GUDS is a 45-item self-report inventory. Each of these items is rated on a 6-point Likert-type scale with the following anchors: 1 = Strongly Disagree to 6 = Strongly Agree. The M-GUDS is composed of 3 subscales: (1) Diversity of Contact; (2) Relativistic Appreciation; and (3) Sense of Connection (or Comfort with Differences). The initial 45-item instrument was developed to measure behavioral, cognitive, and affective components of a Universal-Diverse orientation. These items were based on a review of racism and prejudice literature. Five counseling psychology doctoral students provided feedback regarding the appropriateness and clarity of the initial pool of 78 items and their proposed subscales. A pilot study to examine the item-subscale total-score correlations was conducted. Thirty-three items were deleted as a result of these processes. Initial exploratory factor analysis indicated that the M-GUDS was best conceptualized as a unidimensional measure UDO with behavioral, cognitive, and affective components. Subsequent factor analysis provided support for the originally hypothesized three-factor structure of UDO (see Fuertes, Miville, Mohr, Sedlacek, & Gretchen, 2000).
Samples	Study of the psychometric properties of the M-GUDS included multiple samples. Miville et al. (1999) provided evidence for validity based on four separate samples (Ns = 93, 111, 153, and 135). Fuertes et al. (2000) examined the factor structure of the M-GUDS using a separate sample (N = 335). All samples included male and female college students recruited from nonclinical settings. For all but one study, the samples were ethnically diverse and were recruited from predominantly White institutions. Two additional samples were recruited to establish a short version of the M-GUDS (the M-GUDS-S). One sample was composed of students from a public university (N = 206). The other sample was composed of students from a private university (N = 186).

Scoring	The number of items for the subscales of the M-GUDS and M-GUDS-S are as follows:
	
	    Diversity of Contact: 15 items
	
	    Relativistic Appreciation: 15 items
	
	    Sense of Connection (or Comfort with Differences): 15 items
	
	    Total M-GUDS: 45 items
	
	M-GUDS Short (M-GUDS-S)
	
	    Diversity of Contact: 5 items
	
	    Relativistic Appreciation: 5 items
	
	    Sense of Connection (or Comfort with Differences): 5 items
	
	    Total M-GUDS-S: 15 items

(Continued)

(Continued)

	Three items are reverse scored. Scoring the subscales consists of summing subscale items. Higher scores indicate higher levels of each subscale. No transformations are required.
Reliability	Cronbach's alpha for the score of total full scale was as follows: Total M-GUDS: Alpha = .92 Cronbach's alpha for the subscales scores on the Short version were as follows: Diversity of Contact: Alpha = .82 Relativistic Appreciation: Alpha = .59 Sense of Connection (or Comfort with Differences): Alpha = .92 Total M-GUDS-S: Alpha = .77 2-Week Test-Retest reliability for the total full scale score was: $r = .94$.
Validity	Convergent validity of M-GUDS was established through expected correlations with White racial identity attitudes (Helms & Carter, 1990), homophobia (Hansen, 1982), dogmatism (Troldahl & Powell, 1965), perspective taking (Davis, 1983), and healthy narcissism (Goldman & Gelso, 1997). Discriminant validity was established through the lack of correlation with SAT scores and through mixed findings with a measure of social desirability (Crowne & Marlowe, 1964). Contrary to expectations, no significant correlations were found between the M-GUDS and fantasy or personal distress (Davis, 1983) or defensive narcissism (Goldman & Gelso, 1997). For the M-GUDS-S, convergent validity was demonstrated through significant correlations, in the expected directions, with single items centered on diversity-related issues. Results also indicate no significant effect of race on the M-GUDS-S or its subscales.
Related References	Fuertes, J. N., Miville, M. L., Mohr, J. J., Sedlacek, W. E., & Gretchen, D. (2000). Factor structure and short form of the Miville-Guzman Universality-Diversity Scale. *Measurement and Evaluation in Counseling and Development, 33,* 157–169. Spanierman, L. B., Todd, N. R., & Anderson, C. J. (2009). Psychosocial costs of racism to Whites: Understanding patterns among university students. *Journal of Counseling Psychology, 56,* 239–252.
Language Versions	English
Contact	Marie L. Miville Teachers College Columbia University Counseling and Clinical Psychology 525 West 120th Street Box 73 New York, NY 10027–6696 (212) 678-3343 Email: miville@exchange.tc.columbia

7.9.10 Name of the Measure	Color-Blind Racial Attitudes Scale CoBRAS
Primary Reference	Neville, H. A., Lilly, R. L., Duran, G., Lee, R. M., & Browne, L. (2000). Construction and initial validation of the Color-Blind Racial Attitudes Scale (CoBRAS). *Journal of Counseling Psychology, 47*, 59–70.
Purpose	The CoBRAS is intended to measure the cognitive aspects of color-blind racial attitudes.
Description	The CoBRAS is a 20-item self-report inventory. The measure utilizes a 6-point Likert-type scale with the following anchors: 1 = Strongly Disagree to 6 = Strongly Agree.
	The CoBRAS is composed of three subscales: (1) Racial Privilege; (2) Institutional Discrimination; and (3) Blatant Racial Issues.
	The initial 17 items of the CoBRAS were developed based on current definitions of color-blind racial attitudes, interdisciplinary literature, consultation with scholars of racial attitudes, and discussions with diverse graduate and undergraduate students as well as with individuals from the community. These items were written by a team of researchers from diverse backgrounds. In order to assess content validity, a panel of five experts rated the items for appropriateness and clarity. This panel rated two items as inappropriate or unclear. These items were deleted. Seven items were reworded and 11 items were added. These 26 items were rated for clarity and appropriateness by the original team of researchers. Four items were reworded for greater clarity based on the ratings of clarity and appropriateness by individuals from the community.
	Using a computer software program, the scale was rated to be appropriate for individuals with more than a 6th-grade reading level.
	A principal components analysis resulted in five factors with eigenvalues greater than 1.00. Using both oblique and orthogonal rotations, data were reanalyzed for a five-, four-, three-, two-, and one-factor solution. Using an equimax rotation, a three-factor solution was found to be the most interpretable. Six items were deleted from this process. Confirmatory factor analysis provided support for this three-factor solution.
Samples	The psychometric properties of this measure were established over the course of five studies. The first sample involved 302 college students and community members from the Midwest and West Coast. Participants' ages ranged from 17–52 (*M* = 20.57; *SD* = 8.56). With respect to gender, women (*n* = 212) constituted the majority of this sample. There also are 86 men in the sample, leaving 4 individuals who did not report their gender. A majority of the sample was White Americans (*n* = 256), with 24 African Americans, 3 Native Americans, 10 Asian Americans, and 9 Latino/a Americans. Four percent of the sample either did not indicate a race or reported "other."
	The second sample was composed of 594 college students or community members from the Midwest and West Coast. The sample was more evenly composed of women (*n* = 304) and men (*n* = 289). One participant did not report gender.

(Continued)

(Continued)

	Participants' ages ranged from 14–88 ($M = 22.78$; $SD = 9.14$). Sixty-seven percent of the sample identified as White American, nearly 20% identified as African American, 5% as Chicano/a American, 2% as Asian American, and 1% as Native American. The remaining 6% did not specify a racial or ethnic classification.
	The third sample was composed of 102 college students (74 women; 28 men) attending a predominantly White university in the Midwest. Ninety percent of the sample identified as White American. Eighty-three percent of the sample was undergraduate students.
	The fourth sample was composed of 89 women, 55 men, and one individual who did not indicate his or her gender. These participants were college students and community members from the Midwest and West Coast. Their ages ranged from 18–85 ($M = 31.37$; $SD = 16.88$). Seventy percent of the sample identified as White Americans.
	In the fifth study, 28 undergraduate students at a major West Coast university (21 women; 7 men). The mean age was 19.57 years ($SD = 1.50$). With respect to racial background, the sample was composed of 7 African American, 7 Asian Americans, Latino/a American or 5 Latino/a American or Chicano/a Americans, 3 White Americans, 1 Native American, and 5 multiracial individuals.

Scoring	There are a total of 20 items on the measure.
	
	    Racial Privilege: 7 items
	
	    Institutional Discrimination: 7 items
	
	    Blatant Racial Issues: 6 items
	
	    Total CoBRAS: 20 items
	
	Half of the items are reverse scored. Scoring the CoBRAS consists of summing subscale items. Higher scores indicated higher levels of color-blind racial attitudes. No transformations are required.

Reliability	Cronbach's coefficient alpha for the scores on the total and subscales were as follows:
	
	    Racial Privilege: Alpha = .71 to .83
	
	    Institutional Discrimination: Alpha = .73 to .81
	
	    Blatant Racial Issues: Alpha = .70 to .76
	
	    Total CoBRAS: Alpha = .84 to .91
	
	Two-week test-retest reliability coefficients for the total and subscales were as follows:
	
	    Racial Privilege: $r = .80$
	
	    Institutional Discrimination: $r = .80$
	
	    Blatant Racial Issues: $r = .34$
	
	    Total CoBRAS: $r = .68$
	
	Guttman split-half reliability coefficient:
	
	    Total CoBRAS: $r = .72$

Validity	Convergent validity was determined through significant relationships in the expected direction with measures of Ambivalent Sexism (Glick & Fiske, 1996) and Subtle Prejudice (Pettigrew & Meertens, 1995).
	Concurrent validity was established through significant correlations between each of the three CoBRAS subscales and the two subscales of the Global Belief in a Just World Scale (GBJWS; Lipkus, 1991), the Multidimensional Belief in a Just World Scale (MBJWS; Furnham & Procter, 1988), the Quick Discrimination Index (Ponterotto et al., 1995), and the Modern Racism Scale (McConahay, 1986).
	Criterion validity was established through the use of multivariate analysis of variance (MANOVA) to compare responses from the different racial groups on the three CoBRAS subcales. In one study, MANOVA indicated that Black individuals reported lower scores on the Institutional Discrimination subscale than did Latino/a American and White American participants. White American participants reported significantly lower scores on the Blatant Racism subscale than did Black participants. Latino/a participants reported significantly lower Racial Privilege and Blatant Racial Issues subscales than did Black American and White American participants. In a second study, White American participants were found to have higher Institutional Discrimination subscale scores than did an aggregated "racial minority" group.
	MANOVA also was used to test for significant differences based on gender. Results from several MANOVA did not indicate a consistent pattern of expected differences. In two of the three studies, women were found to have significantly lower CoBRAS scores than did men. No significant effect of gender on the three CoBRAS scores was found in a third study.
	Discriminant validity was demonstrated through lack of significant correlations between the three CoBRAS subscales and Marlowe-Crowne Social Desirability Scale–Short (Reynolds, 1982).
Related References	Spanierman, L. B., Poteat, V. P., Beer, A. M., & Armstrong, P. I. (2006). Psychosocial costs of racism to Whites: Exploring patterns through cluster analysis. *Journal of Counseling Psychology, 53,* 434–441.
	Worthington, R. L., Navarro, R. L., Loewy, M., & Hart, J. (2008). Color-blind racial attitudes, social dominance orientation, racial ethnic group membership and college students' perceptions of campus climate. *Journal of Diversity in Higher Education, 1,* 8–19.
Language Versions	English
Contact	Helen A. Neville Educational Psychology 188f Education 1310 S. Sixth M/C 708 Champaign, IL 61820 Email: hneville@illinois.edu

7.9.11 Name of the Measure	The White Privilege Attitudes Scale WPAS
Primary Reference	Pinteritis, E. J., Poteat, V. P., & Spanierman, L. B. (2009). The White Privilege Attitudes Scale: Development and initial validation. *Journal of Counseling Psychology, 56,* 417–429.
Purpose	The WPAS is designed to measure the cognitive, behavioral, and affective dimensions of an individual's White privilege attitudes.
Description	The WPAS is a 28-item Likert-type self-report inventory. Each of these items is rated on a 6-point Likert-type scale with the following anchors: 1 = Strongly Disagree to 6 = Strongly Agree.
	The WPAS is composed of four subscales: (1) Willingness to Confront White Privilege; (2) Anticipated Costs of Addressing White Privilege; (3) White Privilege Awareness; and (4) White Privilege Remorse.
	The instrument was developed through several steps. An initial pool of 111 items was created based on a review of research literature regarding White privilege and a consideration of the tripartite models of attitudes that include cognitive, behavioral, and affective components. The authors also consulted leading scholars in the area of critical Whiteness studies. In the first phase, five faculty and four graduate students with experience in multicultural counseling, White attitudes toward race, and the study of racism generated 160 items. The authors then consulted five scholars of White privilege who rated each item for appropriateness and clarity. This resulted in 111 items.
	Experts in scale construction then edited items that were double-barreled and deleted redundant items. This resulted in 81 items, of which 15 were reverse coded.
	The authors first tested their data to ensure their sample was appropriate for factor analysis. An exploratory factor analysis, using maximum likelihood extraction with oblique rotation, was used. Items correlating with multiple factors with values of .25 or greater and those with structure coefficients less than .45 were deleted. This resulted in a 28-item measure with four factors. Confirmatory factor analysis, using LISREL 8.7 (Jöreskog & Sörbom, 2006), was used to test for stability of the factor structure. Their data fit a four-factor solution best.
Samples	A sample of 501 White Americans was recruited from several colleges and universities from across the United States. The sample was split into two in order to explore and confirm the structure of the WPAS and establish validity. In the first sample of 250 individuals, 78% were undergraduate students, 18% were graduate students, with 4% not indicating their school standing. In terms of gender, 65% of the sample identified as women, 34% were men, and one individual identified as transgender. With respect to age, the sample ranged in age from 18–70 years ($M = 22.45$; $SD = 7.43$). In the second study, which was designed to confirm the factor structure of the WPAS, 251 individuals participated. This sample's composition was nearly identical to the first sample.

Scoring	The number of items in each subscale of the WPAS is as follows:
	Willingness to Confront White Privilege: 12 items
	Anticipated Costs of Addressing White Privilege: 6 items
	White Privilege Awareness: 4 items
	White Privilege Remorse: 6 items
	Total WPAS: 28 items
	Four of the items are reverse scored. Scoring the subscales consists of summing subscale items and dividing by the number of items of which it is composed. Higher scores indicate higher levels of cognitive, affective, or behavioral dimensions of White privilege attitudes. No transformations are required.
Reliability	Cronbach's alpha for the subscale scores were as follows:
	Willingness to Confront White Privilege: Alpha = .95
	Anticipated Costs of Addressing White Privilege: Alpha = .81
	White Privilege Awareness: Alpha = .84
	White Privilege Remorse: Alpha = .91
	Two-week Test-retest reliability coefficients were as follows:
	Willingness to Confront White Privilege: $r = .83$
	Anticipated Costs of Addressing White Privilege: $r = .70$
	White Privilege Awareness: $r = .87$
	White Privilege Remorse: $r = .78$
Validity	Convergent validity of WPAS subscales was established through expected findings of significant correlations with subscales of the Color-Blind Racial Attitude Scale (Neville et al., 2000), Modern Racism Scale (McConahay, 1986), Psychological Costs of White Racism Scale (Spanierman & Heppner, 2004), and Social Dominance Orientation (Pratto, Sidanius, Stallworth, & Malle, 1994).
	Discriminant validity was established through the lack of significant correlations with the Marlowe-Crowne Social Desirability Scale—Form C (Reynolds, 1982).
Related References	
Language Versions	English
Contact	E. Janie Pinteritis
	Department of Counseling Psychology and Community Services
	University of North Dakota
	290 Centennial Drive Stop 8255
	Grand Forks, ND 58202–8255
	Email: Janie.pinterits@und.edu

7.9.12 Name of the Measure	Internal Motivation to Respond Without Prejudice Scale and External Motivation to Respond Without Prejudice Scale IMS and EMS
Primary Reference	Plant, E. A., & Devine, P. G. (1998). Internal and external motivation to respond without prejudice. *Journal of Personality and Social Psychology, 75,* 811–832.
Purpose	The IMS and EMS were designed to measure individuals' internal and external motivation to respond without prejudice. Internal motivation to respond without prejudice reflects nonprejudiced standards that are internalized. External motivation to respond without prejudice reflects motivations that result from societal pressure.
Description	The 10-item measure is rated on a Likert-type self-report inventory. Each item is rated on a 9-point Likert-type scale with the following anchors: 1 = Strongly Disagree to 9 = Strongly Agree. The IMS and EMS are two distinct scales: (1) Internal Motivation Scale, (2) External Motivation Scale. Based on a review of literature on prejudice, the authors developed an initial 19-item instrument to measure external and internal motivations to respond without prejudice. Principal components analysis with oblimin rotation resulted in a 15-item, two-factor measure. Using LISREL 7, confirmatory factor analysis indicated that a two-factor solution provided the best fit to their data. Confirmatory factor analysis also resulted in the deletion of 5 additional items, resulting in a 10-item, two-factor measure.
Samples	Validation of the measure was established using three samples. The first sample was composed of 135 introductory psychology undergraduate students. The second sample included 247 introductory psychology undergraduate students and a separate additional sample of 119 students. The final sample was composed of 1,363 introductory psychology students. The first sample was composed primarily of females (76%) and White Americans students (94%). The second sample was similarly composed primarily of females (74%) and White Americans students (84%). The additional sample of 119 students also was composed primarily of females (62%) and White Americans (90%). A majority of the final sample were females (60%) and primarily White Americans (85%).
Scoring	The number of items in each subscale is as follows: Internal Motivation: 5 items External Motivation: 5 items One of the items on the Internal Motivation Scale requires reverse scoring. Scoring the scales consists of summing subscale items. Higher scores on each of these scales indicate higher levels of that type of motivation. No transformations are required.
Reliability	Cronbach's alpha for each of the scales were as follows: Internal Motivation Scale: Alpha = .81 to .85 External Motivation Scale: Alpha = .76 to .80

	Nine-week test-retest reliability coefficients were as follows:
	Internal Motivation Scale: $r = .77$
	External Motivation Scale: $r = .60$
Validity	Convergent validity for the IMS was established through significant inverse correlations with the Modern Racism Scale (MRS; McConahay, 1986) and the Anti-Black Scale (ABS; Katz & Hass, 1988) and positively correlated with Attitudes Toward Blacks (ATB; Brigham, 1993), the Pro-Black Scale (PBS; Katz & Hass, 1988), Humanitarianism-Egalitarianism Scale (HE; Katz & Hass, 1988), and concern with acting prejudiced (Dunton & Fazio, 1997). The IMS also was established through negative correlations with Right Wing Authoritarianism (RWA; Altemeyer, 1981), Protestant Ethic Scale (PE; Katz & Hass, 1988), and restraint to avoid dispute (Dunton & Fazio, 1997). The EMS was found to be positively correlated with the MRS and negatively correlated with the ATB. A significant small positive correlation between EMS and RWA was also found. Finally, a modest positive correlation was found with concern with acting prejudiced and restraint to avoid dispute.
	Discriminant validity was demonstrated through the lack of significant relationships between the IMS and EMS with social desirability (Crowne & Marlowe, 1960) and self-monitoring (Snyder & Gangestad, 1986). The IMS also was not significantly related to fear of negative self-evaluation (FNE; Leary, 1983; Watson & Friend, 1969) and social anxiety (IAS; Leary, 1983). The EMS only was modestly correlated with the FNE and the IAS.
	Predictive validity was established such that large discrepancies between what a person's own beliefs about what one should (i.e., self-standards) and would do was associated with feelings of guilt and self-criticism for individuals who reported being more internally motivated to respond without prejudice. Large discrepancies between what one would do and perceptions of other-standards were associated with threatened affect for individuals who were highly externally motivated to respond without prejudice.
Related References	Plant, E. A., & Devine, P. G. (2009). The active control of prejudice: Unpacking the intentions guiding control efforts. *Journal of Personality and Social Psychology, 96,* 640–652.
Language Versions	English
Contact	Ashby Plant A2500 University Center Florida State University B332 PDB Tallahassee, FL 32306 (850) 644–5533 Email: plant@psy.fsu.edu

7.9.13 Name of the Measure	Quick Discrimination Index QDI
Primary Reference	Ponterotto, J. G., Burkard, A., Rieger, B. P., Grieger, I., et al. (1995). Development and initial validation of the Quick Discrimination Index (QDI). *Educational and Psychological Measurement, 55*, 1016–1031.
Purpose	The QDI is a measure of the cognitive component of attitudes toward women and racial minorities and the affective component of attitudes regarding comfort in interpersonal interactions with racially diverse populations.
Description	The QDI is a 30-item, Likert-type self-report inventory. Each item is rated on a 5-point Likert-type scale with the following anchors: 1 = Strongly Disagree to 5 = Strongly Agree. The QDI is composed of a total score on three subscales: (1) Cognitive Racial Attitudes; (2) Affective Racial Attitudes; (3) Cognitive Gender Attitudes. After an intensive literature review on discrimination, prejudice, and racism, the authors developed 40 statements measuring cognitive and affective components of prejudicial attitudes. Twelve items were removed after a review (by the authors) of those statements for redundancy and clarity. The remaining 28 items were then reviewed by a panel of five experts for clarity and appropriateness. This resulted in a final pool of 25 items. A focus group was then facilitated to learn the reactions of participants to the measure. Based on the results of initial item and factor analyses, the authors reworded two items and added five new items to refine Factor 2 and 3. These procedures resulted in a 30-item measure. A principal components analysis with varimax rotation yielded seven factors. However, a scree test indicated up to three factors. Using orthogonal and oblique rotations, a three-factor solution was found to have the best fit. Analyses using the Lix Readability Index (Anderson, 1983) indicate that a 9th-grade reading level is needed.
Samples	Initial validation of the 30-item measure was established using two samples. The first sample, composed of 220 participants, ranged in age from 16–58 years of age ($M = 22$, $SD = 9.3$). Fifty-nine percent of the sample was female, 41% was male. Educational levels were as follows: 33% in high school, 23% held a high school diploma, 1% held a high school equivalency degree, 2% held an associate's degree, 19% held a bachelor's degree, 7% held a master's degree, and 1% held a doctoral degree. The racial and ethnic composition of the sample was 60% White American, 23% Latino/a American, 10% African American, 4% Asian American, and 4% "Other." The second sample, composed of 333 participants from the New York City metropolitan area, ranged in age from 16 to 63 years ($M = 26.9$, $SD = 10.0$). With respect to gender, women composed 79% of the sample and men, 21%. Educational levels were as follows: 33% high school, 23% held a high school diploma, 1% held a high school equivalency, 2% held an associate's degree, 19% a bachelor's degree, 7% a master's degree, and 1% a doctoral degree. The racial and ethnic composition of the sample was 76% White American, 8% Latino/a American, 5% African American, 5% Asian American, and 6% were "Other." The measure has been utilized in samples comprised of White American individuals (e.g., Green, Kiernan-Stern, & Baskind, 2005), Asian Americans (Lam, 2008; Liu, 2002;

	Liu, Pope-Davis, Nevitt, & Toporek, 1999), and African Americans (Fujioka, 2005). Reliability coefficients have been adequate.
Scoring	The number of items for each of the three subscales of the QDI are as follows:
	Cognitive Racial Attitudes: 9 items
	Affective Racial Attitudes: 7 items
	Cognitive Gender Attitudes: 9 items
	Total QDI: 30 items
	Half of the items are negatively worded, which requires reverse scoring. Scoring the QDI consists of summing subscale items and dividing by the number of items in the specific subscale. Higher scores indicate more positive affective and cognitive attitudes toward women and racial minorities. No transformations are required.
Reliability	Cronbach's alpha for the subscale scores ranged from .76 to .83.
	Cognitive Racial Attitudes: Alpha = .80
	Affective Racial Attitudes: Alpha = .83
	Cognitive Gender Attitudes: Alpha = .76
	Total QDI: Alpha = .88
	Fifteen-week test-retest reliability coefficients ranged from .65 to .96 across three different groups.
	Cognitive Racial Attitudes: r = .82, .92, and .96
	Affective Racial Attitudes: r = .65, .95, and .87
	Cognitive Gender Attitudes: r = .82, .78, and .84
Validity	Criterion-related validity was evidenced through the significant main effect for gender, race, geographic region, and political affiliation on QDI scores. Convergent validity was evidenced through significant correlations with the New Racism Scale (Jacobson, 1985) and the Multicultural Counseling Awareness Scale (Ponterotto et al., 1993).
	Evidence for discriminant validity was demonstrated through nonsignificant correlations with the Social Desirability Scale (Crowne & Marlowe, 1960).
Related References	Utsey, S. O., & Ponterotto, J. G. (1999). Further factorial validity assessment of scores on the Quick Discrimination Index (QDI). *Educational and Psychological Measurement, 59,* 325–335.
	Ponterotto, J. G., Potere, J. C., & Johansen, S. A. (2002). The Quick Discrimination Index: Normative data and user guidelines for counseling researchers. *Journal of Multicultural Counseling and Development, 30,* 192–206.
Language Versions	English
Contact	Joseph G. Ponterotto Graduate School of Education Fordham University Division of Psychological and Educational Services 113 West 60th Street, RM 1016D New York, NY 10023

7.10 PERCEPTIONS OF DISCRIMINATION

7.10.1 Name of the Measure	Intragroup Marginalization Inventory IMI
Primary Reference	Castillo, L. G., Conoley, C. W., Brossart, D. F., & Quiros, A. E. (2007). Construction and validation of the Intragroup Marginalization Inventory. *Cultural Diversity and Ethnic Minority Psychology, 13*, 232–240.
Purpose	The IMI is designed to measure an individual's awareness of interpersonal distancing between self and family, friends, and own-ethnic group community.
Description	The IMI is a 42-item Likert-type self-report inventory grounded in social identity theory. Each of these items is rated on a 6-point Likert-type scale with the following anchors: 1 = Strongly Disagree to 6 = Strongly Agree. The IMI is composed of 3 scales: (1) Family Scale (four factors); (2) Friends Scale (five factors); and (3) Ethnic Group Scale (four factors). The instrument was developed through several steps. An initial pool of 14 items was created based on a review of research literature regarding acculturation and the personal experiences of the research team members. These items were then reviewed by a panel of six experts, who suggested the addition of 22 more items and edited 14. A focus group of 31 undergraduate students then reviewed the items for their clarity and appropriateness. Based on their feedback, two items were removed. This resulted in a 34-item measure. Two additional faculty members then reviewed the document for grammatical errors and clarity. Three exploratory factor analyses with promax rotation were conducted to estimate the number of factors in each predetermined scale (i.e., family, friends, own ethnic group). The authors reported that the selection of items was based on (a) items correlating high on only one factor; (b) items being logically related to other items on the same factor; and (c) each factor having at least three items. The authors, however, did not define what constituted a structure coefficient. On more than half of the items that appear to have to been retained, structure coefficients above .40 were observed on more than one factor. Confirmatory factor analytic strategies were employed to provide further evidence of construct validity. Using AMOS 5.0 (Arbuckle, 2003), the authors found that their data fit their hypothesized model well.
Samples	A sample of 386 racial/ethnic minority college students was recruited through introductory psychology courses and through Web-based technology. The sample was composed of 224 females and 160 males. The ethnic composition of the sample was as follows: 196 Latino/a American, 85 Asian/Asian American, 75 African American, 9 Native American, and 21 Biracial. The sample ranged in age from 17–49 years ($M = 20.8$; $SD = 4.6$).

Scoring	The IMI is composed of three scales, each with 4 to 5 subscales. The number of items for each subscale is as follows:
	Family Scale: 12 items
	Friend Scale: 17 items
	Ethnic Group Scale: 13 items
	Total IMI: 42 items
	The items on the Ethnic Group Scale require reverse scoring. No other items are reverse worded. Scoring the subscales consists of summing subscale items. Higher scores indicate higher levels of the subscale. No transformations are required.
Reliability	Cronbach's coefficient alpha for the scores on the subscales ranged from .80 to .92:
	Family Scale: Alpha = .82
	Friend Scale: Alpha = .80
	Ethnic Group Scale: Alpha = .82
	Total IMI: Alpha = .92
Validity	Convergent validity of the Family Scale was established through expected positive correlations with the scale and acculturation (Tropp, Erkut, García-Coll, Alarcón, & Vásquez-García, 1999), acculturative stress (Fuertes & Westbrook, 1996), family conflict (Lee, Cho, Kim, & Ngo, 2000), and negative social interactions (Ruehlman & Karoly, 1991). Convergent validity for the Friend Scale was significantly and positively correlated with acculturative stress. Furthermore, no significant correlation between Friend Scale and social desirability (Reynolds, 1982) was found. The Ethnic Group Scale was found to be related to acculturative stress. No significant correlations were found between scores on the Ethnic Group Scale and social desirability.
Related References	
Language Versions	English
Contact	Linda G. Castillo Department of Educational Psychology Texas A & M University College Station, TX 77843–4225 Email: lcastillo@tamu.edu

7.10.2 Name of the Measure	Own-Group Conformity Pressure Scale OGCPS
Primary Reference	Contrada, R. J., Ashmore, R. D., Gary, M. L., Coups, E., Egeth, J. D., Sewell, A., Ewell, K., Goyal, T. M., & Chasse, V. (2001). Measures of ethnicity-related stress: Psychometric properties, ethnic group differences, and associations with well-being. *Journal of Applied Social Psychology, 31,* 1775–1820.
Purpose	The OGCPS is designed to measure an individual's perceptions that members of their own ethnic group do not approve of them or their behavior over the past 3 months.
Description	The OGCPS is a 12-item self-report inventory. Each of these items is rated on a 7-point Likert-type scale with the following anchors: 1 = Not at all Pressured to 7 = Quite a Bit Pressured. The OGCPS is composed of two subscales: (1) Style/Interests and (2) Social Relations. The instrument was developed through the findings of a pilot study involving a sample of college students from diverse backgrounds who described both the prescriptions and proscriptions of being a member of their ethnic group expressed by members of their ethnic group. The factor structure of an initial 16-item measure was then examined. The results of factor analysis with varimax rotation yielded a five-factor solution that was deemed to be unsatisfactory. Items were deleted and data were reanalyzed. This resulted in an interpretable 12-item, two-factor solution.
Samples	A sample of 361 first-year undergraduate college students from a university in the Northeastern portion of the United States was recruited to establish validity and explore the factor structure of the OGCPS. The sample was composed entirely of students fulfilling a requirement for their Introduction to Psychology course. Twenty-eight participants did not indicate their gender or ethnicity and, as a result, were not included in subsequent analyses. Of these 333 participants (91 male; 242 female), 208 were White American, 34 were African American, 31 were Latino/a American, and 60 were Asian American or Pacific Islander. The sample ranged in age from 16 to 29 years ($M = 17.9$).
Scoring	The total number of items for each subscale of the OGCPS is as follows: Style/Interests: 7 items Social Relations: 5 items Total OGCPS: 12 items None of the items are reverse scored. Scoring the subscales consists of summing subscale items and dividing by the number of items of which it is composed. Higher scores indicate higher concerns over conforming to known stereotypes of own ethnic group. No transformations are required.
Reliability	Cronbach's coefficient alpha for the scores of ethnic minorities were as follows: Style/Interests: Alpha = .89 Social Relations: Alpha = .84

	Cronbach's coefficient alpha for the scores of White Americans were as follows: Style/Interests: Alpha = .87 Social Relations: Alpha = .79
Validity	Convergent validity of OGCPS was established through significant relationships, in the expected direction, with measures of generic life stress (Crandall, Preisler, & Aussprung, 1992), global self-esteem (Rosenberg, 1965), negative mood (Usala & Hertzog, 1989), life satisfaction (Diener, Emmons, Larsen, & Griffin, 1985). Known-groups validity also was demonstrated through a significant main ethnic group effect on the OGCPS.
Related References	
Language Versions	English
Contact	Richard J. Contrada Department of Psychology Rutgers University 53 Avenue E Piscataway, NJ 08854–8040 (732) 445–3195 Email: contrada@rci.rutgers.edu

7.10.3 Name of the Measure	Perceived Ethnic Discrimination Questionnaire PEDQ
Primary Reference	Contrada, R. J., Ashmore, R. D., Gary, M. L., Coups, E., Egeth, J. D., Sewell, A., Ewell, K., Goyal, T. M., & Chasse, V. (2001). Measures of ethnicity-related stress: Psychometric properties, ethnic group differences, and associations with well-being. *Journal of Applied Social Psychology, 31*, 1775–1820.
Purpose	The PEDQ is designed to measure individuals' perceptions of seven forms of discrimination over a period of 3 months.
Description	The PEDQ is a 17-item self-report inventory. Each of these items is rated on a 7-point Likert-type scale with the following anchors: 1 = Never to 7 = Very Often.
	The PEDQ is composed of four subscales: (1) Disvaluing Action; (2) Threat and Aggression; (3) Verbal Rejection; (4) Avoidance.
	The instrument was developed through conceptual analysis, journalistic descriptions, qualitative analysis, and the use of a pilot study involving a sample of college students from diverse backgrounds who shared descriptions of their earliest, worst, and most recent experiences of ethnic discrimination.
	The factor structure of an initial 22-item measure was then examined. This resulted in the deletion of 5 items. Specifically, the results of factor analysis with varimax rotation yielded a four-factor solution.
	In a follow-up paper, Brondolo et al. (2005) developed the PEDQ-Community Version (PEDQ-CV) based on the PEDQ for use with community individuals. A brief version of the PEDQ-CV also was reported by Brondolo et al.
Samples	A sample of 361 first-year undergraduate college students from a university in the northeastern portion of the United States was recruited to establish validity and explore the factor structure of the PEDQ. The sample was composed entirely of students fulfilling a requirement for their Introduction to Psychology course. Twenty-eight participants did not indicate their gender or ethnicity and, as a result, were not included subsequent analyses. Of these 333 participants (91 male; 242 female), 208 were White, 34 were Black, 31 were Latino/a, and 60 were Asian American or Pacific Islander. The sample ranged in age from 16 to 29 years (*M* = 17.9).
Scoring	The number of items for each subscale of the PEDQ is as follows:
	Disvaluing Action: 6 items
	Threat and Aggression: 5 items
	Verbal Rejection: 3 items
	Avoidance: 3 items
	Total PEDQ: 17 items
	None of the items are reverse scored. Scoring the subscales consists of summing subscale items and dividing by the number of items of which it is composed. Higher scores indicate higher experience of each form of racism. No transformations are required.

Reliability	Cronbach's coefficient alpha for the subscale scores for ethnic minorities are as follows:
	Disvaluing Action: Alpha = .90
	Threat and Aggression: Alpha = .85
	Verbal Rejection: Alpha = .77
	Avoidance: Alpha = .73
	Cronbach's coefficient alpha for the subscale scores for White Americans are as follows:
	Disvaluing Action: Alpha = .71
	Threat and Aggression: Alpha = .78
	Verbal Rejection: Alpha = .75
	Avoidance: Alpha = .65
Validity	Convergent validity of PEDQ subscales was established through significant relationships, in the expected direction, with measures of generic life stress (Crandall, Preisler, & Aussprung, 1982), global self-esteem (Rosenberg, 1965), negative mood (Usala & Hertzog, 1989), life satisfaction (Diener, Emmons, Larsen, & Griffin, 1985), depressive symptoms (Beck, Ward, Mendelson, Mock, & Erbaugh, 1961), and physical symptoms (Jenkins, Kreger, Rose, & Hurst, 1980).
	Known-groups validity also was demonstrated through a significant main ethnic group effect on each of the scales of the PEDQ.
Related References	Brondolo, E., Kelly, K. P., Coakley, V., Gordon, T., Thompson, S., Levy, E., Cassells, A., Tobin, J. N., Sweeney, M., & Contrada, R. J. (2005). The Perceived Ethnic Discrimination Questionnaire: Development and preliminary validation of a community version. *Journal of Applied Social Psychology, 35,* 335–365.
Language Versions	English
Contact	Richard J. Contrada Department of Psychology Rutgers University 53 Avenue E Piscataway, NJ 08854–8040 (732) 445–3195 Email: contrada@rci.rutgers.edu

7.10.4 Name of the Measure	Perceptions of Racism Scale PRS
Primary Reference	Green, N. L. (1995). Development of the Perceptions of Racism Scale. *Journal of Nursing Scholarship, 27,* 141–146.
Purpose	The PRS is a measure of the cognitive component of attitudes toward women and racial minorities and the affective component of attitudes regarding comfort in interpersonal interactions with racially diverse populations.
Description	The PRS is a 20-item self-report inventory that utilizes a 4-point Likert-type scale (1 = Strongly Disagree, 2 = Disagree, 3 = Agree, 4 = Strongly Agree). The PRS is composed of one total score of perception of racism. Items regarding the perceptions of health and racism were developed through interviews with eight African American women. Contents of these interviews were subjected to domain analysis (Spradley, 1979). Items regarding general perceptions of racism were based on items appearing on the Business Week/Harris Poll (Jackson & Collingswood, 1988). The contents of the scale were reviewed for appropriateness and clarity by a group of six African American nurse-midwives and one teacher. A principal components analysis with varimax rotation yielded one interpretable factor.
Samples	Initial validation of the 20-item measure was established using a sample of 165 African American women. The age of the sample ranged from 18–39 (*M* = 24.4 years; *SD* = 5.24). The women completed between 8–18 years of education (*M* = 13.55; *SD* = 1.78).
Scoring	The PRS is composed of 20 items. Nine of the items require reverse scoring. Scoring the PRS consists of summing the items. Higher scores indicate more perceptions of racism. No transformations are required.
Reliability	Cronbach's coefficient alpha for full scale score was .91.
Validity	Concurrent validity was established through a significant relationship with a measure of stress.
Related References	
Language Versions	English
Contact	The PRS is presented in Green (1995).

7.10.5 Name of the Measure	Experience of Discrimination EOD
Primary Reference	Krieger, N., Smith, K., Naishadham, D., Hartman, C., & Barbeau, E. M. (2005). Experiences of discrimination: Validity and reliability of a self-report measure for population health research on racism and health. *Social Science & Medicine, 61,* 1576–1596.
Purpose	The EOD is a measure of self-reported exposure to racial discrimination.
Description	The EOD is an 11-item self-report inventory. The measure uses several response formats. *Experience of Discrimination* is scored by counting the number of situations in which a participant reported having experienced racial discrimination. *Frequency* is measured through participant self-report of number of occurrences of an event (i.e., 0 = "never," 1 = "once," 2.5 = "2–3 times," and 5 = "4 or more times." *Response to unfair treatment* items were scored based on one of the two following response choices: "Accept It as a Fact of Life" or "Try to Do Something About It"; "Talk to Other People About It" or "Keep It to Yourself."
	The EOD is composed of items assessing for (1) Discrimination Situation, (2) Frequency of Occurrence, and (3) Response to Unfair Treatment.
	The EOD questionnaire is based on closed-format questions previously developed by Krieger (1990). Results of structural equation modeling indicated excellent fit of the data to the hypothesized model.
Samples	The sample was composed of 616 participants, who ranged in age from 25–64 years. The authors reported the gender composition of ethnic groups separately. The racial and ethnic composition of the sample was 208 White Americans (57.2% women), 249 Latino/a Americans (44.9% women), 159 African Americans (40% women).
Scoring	The number of items for each subscale are as follows:
	Response to Unfair Treatment: 2 items
	Experiences of Discrimination: 9 items
	Frequency of Discrimination: Dependent on number of affirmative responses to Experiences of Discrimination items.
	No reverse scoring is required. Responses to Unfair Treatment scores are based on the combination of the response types provided by the participant. Specifically, a score of "2" or "Engaged" is given to individuals who responded with "Try to Do Something About It"/"Talk to Others"; a score of "1" or "Moderate" is given to participants who responded with either "Try to Do Something About It"/"Keep to Self" or "Accept It as a Fact of Life"/"Talk to Other People About It"; a score of "0" or "Passive" is given to participants who "Accept It as a Fact of Life"/"Keep it to Yourself."

(Continued)

(Continued)

	Situation score is derived by summing the number of situations in which a participant reported experiencing racial discrimination.
	Frequency score is obtained by summing across the number of items.
Reliability	Cronbach's coefficient alpha were as follows:
	Response to Unfair Treatment: Alpha = .56
	EOD Situation: Alpha = .81
	EOD Frequency: Alpha = .86
	Test-retest reliability coefficients for African American and Latino/a American participants was reported to be .69 or higher.
Validity	Suggesting criterion validity, EOD was statistically significantly associated with psychological distress such that higher levels of EOD were related to poorer psychological health. EOD also tended to be associated with cigarette smoking.
	Suggesting discriminant validity, EOD was not statistically significantly related to social desirability.
Related References	
Language Versions	English and Spanish
Contact	The measure can be found in Krieger et al. (2005).

7.10.6 Name of the Measure	Schedule of Racist Events SRE
Primary Reference	Landrine, H., & Klonoff, E. A. (1996). The Schedule of Racist Events: A measure of racial discrimination and a study of its negative physical and mental health consequences. *Journal of Black Psychology, 22,* 144–168.
Purpose	The SRE is designed to measure the frequency of perceived race-based discrimination experienced by African Americans.
Description	The SRE is an 18-item self-report inventory. The first 17 items assess the frequency of specific occurrences of race-based discrimination encountered by African Americans. Respondents answer these questions with respect to frequency of experiences during the past year and entire life, respectively. Each of these items is rated on a 6-point Likert-type scale with the following anchors: 1 = Never Happened; 2 = Once in a While (less than 10% of the time); 3 = Sometimes (10–25% of the time); 4 = A Lot (26–49% of the time); 5 = Most of the Time (50–70% of the time); and 6 = Almost all of the Time (more than 70% of the time). Respondents also are asked to report how stressful they perceived the event to be on a scale (1 = Not at all to 6 = Extremely). The final question of the SRE measures how different a respondent perceives his or her life to be now had it not been for race-based discrimination experiences during the past year and entire life, respectively. The SRE is composed of three subscales: (1) Recent Racist Events; (2) Lifetime Racist Events; and (3) Appraised Racist Events. The authors developed items on their measure based upon a review of the literature on racism and grounded their scale on stress and coping theory. The scale was modeled after the PERI-Life Events Scale (Dohrenwend, Krasnoff, Askenasy, & Dohrenwend, 1978), the Hassles Frequency Scale (Kanner, Coyne, Schaeffer, & Lazarus, 1981), and the Perceived Stress Scale (Cohen, Kamarck, & Mermelstein, 1983). Klonoff and Landrine (1999) also conducted a factor analysis, using principal components analysis with orthogonal rotation, on each of the three subscales of the SRE. Analysis of eigenvalues and scree plot indicated that items correlated with their respective subscales strongly. The measure has been adapted for use with other groups. For example, Moradi and Hasan (2004) adapted the measure for use in a study involving Arab Americans. In their study, the word "Black" was replaced with "Arab."
Samples	Initial validation of the 18-item measure was established using a sample composed of 153 African American participants who ranged in age from 15 to 70 years of age (M = 30.14, SD = 11.66). The participants were recruited at a meeting of University's Black Student Union and as a meeting of the Black Faculty and Staff Organization. Eighty-three of the participants were women, 66 are men, with four choosing not to disclose their gender. Educational levels were as follows: 22.8% held a high school diploma, 44.3% were college students, 25.5% had college degrees, and 7.4% held master's or doctorate degrees.

(Continued)

(Continued)

	Follow-up validation studies involved 520 African Americans (277 women, 243 men) who ranged in age from 18 to 79 years ($M = 28.2$ years, $SD = 10.01$). Their educational levels were as follows: 11.5% had not completed high school; 28.2% graduated high school; 47.3% had some college classes; 12.5% had earned a college degree or higher. Participants were recruited through in-person contact in four randomly selected middle and working class census tracts in San Bernardino County, California.
Scoring	The number of items for each subscale of the SRE is as follows: Recent Racist Events: 18 items Lifetime Racist Events: 18 items Appraised Racist Events: 17 items Items do not need to be reverse scored. Scoring the subscales consists of summing subscale items. Higher scores on the first two subscales indicate more frequent experiences with racism in the recent past and during one's lifetime. Higher scores on the remaining subscale, Appraised Racist Events, indicate higher levels of stress appraised to the event.
Reliability	Cronbach's alpha for the subscale scores ranged from .94 to .95. Recent Racist Events: Alpha = .95 Lifetime Racist Events: Alpha = .95 Appraised Racist Events: Alpha = .94 Split-half reliability for the subscales ranged from .91 to .93. Recent Racist Events: $r = .93$ Lifetime Racist Events: $r = .91$ Appraised Racist Events: $r = .92$ Test-Retest reliability for the subscales ranged from .95 to .96.
Validity	Concurrent validity was established through significant relationships with symptoms of psychological distress. Specifically, each of the three subscales was found to be significantly correlated with symptoms associated with obsessive-compulsive disorder, interpersonal sensitivity, depression, anxiety, and somatization. Multivariate analysis of variance also indicated a significant effect of recent racist events, lifetime racist events, and appraised racist events on smoking behavior. Smokers were found to report having experienced significantly more racist events and appraised these events as more stressful than did non-smokers. Cluster analysis also indicated traditional African Americans, as measured by the African American Acculturation Scale (Landrine & Klonoff, 1994), reported significantly more experiences with racist events in their recent past and lifetime than did more acculturated African Americans. Traditional African Americans also appraised events of racial discrimination as more stressful than acculturated African Americans.

	Klonoff and Landrine (1999) presented further validation of concurrent validity. They found significant positive correlations between SRE subscales and the total score on the Hopkins Symptom Checklist–59 (Derogatis et al., 1974).
Related References	Fischer, A. R., & Shaw, C. M. (1999). African Americans' mental health and perceptions of racist discrimination: The moderating effects of racial socialization experiences and self-esteem. *Journal of Counseling Psychology, 46,* 395–407. Klonoff, E. A., & Landrine, E. (1999). Cross-validation of the Schedule of Racist Events. *Journal of Black Psychology, 25,* 231–254. Moradi, B., & Hasan, N. T. (2004). Arab American persons' reported experiences of discrimination and mental health: The mediating role of personal control. *Journal of Counseling Psychology, 51,* 418–428.
Language Versions	English
Contact	Hope Landrine American Cancer Society 250 Williams Street Atlanta, GA 30303 (404) 329–4425 Email: Hope.Landrine@cancer.org

7.10.7 Name of the Measure	General Ethnic Discrimination Scale GEDS
Primary Reference	Landrine, H., Klonoff, E. A., Corral, I., Fernandez, S., & Roesch, S. (2006). Conceptualizing and measuring ethnic discrimination in health research. *Journal of Behavioral Medicine, 29,* 79–94.
Purpose	The GEDS is an instrument intended to measure perceived ethnic discrimination experienced among a general group of racial or ethnic minorities.
Description	The GEDS is an 18-item self-report inventory. On the first 17 items, respondents rate the frequency of perceived racist events during the past year and entire life, respectively. Recent and life events of racism are rated on a 6-point Likert-type scale: 1 = Never; 2 = Once in a While; 3 = Sometimes; 4 = A Lot; 5 = Most of the Time; and 6 = Almost All the Time. Respondents also indicate their appraisal of stress on a 6-point scale with 1 = Not at All Stressful to 6 = Extremely Stressful. The last item measures how different one perceives his or her life to be had he or she not been treated in a racist manner. Respondents indicate their response for Recent Racist Events and Lifetime Racist Events on a 6-point Likert-type scale with the following anchors: 1 = The same as it is now; 2 = A little different; 3 = Different in a few ways; 4 = Different in a lot of ways; 5 = Different in most ways; and 6 = Totally different.
	A maximum likelihood estimation procedure in EQS was used to estimate the goodness of fit of their data to their model. Results indicated good fit of their data to the model.
	Confirmatory factor analysis was used to test whether the factor structure of the GED was similar to the SRE, the measure upon which it is based. The structure coefficients of each subscale ranged from .77 to 1.0 for four of the groups (African American, Asian American, White American, Latino/a American). Confirmatory factor analysis also indicated that the structure coefficients of each subscale were equally strong and significant for community and college-student samples.
	The GEDS is composed of three unidimensional subscales: (1) Recent Discrimination; (2) Lifetime Discrimination; (3) Appraised Discrimination.
	Landrine, Klonoff, Corral, Fernandez, and Roesch (2006) indicated that the GEDS is modeled on the Schedule of Racist Events (SRE; Landrine & Klonoff, 1996). The SRE was chosen as a model because of its theoretical grounding in the stress-coping literature. The GEDS is a slightly modified version of the SRE that can be employed with diverse groups of ethnic minorities.
Samples	Initial validation of the 18-item measure was established using a sample of 1,569 adults who ranged in age from 18 to 86 years (*M* = 30.24, *SD* = 11.66). The sample was composed of 1,133 women (72.2%). The remaining participants are men. The sample included undergraduate and graduate students (55.3%) who were in classrooms, libraries, or student union buildings and community adults (44.7%) who were recruited while shopping, waiting for a bus, or at a bank.
	The racial and ethnic composition of the sample was 49.7% White American, 25.9% Latino/a American, 11.1% African American, 6% Asian American, and 6.1% "Other."

Scoring	There are a total of 18 items on the measure. Each of the first 17 items requires a response for Recent, Lifetime, and Appraised Discrimination. The remaining item requires only a response for Recent and Lifetime Discrimination.
	Recent Discrimination: 18 items
	Lifetime Discrimination: 18 items
	Appraised Discrimination: 17 items
	None of the items are negatively worded. Scoring the GEDS consists of summing subscale items. Higher scores on the Recent Discrimination and Lifetime Discrimination subscales indicate more frequent encounters with discrimination in the past 12 months and lifetime, respectively. Higher scores on the Appraised Discrimination subscale indicate greater levels of stress associated with those events. No transformations are required.
Reliability	Cronbach's alpha for the scores on the subscales were as follows:
	Recent Discrimination: Alpha = .94
	Lifetime Discrimination: Alpha = .94
	Appraised Discrimination: Alpha = .94
	Split-half reliability coefficients for the subscales were as follows:
	Recent Discrimination: $r = .91$
	Lifetime Discrimination: $r = .91$
	Appraised Discrimination: $r = .91$
Validity	Concurrent validity was established through the use of this procedure, which indicated the latent construct of perceived discrimination was related to the latent construct of psychiatric symptoms (Hopkins Symptoms Checklist–58; Derogatis, Lipman, Rickles, Uhlenhuth, & Covi, 1974) in the expected direction.
	Multiple group analysis indicated that data fit the model well across different racial groups.
	Concurrent validity also was established through three stepwise logistic regression analyses. Results indicated that individuals experiencing moderate and high levels of lifetime discrimination were more likely to smoke than those who experienced lower levels of lifetime discrimination. Results of these analyses did not indicate similar patterns for recent events or appraised events.
Related References	Hwang, W., & Goto, S. (2008). The impact of perceived racial discrimination on the mental health of Asian American college students. *Cultural Diversity and Ethnic Minority Psychology, 14,* 326–335.
Language Versions	English
Contact	Hope Landrine American Cancer Society 250 Williams Street Atlanta, GA 30303 (404) 329–4425 Email: Hope.Landrine@cancer.org

7.10.8 Name of the Measure	Scale of Ethnic Experience SEE
Primary Reference	Malcarne, V. L., Chavira, D. A., Fernandez, S., & Liu, P.-J. (2006). The Scale of Ethnic Experience: Development and psychometric properties. *Journal of Personality Assessment, 86*(2), 150–161.
Purpose	The SEE is designed to measure multiple aspects of ethnicity-related cognitive constructs across diverse ethnic groups.
Description	The SEE is a 32-item self-report inventory. These items are rated on a 5-point Likert-type scale with the following anchors: 1 = Strongly Disagree and 5 = Strongly Agree. The SEE is composed of four factors: (1) Ethnic Identity, (2) Perceived Discrimination, (3) Mainstream Comfort, and (4) Social Affiliation. Two focus groups, composed of diverse undergraduate and graduate students, were conducted. Approximately 100 items were developed from the contents of the focus groups, a review of literature, and expert consultation. Focus group members then reviewed the items for content clarity, relevance, and wording. As a result of this process, 73 items were included in the pilot version of the measure. The 73-item version was administered to two separate groups of undergraduate psychology students from San Diego State University. Data from the first sample were submitted to a principal components analysis (PCA) using promax rotation. Items with structure coefficients greater than or equal to .45 that did not correlate with any other factor at .45 or above were retained. Fifty-seven items were retained through this process. A PCA with promax rotation for the total second sample, as well as by ethnic group, was then performed. Items were retained if their structure coefficient, across the total sample and the ethnic specific samples was equal to or greater than .40 and did not correlate with any other factor at .30 or above. Twenty-five items were dropped as a result of this process. This resulted in a final 32-item, four-factor SEE. Confirmatory factor analysis, which was then performed on a separate sample, indicated that data fit the model well.
Samples	Four samples of undergraduate psychology students participated in three studies of the psychometric properties of the SEE. The first sample (N_1 = 638; 60% women) was composed of African Americans (13%), White Americans (44%), Filipino/a Americans (15%), and Mexican Americans (28%). The mean age was 20.12 years (SD = 4.35). A second sample was (N_2 = 1,727; 66% women) with a mean age of 18.73 years (SD = 2.38). This sample was composed of African Americans (12%), White Americans (52%), Filipino/a Americans (14%), and Mexican Americans (22%). A third sample (N_3 = 228) was used to assess the temporal stability of the SEE. The gender composition of the sample was not reported. With respect to ethnic background, the sample was composed of African Americans (12%), White Americans (24%), Filipino/a Americans (36%), and Mexican Americans (28%). In the final sample (N_4 = 940; 72% women), the mean age was 18.68 (SD = 1.09). This sample was composed of African Americans (8.7%), White Americans (46.9%), Filipino/a Americans (18.0%), and Mexican Americans (25.4%).

Scoring	The number of items for each subscale is as follows:
	
	    Ethnic Identity: 12 items
	
	    Perceived Discrimination: 9 items
	
	    Mainstream Comfort: 6 items
	
	    Social Affiliation: 5 items
	
	    Total SEE: 32 items
	
	Twelve items require reverse scoring. Scoring the SEE consists of summing the scores of items on each subscale and dividing by the number of items for the corresponding subscale. Higher scores indicate higher levels of ethnic identity, perceptions of discrimination, comfort with the dominant culture, and comfort with members of one's own group. No transformations are required.

Reliability	Cronbach's alpha for the subscale scores ranged across several studies. They were as follows:
	
	    Ethnic Identity: Alpha = .81 to .91
	
	    Perceived Discrimination: Alpha = .76 to .91
	
	    Mainstream Comfort: Alpha = .76 to .87
	
	    Social Affiliation: Alpha = .81 to .84
	
	Six-Week Test-retest reliability coefficients were as follows:
	
	    Ethnic Identity: $r = .86$
	
	    Perceived Discrimination: $r = .82$
	
	    Mainstream Comfort: $r = .81$
	
	    Social Affiliation: $r = .77$

Validity	Evidence for concurrent validity was demonstrated through statistically significant relationships between the ethnic identity, mainstream comfort, and/or social affiliation subscales of the SEE with ethnic identity and other group orientation (Phinney, 1992) and scores on acculturation measures for African Americans (Klonoff & Landrine, 2000), Mexican Americans (Cuellar et al., 1980), and Filipino/a Americans (Suinn et al., 1987).
Related References	
Language Versions	English
Contact	Vanessa L. Malcarne Department of Psychology College of Sciences San Diego State University 6363 Alvarado Court, Suite 103 San Diego, CA 92120–4913 Phone: (619) 594–6495 Fax: (619) 594–6780 Email: malcarne@psychology.sdsu.edu

7.10.9 Name of the Measure	Perceived Racism Scale PRS
Primary Reference	McNeilly, M. D., Anderson, N. B., Armstead, C. A., Clark, R., Corbett, M., Robinson, E. L., Pieper, C. F., & Lepisto, E. M. (1996). The Perceived Racism Scale: A multidimensional assessment of the experience of White racism among African Americans. *Ethnicity & Disease, 6,* 154–166.
Purpose	The PRS is designed to measure both the frequency of perceived experiences of multiple forms of racism among African Americans as well as their emotional and behavioral coping responses used in those events.
Description	The PRS is a 51-item self-report inventory with multiple response formats. On the first 43 items, respondents report their own perceived exposure to racist events and statements during the past year and during their lifetime. These items are rated on a 5-point Likert-type scale (0 = Not Applicable, 1 = Almost Never, 2 = Several Times a Year, 3 = Several Times a Month, 4 = Several Times a Week, and 5 = Several Times a Day). Respondents utilize a 5-point Likert-type scale (0 = Not at All, 3 = Moderately, 5 = Extremely) to indicate how they feel (i.e., Angry, Hurt, Frustrated, Sad, Powerless, Hopeless, Ashamed, Strengthened) during an encounter with a racist event in four different domains (i.e., On the Job, Academic Settings, Public Realm, Racism Statements). Respondents also are instructed to mark behaviors they engage in in response to racist events or statements. An affirmative response, indicated by a checkmark, is coded as "1" while a "0" indicates a no response. The PRS is composed of five factors for frequency: (1) On the Job; (2) In Academic Settings; (3) Overt Racism in Public Settings; (4) Subtle Racism in Public Settings; (5) Exposure to Racist Statements; and nine factors of emotional and behavioral coping responses: (1) Anger/Frustration; (2) Depressed Affect; (3) Feeling Strengthened; (4) Working Harder/Trying to Change Things; (5) Avoiding/Ignoring; (6) Praying; (7) Forgetting It; (8) Getting Violent; and (9) Speaking Up. The items making up the measure were constructed based on instructions made up of 190 college students and community members to list the types of personal experiences of racism they encountered as well as their feelings and coping responses. These responses were content analyzed into four domains (on the job, in academic settings, in the public realm, and exposure to racist statements). Items showing the highest frequency were included in the measure. Twenty African American individuals, selected for a pilot study of the measure, provided feedback for content, wording, response format, and instructions. Principal component, analyses with both oblique and orthogonal rotations were performed on a sample of college students and individuals from the community. The scale was divided into two portions based on question type (frequency; emotional and coping responses). The result of principal components analysis using oblique rotation reportedly was nearly identical to one using an orthogonal rotation. These analyses yielded five factors for items addressing frequency and nine factors concerning emotional coping responses.

Samples	The factor structure of the 51-item measure was established using a sample of 273 participants (67 males, 123 females) across two studies from the university and the community. The range of ages for the two samples of university students and the community was 18 to 35 years ($M = 21.2$; $SD = 2.9$), 18 to 38 years ($M = 21.6$; $SD = 4.17$), and 18 to 39 years ($M = 21.6$; $SD = 4.17$), respectively. With respect to gender, 75 were male and 198 were female. Data from 67 participants were not included in the final sample.

Scoring	The number of items for each subscale is as follows:
	
	Factors for Frequency of Exposure to Racism
	    Racism on the Job: 9 items
	    Racism in Academic Settings: 9 items
	    (overt) Racism in Public Settings: 9 items
	    (subtle) Racism in Public Settings: 4 items
	    Racist Statements: 7 items
	
	Factors for Emotional Responses
	    Anger/Frustration: 8 items
	    Depressed Affect: 16 items
	    Feeling Strengthened: 4 items
	
	Factors for Behavioral Coping Responses
	    Working Harder/Trying to Change Things: 8 items
	    Avoiding/Ignoring: 7 items
	    Praying: 4 items
	    Forgetting It: 4 items
	    Getting Violent: 3 items
	    Speaking Up: 4 items
	
	Scoring the PRS consists of summing subscale items. Higher scores indicate more frequent exposure to racism and more experiences of specific emotional responses or behavioral coping strategies. No transformations are required.

Reliability	Cronbach's alpha for the subscale scores ranged from .64 to .95.
	
	Factors for Frequency of Exposure to
	    Racism on the Job: Alpha = .91
	    Racism in Academic Settings: Alpha = .93
	    (overt) Racism in Public Settings: Alpha = .84
	    (subtle) Racism in Public Settings: Alpha = .84
	    Racist Statements: Alpha = .89
	    Total Frequency of Exposure: Alpha = .96

(Continued)

	Factors for Emotional and Behavioral Coping Responses
	Anger/Frustration: Alpha = .95
	Depressed Affect: Alpha = .90
	Feeling Strengthened: Alpha = .85
	Working Harder/Trying to Change Things: Alpha = .82
	Avoiding/Ignoring: Alpha = .79
	Praying: Alpha = .91
	Forgetting It: Alpha = .77
	Getting Violent: Alpha = .64
	Speaking Up: Alpha = .70
	Total Emotional and Coping Responses: Alpha = .94
	Test-retest coefficients ranged from .50–.80.
Validity	
Related References	Moody-Ayers, S. Y., Stewart, A. L., Covinsky, K. E., & Inouye, S. K. (2005). Prevalence and correlates of perceived societal racism in older African-American adults with Type 2 diabetes mellitus. *Journal of the American Geriatrics Society, 53*, 2202–2208.
Language Versions	English
Contact	Maya D. McNeilly Box 3003 Duke University Medical Center Durham, NC 27710

7.11 PSYCHOLOGICAL RESPONSES TO RACISM

7.11.1 Name of the Measure	Hispanic Stress Inventory HIS
Primary Reference	Cervantes, R. C., Padilla, A., & de Snyder, N. S. (1991). The Hispanic Stress Inventory: A culturally relevant approach to psychological assessment. *Psychological Assessment, 3,* 438–447.
Purpose	The HSI is designed as a measure of the occurrence and cognitive appraisal of psychosocial stress experienced by immigrant or U.S.-born Latino/a Americans.
Description	The HSI-Immigrant version is a 73-item self-report inventory. Each of these items is rated on a 5-point Likert-type scale: 1 = Not at all Stressful, 2 = Somewhat Stressful, 3 = Moderately Stressful, 4 = Very Stressful, 5 = Extremely Stressful. The HSI-Immigrant version is composed of 5 subscales: (1) Occupational/Economic Stress, (2) Parental Stress, (3) Marital Stress, (4) Immigration Stress, and (5) Cultural/Family Conflict. The HSI-U.S. Born version is a 59-item self-report inventory. Each of these items is rated on a 5-point scale with the following anchors 1 = Not at all Stressful, 2 = Somewhat Stressful, 3 = Moderately Stressful, 4 = Very Stressful, 5 = Extremely Stressful. The HSI-U.S. Born version is composed of 4 subscales: (1) Occupational/Economic Stress, (2) Parental Stress, (3) Marital Stress, and (4) Cultural/Family Conflict. Items of HSI were developed based on the contents of semistructured interviews with a sample of 105 Latino/a American individuals who could trace their family history to Mexico or countries in Central America. Interview questions were designed to elicit responses regarding stress in five domains (marital stress, family stress, occupational stress, discrimination stress, and acculturation stress). Based upon the contents of the responses, 176 statements reflecting acute and chronic stress experiences of U.S.-born and immigrant Latino/a Americans were composed. Five Latino/a American judges familiar with Latino/a American mental health issues then were instructed to categorize these statements into one of six categories. These judges also provided feedback regarding the appropriateness and clarity of wording in the items. This resulted in 133 items. Items were then subjected to back translation procedures (Brislin, 1986). Additional procedures for item refinement were engaged for U.S. Born and Immigrant Latino/a American samples separately. For example, items not yielding a mean score more than 2.0 or reported by less than 5% of the entire subsample were eliminated. Factor analysis with oblique rotation was then conducted on data from immigrant Latino/a Americans and U.S.-born Latino/a Americans separately. Based on eigenvalues greater than 1.0 and scree-test procedures, these factor analyses yielded a final five-factor solution for the immigrant Latino/a American sample and a four-factor solution

(Continued)

(Continued)

	for the U.S.-born sample. Items were retained if their structure coefficients was greater than .30. These procedures resulted in a 73-item measure for immigrant Latino/a Americans and a 59-item measure for U.S.-born Latino/a Americans. The measure has been adapted for use to assess social stressors experienced specifically by Latina American women (Goodkind, Gonzales, Malcoe, & Espinosa, 2008). A shortened version for use with immigrants has been developed (Cavazos-Rehg, Zayas, Walker, & Fisher, 2006).
Samples	This measure was developed based on studies involving samples of Latino/a American immigrants ($n = 305$; 58.0% male, 42% female) and U.S.-born Latino/a Americans ($n = 188$; 41.5% male, 58.5% female). The mean age of the immigrant group and U.S.-born group was 24.3 years and 21.6 years, respectively. The participants were recruited from adult community schools or a community college located in the Los Angeles metropolitan area.

Scoring	The number of items for each subscale of each version of the HSI are as follows:
	
	Immigrant Version
	    Occupational/Economic Stress: 13 items
	    Parental Stress: 13 items
	    Marital Stress: 16 items
	    Immigration Stress: 18 items
	    Cultural/Family Conflict: 13 items
	    HSI-Immigrant: 73 items
	
	U.S.-Born Version
	    Occupational/Economic Stress: 14 items
	    Parental Stress: 9 items
	    Marital Stress: 14 items
	    Cultural/Family Conflict: 22 items
	    HIS-U.S. Born: 59 items
	
	None of the items are reverse scored. Scoring the subscales consists of summing items on the subscale. No transformations are required.

Reliability	The Cronbach alpha coefficients have been reported for the scores on the immigrant and U.S. born versions. They were as follows:
	
	Immigrant Version
	    Occupational/Economic Stress: Alpha = .91
	    Parental Stress: Alpha = .88
	    Marital Stress: Alpha = .86
	    Immigration Stress: Alpha = .85
	    Cultural/Family Conflict: Alpha = .77

	Two-Week Test-Retest reliability coefficients were as follows:
	
	    Occupational/Economic Stress: $r = .79$
	
	    Parental Stress: $r = .73$
	
	    Marital Stress: $r = .61$
	
	    Immigration Stress: $r = .80$
	
	    Cultural/Family Conflict: $r = .86$
	
	U.S. Born Version
	
	    Occupational/Economic Stress: Alpha = .90
	
	    Parental Stress: Alpha = .88
	
	    Marital Stress: Alpha = .85
	
	    Cultural/Family Conflict: Alpha = .85

Validity	Criterion-related validity was established through significant correlations between the subscales of the HSI immigrant version and measures of self-esteem (Rosenberg, 1965) as well as depression, anxiety, somatization (Derogatis, 1977). Other evidence for criterion-related validity was established through the authors' failure to find an interpretable factor structure of the HSI with data from a sample of 141 White American participants.
Related References	Cavazos-Rehg, P. A., Zayas, L. H., Walker, M. S., & Fisher, E. B. (2006). Evaluating an abbreviated version of the Hispanic Stress Inventory for Immigrants. *Hispanic Journal of Behavioral Sciences, 28,* 498–515. Goodkind, J. R., Gonzales, M., Malcoe, L. H., & Espinosa, J. (2008). The Hispanic Women's Social Stressor Scale: Understanding the multiple social stressors of U.S.- and Mexico-born Hispanic women. *Hispanic Journal of Behavioral Sciences, 30,* 200–229.
Language Versions	English and Spanish
Contact	Richard C. Cervantes Behavioral Assessment, Inc. 291 South La Cienega Blvd, Suite 305 Beverly Hills, CA 90211 (310) 652–6449 Email: cervantes@bai-eval.com

7.11.2 Name of the Measure	Stereotype Confirmation Concern Scale SCCS
Primary Reference	Contrada, R. J., Ashmore, R. D., Gary, M. L., Coups, E., Egeth, J. D., Sewell, A., Ewell, K., Goyal, T. M., & Chasse, V. (2001). Measures of ethnicity-related stress: Psychometric properties, ethnic group differences, and associations with well-being. *Journal of Applied Social Psychology, 31,* 1775–1820.
Purpose	The SCCS is designed to measure individuals' experience of having concern over confirming stereotypes during the past three months.
Description	The SCCS is an 11-item Likert-type self-report inventory. Each of these items is rated on a 7-point Likert-type scale with the following anchors: 1 = Never to 7 = Always. The SCCS is composed of one total scale score. The instrument was developed through a review of the research literature on stereotypes and stereotype threat and the use of a pilot study involving a sample of college students from diverse backgrounds who shared description of their concerns over conforming to a stereotype of their ethnic group. The factor structure of an initial 11-item measure was then examined. The results of factor analysis with varimax rotation yielded a two-factor solution that lacked conceptual clarity. Examination of the scree plot indicated one single interpretable factor.
Samples	A sample of 361 first-year undergraduate college students from a university in the Northeastern portion of the United States was recruited to establish validity and explore the factor structure of the SCCS. The sample was composed entirely of students fulfilling a requirement for their Introduction to Psychology course. Twenty-eight participants did not indicate their gender or ethnicity and, as a result, were not included subsequent analyses. Of these 333 participants (91 male; 242 female), 208 were White American, 34 were African Americans, 31 were Latino/a American, and 60 were Asian American or Pacific Islander. The sample ranged in age from 16 to 29 years (*M* = 17.9).
Scoring	There are 11 items in the SCCS. None of the items are reverse scored. Scoring the scale consists of summing the scale items and dividing by the number of items of which it is composed. Higher scores indicate higher concerns over conforming to known stereotypes of own ethnic group. No transformations are required. The Mean scores for SCCS for African Americans, Latino/a Americans, Asian Americans, and White Americans, respectively, were as follows: 2.34, 1.81, .207, and 1.48.

Reliability	Cronbach's alpha for the total SCCS scale score for ethnic minorities was .91.
	Cronbach's alpha for the SCCS scale score for White Americans was .89.
Validity	Convergent validity of SCCS was established through significant relationships, in the expected direction, with measures of generic life stress (Crandall, Preisler, & Aussprung, 1982), global self-esteem (Rosenberg, 1965), negative mood (Usala & Hertzog, 1989), life satisfaction (Diener, Emmons, Larsen, & Griffin, 1985).
	Known-groups validity also was demonstrated through a significant main ethnic group effect on the SCCS.
Related References	
Language Versions	English
Contact	Richard J. Contrada
	Department of Psychology
	Rutgers University
	53 Avenue E
	Piscataway, NJ 08854–8040
	(732) 445–3195
	Email: contrada@rci.rutgers.edu

7.11.3 Name of the Measure	Colonial Mentality Scale CMS
Primary Reference	David, E. J. R., & Okazki, S. (2006). The Colonial Mentality Scale (CMS) for Filipino Americans: Scale construction and psychological implications. *Journal of Counseling Psychology, 53,* 241–252.
Purpose	The CMS is designed to be a measure of internalized oppression among Filipino/a Americans.
Description	The CMS is a 36-item self-report inventory. Each of these items is rated on a 6-point Likert-type scale with the following anchors: 1 = Strongly Disagree to 6 = Strongly Agree.
	The CMS is composed of 5 subscales: (1) Within-Group Discrimination; (2) Physical Characteristics; (3) Colonial Debt; (4) Cultural Shame and Embarrassment; and (5) Internalized Cultural/Ethnic Inferiority.
	The principal author developed an initial 53-item instrument to measure colonial mentality based on a review of the literature on internalized oppression of Filipino/a Americans. A research assistant reviewed these items and provided feedback regarding the measure's clarity and readability.
	An exploratory factor analysis (EFA) with direct oblimin rotation was conducted on data from 292 cases. The EFA resulted in 13 factors with eigenvalues greater than 1.00. Examination of scree plot indicated a six-factor solution. A one-, two-, three-, four-, five-, and six- factor solution were forced to indicate the best factor structure for the measure. The authors chose a five-factor solution because it produced the least amount of cross-correlated items and was consistent with theory. This resulted in a 36-item CMS.
	Confirmatory factor analysis was performed using AMOS 5.0 (Arbuckle, 2003). The five-factor solution proved to fit their data best. Organization of the five factors into three types of colonial mentality also was supported.
Samples	The factor structure of the CMS was explored, confirmed, and validated based on data collected from one large national sample of Filipino/a Americans (N = 603) recruited through the use of email snowball sampling. This sample was split into two smaller samples of 292 and 311 Filipino/a Americans for exploratory and confirmatory analyses, respectively.
	The sample was composed of 397 women and 206 men. The sample ranged in age from 18 to 72 years (M = 28.90; SD = 10.43). With respect to generational status, 371 reported being second generation, 220 first generation, 6 third generation, and 1 fourth generation. Thirty-eight percent of the sample held college degrees.
Scoring	The number of items for each of the subscales of the CMS are as follows:
	Within-Group Discrimination: 11 items
	Physical Characteristics: 8 items
	Colonial Debt: 7 items
	Cultural Shame and Embarrassment: 5 items
	Internalized Cultural/Ethnic Inferiority: 5 items
	Total CMS: 36 items

	The authors also argue that the subscales can be categorized into three general types of manifestations of colonial mentality: Cultural Shame and Internalized Inferiority, Within-Group Discrimination and Physical Characteristics, and Colonial Debt.
	None of the items are reverse scored. Scoring the subscales consists of summing subscale items. Higher scores indicate higher levels of Colonial Mentality. No transformations are required.
Reliability	Cronbach's alpha for the scores on the subscales were as follows: Within-Group Discrimination: Alpha = .89 Physical Characteristics: Alpha = .89 Colonial Debt: Alpha = .87 Cultural Shame and Embarrassment: Alpha = .78 Internalized Cultural/Ethnic Inferiority: Alpha = .81 Gutman split-half reliability of .80 also was reported.
Validity	Discriminant validity was established through the lack of significant correlation between the Colonial Debt subscale and self-esteem (Rosenberg, 1965). Concurrent validity of CMS subscales was established through expected significant negative correlations with a measure of personal self-esteem (Rosenberg, 1965), collective self-esteem (Luthanen & Crocker, 1992), and acculturation (Ryder, Alden, & Paulhus, 2000). The CMS subscales also were found to be positively correlated with a measure of depression (Radloff, 1977). The subscale of Colonial Debt also was found to be negatively correlated with the perception and appraisal of racist events (Landrine & Klonoff, 1996).
Related References	
Language Versions	English
Contact	E. J. R. David Department of Psychology University of Illinois at Urbana-Champaign 603 East Daniel Street Champaign, IL 61820 Email: edavid@psyc.uiuc.edu

7.11.4 Name of the Measure	Asian American Racism-Related Stress Inventory AARRSI
Primary Reference	Liang, C. T. H., Li, L. C., & Kim, B. S. K. (2004). The Asian American Racism-Related Stress Inventory: Development, factor analysis, reliability, and validity. *Journal of Counseling Psychology, 51,* 103–114.
Purpose	The AARRSI is designed to be a multidimensional measure of racism-related stress experienced by Asian Americans.
Description	The AARRSI is a 29-item self-report inventory. Each of these items is rated on a 5-point Likert-type scale with the following anchors: 1 = This Event has Never Happened to Me or Someone I know; 2 = This Event Happened but Did Not Bother Me; 3 = This Event Happened and I Was Slightly Bothered; 4 = This Event Happened and I Was Upset; 5 = This Event Happened and I Was Extremely Upset. The AARRSI is composed of 3 subscales: (1) socio-historical racism; (2) general racism; and (3) perpetual foreigner. Items were initially developed based on a review of interdisciplinary literature on Asian American experiences, stress and coping theory, the psychological literature regarding racism, and the contents of a focus group of eight Asian American university students enrolled in Asian American Studies courses. Redundant items were deleted. This process resulted in an initial 62 items. These items were then reviewed for clarity and representativeness by a group of 10 counseling psychology doctoral students who were enrolled in a course on psychometrics. An exploratory factor analysis with direct oblimin rotation resulted in 15 factors with eigenvalues greater than 1.00. Examination of the interpretability and composition of those factors led to the retention of 29 items correlating with three factors. Confirmatory factor analysis indicated that their data adequately fit the three-factor model.
Samples	The factor structure of the AARRSI was explored based on a sample of 161 participants (88 women, 73 men). The sample was composed of a college sample and a community sample who ranged in age from 17 to 41 years ($M = 20.33$, $SD = 2.83$), and 24 to 57 years ($M = 38.14$, $SD = 10.60$). Both samples were diverse with respect to Asian ethnic background. A second sample of 142 undergraduate students (83 men, 58 women, 1 did not indicate gender) participated in a study confirming the factor structure of the AARRSI. Their age ranged from 17 to 65 years ($M = 19.73$; $SD = 5.39$). There was a diverse group of Asian ethnic groups represented in the sample.
Scoring	The number of items for each of the three subscales of the AARRSI are as follows: Socio-Historical: 14 items / General Racism: 8 items / Perpetual Foreigner: 7 items / Total AARRSI: 29 items / None of the items are reverse scored. Scoring the subscales consists of summing subscale items and dividing by the number of items. Higher scores indicate higher levels of racism-related stress. No transformations are required.

Reliability	Cronbach's alpha for the scores on the subscales and total scale were as follows: Socio-Historical: Alpha = .93 General Racism: Alpha = .86 Perpetual Foreigner: Alpha = .84 Total AARRSI: Alpha = .95 Two-Week Test-Retest Reliability Socio-Historical: $r = .87$ General Racism: $r = .82$ Perpetual Foreigner: $r = .73$ Total AARRSI: $r = .84$
Validity	Discriminant validity was established through the lack of significant correlation between the AARRSI, its subscales, and the Asian Value Scale (Kim, Atkinson, & Yang, 1999). Concurrent validity of AARRSI subscales was established through expected significant positive correlations with a measure of perceived racism (Landrine & Klonoff, 1996; McNeilly et al., 1996) and minority status stress (Smedley, Myers, & Harrell, 1993). The AARRSI, however, was not found to be significantly related to measures of psychological distress (Derogatis et al., 1974), stress (Cohen, Kamarck, & Mermelstein, 1983), or self-esteem (Rosenberg, 1965).
Related References	Liang, C. T. H., Alvarez, A. N., Juang, L., & Liang, M. (2007). The role of coping in the relationship between perceived racism and racism-related stress for Asian Americans: Gender differences. *Cultural Journal of Counseling Psychology, 54,* 132–142. Liang, C. T. H., & Fassinger, R. E. (2008). Collective self-esteem in the relationship between racism-related stress and psychological adjustment: A test of moderator and mediator hypotheses. *Cultural Diversity and Ethnic Minority Psychology, 14,* 19–28. Patel, S. G., Salahuddin, N. M., & O'Brien, K. M. (2008). Career decision-making self-efficacy of Vietnamese adolescents: The role of acculturation, social support, socioeconomic status, and racism. *Journal of Career Development, 34,* 218–240.
Language Versions	English
Contact	Christopher T. H. Liang 1950 Third Street University of La Verne Department of Psychology La Verne, CA 91750

7.11.5 Name of the Measure	Race-Related Stressor Scale RRSS
Primary Reference	Loo, C. M., Fairbank, J. A., Scurfield, R. M., Ruch, L. O., King, D. W., Adams, L. J., & Chemtob, C. M. (2001). Measuring exposure to racism: Development and validation of a Race-Related Stressor Scale (RRSS) for Asian American Vietnam Veterans. *Psychological Assessment, 13*, 503–520.
Purpose	The RRSS is designed to measure exposure to race-related stressors in the military or a war zone by Asian Americans.
Description	The RRSS is a 33-item self-report inventory. Each of these items is rated on a 5-point Likert-type scale: 0 = Never; 1 = Rarely; 2 = Sometimes; 3 = Frequently; 4 = Very Frequently. The RRSS is composed of three subscales: (1) Racial Prejudice and Stigmatization; (2) Bicultural Identification and Conflict; and (3) Racist Environment. Four methods were used to develop the items of the RRSS: (a) a review of the literature on race-related stressors among minority Vietnam War veterans; (b) clinical interviews with Asian American Vietnam War veterans who had symptoms of PTSD; (c) focus groups; and (d) input from clinicians with experience working with Asian American Vietnam War veterans. Items were sorted into three categories: Racial Prejudice and Stigmatization, Bicultural Identification and Conflict, and Racist Environment. As a result of these four steps, an initial pool of 94 items was included in a pilot study to test for variability in responses for each of the aforementioned dimensions. Results of their analyses also indicated differences in mean scores between clinical and nonclinical veterans. After further examination of the measure, the item pool was reduced to 39. The scale was then subjected to an exploratory factor analysis using maximum-likelihood estimation with oblimin rotation. Items with a structure coefficients less than .50 were omitted. This resulted in a 33-item measure.
Samples	The psychometric properties of the RRSS were established based on several samples. The primary sample was composed of 300 veterans of Asian American descent who served in the U.S. military during the Vietnam War. The mean age of the sample was 55.07 years (*SD* = 6.53). The average number of years of education was 14.18 (*SD* = 2.74). This sample was composed of Asian Americans of several different ethnic backgrounds, including Mixed Asian or mixed race (37%), Japanese/Okinawan (21%), Chinese (14%), Chamorro (13%), Filipino (12%), and Korean (3%). Multiple sampling methods were utilized to recruit those participants who were in treatment for medical or mental health and those who were not in treatment.

Scoring	The number of items for each subscale is as follows:
	
	    Racial Prejudice and Stigmatization: 19 items
	    Bicultural Identification and Conflict: 7 items
	    Racist Environment: 7 items
	    Total RRSS: 33 items
	
	None of the items are reverse scored. Scoring the subscales consists of summing subscale. No transformations are required.

Reliability	Cronbach's coefficient alpha for scores of the total scale and the three subscale scores were as follows:
	Racial Prejudice and Stigmatization: Alpha = .97
	Bicultural Identification and Conflict: Alpha = .93
	Racist Environment: Alpha = .93
	Total RRSS: Alpha = .97
	Test-Retest coefficients are based on data collected within a 5- to 16-week interval between test administrations. The Pearson coefficients were as follows:
	Racial Prejudice and Stigmatization: $r = .84$
	Bicultural Identification and Conflict: $r = .84$
	Racist Environment: $r = .69$
	Total RRSS: $r = .85$
Validity	Convergent validity was indicated through significant correlations between the RRSS total, RRSS subscale scores, and scores of the Brief Symptom Inventory (Derogatis, Rickles, & Rock, 1976) and the measure of combat-related post-traumatic stress disorder (Keane, Caddell, & Taylor, 1988).
Related References	Rippy, A. E., & Newman, E. (2008). Adaptation of a scale of race-related stress for use with Muslim Americans. *Journal of Muslim Mental Health, 3*, 53–68.
Language Versions	English
Contact	Chalsa M. Loo 1164 Bishop Street, Suite 1502 Honolulu, HI 96813 (808) 526–2008 Email: chalsa@earthlink.net

7.11.6 Name of the Measure	Psychosocial Costs of Racism for Whites PCRW
Primary Reference	Spanierman, L. B., & Heppner, M. J. (2004). Psychosocial Costs of Racism to Whites Scale (PCRW): Construction and initial validation. *Journal of Counseling Psychology, 51,* 249–262.
Purpose	The PCRW is designed to measure an individual's awareness and acceptance of similarities and differences in others.
Description	The PCRW is a 16-item self-report inventory. Each of these items is rated on a 6-point Likert-type scale with the following anchors (1 = Strongly Disagree to 6 = Strongly Agree).
	The PCRW is composed of three subscales: (1) White Empathic Reactions Toward Racism; (2) White Guilt; and (3) White Fear of Others.
	The instrument was developed through several steps. An initial pool of 39 items was created based on a review of research literature regarding Whiteness to reflect behavioral, cognitive, and affective costs of racism for Whites. Five counseling psychology doctoral students provided feedback regarding the appropriateness of content, clarity, and parsimony of the items. An additional panel of five faculty members with expertise with race, multiculturalism, and scale construction was consulted to further ensure the appropriateness of the items. As a result of this process, several items were reworded, four items were deleted, and one new item was created.
	The authors first tested their data to ensure their sample was appropriate for factor analysis. Principal components analysis was conducted to estimate the number of factors to specify in the exploratory factor analysis. Two-, three-, and four-factor solutions were tested. Based on eigenvalues and examination of scree plot, a three-factor solution emerged as the best fit for their data. An exploratory factor analysis, using maximum likelihood extraction with oblique rotation, was used. Items correlating with multiple factors or with structure coefficients less than .35 were deleted. This resulted in a 16-item measure. Confirmatory factor analysis, using AMOS (Arbuckle, 1999), was used to test for stability of the factor structure. Their data fit a three-factor solution best.
Samples	A sample of 361 White American undergraduate college students from a university in the Midwestern portion of the United States was recruited to explore the factor structure of the PCRW. A second sample of 366 undergraduate students attending either a large or a midsized university in the Midwestern portion of the United States was used to confirm the factor structure and further establish validity of the measure.
Scoring	The number of items for the subscales are follows:
	White Empathic Reactions Toward Racism: 6 items
	White Guilt: 5 items
	White Fear of Others: 5 items
	Total PCRW: 16 items

	Three of the items are reverse scored. Scoring the subscales consists of summing subscale items and dividing by the number of items of which it is composed. Higher scores indicate higher experience of the psychosocial costs of racism. No transformations are required.
Reliability	Cronbach's alpha for the subscale scores ranged from .63 to .78.
	White Empathic Reactions Toward Racism: Alpha = .78, .79, .85 White Guilt: Alpha = .70, .73, .81 White Fear of Others: Alpha = .63, .69, .78
	Two-week Test-retest reliability coefficients were as follows: White Empathic Reactions Toward Racism: Alpha = .84 White Guilt: Alpha = .69 White Fear of Others: Alpha = .95
Validity	Convergent validity of PCRW subscales was established through expected findings of significant negative and positive correlations with subscales of the Color-Blind Racial Attitude Scale (Neville et al., 2000), Scale of Ethnocultural Empathy (SEE; Wang et al., 2003). None of the SEE subscales were found to be related to White Guilt. Furthermore, contrary to expectations, White Fear of Others was negatively related to three of the four SEE subscales.
	Additional convergent validity was established through significant positive correlations between White Emphatic Reactions Toward Racism, White Guilt, and the Quick Discrimination Index (Ponterotto et al., 1995) and through significant negative correlations between White Fear of Others and the QDI. The Oklahoma Racial Attitudes Scale (LaFleur, Leach, & Rowe, 2002) also was used to establish convergent validity. Its subscales were found to be related to PCRW subscales in the expected directions.
	Discriminant validity was established through the lack of significant correlations with the Marlowe-Crowne Social Desirability Scale–Form C (Reynolds, 1982) and Negative Affectivity (Watson, Clark, & Tellegen, 1988).
Related References	Poteat, V. P., & Spanierman, L. B. (2008). Further validation of the Psychosocial Costs of Racism to White Scale among employed adults. *Journal of Counseling Psychology, 36,* 871–894.
	Spanierman, L. B., Poteat, V. P., Beer, A. M., & Armstrong, P. I. (2006). Psychosocial costs of racism to Whites: Exploring patterns through cluster analysis. *Journal of Counseling Psychology, 53,* 434–441.
	Spanierman, L. B., Todd, N. R., & Anderson, C. J. (2009). Psychosocial costs of racism to Whites: Understanding patterns among university students. *Journal of Counseling Psychology, 56,* 239–252.
Language Versions	English
Contact	Lisa B. Spanierman Department of Educational Psychology University of Illinois at Urbana-Champaign 226 Education Building MC–708 Champaign, IL 61820 Email: lbspan@illinois.edu

7.11.7 Name of the Measure	Cultural Mistrust Inventory CMI
Primary Reference	Terrell, F., & Terrell, S. (1981). An inventory to measure cultural mistrust among Blacks. *The Western Journal of Black Studies, 5*, 180–185. Whaley, A. L. (2002). Psychometric analysis of the Cultural Mistrust Inventory with a Black psychiatric inpatient sample. *Journal of Clinical Psychology, 58*, 383–396.
Purpose	The CMI is a measure of the personality characteristics among Black individuals to perceive mistrust of White people and institutions that are perceived to reflect White culture.
Description	The CMI is a 48-item self-report inventory. Each item is rated on a 9-point Likert-type scale: 0–1 = Not in the Least Agree; 2–3 = Slightly Agree; 4–5 = Moderately Agree; 6–7 = Very Much Agree; and 8–9 = Entirely Agree. Respondents are instructed that selection of the higher value within each response option indicates stronger agreement with the statement. The CMI is composed of four subscales: (1) Education and Training, (2) Interpersonal Relations, (3) Business and Work, and (4) Politics and Law. These four subscales were developed based on a review of the literature that indicated that African Americans make decisions in life based on a tendency to be suspicious of White individuals. Items were then developed for each subscale by the original authors. A team of four African American psychologists then rated each scale for clarity and appropriateness. Items deemed to not meet these criteria were rewritten or eliminated. This procedure was followed for all items that required rewriting. Eighty-one items composed the initial CMI. A total of 23 items were eliminated from further consideration after a three-step process including the elimination of items that were endorsed by a majority of the participants, as well as analyses of relationships between items and of each item's relationship to social desirability (Jackson, 1970). Items yielding significant correlations of .50 or higher with other items on the scale or with the measure of social desirability were eliminated.
Samples	Initial validation of the measure was established using two samples. The first sample was composed of 172 African American first- and second-year college students. A second sample composed of 69 African American individuals similar to those in the first sample. In a study that further analyzed the psychometric properties of the CMI, Whaley (2002) sampled 154 participants who were patients of a state psychiatric hospital. In this sample, there were 116 males (75%) and 38 females (25%). The mean age of the sample was 38.88 (SD = 9.89).

Scoring	The number of items for each of the subscales are as follows:
	
	    Education and Training: 7 items
	    Interpersonal Relations: 14 items
	    Business and Work: 15 items
	    Politics and Law: 12 items
	    Total CMI: 48 items

	Twenty of the 48 items are negatively worded, which requires reverse scoring. Scoring the CMI consists of summing subscale items and dividing by the number of items in the specific subscale. Scores for the full scale are obtained similarly. Higher scores indicate higher levels of cultural mistrust.

Reliability	Cronbach's alpha for the full or subscale scores were not reported by Terrell and Terrell (1981).
	
	 Whaley (2002) reported Cronbach's alpha coefficients for the full and subscale scores.
	
	    Full Scale: Alpha = .85
	
	    Education and Training: Alpha = .63
	
	    Interpersonal Relations: Alpha = .43
	
	    Business and Work: Alpha = .71
	
	    Politics and Law: Alpha = .63
	
	 A two-week test-retest reliability coefficient of .86 was reported for the full scale score.

Validity	In the initial college sample, convergent validity was established through the demonstration that individuals reporting higher incidences of racial discrimination (Terrell & Miller, 1980) also would report higher levels of cultural mistrust. Whaley (2002) reported convergent validity through significant relationships with nonclinical paranoia (Fenigstein & Vanable, 1992), criterion validity with self-esteem (Rosenberg, 1989), and discriminant validity with social desirability (measured through an instrument adapted by the author from the Crowne and Marlowe [1960] Social Desirability Scale). Whaley (2002) also conducted a principal components analysis to examine the structure of the total scale and its subscales. Results of their analyses indicated a different CMI factor structure. High intercorrelations between subscales also suggest the possibility of a unidimensional structure of the CMI for clinical samples.
Related References	Bell, T. J., & Tracey, T. J. G. (2006). The relation of cultural mistrust and psychological health. *Journal of Multicultural Counseling and Development, 34,* 2–14.
Language Versions	English
Contact	Francis Terrell University of North Texas Department of Psychology 1611 W. Mulberry Terrill Hall Room 359 Denton, TX 76203 940–565–2678 Email: terrellf@unt.edu

7.11.8 Name of the Measure	Africultural Coping Systems Inventory ACSI
Primary Reference	Utsey, S. O., Adams, E. P., & Bolden, M. (2000). Development and initial validation of the Africultural Coping Systems Inventory. *Journal of Black Psychology, 26,* 194–215.
Purpose	The ACSI is a 30-item measure of the culture-specific coping strategies and behaviors used by African Americans in stressful situations. The ACSI is grounded in an African-centered conceptual framework.
Description	The ACSI contains the following four subscales: Cognitive/Emotional Debriefing (CED), Spiritual-Centered Coping (SC), Collective Coping (CC), and Ritual-Centered Coping (RC). To complete the ACSI, respondents are asked to "recall a stressful situation that occurred within the past week or so." Respondents are then asked to describe the stressful situation. Lastly, using a 4-point Likert-type scale (0 = Did Not Use, 1 = Used a Little, 2 = Used a Lot, 3 = Used a Great Deal), respondents are asked to indicate which coping strategies they employed with this particular stressful situation. A confirmatory factor analysis with a separate sample ($N = 220$) provided evidence that the four-factor model of coping adequately fit the data.
Samples	The convenience sample consisted of 180 African American adults (104 women and 75 men) from the northeastern United States. Ages ranged from 16 to 66 years ($M = 29.87$, $SD = 11.07$). Marital status of the sample was 69% single, 24% married/committed relationship, 3% separated, 3% divorced, and 1% widowed. Mean educational level was $M = 13.75$, $SD = 1.99$. Mean annual income was $M = \$28,043$, $SD = \$17,480$.
Scoring	The number of items in each of the four subscales is as follows: Cognitive/Emotional Debriefing: 11 items Spiritual-Centered Coping: 8 items Collective Coping: 8 items Ritual-Centered Coping: 3 items Total ACSI: 30 items Scoring the ACSI consists of adding the respondent's ratings on each item in the subscale and dividing by the number of subscale items to obtain a subscale mean. No reverse coding or transformations are required.
Reliability	Cronbach's alpha ranged from .76 to .82 across the scores of the four subscales. Cognitive/Emotional Debriefing (CED): Alpha = .79 Spiritual-Centered Coping (SC): Alpha = .78 Collective Coping (CC): Alpha = .78 Ritual-Centered Coping (RC): Alpha = .76

Validity	Concurrent validity was established by correlating the ACSI subscales with the subscales of the Ways of Coping Questionnaire (Folkman & Lazarus, 1988) subscales.
Related References	Constantine, M. G., Donnelly, P. C., & Myers, L. J. (2002). Collective self-esteem and Africultural coping styles in African American adolescents. *Journal of Black Studies, 32*(6), 698–710.
	Utsey, S. O., Bolden, M. A., Williams, O., III, Lee, A., Lanier, Y., & Newsome, C. (2007). Spiritual well-being as a mediator of the relation between culture-specific coping and quality of life in a community sample of African Americans. *Journal of Cross-Cultural Psychology, 38*(2), 123–136.
Language Versions	English
Contact	Shawn Utsey Virginia Commonwealth University Department of Psychology and African American Studies 915 W. Franklin St., Stark House, Rm. 102 P.O. Box 842509 Richmond, VA 23284–2509 (804) 828–1384 (Office) (804) 828–1665 (Fax) Email: soutsey@vcu.edu

7.11.9 Name of the Measure	Index of Race-Related Stress IRRS IRRS-B
Primary Reference	Utsey, S. O., & Ponterotto, J. G. (1996). Development and validation of the Index of Race-Related Stress (IRRS). *Journal of Counseling Psychology, 43,* 490–501.
Purpose	The IRRS is designed as a measure of the stress experienced by African Americans as a result of their encounters with racism.
Description	The IRRS is a 46-item self-report inventory. Each of these items is rated on a 5-point Likert-type scale with the following anchors: 1 = This Event Has Never Happened to Me or Someone I Know to 5 = This Event Happened and I Was Extremely Upset. The IRRS is composed of 4 subscales: (1) Cultural Racism, (2) Institutional Racism, (3) Individual Racism, and (4) Collective Racism. The instrument was developed through (1) a review of the literature, (2) informal interviews with African American from diverse backgrounds, (3) the personal life experiences of the primary author, an African American male, (4) comments from a focus group of five individuals regarding their reactions to the content of the IRRS, and (5) a second focus group with five experts who rated the measure for clarity and appropriateness. As a result of these steps, several items were reworded to add more clarity. Additionally, the original Likert-type scale was changed. Efforts also were made to ensure that individuals with an 8th-grade reading level could complete the survey. A pilot study utilizing the 67-item IRRS was administered to a sample of 377 participants (203 women, 163 men). Based on the results of the study, the Likert-type response was changed again (to its final format). Based on principal components analysis with orthogonal and oblique rotations and evaluation of scree test, a three-factor model was found to be most interpretable. Based on the principal components analysis and a review by the researchers, the IRRS was reduced to 59 items. A principal components analysis with orthogonal rotation and analysis of scree test yielded a four-factor structure. The authors reported that items were required to have a structure coefficient of at least .40. Confirmatory factor analysis, using LISREL (Jöreskog & Sörborn, 1989), was used to test for stability of the factor structure. Their data indicated a four-component oblique model to be the best fit. Utsey developed and tested the psychometric properties of a 22-item version of the IRRS-Brief. Because some of the items on the Collective Racism subscale were found to be geographically specific, it was eliminated from the IRRS-Brief. The IRRS-Brief was found to have adequate reliability, construct validity, criterion validity, and concurrent validity. Seaton (2003, 2006) tested the psychometric properties of the IRRS for use with adolescents.

Samples	Principal components analysis was conducted with a sample of 302 participants from Greensboro, NC ($n = 113$), and New York City ($n = 188$). The ages ranged from 18–61 years of age ($M = 26.77$, $SD = 9.02$) and were composed primarily of American-Born Blacks (92%). Thirty-five percent of the participants were from the community, 51% were college students, and 13% were residents in a substance abuse treatment facility.
	A group of 310 African American participants (207 women, 92 men), who ranged in age from 17–76 ($M = 23.38$, $SD = 7.74$), was sampled. The sample was composed of 153 participants from Washington, DC, and 157 from the New York City area. Sixteen percent were individuals from the community, with the remaining from colleges and universities. Thirty-one additional non-Black participants were recruited as well. They ranged in age from 19 to 47 years ($M = 27.97$, $SD = 7.64$).
Scoring	Cultural Racism: 16 items
	Institutional Racism: 11 items
	Individual Racism: 11 items
	Collective Racism: 8 items
	Total IRRS: 46 items
	None of the items are reverse scored. Scoring the subscales consists of summing subscale items and dividing by the number of items of which it is composed. Higher scores indicate higher experience of each component of race-related stress. No transformations are required.
Reliability	Cronbach's alpha for the scores on the subscales were as follows:
	Cultural Racism: Alpha = .87
	Institutional Racism: Alpha = .85
	Individual Racism: Alpha = .84
	Collective Racism: Alpha = .79
	Three-Week Test-Retest reliability coefficients for the subscales were as follows:
	Cultural Racism: $r = .77$
	Institutional Racism: $r = .69$
	Individual Racism: $r = .61$
	Collective Racism: $r = .79$
	Two-Week Test-Retest reliability coefficients for the subscales were as follows:
	Cultural Racism: $r = .58$
	Institutional Racism: $r = .71$
	Individual Racism: $r = .54$
	Collective Racism: $r = .75$

(Continued)

Validity	Concurrent validity was established through significant correlations with the total scale and IRRS subscales scores and another measure of perceived discrimination (Harrell, 1994) and perceived stress (Cohen, Karmarck, & Mermelstein, 1983).
	Criterion-related validity was tested using one-way MANOVAs to examine the effects of race on the IRRS subscales. Results indicated that Blacks reported higher levels of each form of racism than did an aggregated group of Asian Americans and White Americans.
Related References	Seaton, E. K. (2003). An examination of the factor structure of the Index of Race-Related Stress among a sample of African American adolescents. *Journal of Black Psychology, 29,* 292–307.
	Seaton, E. K. (2006). Examination of a measure of racial discrimination among African American adolescents. *Journal of Applied Social Psychology, 36,* 1414–1429.
	Utsey, S. O. (1999). Development and validation of a short form of the Index of Race-Related Stress (IRRS)–Brief Version. *Measurement and Evaluation in Counseling and Development, 32,* 149–167.
	Utsey, S. O., Ponterotto, J. G., Reynolds, A. L., & Cancelli, A. A. (2000). Racial discrimination, coping, life satisfaction, and self-esteem among African Americans. *Journal of Counseling and Development, 78,* 72–80.
Language Versions	English
Contact	Shawn O. Utsey Virginia Commonwealth University Department of Psychology 806 West Franklin Street Richmond, VA 23284–2018 (804) 828–1144 Email: soutsey@vcu.edu

7.11.10 Name of the Measure	Internalization of the Model Minority Myth Measure IM-4
Primary Reference	Yoo, H. C., Burrola, K. S., & Steger, M. F. (2010). A preliminary report on a new measure: Internalization of the Model Minority Myth Measure (IM-4) and its psychological correlates among Asian American college students. *Journal of Counseling Psychology, 57,* 114–127.
Purpose	The IM-4 is designed to measure Asian Americans' internalization of the model minority myth, a stereotype of the group as being successful compared to other racialized groups and that this achievement is associated with the groups' work and effort.
Description	The IM-4 is a 15-item self-report inventory. Each of these items is rated on a 7-point Likert-type scale with the following anchors: 1 = Strongly Disagree to 7 = Strongly Agree.
	The IM-4 is composed of two subscales: (1) Model Minority—Achievement Orientation (MM-AO) and (2) Model Minority—Unrestricted Mobility (MM-UM).
	The instrument was developed through (1) a review of the literature regarding the model minority myth and feedback from six experts, representing multiple academic disciplines, in the field of Asian American studies. Specifically, an initial pool of 49 items that were based on the literature was developed by the primary author and his team of research assistants. Fifteen items were deleted based on feedback from the experts.
	The 34-items were then submitted for exploratory factor analysis (EFA) with promax rotation. The EFA indicated a clear and interpretable 15-item, two-factor solution. Confirmatory factor analysis (CFA) was then used to test the stability of the proposed factor structure. Results of the CFA indicated good fit of the data to the model.
Samples	Asian American undergraduate college students ($N = 206$) participated in a study that explored the IM-4's factor structure. Their mean age was 20 ($SD = 2.1$). There were 94 women and 111 men with one not responding. The respondents represented first- ($n = 78$), second- ($n = 73$), and third- ($n = 55$) generation students. In terms of ethnic background, the sample was composed of 61 Chinese, 38 Vietnamese, 30 multiracial/multiethnic, 29 Filipino/a, 21 Korean, 8 Japanese, 6 Asian Indian, 3 Hawaiian/Pacific Islander, 2 Cambodian, 2 Taiwanese, 1 Thai, and 1 Bengali with four individuals not responding.
	A second sample of 187 college students (79 women, 99 men) with a mean age of 21 ($SD = 2.5$) participated in a study to confirm the factor structure of the IM-4. In terms of ethnic background, the sample was composed of 45 Chinese, 15 Vietnamese, 13 multiracial/multiethnic, 19 Filipino/a, 34 Korean, 19 Japanese, 15 Asian Indian, 16 other Asian with 11 individuals not responding.

(Continued)

(Continued)

Scoring	The number of items in each of the two subscales is as follows:
	MM-AO: 10 items
	MM-UM: 5 items
	Total IM-4: 15 items
	None of the items are reverse scored. Scoring the subscales consists of summing subscale items and dividing by the number of items of which it is composed. Higher scores indicate greater levels of internalizing these two components of the model minority myth. No transformations are required.
Reliability	Cronbach's alpha for the scores on the subscales were as follows:
	MM-AO: Alpha = .91
	MM-UM: Alpha = .77
	Two-Week Test-Retest reliability coefficients were as follows:
	MM-AO: r = .72
	MM-UM: r = .70
Validity	Evidence for discriminant validity was demonstrated through small positive or nonstatistically significant relations between the IM-4 subscales and Asian American values (Kim et al., 2005). Convergent validity was demonstrated through some statistically significant relationships found between the IM-4 subscales and ethnic identity (Phinney, 1992), psychological distress (Green, Walkey, McCormick, & Taylor, 1988), and through statistically significant correlations between MM-UM and negative affect (Thompson, 2007).
Related References	
Language Versions	English
Contact	Hyung Chol Yoo
	Asian Pacific American Studies
	Arizona State University
	P.O. Box 874902
	Tempe, AZ 85287–4902
	Email: yoo@asu.edu

7.12 ADOLESCENT EXPERIENCES

7.12.1 Name of the Measure	Everyday Discrimination Scale—Modified EDS–M
Primary Reference	Clark, R., Coleman, A. P., & Novak, J. D. (2004). Brief report: Initial psychometric properties of the everyday discrimination scale in Black adolescents. *Journal of Adolescence, 28*, 363–368.
Purpose	The EDS–M is designed to measure perceptions of racism among African American adolescents.
Description	The EDS–M is a 9-item self-report measure. It utilizes a 6-point Likert scale with the following anchors: 1 = Almost Every Day and 6 = Never. The EDS-M is a unidimensional measure. The EDS-M is a modified version of the Everyday Discrimination Scale (Forman, Williams, & Jackson, 1997). One component, accounting for 49.34% of the standardized variance, emerged from a principal components analysis using varimax rotation.
Samples	A sample of 120 African American adolescents (55 females, 65 males) in grades 9–12 participated in the study. The sample's mean age was 15.70 years (*SD* = 0.95).
Scoring	Total EDS-M: 9 items All of the items are reverse scored. Scoring consists of summing nine items. Higher scores indicate greater perceptions of perceived racism. No transformations are required.
Reliability	Cronbach's coefficient alpha for the total scale score was .87.
Validity	Criterion-related validity of the EDS-M was evidenced through significant positive relationships with both internalizing and externalizing symptoms, as measured by the Child Behaviour Checklist-Youth Self-Report Form (Achenbach, 1991).
Related References	Forman, T. A., Williams, D. R., & Jackson, J. S. (1997). Race, place, and discrimination. *Perspectives on Social Problems, 9*, 231–261.
Language Versions	English
Contact	Items of the EDS-M are published in Clark et al. (2004).

7.12.2 Name of the Measure	Adolescent Discrimination Distress Index ADDI
Primary Reference	Fisher, C. B., Wallace, S. A., & Fenton, R. E. (2000). Discrimination distress during adolescence. *Journal of Youth and Adolescence, 29,* 679–695.
Purpose	The ADDI is designed to measure experiences of distress in response to perceived race-based discrimination experiences among multi-ethnic American adolescents.
Description	The ADDI is a 15-item self-report measure. It utilizes Yes/No response format to measure the frequency of perceived discrimination and a 5-point Likert scale with the following anchors: 1 = Not at All and 5 = Extremely to assess for distress. The ADDI is composed of three subscales: (1) Institutional Discrimination Subscale, (2) Educational Discrimination Subscale, and (3) Peer Discrimination Subscale. For each subscale, an "experience" and "distress" score can be derived. Nineteen items originally composed the ADDI. Items were constructed based on existing literature, news reports, personal experiences of the research team members, and the Racial Discrimination Index (Terrell & Miller, 1988). Items were reviewed for clarity, relevance, and appropriateness of terminology by a multi-ethnic group of 28 high school students. A final three-factor, 15-item ADDI emerged from their feedback and the results of a principal-components analysis (rotation unspecified). The ADDI is a modified version of the Everyday Discrimination Scale (Forman, Williams, & Jackson, 1997).
Samples	A sample of 177 high school students ranging from 13–19 years of age (*M* = 16 years) from an academically competitive and ethnically diverse urban school participated in the study. There were 78 males, 98 females, as well as one person who did not identify her or his gender in the sample. With respect to race, 21% reported African American (American, African, Caribbean), 23% Latino/a American (Caribbean, Central or South American), 25% East Asian (Chinese or Korean), 8% South Asian (Indian), and 23% White American (Europe, Russia, and Mid-East).

Scoring	The number of items for each of the three subscales of the ADDI are as follows:
	
	    Institutional Discrimination Subscale: 6 items
	
	    Educational Discrimination Subscale: 4 items
	
	    Peer Discrimination Distress: 5 items
	
	    Total ADDI: 15 items
	
	None of the items are reverse scored. Scoring for "experience" can be derived by summing the "yes" responses. Higher scores indicate more perceived experiences of discrimination. Scoring of "distress" can consists of summing the items on the corresponding subscale. Higher scores indicate greater levels of distress experienced in response to perceived race-based discrimination. No transformations are required.

Reliability	Cronbach's alpha for the scores on the subscale are as follows:
	Institutional Discrimination Distress Subscale: Alpha = .72
	Educational Discrimination Distress Subscale: Alpha = .60
	Peer Discrimination Distress Subscale: Alpha = .60
	Two-week test-retest reliability coefficients were calculated for a subsample ($n = 52$) of the total participants. The reliability coefficients were as follows:
	Institutional Discrimination Distress Subscale: $r = .76$
	Educational Discrimination Distress Subscale: $r = .53$
	Peer Discrimination Distress Subscale: $r = .75$
Validity	Evidence for known-groups validity was demonstrated through statistically significantly higher levels of distress in institutional and educational settings among African American, Latino/a American, and South Asian Americans, and East Asian Americans than White Americans. Higher levels of peer racial discrimination were reported by East Asian American and White American participants.
	Evidence for criterion-related validity was demonstrated through statistically significant inverse relationships between self-esteem (Rosenberg, 1986) and scores on the peer discrimination distress and educational discrimination distress subscales of the ADDI.
Related References	
Language Versions	English
Contact	Celia B. Fisher Center for Ethics Education Fordham University 441 E. Fordham Road Dealy Hall Bronx, NY 10458 Phone: 718–817–3793 Email: fisher@fordham.edu

7.12.3 Name of the Measure	The Racial Bias Preparation Scale RBPS
Primary Reference	Fisher, C. B., Wallace, S. A., & Fenton, R. E. (2000). Discrimination distress during adolescence. *Journal of Youth and Adolescence, 29,* 679–695.
Purpose	The RBPS is designed to measure the frequency with which adolescents perceive receiving messages about living in a multiethnic society from primary caretakers.
Description	The RBPS is a 20-item self-report measure. It utilizes a 3-point Likert scale (1 = Never, 2 = A Few Times, 3 = A Lot). The RBPS is composed of two dimensions: (1) Reactive Messages and (2) Proactive Messages. Items of the RBPS were constructed based on the Teenager Experience of Racial Socialization Scale (Stevenson, Cameron, Herrero-Taylor, & Davis, 2002) and a review of the related literature. Items were reviewed for clarity, relevance, and appropriateness of terminology by a multi-ethnic group of 28 high school students. A final two-factor, 20-item RBPS emerged from their feedback and the results of a principal-components analysis (rotation unspecified).
Samples	A sample of 177 high school students ranging from 13–19 years of age (*M* = 16 years) from an academically competitive and ethnically diverse urban school participated in the study. There were 78 males, 98 females, as well as one person who did not identify her or his gender in the sample. With respect to race, 21% reported African American (American, African, Caribbean), 23% Latino/a American (Caribbean, Central or South American), 25% East Asian (Chinese or Korean), 8% South Asian (Indian), and 23% White American (Europe, Russia, and Mid-East).
Scoring	The number of items in each of the subscales is as follows: Reactive Messages: 10 items Proactive Messages: 10 items Total RBPS: 20 items None of the items are reverse scored. Scoring consists of dividing the summed score by the number of the items on the corresponding subscale. Higher scores indicate greater levels of racial bias preparation by primary caretakers. No transformations are required.
Reliability	Cronbach's alpha for the scores on the subscale are as follows: Reactive Messages: Alpha = .86 Proactive Messages: Alpha = .83 Total RBPS: 20 items Two-week test-retest reliability coefficients were calculated for a subsample (*n* = 52) of the total participants. The reliability coefficients were as follows: Reactive Messages: *r* = .87 Proactive Messages: *r* = .76

Validity	Evidence for concurrent validity was demonstrated through statistically significant positive relationships between the ADDI and the RBPS.
Related References	
Language Versions	English
Contact	Celia B. Fisher Center for Ethics Education Fordham University 441 E. Fordham Road Dealy Hall Bronx, NY 10458 Phone: 718–817–3793 Email: fisher@fordham.edu

7.12.4 Name of the Measure	Scale of Racial Socialization—Adolescents SORS–A
Primary Reference	Stevenson, H. C. (1994). Validation of the Scale of Racial Socialization for African American Adolescents: Steps toward multidimensionality. *Journal of Black Psychology, 20,* 445–468.
Purpose	The SORS–A is designed to measure the level of acceptance of racial socialization attitudes or race-related messages.
Description	The SORS–A is a 45-item self-report inventory. Each of these items is rated on a 5-point Likert-type scale with the following anchors: 1 = Strongly Disagree to 5 = Strongly Agree. The SORS–A is composed of 4 subscales: (1) Spiritual and Religious Coping, (2) Extended Family Caring, (3) Cultural Pride Reinforcement, and (4) Racism Awareness Teaching. One hundred items were initially developed based on a review of the interdisciplinary literature pertaining to African American family functioning and on literature on racial socialization. These were revised to form a 45-item measure. A principal components analysis using varimax rotation was conducted on the SORS-A. A four-factor solution was found to be most meaningful and interpretable. A principal axis factor analysis with oblique and equamax rotations was conducted and yielded a five-factor solution. The fifth factor, however, was not found to have strong internal consistency and was not included in subsequent analyses. Factors were deemed acceptable based on a scree test, its ability to retain five or more items with structure coefficients greater than or equal to .30, yielded satisfactory internal consistency coefficients, included only items that correlated onto one factor, and made psychological sense. The four factors were subjected to higher-order principal components factor analysis. This resulted in two second-order factors: Proactive and Protective.
Samples	The factor structure of the SORS–A was explored based on a sample of 236 African American adolescents (156 females, 80 males). The sample's mean age was 14.6 years. Only 200 of these participants were included in the final sample.
Scoring	The number of items in each of the four subscales is as follows: Spiritual and Religious Coping: 7 items Extended Family Caring: 10 items Cultural Pride Reinforcement: 10 items Racism Awareness Teaching: 9 items Total SORS-A: 45 items None of the items are reverse scored. Scoring the subscales consists of summing subscale items. Higher scores indicate higher levels of agreement with racial socialization practices. No transformations are required.

Reliability	Cronbach's alpha for the subscale and total scale scores were as follows:
	Spiritual and Religious Coping: Alpha = .74
	Extended Family Caring: Alpha = .70
	Cultural Pride Reinforcement: Alpha = .63
	Racism Awareness Teaching: Alpha = .60
	Total Scale: Alpha = .75
Validity	Concurrent validity of SORS–A subscales was established through expected significant positive correlations with self-reports of how often one's family talked about racism.
Related References	Bennett, A. D., Jr. (2006). Culture and context: A study of neighborhood effects on racial socialization and ethnic identity content in a sample of African American adolescents. *Journal of Black Psychology, 32,* 479–500.
	Wilson, D., Foster, J., Anderson, S., & Mance, G. (2009). Racial socialization's moderating effect between poverty stress and psychological symptoms for African American youth. *Journal of Black Psychology, 35,* 102–124.
Language Versions	English
Contact	Howard C. Stevenson Jr. Graduate School of Education University of Pennsylvania 3700 Walnut Street Philadelphia, PA 19104–6216 Email: howards@nwfs.upenn.gse.edu

7.12.5 Name of the Measure	Teenager Experience of Racial Socialization Scale TERS
Primary Reference	Stevenson, H. C., Jr., Cameron, R., Herrero-Taylor, T., & Davis, G. Y. (2002). Development of the Teenager Experience of Racial Socialization Scale: Correlates of race-related socialization frequency from the perspective of Black youth. *Journal of Black Psychology, 28*, 84–106.
Purpose	The TERS is designed to measure the frequency of messages or practices regarding race that teenagers have received or experienced from their parents or guardians.
Description	The TERS, a 39-item self-report inventory, is an empirically supported measure developed based on the theoretical tenets of African-centered psychology. Each of these items is rated on a 3-point Likert-type scale: 1 = Never; 2 = A Few Times; 3 = Lots of Times. The TERS is composed of five subscales: (1) Cultural Coping With Antagonism; (2) Cultural Pride Reinforcement; (3) Cultural Appreciation of Legacy; (4) Cultural Alertness to Discrimination; (5) Cultural Endorsement of the Mainstream. A principal components analysis with equamax rotation yielded a five-factor solution as most interpretable. The five-factor solution was evaluated by (a) scree test, (b) a factor's ability to retain at least five items where structure coefficients were greater than or equal to .30, (c) the demonstration of strong internal consistency for items within a factor, (d) the inclusion of items correlating only onto one factor, and (e) the psychological and conceptual clarity of factor. Second-order factor analysis indicated that with the exception of Cultural Endorsement of the Mainstream, all factors correlated with one higher-order factor of racial socialization. This higher-order factor is called Cultural Socialization Experience.
Samples	Initial validation of the 39-item measure was established using a sample composed of 260 African American adolescents (*M* = 14.3 years) who were enrolled in a summer job preparation program. The sample was comprised of 136 females and 124 males.
Scoring	The number of items in each of the subscaless of the TERS are as follows: Cultural Coping With Antagonism: 13 items Cultural Pride Reinforcement: 9 items Cultural Appreciation of Legacy: 5 items Cultural Alertness to Discrimination: 6 items Cultural Endorsement of the Mainstream: 6 items Total TERS: 39 items None of the items are reverse scored. Scoring the subscales consists of summing subscale items. No transformations are required.

Reliability	Cronbach's alpha for the scores ranged from .71 to .85.
	Cultural Coping with Antagonism: Alpha = .85
	Cultural Pride Reinforcement: Alpha = .83
	Cultural Appreciation of Legacy: Alpha = .74
	Cultural Alertness to Discrimination: Alpha = .76
	Cultural Endorsement of the Mainstream: Alpha = .71
	Total TERS: Alpha = .91
Validity	Convergent validity was established through multivariate analysis of variance. Specifically, MANOVA indicated a significant effect of family communication about race on all of the subscales of the TERS, such that adolescents who reported that their family talked about the least reported lower levels of each of the subscales of the TERS.
	Discriminant validity was determined through correlation analysis. Specifically, a measure of Racial Socialization Beliefs (Stevenson, 1996) was not found to be strongly related to the subscales of the TERS.
Related References	Barr, S. C., & Neville, H. A. (2008). Examination of the link between parental racial socialization message and racial ideology among Black college students. *Journal of Black Psychology, 34,* 131–155.
	Fischer, A. R., & Shaw, C. M. (1999). African Americans' mental health and perceptions of racist discrimination: The moderating effects of racial socialization experiences and self-esteem. *Journal of Counseling Psychology, 46,* 395–407.
Language Versions	English
Contact	Howard C. Stevenson Jr. 3700 Walnut Street University of Pennsylvania Philadelphia, PA 19104–6216 Email: howards@gse.upenn.edu

8

Gender-Related Measures

8.1 THE IMPORTANCE OF GENDER

The role of gender in the daily lives of individuals is ubiquitous. Along with race, gender is a visible trait upon which individuals make judgments of others and that impact their relationships with others and themselves. From the moment a young boy or girl is born, she or he and her or his parent(s) are inculcated with messages of appropriate behaviors and style of dress. Throughout their lives, boys and girls are reminded of the roles to perform and the ways to look and express oneself lest they be marginalized (e.g., Brannon, 1976; Chrisler, 2008). Women must contend with both role overload (i.e., being the "supermom") and pervasive sexism at cultural, institutional, and interpersonal levels and threats to their physical safety and economic well-being. In addition to coping with sexism, women and men are socialized to expect certain behaviors from women and girls (e.g., meeting the standards of the ideal body; being nurturing). Men, on the other hand, must negotiate their privilege with the restrictions and expectations that are embedded in the system of patriarchy. For instance, Brannon (1976) used the terms "*No Sissy Stuff,*" "*The Big Wheel,*" "*The Sturdy Oak,*" and "*Give 'Em Hell*" to illustrate how men are expected to (1) avoid engaging in feminine behaviors (e.g., expressing feelings); (2) become successful in sports, work, and sexual relations with women; (3) be independent and in control of one's own emotions; and (4) to be adventurous, respectively. As a result of attempting to conform to gender role expectations, men and women may experience gender role strain (Levant & Philpot, 2002; Pleck, 1981), gender role conflict (O'Neil et al., 1986), gender role stress (Eisler & Skidmore, 1987), and role overload (Hochschild, 1989) as well as threats to health behaviors and psychological well-being (e.g., Addis & Mahalik, 2003; Kilmartin, 2009; Yoder, 2009). Needless to say, gender is indeed an important dimension of identity. The purpose of this chapter is to offer a brief overview of the study of gender and provide a summary of measures currently in use.

8.2 GENDER DEFINED

A brief overview of the history of the psychological study of sex and gender is provided here. It is worthwhile, however, to first provide some discussion of terminology. The terms *sex* and *gender* often are used interchangeably but reflect two different meanings (Wester & Trepal, 2008). While *sex* refers to biological characteristics, *gender* reflects the psychological, social, and cultural characteristics associated with being a woman or man. That scholars and laypeople use the terms interchangeably is an indication of the power of essentialist (biological and psychological) perspectives on gender. Although most social scientists today view gender as something people *do* as opposed to some collection of biological and psychological traits with which people are born, popular media and a long history of gender-differences research provide "evidence" of essential characteristics of women and men.

8.3 THE EVOLUTION OF THE PSYCHOLOGICAL STUDY OF GENDER

The psychological study of gender began with the formation of American schools of psychology. With the emergence of the field of psychology in the United States at the end of the 19th century, U.S.-based psychologists sought to understand individual differences. They did so, in part, by focusing their efforts to examine how men and women differed on intellectual, motor, and emotional functioning (Milar, 2000). As a result of these studies *and* androcentric views, which held that the characteristics of males were superior to those of women, women were deemed to be inferior to men. Early women psychologists (e.g., Mary Whiton Calkins, Karen Horney) challenged these androcentric interpretations of research findings and theory (Russo & Dumont, 1997). Despite those challenges, assumptions of innate differences between men and women have become embedded in our popular culture and scholarly literature. While firmly entrenched in popular discussions of gender differences, 78% of the effect sizes in gender-difference research are small to nonexistent (Hyde, 2007). Thus, while there is evidence for between-group differences, the evidence does not provide strong support for the existence of between-group variability on a number of constructs.

Women psychologists formed Division 35, Society for the Psychology of Women, of the American Psychological Association in 1973 to address the androcentric bias and to promote the psychological study of women and gender (Mednick & Urbanski,

1991). Common topics of study include perceived sexism, career development, identity development, disordered eating behavior, mental, sexual and physical health problems, interpersonal violence, sexuality, role overload, marriage, and motherhood. In short, these lines of research highlight the importance of gender, gender roles, and power dynamics in the lives of women.

Division 35 was founded on feminist principles and would later help the formation of Division 51, Society for the Psychological Study of Men and Masculinity, also of the American Psychological Association. For some, the need for the psychological study of men may be questioned; they may wonder whether, if there is an androcentric bias in psychology, there is anything to be learned from this research. To answer this skepticism, scholars of men's studies have argued that although men have been treated as a normative referent, the gendered lives of men have not been examined (e.g., Kilmartin, 2009; Pleck, 1981) and that masculinity is an organizing principle for how men engage in relationships with self, intimate others, work, health behaviors, and society (e.g., Addis & Mahalik, 2003; Jakupcak, Lisak, & Roemer, 2002; Pollack & Levant, 1998). Together, these divisions serve the role of promoting the development of gender-aware theory and science to guide the clinical and research practice of psychologists.

As an area of study, gender has garnered much attention from social scientists. This may be evidenced by the number of reviews of measurement alone. For instance, Smiler and Epstein (2010) indicate that there have been at least six separate reviews of gender-related measures. Their chapter represented the seventh. This current chapter is the eighth. Like Smiler and Epstein, we do not purport to provide an exhaustive review of all measures. Instead, we summarize the development, contents, and psychometric properties of 41 measures. We selected measures for which a researcher has demonstrated, in at least one study, the instrument's psychometric properties—inclusive of some evidence for factorial validity. For the purposes of this chapter, the body of gender-related research and measures is grouped into the following domains:

Gender Traits and Gender Role Ideology; Psychological Costs of Gender Role Conformity; Gender Prejudice and Sexism; Identity Development; Parental Attitudes and Gender Role Socialization; and Gender Identity.

8.4 GENDER TRAITS AND GENDER ROLE IDEOLOGY

A major area of gender-related research, as indicated by the 15 measures produced, has been the study of gendered personality traits or gender role ideology. The study of psychological traits of men and women has been fairly prominent in the study of gender. Before the introduction of the Bem Sex Role Inventory (BSRI; Bem, 1974), personality traits were argued to be either male or female. Bem's work on androgyny played a major role in shifting the field from a dichotomous and unidimensional view of masculinity and femininity to one in which each was seen as a unique construct whereby men and women could be high or low in one or both. From this, the study of gender evolved to further contextualize the personality characteristics noted in men and women. Specifically, scholars began to frame gender as a set of behaviors and characteristics learned in the context of powerful socializing agents (e.g., parents, teachers, media). Social constructionists furthered this line of thinking by suggesting that these behaviors are not immutable but constructed based on a culture's values and tradition. As such, individuals interact with and inform the rules of gender and can, therefore, deconstruct and create new ideologies of masculinity and femininity.

Measurement has reflected the increased acknowledgment of the complexity of the gendered lives of women and men from diverse backgrounds. Gender trait or gender role ideology measures can be grouped into three subcategories. In the first subcategory, the Bem Sex Role Inventory (Bem, 1981) and Extended Personal Attributes Questionnaire (EPAQ; Spence, Helmreich, & Holahan, 1979) address psychological traits theorized to be associated with each gender. The second group addresses instruments that measure ideology or conformity associated with masculinities. They are the Auburn

Differential Masculinity Inventory (ADMI; Burk, Burkhart, & Sikorski, 2004), the Adolescent Masculinity Ideology in Relationships Scale (AMIRS; Chu, Porche, & Tolman, 2005), the Male Role Norms Inventory—Revised (MRNI-R; Levant, Rankin, Williams, Hasan, & Smalley, 2010), Conformity to Masculine Norms Inventory (CMNI; Mahalik et al., 2003), Hypermasculinity Inventory (HMI; Mosher & Sirkin, 1984); the Male Role Attitudes Scale (MRAS; Pleck, Sonenstein, & Ku, 1993), the Macho Belief Inventory (MBI; Strong, McQuillen, & Hughey, 1994), and the Male Role Norms Scale (MRNS; Thompson & Pleck, 1986). The third group, composed of the Femininity Ideology Scale (FIS; Levant et al., 2007), the Conformity to Feminine Norms Inventory (CFNI; Mahalik, Morray et al., 2005), and the Adolescent Femininity Ideology Scale (AFIS; Tolman, Impett, Tracy, & Michael, 2006; Tolman & Porche, 2000), addresses instruments that measure ideology or conformity associated with Western notions of femininity. Finally, the last group addresses measures that allow for further study of multicultural masculine ideologies, an area O'Neil (2008) argued was needed. Although some measures have been used (e.g., the Mirandé's Sex Role Inventory, Mirandé, 1997), only two instruments, the Machismo Measure (M-Measure; Arciniega, Anderson, Tovar-Blank, & Tracey, 2008) and the Multicultural Masculinity Ideology Scale (MMIS; Doss & Hopkins, 1998), met our criteria for inclusion.

8.5 PSYCHOLOGICAL COSTS OF GENDER ROLE CONFORMITY

Conforming to gender role ideology has been argued to be associated with stress, strain, conflict, and overload for men and women (Chrisler, 2008; Levant & Philpot, 2002; O'Neil, 1982; Pleck, 1981). These costs can be seen in the way men and women negotiate socially prescribed roles. Messages of the appropriate physical appearance, and in turn self-worth, as women and men can be seen in video games, television shows, cartoons, movies, and so forth. Men and women also are socialized to behave in certain manners (e.g., men control sadness; women control anger and own needs) and to engage in certain roles (e.g., men as providers; women as nurturers). However, these gender role expectations are impossible to meet. Pleck (1995) argued that many individuals are unable to meet the demands. He proposed that as a result of striving and failing to meet gender expectations, women and men experience discrepancy strain, dysfunction strain, and trauma strain. In highlighting his 10 propositions regarding gender role strain, Pleck also argued that there are negative psychological consequences for individuals who do not meet the expectations.

In a similar vein, O'Neil, Helms, Gable, David, and Wrightsman (1986) proposed that men, as a result of gender role conformity, may strive to be competitive, gain wealth, experience challenges in balancing the demands of work and family, and have difficulty expressing their emotions and in being affectionate with other men. Levant and Philpot (2002) noted the lack of existing theory to guide the empirical study of and clinical practice in cases involving potential gender role strain of women. They noted that women's discrepancy strain can be seen in how women must (1) strive to meet established western beauty ideals, (2) choose between a career and motherhood, and (3) manage multiple role responsibilities. Dysfunction strain, they argued, could be seen in the types of psychological problems often associated with women (i.e., depression, eating disorders, histrionic personality disorders, self-limiting behaviors, role overload, etc.). Finally, they also argued that women experienced trauma as a result of gender socialization. They cited the following as examples of trauma: strain, devaluation, role restriction, sexual objectification, and sexual abuse. Physical abuse also is evident in the lives of women. The following five instruments measure stress, strain, conflict, and other behavioral, cognitive, or attitudinal outcomes of striving to meet gender role expectations. They are the Masculine Gender Role Stress Scale (MGRS; Eisler & Skidmore, 1987), Feminine Gender Role Stress Scale (FGRS; Gillespie & Eisler, 1992), Gender Role Conflict Scale (GRCS; O'Neil et al., 1986), Normative Male Alexithymia Scale (NMAS; Levant, Richmond, Cook, Hous, & Aupont,

2007), and Barriers to Help Seeking Scale (BHS; Mansfield, Addis, & Courtenay, 2005).

8.6 GENDER PREJUDICE AND PERCEIVED SEXISM

Given the long history of subordination of women, it stands to reason that a major area of gender-related research would be to understand prejudice and perceptions of sexism. We identified three subcategories from the nine instruments found for this category. The first group of five instruments addresses prejudicial attitudes and beliefs in stereotypes of women and men. As with other forms of discrimination, social scientists have invested their time to study the attitudes held of a targeted group. Through our search process, four instruments were identified. The oldest measure, the Attitudes Toward Women Scale (AWS; Spence, Helmreich, & Stapp, 1973), still is currently in use. Spence and her colleagues developed an original 55-item version and also have published a 15-item AWS. We elected to summarize the 25-item version, which is the shortest of the three measures to have undergone tests of factorial validity. The Ambivalent Sexism Inventory (ASI; Glick & Fiske, 1996), Modern and Old Fashioned Sexism Scale (MOFSS; Swim, Aiken, Hall, & Hunter, 1995), and Neosexism Scale (NS; Tougas, Brown, Beaton, & Joly, 1995) are instruments designed to measure the attitudinal, cognitive, or behavioral dimensions of old and/or modern forms of sexism. Interestingly, Glick and Fiske (1999) also developed the Ambivalence Toward Men Inventory (AMI) as a measure of benevolent or hostile attitudes and beliefs about men. The third subcategory consists of prejudiced attitudes toward transgender individuals. Transgender issues often are subsumed under the general study of lesbian, gay, and bisexual issues. However, we view transgender issues as more consistent with gender nonconformity than sexual orientation nonconformity. The two measures of transgender issues were the Genderism and Transphobia Scale (GTS; Hill & Willoughby, 2005) and the Transphobia Scale (TS; Nagoshi, Adams, Terrell, Hill, Brzuzy, & Nagoshi, 2008).

There is a long history in the social sciences of focusing attention on the attitudes of the perpetrator. Doing so allows for greater understanding of how and under what conditions stereotypes form (Corning, 2002), which in turn should ostensibly facilitate the development of interventions that allow for challenging stereotypes. Since the 1980s, there has been increased attention to studying the role of perceived sexism in the psychological health and interpersonal relationships of women. In the second subcategory, for which there were two, the instruments measure perceived sexism or inequitable treatment because of gender. Under a stress framework, Klonoff and Landrine (1995) argued that sexism is a source of chronic stress that is gender specific that results in lower levels of self-esteem and other psychological problems. In order to facilitate the testing of their theory, they developed the Schedule of Sexist Events (SSE; 1995). In taking a relative-deprivation framework (Davis, 1959), Corning (2000) developed the Perceived Social Inequity Scale—Woman's Form (PSIS-W) to assess women's perceptions of unfairness between their own situation and those of others.

8.7 IDENTITY DEVELOPMENT

As a way to understand how individuals develop in the context of a patriarchal environment, some sought to develop instruments to learn more about the identity development of women. In total, we identified six measures of identity development, one of which addresses the identity development of men. Heavily influenced by Downing and Roush's model of feminist identity development, several groups of authors developed instruments to measure the development of women. Specifically, Rickard (1989) and Bargard and Hyde (1991) developed the Feminist Identity Scale (FIS) and Feminist Identity Development Scale (FIDS), respectively. The Feminist Identity Composite (FIC; Fischer, Tokar, Good, Hill, & Blum, 2000), which was developed to address the psychometric limitations of the FIS and FIDS, and the Feminist Perspectives Scales (FPS; Henley, Meng, O'Brien, McCarthy, & Sockloskie; 1998) also were published. In order to measure how African American

women develop, Ossana, Helms, and Leonard (2001) developed the Womanist Identity Attitudes Scale (WIAS). In our search for gender-related measures, we identified the Reference Group Identity Dependence Scale (RGIDS; Wade & Gelso, 1998) to measure men's identity.

8.8 PARENTAL ATTITUDES AND GENDER SOCIALIZATION

In the gender literature, there has been much attention on attitudes of gender roles and on what adolescents learn about sexuality (Epstein & Ward, 2008; Owen Blakemore & Hill, 2008). However, the development of psychometrically sound instruments to measure parental gender role attitudes as they pertain to their children or the socialization of children and adolescents has not been a focus. In our review of the literature, we were able to identify the Parent Gender-Based Attitudes Scale (PGBAS; Hoffman & Kloska, 1995) and the Child Gender Socialization Scale (CGSS; Owen Blakemore & Hill, 2008) as two measures in this emerging field of study.

8.9 GENDER IDENTITY

The study of gender identity also is a major area of gender-related research. In our search, we identified four instruments that help aid the study of gender identity disorders. Specifically, the Recalled Childhood Gender Questionnaire—Revised (RCGQR; Meyer-Bahlburg et al., 2006), the Gender Identity/Gender Dysphoria Questionnaire—Adolescents and Adults (GIDYQ-AA; Deogracias et al., 2007), and the Gender Identity Questionnaire for Children (GIQ; Johnson et al., 2004) are summarized here. One instrument, Gender Identity (GI; Egan & Perry, 2001), measures feelings of gender/biological sex congruency, feelings of pressure from others to conform to gender role norms, and intergroup bias.

8.10 FUTURE RESEARCH

This summary represents but one of many reviews of the gender-related measures developed during the past

50 years. The focus has been to study attitudes regarding gender traits or roles; gender-related stress, strain, or conflict; sexual prejudice and perceived sexism; identity development; gender identity; and, more recently, gender socialization. We provide several recommendations for future research—with particular attention to further efforts at measurement development.

1. We found that there is a need for greater attention to the messages boys and girls are receiving about gender and sexuality through their parents, peers, and media. Only two studies for which the purpose was to develop a measure addressing these issues were identified.

2. Attention to the racialized experiences of women of color also may provide a fruitful area of inquiry for researchers. For instance, our review of the literature indicates much development of theory regarding the gendered experiences of women. Less attention has been given to the development of instrumentation to test theory.

3. We also found there to be a lack of attention to how gender role expectations and perceived racism may influence the lives of men of color. Thus, we recommend the development of theory and measurement to address this gap in the literature.

4. Finally, several of these instruments were either long or potentially dated (e.g., language). We encourage researchers to further refine, revise, and provide additional evidence for the validity of existing measures for use in future research as well as in clinical settings.

8.11 GENDER TRAITS AND GENDER ROLE IDEOLOGY

8.11.1 Name of the Measure	Machismo Measure M-Measure
Primary Reference	Arciniega, G. M., Anderson, T. C., Tovar-Blank, Z. G., & Tracey, T. J. G. (2008). Toward a fuller conception of Machismo: Development of a Traditional Machismo and Caballerismo Scale. *Journal of Counseling Psychology, 55,* 19–33.
Purpose	The M-Measure was developed to measure behavioral or cognitive aspects of machismo.
Description	The M-Measure is a 20-item measure that employs a 7-point Likert-type self-report scale (1 = Very Strongly Disagree to 7 = Very Strongly Agree). The M-Measure has two components: (1) Machismo and (2) Caballerismo. The M-Measure was developed, in part, using an explicit deductive scale construction strategy. Items also were generated based on literature addressing machismo and on interviews with seven Mexican American men in the southwest of the United States. A preliminary 84-item measure was generated and pilot tested on 20 Mexican American men. Several items were deleted or clarified based on their feedback. Four Mexican American men who are experts in either culture or masculinity independently rated each item to determine how well they reflected machismo. They used a scale with the following anchors: 1 = Not At All to 7 = Very Much So. A 71-item measure emerged from these procedures. Principal axis factor analyses with both and varimax and oblimin rotations were used to examine the factor structure of the measure. Results of these two analyses yielded a similar two-factor solution. Thus, the authors chose to use the results from the varimax rotation. Forty-one items correlated with one of the first two factors. Items on the first two factors were then correlated with the expert ratings described earlier. Results indicated evidence for construct validity. The authors chose the best 10 items for each factor, resulting in a 20-item measure. Items had structure cofficients of greater than .30 and did not correlate with more than one factor with a value greater than .30. Confirmatory factor analysis with item parceling was used to further establish construct validity and indicated good fit of their data to the hypothesized model.
Samples	Validation of the measure was established using a sample of 403 Mexican American men (*M* = 31 years old; *SD* = 12 years) and 74 non-Mexican American Latino men (*M* = 32 years old; *SD* = 12 years). Among the Mexican American sample, 84% were born in the United States. Fifty-four percent of the non-Mexican American Latino men were born in the United States. A majority of the samples received at least a high school degree.

(Continued)

(Continued)

Scoring	The number of items in each subscale of the M-Measure are as follows:
	Machismo: 10 items
	Caballerismo: 10 items
	Total M-Measure: 20 items
	The scores on the two subscales are calculated by summing the scores and dividing by the number of corresponding items. Higher scores indicate greater levels of endorsement of either machismo or caballerismo.
Reliability	Cronbach's alpha for the scores were as follows:
	Machismo: Alpha = .84
	Caballerismo: Alpha = .71
Validity	Convergent and discriminant validity of the machismo and caballerismo subscales were established through expected correlations or null relationships with number of arrests and number of fights. Machismo also was significantly positively correlated with aggressive masculine behaviors (Lara-Cantú, 1989) but not with life satisfaction (Diener et al., 1985) or affiliation with others (Paulhus & Martin, 1987). Caballerismo was found to be significantly related to affiliation with and emotional connection to others and satisfaction with life.
	Structural equation modeling was used to further establish validity of the two subscales. The Machismo subscale was found to be positively associated with alexithymia (Bagby, Parker, & Taylor, 1994), wishful thinking (Hatton & Emerson, 1995), alcohol use, fights, and arrests. Machismo also was found to be negatively associated with ethnic identity and other group orientation (Phinney, 1992). The Caballerismo subscale was found to be associated with problem solving (Hatton & Emerson, 1995) and ethnic identity (Phinney, 1992).
Related References	
Language Versions	English, dialects of Spanish
Contact	G. Miguel Arciniega 302 Payne Hall MC 0611 Arizona State University Tempe, AZ 85287–0611 Email: m.arciniega@asu.edu

8.11.2 Name of the Measure	Bem Sex Role Inventory—Short BSRI-S
Primary Reference	Bem, S. L. (1981). *A manual for the Bem Sex Role Inventory*. Palo Alto, CA: Consulting Psychologist Press.
Purpose	The BSRI-S is designed to measure personality characteristics associated with masculinity and femininity.
Description	The BSRI-S is an 18-item self-report inventory. Each of these items is rated on a 7-point Likert-type scale ranging from 1 = Never or Almost Never True to 7 = Always or Almost Always True. The BSRI-S was initially composed of two subscales, (1) Masculinity and (2) Femininity. Ten additional items were used to measure social desirability on the initial BSRI. They later served as filler items. Recent studies of its psychometric properties indicate that the original Masculinity subscale is composed of two dimensions (i.e., Personal Masculinity and Social Masculinity). Thus, a three-factor BSRI-S will be presented. An initial pool of 200 personality characteristics was created by Sandra Bem and her students. These characteristics were seen as positive in value and either masculine or feminine. An additional 200 characteristics were developed that seemed to be neither masculine nor feminine. These items were either positive or negative in value. Items were included for the Masculinity and Femininity Scales if they were judged (i.e., 40 undergraduate students attending Stanford University) to be more desirable for one sex by both males and females. Items were included in the Neutral scale, which originally served as a Social Desirability scale if the characteristic was deemed to be equally desirable for men and women and if the judges did not differ in their overall desirability judgments based on their gender. From this process, 20 items were selected each for the Masculinity and the Femininity Scales, respectively. Ten positive, 10 negative, and 10 neutral characteristics were selected for the Social Desirability scale. Bem (1981) later reported a 30-item short form of the BSRI that was a result of further study of its factor structure. Items were chosen based on the results of factor analysis and item-total correlations. This short form has been found to yield higher reliability coefficients and fit than the long form (Campbell, Gillaspy, & Thompson, 1997). The factor structure of the BSRI has been investigated in many studies. Thompson (1989) reported a meta-analysis of exploratory factor analyses. Similarly, Choi and Fuqua (2003) provided a summary on 23 separate EFA validation studies of the BSRI. Choi, Fuqua, and Newman (2009) conducted the most recent published EFA and CFA of the short form of the BSRI and found that a three-factor model fit data better than the Bem's (1981) proposed two-factor model.

(Continued)

(Continued)

Samples	The psychometric properties of the three-factor BSRI were established based on data gathered from two samples. The first sample of $N = 660$ college students (59% female) was randomly split in half for EFA and CFA. The mean age was 30.29 ($SD = 10.15$ years). The sample's ethnic composition was 77% White American; 14% African American; 4% other; 3% Asian American; and 2% Latino/a Americans. A sample of 312 certified public accountants also was included in this study to further establish structural validity. The mean age was 44.34 years ($SD = 10.42$). Males comprised 59% of the sample.
Scoring	The number of items in each subscale is as follows: Femininity: 9 items Personal Masculinity: 5 items Social Masculinity: 4 items Total BSRI-S: 18 items Scoring the subscales consists of summing subscale items and dividing by the number of items of which it is composed.
Reliability	Cronbach's alpha for the subscale scores were as follows: Masculinity: Alpha = .84–.86 Personal Masculinity: Alpha = Not Reported Social Masculinity: Alpha = Not Reported Femininity: Alpha = .84–.87
Validity	Although the validity of the two-factor BSRI has been established in a number of studies, the construct validity of the three-factor BSRI has not been tested.
Related References	Campbell, T., Gillaspy, J. A., Jr., & Thompson, B. (1997). The factor structure of the Bem Sex-Role Inventory (BSRI): Confirmatory factor analysis of long and short forms. *Educational and Psychological Measurement, 57,* 118–124. Choi, N., & Fuqua, D. R. (2003). The structure of the Bem Sex Role Inventory: A summary report of 23 validation studies. *Educational and Psychological Measurement, 63,* 872–887. Choi, N., Fuqua, D. R., & Newman, J. L. (2009). Exploratory and confirmatory studies of the structure of the Bem Sex Role Inventory Short Form with two divergent samples. *Educational and Psychological Measurement, 69,* 696–705.
Language Versions	English
Contact	http://www.mindgarden.com/products/bemss.htm

8.11.3 Name of the Measure	Auburn Differential Masculinity Inventory—60 ADMI-60
Primary Reference	Burk, L. R., Burkhart, B. R., & Sikorski, J. F. (2004). Construction and preliminary validation of the Auburn Differential Masculinity Inventory. *Psychology of Men & Masculinity, 5*, 4–17.
Purpose	The ADMI-60 was developed to measure conformity to attitudinal and behavioral components of hypermasculinity.
Description	The ADMI-60 is a 60-item self-report inventory. Each item is rated on a 5-point Likert-type scale with the following anchors: 0 = Not at All Like Me to 4 = Very Much Like Me. There are five subscales to the ADMI-60: (1) Hypermasculinity, (2) Sexual Identity, (3) Dominance and Aggression, (4) Conservative Masculinity, and (5) Devaluation of Emotion. Based on literature and theory of hypermasculinity, a group of graduate students and faculty rationally constructed 180 face-valid items of the ADMI. An additional group of 27 doctoral students of psychology rated the items for appropriateness to the construct of hypermasculinity. The 100 items that received more than 50% rating of very good or good were retained. Data from 114 male undergraduate students of the 100-item ADMI were then analyzed. Forty items judged not to be adequately discriminative were eliminated. With data from 347 participants, the resultant 60-item ADMI was then subjected to principal-axis factor analysis with varimax rotation. Five factors emerged from this analysis. Items with structure coefficients greater than .29 were retained. Furthermore, an unacceptable reliability coefficient of .19 was yielded for the Sexual Identity factor.
Samples	Two separate samples of male undergraduate students participated in the validation studies. The first sample (*N* = 114) had an average age of 20.6 years (*SD* = 1.32 years) and was used to establish construct validity. The average age of the second sample (*N* = 347) was 20.1 years (*SD* = 1.3 years). Data from the second sample were used to further study the underlying structure of the ADMI. Data regarding the ethnic background were not collected. However, the authors estimate that 85% of the sample was composed of White Americans. The remaining 15% was estimated to be African Americans.
Scoring	The number of items in each subscale of the ADMI is as follows: Hypermasculinity: 17 items Sexual Identity: 14 items Dominance and Aggression: 18 items Conservative Masculinity: 14 items Devaluation of Emotion: 5 items Total ADMI: 60 items Some items require reverse scoring. Subscale and Total Scale Scores are obtained by summing the corresponding item scores. Higher scores indicate more agreement with hypermasculinity attitudes and behaviors.

(Continued)

(Continued)

Reliability	Cronbach's alpha for the scores were as follows:
	
	    Hypermasculinity: Alpha = .88
	
	    Sexual Identity: Alpha = .19
	
	    Dominance and Aggression: Alpha = .65
	
	    Conservative Masculinity: Alpha = .78
	
	    Devaluation of Emotion: Alpha = .73
	
	    Total ADMI: Alpha = .85
	
	Cronbach's alpha also was calculated for scores on scales with only items that yielded factor structure coefficients of greater than .40 on their respective subscales. The alpha coefficients were as follows:
	
	    Hypermasculinity: Alpha = .85 (10 items)
	
	    Sexual Identity: Alpha = .78 (11 items)
	
	    Dominance and Aggression: Alpha = .79 (11 items)
	
	    Conservative Masculinity: Alpha = .83 (11 items)
	
	    Devaluation of Emotion: Alpha = .73 (4 items)

Validity	Construct validity was demonstrated through statistically significant positive relationships found between its subscales and an older measure of hypermasculinity (Mosher & Sirkin, 1984). The measure also was found to be significantly positively associated with hostility toward women (Marshall & Moulden, 2001) and antisocial practices (Gynther, Burkhart, & Hovanitz, 1979). Social desirability (Crowne & Marlowe, 1960) also was found to be significantly negatively associated with hypermasculinity, sexual identity, and dominance and aggression. Social desirability was not associated with conservative masculinity and devaluation of emotion. The subscales of the ADMI were not found to be associated with empathy. Self-esteem was significantly negatively associated with hypermasculinity and sexual identity but not the other subscales of the ADMI. Sensation seeking (Zuckerman, 1976) was positively associated with sexual identity, conservative masculinity, and devaluation of emotion but not dominance and aggression or hypermasculinity.
Related References	Joseph, M., Struckman-Johnson, C., Quevillon, R., & Banka, S. R. (2008). Heterosexual men's attitudes toward gay men: A hierarchical model including masculinity, openness, and theoretical explanations. *Psychology of Men & Masculinity, 9,* 154–166.
Language Versions	English
Contact	Barry R. Burkhart 226 Thach Hall Department of Psychology Auburn, AL 36849-5214 Email: burkhbr@auburn.edu The measure was published in Burk et al. (2004).

8.11.4 Name of the Measure	Adolescent Masculinity Ideology in Relationships Scale AMIRS
Primary Reference	Chu, J. Y., Porche, M. V., & Tolman, D. L. (2005). The Adolescent Masculinity Ideology in Relationships Scale: Development and validation of a new measure for boys. *Men and Masculinities, 8,* 93–115.
Purpose	The AMIRS was developed to measure adolescent boys' internalization of traditional masculine norms.
Description	The AMIRS is a 12-item self-report inventory. Each item is rated on a 4-point Likert-type scale with the following anchors: 1 = Disagree a Lot to 4 = Agree a Lot. The AMIRS is a unidimensional measure. The AMIRS is grounded on Pleck, Sonenstein, and Ku's (1993) theory of masculine ideology and a relational paradigm. Items on the AMIRS were developed based on qualitative data involving adolescent boys' reports and observations of how they negotiate masculine norms in the context of relationships with peers. These data were content analyzed. A pool of more than 50 items was generated from these analyses and reflects language and words adolescent boys might be more apt to use. A focus group of adolescent boys was convened and resulted in the deletion, rewording, or addition of items. This process resulted in a 17-item version of the scale. Several pilot studies involving a group of eighth-grade and ninth-grade boys, respectively, were conducted. Based on the eighth-grade sample, items were deleted or reworded to add more clarity. The measure was then tested on a sample of ninth-grade boys. Based upon feedback offered by the sample, items were refined or deleted, resulting in a 12-item measure. A single-factor solution that was deemed to be consistent with the scale's theoretical underpinnings emerged from a factor analysis.
Samples	Validation of the measure was established using a sample of 114 seventh-grade boys ($M = 12.2$ years of age), 133 eighth-grade boys ($M = 13.5$ years of age), and 31 high school participants ($M = 16.8$ years of age). The demographic makeup of the seventh-grade sample is as follows: 61% White American, 19% Latino/a American, 4% African American, 9% biracial, and 7% other (including Asian Americans and Native Americans). The demographic composition of the eighth-grade sample was 62% White American, 20% Latino/a American, 2% African American, and 7% other (including Asian Americans and Native Americans). The composition of the high school boys was 79% White Americans, 4% Latino/a Americans, and 17% biracial.
Scoring	5 negatively worded items require reverse scoring. The score on the 12-item AMIRS is calculated by summing the scores and dividing by the number of items on the measure. Higher scores indicate greater levels of endorsement of hegemonic masculine norms.

(Continued)

(Continued)

Reliability	Cronbach's alpha for the score is .70.
Validity	Construct validity for the AMIRS was established through significant positive relationships with measures of male role attitudes (Pleck, Sonenstein, & Ku, 1993) and masculine behaviors (Snell, 1989). Discriminant validity was established through significant inverse relationships between the AMIRS and attitudes toward women (Galambos, Peterson, Richards, & Gitelson, 1985). Concurrent validity was established through significant positive relationship found between the AMIRS and acting out and an inverse relationship indicated with self-esteem (Rosenberg, 1965).
Related References	
Language Versions	
Contact	Judy Chu 370 Arkansas Street San Francisco, CA 94107 Email: judy.chu@stanfordalumni.org

8.11.5 Name of the Measure	Multicultural Masculinity Ideology Scale MMIS
Primary Reference	Doss, B. D., & Hopkins, J. R. (1998). The Multicultural Masculinity Ideology Scale: Validation from three cultural perspectives. *Sex Roles, 38,* 719–741.
Purpose	The MMIS was developed to measure men's masculine ideology.
Description	The MMIS is a 21-item self-report inventory that utilizes a Likert-type scale response format with the following anchors: 1 = Strongly Disagree and 5 = Strongly Agree. The authors describe the MMIS as being composed of the following two etic components of ideology and behavior: (1) Hypermasculine Posturing and (2) Achievement. Emic components also were presented for Chilean, White American, and African American samples. The MMIS is composed of three emic components for Chileans: (1) Toughness, (2) Pose, and (3) Responsibility. For White Americans, there is one emic component of the MMIS. One emic component also was found when studying responses from African Americans. This one component was named Sexual Responsibility. Items of the MMIS were developed based on previous literature concerning masculinity of Latino men, African American men, and White American men. Thirty-nine items were selected for inclusion in the initial MMIS if the item reflected a masculinity ideology common in at least one culture or was distinct. Additionally, behavioral items were developed that directly related to the masculinity ideology underlying each item. Principal components analysis (PCA) with varimax rotation were performed and items were selected for inclusion if it yielded a structure coefficient greater than .40 on the component in a sample equally composed of Chileans, African Americans, and White Americans, and above .25 or greater in analyses conducted on each group separately. PCA conducted on data from a sample of equally represented ethnic groups resulted in a 13-item Hypermasculine Posturing component and an 8-item Achievement component. PCA with specific groups resulted in different factor structures. Items were retained if they correlated with other items with values greater than .30, were interpretable, and tapped aspects of masculinity different from the two etic components (i.e., Hypermasculine Posturing and Achievement). PCA with the Chilean, White American, and African American sample yielded a three-factor solution (toughness, pose, and responsibility), a one-factor solution (sensitivity), and a one-factor solution (sexual responsibility).
Samples	The sample was composed of 769 undergraduate students (503 men and 299 women) representing Chilean, African American, and White Americans. The Chilean sample was recruited from two universities located in Chile.
Scoring	The MMIS can be used as an Etic measure or an Emic measure for three ethnic groups. The structure of the MMIS changes based on an Etic or Emic approach.

(Continued)

(Continued)

	The number of items in each version of the MMIS is as follows:
	
	Etic
	    Hypermasculine Posturing: 13 items
	    Achievement: 8 items
	    Total MMIS: 21 items
	Chilean Emic
	    Toughness: 8 items
	    Pose: 5 items
	    Responsibility: 5 items
	    Total MMIS: 18 items
	White American Emic
	    Sensitivity: 6 items
	African American Emic
	    Sexual Responsibility: 4 items
	
	A score on the MMIS subscales can be calculated by summing its corresponding items. Higher scores indicate more agreement with masculinity ideologies reflected in this scale.

Reliability	Reliability coefficients were calculated for the subscales for Chilean, White American, and African American samples, respectively.
	
	    Hypermasculine Posturing: Alpha = .81, .88, .76
	    Achievement: Alpha = .60, .73, .79
	
	Three-Week Test-retest reliability coefficients also were presented for data collected with a mostly White American sample.
	
	    Hypermasculine Posturing: $r = .98$
	    Achievement: $r = .82$

Validity	Construct validity was established through a significant relationship with dimensions of masculinity norms (Thompson & Pleck, 1986). Divergent validity was established through the lack of significant relationships with social desirability (Fisher & Fick, 1993).
Related References	Janey, B. A., Janey, N. V., Goncherova, N., & Savchenko, V. (2006). Masculinity ideology in Russian society: Factor structure and validity of the Multicultural Masculinity Ideology Scale. *The Journal of Men's Studies, 14,* 93–108.
Language Versions	English, Russian, Spanish
Contact	J. Roy Hopkins Department of Psychology St. Mary's College of Maryland St. Mary's City, MD 20686 Email: jrhopkins@smcm.edu (240) 895–4458

8.11.6 Name of the Measure	Male Role Norm Inventory—Revised MRNI-R
Primary Reference	Levant, R. F., Rankin, T. J., Williams, C. M., Hasan, N. T., & Smalley, K. B. (2010). Evaluation of the factor structure and construct validity of scores on the Male Role Norms Inventory—Revised (MRNI-R). *Psychology of Men & Masculinity, 11,* 25–37.
Purpose	The MRNI-R is an updated version of the MRNI (Levant et al., 1992), which was developed to measure traditional and nontraditional masculinity ideologies.
Description	The MRNI-R is a 39-item self-report inventory. Each item is rated on a 7-point Likert-type scale with the following anchors: 1 = Strongly Agree to 7 = Strongly Disagree. There are seven subscales to the MRNI-R: (1) Restrictive Emotionality; (2) Self-Reliance Through Mechanical Skills; (3) Negativity Toward Sexual Minorities; (4) Avoidance of Femininity; (5) Importance of Sex; (6) Toughness; and (7) Dominance. One hundred seven items were developed based on a review of literature on the male role and included 49 original items from the MRNI (Levant, Smalley, Aupont, House, Richmond, & Noronha, 2007). Through examination of item-subscale correlations, 53 items were deleted. Levant et al. (2010) submitted data for these 53 items to an exploratory factor analysis (EFA) with oblimin rotation. The EFA yielded a 39-item, seven-factor MRNI-R and resulted in the removal of 13 items that did not yield a structure coefficient greater than .35 and was correlated highly on more than one factor or did not make conceptual sense.
Samples	A sample of 593 undergraduate students was recruited from psychology, computer science, and physics courses. With respect to gender, 58% identified as male, 42% identified as female, with less than 1% identifying as "other" (*n* = 1). The sample ranged in age from 18 to 51 years (*M* = 21.4). Eighty-three percent of the participants reported being White American. The ethnic composition of the sample was not otherwise provided.
Scoring	The number of items in each subscale is as follows: Restrictive Emotionality: 7 items Self-Reliance Through Mechanical Skills: 3 items Negativity Toward Sexual Minorities: 8 items Avoidance of Femininity: 7 items Importance of Sex: 3 items Toughness: 4 items Dominance: 7 items Total MRNI-R: 39 items Scores are summed and divided by the number of items of the subscale. Higher scores indicate higher levels of endorsement of traditional masculinity ideology.
Reliability	Cronbach's alpha for the scores on the subscales and total scale for men were as follows: Restrictive Emotionality: Alpha = .88 Self-Reliance Through Mechanical Skills: Alpha = .88

(Continued)

	Negativity Toward Sexual Minorities: Alpha = .85
	Avoidance of Femininity: Alpha = .89
	Importance of Sex: Alpha = .84
	Toughness: Alpha = .75
	Dominance: Alpha = .88
	Total MRNI-R: Alpha = .96
	Cronbach's alpha for the scores on the subscales and total scale also were reported for women and were as follows:
	Restrictive Emotionality: Alpha = .89
	Self-Reliance Through Mechanical Skills: Alpha = .86
	Negativity Toward Sexual Minorities: Alpha = .92
	Avoidance of Femininity: Alpha = .87
	Importance of Sex: Alpha = .82
	Toughness: Alpha = .78
	Dominance: Alpha = .90
	Total MRNI-R: Alpha = .96
Validity	Known-groups validity was established. Specifically, men and women differed significantly on the subscales as well as on the total MRNI-R, with men reporting higher levels of each male role norm.
	Evidence for convergent validity was established through expected statistically significant positive relationships between the MRNI-R and the Male Role Attitudes Scale (Pleck et al., 1993).
	Discriminant validity was evidenced through an expected nonstatistically significant relationship between the MRNI-R and the Personal Attributes Questionnaire—Masculinity Scale (Spence & Helmreich, 1978).
	Concurrent validity was evidenced through statistically significant positive associations between the MRNI-R and the Gender Role Conflict Scale (O'Neil, Good, & Holmes, 1995), Conformity to Masculinity Norms Inventory (Mahalik et al., 2003), as well as the Normative Male Alexithymia Scale (Levant et al., 2006).
Related References	Levant, R. F., Smalley, K. B., Aupont, M., House, A. T., Richmond, K., & Noronha, D. (2007). Initial validation of the Male Role Norms Inventory—Revised (MRNI-R). *The Journal of Men's Studies, 15,* 83–100.
Language Versions	English
Contact	Ronald F. Levant Department of Psychology Butchel College of Arts and Sciences The University of Akron Akron, OH 44325 Email: Levant@uakron.edu

8.11.7 Name of the Measure	Femininity Ideology Scale FIS
Primary Reference	Levant, R., Richmond, K., Cook, S., House, A. T., & Aupont, M. (2007). The Femininity Ideology Scale: Factor, structure, reliability, convergent, and discriminant validity, and social contextual variation. *Sex Roles, 57,* 373–383.
Purpose	The FIS is designed to measure the degree to which women endorse traditional beliefs about how women should act.
Description	The FIS is a 45-item self-report inventory that assesses the level of agreement with traditional norms for women. Each item is rated on a 5-point Likert-type scale with the following anchors: 1 = Strongly Agree to 5 = Strongly Disagree. The FIS is composed of five components: (1) Stereotypic Image and Activities; (2) Dependence/Deference; (3) Purity; (4) Caretaking; and (5) Emotionality. An initial pool of 166 items was developed regarding traditional feminine norms. These statements were given to 292 male and female individuals. Their responses were submitted to a principal components analysis with varimax rotation. A five-factor solution emerged. Their criteria were (1) a structure coefficient greater than .45 and (2) did not have a strong structure coefficient on more than one factor. This resulted in a 45-item measure. This factor structure was replicated through a principal components analysis with varimax rotation.
Samples	Validation of the measure was established using a sample of 407 undergraduate students: 192 men and 210 women. Nearly 90% of the sample reported being between the ages of 17 and 20, 7.5% between the ages of 21 and 24, and 1.1% were between the ages of 25 and 45 years. With respect to race, they were 331 White American, 10 Asian American, 10 Latino/a American, 41 African American, with 10 identifying as "other."

Scoring	The number of items in each subscale is as follows:
	
	    Stereotypic Image and Activities: 11 items
	    Dependence/Deference: 10 items
	    Purity: 9 items
	    Caretaking: 7 items
	    Emotionality: 8 items
	    Total FIS: 45 items
	
	The total score and the scores for each subscale are calculated by summing items and dividing by the number of items associated with the factor. Higher scores indicate higher levels of agreement with traditional femininity ideology.

(Continued)

Reliability	Cronbach's alpha ranged from .76 to .92 for women. They were as follows:
	
	    Stereotypic Image and Activities: Alpha = .79
	
	    Dependence/Deference: Alpha = .76
	
	    Purity: Alpha = .85
	
	    Caretaking: Alpha = .80
	
	    Emotionality: Alpha = .81
	
	    Total FIS: Alpha = .92
	
	Cronbach's alpha ranged from .72 to .93 for men. They were as follows:
	
	    Stereotypic Image and Activities: Alpha = .84
	
	    Dependence/Deference: Alpha = .85
	
	    Purity: Alpha = .84
	
	    Caretaking: Alpha = .72
	
	    Emotionality: Alpha = .79
	
	    Total FIS: Alpha = .93

Validity	Discriminant validity was indicated through the lack of significant correlation between the FIS-Total and the Bem Sex Role Inventory—Femininity Score (Bem, 1981) or the Bem Sex Role Inventory—Masculinity Score (Bem, 1981). The FIS-Caretaking subscale did correlate positively with the BSR-Femininity Score. Convergent validity was established through a significant positive correlation between the FIS-Total and agreement with traditional masculine role norms (MNRI-49; Berger, Levant, McMillan, Kelleher, & Sellers, 2005). Furthermore, only one of the FIS subscales did not correlate with the subscales of the MNRI-49. The FIS-Total score also was found to be significantly positively correlated with the subscales of the Feminist Identity Development Scale (FIDS)—Passive Acceptance Stage, and the FIDS—Revelations Stage. The FIS-Total also was significantly negatively correlated with FIDS—Active Commitment Stage. Known-group validity was demonstrated through Analysis of Covariance procedures. Men endorsed traditional femininity ideology more than women.
Related References	Lehman, P. (2000). A validity study of the Femininity Ideology Scale. Master's thesis, Florida Institute of Technology.
Language Versions	English
Contact	Ronald Levant Buchtel College of Arts and Sciences The University of Akron Akron, OH 44325–1901 Email: levant@uakron.edu

8.11.8 Name of the Measure	Conformity to Masculine Norms Inventory CMNI
Primary Reference	Mahalik, J. R., Locke, B. D., Ludlow, L. H., Diemer, M. A., Scott, R. P. J., Gottfried, M., & Freitas, G. (2003). Development of the Conformity to Masculine Norms Inventory. *Psychology of Men and Masculinity, 4*, 3–25.
Purpose	The CMNI is designed to measure the extent to which an individual male conforms to the actions, thoughts, and feelings associated with hegemonic masculinity in the United States.
Description	The CMNI is a 94-item self-report inventory. Each of these items is rated on a 4-point Likert-type scale with the following anchors: 1 = Strongly Disagree to 4 = Strongly Agree. The CMNI is composed of 11 subscales: (1) Dominance; (2) Emotional Control; (3) Disdain for Homosexuals; (4) Playboy; (5) Power over Women; (6) Pursuit of Status; (7) Risk Taking; (8) Self-Reliance; (9) Violence; (10) Winning; and (11) Work Primacy. The instrument was developed through several steps. An initial pool of 144 items was created based on a review of literature regarding masculine norms and two focus groups consisting of men and women receiving graduate education in counseling psychology. These groups discussed masculine norms for 90 minutes weekly over an 8-month period. The focus groups identified 12 masculine norms and crafted 12 statements for each norm. The measure was then piloted at three different times with samples ranging from 20 to 30 people in size. Data from these participants were analyzed and individual items were revised to improve their readability. Items were then given to three graduate students to establish face and content validity. Sampling adequacy was first established. Principal axis extraction with oblique rotation was then conducted and yielded 11 interpretable factors. Based on these findings, 12 items were deleted. Items with structure coefficients of .40 or greater on only one factor were retained. All other items were deleted. This resulted in a 94-item CMNI.
Samples	The psychometric properties of the CMNI were established based on data gathered from a sample of 752 men and 245 women. The sample was composed mostly of White American men (nearly 85%). Most of the men were single ($n = 728$). All participants were in college or graduate school from across the United States. The average age of the sample was 20 years ($SD = 3.42$). A median age of 27 years was used to conduct an exploratory factor analysis and to establish convergent validity.
Scoring	The number of items in each of the subscales is as follows: Dominance: 4 items Emotional Control: 11 items Disdain for Homosexuals: 10 items Playboy: 12 items Power over Women: 9 items

(Continued)

(Continued)

	Pursuit of Status: 6 items
	Risk Taking: 10 items
	Self-Reliance: 6 items
	Violence: 8 items
	Winning: 10 items
	Work Primacy: 8 items
	Total CMNI: 94 items
	Forty-seven items require reverse scoring. Scoring the subscales consists of summing the scores of the items of which they are composed. Higher scores indicate higher levels of conformity to total or specific masculine norm.
Reliability	Cronbach's alpha for the subscale scores ranged from .72 to .91.
	Dominance: Alpha = .73
	Emotional Control: Alpha = .91
	Disdain for Homosexuals: Alpha = .90
	Playboy: Alpha = .88
	Power over Women: Alpha = .87
	Pursuit of Status: Alpha = .72
	Risk Taking: Alpha = .82
	Self-Reliance: Alpha = .85
	Violence: Alpha = .84
	Winning: Alpha = .88
	Work Primacy: Alpha = .76
	Total CMNI: Alpha = .94
	Two-three week Test-retest reliability coefficients were as follows:
	Dominance: $r = .91$
	Emotional Control: $r = 75$
	Disdain for Homosexuals: $r = .96$
	Playboy: $r = .91$
	Power over Women: $r = .74$
	Pursuit of Status: $r = .51$
	Risk Taking: $r = .88$
	Self-Reliance: $r = .80$
	Violence: $r = .76$
	Winning: $r = .87$
	Work Primacy: $r = .67$
	Total CMNI: $r = .95$

Validity	Convergent validity of CMNI and most of its subscales was established through expected correlations with the Gender Role Conflict Scale (GRCS; O'Neil et al., 1986), Brannon Masculinity Scale—Short Form (BMSl; Brannon & Juni, 1984), Drive for Muscularity Scale (McCreary & Sasse, 2000), Social Dominance Orientation Scale (Pratto et al., 1994), the Aggression Questionnaire (Buss & Perry, 1992), Attitudes toward Professional Psychological Help Seeking (Fischer & Turner, 1970), Social Desirability (Crowne & Marlowe, 1960), and the Global Severity Index of the Brief Symptom Inventory (Derogatis, 1993).
	Known-group validity was demonstrated on 9 of 11 scales. Specifically, men scored higher than women on all but the Primacy of Work or Pursuit of Status subscales.
Related References	Burn, S. M., & Ward, Z. (2005). Men's conformity to traditional masculinity and relationship satisfaction. *Psychology of Men & Masculinity, 6,* 254–263.
	Mahalik, J. R., Talmadge, W. T., Locke, B. D., & Scott, R. P. J. (2005). Using the Conformity to Masculine Norms Inventory to work with men in a clinical setting. *Journal of Clinical Psychology, 61,* 661–674.
	Smiler, A. P. (2006). Conforming to masculine norms: Evidence for validity among adult men and women. *Sex Roles, 54,* 767–775.
Language Versions	English
Contact	James R. Mahalik Campion Hall 312 Boston College Chestnut Hill, MA 02467 Email: Mahalik@bc.edu

(Continued)

Validity	One tail *t*-tests indicated a significant main effect of gender on the total score and six of the eight subscales. As expected, women were found to have higher levels of conformity to feminine roles than men for all but modesty and romantic relationships.
	Convergent validity was indicated through significant positive relationships with the Bem Sex Role (BSR) Inventory—Femininity Score (Bem, 1981) and Feminist Identity Composite—Passive Acceptance subscale (FIC; Fischer et al., 2000), and significant negative relationships with the BSR Inventory—Masculinity Score (Bem, 1981). The CFNI and its subscales also correlated with some (but not all) of the subscales of the FIC and an eating disorder inventory (Garner, 1991).
Related References	Hurt, M. M., Nelson, J. A., Turner, D. L., Haines, M. E., Ramsey, L. R., Erchull, M. J., & Liss, M. (2007). Feminism: What is it good for? Feminine norms and objectification as the link between feminist identity and clinically relevant outcomes. *Sex Roles, 57,* 355–363.
	Smiler, A. P., & Gelman, S. A. (2008). Determinants of gender essentialism in college students. *Sex Roles, 58,* 864–874.
Language Versions	English
Contact	James R. Mahalik Campion Hall 312 Boston College Chestnut Hill, MA 02467 Email: Mahalik@bc.edu

8.11.10 Name of the Measure	Hypermasculinity Inventory HMI
Primary Reference	Mosher, D. L., & Sirkin, M. (1984). Measuring a macho personality constellation. *Journal of Research in Personality, 18,* 150–163.
Purpose	The HMI was designed to measure a macho personality.
Description	The HMI is composed of 30 forced-choice self-report items. The HMI is composed of three factors: (1) Calloused Sex Attitudes toward Women, (2) Violence as Manly, and (3) Danger as Exciting. A total of 221 items were developed based on theory (e.g., Izard, 1977) and from discussions involving men. With a sample of 60 college men, the 30 items with the highest item-total correlation coefficients were selected for each subscale. This 90-item measure was then administered to a sample of 135 college men. The 10 items (per subscale) with the highest item-total correlation were then selected to form the final 30-item HMI. These items were then submitted to a principal axis factor analysis (rotation method not indicated). The authors indicate that nine factors emerged from this analysis but that one factor solution accounted for 24% of the variance. Eigenvalues and structure coefficients were not reported. Thus, the final structure of the HMI is based on item-total correlation coefficients and not on results of factor analysis.
Samples	135 undergraduate students from the University of Connecticut from a psychology research pool participated in this study. The majority of the students were 19 years of age and from middle-class backgrounds.

Scoring	The number of items in each subscale is as follows:
	
	    Calloused Sex Attitudes toward Women: 10 items
	
	    Violence as Manly: 10 items
	
	    Danger as Exciting: 10 items
	
	    Total HMI: 30 items
	
	Scores on the subscales are obtained by calculating the sum of all items of the subscale. Higher scores indicate greater levels of hypermasculinity.

Reliability	A Cronbach's alpha coefficient for the three subscale scores was as follows:
	
	    Calloused Sex Attitudes Toward Women: Alpha = .79
	
	    Violence as Manly: Alpha = .79
	
	    Danger as Exciting: Alpha = .71
	
	    Total HMI: Alpha = .89

(Continued)

(Continued)

Validity	Validity was established through significant positive relationships between the HMI subscales and use of all types of drugs (Kopplin, Greenfield, & Wong, 1977). With respect to specific substances, use of alcohol and use of stimulants were found to be related to each of the three subscales. The Danger as Exciting subscale also was correlated with use of the following substances: codeine, depressants, opium, hashish, and hallucinogens. A number of correlations also were established between the three subscales and dimensions of personality (Jackson, 1974). All three subscales were found to be significantly positively associated with exhibition, impulsivity, and play. Other significant relationships were reported between one or two of the subscales and other personality traits.
Related References	Parrott, D. J., & Zeichner, A. (2005). Effects of sexual prejudice and anger on physical aggression toward gay and heterosexual men. *Psychology of Men & Masculinity, 6,* 3–17.
	Saez, P. A., Casado, A., & Wade, J. C. (2009). Factors influencing masculinity ideology among Latino men. *Journal of Men's Studies, 17,* 116–128.
Language Versions	English
Contact	Donald L Mosher Department of Psychology 406 Babbidge Road, Unit 1020 Storrs, CT 06269-1020

8.11.11 Name of the Measure	Male Role Attitude Scale MRAS
Primary Reference	Pleck, J. H., Sonenstein, F. L., & Ku, L. C. (1993). Attitudes toward male roles among adolescent males: A discriminant validity analysis. *Sex Roles, 30*, 481–501.
Purpose	The MRAS is designed to measure beliefs about the importance of men conforming to traditional male roles.
Description	The MRAS is an 8-item measure that employs a 4-point Likert-type self-report scale (0 = Disagree A Lot to 3 = Agree A Lot). The MRAS is composed of one factor. Seven of the eight items were adapted from the MRNS (Thompson & Pleck, 1986). The eighth item addressed the topic of sex, an issue not addressed in the MRNS. Based on eigenvalues, factor analysis indicated the possibility of a two-factor solution. However, the authors reasoned that because of the relatively weak coefficient alpha ($\alpha = .50$) found for the second subscale score, a one-factor solution would be a better fit.
Samples	Validation of the measure was established using a sample of 676 African American, 386 Latino American, 755 White American, and 63 men identifying as "other." Participants ranged in age (15–19 years).
Scoring	The MRAS is composed of eight items. The total score is calculated by summing the scores. Higher scores indicate greater levels of traditional or conservative attitudes regarding men.
Reliability	Cronbach's alpha for the MRAS score was .56.
Validity	Discriminant validity was indicated by the lack of significant relationships between the MRAS and an item assessing the attitudes toward female roles. Convergent validity was established through significant relationships found between the MRAS and several items assessing the attitudes toward gender roles and relationships. Criterion validity also was established. MRAS was found to be positively associated with the scores of several items measuring homophobic attitudes, traditional male procreative attitudes, and beliefs that impregnation validates masculinity.
Related References	Doss, B. D., & Hopkins, J. R. (1998). The Multicultural Masculinity Ideology Scale: Validation from three cultural perspectives. *Sex Roles, 38*, 719–741. Ojeda, L., Rosales, R., & Good, G. E. (2008). Socioeconomic status and cultural predictors of male role attitudes among Mexican American men: Son más machos? *Psychology of Men & Masculinity, 9*, 133–138.
Language Versions	English
Contact	Joseph H. Pleck Christopher Hall 2033 (MC-081) 904 W. Nevada University of Illinois Urbana, IL 61801 office: (217) 244–8834 fax: (217) 333–9061 Email: jhpleck@uiuc.edu

8.11.12 Name of the Measure	Extended Personal Attributes Questionnaire EPAQ
Primary Reference	Spence, J. T., Helmreich, R. L., & Holahan, C. K. (1979). Negative and positive components of psychological masculinity and femininity and their relationships to self-reports of neurotic and active out behaviors. *Journal of Personality and Social Psychology, 37,* 1673–1682.
Purpose	The EPAQ is an extension of the PAQ (Spence & Helmreich, 1978) that was developed to measure socially desirable and undesirable feminine and masculine traits.
Description	The EPAQ is a 40-item, Likert-type self-report inventory. Participants are instructed to rate how well a trait is reflective of their own personality. Each item is rated on a 5-point Likert-type scale with opposing statements for each trait (e.g., 1 = Not At All Aggressive to 5 = Very Aggressive Like Me). There are six subscales to the EPAQ: (1) Positive Masculine; (2) Positive Feminine; (3) Masculine-Feminine; (4) Negative Masculine; (5) Feminine—Unmitigated Communality; and (6) Feminine—Verbal Aggression. In practice, the Masculine-Feminine subscale has been excluded because of its inclusion of both masculine and feminine traits. The EPAQ consists of the original PAQ (Helmreich, Spence, & Wilhelm, 1981), which measures desirable masculine and feminine traits and newly developed items that measure socially undesirable masculine and feminine traits. The authors grounded their instrument in the theoretical work of Bakan (1966). The newly developed items were derived through the same processes as the original "positive" traits of the PAQ. As such, items were drawn from a pool of items that were identified as (a) socially undesirable for both sexes, (b) attributed more frequently to one sex over the other, and (c) agentic or communal in nature. Because of the difficulties encountered in identifying negative communal traits of women, the authors chose to study two specific undesirable feminine traits (i.e., unmitigated communion and verbal passive-aggressiveness). These 16 items were combined with the original 24-item PAQ to form a six-scale EPAQ. A series of *t*-tests was conducted to compare the means on those scales by gender. With the exception of the masculinity-femininity subscale, which is hardly used (Smiler & Epstein, 2010), the expected significant differences were found. Helmreich et al. (1981) performed a series of factor analyses with oblique rotation to study the underlying structure of a 16-item PAQ, measuring only masculine and feminine items; the 24-item PAQ, which includes the masculinity-femininity subscale; and, finally, the EPAQ, which measures both socially desirable and undesirable traits of women and men. Twelve factor analyses were conducted for men and women of three age groups (i.e., high school, college, parents in the community) separately for the 16- and 24-item PAQ. The factor structure of the negative items of the EPAQ was studied for men and women separately using only a college student population. A two-factor solution, reflecting masculine and feminine traits, emerged from factor analyses of the 16-item PAQ and from the 24-item PAQ. The factor structure of the negative items from the EPAQ differed for women and men. For men, feminine verbal aggression and negative masculine items correlated on one factor. Other items correlated with another factor that reflected the proposed Feminine Unmitigated

	Communion dimension of negative feminine traits. A three-factor solution emerged in factor analysis using data from only women. These three factors reflected the proposed three subscales of socially undesirable traits of women and men.
Samples	The factor structure of the PAQ was examined based on data gathered from 1,465 female and 854 male undergraduate college students attending the University of Texas, Austin. Validity of the EPAQ was demonstrated based on data gathered from 220 male and 363 female undergraduate students, also from the University of Texas, Austin.
Scoring	Scale scores are obtained by summing the corresponding item scores. Higher scores indicate more agreement with positive or negative components of psychological masculinity or femininity as reflective of self.

Reliability	Cronbach's alpha for the subscale scores were as follows:
	
	    Positive Masculine: Alpha = .74 (males) and .74 (females)
	    Positive Feminine: Alpha = .75 (males) and .75 (females)
	    Masculine-Feminine: Alpha = .54 (males) and .63 (females)
	    Negative Masculine: Alpha = .69 (males) and .70 (females)
	    Unmitigated Communality: Alpha = .46 (males) and .41 (females)
	    Verbal Aggression: Alpha = .60 (males) and .63 (females)

Validity	Spence et al. (1979) reported generally expected correlations between the subscales of the EPAQ and self-esteem (Helmreich & Stapp, 1974), and neuroticism, and acting out. Known-groups validity was demonstrated through significant gender differences in the subscales scores.
Related References	Conway, M., Alfonsi, G., Pushkar, D., & Giannopoulos, C. (2008). Rumination on sadness and dimensions of communality and agency: Comparing White American and visible minority individuals in a Canadian context. *Sex Roles, 58,* 738–749. Helmreich, R. L., Spence, J. T., & Wilhelm, J. A. (1981). A psychometric analysis of the Personal Attributes Questionnaire. *Sex Roles, 7,* 1097–1108. Hoffmann, M. L., Powlishta, K. K., & White, K. J. (2004). An examination of gender differences in adolescent adjustment: The effect of competence on gender role differences in symptoms of psychopathology. *Sex Roles, 50,* 795–810.
Language Versions	English
Contact	The items can be found in Helmreich et al. (1981).

8.11.13 Name of the Measure	Macho Belief Inventory MBI
Primary Reference	Strong, W. F., McQuillen, J. S., & Hughey, J. D. (1994). En el laberinto de machismo: A comparative analysis of macho attitudes among Hispanic and Anglo college students. *Howard Journal of Communications, 5,* 18–35.
Purpose	The MBI was developed to measure attitudes toward the male sex role.
Description	The MBI is a 41-item self-report inventory. Each item is rated on a 7-point Likert-type scale with the following anchors: 1 = Strongly Disagree to 7 = Strongly Agree.
	There are 11 subscales to the MBI: (1) Chauvinism; (2) Role Liberation; (3) Cultural Propriety; (4) Promiscuity; (5) Premarital Experience; (6) Tolerance; (7) Possessiveness; (8) Security; (9) Dependency; (10) Permissiveness; and (11) Male Supremacy.
	Fifty-one items were developed based on a review of relevant literature (e.g., Lara-Cantú, 1989) and on feedback from 10 faculty and graduate students who were identified as experts of Latino/a culture. Ten items were discarded based on pilot test data. The remaining 41 items were submitted to principal component analysis (PCA) with varimax rotation. Results of the PCA indicated 11 factors with eigenvalues greater than 1.0.
Samples	A sample of 171 Latino/a American students (111 females, 60 males) attending a predominantly Hispanic institution and 130 White Americans (72 females, 58 males) attending a predominantly White institution participated in the factor analytic study of the MBI.
Scoring	The number of items per subscales are as follows:
	Chauvinism: 9 items
	Role Liberation: 4 items
	Cultural Propriety: 4 items
	Promiscuity: 4 items
	Premarital Experience: 2 items
	Tolerance: 2 items
	Possessiveness: 3 items
	Security: 2 items
	Dependency: 2 items
	Permissiveness: 2 items
	Male Supremacy: 3 items
	Total MBI: 41 items
	About a third of the items require reverse scoring (William Strong, personal communication, March 18, 2010). Scores are summed and divided by the number of items of the subscale. Higher scores indicate lower levels of agreement with macho beliefs.

Reliability	Cronbach's alpha for the total score on the MBI was .84. Cronbach's alpha for subscale scores was not reported.
Validity	Discriminant validity was evidenced through differences found in mean scores of men and women from both Latino/a American and White American samples.
Related References	
Language Versions	English
Contact	The MBI is published in Strong et al. (1994).

8.11.14 Name of the Measure	Male Role Norms Scale MRNS
Primary Reference	Thompson, E. H., Jr., & Pleck, J. H. (1986). The structure of male role norms. *American Behavioral Scientist, 29,* 531–534.
Purpose	The MRNS was developed to measure attitudes toward the male sex role.
Description	The MRNS is a 26-item self-report inventory. Each item is rated on a 7-point Likert-type scale with the following anchors: 1 = Strongly Disagree to 7 = Strongly Agree. There are three subscales to the MRNS: (1) Status, (2) Toughness, and (3) Antifemininity. Items were taken directly from Brannon and Juni's (1984) conceptualization of male role norms. Principal factor analyses with oblique and oblimin rotation were performed. An oblimin rotation was selected because it produced a clearer factor solution. Items were chosen if the analysis yielded structure coefficients greater than .40 on only one factor.
Samples	A random sample of 233 men attending one of two liberal arts colleges in New England participated. With respect to academic class standing, 24% were first-year students, 29% were sophomores, 28% juniors, and 19% seniors. The sample was composed predominantly of White Americans (96%). Eighty-four percent identified as Catholic. The sample was composed of children from middle- to upper-middle-class parents. Nearly 75% of the fathers completed an undergraduate degree and nearly half completed some graduate or professional training. Forty-five percent of the mothers completed college and 20% held a graduate or professional degree.

Scoring	The number of items in each subscale is as follows:
	
	    Status: 11 items
	
	    Toughness: 8 items
	
	    Antifemininity: 7 items
	
	    Total MRNS: 26 items
	
	Two items require reverse scoring. Scores are summed and divided by the number of items of the subscale. Higher scores indicate higher levels of agreement with male role norms.

Reliability	Cronbach's alpha for the scores were as follows:
	
	    Status: Alpha = .81
	
	    Toughness: Alpha = .74
	
	    Anti-femininity: Alpha = .76

Validity	Validity was established through significant positive correlations between MRNS subscales and negative attitudes toward the Equal Rights Amendment and for preference for a virgin wife.

Related References	Fischer, A. R., Tokar, D. M., Good, G. E., & Snell, A. F. (1998). More on the structure of male role norms: Exploratory and multiple sample confirmatory analyses. *Psychology of Women Quarterly, 22,* 135–155.
	Magovcevic, M., & Addis, M. E. (2008). The Masculine Depression Scale: Development and psychometric evaluation. *Psychology of Men and Masculinity, 9,* 117–132.
	Parrott, D. J. (2009). Aggression toward gay men as gender role enforcement: Effects of male role norms, sexual prejudice, and masculine gender role stress. *Journal of Personality, 77,* 1137–1166.
Language Versions	English
Contact	Edward H. Thompson, Jr. Department of Sociology and Anthropology 1 College Street Holy Cross College Worcester, MA 01610–2395 Phone: (508) 793–3468 Fax: (508) 793–3088 Email: ethompson@holycross.edu

8.11.15 Name of the Measure	Adolescent Femininity Ideology Scale AFIS
Primary Reference	Tolman, D. L., Impett, E. A., Tracy, A. J., & Michael, A. (2006). Looking good, sounding good: Femininity ideology and adolescent girls' mental health. *Psychology of Women Quarterly, 30,* 85–95.
Purpose	The AFIS was developed to measure adolescent girls' internalization of and resistance to two dimensions of hegemonic femininity ideology: body image and relationships with others.
Description	The AFIS is a 17-item self-report inventory. Each item is rated on a 6-point Likert-type scale with the following anchors: 1 = Strongly Disagree to 6 = Strongly Agree. There are two subscales to the AFIS: (1) Inauthentic Self in Relationship (ISR) and (2) Objectified Relationship with Body (ORB). The AFIS is grounded upon the findings of research on female adolescent development (e.g., Bartky, 1990; Brown & Gilligan, 1992; Taylor, Gilligan, & Sullivan, 1995; Tolman & Debold, 1993) and on the findings of eight focus groups involving a racially and economically diverse group of 55 adolescent girls who ranged in age from 13 to 19 years. These girls also evaluated the items for appropriateness. One hundred twenty-six items were developed from these focus groups. Items were deleted if they yielded limited variability in responses or if focus group members offered significant negative feedback. Items also were deleted if they yielded an interitem correlation coefficient less than .15. From this process, 42 items were selected for the AFIS. Tolman, Impett, Tracy, and Michael (2006) conducted confirmatory factor analysis with a sample of younger adolescent girls. The results of their analysis indicated that data did not fit the hypothesized factor structure of the AFIS. Thus, the AFIS is composed of 17 items.
Samples	One hundred forty-eight girls attending the eighth grade in an urban middle school located in the Northeast (U.S.) participated in the study. The sample was composed of White Americans (52%), Latina Americans (20%), multiracial Americans (16%), African Americans (4%), Asian Americans (3%), and those for which data were missing or reported as "other" (5%).
Scoring	The number of items in each subscale is as follows: ISR: 9 items ORB: 8 items Total AFIS: 17 items Six items require reverse scoring. Scores are summed and divided by the number of items of the subscale. Higher scores indicate lower levels of authenticity and higher levels of self-objectification.
Reliability	Cronbach's alpha for the scores were as follows: Status: Alpha = .81 Toughness: Alpha = .74 Anti-femininity: Alpha = .76

Validity	Evidence for validity was indicated through significant positive correlations between ISR and ORB and depression (Kovacs, 1992) and significant inverse relationships with the subscales yielded with self-esteem (Rosenberg, 1965).
Related References	Tolman, D. L., & Porche, M. V. (2000). The Adolescent Femininity Ideology Scale: Development and Validation of a new measure for girls. *Psychology of Women Quarterly, 24,* 365–376.
Language Versions	English, Spanish
Contact	Deborah L. Tolman Center for Research on Gender and Sexuality San Francisco State University 2017 Mission Street, Suite 300 San Francisco, CA 94110 Email: dtolman@sfsu.edu

8.12 PSYCHOLOGICAL COSTS OF GENDER ROLE CONFORMITY

8.12.1 Name of the Measure	Masculine Gender Role Stress Scale MGRS
Primary Reference	Eisler, R. M., & Skidmore, J. R. (1987). Masculine gender role stress: Scale development and component factors in the appraisal of stressful situations. *Behavior Modification, 11*, 123–136.
Purpose	The MGRS is designed to measure stress associated with conforming to masculine gender roles.
Description	The MGRS is a 40-item, Likert-type self-report inventory. Each item is rated on a 7-point Likert-type scale with the following anchors: 1 = Not at all Stressful to 7 = Extremely Stressful. The MGRS is composed of five components: (1) Physical Inadequacy; (2) Emotional Inexpressiveness; (3) Subordination to Women; (4) Intellectual Inferiority; and (5) Performance Failure. The initial pool of 105 items was developed empirically through sentence completion tasks that elicited responses to stressful attributes of being a man. The sample was composed of 205 undergraduates at a large public university in Virginia. These items were then judged by 50 trained raters for the level of stress for women and men. Sixty-six items were included because they were rated (1) as significantly more stressful for men than for women and (2) had a mean rating above the median. An additional 23 items were deleted because of their correlation with the total score. A five-component solution emerged from a principal components analysis with direct oblimin rotation. The authors required that each factor contain at least six structure coefficients of .30 or greater. Three of those structure coefficients were required to be .50 or greater. Finally, a minimum eigenvalue of 1.50 was established. This resulted in a 40-item MGRS scale.
Samples	Validation of the measure was established using a sample of 173 college students attending a public university. The sample was composed of 82 males and 91 females who ranged in age from 18 to 23 years.

Scoring	The number of items in each subscale is as follows:
	
	    Physical Inadequacy: 9 items
	    Emotional Inexpressiveness: 7 items
	    Subordination to Women: 9 items
	    Intellectual Inferiority: 7 items
	    Performance Failure: 8 items
	    Total MGRS: 40 items
	
	Total and each subscale score are determined by summing the responses for each item with the subscale. Higher scores indicate greater masculine gender role stress.

Reliability	Cronbach's alpha for the scale was not reported in the development of the MGRS.
Validity	Known-group differences and convergent validity were demonstrated to further indicate the psychometric properties of the MGRS. First, men were found to have higher levels of MGRS than women. Convergent validity was demonstrated, among the sample of men, through significant positive relationships between the MGRS and anxiety (Spielberger, Gorsuch, Lushene, Vagg, & Jacobs, 1983) and anger (Siegel, 1986). Finally and as expected, MGRS was not found to be related to masculine ideology (Spence, Helmreich, & Stapp, 1974).
Related References	Parrott, D. J., Peterson, J. L., Vincent, W., & Bakeman, R. (2008). Correlates of anger in response to gay men: Effects of male gender role beliefs, sexual prejudice, and masculine gender role stress. *Psychology of Men & Masculinity, 9,* 167–178.
	Wade, J. C. (2008). Masculinity ideology, male reference group identity dependence, and African American men's health-related attitudes and behaviors. *Psychology of Men & Masculinity, 9,* 5–16.
Language Versions	English, Chinese
Contact	Richard M. Eisler 200 Southpark Drive, Suite 4 Blacksburg, VA 24060

8.12.2 Name of the Measure	Feminine Gender Role Stress Scale FGRS
Primary Reference	Gillespie, B. L., & Eisler, R. M. (1992). Development of the Feminine Gender Role Stress Scale: A cognitive-behavioral measure of stress, appraisal, and coping for women. *Behavior Modification, 16,* 426–438.
Purpose	The FGRS is designed to measure the gender role-related stress experienced by women.
Description	The FGRS is a 39-item self-report inventory. Each of these items is rated on a 6-point Likert-type scale with the following anchors: 0 = Not at all Stressful to 5 = Extremely Stressful.
	The FGRS is composed of 5 subscales: (1) Fear of Unemotional Relationships; (2) Fear of Physical Unattractiveness; (3) Fear of Victimization; (4) Fear of Behaving Assertively; and (5) Fear of Not Being Nurturant.
	The instrument was developed through several steps. An initial pool of 99 items was created based on a review of literature regarding gender roles, interviews with 16 women aged 24–56 years, and the contents of a sentence-completion task administered to 205 undergraduate college students (87 males and 118 females). Their ages ranged from 18 to 24 years old. Items were then given to 43 male and female faculty and graduate students of psychology. These individuals rated each situation on stressfulness. Items rated by both female and male raters as significantly more stressful for women than for men were retained. This resulted in the deletion of 34 items.
	Factor analysis with orthogonal rotation was conducted to understand the factor structure of the FGRS. A five-factor solution was deemed to be the most interpretable. Twenty-six items were deleted because they did not yield a structure coefficient greater than .35. These procedures resulted in a 39-item measure.
Samples	The psychometric properties of the FGRS were established based on data gathered from a sample of 253 women who ranged in age from 17 to 51 ($M = 19$). Ninety-seven of these women also provided data to establish temporal stability.
Scoring	The number of items in each subscale is as follows:
	Fear of Emotional Relationships: 10 items
	Fear of Physical Unattractiveness: 8 items
	Fear of Victimization: 6 items
	Fear of Behaving Assertively: 7 items
	Fear of Not Being Nurturant: 8 items
	Total FGRS: 39 items
	Scoring the subscales consists of summing subscale items and dividing by the number of items of which it is composed. Higher scores indicate higher levels of gender role stress for women. No transformations are required.

Reliability	Cronbach's alpha for the scores on the subscales ranged from .73–.83.
	Fear of Emotional Relationships: Alpha = .83
	Fear of Physical Unattractiveness: Alpha = .81
	Fear of Victimization: Alpha = .77
	Fear of Behaving Assertively: Alpha = .80
	Fear of Not Being Nurturant: Alpha = .73
	Two-week test-retest reliability was .82 for the total FGRS score.
Validity	Convergent validity of FGRS and its factors was established through expected correlations with the Hassles Scale (Kanner, Coyne, Shaefer, & Lazarus, 1981). Discriminant validity was established through the lack of significant correlations with the femininity (Spence, Helmreich, & Stapp, 1974).
	Known-group validity was evidenced by demonstrating that women scored higher than men on the FGRS.
Related References	Bekker, M. H. J., & Boselie, K. A. H. M. (2002). Gender and stress: Is gender role stress? A re-examination of the relationship between feminine gender role stress and eating disorders. *Stress and Health, 18,* 141–149.
	van Well, S., Kolk, A. M., & Arrindell, W. A. (2005). Cross-cultural validity of the Masculine and Feminine Gender Role Stress Scales. *Journal of Personality Assessment, 84,* 271–278.
Language Versions	English, Chinese
Contact	Betty L. Gillespie 2117 Maiden Lane South West Roanoke, VA 24015

8.12.3 Name of the Measure	Normative Male Alexithymia Scale NMAS
Primary Reference	Levant, R. F., Good, G. E., Cook, S. W., O'Neil, J. M., Smalley, K., B., . . . Richmond, K. (2006). The Normative Male Alexithymia Scale: Measurement of a gender-linked syndrome. *Psychology of Men & Masculinity, 7,* 212–224.
Purpose	The NMAS is designed to measure normative alexithymia among a general population of men.
Description	The NMAS is a 20-item, Likert-type self-report inventory. Each item is rated on a 7-point Likert-type scale with the following anchors: 1 = Strongly Disagree to 7 = Strongly Agree. The NMAS is composed of one single component. Fifteen items were developed based on a review of literature on normative male alexithymia (i.e., the inability to put emotions into words) and interviews with scholars on the psychology of men. An additional 14 items were adapted from items on the Gender Role Conflict Scale (O'Neil et al., 1986), the Emotional Openness Scale (Komiya, 2000), and the Toronto Alexithymia Scale (Bagby, Parker, & Taylor, 1994). Principal factor analyses with varimax and oblique rotations were performed. A one-component solution was selected based on statistical (i.e., structure coefficient greater than .40) and conceptual clarity. A maximum likelihood confirmatory factor analysis was utilized to confirm the factor structure of the NMAS. This resulted in only modest support for the initial factor structure of the NMAS. The authors performed an exploratory factor analysis (EFA) to replicate its factor structure. This EFA replicated the structure indicated in the first study.
Samples	Validation of the measure was established using two samples of college students attending a public university. The first sample was composed of 266 male undergraduate students. The ages ranged from 18–22 years for 93% of the sample. A majority of the sample identified as White American (84%). The second sample was composed of 407 male (*n* = 192) and female (*n* = 210) undergraduate students. Five individuals did not indicate their sex. The ages ranged from 17–45 with a 91% reporting being ages 17 to 20. This sample was composed of 331 White American, 41 Latino/a American, 10 African American, 10 Asian American, and 9 identified as "other." Sixty-five of the participants also participated in the first study and served to establish test-retest reliability.
Scoring	The NMAS is comprised of 20 items. Ten items of the NMAS require reverse scoring. Scores are summed and divided by the number of items of the measure, with higher scores indicating greater normative male alexithymia.
Reliability	Cronbach's alpha for the scale score was .92 for men and .93 for women. Test-retest reliability coefficients were .91 and .86 for men and women, respectively.

Validity	Validity was established in several ways. First, the NMAS was found to be correlated significantly with the TAS-20 and the total score and Restricted Emotionality subscale score of the MNRI (Levant et al., 1992). Scores on the NMAS also were found to be higher for men than for women.
Related References	Levant, R. F., Halter, M. J., Hayden, E. W., & Williams, C. M. (2009). The efficacy of alexithymia reduction treatment: A pilot study. *Journal of Men's Studies, 17,* 75–84.
Language Versions	
Contact	Ronald F. Levant Butchel College of Arts and Sciences The University of Akron Akron, OH 44325-1901 Phone: 330-972-7882 Email: levant@uakron.edu

8.12.4 Name of the Measure	Barriers to Help Seeking Scale BHSS
Primary Reference	Mansfield, A. K., Addis, M. E., & Courtenay, W. (2005). Measurement of men's help seeking: Development and evaluation of the Barriers to Help Seeking Scale. *Psychology of Men & Masculinity, 6,* 95–108.
Purpose	The BHSS was developed to measure men's reasons for not seeking professional help for psychological and physical health problems.
Description	The BHSS is a 31-item self-report inventory. Each item is rated on a 5-point Likert-type scale with the following anchors: 0 = Not at All to 4 = Very Much.
	There are five subscales to the BHSS: (1) Need for Control and Self-Reliance, (2) Minimizing Problem and Resignation, (3) Concrete Barriers and Distrust of Caregivers, (4) Privacy, and (5) Emotional Control.
	Items were developed based on theories of gender role strain and gender role conflict (e.g., O'Neil, Good, & Holmes, 1995; Pleck, 1995) and literature regarding help seeking (Fischer & Turner, 1970). Based on this review, the authors generated a list of potential barriers to help seeking and created between one and four items for each barrier. Some items were developed to reflect the male gender role socialization process, while others were created to reflect social psychological processes. This process yielded 54 items, which were submitted to a series of principal components factor analyses. In the initial analysis, nine factors emerged. However, the last four of the factors were deemed to not be interpretable. Thus, a five-factor solution was examined further. A second principal components analysis using an oblique rotation, with five factors specified, was conducted. A principal components analysis also was conducted with three factors specified. A five-factor solution was deemed to be the most interpretable.
Samples	A sample of male undergraduate students (*N* = 537) participated in the study of the factor structure of the BHSS. The men attended an all-male college in the Midwest region of the United States. With respect to class standing, 30.2% were first-year students, 27.2% were sophomores, 19.0% were juniors, and 21% were seniors. The sample was composed of White Americans (91.6%), Latino Americans (0.7%), African Americans (0.4%), Native Americans (1.1%), and 1.1% Asian Americans. An additional 1.1% of the sample identified as "other." The mean age was 19.9 years (*SD* = 1.16 years).
Scoring	The number of items in each subscale is as follows:
	Need for Control and Self-Reliance: 10 items
	Minimizing Problem and Resignation: 6 items
	Concrete Barriers and Distrust of Caregivers: 6 items
	Privacy: 5 items
	Emotional Control: 4 items
	Total BHSS: 31 items
	Subscale and Total Scale Scores are obtained by summing the corresponding item scores. Higher scores indicate more barriers to help seeking.

Reliability	Cronbach's alpha for the scores were as follows:
	Need for Control and Self-Reliance: Alpha = .93
	Minimizing Problem and Resignation: Alpha = .89
	Concrete Barriers and Distrust of Caregivers: Alpha = .79
	Privacy: Alpha = .83
	Emotional Control: Alpha = .89
	Total BHSS: Alpha = .95
Validity	Evidence for convergent validity was demonstrated through statistically significant relationships found between the subscale and total of the BHSS and gender role conflict and it subscales (O'Neil, Helms, Gable, David, & Wrightsman, 1986).
	Evidence for criterion-related validity was indicated through expected significant negative relationships found between the BHSS and attitudes toward help seeking (Fischer & Turner, 1970).
Related References	
Language Versions	English
Contact	Abigail Mansfield Department of Psychology Clark University 950 Main Street Worcester, MA 01610 Email: amansfield@clarku.edu

8.12.5 Name of the Measure	Gender Role Conflict Scale GRCS
Primary Reference	O'Neil, J. M., Helms, B. J., Gable, R. K., David, L., & Wrightsman, L. S. (1986). Gender role conflict scale: College men's fear of femininity. *Sex Roles, 14,* 335–350.
Purpose	The GRCS is designed to measure the patterns of gender role conflict experienced by men as a result of rigid gender role socialization.
Description	The GRCS is a 37-item self-report inventory. Each of these items is rated on a 6-point Likert-type scale with the following anchors: 1 = Strongly Disagree to 6 = Strongly Agree. The GRCS is composed of four subscales: (1) Success, Power, Competition; (2) Restrictive Emotionality; (3) Restrictive Affectionate Behavior between Men; and (4) Conflicts between Work and Family Relations. The instrument was developed through several steps. An initial pool of 85 items was created based a review of literature regarding gender role strain and masculine ideology. Factor analysis with oblique rotation and orthogonal rotation was conducted to understand the factor structure of the GRCS. A four-factor solution was deemed to be the most interpretable. Items were deleted because they did not yield a structure coefficient greater than .35 or because of structure coefficients of greater than .30 on more than one factor. An adolescent version of the GRCS has been created to assess gender role conflict in a developmentally appropriate fashion (see Blazina, Pisecco, & O'Neil, 2005).
Samples	The psychometric properties of the GRCS were established based on data gathered from a sample of 527 men attending one of two universities in the Midwest. The mean age was 19.8 years.
Scoring	The number of items in each subscale is as follows: Success, Power, Competition: 13 items Restrictive Emotionality: 10 items Restrictive Affectionate Behavior Between Men: 8 items Conflicts Between Work and Family Relations: 6 items Total GRCS-I: 37 items Scoring the subscales consists of summing subscale items. The total GRCS-I score is derived by summing all items. Higher scores indicate higher levels of gender role conflict for men. No transformations are required.
Reliability	Cronbach's alpha for the subscale scores ranged from .75 to .85. Success, Power, Competition: Alpha = .85 Restrictive Emotionality: Alpha = .82 Restrictive Affectionate Behavior Between Men: Alpha = .83 Conflicts Between Work and Family Relations: Alpha = .75 Four-Week Test-Retest reliabilities ranged from .72 to .86.

Validity	Known-group validity indicated that masculine men scored higher on Success, Power, and Competition, Restrictive Emotionality, and Restrictive Affectionate Behavior between Men.
Related References	Cohn, A. M., Seibert, L. A., & Zeichner, A. (2009). The role of restrictive emotionality, trait anger, and masculinity threat in men's perception of physical aggression. *Psychology of Men & Masculinity, 10,* 218–224.
	O'Neil, J. M. (2008). Summarizing 25 years of research on men's gender role conflict using the Gender Role Conflict Scale: New research paradigms and clinical applications. *The Counseling Psychologist, 36,* 358–445.
	Wester, S. R. (2008). Thinking complexly about men, gender role conflict and counseling psychology. *The Counseling Psychologist, 36,* 462–468.
Language Versions	English, different dialects of Spanish, Turkish
Contact	James O'Neil Family Studies and Educational Psychology School of Family Studies Human Development and Family Studies Box U-2058 University of CT Storrs, CT 06269–2058 (860) 486–4281 http://web.uconn.edu/joneil/

8.13 GENDER PREJUDICE AND SEXISM

8.13.1 Name of the Measure	Perceived Social Inequity Scale—Women's Form PSIS-W
Primary Reference	Corning, A. F. (2000). Assessing perceived social inequity: A relative deprivation framework. *Journal of Personality and Social Psychology, 78,* 463–477.
Purpose	The PSIS-W was designed to measure women's perceptions of perceived social inequity.
Description	The PSIS-W is a 26-item self-report inventory utilizing a Likert-type scale with the response range: 1 = Not At All to 6 = Very Much.
	The authors describe the PSIS-W as being composed of the following six subscales: (1) Physical Appearance; (2) Career Encouragement; (3) Academic Role Models; (4) Harassment/Assault; (5) Career Competence; and (6) Multiple Roles.
	Items for the initial 41-item version of the PSIS-W were created based on a review of literature on sexism against women and on relative deprivation theory (Davis, 1959). Expert reviews from professors and advanced doctoral students of psychology resulted in the elimination of seven items. Feedback also was obtained from a small sample of 10 undergraduate women students. Further refinement of the PSIS-W resulted from two separate factor analyses. In the first effort for refinement, five items were eliminated based on low item–total correlations. Principal-axis factor analysis with oblique rotation yielded a six-factor solution. Two items were deleted due to low structure coefficients. One of the 27 items was retained despite an ambiguous structure coefficient. Before submitting these items for another test of the PSIS-W's factor structure, two experts of test construction were consulted. As a result of this, items were slightly reworded. Principal-axis factor analysis with Harris-Kaiser rotation resulted in a similar six-factor solution. The one item that was retained for further analysis did not correlate with any one factor. This item was deleted, resulting in a 26-item PSIS-W.
Samples	In the last study of factor structure and validity of the PSIS-W, Corning (2000) recruited 232 female undergraduate and graduate students and nonmatriculated adults who ranged in age from 19–48. The sample was composed of White Americans (92.6%), Asian and Asian Americans (3.0%), Latina Americans (1.7%), and 0.9% African Americans. Another 1.3% of the sample reported "other."
Scoring	The number of items in each subscale is as follows: Physical Appearance: 5 items Career Competence: 4 items Academic Role Models: 4 items Harassment/Assault: 6 items Career Competence: 4 items Multiple Roles: 4 items Total PSIS-W: 26 items

	Each item is composed of four sub-items that were written to reflect relative deprivation theory. Specifically, a participant indicates the extent to which she (a) wants a particular resource, (b) believes that another group (i.e., men) has greater access to that resource, (c) feels deserving of the resource, and (d) currently is in possession of the resource. Fourteen questions with 54 subitems require reverse scoring. Responses of the first three subitems are summed and divided by the last subitem to create an item score. The item scores are then summed and divided by the number of items in a subscale or the total score.
Reliability	Reliability coefficients were not reported. However, 1- and 4-month test-retest reliability coefficients were presented: Total PSIS-W: $r = .88$ (for both 1- and 4-month interval)
Validity	Evidence for construct validity was demonstrated through a statistically significant inverse relationship found between it and sexism (Swim, Aiken, Hall, & Hunter, 1995; Tougas, Brown, Beaton, & Joly, 1995) and positive relationships found between it and sexual harassment (Fitzgerald, Gelfand, & Drasgow, 1995), sexual victimization (Koss & Oros, 1982), psychological stress (Derogatis, Lipman, Rickels, Uhlenhuth, & Covi, 1974), and daily hassles (Kanner, Coyne, Schaefer, & Lazarus, 1981). Positive associations also were found with generalized alienation, powerlessness, and social isolation (Dean, 1961) and liberal attitudes toward women (Spence, Helmreich, & Stapp, 1973). An inverse relationship was found between it and beliefs in a just world (Rubin & Peplau, 1975).
Related References	Corning, A. F. (2002). Self-esteem as a moderator between perceived discrimination and psychological distress among women. *Journal of Counseling Psychology, 49,* 117–126.
Language Versions	English
Contact	Alexandra F. Corning Department of Psychology University of Notre Dame Notre Dame, IN 46556 Phone: (574) 247-0403 Email: acorning@nd.edu

8.13.2 Name of the Measure	The Ambivalent Sexism Inventory ASI
Primary Reference	Glick, P., & Fiske, S. T. (1996). The Ambivalent Sexism Inventory: Differentiating hostile and benevolent sexism. *Journal of Personality and Social Psychology, 70*(3), 491–512.
Purpose	The ASI is designed to measure hostile and benevolent attitudes toward women.
Description	The ASI is a 22-item measure that employs a 6-point self-report scale (0 = Disagree Strongly to 5 = Agree Strongly). The ASI has two components: (1) Hostile Sexism (HS) and (2) Benevolent Sexism (BS). The ASI was developed based on theoretical and empirical treatment in the study of benevolent and hostile sexism as well as aversive racism. The ASI was developed and validated over the course of six studies. The initial ASI was composed of 140 statements developed to represent dimensions of hostile sexism (i.e., Dominative Paternalism, Competitive Gender Differentiation, and Heterosexual Hostility) and benevolent sexism (i.e., Protective Paternalism, Complementary Gender Differentiation, and Heterosexual Intimacy). Items addressing modern sexism also were developed based on Katz and Hass's (1988) pro-Black scale. Items measuring recognition of discrimination also were included. Finally, the initial 140-item ASI included six validity items. Before items were submitted for principal components analysis with varimax rotation, 22 items with extreme means and six validity items were deleted. Analysis yielded four interpretable factors: (1) Hostile Sexism; (2) Protective Paternalism; (3) Complementary Gender Differentiation; and (4) Recognition of Discrimination. The second and third factors were reported to have converged into one factor in gender-specific analysis. The fourth was not included in subsequent analyses. Confirmatory factor analysis of the remaining 22 items was conducted with five independent samples. These analyses indicated a two-factor model to fit the data best.
Samples	Validation of the measure was established using four samples of undergraduate college students attending a college in the Northeast or Midwest of the United States and two nonstudent samples. The first sample was composed of 833 undergraduate college students (353 men and 480 women) attending three different institutions. The average ages of the three subsamples were similar and ranged from 19.54 to 20.69 years. A majority of all three of these subsamples were predominantly White American (76%–86%). The second sample was composed of 171 students (77 men and 94 women) from the northeast. The third sample was composed of 937 undergraduate participants (396 men and 541 women). The fourth (72 men and 72 women) and fifth (36 men and 76 women) were composed of nonstudents in the northeast and Midwest. The last sample was composed of 44 men and 41 women.

Scoring	The number of items in each subscale is as follows:
	
	    Hostility: 11 items
	
	    Benevolence: 11 items
	
	    Total ASI: 22 items
	
	Six items require reverse scoring. The score on the two subscales and the total score are obtained by calculating the mean. Higher scores indicate greater levels of hostility or benevolence toward men, respectively.

Reliability	Cronbach's alpha for the scores ranged from .73 to .92:
	
	    Hostility: Alpha = .80 to .92
	
	    Benevolence: Alpha = .73 to .85
	
	    Total ASI: Alpha = .83 to .92

Validity	Discriminant validity was indicated by the finding that Recognition of Discrimination, which emerged as a separate factor through exploratory factor analysis, was weakly associated with Benevolence. Hostility was found to be negatively correlated with Recognition of Discrimination. The ASI scales were not found to be correlated with the self-deception scale and only weakly associated with the impression management scale, both from the balanced inventory of desirable responding (Paulhus, 1988). Convergent validity was demonstrated through moderate positive correlations between the ASI total and its subscales with old-fashioned sexism and modern sexism (Swim et al., 1995), attitudes toward women (Spence & Helmreich, 1972), and rape myth acceptance (Burt, 1980). Hostility was significantly correlated with modern racism (McConahay, 1986). Predictive validity was indicated in analyses that found that Hostile Sexism and Benevolent Sexism would be related to general attitudes toward women, ambivalence toward all traits (masculine/feminine), and ambivalence toward feminine traits in their expected directions among a sample of nonstudent men. College men's scores on Hostile and Benevolent Sexism did not correlate with their general attitudes. The total ASI and Hostile Sexism scores correlated with ambivalence toward all traits and ambivalence toward feminine traits. Similar patterns of relationships emerged for the sample of women. ASI scales also were found to be related to stereotypes about women in the expected direction for the samples of men.
Related References	Glick, P., Lameiras, M., Fiske, S. T., Eckes, T., Masser, B., Volpato, C., . . . & Wells, R. (2004). Bad but bold: Ambivalent attitudes toward men predict gender inequality in 16 nations. *Journal of Personality and Social Psychology, 86,* 713–728.
Language Versions	English
Contact	Peter Glick Psychology Department Lawrence University Appleton, WI 54912 Email: Peter.s.glick@lawrence.edu

8.13.3 Name of the Measure	The Ambivalence Toward Men Inventory AMI
Primary Reference	Glick, P., & Fiske, S. T. (1999). The Ambivalence Toward Men Inventory: Differentiating hostile and benevolent beliefs about men. *Psychology of Women Quarterly, 23,* 519–536.
Purpose	The AMI is designed to measure hostile and benevolent prejudices toward men.
Description	The AMI is a 20-item self-report measure that employs a 7-point Likert-type scale with the following anchors: 0 = Disagree Strongly to 6 = Agree Strongly. The AMI has two components: (1) Hostility toward Men (HM) and (2) Benevolence toward Men (BM). The AMI was developed, in part, based on social identity theory (Tajfel, 1981) and on an informal focus group of women who discussed their attitudes toward men. The initial AMI was composed of 133 statements. Exploratory factor analysis with varimax rotation was used to test the structure of the AMI. A 32-item AMI emerged from this process. The authors decided on a 20-item AMI. Confirmatory factor analysis provided further indication of the fit of their data to their hypothesized model, which contained two factors with three subfactors each.
Samples	Validation of the measure was established using two samples of undergraduate college students attending a college in the Northeast of the United States and a sample of older adults. The first sample was composed of 480 undergraduate students (147 men and 333 women). The second sample was composed of 208 undergraduate participants (74 men and 134 women). The final sample of older adults was made up of 102 men and 164 women. The samples were composed primarily of White Americans.

Scoring	The number of items in each subscale is as follows:
	
	    Hostility: 10 items
	
	    Benevolence: 10 items
	
	    Total AMI: 20 items
	
	The score on the two subscales and the total score are calculated by summing the scores and dividing by the number of corresponding items. Higher scores indicate greater levels of hostility or benevolence toward men, respectively.

Reliability	Cronbach's alpha for the scores were as follows:
	    Hostility: Alpha = .81 to .86
	    Benevolence: Alpha = .79 to .83
	    Total AMI: Alpha = .83 to .87

Validity	Known-groups validity was established through findings indicating that women scored higher on hostility and lower on benevolence than did men. Convergent validity was demonstrated through the AMI total, and its subscales were found to be correlated with two separate measures of attitudes toward men (Downs & Engleson, 1982; Iazzo, 1983).

(Continued)

	BM was found to be positively correlated with benevolent sexism and hostile sexism (Glick & Fiske, 1996). HM was not found to be related to dimensions of ambivalent sexism. Predictive validity also was established. The positive or negative ratings applied to spontaneously generated traits participants associate with men were predicted in their expected directions by BM and HM, respectively.
Related References	Glick, P., Lameiras, M., Fiske, S. T., Eckes, T., Masser, B., Volpato, C., . . . & Wells, R. (2004). Bad but bold: Ambivalent attitudes toward men predict gender inequality in 16 nations. *Journal of Personality and Social Psychology, 86,* 713–728.
Language Versions	English
Contact	Peter Glick Psychology Department Lawrence University Appleton, WI 54912 Email: Peter.s.glick@lawrence.edu

8.13.4 Name of the Measure	Genderism and Transphobia Scale GTS
Primary Reference	Hill, D. B., & Willoughby, B. L. B. (2005). The development and validation of the Genderism and Transphobia Scale. *Sex Roles, 53,* 531–544.
Purpose	The GTS is designed to measure violence, harassment, and discrimination toward people who engage in nonnormative gender behaviors.
Description	The GTS is a 32-item self-report inventory. Each item is rated on a 5-point Likert-type scale with anchors ranging from 1 = Strongly Agree to 5 = Strongly Disagree. The GTS is composed of two subscales: (1) Transphobia/Genderism and (2) Gender-Bashing.
Samples	The measure was established using three samples. The third sample, upon which the final version of the GTS is presented, was composed of 180 undergraduate and graduate students (98 females, 81 males, 1 unknown) enrolled at Concordia University in Montréal, Canada. They ranged in age from 18 to 73 years (*M* = 25 years).
Scoring	The number of items in each subscale is as follows: Transphobia/Genderism: 25 items Gender-Bashing: 7 items Total GTS: 32 items Scoring the GTS consists of summing subscale items and dividing by the number of items in the specific subscale. Higher scores indicate more negative attitudes toward individuals who do not conform to traditional expressions of gender.
Reliability	The range in Cronbach's alpha for the subscale scores and total GTS score are as follows: Genderism/Transphobia: Alpha = .95 Gender-Bashing: Alpha = .87 Total GTS: Alpha = .96
Validity	Convergent validity was established by examining the correlations between the GTS score and the Attitude Function Index (Herek, 1987). Evidence for discriminate validity was provided through nonsignificant correlations with self-esteem (Rosenberg, 1965), Bem Sex Role Inventory—Male, and Bem Sex Role Inventory—Female (Bem, 1974), as well as social desirability (Eysenck & Eysenck, 1975). Known-groups validity also was established. Specifically, individuals who had previous experiences with a transgenderist or cross-dresser scored lower on the GTS than did individuals who had not.
Related References	

Language Versions	English
Contact	Darryl B. Hill Department of Psychology 4S 112 College of Staten Island 2800 Victory Blvd. Staten Island, NY 10314 Phone: (718) 982-3785 Email: darryl.hill@csi.cuny.edu

8.13.5 Name of the Measure	Schedule of Sexist Events SSE
Primary Reference	Klonoff, E. A., & Landrine, H. (1995). The Schedule of Sexist Events: A measure of lifetime and recent sexist discrimination in women's lives. *Psychology of Women Quarterly, 19,* 439–472.
Purpose	The SSE was developed as a measure of perceived lifetime and recent life events of sexism.
Description	The SSE is a 20-item measure in which respondents rate the frequency of perceived sexist events during the past year and entire life, respectively. Recent and life events of sexism are rated on a 6-point Likert-type scale (1 = Never; 2 = Once in a While; 3 = Sometimes; 4 = A Lot; 5 = Most of the Time; and 6 = Almost All the Time). The last item measures how different one perceives her life to be had she not been treated in a sexist manner during her life or recent past. Respondents indicate their response for Recent Sexist Events and Lifetime Sexist Events on a 6-point Likert-type scale with the following anchors: 1 = The Same As It Is Now; 2 = A Little Different; 3 = Different In A Few Ways; 4 = Different In A Lot Of Ways; 5 = Different In Most Ways; and 6 = Totally Different. The 23 items that comprise the SSE were developed based on stress theory and research (e.g., Lazarus & Folkman, 1984). Principal components analysis (PCA) with orthogonal rotation yielded a 20-item measure with four factors for SSE-Lifetime. A nearly identical factor structure emerged from a similar (PCA) for SSE-Recent. The four factors are (1) Sexist Degradation and Its Consequences; (2) Sexist Discrimination in Distant Relationships; (3) Sexist Discrimination in the Workplace; and (4) Sexism in Close Relationships.
Samples	The sample consisted of 631 women who ranged in age from 18 to 73 years ($M = 32.14$; $SD = 11.74$). This sample was composed of 403 White Americans, 117 Latina Americans, 38 African Americans, 25 Asian Americans, and 46 women from other ethnic groups.

Scoring	There are a total of 20 items on the measure.
	
	    SSE-Recent Discrimination: 20 items
	    SSE-Lifetime Discrimination: 20 items
	
	The SSE-Recent is composed of four subscales:
	
	    Sexist Degradation and Its Consequences: 8 items
	    Sexist Discrimination in Distant Relationships: 5 items
	    Sexist Discrimination in the Workplace: 4 items
	    Sexism in Close Relationships: 3 items
	
	The SSE-Lifetime is composed of four subscales:
	
	    Sexist Degradation and Its Consequences: 8 items
	    Sexist Discrimination in Distant Relationships: 5 items

	Sexist Discrimination in the Workplace: 4 items
	Sexism in Close Relationships: 3 items
	Items do not require reverse scoring. The scores on the two subscales are calculated by summing the scores and dividing by the number of corresponding items. Higher scores indicate greater levels of perceived sexism.
Reliability	Cronbach's alpha for the scores were as follows:
	SSE-Recent
	Sexist Degradation and Its Consequences: Alpha = .88
	Sexist Discrimination in Distant Relationships: Alpha = .74
	Sexist Discrimination in the Workplace: Alpha = .70
	Sexism in Close Relationships: Alpha = .61
	Total SSE-Recent: Alpha = .90
	Split-Half: $r = .83$
	SSE-Lifetime
	Sexist Degradation and Its Consequences: Alpha = .90
	Sexist Discrimination in Distant Relationships: Alpha = .82
	Sexist Discrimination in the Workplace: Alpha = .67
	Sexism in Close Relationships: Alpha = .67
	Total SSE-Recent: Alpha = .92
	Split-Half: $r = .87$
	2-week test-retest reliability:
	SSE-Recent: $r = .63$
	SSE-Lifetime: $r = .70$
Validity	Convergent validity was established through positive associations between other measures of stress (e.g., Cohen, Kamarck, & Mermelstein, 1983; Dohrenwend, Krasnoff, Askenasy, & Dohrenwend, 1978; Kanner, Coyne, Schaeffer, & Lazarus, 1981) and the SSE-Recent and SSE-Lifetime as well as their four subscales.
Related References	DeBlaere, C., & Moradi, B. (2008). Structures of the Schedules of Racist and Sexist Events: Confirmatory factor analyses of African American women's responses. *Psychology of Women Quarterly, 32,* 83–94.
	Matteson, A. V., & Moradi, B. (2005). Examining the structure of the Schedule of Sexist Events: Replication and Extension. *Psychology of Women Quarterly, 29,* 47–57.

(Continued)

(Continued)

	Thomas, A. J., Witherspoon, K. M., & Speight, S. L. (2008). Gendered racism, psychological distress, and coping styles of African American women. *Cultural Diversity and Ethnic Minority Psychology, 14,* 307–314.
Language Versions	English
Contact	Elizabeth A. Klonoff Department of Psychology College of Sciences San Diego State University 6363 Alvarado Ct., Ste. 103/11 San Diego, CA 92120–4913 Office: (619) 594–8642 Fax: (619) 594–6780 Email: eklonoff@sunstroke.sdsu.edu

8.13.6 Name of the Measure	Transphobia Scale TS
Primary Reference	Nagoshi, J. L., Adams, K. A., Terrell, H. K., Hill, E. D., Brzuzy, S., & Nagoshi, C. T. (2008). Gender differences in correlates of homophobia and transphobia. *Sex Roles, 59*, 521–531.
Purpose	The TS is designed to measure prejudice against individuals who engage in nonnormative gender behaviors.
Description	The TS is a 9-item self-report inventory. Each item is rated on a 7-point Likert-type scale response options ranging from 1 = Completely Disagree to 7 = Completely Agree. The TS is composed of one factor. The 9-items of the TS were adapted from *My Gender Workbook* (Bornstein, 1998). Principal components analysis with varimax rotation yielded a two-factor solution, with the one item correlating uniquely with the second factor. The first factor accounted for a large amount of the variance, and deletion of the sixth item resulted only in a small increase (.03) in the Cronbach alpha coefficient. As a result, the authors decided that the TS is a measure of a unidimensional construct.
Samples	The measure was established using a sample of undergraduate students ($N = 310$) from Arizona State University. The mean age of the 153 females was 19.45 years ($SD = 3.28$) and 147 males (19.47 years; $SD = 1.76$). With respect to race and ethnicity, 75% were White American, 12% were Latino/a American, 5% were Asian American, 2% African American, 2% Native American, and 4% reported "other." All but six reported being heterosexual.
Scoring	There are nine items in the TS. Scoring the TS consists of summing the items and dividing by the total number of items ($n = 9$). Higher scores indicate more prejudiced attitudes toward transgender individuals.
Reliability	Cronbach's alpha for the total GTS score is as follows A 4-week test-retest reliability coefficient $r = .88$ was presented
Validity	Construct validity was established through nonsignificant correlations between the TS and the Personal Attributes Questionnaire (Spence, Helmreich, & Stapp, 1975) and the Sociosexuality Inventory (Simpson & Gangestad, 1991). Criterion-related validity was established through significant positive relations between transphobia and Ambivalent Sexism Inventory (Glick & Fiske, 1996), Right Wing Authoritarianism (Altemeyer, 1981), and Religious Fundamentalism (Altemeyer & Hunsberger, 1992). Transphobia also was found to be positively related to aggression (Buss & Perry, 1992) among men. Among women, Rape Myth Acceptance Scale (Burt, 1980) was found to be significantly positively correlated with transphobia. Known-groups validity also was established. Specifically, men reported higher levels of transphobia than did women.
Related References	
Language Versions	English
Contact	The TS is published in Nagoshi et al. (2008).

8.13.7 Name of the Measure	Attitudes Toward Women Scale—25 AWS-25
Primary Reference	Spence, J. T., Helmreich, R., & Stapp, J. (1973). A short version of the Attitudes toward Women Scale (AWS). *Bulletin of the Psychonomic Society, 2,* 219–220.
Purpose	The AWS-25 is designed to measure attitudes toward women.
Description	The AWS-25 is a 25-item self-report inventory. Each of these items is rated on a 4-point Likert-type scale with response option ranging from 0 = Strongly Agree to 3 = Strongly Disagree. There are three versions of the measure: AWS (Spence & Helmreich, 1972) and a 15-item AWS (Spence & Helmreich, 1978) in addition to the AWS-25 (reported here). Each version is reported to be unifactorial. The 25-item AWS shorter version was developed to encourage greater use of the measure. The 25 items were selected from the initial 55-item measure through several steps. First, scores for men and women (in a sample of 527 undergraduate students) were divided into quartiles based on the total AWS score. The distribution for each item was then examined. Biserial and point biserial correlation coefficients were calculated. Items that had the highest biserial correlation coefficients and which "had distributions which maximally discriminated among quartile for both sexes" were selected. Results of factor analysis indicated that the scale is unifactorial. The measure has been translated and adapted for use in different parts of the world.
Samples	Tests of structural validity of the 25-item AWS were conducted on two samples. The first was composed of 241 female and 286 male undergraduate college students. The second was composed of 292 mothers and 232 fathers.
Scoring	There are 25 items in the AWS. The scale score is calculated by summing the responses to the individual items. Higher scores indicate egalitarian values. No transformations are needed.
Reliability	The 25-item AWS has been demonstrated to have strong reliability. Daugherty and Dambrot (1986) found a Cronbach's alpha coefficient .89 for the score of AWS. Split-half reliability was calculated to be .86.
Validity	Correlation coefficients between the original 55-item AWS and the 25-item AWS were found to be no lower than .956 for either of the samples. Known-groups validity was established through mean comparisons of male and female responses. Spence et al. (1973) reported that women had more liberal or egalitarian beliefs than did men. The AWS is a widely used measure of sexism. In recent years, the AWS has been found to be correlated with sexism (Forbes, Collinsworth, Jobe, Braun, & Wise, 2007) and rape myth acceptance (Aosved & Long, 2006).
Related References	Forbes, G. B., Collinsworth, L. L., Jobe, R. L., Braun, K. D., & Wise, L. M. (2007). Sexism, hostility toward women, and endorsement of beauty ideals and practices: Are beauty ideals associated with oppressive beliefs? *Sex Roles, 56,* 265–273.

	Khalid, R., & Frieze, I. H. (2004). Measuring perceptions of gender roles: The IAWS for Pakistanis and U.S. immigrant populations. *Sex Roles, 51,* 293–300.
	Spence, J. T., & Helmreich, R. L. (1978). Masculinity and femininity: Their psychological dimensions, correlates and antecedents. Austin, TX: University of Texas Press.
	Twenge, J. M. (1997). Attitudes toward women, 1970–1995: A meta-analysis. *Psychology of Women Quarterly, 21,* 35–51.
Language Versions	English, Arabic, Chinese, Italian, Spanish, Turkish
Contact	Email: spence@mail.utexas.edu Phone: (512) 471-4308

8.13.8 Name of the Measure	Modern and Old Fashioned Sexism Scale MOFSS
Primary Reference	Swim, J. K., Aiken, K. J., Hall, W. S., & Hunter, B. A. (1995). Sexism and racism: Old-fashioned and modern prejudices. *Journal of Personality and Social Psychology, 68,* 199–214.
Purpose	The MOFSS was developed to measure modern and old-fashioned sexism attitudes.
Description	The MOFSS is a 13-item self-report inventory. Each of these items is rated on a 5-point Likert-type scale with the following anchors: 1 = Strongly Disagree to 5 = Strongly Agree. The MOFSS is composed of 2 subscales: (1) Modern Sexism (MS) and (2) Old-Fashioned Sexism (OFS). Items were modeled after the Modern Racism Scale (MRS; McConahay, 1986) and Sears's (1998) conceptualization of symbolic racism. All seven items from the MRS were altered to apply to attitudes toward women to assess for modern sexism. One item from the old-fashioned racism scale (McConahay, 1986) was altered. Additional items were developed to assess for old-fashioned sexism. A two-factor solution emerged when preliminary exploratory principal component factor analyses were conducted. Items representing old-fashioned sexism correlated with one factor. Eight items correlated with the second factor. Of these, several also correlated with the first factor. Confirmatory factor analysis (CFA) indicated that a two-factor solution fit better than a one-factor solution. Using a second sample, an additional CFA confirmed the original factor structure.
Samples	Two samples of college students were utilized to establish the validity of MS. The first sample was composed of 418 women and 265 men (nearly all of whom were White American). The second sample was composed of 477 women and 311 men (nearly all of whom were White American).
Scoring	The total number of items for each subscale are as follows: Old-Fashioned: 5 items Modern: 8 items Total MOFRS: 13 items Scores are derived by calculating the average score of the item responses for each scale. Higher scores indicate more sexist responses.
Reliability	Cronbach's alpha for the scores ranged from .73 to .83. Old-Fashioned: Alpha = .66 Modern: Alpha = .84
Validity	Known-groups validity was established. Men scored higher than women on modern sexism and old-fashioned sexism. Convergent validity also was established through significant inverse relationships found between scores on modern sexism and egalitarianism for women and men. Modern sexism also was found to be related to protestant work ethic for women but not for men. Old-fashioned sexism was found to be related to egalitarianism but not protestant work ethic for women and for men.

	After controlling for political affiliation and liberalism, Modern Sexism did not predict voting preferences.
Related References	Parks, J. B., & Robertson, M. A. (2004). Attitudes toward women mediate the gender effect on attitudes toward sexist language. *Psychology of Women Quarterly, 28,* 233–239.
	Swim, J. K., & Cohen, L. L. (1997). Overt, covert, and subtle sexism: A comparison between the Attitudes Toward Woman and Modern Sexism Scales. *Psychology of Women Quarterly, 21,* 103–118.
Language Versions	English
Contact	Janet K. Swim Department of Psychology The Pennsylvania State University 515 Moore Bldg. University Park, PA 16802 (814) 863–1730 (814) 863–7002

8.13.9 Name of the Measure	Neosexism Scale NS
Primary Reference	Tougas, F., Brown, R., Beaton, A. M., & Joly, S. (1995). Neosexism: Plus ça change, plus c'est pariel. *Personality and Social Psychology Bulletin, 21*, 842–849.
Purpose	The NS was developed to measure subtle gender bias.
Description	The NS is an 11-item self-report instrument in which respondents rate their level of agreement with statements regarding modern and institutional forms of sexism. Each item is rated on a 7-point Likert-type scale (1 = Total Disagreement to 7 = Total Agreement). The NS is composed of one composite score. A complete description of item development is not provided in the original manuscript. However, the authors do explain that while some items were developed specifically for this scale, others were modified from scales measuring covert racism (e.g., Gaertner & Dovidio, 1986; Jacobson, 1985; Kinder & Sears, 1981; McConahay, 1986). Data were submitted for exploratory factor analysis, for which no definite structure emerged.
Samples	The NS was developed based on data from two independent samples. The first consisted of 130 male students enrolled in English or French language psychology courses at the University of Ottawa. They ranged in age from 18 to 43 years ($M = 21.6$ years). The second sample was composed of workers who worked in a firm where an affirmative action hiring program for women and ethnic minorities had been in place for the past 5 years. Of a randomly selected group of 281 male employees, 149 responded. Respondents' ages ranged from 26–60 years ($M = 41.5$).
Scoring	There are a total of 10 items on the measure. Two items require reverse scoring. The score is calculated by summing the scores and dividing by the number of corresponding items. Higher scores indicate greater levels of sexism.
Reliability	Cronbach's alpha for the scale score was .78. Two-week test-retest reliability was $r = .84$.
Validity	Convergent validity was established through expected relationships between the NS and other measures. Specifically, the NS was found to be inversely related to support for affirmative action and to be positively related to old-fashioned sexism (Rombough & Ventimiglia, 1981). NS also was found to be inversely related to evaluations of women's competence, general attitudes toward affirmative action, and attitudes toward affirmative action programs in place.

Related References	Aosved, A. C., Long, P. J., & Voller, E. K. (2009). Measuring sexism, racism, sexual prejudice, ageism, classism, and religious intolerance: The Intolerant Schema Measure. *Journal of Applied Social Psychology, 39,* 2321–2354.
	Leaper, C., & Van, S. R. (2008). Masculinity ideology, covert sexism, and perceived gender typicality in relation to young men's academic motivation and choices in college. *Psychology of Men & Masculinity, 9,* 139–153.
Language Versions	English, French
Contact	Francine Tougas School of Psychology 200 Lees Avenue, C-103 Ottawa, Ontario, Canada K1N 6N5 (613) 562–5799 Email: Francine.tougas@uOttawa.ca

8.14 IDENTITY DEVELOPMENT

8.14.1 Name of the Measure	Feminist Identity Development Scale FIDS
Primary Reference	Bargard, A., & Hyde, J. S. (1991). Women's studies: A study of feminist identity development in women. *Psychology of Women Quarterly, 15,* 181–201.
Purpose	The FIDS was developed to measure feminist identity.
Description	The FIDS is a 39-item self-report inventory that utilizes a 5-point Likert-type response scale with the following anchors: 1 = Strongly Disagree to 5 = Strongly Agree. The authors describe the FIDS as being composed of the following five factors: (1) Passive Acceptance; (2) Revelation; (3) Embeddedness-Emanation; (4) Synthesis; and (5) Active Commitment. Items of the FIDS were developed based on Downing and Roush's (1985) model of feminist identity development. Five women faculty and graduate students of psychology or women's studies composed 200 items reflecting the five stages of the model. These items were reviewed for ambiguity, redundancy, and appropriateness. One hundred and sixty-three items were retained. The face validity of the instrument was then established through evaluations from 10 women faculty and graduates with expertise in feminist identity. These individuals rated each item based on the stage of development they thought it reflected. Items with greater than 70% agreement were retained. This resulted in a 90-item measure, the items in which were then evaluated again for appropriateness, ambiguity, and redundancy. A 73-item measure emerged from these steps. Two separate factor analyses with varimax rotation were conducted on two samples. The factor analyses yielded the same 39-item, five-actor solutions.
Samples	One hundred fifty-six people participated in the first study of the structural properties of the FIDS. This sample was composed of undergraduate women enrolled in a psychology course at the University of Wisconsin, Madison. The sample is composed of 129 White Americans, 9 Asian Americans, 9 Native Americans, 3 African Americans, and 2 who reported other race. The mean age was 18.71 years (SD = 1.45). The second sample was recruited from one of three women's studies courses at the same university. This sample (N = 184) was composed of 177 White Americans, 5 Asian Americans, 1 African American, and 1 Latina American.
Scoring	The number of items per subscale are as follows: Passive Acceptance: 12 items Revelation: 7 items Embeddedness-Emanation: 7 items

	Synthesis: 5 items
	Active Commitment: 8 items
	Total FIDS: 39 items
	A score on the FIDS subscales may be computed by including a sum of all items of the subscale. Higher scores indicate higher levels of the feminist identity attitude corresponding to that subscale.
Reliability	Reliability coefficients were calculated for the scores on the subscales:
	Passive Acceptance: Alpha = .85
	Revelation: Alpha = .75
	Embeddedness-Emanation: Alpha = .82
	Synthesis: Alpha = .65
	Active Commitment: Alpha = .80
	The following 3-month test-retest reliability coefficients were reported by Gerstmann and Kramer (1997):
	Passive Acceptance: $r = .85$
	Revelation: $r = .75$
	Embeddedness-Emanation: $r = .82$
	Synthesis: $r = .69$
	Active Commitment: $r = .85$
Validity	Divergent validity was established through the lack of significant relationships between FIDS subscale scores and social desirability (Crowne & Marlowe, 1960).
Related References	Flores, L. Y., Carrubba, M. D., & Good, G. E. (2006). Feminism and Mexican American women: Examining the psychometric properties of two measures. *Hispanic Journal of Behavioral Sciences, 28,* 48–64.
	Gerstmann, E. A., & Kramer, D. A. (1997). Feminist identity development: Psychometric analyses of two feminist identity scales. *Sex Roles, 36,* 327–348.
Language Versions	English
Contact	Janet Shibley Hyde 1202 West Johnson Street Department of Psychology Brogden Psychology Building University of Wisconsin Madison, WI 53706 Phone: (608) 262–9522 Email: jshyde@wisc.edu

8.14.2 Name of the Measure	Feminist Identity Composite FIC
Primary Reference	Fischer, A. R., Tokar, D. M., Good, G. E., Hill, M. S., & Blum, S. A. (2000). Assessing women's feminist identity development: Studies of convergent, discriminant, and structural validity. *Psychology of Women Quarterly, 24*, 15–29.
Purpose	The FIC was developed to address the psychometric limitations of earlier measures of feminist identity. It is designed to measure women's feminist identity.
Description	The FIC is a 34-item self-report inventory that utilizes a 5-point Likert-type response scale with the following anchors: 1 = Strongly Agree to 5 = Strongly Disagree. The FIC is composed of the following five factors: (1) Active Commitment; (2) Synthesis; (3) Revelation; (4) Embeddedness-Emanation; and (5) Passive Acceptance. Items of the FIC were selected based on a joint factor analysis involving both the Feminist Identity Scale (Rickard, 1989) and Feminist Identity Development Scale (Bargad & Hyde, 1991). Items met the authors' four criteria: "(a) a corrected item-total correlation exceeding correlations with other scales; (b) a minimum corrected item-total correlation of .30; (c) a highest structure coefficient of > .40 on the factor which reflected either the presences or absence of characteristics associated with the feminist identity status for which the item was developed originally; and (d) a minimum item hit rate of 60% across five judges" (Fischer et al., 2000, p. 20). A total of 39 items met these criteria. Results of principal components analysis yielded a five-factor solution as most interpretable. The 39-item FIC was further studied on a separate sample. Confirmatory factor analysis was then performed to further study the structure of the FIC. This analysis indicated that data provided an excellent fit to the model.
Samples	In the first study of the structure of the FIC, the authors sampled 191 female undergraduate students. They ranged in age from 18 to 34 years (*M* = 19.4 years; *SD* = 2.44). With respect to race, 90% of the sample were White Americans, 5% were African Americans, 3% were Asian Americans, 2% were Latina Americans, and 1% international students. Data from 295 women were used to further study the psychometric properties of the FIC. The participants were nonstudent community members (*n* = 92) and undergraduate college students (*n* = 203). The community residents ranged in age from 17 to 67 years (*M* = 37.26 years; *SD* = 13.29 years). In this community sample, there were White Americans (91%), African Americans (4%), Latina Americans (2%), Native Americans (1%), multiracial (1%), and unknown (1%). Of the college sample, students ranged in age from 16 to 50 years

	(M = 22.25; SD = 6.37). In this sample, there were White Americans (82%), African Americans (11%), Latina Americans (1%), Native Americans (1%), multiracial (3%), and "unknown" (2%).
Scoring	The number of items per subscale is as follows: Active Commitment: 9 items Synthesis: 6 items Revelation: 8 items Embeddedness-Emanation: 4 items Passive Acceptance: 7 items Total FIC: 34 items A score on the FIC subscales may be computed by including a sum of all items of the subscale. Higher scores indicate higher levels of the feminist identity attitude corresponding to that subscale.
Reliability	Cronbach's coefficient alpha was calculated for the scores on the subscales across two studies. They ranged from .68 to .86: Passive Acceptance: Alpha = .74 to .75 Revelation: Alpha = .75 to .80 Embeddedness-Emanation: Alpha = .84 to .86 Synthesis: Alpha = .68 to .71 Active Commitment: Alpha = .77 to .81
Validity	Convergent validity of the subscales was demonstrated through expected positive correlations between the FIC subscales and ego identity development (Adams, Bennion, & Huh, 1989) and perceptions of sexism (Klonoff & Landrine, 1995). Significant correlations, in the expected directions, between involvement in women's organizations and all but the Synthesis subscale were found. Discriminant validity was demonstrated through weakly or not correlated with social desirability (Paulhus, 1994).
Related References	Moradi, B., & Subich, L. M. (2002). Feminist identity development measures: Comparing the psychometrics of three instruments. *The Counseling Psychologist, 30,* 66–86.
Language Versions	English
Contact	Ann Fischer Southern Illinois University Carbondale Carbondale, IL 62901–6899 Phone: (618) 453–3560 Fax: (618) 453–3563 Email: arf12@siu.edu

8.14.3 Name of the Measure	Feminist Identity Scale FIS
Primary References	Gerstmann, E. A., & Kramer, D. A. (1997). Feminist identity development: Psychometric analysis of two feminist identity scales. *Sex Roles, 36,* 327–348. Rickard, K. M. (1989). The relationship of self-monitored dating behaviors to level of feminist identity on the Feminist Identity Scale. *Sex Roles, 20,* 213–226.
Purpose	The FIS was developed to measure the social-cognitive components of feminist identity.
Description	The FIS is a 67-item self-report inventory that utilizes a 5-point Likert-type response scale with the following anchors: 1 = Strongly Agree to 5 = Strongly Disagree. The FIS is composed the following four factors: (1) Passive Acceptance; (2) Revelation; (3) Embeddedness-Emanation; (4) Synthesis. Items of the FIS were developed based on Downing and Roush's (1985) model of feminist identity development and intellectual development (Perry, 1970). Principal components analysis with oblimin rotation was conducted in a separate study (Gerstmann & Kramer, 1997) of a 93-item version of the FIS. In that analysis, the solution was restricted to four-factor component structure proposed by Rickard (1989). This procedure yielded a 67-item, four-factor FIS.
Samples	Gerstmann and Kramer (1997) sampled 198 female undergraduate students enrolled in women's studies courses (*n* = 33) or psychology courses (*n* = 165). Of this sample, 129 were White American, 14 were African American, 25 were Asian American, 9 were Latina American, 6 were Native American, and 26 were identified as other races or did not report. The age of the participants ranged from 17–52 years (*M* = 19.05 years, *SD* = 3.42 years).
Scoring	The number of items for each subscale is as follows: Passive Acceptance: 13 items Revelation: 20 items Embeddedness-Emanation: 11 items Synthesis: 23 items Total FIS: 67 items A score on the FIS subscales may be computed by including a sum of all items of the subscale. Higher scores indicate higher levels of the feminist identity attitude corresponding to that subscale.
Reliability	Cronbach alpha coefficients were calculated to be above .85 for the scores on each of the four subscales. Values of the coefficient alpha for each subscale were not provided. The 3-week test retest reliability coefficients were as follows: Passive Acceptance: r = .93 Revelation: r = .90 Embeddedness-Emanation: r = .84 Synthesis: r = .83

Validity	Construct validity was demonstrated through the significant correlations found between the subscales of the FIS and subscales of the FIDS (Bargard & Hyde, 1991) and cognitive development (Kramer, Kahlbaugh, & Goldston, 1992). Discriminant validity also was demonstrated through nonsignificant or low relationships between social desirability (Paulhus, 1981) and FIS subscales.
	Known-groups validity was demonstrated through significantly higher scores on Revelation, Embeddedness-Emanation, and Active Commitment and significantly lower scores on Passive Acceptance by women who were interested in taking a women's studies courses than those who were not interested.
Related References	Fischer, A. R., Tokar, D. M., Mergl, M. M., Good, G. E., Hill, M. S., & Blum, S. A. (2000). Assessing women's feminist identity development: Studies of convergent, discriminant, and structural validity. *Psychology of Women Quarterly, 24,* 15–29.
Language Versions	English
Contact	Kathryn Rickard Psychology Department Colorado State University 1876 Campus Delivery Fort Collins, CO 80523–1876 Phone: (970) 491–6363 Fax: (970) 491–1032 Email: Kathryn.Richard@colostate.edu

8.14.4 Name of the Measure	Feminist Perspectives Scale FPS
Primary Reference	Henley, N. M., Meng, K., O'Brien, D., McCarthy, W. J., & Sockloskie, R. J. (1998). Developing a scale to measure the diversity of feminist attitudes. *Psychology of Women Quarterly, 22,* 317–348.
Purpose	The FPS was developed to measure the behavioral and attitudinal components of different feminist perspectives.
Description	The FPS is a 30-item self-report inventory that utilizes a Likert-type response scale with the following anchors: 1 = Strongly Disagree to 7 = Strongly Agree. The authors describe the FPS as being composed of the following four factors: (1) Radical/Socialist Feminist; (2) Conservative; (3) Women of Color; and (4) Cultural Feminist. An initial 306 items were composed to reflect behavioral (102 items) and attitudinal (204 items) dimensions, from the perspective of six feminist positions, of 17 topics. Behavioral items were not found to yield high item-subscale correlation coefficients. Inclusion of items into the second version of the FPS was based on high item-subscale correlations, low item-other subscale correlations, and clarity (based on participant feedback). Based on these conditions and process, 10 attitudinal items were selected for each of the six proposed feminist perspectives. This resulted in a 60-item measure. The three best behavioral items from each feminist perspective were selected to compose an 18-item behavioral scale. However, only attitudinal items were subjected to subsequent factor analysis. Exploratory factor analysis (EFA) with promax rotation on 301 of the 603 participants was conducted. A six-factor solution was chosen because of the theoretical assumptions underlying the measure. However, results of the EFA indicated the interpretability of four factors. Twenty-one items, including those items making up the proposed Liberal Feminist subscale, were deleted. A second EFA with promax rotation with the remaining 302 participants yielded the same factor structure. The sample was then combined for another EFA with promax rotation. Results indicated a four-factor solution accounting for 95% of the variance. EFA also were run for men and women separately, and this yielded the same four-factor content. However, the factor order of factors 2 and 3 was reversed.
Samples	Data from 603 participants, across several studies, were pooled for tests of factor structure. All but 62 participants were undergraduate students recruited through a large public university in California, United States. The 62 participants were recruited through a psychology of women class at a small liberal arts college in California. There were 336 females, 253 males, and 14 gender unknown.

Scoring	The number of items for each subscale is as follows:
	
	    Radical/Socialist Feminist: 9 items
	
	    Conservative: 9 items
	
	    Women of Color: 6 items
	
	    Cultural Feminist: 6 items
	
	    Total FPS: 30 items

	A score on the FPS subscales may be computed by including a sum of all items of the subscale. Higher scores indicate greater levels of agreement with the feminist perspective reflected in the subscale.
Reliability	Reliability coefficients were calculated for the proposed subscale scores and for the total scale score but not for the factors that emerged from factor analysis.
	Radical/Socialist Feminist: Alpha = .87
	Conservative: Alpha = .76
	Women of Color: Alpha = .76
	Cultural Feminist: Alpha = .66
	Test-retest reliability coefficients were not presented for these four subscales as they were constituted after the second EFA.
Validity	Concurrent validity was established (for an earlier version of the FPS) through significant relationships, in the expected directions, found between its subscales and attitudes toward women (Spence, Helmreich, & Stapp, 1973).
	Known-groups validity also was demonstrated (for an earlier version of the FPS). Specifically, differences on level of agreement on the six proposed feminist perspectives were noted based on gender, political self-identification, self-rated feminist identity, and education through women's studies courses.
	Factors 1, 3, and 4 were correlated with one another in the expected direction. Those factors were not associated with the second factor.
Related References	Rader, J., & Gilbert, L. A. (2005). The egalitarian relationship in feminist therapy. *Psychology of Women Quarterly, 29,* 427–435.
	Schick, V. R., Zucker, A. N., & Bay-Cheng, L. Y. (2008). Safer, better sex through feminism: The role of feminist ideology in women's sexual well-being. *Psychology of Women Quarterly, 32,* 225–232.
Language Versions	English
Contact	Nancy Henley Department of Psychology 1285 Franz Hall Box 951563 Los Angeles, CA 90095–1563 Phone: (310) 825–2961 Fax: (310) 206–5895 Email: nhenley@ucla.edu

8.14.5 Name of the Measure	Womanist Identity Attitudes Scale WIAS
Primary Reference	Ossana, S. M., Helms, J. E., & Leonard, M. M. (2001). Do "Womanist" identity attitudes influence college women's self-esteem and perceptions of environmental bias? *Journal of Counseling and Development, 70,* 402–408.
Purpose	The WIAS was developed to measure womanist identity attitudes that were theorized by Helms (1990c).
Description	The WIAS is a 43-item self-report inventory. Each of these items is rated on a 5-point Likert-type scale with the following anchors: 1 = Strongly Disagree to 5 = Strongly Agree.
	The WIAS is composed of 4 subscales: (1) Pre-encounter; (2) Encounter; (3) Immersion-Emersion; and (4) Internalization.
	Items were developed based on Helms's (1990c) model of womanist identity development. The factor structure of the WIAS was not measured in the initial study. However, Moradi, Yoder, and Berendsen (2004) performed a confirmatory factor analysis (CFA) on the proposed scale. Results of the CFA indicated that data did not fit the proposed model well. Specifically, GFI indicated a good fit, but values on other indices did not suggest the same. Moradi and her colleagues then conducted principal components analysis with varimax rotation and a principal axis factor analysis to identify the structure of the WIAS. Their results indicated a three-factor orthogonal solution, accounting for 22% of the variance. The three-factor solution, however, indicated a departure from the model originally proposed. That is, results of exploratory factor analysis indicated that items designed to reflect on different stages of womanist identity developed correlated onto the same factor.
Samples	A sample of 201 women was recruited by Moradi et al. (2004) to study the structural and convergent validity of the WIAS. Their sample was composed of 101 African American women and 100 White American women. Participants' ages ranged from 19–65 ($M = 22$; $SD = 8.15$).
Scoring	The number of items in each subscale are as follows:
	Preencounter: 8 items
	Encounter: 8 items
	Immersion-Emersion: 16 items
	Internalization: 11 items
	Total WIAS: 43 items
	Scoring the subscales consists of summing subscale items. Higher scores indicate higher levels of gender role stress for women. No transformations are required.
Reliability	Cronbach's alpha for the subscales scores ranged from .31 to .82:
	Preencounter: .44 to .55
	Encounter: .31 to .43
	Immersion-Emersion: .76 to .82
	Internalization: .54 to .77

Validity	Moradi and her colleagues (2004) found evidence of convergent validity of the factors of the WIAS through expected correlations with attitudes toward women (Spence & Helmreich, 1978), modern sexism (Swim, Aiken, Hall, & Hunter, 1995), and hostile and benevolent sexism (Glick & Fiske, 1997).
Related References	Moradi, B., Yoder, J. D., & Berendsen, L. L. (2004). An evaluation of the psychometric properties of the Womanist Identity Attitudes Scale. *Sex Roles, 50,* 253–266.
Language Versions	English
Contact	Janet E. Helms Boston College 318 Campion Hall Phone: 617–552–4080 or 617–552–2482 Fax: 617–552–1003 Email: janet.helms.1@bc.edu

8.14.6 Name of the Measure	Reference Group Identity Dependence Scale RGIDS
Primary Reference	Wade, J. C., & Gelso, C. J. (1998). Reference Group Identity Dependence Scale: A measure of male identity. *The Counseling Psychologist, 26,* 384–412.
Purpose	The RGIDS is designed to measure the extent to which a man's gender role self-concept is dependent on a male reference group.
Description	The RGIDS is a 30-item self-report inventory grounded on Wade's (1998) theory of male reference group identity dependence. Each item is rated on a 6-point Likert-type scale with the following anchors: 1 = Strongly Disagree to 6 = Strongly Agree. The RGIDS is composed of four components: (1) No Reference Group (NRG); (2) Reference Group Nondependent Diversity (RGND); (3) Reference Group Nondependent Similarity (RGNS); and (4) Reference Group Dependent (RGD). An initial pool of 20 items was theoretically derived (i.e., Wade, 1998). These items were examined by an expert on the theory and psychology of men. These items were exposed to a pilot study in which undergraduate males completed the measure. Four items, with item-total score correlation coefficients of .20 or lower, were deleted. An additional 34 items were developed based on theory. Face validity was then established for the remaining 50 items through the use of seven doctoral students who determined the male reference group identity status represented by each item. Three items were deleted because three or more judges did not agree on the status each reflected. This resulted in a 47-item scale. Principal factor analyses with varimax and oblimin rotations were performed. A four-factor solution based on varimax rotation was determined to be the most interpretable. Eleven items were deleted because they did not yield structure coefficients of .30 or greater. Two more items failed to correlate above .30 on any factor. All remaining items yielded structure coefficients above .30 on their respective factor and less than a .30 on all other factors. An additional factor analysis with varimax rotation was performed, resulting in the deletion of four items because of their failure to correlate with a value greater than .30. The final 30 items were factor analyzed with principal factors analysis with varimax rotation.
Samples	Validation of the measure was established using a sample of 344 male college students attending a public university. The sample was composed of men who ranged in age from 17–35 years ($M = 19.23$; $SD = 1.64$). This sample was composed of 223 White American individuals, 47 Asian American or Pacific Islander individuals, 39 African American individuals, 14 Latino/a American individuals, and 13 biracial individuals.
Scoring	The number of items for each subscale is as follows: No Reference Group: 10 items Reference Group Dependent: 7 items Reference Group Nondependent Diversity: 6 items Reference Group Nondependent Similarity: 7 items Total RGIDS: 30 items

	One item requires reverse scoring. Scores for each subscale are calculated by summing items associated with the factor. Higher scores indicate higher levels of beliefs and attitudes toward that factor.
Reliability	Cronbach's alpha for the scale scores ranged from .70 to .78. No Reference Group: Alpha = .78 Reference Group Dependent: Alpha = .70 Reference Group Nondependent Diversity: Alpha = .70 Reference Group Nondependent Similarity: Alpha = .73 Test-retest reliability coefficients were as follows: No Reference Group: $r = .67$ Reference Group Dependent: $r = .30$ Reference Group Nondependent Diversity: $r = .68$ Reference Group Nondependent Similarity: $r = .60$
Validity	Construct validity was established through a series of statistically significant correlations, in the expected directions, between its subscales and subscales of the Extended Objective Measure of Ego Identity Status (MEIS; Grotevant & Adams, 1984), Self-Esteem (Coopersmith, 1967), Social Anxiety (Fenigstein, Scheier, & Buss, 1975), Depression (Hesbacher, Rickels, Morris, Newman, & Rosenfeld, 1980), and Gender Role Conflict (O'Neil et al., 1986). Unexpected correlations between its subscales and subscale scores of other these measures also emerged, however.
Related References	Wade, J. C. (1998). Male reference group identity dependence: A theory of male identity. *The Counseling Psychologist, 26,* 349–383. Wade, J. C. (2008). Masculinity ideology, male reference group identity dependence, and African American men's health-related attitudes and behaviors. *Psychology of Men & Masculinity, 9,* 5–16.
Language Versions	English
Contact	Jay C. Wade Psychology Department Fordham University Bronx, NY 10458 (718) 817–3885 Email: jwade@murray.fordham.edu

8.15 PARENTAL ATTITUDES AND GENDER ROLE SOCIALIZATION

8.15.1 Name of the Measure	Parent Gender-Based Attitudes Scale PGBAS
Primary Reference	Hoffman, L. W., & Kloska, D. D. (1995). Parents' gender-based attitudes toward marital roles and child rearing: Development and validation of new measures. *Sex Roles, 32,* 273–295.
Purpose	The PGBAS is designed to measure parents' gender-based attitudes toward child rearing and marital roles.
Description	The PGBAS is a 13-item self-report inventory. Each of these items is rated on a 4-point Likert-type scale with the following anchors: 1 = Strongly Agree and 4 = Strongly Disagree. The PGBAS is composed of two factors: (1) Gender-based Attitudes Toward Marital Roles and (2) Gender-based Attitudes Toward Child Rearing. An 18-item instrument was initially developed to measure (1) the division of labor between a married couple; (2) the division of power between them; and (3) gender-based attitudes toward child rearing. Principal factor analyses (PFA) with oblimin rotation were conducted for the samples of married mothers, single mothers, and fathers separately. The emergent two-factor solution for each of the samples was similar. Based on PFA, five items were removed.
Samples	Three hundred sixty-four families with a child in third or fourth grade from a large industrial city in the Midwestern portion of the United States participated in the validation study. Analyses included 253 married mothers, 111 single mothers, and 213 fathers.

Scoring	The number of items for the two subscales is as follows:
	
	    Gender-based Attitudes Toward Marital Roles: 6 items
	    Gender-based Attitudes Toward Child Rearing: 7 items
	    Total PGBAS: 13 items
	
	Three items require reverse scoring. Deriving the subscale consists of summing subscale items. Higher scores indicate less gender stereotyping. No transformations are required.

Reliability	Cronbach's alpha for the subscale scores ranged from .77 to .85.
	    Gender-based Attitudes Toward Marital Roles: Alpha = .85
	    Gender-based Attitudes Toward Child Rearing: Alpha = .77

Validity	Known-groups validity was established through analyses indicating the expected main effect of social class, higher educational achievement, gender, and mother's employment status on both dimensions of the PGBA scale. GATMR also was found to be statistically significantly correlated with self-report, child report, and husband report (on a 48-item questionnaire developed for the purposes of the validation study) of mothers' engagement in traditional feminine tasks.

	GATMR and GATCR were also both statistically significantly positively correlated with their children's perception, as indicated on an instrument modified from Miller (1975) and Signorella and Liben (1985), that men were capable of engaging in tasks associated with traditional femininity. Mother's GATCR was positively and statistically significantly associated with teacher ratings of daughter's level of assertiveness (Hightower, Work, Cowen, Lotyczewski, Spinell, Guare, & Rohrbeck, 1986).
	GATCR scores of middle-class mothers were statistically significantly positively associated with daughters' scores on math and language components of standardized achievement measures (i.e., Metropolitan Achievement Test; Otis-Lennon Ability Test). No statistically significant relationship was found for boys. This relationship also was not indicated for families in the lower class.
Related References	Adams, M., Coltrane, S., & Parke, R. D. (2007). Cross-ethnic applicability of the Gender-Based Attitudes Toward Marriage and Child Rearing scales. *Sex Roles, 56,* 325–339.
Language Versions	English
Contact	Lois Hoffman Department of Psychology University of Michigan Ann Arbor, MI 48109–1027 (734) 647–3929 Email: lhoffman@umich.edu

8.15.2 Name of the Measure	The Child Gender Socialization Scale CGSS
Primary Reference	Owen Blakemore, J. E., & Hill, C. A. (2008). The Child Gender Socialization Scale: A measure to compare traditional and feminist parents. *Sex Roles, 58,* 192–207.
Purpose	The CGSS is designed to measure parents' attitudes about the gendered behaviors of their children.
Description	The CGSS is a 28-item self-report inventory. Each of the first 22 items is rated on a 7-point Likert-type scale with the following anchors: 1 = Very Negative and 7 = Very Positive. The remaining six items are scored on a 7-point Likert-type scale with the following anchors: 1 = Disagree Strongly and 7 = Agree Strongly. The CGSS is composed of five factors: (1) Toys and Activities Stereotyped for Girls; (2) Toys and Activities Stereotyped for Boys; (3) Helping at Home; (4) Education for Marriage and Family; and (5) Disapproval of Other Gender Characteristics. Two filler items are also included in the measure. Two different forms of the CGSS were constructed so that parents could respond for the gender of their child. The CGSS was developed over the course of four studies through a series of principal components factor analyses using oblique rotation, which reduced the number of items from the 84 items originally constructed to the final 28-item measure. Items with a structure coefficient greater than .40 and those that yielded significant statistical difference between the responses for boys and girls were included in the final CGSS.
Samples	The measure was developed with data from four samples. The demographic information of the samples from the third and fourth studies for which the authors utilized a 7-point scale is reported here. The sample in study three was composed of 267 males and 153 females enrolled in an introduction to psychology course at a university in the United States. Seventy-three percent of the sample were not parents of a 2- to 8-year-old child and were thus asked to pretend to be such. Their ages ranged from 18 to 54 years ($M = 21.97$; $SD = 5.58$). The sample in study four was composed of 339 females and 97 males who were parents of a child between the ages of 2 and 8 years who were either enrolled in an introduction to psychology course at a university ($n = 310$) or from the community ($n = 126$). Parents with more than one child were asked to respond to the questionnaire with only one child in mind (chosen randomly by experimenter). Parents reported on their children (219 boys; 217 girls). The racial background of the sample was as follows: 85% White American; 7% African American; 2.5% Latino/a American; 1.5% Asian American; 1% Native American; and 1% biracial. Two percent of the sample reported "other."

Scoring	The number of items for each subscale is as follows:
	
	    Toys and Activities Stereotyped for Girls: 8 items
	
	    Toys and Activities Stereotyped for Boys: 7 items

	Helping at Home: 7 items
	Education for Marriage and Family: 2 items
	Disapproval of Other Gender Characteristics: 2 items
	Two Filler Items
	Total CGSS: 28 items
	Deriving the subscale consists of summing and dividing by the number of items in the subscale. Higher scores indicate greater levels of agreement with attitudes of gender role socialization.
Reliability	Cronbach's coefficient alpha for the subscale scores ranged across three studies. They were as follows:
	Toys and Activities Stereotyped for Girls: Alpha = .93 to .95
	Toys and Activities Stereotyped for Boys: Alpha = .82 to .89
	Helping at Home: Alpha = .82 to .86
	Education for Marriage and Family: Alpha = .79 to .85
	Disapproval of Other Gender Characteristics: Alpha = .60 to .77
	4- to 8-week test-retest reliability coefficients were as follows:
	Toys and Activities Stereotyped for Girls: $r = .76$
	Toys and Activities Stereotyped for Boys: $r = .67$
	Helping at Home: $r = .65$
	Education for Marriage and Family: $r = .76$
	Disapproval of Other Gender Characteristics: $r = .64$
Validity	Evidence for convergent validity was provided through significant correlations in the expected directions with Attitudes toward Women (Spence & Helmreich, 1972), Old Fashioned Racism (Swim et al., 1995), and Ambivalent Sexism (Glick & Fiske, 1996).
	Known-groups differences validity was demonstrated through more positive attitudes toward cross-gender behaviors for sons and daughters by women when compared to men.
Related References	
Language Versions	English
Contact	Judith E. Owen Blakemore Department of Psychology Indiana University–Purdue University Fort Wayne Fort Wayne, IN 46805 Email: Blakemore@ipfw.edu

8.16 GENDER IDENTITY

8.16.1 Name of the Measure	Gender Identity/Gender Dysphoria Questionnaire—Adolescents and Adults GIDYQ-AA
Primary Reference	Deogracias, J. J., Johnson, L. L., Meyer-Bahlburg, H. F. L., Kessler, S. J., Schober, J. M., & Zucker, K. J. (2007). The Gender Identity/Gender Dysphoria Questionnaire for Adolescents and Adults. *Journal of Sex Research, 44,* 370–379.
Purpose	The GIDYQ-AA is designed as an assessment tool for use with children with potential problems in their gender identity development.
Description	The GIDYQ-AA is a 27-item parent-report inventory. Each of these items is rated on a 5-point Likert-type scale with the following anchors: 1 = Always and 5 = Never. The GIDYQ-AA is composed of one factor. Items were developed based on clinical experiences of members of the North American Task Force on Intersexuality Research Protocol Working Group and the diagnostic criteria from the *DSM-IV-TR.* Principal factor analysis indicated a 27-item, one-factor solution for the GIDYQ-AA to be the most interpretable.
Samples	The psychometric properties of the GIDYQ-AA were established based on data gathered from 462 (197 males, 265 females) undergraduate students. Three hundred eighty-nine were recruited through undergraduate psychology courses at the University of Toronto (Mississauga Campus). The remaining participants were recruited through the use of listservs of lesbian, gay, bisexual, transgendered, and queer student groups at all three University of Toronto campuses. With respect to sexual orientation, 304 identified as heterosexual, 49 identified as gay or lesbian, 18 identified as bisexual, 9 did not identify their sexual orientation, 6 identified as transgendered, and 3 reported "other."
Scoring	Three items require reverse scoring. Scoring consists of summing and dividing by the total number of items in the measure. Lower scores indicate more frequent cross-gendered behavior. No transformations are required.
Reliability	The Cronbach alpha for the scale score was reported to be .97.
Validity	Discriminant validity was established. Specifically, gender identity patients had significantly more gender dysphoria than did both heterosexual and nonheterosexual university students.
Related References	
Language Versions	English
Contact	Kenneth J. Zucker Centre for Addiction and Mental Health 250 College St. Toronto, Ontario M5T 1R8 Canada Email: ken_zucker@camh.net

8.16.2 Name of the Measure	Gender Identity GI
Primary Reference	Egan, S. K., & Perry, D. G. (2001). Gender identity: A multidimensional analysis with implications for psychosocial adjustment. *Developmental Psychology, 37,* 451–463.
Purpose	The GI is designed as a self-report measure of gender identity among children.
Description	The GI is a 30-item self-report inventory. Each of these items is worded to assess a participant's beliefs about the similarity of self to others (boys or girls) who feel one way as well as similarity of self to other (girls or boys) who feel the opposite way. Respondents rate 1 = Very True for Me or 2 = Sort of True for Me for each item. The GI is composed of four subscales: (1) Gender Typicality Scale; (2) Gender Connectedness Scale; (3) Felt Pressure Scale; and (4) Intergroup Bias Scale. The authors developed three measures to assess for felt gender compatibility, psychological gender identity, and intergroup bias/same-sex favoritism. Data from the 15-item instrument to assess for felt gender compatibility were submitted for principal components analysis with varimax rotation. This yielded two 6-item subscales named Gender Contentedness and Gender Typicality. Each of the items yielded a structure coefficient greater than .50 and lower than .40 on any other factor. Sixteen items measuring psychological gender identity also were submitted for factor analysis. Only one 10-item factor was deemed interpretable. A factor analysis was not performed on the intergroup bias scale, but three items were deleted as a result of low item-total correlations.
Samples	The sample consisted of 182 children in grades 4 through 8 in the state of Florida. There were 81 boys and 101 girls. The sample was composed of White Americans (68%), African Americans (18%), Latino/a Americans (13%), and Asian American (1%). There were 39 fourth graders, 42 fifth graders, 35 sixth graders, 35 seventh graders, and 31 eighth graders.
Scoring	The number of items in each subscale is as follows: Gender Typicality Scale: 6 items Gender Contentedness Scale: 6 items Felt Pressure Scale: 10 items Intergroup Bias: 8 items Total GI: 30 items Scoring consists of summing and dividing by the total number of items in the measure. Higher scores indicate more gender typicality, gender contentedness, felt pressure, and intergroup bias.

(Continued)

(Continued)

Reliability	Cronbach's alpha for the subscale scores was as follows:
	
	    Gender Typicality Scale: Alpha = .78
	
	    Gender Contentedness Scale: Alpha = .79
	
	    Felt Pressure Scale: Alpha = .92
	
	    Intergroup Bias: Alpha = .73
	
	6-month test-retest reliability was as follows:
	
	    Gender Typicality Scale: $r = .64$
	
	    Gender Contentedness Scale: $r = .56$
	
	    Felt Pressure Scale: $r = .82$
	
	    Intergroup Bias: $r = .65$

Validity	Construct validity was evidenced through significant positive correlations between gender typicality and global self-worth and self-perceived social competence (Harter, 1998) for both boys and girls. Gender typicality was statistically significantly related to acceptance from male peers among girls but not boys. Gender typicality was significantly related to acceptance from female peers by girls and boys. Construct validity also was demonstrated through evidence of statistically significant relations between gender contentedness and global self-worth for both boys and girls and self-perceived peer social competence among boys. Evidence for some of the scales also was demonstrated through significant relations between gender typicality and both agentic traits and communal traits for both boys and girls.
Related References	Carver, P. R., Egan, S. K., & Perry, D. G. (2004). Children who question their heterosexuality. *Developmental Psychology, 40,* 43–53. Corby, B. C., Hodges, E. V. E., & Perry, D. G. (2007). Gender identity and adjustment in Black, Hispanic, and White American preadolescents. *Developmental Psychology, 43,* 261–266. Yunger, J. L., Carver, P. R., & Perry, D. G. (2004). Does gender identity influence children's psychological well-being? *Developmental Psychology, 40,* 572–582.
Language Versions	English
Contact	David G. Perry Department of Psychology Florida Atlantic University Boca Raton, FL 33431 Email: perrydg@fau.edu

8.16.3 Name of the Measure	Gender Identity Questionnaire for Children GIQ
Primary Reference	Johnson, L. L., Bradley, S. J., Birkenfeld-Adams, A. S., Kuksis, M. A. R., Maing, D. M., Mitchell, J. N., & Zucker, K. J. (2004). A parent-report Gender Identity Questionnaire for children. *Archives of Sexual Behavior, 33*, 105–116.
Purpose	The GIQ is designed as a parent-report assessment tool for use with children with potential problems in their gender identity development.
Description	The GIQ is a 14-item parent-report inventory. Each of these items is rated on a 5-point scale for frequency of occurrence.
	The GIQ is composed of one factor.
	The instrument was a revised version of a parent-report behavior preference questionnaire (Elizabeth & Green, 1984).
	Principal factor analysis with varimax rotation was conducted to examine the factor structure of the GIQ. A 14-item, one-factor solution was deemed to be the most interpretable.
Samples	The psychometric properties of the GIQ were established based on data gathered from the parents of 325 "gender-referred" individuals and 504 "controls."
Scoring	Scoring consists of summing and dividing by the 14 items in the measure. Lower scores indicate more frequent cross-gendered behavior. No transformations are required.
Reliability	No reliability data were provided.
Validity	Known-group validity indicated that the parents of "gender-referred" individuals scored higher on the GIQ than did parents of the "controls."
Related References	Cohen-Kettenis, P. T., Wallien, M., Johnson, L. L., Owen-Anderson, A. F. H., Bradley, S. J., & Zucker, K. J. (2006). A Parent-report Gender Identity Questionnaire for Children: A cross-national, cross-clinic comparative analysis. *Clinical Child Psychology and Psychiatry, 11*, 397–405.
Language Versions	English
Contact	Kenneth Zucker Gender Identity Clinic Child, Youth, and Family Program Center for Addiction and Mental Health–Clarke Division Toronto, Ontario, Canada M5T 1R8 Email: Ken.zucker@camh.net

8.16.4 Name of the Measure	The Recalled Childhood Gender Questionnaire—Revised RCGQ-R
Primary Reference	Meyer-Bahlburg, H. F. L., Dolezal, C., Zucker, K. J., Kessler, S. J., Schober, J. M., & New, M. I. (2006). The Recalled Childhood Gender Questionnaire—Revised: A psychometric analysis in a sample of women with congenital adrenal hyperplasia. *Journal of Sex Research, 43*, 364–367.
Purpose	The RCGQ-R is designed to measure gender-related behaviors that are associated with gender identity disorder.
Description	The RCGQ-R is an 18-item self-report inventory. Each of these items is rated on a Likert-type scale. The anchors for the 18 items vary, with some items utilizing a 4-point scale and others a 5-point scale. The RCGQ-R is composed of three subscales: (1) Gender Role, (2) Physical Activity, and (3) Cross-Gender Desire. The RCGQ-R is a modified version of the original 23-item RCGQ (Zucker, Mitchell, Bradley, Tkachuk, Cantor, & Allin, 2006). Based on the recommendations of the Research Protocol Work Group of the North American Task Force on Intersexuality, five items were deleted because they were deemed to not differentiate between men and women. The items of the RCGQ-R were submitted for principal components analysis, which generated three components.
Samples	The structure and validity of the RCGQ-R was examined using a sample of 147 women representing different degrees of prenatal androgenization.
Scoring	The number of items for each subscale is as follows: Gender Role: 13 items Physical Activity: 3 items Cross-Gender Desire: 2 items Total RCGQ-R: 18 items Scoring consists of summing and dividing by the total number of items in the measure. Higher scores indicate more cross-gender behavior.
Reliability	Cronbach's alpha for the subscale scores were as follows: Gender Role: Alpha = .91 Physical Activity: Alpha = .64 Cross-Gender Desire: Alpha = .47 Total RCGQ-R: Alpha = .90

Validity	Known-groups validity was demonstrated through a comparison of means of the groups formed in the sample based on prenatal androgenization.
Related References	Zucker, K. J., Mitchell, J. N., Bradley, S. J., Tkachuk, J., Cantor, J. M., & Allin, S. M. (2006). The Recalled Childhood Gender Identity/Gender Role Questionnaire: Psychometric properties. *Sex Roles, 54*, 469–483.
Language Versions	English
Contact	Kenneth Zucker Gender Identity Clinic Child, Youth, and Family Program Center for Addiction and Mental Health–Clarke Division Toronto, Ontario, Canada M5T 1R8 Email: Ken.zucker@camh.net

9

Sexual Orientation–Related Measures

9.1 TERMINOLOGY

The focus of this chapter is to present measures that purport to address matters related to sexual orientation. Given the number of terms used in research and lay discussion, an overview of terminology used in this field of study is needed. Through Herek, Kimmel, Amaro, and Melton (1991), the Committee on Lesbian and Gay Concerns of the American Psychological Association (APA) provided clarity and caution with respect to the terms used for gay men, lesbian individuals, and bisexual men and women. In the report, the APA suggested that because of the fluidity of language and the shifts inherent in the sociopolitical milieu, terms may fall in or out of favor. In the same vein, we provide an overview of some past and current-day terminology. First, the term *homosexual* as a noun or adjective is, because of (1) the stigma of pathology and criminality attached to the word, (2) its association with men as opposed to women in same-sex relationships, (3) its focus on sexual (as opposed to emotional and relational) dimensions of relationships, and (4) its exclusion of other sexual minority orientations (e.g., bisexual men and women), not viewed as appropriate. Second, the term *gay* alone also is not recommended as it is an adjective that can refer to both males and females. Instead, it is recommended that the terms *lesbian, gay male, bisexual female,* or *bisexual male* be

used. The commonly used acronyms to describe this group as a whole are LGBQ or GLBQ; the first three letters represent the three major groups within this social identity category. The last letter, Q, may represent *questioning* (one's sexual orientation) or *queer*. *Queer* was once exclusively a pejorative term for sexual minorities. However, some sexual minorities, especially youth, have reclaimed this term as one that inclusively and positively describes nonheterosexual people and transgendered individuals. On a related note, we made a conscious decision to not include measures addressing transgender issues in this chapter. Although LGB and transgender individuals share similar experiences because of their lack of conformity to heterosexual norms (Fassinger & Arseneau, 2007), they may experience distinct forms of oppression. Thus, we felt it necessary to distinguish measures addressing experiences primarily based on gender expression (see Chapter 8) from those interpersonal and intrapersonal experiences that manifest as a result of one's expression of sexual and relational desires.

Terms such as *men who have sex with men* (MSM) and *women who have sex with women* (WSW) have been commonly used by epidemiologists in the public health literature (see Young & Meyer, 2005). First introduced in the 1980s, the terms were developed and used to shift focus in HIV/AIDS prevention efforts from targeting an identity (i.e., those men who identified as gay) to behavior (i.e., men who had sex with other men). Young and Meyer also point out that the term was adopted by social constructionists who seek to provide more complex understandings of sexual identity, behavior, and intimate desire. Irrespective of the perspective, Young and Meyer argued that *MSM* and *WSM* are problematic to prevention efforts because of their (1) undermining of self-determination among sexual minorities, (2) exclusion of social dimensions of sexuality, and (3) lack of precision in the terms to describe the full range of sexual behaviors. In short, the terms *MSM* and *WSW* may not be appropriate for use. Instead, they urged researchers and practitioners to utilize more culturally relevant and specific terms (e.g., *down-low, queer, sexual minority, two-spirit people,* or *Black men who identify as gay*; see Baez, Howd, & Pepper, 2007). The lack of consistent use of terminology to describe members of this social identity group reflects the (1) diversity of members who occupy these social identities as well as (2) social constructionist perspectives on sexual identity. For the purposes of this chapter, the terms *LGB* or *sexual minority* (i.e., a person who is, as a result of his/her sexual orientation, in a position of less political power) will be used interchangeably unless otherwise presented by authors of respective summarized scales.

Heteronormative ideology, the cultural belief and assumption that heterosexuality is normal and that all other forms of sexuality are abnormal, sick, or immoral, serves as a foundation for *homophobia, sexual stigma, heterosexism,* and *sexual prejudice.* The term *homophobia* was coined by George Weinberg (1972), a psychologist trained as a psychoanalyst, to describe the fear and prejudice that heterosexual individuals, particularly men, held toward gay men. The term has been used in the popular press, research articles, and by lay people. Offshoots of the term such as *biphobia, transphobia,* and *lesbophobia* have also been developed to describe fear associated with bisexual, transgender, and lesbian individuals, respectively

(Herek, 2004). *Internalized homophobia* also was developed by Weinberg to describe the feelings individuals have internalized about what it means to be a sexual minority. Herek argues that while the term *homophobia* has been useful, it lacks precision and clarity as well as its focus on describing anti-LGB attitudes as individually based pathology or fear. The term *homonegative* was developed (Hudson & Ricketts, 1980) in order to shift focus on the negative attitudes, beliefs, and feelings individuals may have about LGB individuals. *Internalized homonegativity,* like *internalized homophobia,* refers to the negative attitudes, beliefs, and feelings a person may have about being LGB (Mayfield, 2001).

Herek (2004) offered that the terms *sexual stigma, heterosexism,* and *sexual prejudice* provide a more complex understanding of antigay attitudes than that offered by *homophobia.* He explained that *sexual stigma* is the "shared knowledge of society's negative regard for any nonheterosexual behavior, identity, relationship, or community" (p.15, 2004). He further explained that sexual stigma results not only in the labeling of sexual minorities as deviants who engage in immoral, criminal, and shameful acts but also in the power differential between heterosexual individuals and LGB individuals. *Heterosexism,* which is inappropriately used as a synonym of *homophobia,* reflects the socio-cultural depictions (e.g., media depictions of two men kissing as disgusting) or practices (e.g., gendered language) and institutional policies (e.g., marriage only for heterosexual individuals) that privilege heterosexual orientations, behaviors, and practices and that engender hostility toward sexual minorities. Szymanski (2004) proposed the term *internalized heterosexism* to underscore how beliefs, attitudes, and feelings are situated within a sociopolitical context. *Sexual prejudice* is defined as the "internalized sexual stigma that results in the negative evaluation of sexual minorities" (Herek, 2009, p.74). Given this definition, prejudice may be held by those with power (i.e., heterosexual individuals) or sexual minorities. Much of the study of sexual prejudice, however, has focused on the attitudes held among individuals identifying as heterosexual toward those perceived to be a sexual minority.

9.2 HISTORY OF STUDY OF SEXUAL MINORITY ISSUES

Homosexuality has a long history of being seen as a pathology or mental illness by mental health professionals, who held a focus of finding a cure (Croteau, Bieschke, Fassinger, & Manning, 2008). It was not until 1973 that the American Psychiatric Association removed homosexuality as a mental disorder from the second edition of the *Diagnostic and Statistical Manual of Mental Disorders* (DSM). Today, it is widely accepted among mental health professionals that LGB individuals, while at risk for mental and physical health problems because of rampant discrimination experienced by members of the group, are no less capable of forming healthy relationships or of being happy or satisfied with life.

In providing a historical overview of LGB mental health, Rothblum (2000) explained that before Evelyn Hooker's landmark study comparing psychologists' evaluation of assessment data of the psychological health of nonclinical samples of gay men and heterosexual men, studies addressing homosexuality employed samples obtained from prisons or psychotherapy (i.e., individuals who wanted to change their sexual orientation). In her landmark study, Hooker (1957) found that contrary to widely held beliefs, gay men could not be identified by psychological experts from their responses on projective assessments. Her study, which demonstrated that gay men were just as healthy as heterosexual men, shifted psychology's focus on pathology to one in which identity is affirmed. Since that time, researchers have examined the attitudes of heterosexual men and women (e.g., Herek & Capitanio, 1996; Herek & Gonzalez-Rivera, 2006), coming-out experiences (e.g., Mohr & Fassinger, 2003), the impact of sexual prejudice on the health of LG individuals (e.g., Meyer, 2003), identity development (Rosario, Schrimshaw, & Hunter, 2004, 2008), and relationships (e.g., Todosijevic, Rothblum,

& Solomon, 2005). While LGB issues have received more attention in the empirical literature, Phillips, Ingram, Smith, and Mindes (2003) found that LGB-related articles represented only 2% of the total number of articles published between 1990 and 1999. In their content analysis, Phillips et al. also reported that more attention regarding bisexual men and bisexual women is needed. Furthermore, Riggle, Whitman, Olson, Rostosky, and Strong (2008) have argued that, because the majority of research has focused on negative outcomes, a shift to the study of strengths of the community must take place.

9.3 THEORETICAL FOUNDATIONS

The study of sexual minority–related issues is informed by several different theoretical perspectives. The study of attitudes toward this stigmatized group is grounded in the social-cognitive perspectives of prejudice. The impact of prejudice on self-concept and behaviors has been informed by feminist perspectives as well as social identity theory (e.g., Tajfel & Turner, 1986), identity development theory (e.g., Cass, 1979), and minority stress theory (Meyer, 2003). In this review, we identified four interrelated categories of measures: (1) Sexual Prejudice and Attitudes; (2) Identity Development; (3) Internalized Prejudice and Attitudes; and (4) Environments and Climates.

9.4 SEXUAL PREJUDICE AND ATTITUDES

Although attitudes do not always result in behavior, LGB individuals have been demonstrated to be victims of hate crimes based on sexual orientation (see http://www.fbi.gov/hq/cid/civilrights/hate.htm). While attitudes toward sexual minorities have become more positive since the 1970s (Herek, 2009), an examination of data collected by the Federal Bureau of Investigation indicates a rise in the percentage of single-bias incidents related to sexual orientations in each year between 2005 and 2008. The study of sexual prejudice and attitudes has focused on understanding the attitudes of heterosexual-identified people toward LGB individuals. While some measures assess for overt negative attitudes, some reflect the movement toward assessing modern forms of discrimination. The following 12 measures assess for attitudes of LGB individuals. Those meeting our criteria are Attitudes Toward Lesbians and Gay Men Scale (ATLG; Herek, 1984); Kite Homosexuality Attitude Scale (KHAS; Kite & Deaux, 1986); Modern Heterosexism and Queer/Liberationist Scales (MHQ/LS; Massey, 2009); Attitudes Regarding Bisexuality Scale (ARBS; Mohr & Rochlen, 1999); Modern Homonegativity Scale (MHS; Morrison & Morrison, 2002); Homonegativity Scale (HNS; Morrison, Parriag, & Morrison, 1999); Attitudes Toward Same-Sex Marriage Scale (ATSMS; Pearl & Galupo, 2007); Modern Homophobia Scale—Lesbian (MHS-L; Raja & Stokes, 1998); Modern Homophobia Scale—Gay (MHS-G; Raja & Stokes, 1998); Lesbian, Gay, and Bisexual Knowledge and Attitudes Scale for Heterosexuals (LGB-KASH; Worthington, Dillon, & Becker-Schutte, 2005), and Homophobia Scale (HS; Wright Jr., Adams, & Bernat, 1999). Some authors have developed positive beliefs of the group (i.e., Homopositivity Scale; Morrison & Bearden, 2007).

9.5 IDENTITY DEVELOPMENT

The identity development of individuals from a variety of stigmatized groups has been a main area of interest to mental health professionals and researchers, particularly counseling psychologists. The interest in the development of a healthy self-concept among sexual minorities is no different (see Croteau et al., 2008). Vivienne Cass's (1979) model, which was based on earlier models of ethnic identity, was the first to address the identity development of sexual minorities. Now understood as lacking in complexity, scholars have studied and expanded theoretical formulations of sexual identity development theory of sexual minorities (e.g., Fassinger & Miller, 1996; McCarn & Fassinger, 1996) as well as heterosexual individuals (e.g., Mohr, 2002; Worthington, Savoy, Dillon, & Vernaglia, 2002). In our review, we identified three instruments

that address development of sexual identity. They are Outness Inventory (OI; Mohr & Fassinger, 2000); Lesbian, Gay, and Bisexual Identity Scale (LGBIS; Mohr & Fassinger, 2000); and the Measure of Sexual Identity Exploration and Commitment (MoSIEC; Worthington, Navarro, Savoy, & Hampton, 2008).

9.6 INTERNALIZED PREJUDICE AND ATTITUDES

Early on, scholars proposed that sexual minorities would internalize sexual stigma as well as sexual prejudice (Weinberg, 1972). Internalization of the stigma attached to being a sexual minority has been theorized to be a central component in identity development models (see Cass, 1979) because it can result in self-hatred. Over the past 30 years, researchers have found that this internalization of negative attitudes and beliefs regarding homosexuality would be inversely correlated with self-esteem, outness, health, and behaviors of LGB individuals (e.g., Herek, Cogan, & Gillis, 2002; Herek, Gillis, & Cogan, 2009; Meyer, 2003; Szymanski & Gupta, 2009; Szymanski, Kashubeck-West, & Meyer, 2008). The following three measures were developed to measure individuals' internalization of homophobia and homonegativity: the Short Internalized Homonegativity Scale (SIHS; Currie, Cunningham, & Findlay, 2004); Internalized Homonegativity Inventory (IHNI; Mayfield, 2001); and Internalized Homophobia Scale (HIS; Ross & Rosser, 1996).

9.7 ENVIRONMENTS AND CLIMATES

As stated earlier, a major focus of research addressing sexual minorities has been the attitudes of heterosexuals. Because they represent an important dimension of the experiences sexual minorities have, studying the attitudes of heterosexuals is important. However, the study of the experiences of members of target groups also is needed. In order to further study these experiences, several measures have been developed to assess the climates in which lesbian, gay male, and bisexual individuals live, go to school, and work. These three measures are the Lesbian, Gay, Bisexual, and Transgendered Climate Inventory (LGBTCI; Liddle, Luzzo, Hauenstein, & Schuck, 2004); Homophobia Content Agent Target Scale (HCATS; Poteat & Espelage, 2005); and the Heterosexist Harassment, Rejection, and Discrimination Scale (HHRDS; Szymanski, 2006).

9.8 FUTURE RESEARCH

Nearly 40 years after homosexuality was removed from the *DSM* as a disorder, the study of sexual minorities has grown in breadth and depth (Phillips et al., 2003). The following are some recommendations based on our review of the existing sexual minority-related measures.

1. New theory has replaced old. For instance, the work on identity development has moved beyond Cass's original formulations to include multiple dimensions (e.g., McCarn & Fassinger, 1996) and heterosexual individuals (e.g., Mohr, 2002). However, instruments to test those theories have either not been developed or not been subjected to tests of factorial validity. Without such measurement devices, study of these newer theories is hampered. As such, we recommend the development and/or testing of the factorial validity of instruments developed that purport to measure identity development.

2. With a few notable exceptions (e.g., ATLG scale), many of the measures reviewed in this chapter were developed relatively recently and require more testing of their psychometric properties. To those ends, we recommend further study to establish evidence of validity for those measures.

3. Because many of the measures summarized in this chapter were developed primarily on White American or White Canadian samples, tests of structural equivalence (invariance) may be necessary to determine the instruments' utility with ethnic minority samples.

4. Many of the authors did not provide evidence for temporal stability of their measures or their subscales. Thus, we encourage authors to work to establish test-retest reliability of these measures.

5. Given the complexity of social identity and social stigma, it may be necessary to develop instruments to measure the prejudice or attitudes toward or experiences of individuals who occupy more than one stigmatized social group (e.g., racism experiences of Black men who identify as gay).

9.9 ATTITUDES TOWARD LESBIANS, GAY MEN, AND BISEXUALS

9.9.1 Name of the Measure	Attitudes Toward Lesbians and Gay Men Scale ATLG
Primary Reference	Herek, G. M. (1984). Attitudes toward lesbians and gay men: A factor analytic study. *Journal of Homosexuality, 10*, 39–51.
Purpose	The ATLG was designed to be a measure of attitudes toward lesbians and gay men.
Description	The ATLG is a 20-item self-report measure that was originally developed with a 9-point Likert-type scale but has since employed a 5- or 7-point response format with the following anchor points: Strongly Disagree and Strongly Agree. In oral administrations of the ATLG, a 4-point Likert-type response format with the same anchors is recommended. The ATLG is composed of two 10-item subscales: (1) Attitudes toward Lesbians and (2) Attitudes toward Gay Men. A series of four exploratory factor analyses (EFA), all with oblique rotation, was conducted on data collected from college students from several universities and colleges from across the United States. In the first study, items from the Attitudes toward Homosexuality Scale (ATHS-Form G; MacDonald, Huggins, Young, & Swanson, 1973) were administered to 72 respondents. Several factors, with one major component (i.e., Condemnation-Tolerance), emerged from this EFA. In a second EFA, items from the ATHS-Form G as well as items used by Levitt and Klassen (1974) and Smith (1971) and newly constructed items were administered to 104 undergraduate students. The Condemnation-Tolerance factor emerged from this EFA with three smaller factors. From this procedure, along with the addition of newly developed items, a 59-item version of the questionnaire was administered to 130 undergraduates. Data were then submitted for another EFA and the same one-factor solution emerged. Because the items of the questionnaire did not differentiate between gay male and lesbian targets, a fourth EFA was conducted on data from 906 undergraduate students. In this study, participants were administered either a questionnaire with a gay target or a lesbian target. The questionnaire was composed of the items from the previous studies along with some newly constructed items. A total of four EFA were conducted, with separate analyses conducted for male and female participants with either a gay male or lesbian target. The four EFA yielded the same 37-item Condemnation-Tolerance factor. Smaller factors also emerged but did not account for a large amount of the variance and were subsequently omitted from the ATLG. The 10 items with the highest item-total correlations among items with a gay male and lesbian as a target were selected for the final 20-item ATLG. Shorter versions (10-item, 6-item) of the ATLG have also been used (see Herek & McLemore, 2010). Stoever and Morera (2007) conducted further study of the structure of the ATLG. In their confirmatory factor analysis, they found a two-factor structure similar to that found initially through EFA. However, data from four items of the ATL were not found to be a good fit for the proposed 10-item model.

Samples	Four samples ($N_1 = 72$; $N_2 = 104$; $N_3 = 130$; $N_4 = 906$) were utilized to develop the 20-item ATLG. In the first sample, there were 40 females and 32 males. In the second sample, there were 57 females and 47 males. The third sample was composed of 66 females and 64 males. In the final sample, there were 558 females and 348 males.
Scoring	The number of items for each of the two subscales is as follows: ATL: 10 items ATG: 10 items Total ATLG: 20 items Seven of the items require a reverse score. Total scale and subscale scores are calculated by summing the responses to the corresponding items. Higher scores indicate more negative attitudes.
Reliability	Cronbach's alpha coefficient for the scores of the subscales and total scale were reported to be: ATL: Alpha = .77 ATG: Alpha = .89 Total ATLG: Alpha = .90
Validity	Known-groups validity was established through statistically significantly more negative attitudes held by heterosexual men toward gay men (Herek, 1988). Evidence for criterion-related validity was established through statistically significant correlations, in the expected directions, between the ATL and ATG scores and attitudes toward sex roles (Spence, Helmreich, & Stapp, 1973), traditional family ideology (Levinson & Huffman, 1955), dogmatism (Troldahl & Powell, 1965), number of gay male or lesbian friends, and positive contact with any lesbians and gay men. Religiosity and ambiguity tolerance also were found to be statistically significantly correlated, in the expected directions, with scores on the ATG and ATL for female participants.
Related References	Cardenas, M., & Barrientos, J. (2008). The Attitudes Toward Lesbians and Gay Men Scale (ATLG): Adaptation and testing the reliability and validity in Chile. *Journal of Sex Research, 45,* 140–149. Herek, G. M., & McLemore, K. A. (2010). The Attitudes Toward Lesbians and Gay Men (ATLG) scale. In T. Fisher, C. M. Davis, W. L. Yarber, and S. L. Davis, *Handbook of sexuality-related measures* (3rd ed.). New York: Taylor & Francis. Herek, G. M., & Gonzalez-Rivera, M. (2006). Attitudes toward homosexuality among U. S. residents of Mexican descent. *Journal of Sex Research, 43,* 122–135. Stoever, C. J., & Morera, O. F. (2007). A confirmatory factor analysis of the Attitudes Toward Lesbians and Gay Men (ATLG) measure. *Journal of Homosexuality, 52,* 189–209.
Language Versions	English, Dutch, Spanish, Turkish, Brazilian Portuguese, Mandarin, Malay
Contact	The ATLG has been published in Herek (1988). Shorter versions can be found in Herek and McLemore (in press).

9.9.2 Name of the Measure	Kite Homosexuality Attitude Scale KHAS
Primary Reference	Kite, M. E., & Deaux, K. (1986). Attitudes toward homosexuality: Assessment and behavioral consequences. *Basic and Applied Social Psychology, 7*(2), 137–162.
Purpose	The purpose of the measure is to assess attitudes toward homosexuality.
Description	The KHAS is a 21-item self-report measure that utilizes a 5-point Likert-type response format with the following anchors: (1) Strong Agreement to (5) Strong Disagreement. The KHAS is a unidimensional measure. A pool of 40 items was developed to measure attitudes, beliefs, and anxieties people hold toward gay men or lesbians. These items were pilot tested with a sample of 40 undergraduate college students. Based on their feedback and item-total correlations, 15 items were removed from the KHAS. The remaining 25 items were submitted for factor analysis with oblique rotation. The eigenvalues of five factors were greater than 1.0. Based on scree-plot and coefficient alpha on the scores, a one-factor solution was selected. These processes resulted in a 21-item measure. Alternate forms, with *gay* or *lesbian* used as terms to replace *homosexual*, were administered. Only small differences were observed when total scores of these two forms were compared.
Samples	The KHAS was developed based on data from a sample of 569 students attending either the University of Texas at Austin (*n* = 317) or Purdue University (*n* = 252). An additional sample of 1,342 students from Purdue University provided responses to study the internal consistency of the KHAS. Data from a sample of 630 students from Purdue University were used to provide evidence for validity of the KHAS. Finally, a sample of 144 undergraduate men participated in an experiment that served to establish evidence for the predictive validity of the KHAS.
Scoring	There are 21 items in the KHAS. Ten items require reverse scoring. The Total KHAS score is derived by summing the responses to each item. Higher scores indicate more positive attitudes.
Reliability	The Cronbach's alpha coefficient for the KHAS score was reported to be .94. 1-month test-retest reliability was reported to be .71.
Validity	Known-groups validity was demonstrated through statistically significantly more negative attitudes among men than women. Construct validity was evidenced through statistically significant positive correlations between the KHAS and a measure of attitudes toward feminism (Smith, Ferree, & Miller, 1975) and a small but significant correlation with femininity (Spence, Helmreich, & Stapp, 1974).

	Predictive validity was evidenced through an experiment involving male undergraduate students ($N = 144$). Men with higher scores on the KHAS reacted more positively toward a person they learned was gay.
Related References	Cowan, G., Heiple, B., Marquez, C., Khatchadourian, D., & McNevin, M. (2005). Heterosexuals' attitudes toward hate crimes and hate speech against gays and lesbians: Old-fashioned and modern heterosexism. *Journal of Homosexuality, 49,* 67–82.
Language Versions	English
Contact	The KHAS is published in Kite and Deaux (1986).

9.9.3 Name of the Measure	Modern Heterosexism and Queer/Liberationist Scales MHQ/LS
Primary Reference	Massey, S. G. (2009). Polymorphous prejudice: Liberating the measurement of heterosexuals' attitudes toward lesbians and gay men. *Journal of Homosexuality, 56*, 147–172.
Purpose	The MHQ/LS was developed to assess heterosexuals' attitudes toward gay men and lesbians.
Description	The MHQ/LS is a 70-item measure that utilizes a 5-point Likert-type response format with the following anchors: (1) = Totally Disagree to (5) = Totally Agree. The MHQ/LS is composed of seven factors: (1) Traditional Heterosexism, (2) Denial of Continued Discrimination, (3) Aversion toward Gay Men, (4) Aversion toward Lesbians, (5) Value Gay Progress, (6) Resist Heteronormativity, and (7) Positive Beliefs. The author conceived the measure through a review of literature regarding prejudice against sexual minorities as well as heteronormativity (e.g., Butler, 1990). As such, items were developed or selected from other measures to reflect both modern heterosexism and queer/liberationist literature. Specifically, 79 items of the initial Modern Heterosexism Scale (MHS) were selected from the Attitudes Toward Lesbians and Gay Men Scale (Herek, 1984) or the Homosexual Attitude Scale (Kite & Deaux, 1986), modified from the Modern and Old Fashioned Sexism Scale (Swim et al., 1995), the Multidimensional Inventory of Black Identity, or based on a study of racial ambivalence (Katz & Hass, 1988). Seventy-three items were developed for the Queer/Liberationist Consciousness (Q/LC) scale to reflect queer/liberationist literature (e.g., Jagose, 1996; Kitzinger, 1987) as well as from a measure of beliefs of the mutability and fundamentality of sexual orientation (Hegarty, 2002). The 73- and 79-item measures were submitted for exploratory factor analysis (EFA) with oblique rotation separately. A three-factor solution emerged from both sets of EFA. The factors that emerged for the MHS were (1) Moral Condemnation, (2) Aversion, and (3) Denial of Continued Discrimination. The factors that emerged for the Q/LC scale were (1) Value Gay Progress, (2) Resist Heteronormativity, and (3) Positive Beliefs. Thirty-two and 24 items were deleted from the MHS and Q/LC, respectively, due to low item-total correlations calculated for each subscale. Before submitting additional data from a different sample for confirmatory factor analysis (CFA), the aversion scale was revised so that it could assess for aversion toward gay men and aversion toward lesbians separately. Internal consistency was assessed for each subscale to determine if additional items should be removed. Two items with low estimates were removed. CFA were then conducted and results indicated close to adequate fit. To test the model further, Massey (2009) created composite variables for each subscale. The model fit was better but still statistically significantly different from the data. Massey then conducted another CFA with contact with gay men or lesbians included in the model. The overall model fit improved.

Samples	The MHQ/LS was established based on data collected from 269 undergraduate psychology students from central Texas, U.S. The sample (46% female, 54% male) ranged in age from 17 to 59 years ($Mdn = 19$). With respect to race and ethnicity, 69% identified as White American, 18% identified as Asian or Pacific Islander American, 14% identified as Latino/a American, 9% identified as multiracial, 3% identified as African American, with less than 1% identified as Native American.
	A sample of 592 undergraduate students (61% female; 39% male) was recruited for studies of validity and to confirm the factor structure of the MHQ/LS. Participants' ages ranged from 17 to 47 years ($Mdn = 19$). With respect to race and ethnicity, 69% identified as White American, 20% identified as Asian or Pacific Islander American, 10% identified as Latino/a American, 7% identified as multiracial, 4% identified as African American, with less than 1% identified as Native American.

Scoring	The number of items for each subscale is as follows:
	
	  Traditional Heterosexism: 19 items
	  Denial of Continued Discrimination: 9 items
	  Aversion toward Gay Men: 8 items
	  Aversion toward Lesbians: 8 items
	  Value of Gay Progress: 8 items
	  Resist Heteronormativity: 8 items
	  Positive Beliefs: 10 items
	  Total MHQ/LS: 70 items
	
	Scores on the subscales are obtained by summing and dividing the scores by the number of items of the subscale. Higher scores on the Traditional Heterosexism, Denial of Continued Discrimination, and Aversion Toward Gay Men and Lesbians scales indicated higher levels of antigay/antilesbian attitudes. Higher scores on the Value Gay Progress, Resist Heteronormativity, and Positive Beliefs scales indicate higher levels of progay/prolesbian attitudes.

Reliability	Cronbach's alpha coefficient for the subscale scores were as follows:
	
	  Traditional Heterosexism: Alpha = .95
	  Denial of Continued Discrimination: Alpha = .83
	  Aversion toward Gay Men: Alpha = .90
	  Aversion toward Lesbians: Alpha = .88
	  Value of Gay Progress: Alpha = .94
	  Resist Heteronormativity: Alpha = .90
	  Positive Beliefs: Alpha = .86
	
	One-week test-retest reliability was reported to range from .67 (Positive Beliefs) to .93 (Traditional Heterosexism).

(Continued)

(Continued)

Validity	Known-groups validity was established through statistically significant more negative attitudes among men, as compared to women, on Aversion toward Gay Men, Traditional Heterosexism, and Denial of Continued Discrimination. Women were more likely to report more positive attitudes, as compared to men, on Value of Gay Progress and Positive Beliefs. Furthermore, individuals who reported greater contact with someone who identified as gay or lesbian reported lower levels of Aversion toward Gay Men, and Aversion toward Lesbians.
Related References	
Language Versions	English
Contact	Items of the MHQ/LS are presented in Massey (2009).

9.9.4 Name of the Measure	Attitudes Regarding Bisexuality Scale ARBS
Primary Reference	Mohr, J. J., & Rochlen, A. B. (1999). Measuring attitudes regarding bisexuality in lesbian, gay male, and heterosexual populations. *Journal of Counseling Psychology, 46,* 353–369.
Purpose	The ARBS-FM, ARBS-F, and ARBS-M were developed to assess attitudes about female and male bisexuality, female bisexuality, and male bisexuality, respectively.
Description	The ARBS-FM is composed of 18 items. The ARBS-F and ARBS-M each are composed of 12 items. All three forms of the ARBS are self-report and utilize a Likert-type response format with following anchors: 1 = Strong Disagree to 5 = Strongly Agree. There are two subscales to each version of the ARBS: (1) Stability and (2) Tolerance. Items of the ARBS were derived after a review of the empirical and theoretical literature of attitudes regarding sexual minorities. Based on their review, the authors hypothesized that Stability and Tolerance are two domains of attitudes toward bisexual individuals. They developed 46 items. Two separate versions were created out of each item, with one version addressing attitudes toward men and the other addressing attitudes toward women. These 92 items were assessed for appropriateness and clarity by three doctoral-level graduate students and one master's-level social worker, all of whom had extensive experience as researchers or clinicians in sexual orientation issues. The measure was then pilot-tested on a sample of nine undergraduate students who were asked to provide comments regarding the instrument's clarity. Twelve items were deleted based on this feedback. A principal-axis factor analysis with varimax rotation was performed. This resulted in a three-factor solution. The third factor, however, was composed of items with structure coefficients greater than .40 on at least one other factor. Thus, a two-factor solution was selected as most interpretable. The authors made an a priori decision to create a measure that could be administered easily, one in which the each of the male and female subscales of the ARBS would be composed of no more than 10 items each. For the first item, they selected the item with the highest structure coefficient. The item with the next highest structure coefficient and that had a different gender as the target (male or female) then was selected. Each subsequent item followed this same decision rule but could not be the opposite-sex parallel of the previous item. This resulted in an 18-item ARBS-FM. The ARBS-F and ARBS-M were designed to be identical to each other but with a different gender for the target. Thus, items with a structure coefficient greater than .40 and that had a parallel item (also with a loading of greater than .40) were selected. A total of 24 items (12 pairs) was selected for the ARBS-F and ARBS-M. Confirmatory factor analysis (CFA) indicated good fit of the ARBS-FM to the data. CFA indicated excellent fit of the ARBS-F and ARBS-M to the data. CFA also indicated that a two-factor model to be a better fit to the data than a one-factor model.

(Continued)

(Continued)

Samples	The initial psychometric properties of the ARBS measures were developed across five studies. The first study on which the structures of the ARBS measures were found was composed of 110 lesbians and 141 gay men. These participants ranged in age (15–52; $M = 27.71$ years, $SD = 8.98$). With respect to racial background, 83% percent of this sample identified as White American, 6% Latino/a American, 6% Asian American, 2% African American, 2% Native American, and 1% Middle Eastern. CFA were performed on data gathered from 288 students attending three different colleges or universities in the mid-Atlantic (U.S.). This sample was composed of 55% White American, 20% African American, 12% Asian American, 7% Latino/a American, and 6% reporting "other." Only data from heterosexual participants were included in the analyses.

Scoring	The number of items in each subscale for each of the three versions of the ARBS is as follows:
	
	ARBS-FM
	
	    Stability: 9 items
	
	    Tolerance: 9 items
	
	ARBS-M
	
	    Stability: 6 items
	
	    Tolerance: 6 items
	
	ARBS-F
	
	    Stability: 6 items
	
	    Tolerance: 6 items
	
	Thirteen items require reverse scoring. Scores are then obtained by summing and dividing the number of items in the corresponding subscale. Higher scores indicate more positive attitudes toward male or female bisexuality.

Reliability	Cronbach's alpha for the scores ranged across three studies. They were as follows:
	
	    Tolerance: $Alpha_{FM} = .91$ to .93
	
	    $Alpha_F = .86$ to .92
	
	    $Alpha_M = .83$ to .93
	
	    Stability: $Alpha_{FM} = .89$ to .94
	
	    $Alpha_F = .85$ to .89
	
	    $Alpha_M = .84$ to .90

	3-week test-retest reliability:
	Tolerance: $r_{FM} = .91$
	$r_F = .92$
	$r_M = .83$
	Stability: $r_{FM} = .84$
	$r_F = .69$
	$r_M = .85$
Validity	Among heterosexual participants, evidence for convergent validity was demonstrated through statistically significant positive relationship between the ARBS subscales and attitudes toward lesbians and gay men (Herek, 1994) as well as statistically significant inverse relationship with the need for simple structure (Webster & Kruglanski, 1994). Divergent validity also was demonstrated through the lack of statistically significant relationship between the ARBS and social desirability (Reynolds, 1982).
	Among a sample of lesbian and gay male participants, convergent validity was evidenced through statistically significant positive correlations between the ARBS-FM and personal contact with a bisexual person, willingness to have a best friend who is bisexual, willingness to date a bisexual person, and level of contact with heterosexual people (Phinney, 1992). Discriminant validity was demonstrated through the lack of statistically significant associations found between the ARBS-FM subscales and self-monitoring (Snyder & Gangestad, 1986), need to evaluate (Jarvis & Petty, 1996), or age.
Related References	Worthington, R. L., Dillon, F. R., & Becker-Schutte, A. M. (2005). Development, reliability, and validity of the Lesbian, Gay, and Bisexual Knowledge and Attitudes Scale for Heterosexuals (LGB-KASH). *Journal of Counseling Psychology, 52,* 104–118.
Language Versions	English
Contact	Jonathan Mohr Department of Psychology MSN 3F5 George Mason University Fairfax, VA 22030 Phone: (703) 993-1279 Email: jmohr@gmu.edu

9.9.5 Name of the Measure	Homopositivity Scale HPS
Primary Reference	Morrison, T. G., & Bearden, A. G. (2007). The construction and validation of the Homopositivity Scale: An instrument measuring endorsement of positive stereotypes about gay men. *Journal of Homosexuality, 52,* 63–89.
Purpose	The HPS is designed as a measure of endorsement of positive stereotypes of gay men.
Description	The HPS is a 9-item self-report inventory. Each item is rated on a 5-point Likert-type scale with anchors ranging from 1 = Strongly Disagree to 5 = Strong Agree. The HPS is composed of one factor. The HPS was initially composed of 24 items. In order to reduce the length of the instrument and to provide the best items, the 10 items of the HPS with the highest correlation coefficients were submitted to a maximum-likelihood factor analysis (unspecified method of rotation). Only one factor yielded an eigenvalue greater than 1.00. Structure coefficients ranged from .59 to .72. Thus, the HPS is unidimensional.
Samples	The measure was established using a sample of 176 female and 36 male college students enrolled in introductory and social psychology courses. Their ages ranged from 17 to 53 years ($M = 22.2$ years; $SD = 6.4$ years). However, only data from 175 of the students were utilized. The remaining participants were not used because those participants did not identify as "exclusively heterosexual."
Scoring	There are nine items in the HPS. Scoring the HPS consists of summing scores on the scale's items. Higher scores indicate greater levels of homopositivity.
Reliability	The Cronbach's coefficient alpha for the total HPS score ranged from .73 to .78.
Validity	Evidence for discriminant validity was provided through two factor analyses. In the first factor analysis with oblique rotation, items from the HPS and the Homonegativity Scale (Morrison, Parriag, & Morrison, 1999) were entered for analysis. The results indicated two distinct factors with items loading onto their respective scales. In the second factor analysis with oblique rotation, items from the Modern Homonegativity Scale (Morrison & Morrison, 2002) and the HPS were entered. Results indicated two distinct and interpretable factors with items loading onto their respective scales. Criterion-related validity was demonstrated through statistically significant relationships between the scores on the HPS and scores on the Attitude towards Gay Men Scale (Herek, 1988), Ambivalent Sexism Inventory (Glick & Fiske, 1996) as well as media contact. Inverse relationships between the HPS and need for cognition (Cacioppo, Petty, & Kao, 1984) and need for uniqueness (Snyder & Fromkin, 1977) also were found. Known-groups validity also was established. Specifically, females evidenced higher levels of homopositivity than did males.

Related References	
Language Versions	English
Contact	Todd G. Morrison Department of Psychology National University of Ireland, Galway University Road Galway, Ireland Phone: 353-91 495122 Email: todd.morrison@nuigalway.ie

9.9.6 Name of the Measure	Modern Homonegativity Scale MHS
Primary Reference	Morrison, M. A., & Morrison, T. G. (2002). Development and validation of a scale measuring modern prejudice toward gay men and lesbian women. *Journal of Homosexuality, 43*, 15–126.
Purpose	The MHS is designed as a measure of contemporary forms of homonegativity.
Description	The MHS is a 13-item self-report inventory. Each item is rated on a 5-point Likert-type scale with anchors ranging from 1 = Strongly Disagree to 5 = Strong Agree. The MHS-Gay (MHS-G) and MHS-Lesbian (MHS-L) utilize the same response format but are each composed of 12 items.
	The MHS is composed of one factor. Depending on the interests of the administrator of the measure, the target group may be gay or lesbian.
	The MHS was developed using the theoretical frameworks of modern racism (McConahay, 1986) and modern sexism (Swim, Aiken, Hall, & Hunter, 1995). Items were developed through consultation with several gay male and lesbian graduate students. An initial measure of the MHS was then analyzed by members of a local gay and lesbian organization for its content. Several items were revised as a result of their feedback. An initial 50-item MHS was then reduced through several criteria: (1) if one of the response categories on an item was higher than 50%, (2) if the item yielded more than two responses with less than 10%, and (3) the "don't know" response category yielded a response of 30% or more. This resulted in the deletion of 25 items. The resulting 25-item MHS was then submitted to principal components factor analysis with oblique rotation. Using a scree plot, a one-factor solution was selected. Items with a structure coefficient of .30 or greater were included in the final version of the 13-item MHS. The MHS-G and MHS-L were developed as parallel forms to assess the modern negative attitudes toward gay men and lesbians, respectively. The forms were the same as the MHS except for the inclusion of the target group (i.e., gay men or lesbian).
	In order to test the structure of the MHS-G and MHS-L, maximum-likelihood factor analyses with oblique rotation were conducted. A one-factor solution for both the MHS-G and MHS-L was supported. However, one item was deleted because it was found to have high structure coefficients on two factors. This resulted in a 12-item MHS-G and 12-item MHS-L.
Samples	The factor structure of the MHS was established using a sample of 353 university students in British Columbia, Canada. The sample was composed of 204 females and 149 males who ranged in age from 17 to 45 years ($M = 21.8$ years; $SD = 4.9$ years).
	In developing the MHS-G and MHS-L, the authors recruited 308 (148 males and 160 females) university students in British Columbia, Canada. The participants' ages ranged from 18 to 51 ($M = 22.5$; $SD = 4.8$).
	In further study of the MHS, MHS-G, and MHS-L, the authors sampled 233 (64 males and 169 females) heterosexual students in Alberta, Canada.

Scoring	The MHS is composed of 13 items. The MHS-G and MHS-L are each composed of 12 items. Three items require reverse scoring. Scoring the MHS, MHS-G, and MHS-L consists of summing scores on the scale's items. Higher scores indicate greater levels of modern homonegativity toward gay individuals in general, gay men specifically, and lesbians, respectively.
Reliability	Cronbach's alpha for the total scale scores were as follows: Total MHS: Alpha = .93 Total MHS-G: Alpha = .91 Total MHS-L: Alpha = .89
Validity	Construct validity for the MHS was demonstrated through statistically significant positive correlations with one-item measures of self-reported conservatism, self-reported religious behavior, and self-reported religious self-schema. Discriminant validity of the MHS-G and MHS-L was established through the use of separate factor analysis with oblique rotation. Results of the procedure produced a three-factor solution with items from the MHS-G loading onto its own factor. Items from a measure of homonegativity toward gay men (Morrison, Parriag, & Morrison, 1999) did not load onto that factor. The same results were indicated in factor analysis with items from MHS-L and homonegativity-lesbian (Morrison et al.). Evidence for criterion-related validity was demonstrated through statistically significant positive correlations with modern sexism (Tougas, Brown, Beaton, & Joly, 1995). Discriminant validity was demonstrated through nonstatistically significant correlations with social desirability (Reynolds, 1982). Known-groups validity also was established through two methods. First, in an experimental study, the authors found that high scorers on the MHS were more likely to avoid sitting with a person who was presumed to be gay or lesbian (based on a slogan indicated on their T-shirt). Second, the strength of correlations between the MHS and other measures were stronger for males than they were for females.
Related References	Morrison, M. A., Morrison, T. G., & Franklin, R. (2009). Modern and old-fashioned homonegativity among samples of Canadian and American university students. *Journal of Cross-Cultural Psychology, 40,* 523–542.
Language Versions	English
Contact	Melanie A. Morrison Department of Psychology University of Saskatchewan 9 Campus Drive Saskatoon, SK, S7N5A5 Email: melanie.morrison@usask.ca

9.9.7 Name of the Measure	Homonegativity Scale HS
Primary Reference	Morrison, T. G., Parriag, A. V., & Morrison, M. A. (1999). The psychometric properties of the Homonegativity Scale. *Journal of Homosexuality, 37,* 111–126.
Purpose	The HS is designed as a measure of endorsement of negative attitudes toward gay men and lesbians.
Description	The HS is a 6-item self-report inventory. Each item is rated on a 5-point Likert-type scale with anchors ranging from 1 = Strongly Disagree to 5 = Strong Agree.
	The HS is composed of one factor. Depending on the interests of the administrator of the measure, the target group may be gay or lesbian.
	A principal components factor analysis was performed to test the structure of the HS. Results indicated that the HS is composed of one factor. Alternate forms measuring attitudes toward gay men and lesbians separately were created by simply replacing *homosexual* with either *gay men* or *lesbian*.
Samples	The factor structure of the HS was established using a sample of 1,045 Canadian adolescents (514 females and 531 males). The mean age was 16.5 years (*SD* = 2.3 years). Criterion-related validity was established through a sample of 64 college and high school students as well as a sample of 312 Canadian university students.
Scoring	The number of items in the different versions of the HS is as follows:
	Total HS: 6 items
	Total HS-G: 6 items
	Total HS-L: 6 items
	Scoring the HS consists of summing scores on the scale's items. Higher scores indicate greater levels of homonegativity.
Reliability	Cronbach's coefficient alpha for the total HS, HS-G, and HS-L scores are as follows:
	Total HS: Alpha = .84
	Total HS-G: Alpha = .86
	Total HS-L: Alpha = .87
Validity	Evidence for criterion-related validity was demonstrated through statistically significant positive correlations with the Heterosexual Attitudes Toward Homosexuality Scale (Larson, Reed, & Hoffman, 1980), authoritarianism (Lutterman & Middleton, 1970), and Modern Sexism (Swim et al., 1995) as well as two single-item measures of political conservatism and religiosity.
	Discriminant validity was demonstrated through nonstatistically significant correlations with social desirability (Reynolds, 1982).
	Known-groups validity also was established. Specifically, males reported higher levels of homonegative attitudes than did females.

Related References	
Language Versions	English
Contact	Todd G. Morrison Department of Psychology National University of Ireland, Galway University Road Galway, Ireland Phone: 353-91 495122 Email: todd.morrison@nuigalway.ie

9.9.8 Name of the Measure	Attitudes Toward Same-Sex Marriage Scale ATSMS
Primary Reference	Pearl, M. L., & Galupo, M. P. (2007). Development and validation of the Attitudes Toward Same-Sex Marriage Scale. *Journal of Homosexuality, 53,* 117–134.
Purpose	The ATSMS was developed to measure attitudes toward same-sex marriage.
Description	The ATSMS is composed of 17 items and utilizes a 5-point Likert-type response format with the following anchors: 1 = Strong Disagree to 5 Strongly Agree. The ATSMS is a unidimensional measure. A 22-item ATSMS was originally developed to represent 11 separate dimensions of the debate on same-sex marriage. The method for item development is not clear. However, it appears that the items were developed based on the authors' understanding of the debate on attitudes toward same-sex marriage. Data collected from the 22-item ATSMS were submitted for a principal component analysis with oblimin rotation. A one-factor solution emerged as most interpretable. A one-factor solution emerged from two additional PCA with oblimin rotation with data from a separate sample. All structure coefficients were above .56.
Samples	The initial psychometric properties of the ATSM were developed across three studies. The first study on which the structure of the ATSM measures was identified was composed of 148 heterosexual undergraduate students enrolled at a university in the mid-Atlantic (U.S.). The sample included 100 women and 48 men. These participants ranged in age (17 to 51 years; $M = 19.28$, $SD = 3.86$). With respect to racial background, 81.8% percent of this sample identified as White American, 0.7% Latino/a American, 7.4% Asian American, 8.8% African American, 0.7% Native American, and 0.7% were unidentified. A second sample of 255 undergraduate students from 30 different 2- or 4-year institutions responded to the survey. These participants ranged in age (17 to 50 years; $M = 20.90$, $SD = 4.45$). The sample included 173 women and 52 men. With respect to racial background, 82.2% percent of this sample identified as White American, 3.1% Latino/a American, 2.7% Asian American, 8.0% African American, 3.6% Multiracial American, and 0.4% were unidentified. A third sample of 242 community-based heterosexual adults participated in further study of the ATSM's psychometric properties. These participants ranged in age (17 to 87 years; $M = 35.88$, $SD = 12.55$). With respect to racial background, 89.7% percent of this sample identified as White American, 1.7% Latino/a American, 1.7% Asian American, 4.1% African American, 2.1% Multiracial American, 0.4% Native American, and 0.4% were unidentified.
Scoring	ATSM is composed of 17 items. Eight items require reverse scoring. Scores are then obtained by summing the scores on the items of the scale. Higher scores indicate more positive attitudes toward same-sex marriage.

Reliability	Data from the three samples ($N = 467$) were pooled and revealed a Cronbach's alpha for the ATSM score of .96.
Validity	Known-groups validity was established through statistically significant differences found in the attitudes toward same-sex marriage held by men when compared to women. Specifically, men had statistically significantly more negative attitudes than did women.
	Evidence for construct validity was demonstrated through statistically significant inverse relationships found between the ATSM and attitudes toward lesbians and gay men (Herek, 1988), self-described political conservatism, and religiosity. Finally, ATSM was found to be statistically significantly correlated with educational attainment.
Related References	
Language Versions	English
Contact	M. Paz Galupo Multicultural Institute Admin 210 Towson University 8000 York Road Towson, MD 21252-0001 Email: pgalupo@towson.edu

9.9.9 **Name of the Measure**	The Modern Homophobia Scale—Lesbian MHS-Lesbian
Primary Reference	Raja, S., & Stokes, J. P. (1998). Assessing attitudes toward lesbians and gay men: The Modern Homophobia Scale. *Journal of Gay, Lesbian, and Bisexual Identity, 3,* 113–134.
Purpose	The MHS-L is designed as a measure of attitudes toward lesbians.
Description	The MHS-L is 24-item Likert-type self-report inventory. Each item is rated on a 5-point Likert-type scale with anchors ranging from 1 (Strongly Agree) to 5 (Strongly Disagree). The MHS-L is composed of three factors: (1) Institutional Homophobia toward Lesbians (IHL); (2) Personal Discomfort (PD); and (3) Belief that Female Homosexuality is Deviant and Changeable (BFHDC). The MHS was initially composed of 97 items. Nineteen of these items were excluded because of highly skewed distributions (more than 50% either "strongly agree" or "strongly disagree"). Principal factor analysis with oblique rotation yielded seven factors with eigenvalues greater than 1.00. On each factor, an item was deleted if (1) it yielded an item-to-total correlation coefficient of more than .30 smaller than the highest item-to-total correlation or (2) the item-total correlation coefficient was less than .30. Based on these criteria, three items were deleted. Finally, factors with a Cronbach's coefficient alpha of less than .80 were not included in the final scale. This resulted in a three-factor MHS-L.
Samples	The measure was established using a sample of 322 undergraduate students. Responses from 18 individuals who either did not report their sexual orientation or who reported not being exclusively heterosexual were excluded from analyses. The sample equally represented women and men. With respect to racial background, 35% reported White American, 32% were Asian American, 23% were Latino/a American, 7% were African American, and 2% were of mixed race heritage. Their ages ranged from 19 to 22 years.

Scoring	The number of items in each subscale is as follows:
	
	    IHL: 11 items
	    PD: 10 items
	    BFHDC: 3 items
	    Total MHS-L: 24 items
	
	Nine items require reverse scoring. Scoring the subscales consists of summing and dividing scores by the number of the subscale's items. Higher scores indicate greater levels of negative attitudes toward lesbians.

Reliability	Cronbach's coefficient alpha for the total and subscale scores of the MHS-L score were as follows:
	IHL: Alpha = .89
	PD: Alpha = .92
	BFHDC: Alpha = .90
	Total MHS-L: Alpha = .95
Validity	Evidence for criterion-related validity was provided through significant positive relationships between the scores on the MHS-L and scores on the Index of Homophobia (Hudson & Ricketts, 1980) and Attitudes toward Women (Helmreich & Spence, 1978). Finally, participants with higher total MHS-L scores reported significantly more negative affective reactions to a vignette with lesbian and gay characters.
	Known-groups validity also was established. Specifically, participants with at least one lesbian acquaintance or one lesbian friend reported less personal discomfort than did those participants without at least one acquaintance or friend who is lesbian. As further evidence, women were found to be more homophobic toward lesbians than they were toward gay men (MHS-G). Men also were found to be more homophobic toward gay men (MHS-G) than they were toward lesbians.
Related References	
Language Versions	English
Contact	Sheela Raja
	Pediatric Dentistry
	202B DENT, MC 850
	University of Illinois at Chicago
	1007 W. Harrison Street
	Chicago, IL 60607
	Phone: (312) 413-0559
	Email: sraja1@uic.edu

9.9.10 Name of the Measure	The Modern Homophobia Scale—Gay MHS-Gay
Primary Reference	Raja, S., & Stokes, J. P. (1998). Assessing attitudes toward lesbians and gay men: The Modern Homophobia Scale. *Journal of Gay, Lesbian, and Bisexual Identity, 3*, 113–134.
Purpose	The MHS-G is designed as a measure of attitudes toward gay men.
Description	The MHS-G is 22-item self-report inventory. Each item is rated on a 5-point Likert-type scale with anchors ranging from 1 = Strongly Agree to 5 = Strong Disagree.
	The MHS-G is composed of three factors: (1) Personal Discomfort (PD), (2) Belief that Male Homosexuality is Deviant and Changeable (BFHDC), and (3) Institutional Homophobia toward Gay men.
	The MHS was initially composed of 97 items. Nineteen of these items were excluded because of highly skewed distributions (more than 50% either "strongly agree" or "strongly disagree"). Principal factor analysis with oblique rotation yielded seven factors with eigenvalues greater than 1.00. On each factor, an item was deleted if (1) it yielded an item-to-total correlation coefficient of more than .30 smaller than the highest item-to-total correlation or (2) the item-total correlation coefficient was less than .30. Finally, factors with a Cronbach's coefficient alpha of less than .80 were not included in the final scale. This resulted in a three-factor MHS-G.
Samples	The measure was established using a sample of 322 undergraduate students. Responses from 18 individuals who either did not report their sexual orientation or who reported not being exclusively heterosexual were excluded from analyses. The sample equally represented women and men. With respect to racial background, 35% reported White American, 32% were Asian American, 23% were Latino/a American, 7% were African American, and 2% were of mixed race heritage. Their ages ranged from 19 to 22 years.
Scoring	The number of items in each subscale is as follows: PD: 9 items BMHDC: 4 items IHG: 9 items Total MHS-G: 22 items Nine items require reverse scoring. Scoring the subscales consists of summing and dividing scores by the number of the subscale's items. Higher scores indicate greater levels of negative attitudes toward gay men.
Reliability	The Cronbach's coefficient alpha for the total and subscale scores of the MHS-G were as follows: PD: Alpha = .91 BFHDC: Alpha = .85 IHL: Alpha = .90 Total MHS-G: Alpha = .95

Validity	Evidence for criterion-related validity was provided through significant positive relationships between the scores on the MHS-G and scores on the Index of Homophobia (Hudson & Ricketts, 1980) and Attitudes toward Women (Helmreich & Spence, 1978). Finally, participants with higher total MHS-G scores reported significantly more negative affective reactions to a vignette with lesbian and gay characters.
	Known-groups validity also was established. Specifically, participants with at least one gay male acquaintance or one gay male friend reported less personal discomfort than did those participants without at least one acquaintance or friend who is a gay male. As further evidence, women were found to be more homophobic toward lesbians than they were toward gay men. Men also were found to be more homophobic toward gay men than they were toward lesbians (MHS-L). Finally, women held less homophobic attitudes toward gay men than did men.
Related References	
Language Versions	English
Contact	The MHS-G is published in Raja and Stokes (1998).

9.9.11 Name of the Measure	Lesbian, Gay, and Bisexual Knowledge and Attitudes Scale for Heterosexuals LGB-KASH
Primary Reference	Worthington, R. L., Dillon, F. R., & Becker-Schutte, A. M. (2005). Development, reliability, and validity of the Lesbian, Gay, and Bisexual Knowledge and Attitudes Scale for Heterosexuals (LGB-KASH). *Journal of Counseling Psychology, 52,* 104–118.
Purpose	The LGB-KASH was developed to assess attitudes and knowledge of sexual minorities among heterosexual individuals.
Description	The LGB-KASH is a 28-item measure that utilizes a 7-point Likert-type response format with the following anchors: 1 = Very Uncharacteristic of Me or My Views to 7 = Very Characteristic of Me or My Views. The LGB-KASH is composed of five factors: (1) Hate, (2) Knowledge of LGB History, Symbols, and Community, (3) LGB Civil Rights, (4) Religious Conflict, and (5) Internalized Affirmativeness. The LGB-KASH was developed over several studies. First, a 211-item version of the measure was reduced to 32 items over a series of pilot studies. The 211 items were developed based on a review of existing measures of homophobia, racism, and sexism and the literature regarding heterosexuals' attitudes toward sexual minorities. An additional 28 items were added to expand the measure's ability to tap into affirmativeness, conflicting attitudes, and sexual orientation-specific issues. These 60 items then were submitted for analyses. In their initial screening, 18 items were deleted for failure to yield an item-total correlation coefficient of .30 or higher. The factor model was found to be appropriate for factor analysis. A principal-axis factor extraction analysis resulted in the deletion of 14 more items. Factor analyses with oblique rotation with a forced number of factors (one to eight) were conducted. As a result, a five-factor solution containing 28 items was chosen as most interpretable. A confirmatory factor analysis was used to test the factor structure of the LGB-KASH. Results indicated that the five-factor model fit the data best.
Samples	The psychometric properties of the LGB-KASH were developed across four studies. The first study, on which the structure of the LGB-KASH measures was identified, was composed of 422 heterosexually identified undergraduate students attending one of four universities in the Midwest (U.S.). The sample equally represented women and men. The participants' ages ranged from 18 to 57 years ($M = 23.89$ years, $SD = 7.55$). With respect to racial background, 347 identified as White American, 22 African American, 16 Latino/a American, 7 Asian American, 2 Native American, 2 biracial/multiethnic, 6 international, and 20 did not identify a racial background.

Scoring	The number of items in each of the subscales is as follows:
	
	    Hate: 6 items
	
	    Knowledge of LGB History, Symbols, and Community: 5 items
	
	    LGB Civil Rights: 5 items

<table>
<tr><td></td><td>

Religious Conflict: 7 items

Internalized Affirmativeness: 5 items

Total LGB-KASH: 28 items

Nine items require reverse scoring. Scores are then obtained by summing and dividing the scores on the items of the scale. Higher scores indicate greater levels of homophobia.

</td></tr>
</table>

Reliability	Cronbach's alpha for the scores on the subscales were as follows:

Hate: Alpha = .81

Knowledge of LGB History, Symbols, and Community: Alpha = .81

LGB Civil Rights: Alpha = .87

Religious Conflict: Alpha = .76

Internalized Affirmativeness: Alpha = .83

Two-Week Test-retest reliability

Hate: r = .76

Knowledge of LGB History, Symbols, and Community: r = .85

LGB Civil Rights: r = .85

Religious Conflict: r = .77

Internalized Affirmativeness: r = .90

Validity	Known-groups validity was evidenced through significantly different responses on all subscale scores between heterosexual and LGB individuals. All differences were in the expected directions. Specifically, LGB individuals had lower scores on Hate and Religious Conflict with higher scores on Knowledge of LGB History, Symbols, and Community, LGB Civil rights, and Internalized Affirmativeness.

Evidence for convergent validity was provided through significant correlations between some of the subscales of the LGB-KASH and attitudes toward lesbians and gay men (Herek, 1984) and attitudes regarding bisexuals (Mohr & Rochlen, 1999), social dominance orientation (Sidanius & Pratto, 1999), and sexual identity development (Worthington, Savoy, & Navarro, 2002), religiosity, and social desirability (Paulhus & Reid, 1991).

Related References	
Language Versions	English
Contact	Roger L. Worthington Department of Educational, School, and Counseling Psychology 16 Hill Hall University of Missouri-Columbia Columbia, MO 65211 Email: worthingtonR@missouri.edu

9.9.12 Name of the Measure	Homophobia Scale HS
Primary Reference	Wright, L. W., Jr., Adams, H. E., & Bernat, J. (1999). Development and validation of the Homophobia Scale. *Journal of Psychopathology and Behavioral Assessment, 21*, 337–347.
Purpose	The HS was developed to assess the cognitive, affective, and behavioral components of homophobia.
Description	The HS is a 25-item measure that utilizes a 5-point Likert-type response format with the following anchors: 1 = Strong Disagree to 5 = Strongly Agree. The HS is composed of three factors: (1) Behavior/Negative Affect; (2) Affect/Behavioral Aggression; and (3) Cognitive Negativism. An initial 30-item HS was originally developed by a panel of one psychologist and two graduate students. These questions were reviewed for content, readability, and grammar by four graduate students and one psychologist. Five questions were added based on their feedback. The 35-item measure was then submitted for principal components analysis using direct oblimin rotation. The authors selected items for modification or deletion if they yielded item structure coefficients less than .30 on any of the factors, correlated on more than one factor, or if the item was found to be redundant. This process resulted in a three-factor 25-item measure.
Samples	The initial psychometric properties of the HS were developed across two studies. The first study on which the structure of the HS measures was identified was composed of 321 undergraduate students (119 men; 202 women). The average age was 20.86 years (*SD* = 2.90). With respect to racial background, 86.3% of this sample identified as White American, 1.6% Latino/a American, 2.8% Asian American, 8.1% African American, 0.9% Native American, and 0.3% were unidentified. A second sample of 145 undergraduate students (47 men; 98 women) was recruited to further test the properties of the HS. The average age of the participants was 22.38 years (*SD* = 4.12). With respect to racial background, 87.0% percent of this sample identified as White American, 2.0% Latino/a American, 3.0% Asian American, 5.0% African American, and 2.0% reported "other."
Scoring	The number of items in each of the subscales is as follows: Behavior/Negative Affect: 10 items Affect/Behavioral Aggression: 10 items Cognitive Negativism: 5 items HS is composed of 25 items. Nine items require reverse scoring. Scores are then obtained by summing and dividing the scores on the items of the scale. Higher scores indicate greater levels of homophobia.

Reliability	Cronbach's alpha only for the HS total score was reported to be .94.
	1-Week Test-retest reliability coefficient was
	Total HS: $r = .96$
Validity	Known-groups validity was established through significant differences found in levels of homophobia held by men when compared to women. Specifically, men had statistically significantly higher levels of homophobia than did women.
	Evidence for construct validity was demonstrated through statistically significant positive relationships found between the HS and the Index of Homophobia scale (Hudson & Ricketts, 1980). Evidence for construct validity also was established through significant inverse relations with educational level.
Related References	Nagoshi, J. L., Adams, K. A., Terrell, H. K., Hill, E. D., Brzuzy, S., & Nagoshi, C. T. (2008). Gender differences in correlates of homophobia and transphobia. *Sex Roles, 59*, 521–531.
	Zeichner, A., & Reidy, D. E. (2009). Are homophobic men attracted to or repulsed by homosexual men? Effects of gay male erotica on anger, fear, happiness, and disgust. *Psychology of Men & Masculinity, 10*, 231–236.
Language Versions	English
Contact	Lester W. Wright Jr.
	Western Michigan University
	3532 Wood Hall
	Kalamazoo, MI 49008
	Phone: (269) 387-4472
	Email: lester.wright@wmich.edu

9.10 SEXUAL ORIENTATION IDENTITY

9.10.1 Name of the Measure	Lesbian and Gay Identity Scale LGIS
Primary Reference	Mohr, J., & Fassinger, R. (2000). Measuring dimensions of lesbian and gay male experience. *Measurement and Evaluation in Counseling and Development, 33,* 66–90.
Purpose	The LGIS was developed to assess feelings and beliefs related to lesbian and gay identity.
Description	The LGIS is a 27-item measure that utilizes a 6-point Likert-type response format with the following anchors: 1 = Disagree Strongly to 6 = Agree Strongly.
	The LGIS is composed of six factors: (1) Need for Privacy; (2) Need for Acceptance; (3) Internalized Homonegativity; (4) Difficult Process; (5) Identity Confusion; and (6) Superiority.
	Items were developed based on a review of relevant literature. The items were then reviewed for appropriateness and clarity by two doctoral-level graduate students, both of whom identified as lesbian and as White American, as well as one Asian American heterosexual woman. All individuals were knowledgeable about the lesbian and gay identity. Items were revised based on their suggestions. Feedback was then obtained from nine racially diverse undergraduate research assistants. Data from the initial 40-item LGIS were submitted for principal components analysis with varimax rotation. Using data from 251 respondents, confirmatory factor analysis indicated good fit of data to the hypothesized model. Additional exploratory factor analysis, which yielded three second-order factors (i.e., Negative Identity, Identity Confusion, and Superiority), also was conducted.
Samples	The factor structure of the LGIS was established based on data collected from 590 lesbians and 414 gay men who ranged in age from 18 to 69 years ($M = 36.62$; $SD = 9.47$). With respect to racial and ethnic composition, 86% identified as White American, 3% identified as African American, 3% identified as Latino/a American, 1% identified as Asian American or Pacific Islander, 4% identified as biracial or multiethnic, 1% identified as Native American, and 2% identified as other.
Scoring	The number of items in each of the subscales is as follows:
	Need for Privacy: 6 items
	Need for Acceptance: 5 items
	Internalized Homonegativity: 5 items
	Difficult Process: 5 items
	Identity Confusion: 4 items
	Superiority: 2 items
	Total LGIS: 27 items
	Four items require reverse scoring. Scores are then obtained by summing and dividing the scores on the items of the scale. Higher scores indicate greater levels of agreement with the subscale.

Reliability	Cronbach's alpha coefficient for the subscale scores were as follows:
	Need for Privacy: Alpha = .81
	Need for Acceptance: Alpha = .75
	Internalized Homonegativity: Alpha = .79
	Difficult Process: Alpha = .79
	Identity Confusion: Alpha = .77
	Superiority: Alpha = .65
Validity	Evidence for convergent validity was established through significant correlations, in the expected directions, between the subscale scores of the LGIS and the Rosenberg Self-Esteem Scale (Rosenberg, 1965), Same-group and Other-Group orientation (Phinney, 1992), and support from own religious group, as well as a measure of internalization-synthesis and deepening-commitment phases of gay identity (Fassinger, 1997; Fassinger & McCarn, 1997). Known-groups validity was evidenced through significant differences in the way gay men and lesbians scored on the Need for Privacy, Need for Acceptance, Internalized Homonegativity, and Difficult Process subscales. Specifically, gay men scored higher on all four dimensions than did lesbians.
Related References	
Language Versions	English
Contact	Jonathan Mohr Department of Psychology MSN 3F5 George Mason University Fairfax, VA 22030 Email: jmohr@gmu.edu Phone: (703) 993-1279

9.10.2 Name of the Measure	Outness Inventory OI
Primary Reference	Mohr, J., & Fassinger, R. (2000). Measuring dimensions of lesbian and gay male experience. *Measurement and Evaluation in Counseling and Development, 33,* 66–90.
Purpose	The OI was developed to assess the degree to which an individual is open about her or his sexual orientation to others.
Description	The OI is a 10-item measure that utilizes a 7-point Likert-type response format: 1 = person *definitely* does NOT know about your sexual status, 2 = person *might* know about your sexual orientation status, but it is NEVER talked about, 3 = person *probably* knows about your sexual orientation status, but it is NEVER talked about, 4 = person *probably* knows about your sexual status, but it is rarely talked about, 5 = person *definitely* knows about your sexual orientation status, but it is RARELY talked about, 6 = person *definitely* knows about your sexual orientation status, and it is SOMETIMES talked about, 7 = person *definitely* knows about your sexual orientation status, and it is OPENLY talked about. The OI is composed of three factors: (1) Out to Family; (2) Out to World; and (3) Out to Religion. Items were developed based on a review of relevant literature. The items were then reviewed for appropriateness and clarity by two doctoral-level graduate students, both of whom identified as lesbian and as White American, as well as one Asian American heterosexual woman. All individuals were knowledgeable about the lesbian and gay identity. Items were revised based on their suggestions. Feedback was then obtained from nine racially diverse undergraduate research assistants. Responses from gay men and lesbians to the initial 11-item OI were submitted for principal components analysis with varimax rotation. A 10-item, three-factor solution for both gay men and lesbians emerged as the most easily interpretable. One item, assessing for outness to "My Old Straight Friends," did not meet the requirements for the final version of the OI but has been included in subsequent studies (e.g., Solomon, Rothblum, & Balsam, 2004). Confirmatory factor analysis was performed, with data indicated to not be a good fit for the model.
Samples	The OI was established based on data collected from a sample of 1,004 lesbian and gay individuals who ranged in age from 18 to 69 years ($M = 36.62$; $SD = 9.47$). From this, a subsample of 232 lesbians and 179 gay men responded to all items and were included in the analyses of the OI's factor structure.
Scoring	The number of items in each subscale of the OI is as follows: Out to Family = 4 items Out to World = 4 items Out to Religion = 2 items Total OI: 10 items Scores are obtained by summing and dividing the scores on the items of the subscales. Higher scores indicate greater levels of outness to the respective sphere (i.e., family, world, religion) of life.

Reliability	Cronbach's alpha coefficient for the subscale scores were as follows:
	
	    Out to Family = Alpha = .74
	
	    Out to World = Alpha = .79
	
	    Out to Religion = Alpha = .97

Validity	Evidence for convergent validity was established through significant correlations, in the expected directions, between the subscale scores of the OI and Same-group orientation (Phinney, 1992) for gay men and lesbians alike. OI also was found to be related to other-group orientation among gay men. OI was found to be related to a measure of internalization-synthesis phases of gay identity and lesbian identity (Fassinger, 1997; Fassinger & McCarn, 1997) in the expected direction.
Related References	Balsam, K. F., & Szymanski, D. M. (2005). Relationship quality and domestic violence in women's same-sex relationships: The role of minority stress. *Psychology of Women Quarterly, 29,* 258–269. Solomon, S. E., Rothblum, E. D., & Balsam, K. F. (2004). Pioneers in partnership: Lesbian and gay male couples in civil unions compared with those not in civil unions and married heterosexual siblings. *Journal of Family Psychology, 18,* 275–286.
Language Versions	English
Contact	Jonathan Mohr Department of Psychology MSN 3F5 George Mason University Fairfax, VA 22030 Email: jmohr@gmu.edu Phone: (703) 993-1279

9.10.3 Name of the Measure	Measure of Sexual Identity Exploration and Commitment MoSIEC
Primary Reference	Worthington, R. L., Navarro, R. L., Savoy, H. B., & Hampton, D. (2008). Development, reliability, and validity of the Measure of Sexual Identity Exploration and Commitment (MoSIEC). *Journal of Counseling Psychology, 44*, 22–33.
Purpose	The MoSIEC was developed to assess the sexual identity development of gay men and lesbians, as well as of bisexual and heterosexual individuals.
Description	The MoSIEC is a 22-item measure that utilizes a 6-point Likert-type response format with the following anchors: 1 = Very Uncharacteristic of Me to 6 = Very Characteristic of Me. The MoSIEC is composed of four factors: (1) Exploration; (2) Commitment; (3) Sexual Orientation Identity; and (4) Synthesis/Integration. The MoSIEC is grounded in the gay identity development literature (e.g., Cass, 1979; Fassinger & Miller, 1996; McCarn & Fassinger, 1996) as well as heterosexual identity development (Worthington, Savoy, Dillon, & Vernaglia, 2002), bisexual identity literature (e.g., Weinrich & Klein, 2003), and ego-identity development (Marcia, 1966). Forty-eight items were developed based on the dimensions of sexual identity development outlined by Worthington et al. and thus reflected (1) sexual needs, (2) sexual values, (3) characteristics of sexual partners, (4) preferred sexual activities, (5) sexual orientation identity, and (6) modes of sexual expression. Data from the initial 48-item MoSIEC were submitted to four separate principal-axis factor analyses with oblique rotation. A 22-item, four-factor model emerged as most interpretable. Twenty-six items were deleted for one of the following reasons: (1) communalities of less than .30, (2) structure coefficients below .32, (3) and/or cross-correlations with less than a .15 difference. Data from a second study ($N = 1038$) were then submitted for two confirmatory factor analyses. The authors split the sample randomly in two ($n_1 = 517$; $n_2 = 521$) in order to confirm the structure of the MoSIEC. Results of both CFA indicated a good fit of data to the four-factor model.
Samples	The factor structure of the MoSIEC was established based on data collected from 690 participants recruited through (1) university-based classes, (2) email announcements posted on university-based LGBT listservs (in the United States and Canada), and (3) two public-access Internet sites. The sample was composed of 422 women, 256 men, six identified as transgender, and six did not report. They ranged in age from 18 to 66 years ($M = 27.52$; $SD = 9.82$). All but 10 individuals responded to a question regarding their sexual orientation. Of those who responded, 78 identified as bisexual, 86 identified as gay men, 400 identified as heterosexual, 84 identified as lesbian, and 13 identified as "other." With respect to racial and ethnic composition, 87.4% identified as White American, 2.3% identified as African American, 3.5% identified as Latino/a American, 2.6% identified as Asian American or Pacific Islander, 1.3% identified as biracial or multiethnic, 0.3% identified as Native American, 0.6 identified as non-U.S. citizens, and 1.5% identified as other.

	A second sample ($N = 1,038$) was split in two in order to further test the structure of the MoSIEC. This sample ranged in age from 18 to 66 years ($M = 26.13$, $SD = 9.20$). There were 644 women and 366 men, as well as eight individuals who identified as transgender. There were 695 participants who identified as heterosexual, 67 who identified as lesbian, 95 who identified as gay, and 106 who identified as bisexual. With respect to race and ethnicity, 78.8% identified as White American, 5.3% identified as African American, 4.1% identified as Latino/a American, 4.1% identified as Asian American or Pacific Islander, 2.4% identified as biracial or multiethnic, 0.9% identified as Native American, 0.6 identified as non-U.S. citizens, and 2.8% identified as other.
	Evidence for convergent validity was established based on a sample of 851 participants (508 female, 329 male, 10 transgender) who ranged in age from 18 to 80 years ($M = 25.35$, $SD = 8.49$). There were 671 participants who identified as heterosexual, 36 who identified as lesbian, 39 who identified as gay, and 94 who identified as bisexual. With respect to race and ethnicity, 80.2% identified as White American, 3.4% identified as African American, 6.2% identified as Latino/a American, 3.3% identified as Asian American or Pacific Islander, 2.4% identified as biracial or multiethnic, 1.5% identified as Native American, 0.2% identified as non-U.S. citizens, and 2.8% identified as other.

Scoring	The number of items in each subscale of the MoSIEC is as follows:
	
	    Exploration: 8 items
	    Commitment: 6 items
	    Sexual Orientation Identity Uncertainty: 3 items
	    Synthesis/Integration: 5 items
	    Total MoSIEC: 22 items
	
	Four items require reverse scoring. Scores are then obtained by summing and dividing the scores by the number of the items on the scale. Higher scores indicate greater levels of homophobia.

Reliability	Cronbach's alpha coefficient for the subscale scores were calculated six distinct times. The coefficients ranged from .72 to .91:
	
	    Exploration: Alpha = .85 to .91
	    Commitment: Alpha = .78 to .84
	    Sexual Orientation Identity Uncertainty: Alpha = .73 to .87
	    Synthesis/Integration: Alpha =.72 to .80
	2-Week Test-retest reliability coefficients were as follows:
	    Exploration: $r = .85$
	    Commitment: $r = .80$
	    Sexual Orientation Identity Uncertainty: $r = .90$
	    Synthesis/Integration: $r =.71$

(Continued)

(Continued)

Validity	Evidence for convergent validity was established through statistically significant inverse correlations between each of the four subscale scores of the MoSIEC and sexual attitudes (Hudson, Murphy, & Nurius, 1983) whereby higher levels of each dimension were related to more liberal sexual attitudes. Commitment, Exploration, and Synthesis each were found to be positively associated with sexual self-consciousness and sexual assertiveness (Snell, Fisher, & Miller, 1991).
Related References	Worthington, R. L., & Reynolds, A. L. (2009). Within-group differences in sexual orientation and identity. *Journal of Counseling Psychology, 56,* 44–55.
Language Versions	English
Contact	Roger L. Worthington Department of Educational, School, and Counseling Psychology 16 Hill Hall University of Missouri-Columbia Columbia, MO 65211 Email: worthingtonR@missouri.edu

9.11 INTERNALIZED HOMOPHOBIA

9.11.1 **Name of the Measure**	Short Internalized Homonegativity Inventory SIHS
Primary Reference	Currie, M. R., Cunningham, E. G., & Findlay, B. M. (2004). The Short Internalized Homonegativity Scale: Examination of the factorial structure of a new measure of internalized homophobia. *Educational and Psychological Measurement, 64*, 1053–1067.
Purpose	The SIHS was developed to assess contemporary forms of internalized homophobia among men who have sex with men.
Description	The SIHS is a 12-item measure that utilizes a 7-point Likert-type response format with the following anchors: 1 = Strongly Disagree to 7 = Strongly Agree. The SIHS is composed of three factors: (1) Public Identification as Gay, (2) Sexual Comfort with Gay Men, and (3) Social Comfort with Gay Men. The SIHS was developed based items from the Internalized Homophobia Scale (HIS; Ross & Rosser, 1996) and the contention that existing measures contained items that were outdated. All but six of the items (*n* = 20) from the IHS (Perceptions of Stigma Subscale) were included, as were 10 additional items the authors of this measure developed. Eleven items were removed because of problematic skewness and kurtosis. The remaining 19 items were submitted for a three-factor exploratory factor analysis (EFA) with oblique rotation. Six items were removed because they failed to load onto any of the factors. EFA were rerun with the remaining 13 items, which yielded the three-factor solution. Five items from Ross and Rosser's (1996) Public Identification as Gay scale correlated with the first factor. Four newly constructed items comprised the second factor, Sexual Comfort with Gay Men. The last factor was composed of three items originally developed by Ross and Rosser, as well as one newly created item. One-factor models using maximum likelihood-confirmatory factor analysis were tested for each of the three latent constructs. Results of confirmatory factor analysis (CFA) indicated that data did fit not the model for the construct Public Identification as Gay. One redundant item was removed, with the remaining four items submitted for another CFA. Data fit the four-item model for the construct. The fit of the data to the models for the remaining two constructs was acceptable to excellent. This process resulted in a 12-item SIHS. Two additional three-factor models composed of each of the three aforementioned factors were submitted for CFA. In one model, the factors were uncorrelated. In the second model, the correlations between the factors were freely estimated. Results indicated that data fit the second model but not the first. Thus, a second-order factor containing all 12 items may represent the general construct of internalized homonegativity.
Samples	The factor structure of the SIHS was established based on data collected from 677 gay men living in the United States. These men were recruited from the Internet. Their age ranged from 18 to 79 (*M* = 38.53, *SD* = 12.51).

(Continued)

(Continued)

Scoring	The number of items in each subscale of the SIHS is as follows:
	Public Identification as Gay: 4 items
	Sexual Comfort with Gay Men: 4 items
	Social Comfort with Gay Men: 4 items
	Total SIHS: 12 items
	Five items require reverse scoring. Scores on the SIHS and its subscale are obtained by summing the responses from its corresponding items. Higher scores indicate greater levels of internalized homophobia.
Reliability	Cronbach's alpha coefficient for the subscale scores were as follows:
	Public Identification as Gay: Alpha = .77
	Sexual Comfort with Gay Men: Alpha = .71
	Social Comfort with Gay Men: Alpha = .72
	Total SIHS: Alpha = .78
Validity	No evidence for construct validity provided.
Related References	
Language Versions	English
Contact	Items are published in Currie et al. (2004).

9.11.2 Name of the Measure	Internalized Homonegativity Inventory for Gay Men IHNI
Primary Reference	Mayfield, W. (2001). The development of an Internalized Homonegativity Inventory for Gay Men. *Journal of Homosexuality, 41,* 53–75.
Purpose	The IHNI was developed to assess the internalized homophobia among men who have sex with men.
Description	The IHNI is a 23-item measure that utilizes a 6-point Likert-type response format with the following anchors: 1 = Strongly Disagree to 6 = Strongly Agree. The IHNI is composed of three factors: (1) Personal Homonegativity; (2) Gay Affirmation; and (3) Morality of Homosexuality. An initial pool of 40 items was developed by the author and reviewed by four gay male counseling psychology students, one bisexual female counseling psychology student, and three heterosexual male counseling psychology professors. This resulted in an initial 42-item IHNI. Principal factor analyses with oblique rotation were performed specifying a one-, two-, three-, and four-factor solution. A 23-item, three-factor solution was determined to be the most interpretable. Items with structure coefficients of .33 or greater on only one factor were retained. Items with structure coefficients of .30 or greater on more than one factor were eliminated. This three-factor solution best reflected the hypothesized factor structure.
Samples	The factor structure of the IHNI was established based on data collected from 241 gay men living in the United States. These men were recruited from gay bars, churches with large numbers of gay and lesbian members, an adult bookstore, gay pride events, campus organizations, gay choirs, and the Internet. Their age ranged from 18 to 66 (*M* = 33.9, *SD* = 9.6). The racial/ethnic composition was as follows: 88.7% White American, 2.1% African American, 0.8% Latino/a American, 2.8% Native American, 0.8% were not citizens of the United States, and 5.5% multiracial.

Scoring	The number of items in each subscale of the IHNI is as follows:
	
	     Personal Homonegativity: 11 items
	     Gay Affirmation: 7 items
	     Morality of Homosexuality: 5 items
	     Total IHNI: 23 items
	
	 Seven items require reverse scoring. Scores are then obtained by summing and dividing the scores on the items of the subscale. A total score can be obtained by summing and dividing scores on all items and dividing by 26. Higher scores indicate greater levels of internalized homophobia.

(Continued)

(Continued)

Reliability	Cronbach's alpha coefficient for the subscale scores were as follows: Personal Homonegativity: Alpha = .89 Gay Affirmation: Alpha = .82 Morality of Homosexuality: Alpha = .70 Total IHNI: Alpha = .91
Validity	Evidence for convergent validity was established through statistically significant positive correlations between IHNI scores and homosexuality attitudes (Nungesser, 1983). Discriminant validity was evidenced through small statistically significant relationships found between IHNI scores and extroversion and emotional stability (Saucier, 1994) and nonstatistically significant correlations with social desirability (Crowne & Marlowe, 1960). Evidence for construct validity was demonstrated through statistically significant correlations between IHNI scores and gay identity (Brady & Busse, 1994).
Related References	Currie, M. R., Cunningham, E. G., & Findlay, B. M. (2004). The Short Internalized Homonegativity Scale: Examination of the factorial structure of a new measure of internalized homophobia. *Educational and Psychological Measurement, 64,* 1053–1067.
Language Versions	English
Contact	Wayne Mayfield Center for Family Policy and Research 1400 Rock Quarry Road University of Missouri Columbia, MO 65211 (573) 884–9299 Email: mayfieldw@missouri.edu

9.11.3 Name of the Measure	Internalized Homophobia Scale IHS
Primary Reference	Ross, M. W., & Rosser, B. R. S. (1996). Measurement and correlates of internalized homophobia: A factor analytic study. *Journal of Clinical Psychology, 52*, 15–21.
Purpose	The IHS was developed to assess the internalized homophobia among men who have sex with men.
Description	The IHS is a 26-item measure that utilizes a 7-point Likert-type response format with the following anchors: 1 = Strongly Disagree to 7 = Strongly Agree. The IHS is composed of four factors: (1) Public Identification As Gay; (2) Perception of Stigma Associated with Being Gay; (3) Social Comfort with Gay Men; and (4) Moral and Religious Acceptability of Being Gay. The items and factor structure of the IHS were derived from principal components analysis with varimax rotation. This analysis yielded seven factors with eigenvalues great than 1.0. However, examination of structure coefficients indicated only four factors met their three-item-per-factor requirement.
Samples	The factor structure of the IHS was established based on data collected from 202 participants who were recruited from (1) a seminars on man-to-man sexual health, (2) referrals from health service providers, and (3) advertisements in gay-oriented media, venues, and events. The mean age was 37.0 years (*SD* = 9.3 years).

Scoring	The number of items in each subscale of the IHS is as follows:
	
	    Public Identification As Gay: 10 items
	
	    Perception of Stigma Associated with Being Gay: 6 items
	
	    Social Comfort with Gay Men: 6 items
	
	    Moral and Religious Acceptability of Being Gay: 4 items
	
	    Total IHS: 26 items
	
	Thirteen items require reverse scoring. Scores are then obtained by summing and dividing the scores on the items of the subscale. A total score can be obtained by summing and dividing scores on all items and dividing by 26. Higher scores indicate greater levels of internalized homophobia.

Reliability	Cronbach's alpha coefficient for the subscale scores were as follows:
	
	    Public Identification As Gay: Alpha = .85
	
	    Perception of Stigma Associated with Being Gay: Alpha = .69
	
	    Social Comfort with Gay Men: Alpha = .64
	
	    Moral and Religious Acceptability of Being Gay: Alpha = .62

(Continued)

(Continued)

Validity	Evidence for concurrent validity was established through statistically significant relationships, in the expected direction, between Public Identification As Gay with duration of longest relationships, extent of attraction to men, extent of attraction to women, relationship satisfaction, proportion of social time with gays, openly gay/bisexual in personal life, openly gay/bisexual at work, and number of people known with HIV/AIDS. Social Comfort with Gay Men also was statistically significantly correlated with many of these same indicators. Evidence of validity for the remaining subscales is mixed.
Related References	Ross, M. W., Smolenski, D. J., Kajubi, P., Mandel, J. S., McFarland, W., & Raymond, F. H. (2010). Measurement of internalized homonegativity in gay and bisexual men in Uganda: Cross cultural properties of the internalized homonegativity scale. *Psychology, Health & Medicine, 15*, 159–165.
	Sherry, A. (2007). Internalized homophobia and adult attachment: Implications for clinical practice. *Psychotherapy: Theory, Research, Practice, Training, 44*, 219–225.
Language Versions	English, Spanish
Contact	Michael W. Ross University of Texas Health Science Center at Houston School of Public Health UCT 2622, 7000 Fannin Houston, TX 77030 (713) 500–9652 Email: Michael.W.Ross@uth.tmc.edu

9.12 CLIMATE AND EXPERIENCES

9.12.1 Name of the Measure	Lesbian, Gay, Bisexual, and Transgendered Climate Inventory LGBTCI
Primary Reference	Liddle, B. J., Luzzo, D. A., Hauenstein, A. L., & Schuck, K. (2004). Construction and validation of the Lesbian, Gay, Bisexual, and Transgendered Climate Inventory. *Journal of Career Assessment, 12,* 33–50.
Purpose	The LBGTCI was developed to assess the climate at work for LGBT individuals.
Description	The LBGTCI is a 20-item measure that utilizes the following 4-point response options: 1 = Doesn't Describe At All, 2 = Describes Somewhat or a Little, 3 = Describes Pretty Well, and 4 = Describes Extremely Well. The LBGTCI is a unidimensional measure. Items were generated through the use of 62 open-ended questionnaires that were sent to 17 researchers in nine states for distribution. Each collaborating researcher distributed no more than five surveys to acquaintances who occupied a diverse array of occupations. Thirty-nine of these surveys were returned (24 lesbians, 12 gay men, 3 bisexual men, 2 transgendered). These respondents generated 341 phrases that were distilled into meaning units (Giorgi, 1985) by four research team members (two professors, two advanced doctoral students). Fifty-nine items were then developed that reflected every meaning unit. These items were compared to relevant raw data from another study involving LGB psychology professors using the same method. In order to include those items, a few items were reworded with one new addition. This resulted in a 60-item LGBTCI. Several doctoral students and local LGB individuals reviewed the measure for content and clarity. The 60-item measure was then sent out to the same research collaborators as described earlier. Because responses to the survey appeared to lack representativeness, the researchers then oversampled settings they knew would be hostile toward LGB individuals. Based on these responses, 40 items were deleted. This resulted in the retention of 20 items. A principal factor analysis was performed, indicating a single-factor solution.
Samples	The LBGTCI was established based on data collected from 124 participants (51% female; 46% male; 3% indicated other or that gender was not applicable). Twenty-one percent of the sample indicated being transgendered. With respect to sexual orientation, 32% indicated lesbian, 40% indicated gay, 13% bisexual, 13% unspecified (transgendered participants), and 2% heterosexual (transgendered respondents). With respect to race, 87% identified as White American, 6% multiracial, 2% African American, 2% Latino/a American, 1% Asian American, and 1% Native American. Participants' age ranged from 18 to 64 years ($M = 38$ years, $SD = 9$ years).

(Continued)

(Continued)

Scoring	The LGBTCI is composed of 20 items. Eight items require a reverse score. The scale score is obtained by summing responses on each of the items. Higher scores indicate a more positive work climate for LGBT individuals.
Reliability	The Cronbach's alpha coefficient for the LGBTCI score was .96. Six- to 7-month test-retest reliability coefficient for the LGBTCI score was .87.
Validity	Evidence for construct validity was established through expected statistically significant positive relationship between the LGBTCI and job satisfaction (Weiss, Dawis, England, & Lofquist, 1977) and statistically significant inverse relationship with LGB workplace discrimination (Croteau, Anderson, DiStefano, & Chung, 1998).
Related References	
Language Versions	English
Contact	Becky J. Liddle Phone: (647) 989-1555

9.12.2 Name of the Measure	Homophobic Content Agent Target Scale HCAT
Primary Reference	Poteat, V. P., & Espelage, D. L. (2005). Exploring the relation between bullying and homophobic verbal content: The Homophobic Content Agent Target (HCAT) scale. *Violence and Victims, 20,* 513–528.
Purpose	The HCAT was developed to assess the frequency with which adolescents perpetrated and experienced being the victim of homophobic verbal content.
Description	The HCAT is a 10-item measure that utilizes a 5-point Likert-type response format with the following response scale: 1 = Never, 2 = 1 or 2 Times, 3 = 3 or 4 Times, 4 = 5 or 6 Times, 5 = 7 or More Times. The HCAT is composed of two factors: (1) Agent and (2) Target. Data from the 10-item HCAT were submitted to a principal axis factor analysis with varimax rotation. The two-factor model was supported by scree plot and eigenvalues. No item yielded a structure coefficient of greater than .30 on more than one factor.
Samples	The HCAT was established based on data collected from 191 middle school students (99 females, 92 males), which represents a 92% response rate. With respect to race and ethnicity, the sample was composed of White Americans (95.0%), African Americans (0.5%), Asian American (1.0%), Latino/a American (1.6%), Biracial (0.5%) and those who did not report their racial background (1.6%).

Scoring	The number of items in each of the two subscales of the HCAT is as follows:
	
	    Agent: 5 items
	
	    Target: 5 items
	
	    Total HCAT: 10 items
	
	Scores on the subscales are obtained by summing scores on the items of the subscale. Higher scores indicate greater frequency of experiences as an agent or target of homophobic verbal content.

Reliability	Cronbach's alpha coefficient for the subscale scores were as follows:
	
	    Agent: Alpha = .85
	    Target: Alpha = .85

Validity	Known-groups validity was established for the agent and target subscales, with males reporting having experienced both being an agent and target of homophobic verbal content more often than did females. Evidence for construct validity was established through expected statistically significant relationships between the HCAT subscales and relational aggression (Crick, 1996) for agents, victimization (Espelage & Holt, 2001), and relational victimization (Crick, 1996) for targets, empathy (Davis, 1983) for agents, and depression and anxiety (Achenbach, 1991) for targets.

(Continued)

(Continued)

Related References	Poteat, V. P. (2007). Peer group socialization of homophobic attitudes and behavior during adolescence. *Child Development*, 78, 1830–1842.
Language Versions	English
Contact	V. Paul Poteat Boston College Dept. of Counseling, Developmental, and Educational Psychology Lynch School of Education Campion Hall 307 140 Commonweath Ave. Chestnut Hill, MA 02467 Phone: (617) 552-4234 Email: poteatp@bc.edu

9.12.3 Name of the Measure	Heterosexist Harassment, Rejection, and Discrimination Scale HHRDS
Primary Reference	Szymanski, D. M. (2006). Does internalized heterosexism moderate the link between heterosexist events and lesbians' psychological distress? *Sex Roles, 54,* 227–234.
Purpose	The HHRDS was developed to assess the frequency of perceived sexual orientation-based rejection, harassment, and discrimination experienced by lesbians during the past year.
Description	The HHRDS is a 14-item measure that utilizes a 6-point Likert-type response format with the following response scale: 1 = If The Event Has NEVER Happened To You, 2 = If The Event Has Happened ONCE IN A WHILE (less than 10% of the time), 3 = If The Event Happened SOMETIMES (10–25% of the time), 4 = If The Event Happened A LOT (26–49% of the time), 5 = If The Event Happened MOST OF THE TIME (50–70% of the time), 6 = If The Event Happened ALMOST ALL OF THE TIME (more than 70%). The HHRDS is composed of three factors: (1) Harassment and Rejection, (2) Workplace and School Discrimination, and (3) Other Discrimination. Eighteen initial items of the HHRDS were developed based on the items of the Schedule of Sexist Events—Recent (SSE-R; Klonoff & Landrine, 1995) and the Schedule of Racist Events—Recent (SRE-R; Landrine & Klonoff, 1996). Some items of the HHRDS are modified versions of items on the SSE-R and SRE-R. Additional items measuring harassment and rejection by family and friends were added. A three-factor, 14-item HHRDS emerged from factor analysis with oblimin rotation. The author used the following criteria to determine the number of factors to be extracted and rotated: (1) eigenvalues greater than 1.0, (2) scree test, (3) percentage of total variance by each factor, (4) structure coefficient of at least .35 and no cross-correlations greater than or equal to .30, and (5) a minimum of three items on each factor.
Samples	The HHRDS was established based on data collected from 143 predominantly White American (90%) sexual minority women who reported a high level of education (74%). The participants' ages ranged from 19 to 70 years ($M = 41.11$, $SD = 10.18$). Participants were recruited through email announcements on social and academic lesbians' listservs and at a gay pride event in the Midwest (U.S.). All interested participants were given a survey, with 143 of the 460 surveys (31%) distributed returned.
Scoring	The number of items for each of the three subscales of the HHRDS is as follows: Harassment and Rejection: 7 items Workplace and School Discrimination: 4 items Other Discrimination: 3 items Total HHRDS: 14 items

(Continued)

(Continued)

	Scores on the subscales are obtained by summing and dividing the scores on the items of the subscale. Higher scores indicate greater frequency of experiences of harassment and rejection, workplace and school discrimination, and other discrimination in the past year.
Reliability	Cronbach's alpha coefficient for the subscale scores were as follows: Harassment and Rejection: Alpha = .89 Workplace and School Discrimination: Alpha = .84 Other Discrimination: Alpha = .78
Validity	Evidence for criterion-related validity was established through statistically significant relationships with overall psychological distress, somatization, obsessive-compulsiveness, interpersonal sensitivity, depression, and anxiety (Derogatis, Lipman, Rickets, Uhlenhuth, & Covi, 1974).
Related References	
Language Versions	English
Contact	Dawn Szymanski Department of Psychology University of Tennessee Knoxville, TN 37996-0900 Email: dawnszymanski@msn.com

10

Disability Attitude Measures

10.1 HISTORICAL OVERVIEW AND DEFINITION

A report by the U.S Census Bureau (2005) puts the over-all rate of disability in the U.S population for all ages, sexes, and races combined at 18.7%. The rates vary for different racial and ethnic groups: African Americans (20.5%), Asian Americans (12.4%), White Americans (19.7%), and Latino/a Americans (13.1%). Leung (2003) also notes that among African Americans and Latino/a Americans reporting a disability, both groups are more likely to be classified as having a "severe disability" (71.8% and 67.8%, respectively) than White Americans (52%). These disparate rates of disability in the U.S. population and elsewhere have motivated a number of new laws and classification systems.

The Vocational Rehabilitation Act of 1973 and the amendments that followed, the Education for All Handicapped Children Act of 1975 and the Comprehensive Rehabilitation Services Amendments of 1978, have influenced how people with disabilities are treated in the United States. The landmark legislation of the Americans with Disabilities Act (ADA) signed by President George Bush in 1990 further reinforced earlier legislation and was aimed at eliminating discrimination against persons with disabilities and promoting their full participation in society by removing barriers and providing necessary accommodations. These legislative acts have had widespread impact on the lives of individuals with disabilities in all sectors of society from educational to employment settings (e.g., Blanck, 1995; Enright, Conyer, & Szymanski, 1996), especially in light of the fact that disability affects a substantial portion of the American population.

The ADA defines disability as follows:

(A) a physical or mental impairment that substantially limits one or more of the major life activities of such individuals; (B) a record of such impairment; or (C) being regarded as having such an impairment. A person must meet the requirements of at least one of these three criteria to be an individual with a disability under the Act. (Equal Employment Opportunity Commission and the U.S. Department of Justice, 1991)

This broad definition has been the basis for various federal agencies to craft definitions to address their own specific concerns such as employment (Bureau of Labor Statistics), health care (National Center on Health Statistics), or Social Security (Bureau of the Census; National Institute on Disability and Rehabilitation Research, Office of Special Education and Rehabilitation Services, 1993). While this definition looks simple and straightforward, it is ambiguous, and its meaning and implication have been debated, questioned, and expanded in the public discourse from courtrooms to hospital rooms to bedrooms that span the entire realm of bodily dysfunctions, failings, ailments, and diseases, ranging from HIV/AIDS to diabetes to cancer, from mobility challenges to mental competencies to sensory losses (Butler & Parr, 1999; Corker & French, 1999; Davis, 2006; Pothier & Devlin, 2006; Ramanathan, 2010; Sarangi & Roberts, 1998).

Disability has also been addressed globally through the publications of the World Health Organization (WHO) documents *International Classifications of Functioning, Disability and Health (ICF)* (WHO, 2001) and *International Classification of Functioning, Disability and Health for Children and Youth (ICF-CY)* (WHO, 2007). The ICF and ICF-CY are rapidly becoming the standard international classification frameworks to describe functioning in rehabilitation. These classification schemas address health and health-related issues that focus on body functions and structures, activities, and participation. These documents recognize disability as a universal human experience, with emphasis on impact rather than cause. Further, contextual factors (e.g., personal environment) as well as medical or biological components are seen as contributing to the individual's disability status.

10.2 STUDY OF ATTITUDES

The study of attitudes toward persons with disabilities spans some six decades. An overview of the research literature demonstrates that attitudes toward persons with disabilities were negative before the passage of the various rehabilitation acts and the ADA (e.g., Antonak, 1985; Barker, Wright, Meyerson, & Gonick, 1953; Cohen & Struening, 1962; Cowen, Underberg, & Verrillo, 1958; English, 1971; Grand, Benier, & Strohmer, 1982; Hood, 1973; Link, 1987; Mussen & Barker, 1944; Wright, 1975; Yuker, 1965), and continue to be negative afterwards (e. g., Depoy & Gilson, 2010; Link, Yang, Phelan, & Collins, 2004). Although enforcing the law prohibiting discrimination against persons with disabilities has lead to advances in greater participation in society by persons with disabilities, there is a continuing culture of oppression and stigmatization (e.g., Charlton, 2000; Kirkwood & Stamm, 2006; Michalko, 2002).

Historically, disability-related stigma and oppression have been sponsored by three disability viewpoints that have prevailed for several thousand years and that we will briefly examine (Atkinson & Hackett, 2004; Hohenshil & Humes, 1979). Perhaps the historically oldest viewpoint can be construed as the *burdensome view* (Atkinson & Hackett, 2004). Here, individuals with physical disabilities are considered a burden to the group or community. Individuals who could not contribute (or eventually would not be able to contribute) to food procurement or group self-preservation were often abandoned or destroyed. The burdensome viewpoint of people with disabilities is currently evidenced in the discrimination many of these individuals experience while seeking employment (Stefan, 2001).

A second viewpoint is the *charitable view* (Atkinson & Hackett, 2004). This view traces its origins back to the early Christian churches that considered the plight of poor or disabled persons to be a charitable cause, which demanded providing food, shelter, and social support. This subsidization of persons with disabilities was often accompanied by provider attitudes of pity, sympathy, and paternalism (Bowe, 1978), attitudes that are prevalent today. Charitable views of the disabled often were realized through the development of segregated custodial care (e.g., asylums, hospitals) for their protection. Voluntary charitable organizations (e.g., Salvation Army, American Red Cross, Goodwill Industries) and their collective outreach to disabled persons began their ascendancy during the rise of monopoly capitalism in the early 19th century. Workers' struggles for a living wage during this time resulted in the passage of various workers' compensation legislative acts, including the Rehabilitation Act of 1973 (Scotch, 2001).

A final viewpoint noted by Atkinson and Hackett (2004) can be construed as the *egalitarian view*. This viewpoint (beginning in the 1960s) is a fundamental shift from requesting charity to a more militant demand for civil rights. Individuals with disabilities no longer sought help adjusting to their environment but rather demanded that their environments accommodate their needs. This new activism fostered a number of legislative acts including the 1990 Americans with Disabilities Act, the 1998 Crime Victims with Disabilities Awareness Act, and the 2001 No Child Left Behind (NCLB) Act (Atkinson & Hackett, 2004).

As Atkinson and Hackett (2004) note, all three of these views concerning people with disabilities are with us today. These viewpoints also help to inform and reinforce three common models of disability, summarized by Olkin (1999, 2002), that both people with disabilities and their health care providers operate from when considering disability issues. These three models are known as the *moral, medical,* and *social* models of disability. Adherents of the moral model view disability as a defect caused by some moral lapse (past or present). This model is the oldest in origin and very common cross-culturally. This model allows individuals with disabilities to be viewed as specially selected with a greater purpose of the disability or to be shamed and ostracized. The medical model of disability focuses primarily on body malfunctions due to genetics, habits, or behavior. This is the modal model of disability currently favored in the United States. Due to the focus on "medical cures," self-stigma is lessened but still promotes paternalism. The social model of disability argues that environments must accommodate individuals with disabilities. This lack of accommodation and consideration is a form of discrimination and oppression and is a legitimate civil rights issue. This model encourages the development of community and pride and the culture of disability but can also lead to a sense of futility when interfacing with established power structures. These three viewpoints and three models of disability that we have briefly encountered have helped shape the lived experience of discrimination, oppression, and stigma that people with disabilities have experienced for millennia. These same ideas have also helped to construct current attitudes about people with disabilities.

10.3 STIGMA

The seminal works by Goffman (1963), Jones, Farina, Hastorf, Marcus, Miller, and Scott (1984), and Link and Phelan (2001) on conceptualizing stigma have contributed significantly to the theoretical and the empirical literature related to the attitudes toward people with disabilities. While the definitions of stigma vary, there are basic elements that capture the essence of the concept that apply broadly to racial and ethnic groups, people with physical and cognitive disabilities, mental illness, health conditions, persons who display nontraditional expressions of sexuality, and those who have made unusual lifestyle choices. According to Link and Phelan (2001), stigmatization exists "when elements of labeling, stereotyping, separation, status loss and

discrimination co-occur in a power situation that allows them to unfold" (p. 367).

Stigma is associated with being marked in certain ways that discredit a group or an individual. Six categories are used to describe such markers: (1) *concealability* refers to the degree to which undesirable features are detectable by others; (2) *course* refers to the permanence of an undesirable distinctive characteristics; (3) *disruptiveness* refers to attributes that interfere with interpersonal relationships; (4) *aesthetic* refers to differences that are regarded as unattractive or generate disgust; (5) *origin* refers to undesirable differentiating characteristics for which a person may be held responsible; and (6) *peril* refers to possession of attributes considered threatening and potentially dangerous (Jones et al., 1984). According to Goffman (1963), stigmatized groups or individuals possess attributes that are discrediting and lead to being tainted and discounted. These attributes fall into three categories: (1) "abominations" that refer to such attributes as physical disabilities or visible deformities; (2) "character blemishes" such as mental illness or criminal convictions; and (3) "tribal stigma" that may be related to attributes associated with race, sex, and age.

Reflecting the link between all forms of stigma, items of the Mental Retardation Attitudes Inventory (MRAI; Harth, 1971) were based on a measure of racial attitudes toward "Negros," as articulated and measured by Woodmansee and Cook (1967). Moreover, Chesler (1965) showed significant correlations between ethnocentrism and the Attitudes Toward Disabled Persons scale (ATDP; Yuker, Block, & Campbell, 1960). Charlton (2000) affirmed such a parallel in his book *Nothing About Us Without Us: Disability Oppression and Empowerment.*

These conceptualizations and definitions imply that there are those who stigmatize and those who are stigmatized. In this sense, attitudes toward persons with disabilities may reflect dispositions of stigmatizers, and measures of such attitudes may be seen as measures of stigmatization.

10.4 SCOPE OF THE RESEARCH ON ATTITUDES TOWARD PERSONS WITH DISABILITIES

The research literature on attitudes toward persons with disabilities is quite vast and spans cultures and international boundaries, attesting to the pervasive nature of the problems experienced by persons with disabilities everywhere. For example, reviewing the measurement literature related to stigma associated with disability and health conditions, Van Brakel (2006) identified instruments developed in countries across the world. In similar fashion, Angermeyer and Dietrich (2005) identified studies dealing with stigmatization of persons with mental illness in 33 national and 29 local and regional populations, mostly in Europe.

Studies of attitudes toward disabilities have included comparison of different racial and ethnic groups as well as examination of factors within racial and ethnic groups that are related to attitudes toward mental illness. A review of research and theory addressing the intersection of racial and ethnic culture and disabilities can be found in *Culture and Disability: Providing Culturally Competent Services* (Stone, 2005).

Studies have also looked at the interface of disability with expressions of sexuality. In a review of the literature, Schulz (2009) examined disabilities and their intersections with sexuality and development of sexual identity. Also, Harley, Nowak, Gassaway, and Savage (2002) examined the intersections between disability and lesbian, gay, bisexual, and transgender sexual expressions in multiple racial and ethnic groups. Another example is a study by Thomson, Bryson, and de Castell (2001), who examined the myths about sexual expressions among developmentally disabled persons, their impact on the attitudes of caregivers, and how these myths filter into gay and lesbian and disability communities.

Link, Yang, Phelan, and Collins (2004) reviewed 123 empirical articles published between 1995 and 2003 that had studied stigma toward mental illness. They identified different methodologies including experiments, surveys, qualitative analysis, interviews, direct observation, and literature reviews with and without the use of vignettes; populations of study including children and adolescents, general population, professional groups, people with mental illness, and families of people with mental illness; and components of stigma, including behavior, labeling, cognitive separating, stereotyping, emotional reactions, status loss/discrimination, and behavioral responses.

Also, regarding mental illness, Brohan, Slade, Clement, and Thornicroft (2010) reviewed 57 studies and identified 14 survey instruments that measured perceived, experienced, and self-stigma.

The study of attitudes toward persons with disabilities has involved a variety of methods and procedures as well. Antonak and Livneh (2000) reviewed the literature to identify a variety of methods used to study attitudes toward disabilities. They identified 10 direct methods such as ranking, use of adjective checklists, paired comparisons, semantic differential scales, summated rating scales, and social distance scales; 14 indirect methods such as nonobtrusive behavioral observations in public behavior settings (e.g., shopping malls), observation of social interactions, use of confederates who appear to have disabilities, rapid association techniques; and sentence completion methods and expressive techniques such as involving interactions with dolls or other human figures.

Reviewing measures to assess attitudes of children toward peers with disabilities, Vignes, Coley, Grandjean, Godeau, and Arnaud (2008) identified 19 instruments using evidence of reliability and validity as inclusion criteria. These instruments targeted affective, behavioral, and cognitive components of disability attitudes.

The research on attitudes toward disabilities has engaged many researchers and disciplines globally and used varied methodologies and numerous measures. This work has also continued to advance theory building as well as rehabilitation and intervention strategies.

10.5 MEASURES

We realize that we cannot do justice in this handbook by summarizing all the different approaches and instruments used to measure attitudes toward people with disabilities. We have limited ourselves to presenting summated instruments that meet our inclusion criteria of using factor analytic item reduction methods. Moreover, we have not ventured far into the measurement of attitudes toward and stigmatization of a large number of health-related disabilities such as leprosy, HIV/AIDS, cancer, or diabetes. We have focused primarily on measures dealing with mobility and sensory disabilities, epilepsy, cognitive impairments, mental illness, attitudes toward inclusion, and self-stigma. Altogether we summarize 35 measures on attitudes toward people with disabilities. A large group of measures addresses attitudes toward people with at least one disability. A second group of measures addresses the experience of stigma by people with a disability.

10.6 GENERAL MEASURES OF DISABILITY ATTITUDES

The following eight measures of attitudes toward people with disabilities in general are summarized: Attitudes to Sexuality Questionnaire (Individuals with an Intellectual Disability) (ASQ-ID; Cuskelly & Gilmore, 2007); Attitude Toward Disabled Persons Scale (ATDP-O, ATDP-A, ATDP-B; Yuker & Block, 1986); Disability Factor Scales—General (DFS-G; Siller, 1969); Disability Social Relations Generalized Disability (DSRGD; Hergenrather & Rhodes, 2007); Interaction with Disabled Persons Scale (IDP; Gething, 1991, 1994); Multidimensional Attitudes Scale Toward Persons With Disabilities (MAS; Findler, Vilchinsky, & Werner, 2007); Scale of Attitudes Toward Disabled Persons (SADP; Antonak, 1982); and Questions About Disability Survey (QADS; Graf, Blankenship, Sanchez, & Carlson, 2007).

10.7 ATTITUDES TOWARD PEOPLE WITH MENTAL RETARDATION

The following four measures of attitudes toward people with mental retardation are summarized: Attitude Toward Mentally Retarded People Scale (AMRP; Bartlett, Quay, & Wrightsman, 1960); Attitude Toward the Retarded (ATR; Efron & Efron, 1967); Community Living Attitudes Scale—Mental Retardation (CLAS-MR; Henry, Keys, Jopp, & Balcazar, 1996); and Mental Retardation Attitude Inventory—Revised (MRAI-R; Antonak & Harth, 1994).

10.8 ATTITUDES TOWARD PEOPLE WITH EPILEPSY

The following four measures of attitudes toward people with epilepsy are summarized: Attitudes and Beliefs About Living with Epilepsy (ABLE; DiIorio, Kobau, Holder, et al., 2004); Scale of Knowledge and Attitude Toward Epilepsy and Persons with Epilepsy (ATPE; Antonak & Rankin, 1982); Thinking About Epilepsy Questionnaire (TAEQ; Martiniuk, Speechley, Secco, & Campbell, 2007); and Test of Knowledge About Epilepsy (TKAE; Antonak & Livneh, 1995a).

10.9 ATTITUDES TOWARD INCLUSION

The following four measures of attitudes toward inclusion are summarized: Attitude Toward Mainstreaming Scale (ATMS; Berryman & Neal, 1980); Mainstreaming Opinionnaire (MO; Schmelkin, 1981); Multidimensional Attitudes Toward Inclusive Education Scale (MATIES; Mahat, 2008); and Response to Inclusion Survey (RIS; Soodak, Podell, & Lehman, 1998).

10.10 ATTITUDES TOWARD PEOPLE WITH MENTAL ILLNESS

The following five measures of attitudes toward people with mental illness are summarized: Beliefs About Illness (BAI; Norman, Sorrentino, Windall, & Manchanda, 2008a); Community Attitudes Toward the Mentally Ill (CAMI; Taylor & Dear, 1981); Opinion About Mental Illness (OMI; Cohen & Struening, 1962); Participation in Research Attitude Scale (PRAS; McDonald, Keys, & Henry, 2008); and Standardized Stigmatization Questionnaire—Version 1 (SSQ1; Haghighat, 2005).

10.11 ATTITUDES TOWARD PEOPLE WHO ARE BLIND OR DEAF

The following two measures of attitudes toward people who are blind and people who are deaf are summarized: Attitudes Toward Blindness (ATB; Whiteman & Lukoff, 1964a); and Opinion About Deaf People (ODP; Berkay, Gardner, & Smith, 1995).

10.12 ATTITUDES TOWARD SELF-ACCEPTANCE

The extent to which persons with disabilities accept their disabilities and the way they manage the perceptions of others through appearance and attire reflect coping strategies and ways of dealing with stereotyping by others. The following two measures of attitudes toward self-acceptance of disability are summarized: Acceptance of Disability (AD; Linkowski, 1971) and Appearance Management and Social Interaction Scale (AMSI; Kaiser, Wingate, & Freeman, 1987).

10.13 ATTITUDES OF SELF-STIGMA

The following five measures of self-stigma by people with disabilities are summarized: Depression Self-Stigma Scale (DSSS; Kanter, Rusch, & Brondino, 2008); Internalized Stigma of Mental Illness (ISMI; Ritsher, Otilingam, & Grajales, 2003); Perceived Stigma in People with Intellectual Disability (PSPID; Ali, Straydom, Hassiotis, Williams, & King, 2008); Stigma Questionnaire (SQ; Littlewood, Jadhav, & Ryder, 2007); and Stigma Scale (SS; King, Dinos, Shaw, et al., 2007).

10.14 FUTURE RESEARCH

The research related to attitudes toward persons with disabilities spans more than 60 years. It cuts across geographic borders globally and many professional disciplines from medicine to education. The implications and applications of the research range from law, politics, and policy development to counseling, rehabilitation, employment, schooling, and sexual expression. The types of disabilities examined are also quite varied, relating to cognitive disabilities, mental illnesses, mobility, diseases, and developmental and sensory losses or impairments. Stigmatization and internalized stigma have also been studied to understand their impact on the quality of life and well-being of persons with disabilities.

There have also been efforts to integrate the research into theoretical frameworks (e.g., Depoy & Gilson, 2010; Goffman, 1963; Link & Phelan, 2001; Michailakis, 2003; Parker, Schaller, & Hansman; 2003; Siebers, 2008). While work continues in advancing an understanding of how attitudes affect persons with disabilities and their participation in society, we would like to suggest some areas of focus.

1. Continue efforts to strengthen culture-specific validity and the applicability of language of measures developed in the United States and other English-speaking countries that are used in non-English speaking countries.

2. Strengthen the psychometric properties of more recently developed measures.

3. Explore the possibility of adapting existing instruments for generic use across disabilities.

4. Monitor stigmatization and attitude change over time and factors that contribute to change.

5. Continue to investigate the meaning of stigma across cultures and racial and ethnic groups.

6. Examine the differential aspects of pity, sympathy, and fear in stigmatization of persons with disabilities.

7. Study the development of self-stigma and internalization of stigma in children.

8. Develop attitude measures that address racial- and ethnic group–specific issues.

9. Refine old and develop new measures that deal with attitudes toward people who are blind or visually impaired and deaf or hearing impaired.

10. Continue to examine the relationship of the cognitive, affective, and behavioral components of attitudes toward persons with disabilities to socioeconomic, personality, and situational factors, as well as to the visibility and severity of the disabilities.

11. In addition to continuing to study the attitudes of gatekeepers, service providers, and educators, study the attitudes of public officials and policymakers.

12. Develop measures to study self and others' attitudes that involve persons with multiple disabilities.

13. Examine self and others' attitudes toward persons that involve intersections of disabilities with gender, race, ethnicity, sexual orientation, and age.

15. Develop measures of resiliency and other strengths of people with disabilities.

10.15 MEASURES OF ATTITUDES TOWARD PERSONS WITH DISABILITIES IN GENERAL

10.15.1 **Name of the Measure**	Attitudes to Sexuality Questionnaire (Individuals With an Intellectual Disability) ASQ-ID
Primary Reference	Cuskelly, M., & Gilmore, L. (2007). Attitudes to Sexuality Questionnaire (Individuals with an Intellectual Disability): Scale development and community norms. *Journal of Intellectual & Developmental Disability, 32,* 214–221.
Purpose	The purpose of the ASQ-ID is to assess attitudes toward the expression of sexuality by individuals with intellectual disabilities.
Description	The ASQ-ID is a 28-item measure rated on a 6-point Likert-type scale ranging from 1 = Strongly Disagree to 6 = Strongly Agree. The initial items for the ASQ-ID were adopted and somewhat modified from an earlier study by Cuskelly and Bryde (2004) that had 33 items. The identical pool of items was rated separately for men by about half the sample and for women by about another half of the sample. A factor analysis using principal components with a varimax rotation was applied to the combined data for women and men. Seven factors emerged that explained 66% of the total variance. However, three of the factors were discarded either for low internal consistency or for having too few items. The following four factors were retained: (1) Sexual Rights, (2) Parenting, (3) Nonreproductive Sexual Behavior, and (4) Self-control.
Samples	The sample was composed of 261 respondents (135 women, and 126 men) from the general population, the majority of whom lived in the southeastern corner of the Australian state of Queensland. The ages ranged from 20 years to over 70 years, broken down into 10-year age brackets: 20.3% were aged 20–29, 25.3% were aged 30–39, 24.9% were aged 40–49, 14.6% were aged 50–59, 9.2% were aged 60–69, 5.4% were 70 years and older. The distribution of the educational level of the sample was comparable to the general population of the region.

Scoring	The number of items in each of the subscales were as follows:
	
	    Sexual Rights: 13 items
	    Parenting: 7 items
	    Nonreproductive Sexual Behavior: 5 items
	    Self-control: 3 items
	    Total ASQ-ID: 28 items
	
	Sixteen of the items are reverse scored, and higher ratings reflect a more positive attitude toward sexual expression. The subscale scores are obtained by summing the ratings of the items. The items of the ASQ-ID are available in the primary reference.

Reliability	The Cronbach's alphas of the subscales were as follows:
	
	    Sexual Rights: Alpha = .93
	    Parenting: Alpha = .88
	    Non-reproductive Sexual Behavior: Alpha = .84
	    Self-control: Alpha = .67

(Continued)

(Continued)

Validity	Known-group validity: Participants were divided into two age groups, those 60 years and older and those younger than 60. As expected, the older group was less accepting of the sexual rights of individuals with intellectual disabilities, was more negative about their parenthood, scored lower on the Nonreproductive Sexual Behavior subscale, and believed that they were less able to control their sexual urges.
	Criterion validity: A subgroup of 9 items of the ASQ-ID was identified and rated separately for the general population with no intellectual disability and was factor analyzed, yielding one factor with 7 items (Cronbach's alpha of .84) labeled Sexual Openness. The scores on this measure were correlated with the subscale of the ASQ-ID. The Sexual Openness scores were statistically significantly positively correlated with scores of the Sexual Rights subscale, the Parenting subscale, the Nonreproductive Sexual Behavior subscale, and the Self-control subscale. Also, the scores on the Sexual Control subscale were statistically significantly lower for male than female individuals with intellectual disability, suggesting that males have more difficulty controlling their sexual urges. Repeated measure analysis of the four subscales (using mean scores) showed that the respondents were less positive on the Parenting subscale than the other subscales.
Related References	Cuskelly, M., & Bryde, R. (2004). Attitudes towards the sexuality of adults with an intellectual disability: Parents, support staff, and community sample. *Journal of Intellectual & Developmental Disability, 29,* 255–264.
	Gilmore, L., & Chambers, B. (2010). Intellectual disability and sexuality: Attitudes of disability support staff and leisure industry employees. *Journal of Intellectual & Developmental Disability, 35,* 22–28.
Language Versions	English
Contact	Monica Cuskelly Schonell Research Centre, School of Education The University of Queensland QLD 4072 Australia Email: m.cuskelly@uq.edu.au

10.15.2 Name of the Measure	Attitudes Toward Disabled Persons Scale ATDP-O, ATDP-A, and ATDP-B
Primary Reference	Yuker, H. E., & Block, J. R. (1986). *Research with the Attitude Towards Disabled Persons Scales (ATDP) 1960–1985.* Hempstead, NY: Center for the Study of Attitudes Toward Persons with Disabilities, Hofstra University.
Purpose	The purpose of the ATDP scales is to measure attitudes toward persons with disability in general but mainly physical disabilities.
Description	The ATDP is one of the most widely used measures in research dealing with attitudes toward persons with disabilities, both as a direct measure of attitudes and as a criterion for validation of other measures (see Antonak & Livneh, 1988; Hunt & Hunt, 2004; Pruett & Chan, 2006; Seo & Chen, 2009; Yuker & Block, 1986). ATDP-O is a 20-item measure originally published by Yuker, Block, and Campbell (1960), followed by the 30-item equivalent forms ATDP-A and ATDP-B published by Yuker, Block, and Young (1966). While the original scales were published as unrefereed monographs, much research has been conducted using the measures and published in refereed sources.
	All three forms are rated on a 6-point Likert-type scale ranging from −3 = I Disagree Very Much to +3 = I Agree Very Much with no neutral point. The three forms as originally developed were constructed as unidimensional measures of attitudes toward persons with disabilities. Attempts to assess the factor structures of the measures have resulted in mixed and inconsistent findings and have challenged its unidimensional structure. For example, studies by Antonak (1980; Form O), Livneh (1982; Form A), Siller and Chipman (1964; Form O) and Hafer, Wright, and Godley (1983: Form B) reported anywhere from two to four independent factors. However, the ATDP has been most frequently used as a unidimensional measure yielding a single overall score in all three of its forms. The items of the three forms may be found in Yuker and Block (1986) and in Antonak and Livneh (1988).
Samples	No one study is possible to single out for reporting of samples here because of the very different and varied populations used in the development and continued use of ATDP, nationally and internationally. For an extensive early review, see Yuker and Block (1986).
Scoring	Half the items on each form are worded positively and half are worded negatively. To score, first the signs of the positively worded items are reversed, all responses are summed, the sign of the sum is reversed, and a constant is added to eliminate any possible negative values. The scores range from 0 to 120 for Form O and 0 to 180 for Forms A and B. Lower ratings reflect more positive attitudes on individual items. A single overall score is used in each of the forms.
Reliability	Reviewing the development of the ATDP Forms O, A, and B, Antonak and Livneh (1988) provide the following reliability estimates: Test-retest reliability for time intervals of 2 weeks to 18 months: Form O: Range from r = .66 to .89

(Continued)

(Continued)

	Form A: $r = .79$ Form B: Range from $r = .71$ to $.83$ Split-half internal reliability: Form O: Range from $r = .75$ to $.85$ Form A: Range from $r = .73$ to $.89$ Form B: Range from $r = .72$ to $.87$ Additionally, recent examples of Cronbach's alpha are as follows: Form O: Alpha $= .72$ for undergraduates (Thomas, Palmer, Coker-Juneau, & Williams, 2003) Form A: Alpha $= .83$ for rehabilitation counseling volunteers (Pruett & Chan, 2006) Form B: Alpha $= .80$ for undergraduate recreation students (Perry, Ivy, Conners, & Shelar, 2008)
Validity	Reviewing the development of the ADTP Forms O, A, and B, Antonak and Livneh (1988) and Yuker and Block (1986) summarize extensive validity information from different sources. Criterion-related validity is demonstrated as follows: 1. Females show greater acceptance of physical disability than males. 2. Higher educational level is associated with more acceptance of persons with disabilities. 3. Increased contact with persons with disabilities is associated with more favorable attitudes. Convergent validity is demonstrated as follows: 1. ATDP scores are statistically significantly correlated with other measures of attitudes toward persons with disabilities (e.g., Interaction with Disabled Persons scale [IDP], Gething, 1994; the Disability Attitude Implicit Association Test [DA-IAT], Pruett & Chan, 2006; the Contact with Disabled Persons scale [CDP], Pruett, Lee, Chan, Wang, & Lane, 2008). 2. ATDP scores are statistically significantly correlated with attitudes toward other groups such as the elderly, alcoholics, and the mentally ill (Antonak & Livneh, 1988; Yuker & Block, 1986). 3. ATDP scores are statistically significantly positively correlated with personality variables such as low aggressiveness, low anxiety, positive self-esteem, and intraception as reported by Yuker and Block (1986) and Antonak and Livneh (1988).

	Discriminant validity is summarized by Yuker and Block (1986) and Antonak and Livneh (1988) as follows: 1. ATDP scores are unrelated to measures of intelligence or vocational interest. 2. ATDP scores' relationship to social desirability are mixed. 3. ATDP scores do not appear to be influence by acquiescence bias. Additionally, recent examples of validity evidence are as follows: 1. ATDP Form O was statistically significantly positively correlated with discomfort in interactions with persons with disabilities as measured by the Interaction with Disabled Persons Scale (IDP; Gething, 1994), suggestive of convergent validity. 2. ATDP Form A, as expected, was not correlated with the Disability Attitude-Implicit Association Test (DA-IAT), suggestive of discriminant validity (Pruett & Chan, 2006). DA-IAT measures unconscious dispositions toward persons with disability. 3. ATDP Form B mean scores were statistically significantly higher for females than males and for those who had more frequent contact with persons with disabilities (Perry et al., 2008).
Related References	Hunt, C. S., & Hunt, B. (2004). Changing attitudes toward people with disabilities: Experimenting with an educational intervention. *Journal of Managerial Issues, 16,* 266–280. Perry, T. L., Ivy, M., Conners, A., & Shelar, D. (2008). Recreation student attitudes towards persons with disabilities: considerations for future service delivery. *Journal of Hospitality, Leisure, Sport and Tourism, 7,* 4–14. Pruett, S. R., & Chan, F. (2006). The development and psychometric validation of the Disability Attitude Implicit Association Test. *Rehabilitation Psychology, 51,* 202–213. Seo, W., & Chen, R. K. (2009). Attitudes of college students toward people with disabilities. *Journal of Applied Rehabilitation Counseling, 40,* 3–8. Thomas, A., Palmer, J. K., Coker-Juneau, C. J., & Williams, D. J. (2003). Factor structure and construct validity of the Interaction with Disabled Persons Scale. *Educational and Psychological Measurement, 63,* 465–483.
Language Versions	Arabic, Danish, Dutch, English, French, German, Greek, Hebrew, Italian, Japanese, Mandarin, Portuguese, and Russian
Contact	Yuker's collected works are available at the Yuker Reference Library at Hofstra University: Archives Office (516) 463–6158 Geri Solomon, Assistant Dean (516) 463–6407 036 Axinn Library 123 Hofstra University Hempstead, NY 11549

10.15.3 Name of the Measure	Disability Factor Scales—General DFS-G
Primary Reference	Livneh, H. (1985). Factor structure of attitudes toward individuals with disabilities: A replication. *Rehabilitation Counseling Bulletin, 29,* 53–58. Siller, J. (1969). *The general form of the Disability Factors Scales series (DFS-G).* Unpublished manuscript. New York University School of Education, New York. (Cited and reviewed by Antonak & Livneh, 1988.)
Purpose	The purpose of the DFS-G is to measure attitudes toward people with disabilities as a multidimensional construct.
Description	The DFS-G is a 69-item measure rated on a 6-point Likert-type scale ranging from 1 = Strongly Agree to 6 = Strongly Disagree. The content of the items refers to a number of disabilities such as amputation, blindness, deafness, epilepsy, heart trouble, cancer, paralysis, scarring, and hunchback. It is composed of seven factors: (1) Interaction Strain, (2) Rejection of Intimacy, (3) Generalized Rejection, (4) Authoritarian Virtuousness, (5) Inferred Emotional Consequences, (6) Distressed Identification, and (7) Imputed Functional Limitations. The original work by Siller (1969) has not been published. But Livneh (1985) published a study using principal component and maximum likelihood factor analysis with varimax and oblique rotation and confirmed the factor structure proposed by Siller (1969) with some variation in the structure coefficients of the items. Other studies have also supported the original factor structure with variations in the item's correlation to the various subscales (Weisel & Florian, 1990; Weisel, Kravetz, Florian, & Shurka-Zernitsky, 1988). The DFS-G has also been used internationally with Israeli samples (e.g., Rimmerman, Hosmi, & Duvdevany, 2000; Weisel & Florian, 1990) and Italian samples (Johnson & Darrow, 2003).
Samples	Siller's (1969) unpublished original work developed the DFS-G over time with many samples using mostly college students. Livneh's (1985) published factor analytic study used 200 undergraduate (82%) and graduate (18%) students from 19 different academic areas. The ages ranged from 17 to 61 ($M = 23.5$, $SD = 5.5$), and 72% of the participants were women.

Scoring	The number of items in each subscale is as follows:
	
	    Interaction Strain: 9 items
	    Rejection of Intimacy: 11 items
	    Generalized Rejection: 12 items
	    Authoritarian Virtuousness: 10 Items
	    Inferred Emotional Consequences: 8 items
	    Distressed Identification: 12 items
	    Imputed Functional Limitations: 7 items
	    Total DFS-G: 69 items

	Scores on each subscale are obtained by first reversing the ratings of 11 items, then summing the ratings of items in each subscale. Researchers have also used the average of the item ratings in each subscale. Higher scores reflect more accepting and positive attitudes.
Reliability	In their review of the scale, Antonak and Livneh (1988) report internal consistency coefficients for the DFS-G subscales ranging from .73 for the Imputed Functional Limitations subscale to .87 for the Distressed Identification subscale. Roush and Klockars (1988), using a convenience U.S. sample from the general public, and Weisel et al. (1988), using Israeli high school and university students, reported the following Cronbach's alphas, respectively:
	Interaction Strain: Alphas = .78 and .67
	Rejection of Intimacy: Alphas = .88 and .76
	Generalized Rejection: Alphas = .93 and .59
	Authoritarian Virtuousness: Alphas = .89 and .75
	Inferred Emotional Consequences: Alphas = .82 and .74
	Distressed Identification: Alphas = .85 and .81
	Imputed Functional Limitations: Alphas = .64 and .56
Validity	Convergent validity has been shown by the correlation of the DFS-G subscales with scores on Yuker and colleague's (1960) Attitudes Toward Disabled Persons scale (ATDP; Elsberry, 1975). Concerning discriminant validity, Weisel et al. (1988) correlated the Marlowe-Crown Social Desirability Scale (Crowne & Marlowe, 1964) with the DFS-G subscales using Israeli students and showed low but statistically significant correlations with Distressed Identification, Rejection of Intimacy, and Interaction Strain but no correlations with the other subscales.
	Criterion validity was demonstrated by statistically significant positive correlations of educational level with Interaction Strain, Authoritarian Virtuousness, and Distressed Identification (Roush & Klockars, 1988). Berrol (1984) also showed significant interactions of DFS-G scale scores with education, age, and experience with persons with disabilities. Rimmerman et al. (2003) demonstrated known-group validity by showing predictable differences among university students on a number of the DFS-G subscales due to contact with disabled students in a tutoring situation. Also, Berrol (1984) reported differences between pre- and posttests of groups in training programs for special physical education, suggesting predictive validity.
Related References	Berrol, C. F. (1984). Training attitudes toward disabled persons: Effect of a special physical education program. *Archives of Physical Medicine and Rehabilitation, 65,* 760–765.
	Florian, V., Weisel, A., Kravetz, S., & Shurka-Zernitsky, E. (1989). Attitudes in the kibbutz and city toward persons with disabilities: A multifactorial comparison. *Rehabilitation Counseling Bulletin, 32,* 210–218.

(Continued)

	Johnson, C., & Darrow, A.-A. (Winter 2003). Attitudes of junior high school music students from Italy and the USA toward individuals with disability. *Bulletin of the Council for Research in Music Education, 155,* 33–43. Roush, S., & Klockars, A. J. (1988). Construct validation of two scales measuring attitudes toward persons with disabilities. *Journal of Rehabilitation, 54,* 25–30.
Language Versions	English, Hebrew, and Italian
Contact	Jerome Siller New York University, School of Culture, Education, and Human Development 82 Washington Square East New York, NY 10003

10.15.4 Name of the Measure	Disability Social Relations Generalized Disability DSRGD
Primary Reference	Hergenrather, K., & Rhodes, S. (2007). Exploring undergraduate student attitudes toward persons with disabilities: Application of the Disability Social Relationship Scale. *Rehabilitation Counseling Bulletin, 50,* 66–75.
Purpose	The purpose of DSRGD is to measure attitudes toward persons with disabilities in the social contexts of dating, marriage, and work.
Description	The DSRGD is a 17-item measure rated on a 4-point Likert-type scale ranging from 1 = Strongly Disagree to 4 = Strongly Agree. It has three subscales: (1) Dating, (2) Marriage, and (3) Work. The DSRGD is based on the Disability Social Relationship scale (DSR) originally developed by Grand, Bernier, and Strohmer (1982). The DSR consisted of the same three subscales with six items in each subscale. Each subscale of the DSR was written in reference to four different disabilities (amputation, visual impairment, cerebral palsy, and epilepsy), and items were rated on a two-response scale. For the DSRGD, the DSR items were altered to reflect general disability rather than the four specific disabilities and rated on a 4-point Likert-type scale. The alterations were examined by expert panels and piloted with 15 undergraduates, and recommended changes were made, preserving all 18 items. The DSRGD items were subjected to principal axis factor analysis with oblique rotation. Three factors emerged that explained 63.77% of the total variance. The variances explained were 39.97% for the Dating factor, 14.05% for the Marriage factor, and 9.75% for the Work factor. One of the items in the Work subscale was dropped due to it did not low structure coefficients properly. The items of the DSRGD can be found in the primary reference.
Samples	The sample of convenience was composed of 1,013 undergraduate students, 60.2% women and 39.8% men, enrolled at a large southern university. Trained students in a rehabilitation services course recruited the participants by a snowball technique. The mean age of the sample was 22.1 years. The racial/ethnic composition of the sample was 88.2% White American, 9.8% African American, .7% Latino/a American, .4% Native American, and .2% Other. Of the total sample, 3.6% identified as persons with disabilities, and 97.7% reported having had social interactions with a person with a disability.
Scoring	The number of items in the three subscales was as follows: Dating: 6 items Marriage: 6 items Work: 5 items Total DSRGD: 17 items The scores are obtained by summing the ratings of the items in the subscales. One item in the dating subscale is reverse-scored. The authors recommend the use of the total summated score in addition to the subscale scores.

(Continued)

(Continued)

Reliability	The Cronbach's alphas of the subscale scores were as follows: Dating: Alpha = .92 Marriage: Alpha = .83 Work: Alpha = .81 The split-half coefficient with Spearman-Brown correction for the whole scale was .89.
Validity	To demonstrate criterion-related validity, the scores of women and men were compared. As expected, women scored statistically significantly higher than men on the total DSRGD scale as well as on the three subscales. Moreover, as expected, there were statistically significant attitude differences between the subscales, suggesting the effect of social contexts on attitudes toward persons with disabilities. No race/ethnicity or age differences were obtained.
Related References	Grand, S. A., Bernier, J. E., & Strohmer, D. C. (1982). Attitudes toward disabled persons as a function of social context and specific disability. *Rehabilitation Psychology, 27,* 165–173. Gordon, E. D., Minnes, P. M., & Holden, R. R. (1990). The structure of attitudes toward persons with disability, when specific disability and context are considered. *Rehabilitation Psychology, 35,* 79–90.
Language Versions	English
Contact	Keneth C. Hegenrather Department of Counseling, Human and Organizational Studies Graduate School of Education and Human Development The George Washington University 2134 G. St. NW., Room 318 Washington, DC 20037 Email: hegenkc@gwu.edu

10.15.5 Name of the Measure	Interaction With Disabled Persons Scale IDP
Primary Reference	Gething, L. (1991). *The Interaction with Disabled Persons Scale: Manual and kit.* Sydney, Australia: University of Sydney. Gething, L. (1994). The Interaction with Disables Persons Scale. *Journal of Social Behavior and Personality, 9,* 23–42.
Purpose	The IDP measures discomfort in social interactions with people with disabilities.
Description	The IDP is a 20-item measure rated on a 5-point Likert-type scale ranging from 1 = Strongly Disagree to 5 = Strongly Agree with a midpoint of 3 = Not sure. It is composed of six correlated subscales: (1) Discomfort in Social Interactions, (2) Coping/Succumbing Framework, (3) Perceived level of Information, (4) Vulnerability, (5) Coping, and (6) Vulnerability (second scale). The scale was developed over several years in the 1980s using multiple Australian samples. Open-ended responses written by 633 people in 1980 lead to the initial pool of 30 items selected by a panel of expert judges, including persons with disabilities. In early analysis, 10 items were dropped because of low structural coefficients. In a later factor analysis using a very large database ($N = 5468$), two more items were dropped because of low structural coefficients, and three of the items correlated on two factors each. The factor structure of the IDP has varied from one to six factors depending on the populations used. MacLean and Gannon (1995), using Australian university students, reported a 10-item two-factor structure (Discomfort and Sympathy). Forlin, Fogarty, and Caroll (1999), using Australian and South African university students, reported an 18-item, six-factor structure (Discomfort, Sympathy, Uncertainty, Fear, Coping, and Vulnerability). Loo (2001), using Canadian management undergraduates, was unable to support the Gething (1994) six-factor or MacLean and Gannon (1995) two-factor structures with confirmatory factor analysis. Thomas, Palmer, Coker-Juneau, and Williams (2003), using university students from southern United States, reported support for a 14-item, three-factor structure (Discomfort, Empathy, and Fear of Disability). Wallymahmed, McKay-Moffat, and Cunningham (2007), using practicing midwives in the northeast of England, reported an 18-item, five-factor structure (Discomfort, Knowledge & Sensitivity, Disability as Misfortune, Rising to the Occasion, and Vulnerability/Coping). Finally, Iacono, Tracy, Keating, and Brown (2009) report support for a five-item, one-factor structure (Discomfort). In spite of the uncertainty of the IDP's factor structure, it continues to be a popular measure in studies of attitudes and attitude change toward persons with disabilities (e.g., Campbell, Gilmore, & Cuskelly, 2003; Johnson, Bloomberg, & Iacono, 2008; Tracy & Iacono, 2008).
Samples	A large sample ($N = 5,468$) of respondents representing a cross-section of Australians collected between 1988–1990 was combined for standardization purposes.

(Continued)

(Continued)

Scoring	Number of items in IDP scales is as follows:
	
	    Discomfort: 6 items
	    Coping/Succumbing: 4 items
	    Information: 5 items
	    Vulnerability: 2 items
	    Coping: 2 items
	    Vulnerability (second scale): 2 items
	    Total IDPL: 20 items
	
	First three items are reverse scored; then the scores are obtained by summing the responses. The total scores range from 20 to 120. Higher scores indicate more discomfort. The IDP items may be found in Gething (1994).

Reliability	The Cronbach's alpha assessed for the total IDP scores on 15 different samples ranged from .74 to .86. The Cronbach's alpha for the scores using the total standardization Australian sample was .79. Alphas for subscales are not provided. Test-retest reliability of the total IDP scale scores assessed on eight occasions with a variety of samples including the general public, professionals, and students ranged from .51 for 1-year interval to .82 for 2-week interval. The IDP was administered in four translations to international samples in 1992–1993, including, Canada, Croatia, England, Germany, Hong Kong, Poland, Scotland, and United States with acceptable Cronbach's alphas ranging from .68 to .77, except for the Croatian sample, which was .54 (where a civil war was raging at the time).
Validity	Convergent validity was demonstrated with other measures of attitudes toward persons with disabilities using a cross-section of Australians ($n = 227$). The correlation of the IDP total score was significantly correlated with the total score of the Attitude Toward Disabled Persons Form O (ATDP; Yuker, Block, & Campbell, 1960) and with the total score of the Disability Factor Scales (DFS; Siller, Chipman, Ferguson, & Vann, 1967). Those with more frequent contact with persons with disabilities, higher levels of education, older persons, and health and rehabilitation professionals showed more positive attitudes on the IDP than those with less contact and less education and who were members of the general public, respectively, suggesting known-group validity. Also, IDP was used to assess positive attitude change as a result of training and awareness workshops (Gething, 1984), and as a result of taking preservice courses by student teachers (Campbell et al., 2003), suggesting predictive validity.
Related References	Brown, T., Mu, K., Peyton, C. G., et al. (2009). Occupational therapy students' attitudes towards individuals with disabilities: A comparison between Australia, Taiwan, the United Kingdom, and the United States. *Research in Developmental Disabilities: A Multidisciplinary Journal, 30,* 1541–1555.

	Iacono, T., Tracy, J., Keating, J., & Brown, T. (2009). The Interaction with Disabled Persons scale: Revisiting its internal consistency and factor structure, and examining item-level properties. *Research in Developmental Disabilities, 30,* 1490–1501.
	Johnson, H., Bloomberg, K., & Iacono, T. (2008). Student and professional attitudes and interests in working with people with complex communication needs. *International Journal of Speech-Language Pathology, 10,* 286–296.
	Tracy, J., & Iacono, T. (2008). People with developmental disabilities teaching medical students—Does it make a difference? *Journal of Intellectual and Developmental Disabilities, 33,* 345–348.
Language Versions	Croat, English, French, German, Polish, and Urdu
Availability	Lindsay Gething Community Disability and Ageing Program Department of Behavioural and Social Sciences in Nursing The University of Sydney NSW 2006 Australia Email: lgething@mallett.nursing.usyd.edu.au

10.15.6 Name of the Measure	Multidimensional Attitude Scale Toward Persons With Disabilities MAS
Primary Reference	Findler, L., Vilchinsky, N., & Werner, S. (2007). The Multidimensional Attitude Scale Toward Persons with Disabilities (MAS): Construction and validation. *Rehabilitation Counseling Bulletin, 50,* 166–167.
Purpose	The purpose of MAS is to measure attitudes toward persons with disabilities in the domains of affect, cognition, and behavior.
Description	The MAS is a 34-item measure composed of three subscales: (1) Affects, (2) Cognitions, and (3) Behaviors. The items are rated on a 5-point Likert-type scale ranging from 1 = Not at All to 5 = Very Much.
	Participants are asked to read a vignette that describes the interaction between a male and a female in a wheelchair and a "Joseph" or a "Michelle," and then are asked to respond to the scale indicating the degree to which they thought "Joseph" or "Michelle" would feel, think, and act in certain ways based on the scale items. For one half of the respondents, the person in the wheelchair was a male and for the other half a female, thus creating four groups, participant gender X gender of person in wheelchair.
	The initial pool of 79 items was identified through theoretical models in the literature on affect, cognition, and behavior (Izard, 2004; Katz, Hass, & Bailey, 1988; Russell & Barrett, 1999) and adopted from existing measures (Fichten & Amsel, 1988). The vignette and the items were translated into Hebrew using the back-translation method and administered to Jewish Israelis. Through a pilot study with 77 participants, the pool was reduced to 47 items. These items were then subjected to a principal components factor analysis that yielded three distinct factors that explained 47.5% of the total variance with a total of 34 items with the following subscale structure: Affects, Cognitions, and Behaviors.
Samples	The sample was composed of 132 Jewish Israelis, 52% men and 48% women, with a mean age of 29.85 ($SD = 11.28$). The mean years of education was 14 years ($SD = 2.33$), and 69% indicated they had prior acquaintance with a person with disabilities. The sample was obtained through a snowball technique with a group of students and research assistants who asked friends, classmates, and acquaintances to complete the questionnaires. The authors do not indicate if the respondents had the option of completing the questionnaire in Hebrew or English.
Scoring	The number of items in the subscales is as follows:
	Affects: 16 items
	Cognitions: 10 items
	Behaviors: 8 items
	Total MAS: 34 items
	Fifteen of the items are reverse-coded and then the average ratings of the items in each subscale are computed. Higher scores indicate more negative attitude. The items of the MAS may be found in the primary reference.

Reliability	The Cronbach's alphas of the scores of the three subscales were as follows:
	Affects: Alpha = .90
	Cognitions: Alpha = .88
	Behaviors: Alpha = .83
Validity	For convergent validity, the MAS subscale scores were correlated with scores on the Attitude Toward Disabled Persons (ATDP; Yuker, Block, & Young, 1966). The ATDP was correlated positively with the Affects and Behaviors (subscales of the MAS but uncorrelated with Cognitions). Also, higher scores on the Rosenberg Self-Esteem Scale (Rosenberg, 1979) were associated with more positive attitudes on the Affects, Cognitions, and Behaviors subscales of the MAS. Criterion-related validity was shown by the association of increased age with more positive attitudes on the Affects and Behaviors subscales of the MAS. And women, as expected, showed less negative behavioral intentions than men on the Behaviors subscale of the MAS.
Related References	
Language Versions	English and Hebrew
Contact	Liora Findler
	Bar-Ilan University, School of Social Work
	Ramat Gan, 52900
	Israel
	Email: findler@mail.biu.ac.il

10.15.7 Name of the Measure	Scale of Attitudes Toward Disabled Persons SADP
Primary Reference	Antonak, R. F. (1982). Development and psychometric analysis of the Scale of Attitudes toward Disabled Persons. *Journal of Applied Rehabilitation Counseling, 13*, 22–29.
Purpose	The purpose of SADP is to measure generalized attitudes toward disabled persons.
Description	The SADP is a 24-item measure of attitudes toward disabled persons as a group rated on a 6-point Likert-type scale ranging from -3 = I Disagree Very Much to $+3$ = I Agree Very Much with no neutral point. An initial pool of 176 items was generated through a search of the literature, previously published measures, and an analysis of open-ended interviews with experts. Ratings by a panel of 10 expert judges reduced the number of items to 64, which were further reduced to 30 items by a series of item, scale, and factor analyses of responses by 228 graduate and undergraduate students and human service professionals. A second similar sample of 225 individuals was used in a principal components analysis with varimax rotation that yielded the 24-item measure with three factors: (1) Optimism-Human Rights that explained 67% of the total variance; (2) Behavioral Misconceptions that explained 18% of the total variance; and (3) Pessimism-Hopelessness that explained 15% of the total variance. Half the items are negatively stated and half are positively stated.
Samples	The second sample of 225 individuals was composed of 197 women and 28 men enrolled at a northeastern university in undergraduate ($n = 146$), graduate ($n = 46$), and professional-development ($n = 33$) courses. The mean age was 23.90 years ($SD = 6.74$, range from 17 to 53 years).
Scoring	The number of items in the subscales is as follows: Optimism-Human Rights: 11 items Behavioral Misconceptions: 7 items Pessimism-Hopelessness: 6 items Total SADP: 24 items To obtain the total score, the signs of the 12 negative items are reversed, the ratings are summed and then a constant value of 72 is added to eliminate negative scores. Higher scores indicate more favorable attitude, and the scores range from 0 to 144. Subscale scores are obtained similarly.
Reliability	The Cronbach's alpha values are as follows: Optimism-Human Rights: Alpha = .81 Behavioral Misconceptions: Alpha = .71 Pessimism-Hopelessness: Alpha = .82 Total SADP: Alpha = .88

	The Spearman-Brown corrected split-half reliability estimates were as follows:
	
	    Optimism-Human Rights: $r = .71$
	
	    Behavioral Misconceptions: $r = .55$
	
	    Pessimism-Hopelessness: $r = .61$
	
	    Total SADP: $r = .81$

Validity	Convergent validity was demonstrated by correlating the SADP subscale scores with the 18-item reduced version of the Attitude Toward Disabled Persons (ATDP Form O; Yuker, Block, & Campbell, 1960). All the SADP subscales and the total score were found to be statistically significantly correlated with the ATDP Form O. The SADP scores were statistically significantly correlated with educational level and a dummy dichotomous variable representing human service providers and nonproviders, suggesting criterion-related validity.
Related References	Antonak, R. F. (1982). Development and psychometric analysis of the Scale of Attitudes Toward Disabled Persons. *The Journal of Applied Rehabilitation, 13,* 22–29. Chan, F., Hua, M.-S., Ju, J. J., & Lam, C. S. (1984). Factorial structure of the Chinese Scale of Attitude Towards Disabled Persons: A cross-cultural validation. *International Journal of Rehabilitation Research, 7,* 317–319. Chenoweth, L., Pryor, J., Jeon, Y.-H., & Hall-Pullin, L. (2004). Disability-specific preparation programme plays an important role in shaping students' attitudes towards disablement and patients with disabilities. *Learning in Health and Social Care, 3,* 83–91. Wong, D. K. P. (2008). Do contacts make a difference? The effects of mainstreaming on student attitudes toward people with disabilities. *Research in Developmental Disabilities, 29,* 70–82.
Language Versions	English and Chinese
Contact	Dr. Richard F. Antonak Department of Counseling and School Psychology University of Massachusetts Boston, 100 Morrissey Blvd. Boston, MA 02125–3393 Tel: (617) 287–5600 Email: Richard.Antonak@umb.edu

10.15.8 Name of the Measure	Questions About Disability Survey QADS
Primary Reference	Graf, N. M., Blankenship, C. J., Sanchez, G., & Carlson, R. (2007). Living on the line: Mexican and Mexican American attitudes toward disability. *Rehabilitation Counseling Bulletin, 50,* 153–165.
Purpose	The purpose of QADS is to measure the attitudes of Mexican and Mexican Americans toward persons with disabilities in general.
Description	The QADS is 51-item measure rated on a 5-point Likert-type scale ranging from 1 = Always to 5 = Never. An initial pool of 56 items was developed using a review of the literature, focus groups with college students, and three expert judges. Exploratory factor analysis with varimax rotation, using structural coefficients of .40 and higher for retention, yielded five factors that explained 49% of the total variance: (1) Maleficent God, (2) Social Issues-Outer Circle, (3) Expectation, (4) Beneficent God, and (5) Social Issues-Inner Circle. Although five items did not correlate on any factor, the authors present and discuss the responses to those items. Also, the two spirituality factors, Maleficent God and Beneficent God, are not presented in the primary article. However, a reference is provided to an unpublished manuscript where they are discussed (Blankenship & Glover-Graf, 2006).
Samples	The convenience sample of $N = 160$ was composed of the general population who came from the Rio Grande Valley in South Texas and the La Frontera area in the northeast part of the state of Tamaulipas, Mexico. Of the total sample, 51% identified themselves as Mexican and 49% as Mexican American or American; 49% were women and 51% were men; the ages ranged from 18 to 77 years ($M = 33.4$, $SD = 12.6$); the years lived in Mexico ranged from 1 to 62 ($M = 21.4$, $SD = 15.8$) and the years lived in Texas ranged from 1 to 50 ($M = 13.7$, $SD = 14.4$); the years of education ranged from 0 to 17 years ($M = 10.0$, $SD = 3.7$); and 9.4% reported having a disability.

Scoring	The number of items in the five factors are as follows:
	
	    Maleficent God: 17 items
	
	    Social Issues-Outer Circle: 10 items
	
	    Expectations: 12 items
	
	    Beneficent God: 8 items
	
	    Social Issues-Inner Circle: 4 items
	
	    Total QADS: 51 items
	
	Factors were not presented as summated subscale scores. Rather, means of responses to individual items within the three factors (excluding factors 1 and 4) were presented and discussed in the context of demographic differences. Higher scores reflect more positive attitudes. The scale items can be found in the primary reference.

Reliability	The Cronbach's alphas of the factors were as follows:
	Maleficent God: Alpha = .89
	Social Issues-Outer Circle: Alpha = .89
	Expectations: Alpha = .87
	Beneficent God: Alpha = .88
	Social Issues-Inner Circle: Alpha = .22.
Validity	Information about the validity of the whole measure and its factor subscales beyond the factor analysis was not provided. However, the authors reported comparison of item means for nationality, gender, and three age categories: 24 years and younger, between 25 and 34 years, and over the age of 35 years. For the Social Issues-Outer Circle factor, nationality and gender differences on several items were reported, but no age differences were found. For the Expectations factor, nationality and age differences on several items were reported, but no gender differences were found. For the Social Issues-Inner Circle factor, nationality and gender differences on several items were reported, but no age difference was found.
Related References	
Language Versions	English and Spanish
Contact	Noreen M. Graf Department of Rehabilitation The University of Texas-Pan American 1201 W. University Drive Edinburg, TX 78541 Email: nmgraf@panam.edu

10.15.9 Name of the Measure	Contact With Disabled Persons Scale CDP
Primary Reference	Pruett, S. R., Lee, E.-J., Chan, F., Wang, M. H., & Lane, F. J. (2008). Dimensionality of the Contact with Disabled Persons Scale: Results from exploratory and confirmatory factor analysis. *Rehabilitation Counseling Bulletin, 51,* 210–220. Yuker, H. E., & Hurley, M. K. (1987). Contact with and attitudes toward people with disabilities: The measurement of intergroup contact. *Rehabilitation Psychology, 32,* 145–154.
Purpose	The purpose of CDP is to measure negative and positive contact with persons with disabilities.
Description	The CDP is a 16-item measure rated on a 5-point time-frequency scale ranging from 1 = Never to 5 = Very often. The measure was originally developed by Yuker and Hurley (1987) to measure negative and positive contact experiences of nondisabled persons with persons with disabilities based on Allport's (1979) contact hypothesis to reduce intergroup bias. It was composed of 20 items and was conceptualized and used as a unidimensional measure. Pruett, Lee, Chan, Wang, and Lane (2008) subjected the measure to exploratory and confirmatory factor analyses. The exploratory factor analysis using principal axis extraction and oblique rotation yielded three factors that explained 49.5% of the variance. Items with factor correlations of .45 in one and less than .30 in other factors were retained. Four items were eliminated from the original scale. The factors were (1) General Interpersonal Contact, (2) Positive Contact Experiences, and (3) Negative Contact Experiences. Confirmatory factor analysis showed that the three-factor model had the best fit with the Comparative Fit Index (CFI) of .95 and the goodness of fit index (GFI) of .90. The root mean square error of approximation (RMSEA) was .07.
Samples and Norms	The sample was composed of 552 undergraduate and graduate students pooled from a number of research projects that utilized the CDP. The majority ($n = 321$) were rehabilitation counseling or rehabilitation services majors. Majority of participants were female ($n = 480$). Most of the participants were White American ($n = 394$), followed by African American ($n = 46$), Latino/a American ($n = 39$), Asian American ($n = 10$), and other ($n = 35$). Twenty-eight participants did not provide racial background. The majority came from younger age groups (17–21 years, $n = 209$; 22–30 years, $n = 230$). The sample was split into two halves. The first half was used to conduct the exploratory factor analysis, and the second half was used to conduct the confirmatory factor analysis.
Scoring	The number of items in the three subscales is as follows: General Interpersonal Contacts: 9 items Positive Contact Experiences: 4 items Negative Contact Experiences: 3 items Total CDP: 16 items

	It is not indicated if the subscale scores are obtained by summing or averaging the item ratings. Also, no total score is computed.
Reliability	The Cronbach's alphas of the subscale scores were as follows: General Interpersonal Contacts: Alpha = .88 Positive Contact Experiences: Alpha = .86 Negative Contact Experiences: Alpha = .76
Validity	Suggesting evidence of convergent validity, the General Interpersonal Contacts and the Positive Contact Experiences, but not the Negative Contact Experiences, subscale scores were correlated significantly and positively with the Attitudes Toward Disabled Persons Scale—form A (ATDP-A; Yuker & Block, 1986) and the Disability Attitudes Implicit Association Test (DA-IAT; Pruett & Chan, 2006). Suggesting evidence of discriminant validity, the General Interpersonal Contacts and the Positive Contact Experiences subscale scores were uncorrelated with the Marlowe-Crowne Social Desirability Scale—Short Form C (MCSDS-C; Reynolds, 1982). However, the Negative Contact Experiences scores were negatively correlated with the MCDSDS-C, suggesting some social desirability bias. To examine criterion validity, CDP scores were related to demographic factors of age, gender, racial background, number of disability-related courses, and number of disability-related field courses (internships), being with and without disability. Older individuals and those with more courses and field experience scores tended to score higher on all three subscales; males endorsed more general contact than females, persons with disabilities reported more general and more positive contact with persons with disabilities; there were no racial group differences on the General Interpersonal Contacts and Positive Contact Experiences subscales, but non-White Americans scored lower on the Negative Contact Experiences subscale.
Related References	
Language Versions	English
Contact	Steven R. Pruett Ohio State University 480 Medical Center Dr. Columbus, OH 43210 Tel: (614) 293–3830

10.16 MEASURES OF ATTITUDES TOWARD PERSONS WITH MENTAL RETARDATION

10.16.1 Name of the Measure	Attitudes Toward Mentally Retarded People Scale AMRP
Primary Reference	Bartlett, C. J., Quay, L. C., & Wrightsman, L. S., Jr. (1960). A comparison of two methods of attitude measurement: Likert-type and forced choice. *Educational and Psychological Measurement, 20*, 699–704.
Purpose	The purpose of the AMRP is to measure attitudes toward people with mental retardation among attendant employees of state institutions for people with mental retardation
Description	The AMRP is a 24-item measure rated on a 3-point Likert-type scale with "T" = True, "?" = Undecided, and "F" = False.
	An initial pool of 175 items was created and subjected to a factor analysis with a sample of 99 attendants using hierarchical factor solution that generated one general factor and four group factors. The 24 items with structure coefficients of .30 on the general factor were selected for the AMRP. The items of the scale may be found in Antonak and Livneh (1988).
Samples	One sample of 99 attendants at an institution for people with mental retardation was used for factor analysis and item reduction. A second sample of 97 attendants from another institution was used for reliability and validity analysis. In the second sample, 68 attendants participated in a lecture intended to change attitudes toward mentally retarded, and a control group of 17 attendants did not participate in the lecture. Both groups completed the AMRP before and after the lecture (see below for results).
Scoring	Of the 24 items, 14 are worded such that a "T" response indicates an unfavorable attitude, and for 10 of the items a "T" response indicates a favorable attitude. Favorable responses are scored as 2, undecided as 1, and unfavorable responses as 0. The score is the sum of the responses that ranges from 0 to 48.
Reliability	The Spearman-Brown corrected split-half reliability for the second sample that participated in the lecture was .80. The test-retest reliability using the participants in the control group ($n = 17$) was .71.
Validity	The comparison of pre- and postlecture responses showed statistically significantly increased positive attitudes, suggesting predictive validity.
Related References	Quay, L. C., Bartlett, C. J., Wrightsman, L. S., Jr., & Catron, D. (1961). Attitude change in attendant employees. *Journal of Social Psychology, 55*, 27–31.
Language Versions	English
Contact	Contact information of author is unknown.

10.16.2 Name of the Measure	Attitudes Toward the Retarded ATR
Primary Reference	Efron, R. R., & Efron, H. Y. (1967). Measurement of attitudes toward the retarded and an application with educators. *American Journal of Mental Deficiency, 72,* 100–106.
Purpose	The purpose of the ATR is to measure attitudes toward people with mental retardation.
Description	The ATR is a 50-item measure rated on a 6-point Likert-type scale ranging from 1 = Strongly Agree to 6 = Strongly Disagree. An initial pool of 70 items was developed by the investigator covering various conceptual areas of concern, including eight items from the Authoritarian F scale (Adorno, Frankel-Brunswik, Levinson, & Stanford, 1950), three items from the Opinion about Mental Illness scale (Cohen & Struening, 1962), and nine factual knowledge items taken from the Presidential Panel report on mental retardation (Panel on Mental Retardation, 1962). The responses, excluding knowledge items, were subjected to a principal components analysis with varimax rotation that yielded six factors retaining 50 usable items: (1) Segregation via Institutionalization, explained 22% of the variance, (2) Cultural Deprivation, explained 14% of the variance, (3) Noncondemnatory Etiology, explained 14% of the variance, (4) Personal Exclusion, explained 20% of the variance, (5) Authoritarianism, explained 18% of the variance, and (6) Hopelessness, explained 12% of the variance. The following description of retardation was provided at the top of the measure: "By retardation we mean individuals who are in the educable classification, that is, those with IQs of at least 50." The items include language that would be considered sexist.
Samples	The sample was composed of 235 individuals including students, teachers of people who are retarded, and the general public all taking courses at Newark State College: 157 were female and 78 male; 80 were taking undergraduate courses and 155 taking graduate courses; the mean age was 30.0 years (*SD* = 10.6); 9% were educators of individuals with mental retardation, 6% were educators in other fields of special education, 39% were educators in other than special education fields, 17% were students in mental retardation, 3% were students in other fields of special education, 14% were students in other education fields, 1% were students in other fields than education, and 10% came from other occupations; 113 were single, 118 were married, and 4 were in other classifications of marriage.

Scoring	The following are the number of items in the subscales:
	
	    Segregation via Institutionalization: 9 items
	
	    Cultural Deprivation: 6 items
	
	    Noncondemnatory Etiology: 8 items

(Continued)

(Continued)

	Personal Exclusion: 10 items Authoritarianism: 11 items Hopelessness: 6 items Total ATR: 50 items The subscale scores were computed using weighted factor scores. No other scoring information is provided. Items may be found in the primary reference.
Reliability	The internal consistency reliability coefficients (unspecified) were as follows: Segregation via Institutionalization: Alpha = .79 Cultural Deprivation: Alpha = .63 Noncondemnatory Etiology: Alpha = .57 Personal Exclusion: Alpha = .73 Authoritarianism: Alpha = .69 Hopelessness: Alpha = .59
Validity	Known-group validity was shown by expected differences between groups. Comparison of occupation groups found significant differences in the factor scores in the more favorable direction between teachers of students with retardation and people in general education on all subscales except on Noncondemnatory Etiology and Hopelessness. Also, students in retardation scored more favorably than people in general education on all the subscales except on Noncondemnatory Etiology and Personal Exclusion. None of the subscale scores were related to age, sex, marital status, and educational level.
Related References	Aminidav, C., & Weller, L. (1995). Effects of country of origin, sex, religiosity and social class on breadth of knowledge of retardation. *The British Journal of Developmental Disabilities, 41,* 48–55. Overback, D. (1971). Attitude sampling of institutional charge attendant personnel: Cues for intervention. *Mental Retardation 9,* 8–10.
Language Versions	English
Contact	Author contact information unknown.

10.16.3 Name of the Measure	Community Living Attitudes Scale—Mental Retardation CLAS-MR
Primary Reference	Henry, D., Keys, C., Jopp, D., & Balcazar, F. (1996). The Community Living Attitudes Scale, Mental Retardation Form: Development and psychometric properties. *Mental Retardation, 34,* 149–158.
Purpose	The purpose of CLAS-MR is to measure attitudes of the general public toward people with mental retardation, their empowerment, and inclusion in community life.
Description	The CLAS-MR is a 40-item measure rated on a 6-point Likert-type scale ranging from 1 = Strongly Disagree to 6 = Strongly Agree. An initial pool of 67 items was developed by consultation with self-advocates and consumers of mental retardation services, a review of the literature on the self-advocacy movement, and adapting and rewriting several items from the Community Attitudes Toward Mental Illness scale (CATMI; Taylor & Dear, 1981). The factors are (1) Empowerment, (2) Exclusion, (3) Sheltering, and (4) Similarity. An exploratory factor analysis using principal components and varimax rotation yielded a four-factor solution that explained 36.1% of the variance. A confirmatory factor analysis with another sample demonstrated good fit with all 40 items correlating appropriately on their original subscales.
Samples	Three samples were used in the development of the CLAS-MR. The sample for the exploratory factor analysis was composed of 283 participants: 80 were undergraduates and 203 were community members; the ages ranged from 16 to 69 (*Median* = 26); 51.1% were female; 37.3% were students, 31.7% were business or government employees; 11.9% were educators or human service personnel, and 7.1% were laborers; 20.4% reported having a relative or a friend with mental retardation. A second sample of 104 undergraduates was used for test-retest reliability and validity assessment that completed the CLAS-MR and other measures twice with a 1-month interval. For confirmatory factor analysis, a sample of 355 staff members who worked in community agencies that served people with mental retardation was used: 45.3% were direct service providers, 25.5% were first-line supervisors, 22.1% were managers, and the remainder 7.1% had other job titles.

Scoring	The number of items in the subscales is as follows:
	
	   Empowerment: 13 items
	
	   Exclusion: 8 items
	
	   Sheltering: 7 items
	
	   Similarity: 12 items
	
	   Total CLAS-MR: 40 items
	
	Half the items are reverse scored. The subscale scores are obtained by averaging the ratings of items in the subscales. No total score is computed. Higher scores indicated more favorable attitudes.

(Continued)

(Continued)

Reliability	The Cronbach's alphas of the subscale scores were as follows:
	Empowerment: Alpha = .86
	Exclusion: Alpha = .77
	Sheltering: Alpha = .70
	Similarity: Alpha = .75
	The 1-month test-retest reliability indices were as follows:
	Empowerment: $r = .74$
	Exclusion: $r = .71$
	Sheltering: $r = .70$
	Similarity: $r = .75$
Validity	Along with the CLAS-MR, the validation sample also completed the Community Attitudes Toward Mental Illness scale (CATMI; Taylor & Dear, 1981), the Attitudes Toward Disabled Persons scale (ATDP; Antonak, 1982), and the Balanced Inventory of Social Desirability (BISD; Paulhus, 1984).
	Criterion validity was demonstrated as follows: All the subscales of the CLAS-MR were statistically significantly correlated moderately and in the appropriate direction with the ATDP subscales of Optimism-Rights, Behavioral Misconceptions, and Pessimism-Optimism. They were also statistically significantly correlated moderately and in the appropriate direction with the CATMI subscales of Benevolence, Social Restrictiveness, and Community Mental Health Ideology. The Authoritarian subscale of the CATMI was statistically significantly correlated only with the Sheltering and Exclusion subscales of the CLAS-MR.
	Discriminant validity was demonstrated as follows: None of the CLAS-MR subscales were correlated with the two BISD social desirability subscales of Impression Management and Self-Deception.
Related References	Henry, D. B., Duvdevany, I., Keys, C. B., Balcazar, F. E., & Walsh, K. (2004). Attitudes of American and Israeli staff toward people with intellectual disabilities. *Mental Retardation, 42,* 26–36.
	McDonald, K. E., Keys, C. B., & Henry, D. B. (2008). Gatekeepers of science: Attitudes toward the research participation of adults with intellectual disability. *American Journal on Mental Retardation, 113,* 466–478.
	Schwartz, C., & Armony-Sivan, R. (2001). Students' attitudes to the inclusion of people with disabilities in the community. *Disability and Society, 16,* 403–413.
Language Versions	English and Hebrew
Contact	Henry B. David
	Institute of Juvenile Research
	Department of Psychiatry
	University of Illinois at Chicago
	840 S. Wood Street
	Chicago, IL 60612
	Email: dhenry@uic.edu

10.16.4 Name of the Measure	Mental Retardation Attitude Inventory—Revised MRAI-R
Primary Reference	Antonak, R. F., & Harth, R. (1994). Psychometric analysis and revision of the Mental Retardation Attitude Inventory. *Mental Retardation, 32,* 272–280.
Purpose	The purpose of the MRAI-R is to measure attitudes toward people with mental retardation.
Description	The MRAI-R is a 29-item measure with four-subscales rated on a 4-point Likert-type scale ranging from 1 = Strongly Disagree to 4 = Strongly Agree. The MRAI-R is a revised version of the 50-item, five-subscale original measure of Mental Retardation Attitude Inventory (MRAI; Harth, 1971). The MRAI itself was created based on the items of the five subscales of an instrument developed by Woodmansee and Cook (1967) to measure attitudes toward "Negros" by replacing the word "Negros" with "Retarded." Considering the federal legislation in 1974 regarding integration of children with mental retardation in schools and workplace discrimination, items were modified to reflect the law, and sexist language was eliminated. The five subscales of the original MRAI were (1) Integration-Segregation, (2) Overfavorableness, (3) Social Distance, (4) Private Rights, and (5) Subtle Derogatory Beliefs. Through an initial item, scale, and factor analysis, 21 items were deleted, including the entire set of 10 items of the Overfavorableness subscale because of low item-total correlations, correlations on multiple factors, or low structure coefficients. The remaining 29 items were factor analyzed using a principal axis extraction with an oblique rotation to confirm the multidimensional nature of the remaining four subscales. The remaining four subscales were confirmed and explained 59.88% of the total variance. The factors were as follows: (1) Social Distance, explained 28.14% of the variance, (2) Integration-Segregation, explained 14.32% of the variance, (3) Private Rights, explained 9.88% of the variance, and (4) Subtle Derogatory Beliefs, explained 7.54% of the variance. The items of the MRAI-R can be found in the primary reference.
Samples	The sample was composed of 230 participants from three different states (NC, NH, and WI): 184 were female and 46 were male; 84 were university undergraduates, 61 graduate students from a variety of areas, and 85 were nonmatriculated professionals; the mean age was 29.96 (*SD* = 8.42); the years of education ranged from 13 to 21 years. Four professional categories were identified: regular service providers (e.g., teachers), special service providers (e.g., special educators), ancillary service providers (e.g., speech pathologists), and non–human service providers (e.g., business people). Participants were asked to indicate, on six-point scales, their frequency of contact with individuals with mental retardation, the intensity of their contact, and the general knowledge of the life conditions of such individuals. These, together with a five-point measure of intimacy of their relationship with individuals with mental retardation, were used to compute an overall composite familiarity score.

Scoring	The number of items in each of the four subscales is as follows:
	
	    Social Distance: 7 items
	
	    Integration-Segregation: 8 items

(Continued)

(Continued)

	Private Rights: 7 items Subtle Derogatory Beliefs: 7 items Total MRAI-R: 29 items
	Seventeen of the items are reverse scored such that high scores reflect more positive attitudes. The scores are obtained by summing the items in a subscale. The total score is obtained by summing the subscale scores.
Reliability	The Cronbach's alphas of the four subscales were as follows: Social Distance: Alpha = .82 Integration-Segregation: Alpha = .81 Private Rights: Alpha = .76 Subtle Derogatory Beliefs: Alpha = .73 Total MRAI-R: Alpha = .91 The Spearman-Brown corrected split-half reliability coefficients were as follows: Social Distance: $r = .82$ Integration-Segregation: $r = .86$ Private Rights: $r = .68$ Subtle Derogatory Beliefs: $r = .73$ Total MRAI-R: $r = .91$
Validity	Discriminant validity was demonstrated by comparing the subscale and the total scale scores of those who had high and low scores on the Marlowe-Crowne Social Desirability scale (Crowne & Marlowe, 1960). No significant differences were obtained. Known-group validity was demonstrated by comparing special service providers with other groups. Special service providers scored more favorably than all the other professional groups, who did not differ from each other on the subscales and the total scale scores. Criterion validity was demonstrated in a multiple regression analysis. The best predictors of the overall scale score were familiarity and education. The best predictor of all four subscales was the composite familiarity score alone.
Related References	Hampton, N. Z., & Xiao, F. (2007). Psychometric properties of the Mental Retardation Inventory—Revised in Chinese college students. *Journal of Intellectual Disability Research, 52,* 299–308. Rice, G. J. (2009). Attitudes of undergraduate students toward people with intellectual disabilities: Considerations for future policy makers. *College Student Journal, 43,* 207–215.
Language Versions	English and Chinese
Contact	Richard F. Antonak Department of Counseling and School Psychology University of Massachusetts Boston, 100 Morrissey Blvd. Boston, MA 02125–3393 Tel: (617) 287–5600 Email: Richard.Antonak@umb.edu

10.17 MEASURES OF ATTITUDES TOWARD PERSONS WITH EPILEPSY

10.17.1 **Name of the Measure**	Attitudes and Beliefs About Living With Epilepsy ABLE
Primary Reference	DiIorio, C. A., Kobau, R., Holden, E. W., et al. (2004). Developing a measure to assess attitudes toward epilepsy in the U.S. population. *Epilepsy & Behavior, 5,* 965–975.
Purpose	The purpose of ABLE is to measure the attitudes of the U.S. population toward people with epilepsy.
Description	The title of the scale, ABLE, was named by Kobau, DiIorio, Anderson, and Price (2006) in a later publication. The ABLE is a 29-item measure rated on a 6-point Likert-type scale ranging from 1 = Strongly Agree to 6 = Strongly Disagree. An initial pool of 129 items was compiled by reviewing the literature, an environmental scan, and focus groups. Authors reviewed the items and retained 46. Then nine adults were recruited to evaluate the wording and interpretation of the items. Exploratory factor analysis with principal components and varimax rotation yielded 29 items that produced structure coefficients of at least .40 on a factor. Four factors emerged that explained 34.4% of the variance: (1) Negative Stereotypes, (2) Risk and Safety Concerns, (3) Work and Role Expectations, and (4) Personal Fear and Social Avoidance. The Epilepsy Knowledge Questionnaire (Doughty, Baker, Jacoby, & Lavaud, 2003) was administered along with the ABLE to establish criterion validity. A follow-up study by Kobau, DiIorio, Anderson, and Price (2006) further assessed the reliability and validity of two of the subscales, Negative Stereotypes and Risk and Safety Concerns, using a nationally representative sample of more than 4,000. Confirmatory factor analysis using the 13 items in these two subscales confirmed the underlying constructs and explained 61% of the total variance. The Cronbach's alphas were .86 for Negative Stereotypes and .88 for Risk and Safety Concerns.
Samples	The sample was composed of 758 participants who were selected nationwide through a stratified random sampling design. The data were collected by telephone interviews. Of the total sample, slightly more than half were women, the average age was $M = 45.6$ years, and 64% were employed. The sample consisted of 72% White Americans, 15.6% African Americans, 9.8% Latino/a Americans, 2.4% Native Americans or Alaskan Natives, 2% Asian and Pacific Islander Americans, and 8% were of other race or ethnicity. The retest sample of 100 participants was comparable to the whole sample.

Scoring	The number of items in the four factors are as follows:
	
	  Negative Stereotypes: 7 items
	  Risk and Safety Concerns: 6 items
	  Work and Role Expectations: 8 items
	  Personal Fear and Social Avoidance: 8 items
	  Total ABLE: 20 items
	
	Scores on each factor are obtained by averaging the ratings, after reversing positively stated items. A composite attitude score is also obtained by averaging the scores on the four factors. Higher scores indicate more negative attitudes.

(Continued)

(Continued)

Reliability	The Cronbach's alphas were as follows:
	    Negative Stereotypes: Alpha = .73
	    Risk and Safety Concerns: Alpha = .85
	    Work and Role Expectations: Alpha = .76
	    Personal Fear and Social Avoidance: Alpha = .79
	    Total ABLE: Alpha = .71
	4-week test-retest reliability with 100 participants was as follows:
	    Negative Stereotypes: $r = .58$
	    Risk and Safety Concerns: $r = .72$
	    Work and Role Expectations: $r = .58$
	    Personal Fear and Social Avoidance: $r = .62$
	    Total ABLE: $r = .77$

Validity	Criterion validity evidence was shown by moderate statistically significant negative correlations between the knowledge scores and the ABLE subscale scores. The correlation of the knowledge scores with the composite scores was statistically significantly inversely correlated. Known-group evidence validity was demonstrated by predictable known-group differences. Those with more education reported less Negative Stereotypes, less Risk and Safety Concerns, and less negative Work and Role Expectations; men reported higher than women Personal Fear and Social Avoidance. As predicted from the literature, White Americans compared to African Americans reported less Negative Stereotypes, less Risk and Safety Concerns, and less negative Work and Role Expectations. Also, Latino/a Americans compared to non-Latino/a Americans reported more Negative Stereotypes, and more Risk and Safety Concerns.
Related References	Kobau, R., DiIorio, C. A., Anderson, L. A., & Price, P. (2006). Further validation and reliability testing of the Attitudes and Beliefs about Living with Epilepsy (ABLE) components of the CDC epilepsy program instrument on stigma. *Epilepsy & Behavior, 8,* 552–559. Kobau, R., DiIorio, C., Chapman D., Delvecchio P., & SAMHSA/CDC Mental Illness Stigma Panel Members. (2009). Attitudes about mental illness and its treatment: Validation of a generic scale for public health surveillance of mental illness associated stigma. *Community Mental Health Journal, 46,* 164–176.
Language Versions	English
Contact	Rosemarie Kobau Epilepsy Program National Center for Chronic Disease Prevention and Health Promotion Centers for Disease Control and Prevention 4770 Buford Highway NE, Mailstop K-51 Atlanta, GA 30341 Email: RKabau@cdc.gov Fax: +1 770–488–5486

10.17.2 Name of the Measure	Scale of Knowledge and Attitudes Toward Epilepsy and Persons With Epilepsy ATPE
Primary Reference	Antonak, R. F., & Rankin, P.R. (1982). Measurement and analysis of Knowledge and Attitudes Toward Epilepsy and Persons with Epilepsy. *Social Science and Medicine, 16*, 1591–1593.
Purpose	The purpose of ATPE is to measure knowledge of epilepsy and attitudes toward persons with epilepsy.
Description	The ATPE is a 38-item measure composed of 25 items that measure attitudes toward persons with epilepsy and 13 items that measure knowledge of epilepsy. The items are rated on a 6-point Likert-type continuum, ranging from –3 = I Disagree Very Much through +3 = I Agree Very Much, with no neutral point. Six of the items are used in the scoring of both knowledge and attitude. An initial pool of 106 items was compiled by reviewing the published research literature and by analyzing open-ended interviews with experts. The pool was reduced to 38 items by a panel of 10 experts and then reduced further to 32 items by item, scale, and factor analysis. The final version included 16 positive and 16 negative items. A principal components analysis with varimax rotation of the attitude items yielded three factors that explained 68% of the variance: (1) Prejudice Stereotypes, (2) Behavioral Misconceptions, and (3) Behavioral Optimism. These factors are not scored separately. The factor analysis of the knowledge items yielded one nontrivial factor that explained 19% of the variance.
Samples	The sample was composed of 253 students (203 females and 50 males) enrolled in a variety of undergraduate ($n = 122$), graduate ($n = 87$), and professional-development ($n = 44$) courses in a northeastern university. The mean age of the sample was 26.41 years ($SD = 7.62$, range from 17 to 62 years).
Scoring	The number of items in the subscales is as follows: Attitude: 25 items Knowledge: 13 items *Note:* Six items are score on both subscales The attitude and knowledge items are scored separately. On the attitude scale, the sign of the negative items (13) is reversed. The score is obtained by adding the responses on all 25 items plus a constant value of 75. The attitude scores range from 0 to 150. The 13 knowledge items are scored dichotomously. First the three agree response options are collapsed into one category (True) and disagree response options into another category (False). Then the number of correct responses is summed. The knowledge scores range from 0 to 13.

(Continued)

Reliability	The reliability scores were as follows:
	
	    Attitude: Alpha = .87; Spearman-Brown = .81
	
	    Knowledge: Alpha = .97; Kuder-Richardson = .97

Validity	Evidence for criterion validity information was provided by a multiple regression analysis using age, sex, professional specialization, and educational level as predictors. The best predictor of both attitude and knowledge was level of education. Females scored higher than males on the attitude portion but no differently on the knowledge portion. Also, respondents in the professional human service areas were more knowledgeable and had more positive attitude scores compared to respondents in other areas.
Related References	Antonak, R. F. (1990). Psychometric analysis and validation of the Scale of Attitudes toward Persons with Epilepsy. *Journal of Epilepsy, 3,* 11–16. Antonak, R. F., & Livneh, H. (1995a). Development, psychometric analysis, and validation of an error-choice test to measure attitude toward persons with epilepsy. *Rehabilitation Psychology, 40,* 25–38. Bishop, M., & Boag, E. M. (2006). Teacher's knowledge about epilepsy and attitudes toward students with epilepsy: Results of a national survey. *Epilepsy and Behavior, 8,* 397–405.
Language Versions	English
Contact	Dr. Richard F. Antonak Department of Counseling and School Psychology University of Massachusetts, Boston 100 Morrissey Blvd. Boston, MA 02125–3393 Tel: (617) 287–5600 Email: Richard.Antonak@umb.edu

10.17.3 Name of the Measure	Thinking About Epilepsy Questionnaire TAEQ
Primary Reference	Martiniuk, A. L. C, Speechley, K., Secco, M., & Campbell, M. K. (2007). Development and psychometric properties of the Thinking about Epilepsy Questionnaire assessing children's knowledge and attitudes about epilepsy. *Epilepsy & Behavior, 10,* 595–603.
Purpose	The purpose of the TAEQ is to measure knowledge and attitudes of children about epilepsy.
Description	The TAEQ is a 25-item measure composed of two domains: Knowledge and Attitudes. The Attitudes items are rated on a 5-point Likert-type scale ranging from 1 = Strongly Disagree to 5 = Strongly Agree. Six of the eight items are reverse scored. The questionnaire was read aloud in classes while students had the TAEQ in front of them to follow along and then respond.
	The Knowledge domain has five subscales: (1) Epilepsy (what it is, types, causes), (2) Epilepsy (manifestation), (3) First aid, (4) Diagnosis and Treatment, and (5) Role of the Brain. The Attitudes domain has two subscales: (1) Contagiousness and (2) Epilepsy Should not Limit Achievement. Eleven of the Knowledge items are rated using True, False, and Don't Know options, and the rest have multiple correct responses, such as different types of actions taken when someone is having a seizure. "Sleeper" (incorrect) options are included in items with multiple correct response options.
	The TAEQ was developed to evaluate the Thinking About Epilepsy Program in Canada. An initial pool of 36 items was developed. Nine of the items were taken from already existing surveys, and the rest were developed specifically for the TAEQ. After a pilot test in five classes, the items were revised for reading level, font size, numbering, item wording, etc.
	The items in the Knowledge and Attitude domains were factor analyzed separately using principal components and varimax rotation. Items correlating .30 and greater on a factor were retained. The knowledge domain yielded 17 items and five factors. The Attitude domain yielded eight items and two factors. The TAEQ items may be found in the primary reference. Supplemental data and the measure may be found at doi: 10.1016/j.yebeh.2007.01.011.
Samples	The sample was composed of 783 students in grade 5 from two school boards in southwestern Ontario, Canada. The ages ranged from 9 to 11. There was an equal balance of females and males; 73% had English as their first language; about 60% had heard of epilepsy (at baseline before the Thinking About Epilepsy Program was delivered); 24% came from high SES schools, 20% from medium SES schools, 36% from low SES schools, and 20% from very low SES schools.
Scoring	The number of items in the two domains are as follows: Knowledge Domain: 17 items

(Continued)

(Continued)

	The subscales are as follows:
	
	    Epilepsy (what it is, types, causes): 7 items
	    Epilepsy (manifestation): 2 items
	    First aid: 2 items
	    Diagnosis and treatment: 3 items
	    Role of the brain: 3 items
	
	For items with True, False, and Don't Know options, the Don't Know choice is scored as False. For items with multiple correct responses, the score is the number of correct choices, which vary across items. Individual item scores are summed to obtain a subscale score. A total Knowledge score is also obtained by summing the responses to the 17 items.
	
	    Attitude Domain: 8 Items
	
	The subscales are as follows:
	
	    Contagiousness: 4 items
	    Epilepsy should not limit Achievement: 4 items
	
	Six of the eight items are reverse scored. Individual item scores are summed to obtain a subscale score. A total Attitude score is obtained by summing the responses to the eight items. Higher scores reflect more positive attitudes.

Reliability	The Cronbach's alphas for the Knowledge domain were as follows:
	
	    Epilepsy (what it is, types, causes): Alpha = .74
	    Epilepsy (manifestation): Alpha = .57
	    First aid: Alpha = .47
	    Diagnosis and Treatment: Alpha = .52
	    Role of the brain: Alpha = .26
	    Total Knowledge domain: Alpha = .65
	
	The Cronbach's alphas for the Attitudes domain were as follows:
	
	    Contagiousness: Alpha = .77
	    Epilepsy should not limit achievement: Alpha = .65
	    Total Attitude domain: Alpha = .82

Validity	Evidence of known-group validity of the knowledge domain was demonstrated as follows: Those who had heard of epilepsy scored higher on the Knowledge domain than those who had not. Those who knew someone with epilepsy scored higher on the Knowledge domain than those who did not. Evidence of construct validity of the Attitude domain was demonstrated by showing statistically significant correlations between the belief that one can catch epilepsy and the believe that people with epilepsy should not go to school, and that one should not sit beside someone who has epilepsy.

Related References	Bozkaya, I. O., Arhan, E., Sedaroglu, A., Soysal, A. S., Ozkan, S., & Gucuyener, K. (2009). Knowledge of, perception of, and attitude toward epilepsy of schoolchildren in Ankara and the effect of an educational program. *Epilepsy & Behavior, 17,* 56–63. Martiniuk, A. L. C., Speechley, K. N., Secco, M., Campbell, M. K., & Donner, A. (2007). Evaluation of an epilepsy education program for Grade 5 students: A cluster randomized trial. *Epilepsy & Behavior, 10,* 604–610.
Language Versions	English and Turkish
Contact	Alexander L. C. Martiniuk The George Institute for International Health at the University of Sydney M201 Missenden Road Camperdown, NSW 2050 Australia Fax: +61–2-9657–0301 Email: amartiniuk@george.org.au

10.17.4 Name of the Measure	Test of Knowledge About Epilepsy KAE
Primary Reference	Antonak, R. F., & Livneh, H. (1995a). Development, psychometric analysis, and validation of an error-choice test to measure attitudes toward persons with epilepsy. *Rehabilitation Psychology, 40,* 25–38.
Purpose	The purpose of the KAE is to measure attitudes toward epilepsy indirectly.

Description	The KAE was developed using the error-choice method, an uncommon way of measuring attitudes indirectly. The error-choice method as described by Antonak and Livneh (1995b) involves a multiple-choice test with factual information items where none of the alternatives are correct. The response options are set up such that the choices reflect positive or negative attitudes. For example,
	
	"The frequency of psychoses among persons with epilepsy is ___ than the frequency of psychoses in the general population.
	
	    a. Considerably greater
	    b. Somewhat greater
	    c. Somewhat lesser
	    d. Considerably lesser"
	
	The choice of (a) or (b) would reflect a negative attitude and the choice of (c) or (d) would reflect a positive attitude. In this example, the actual risk of psychoses is about the same in both populations. Thus, the biased guessing determines the attitude.
	
	The KAE is composed of two scales with 20 items each randomly arranged: (1) KAE-A, the attitude scale, uses the error-choice method with three types of factual questions: (a) ones where the truth can be determined but no correct options are provided, (b) ones where the truth is indeterminable because no data are provided, and (c) ones where the truth is indeterminable; (2) KAE-GK, the knowledge scale, includes very difficult general knowledge questions with correct options provided.
	
	An original pool of 67 items was composed and then reduced using expert judges, factor analysis, and item analysis. Principal components analysis of the KAE-A yielded a single factor that explained 14% of the variance with item structure coefficients ranging from .20 to .49.

Samples	Two samples were used in the study. The first one was used to develop the KAE and the second one was used to further establish validity. The first sample was composed of 406 graduate and undergraduate students at two universities: 310 were female; 331 were White American, 31 were Asian American, 23 were African American, and 13 were Latino/a American and 8 were other; the ages ranged from 18 to 58 ($M = 28.72$, $SD = 8.79$); professional specializations included regular educators ($n = 78$), special educators ($n = 47$), special service providers ($n = 130$), and non–human service providers ($n = 151$); different degrees of contact were reported, with an $n = 200$ indicating none.

	The second sample was composed of 325 graduate and undergraduate students at two universities: 250 were female; 386 were White American, 13 were Asian American, 12 were African American, 5 were Latino/a American, and 9 were other; the ages ranged from 18 to 64 ($M = 29.40$, $SD = 9.67$); professional specializations included 24 health care providers, 53 special service providers, 17 special educators, 96 regular educators, and 135 non–human service providers; different degrees of contact were reported, with an $n = 170$ indicating none.
Scoring	The number of items in the subscales is as follows:
	KAE-A: 20 items
	KAE-GK: 20 items
	Total KAE: 40 items
	The scores for the KAE-A and the KAE-GK are obtained by summing the scores on each of the items. Higher scores on the KAE-A reflect more positive attitudes, and higher scores on KAE-GK reflect greater knowledge.
Reliability	In study 1, the Spearman-Brown split-half reliability estimate of the KAE-A was .63. The mean item difficulty of the KAE-GK was .33. In study 2, the Spearman-Brown split-half reliability estimate of the KAE-A was .57. The mean item difficulty of the KAE-GK was .32.
Validity	Evidence of discriminant validity was provided. The correlations of the KAE-A with the KAE-GK were not significant in the two studies, respectively, indicating that the two scales are measuring different constructs. In study 2, KAE-A was uncorrelated with the Marlowe-Crowne Social Desirability Scale (Crowne & Marlowe, 1960).
	Evidence of convergent validity was provided. The two scales of the direct measure of the Attitude Toward Persons with Epilepsy (ATPE; Antonak & Rankin, 1982), Attitude (ATPE-A) and Knowledge (ATPE-K), were administered to the second sample. The correlation between KAE-A and ATPE-A was significant and the correlation between KAE-GK and ATPE-K was not significant.
	There was also evidence of criterion validity. As expected, KAE-A was positively correlated with age, education, and familiarity with epilepsy. As expected, KAE-GK was positively correlated with age, education, and familiarity with epilepsy.
Related References	Bishop, M., & Slevin, B. (2004). Teachers' attitudes toward students with epilepsy: Results of a survey of elementary and middle schoolteachers. *Epilepsy & Behavior, 5*, 308–315.
Language Versions	English
Contact	Richard F. Antonak Department of Counseling and School Psychology University of Massachusetts, Boston 100 Morrissey Blvd. Boston, MA 02125–3393 Tel: (617) 287–5600 Email: Richard.Antonak@umb.edu

10.18 MEASURES OF ATTITUDES TOWARD INCLUSION AND MAINSTREAMING

10.18.1 **Name of the Measure**	Attitudes Toward Mainstreaming Scale ATMS
Primary Reference	Berryman, J. D., & Neal, R. Q., Jr. (1980). The cross validation of the Attitude Toward Mainstreaming Scale (ATMS). *Educational and Psychological Measurement, 40,* 469–474.
Purpose	The purpose of the ATMS is to measure attitudes toward mainstreaming children with a disability into public schools.
Description	The ATMS is a 18-item measure rated on a 6-point Likert-type scale with the points on the anchors not reported. Three factors were identified: (1) Learning Capability, (2) General Mainstreaming, and (3) Traditional Limiting Disability. An initial pool of 22 items was developed and the responses were factor analyzed using principal components with varimax rotation. In a second sample, the factor structure was confirmed. Reliability estimates and intercorrelations of factors were reported for both samples.
Samples	The first sample was composed of 159 students including 78% females and 22% males. The second sample was composed of 164 students including 84% females and 16% males. Participants were students in preservice and in-service introductory education courses representing 17 different teaching fields including K–12 levels. No ages were reported.

Scoring	The number of items in the three factors is as follows:
	
	    Learning Capability: 9 items
	
	    General Mainstreaming: 7 items
	
	    Traditional Limiting Disability: 4 items
	
	    Total ATMS: 18 items
	
	From the reported descriptive statistics, it is presumed that the scores are obtained by summing the items in each factor. Total scores are also reported. Items are worded such that an agreement with a statement indicates a favorable attitude.

Reliability	The Cronbach's alphas of the scores in the two samples were as follows:
	    Learning Capability: Alphas = .84 and .82, respectively
	    General Mainstreaming: Alphas = .81 and .81, respectively
	    Traditional Limiting Disability: Alphas = .78 and .76, respectively
	    Total ATMS: Alphas = .88 and .88, respectively.

Validity	The confirmation of the factor structure in the second cross-validation sample suggests construct validity. The intercorrelations of the three factors were moderate, ranging from .42 to .50 in the first sample and from .46 to .55 in the second sample, suggesting the relative independence of the factors. No evidence of criterion, discriminant, or convergent validity was reported.

Related References	Berryman, J. D. (1989). Attitudes of the public toward educational mainstreaming. *Remedial and Special Education, 10,* 44–49.
	Berryman, J. D., Neal, W. R., Jr., & Robinson, J. E. (1980). The validation of a scale to measure attitudes toward the classroom integration of disabled students. *Journal of Educational Research, 73,* 199–203.
	Eiserman, W. D., Shisler, L., & Healey, S. (1995). A community assessment of preschool providers' attitudes toward inclusion. *Journal of Early Intervention, 19,* 149–167.
	Green, K., & Harvey, D. (1983). Cross-validation of the Attitude Toward Mainstreaming Scale. *Educational and Psychological Measurement, 43,* 1255–1261.
	Yuen, M., & Westwood, P. (2002). Teachers' attitude toward integration: Validation of a Chinese version of the Attitude Toward Mainstreaming Scale (ATMS). *Psychologia, 45,* 1–11.
Language Versions	English and Chinese
Contact	Joan D. Berryman 570 Aderhold Hall University of Georgia Athens, GA 30602

10.18.2 Name of the Measure	Mainstreaming Opinionnaire MO
Primary Reference	Schmelkin, L. P. (1981). Teachers' and nonteachers' attitudes toward mainstreaming. *Exceptional Children, 48*, 42–47.
Purpose	The purpose of the MO is to measure attitudes of teachers and nonteachers toward the mainstreaming of students with disabilities.
Description	The MO is a 30-item measure of attitudes toward mainstreaming of disabled students. The items are rated on a 7-point Likert-type scale ranging from +3 = Very Strong Agreement to –3 = Very Strong Disagreement with a neutral zero point. A large pool of items was developed by reviewing the literature on issues related to mainstreaming of children with a disability. Items were both negatively and positively phrased. Of these items, 67 were included in a principal axis factor analysis using orthogonal as well as oblique rotation. Two correlated factors that explained 60% of the variance were retained, each factor included 15 items: (1) Academic Costs of Mainstreaming and (2) Socio-Emotional Costs of Segregation.
Samples	Two samples were used: one for factor analysis and one for validation purposes. The sample used for factor analysis was composed of 222 graduate students in the School of Education, Health, Nursing, and Arts Professions at New York University and at Fordham University Graduate School of Education. The sample used for validation came from the same schools and was composed of three groups, each composed of 40 students: special education teachers, regular teachers, and nonteachers. The mean age of the validation sample was 30.65 (*SD* = 6.22). The mean years of experience by teachers was 7.24 (*SD* = 4.48). Of the regular teachers, 65% said they had one or more students with a disability in their classes.

Scoring	The number of items for each subscale are as follows:
	
	    Academic Cost of Mainstreaming: 15 items
	    Socio-emotional Costs of Segregation: 15 items
	    Total MO: 30 items
	
	The subscale scores are obtained by averaging the responses to the 15 statements in each factor without reversal of ratings.

Reliability	The Cronbach's alphas of the scores of the two subscales of the MO were as follows:
	    Academic Costs of Mainstreaming: Alpha = .90
	    Socio-Emotional Costs of Segregation: Alpha = .88

Validity	The criterion group validity of the MO was demonstrated by comparing the three groups of special education teachers, regular teachers, and nonteachers. As expected, the special education teachers scored significantly lower on the Academic Costs of Mainstream subscale than the regular teachers and the nonteachers, who did not score differently. There were no differences between the groups on the Socio-Emotional Costs of Segregation.

Related References	Antonak, R. F., & Larrivee, B. (1995). Psychometric analysis and revision of Opinions Relative to Mainstreaming Scale. *Exceptional Children, 62,* 139–149.
	Garvar-Pinhas, A., & Schmelkin, L. P. (1989). Administrators' and teachers' attitudes toward mainstreaming. *Remedial and Special Education, 10,* 38–43.
Language Versions	English
Contact	Liora Pedhazur Schmelkin Office of the Provost 200 West Library Wing Hofstra University Hempstead, NY 11549–1440 Email: Liora.P.Schmelkin@hofstra.edu Tel: (516) 463–4680 Fax: (516) 463–6505

10.18.3 Name of the Measure	Multidimensional Attitudes Toward Inclusive Education Scale MATIES
Primary Reference	Mahat, M. (2008). The development of a psychometrically sound instrument to measure teachers' multidimensional attitudes toward inclusive education. *International Journal of Special Education, 23*, 82–92.
Purpose	The purpose of MATIES is to measure teachers' cognitive, behavioral, and affective attitudes toward physical, social, and curricular inclusion of students with disabilities into regular classrooms.
Description	The MATIES is an 18-item measure composed of three subscales: (1) Cognitive, (2) Affective, and (3) Behavioral. The items are rated on a 6-point Likert-type scale with no neutral midpoint ranging from Strongly Agree to Strongly Disagree (no numerical values associated with the scale were provided). The Cognitive subscale reflects perceptions and beliefs about inclusive education. The Affective subscale reflects feelings and emotions about inclusive education. The Behavioral subscale reflects behavioral intentions to act in certain ways to accommodate students with disabilities. An initial pool of 100 items was composed from the literature and then reduced to 41 items that fit the three dimensions. Using experts and teachers as judges, the number of items was further reduced to 36 items. Then through exploratory and confirmatory factor analyses using orthogonal and oblique rotations, 18 items and three factor subscales were identified. Items correlating .50 and over were retained in the factors.
Samples	The sample was composed of 115 primary and secondary school teachers in Victoria, Australia, 74% female and 26% male. The ages ranged from under 30 years to over 60 years with a median of 45 years. The years of experience ranged from under 2 years to over 30 years with a median of 15 years.
Scoring	The number of items for each subscale are as follows: Cognitive: 6 items Affective: 6 items Behavioral: 6 items Total MATIES: 18 items Each subscale includes six items. No numerical weights associated with the Likert-type scale are identified, but it can be inferred from the discussion that higher scores reflect more positive attitudes, after reversing negatively stated items. The author does not recommend the use of a total score. In the Cognitive subscale, half the items are stated negatively; in the Affective subscale, all six items are negatively stated; and in the Behavioral subscale, all items are positively stated. The author does not indicate if the sum or average of the item ratings is used in scoring the subscales. The items of the scale can be found in the primary reference.

Reliability	The Cronbach's alphas were as follows: Cognitive: Alpha = .77 Affective: Alpha = .78 Behavioral: Alpha = .91 Item separation indices were over .91, indicating strong unique contribution of items to the subscales.
Validity	Some evidence of predictive validity was provided. As expected, teachers with more positive Cognitive and Affective attitudes tended to be more willing to make behavioral changes in their classrooms to accommodate students with disabilities. The internal consistency indices, the factorial structure, and the subscale correlations were taken to reflect construct and criterion validity. No independent criteria were used for validation purposes.
Related References	
Language Versions	English
Contact	Marian Mahat Monash University Clayton Campus Wellington Road, Building 3A Clayton, Victoria 3800 Australia Tel: +61–3-9905–9317 ext. 53276

10.18.4 Name of the Measure	Opinion Related to Integration ORI (Original version is called Opinion Relative to Mainstreaming-ORM)
Primary Reference	Antonak, R. F., & Larrivee, B. (1995). Psychometric analysis and revision of the Opinion Relative to Mainstreaming scale. *Exceptional Children, 62,* 139–149. (For ORI) Larrivee, B., & Cook, L. (1979). Mainstreaming: A study of the variables affecting teacher attitude. *Journal of Special Education, 13,* 315–324. (For ORM)
Purpose	The purpose of the ORI is to measure attitudes of regular classroom teachers toward mainstreaming children with special needs.
Description	The ORI is a revised and updated version of the ORM. The ORM was a 30-item measure reduced from a pool of 41 items, maintaining items with item-total correlation of .30. No factor analysis was conducted in this item-reduction process. The items were rated on a 5-point Likert-type scale ranging from 1 = Strongly Agree to 5 = Strongly Disagree, including a 3 = Undecided midpoint category. On 12 of the items, agreement indicated endorsement of mainstreaming, and on 18 items, disagreement indicated endorsement of mainstreaming. The content of the items dealt with the following seven domains: views of education in general, philosophy of mainstreaming, effect of classroom placement to the development of students with disabilities, classroom behavior of students with disabilities, cognitive functioning of students with disabilities, views of the parents of students with disabilities, and teachers' perception of their ability to teach students with disabilities. A multiple regression analysis showed that as teachers' grade level increased, their attitudes became more negative. Antonak and Larrivee (1995) reworded the original items of the ORM to reflect more inclusive, contemporary, and appropriate terminology and renamed the scale Opinion Relative to Integration (ORI). The wording of 10 items was changed to yield 15 positive and 15 negative items. They also changed the rating scale to a six-point continuum with no midpoint ranging from –3 = I Disagree Very Much to +3 = I Agree Very Much. Item, scale, and factor analyses with varimax rotation reduced the scale to 25 items and yielded four factors and accounted to 41% of the total variance: (1) Benefits of Integration, (2) Integrated Classroom Management, (3) Perceived Ability to Teach Students with Disabilities, and (4) Special Versus Integrated General Education.
Samples	The sample was composed of 376 special education (16%) and general education (84%) undergraduate students. Of the total sample, 21% were males and 79% female, and the mean age was 23.30 (*SD* = 7.05). Reported relationship with people of disability ranged from none (21%), acquaintance (39%), casual (15%), and close (15%) to intimate (7%). The ethnic breakdown of the sample was 30% White American, 6% African American, 2% Asian American, 1% Latino/a American, and 1% other, and the rest unknown.
Scoring	Antonak and Larrivee (1995) did not recommend the use of the four factor scores as subscale scores because their independent validity was not examined. The number of items in the four factors is as follows: Benefits of Integration: 8 items Integrated Classroom Management: 8 items

	Perceived Ability to Teach Students with Disabilities: 5 items Special Versus Integrated General Education: 4 items Total ORI: 26 items The total score of the ORI is obtained by reversing the negative items, then summing the ratings and adding a constant of 25 to eliminate negative scores.
Reliability	For the total score, the Spearman-Brown corrected split-half reliability was .87, and Cronbach's alpha was .83.
Validity	For criterion validity, the Attitude Toward Disabled Persons (SADP; Antonak, 1982) was used as a predictor in a regression analysis along with demographic and experiential variables. The ORI scores were significantly related to the SADP scores as expected and unrelated to respondent sex, age, ethnicity, or educational level. ORI scores were also unrelated to the professional areas or to the closeness of relationships to persons with disabilities.
Related References	Avramidis, E., Bayliss, P., & Burden, R. (2000). A survey into mainstreaming teachers' attitudes toward the inclusion of children with special education needs in the ordinary school in one local education authority. *Educational Psychology, 20,* 191–211. Dupoux, E., Wolman, C., & Estrada, E. (2005). Teachers' attitudes toward integration of students with disabilities in Haiti and the United States. *International Journal of Disability, Development and Education, 52,* 43–58. Leyser, Y., & Kirk, R. (2004). Evaluating inclusion: An examination of parent views and factors influencing their perspectives. *International Journal of Disability, Development and Education, 51,* 271–285. Monsen, J. J., & Frederickson, N. (2004). Teachers' attitudes towards mainstreaming and their pupils' perceptions of their classroom learning environment. *Learning Environment Research, 7,* 129–142.
Language Versions	English
Contact	Richard F. Antonak Department of Counseling and School Psychology University of Massachusetts, Boston 100 Morrissey Blvd. Boston, MA 02125–3393 Tel: (617) 287–5600 Email: Richard.Antonak@umb.edu

10.18.5 Name of the Measure	Response to Inclusion Survey RIS (AKA-Preservice Inclusion Survey [PSIS] as modified)
Primary Reference	Soodak, L. C., Podell, D. M., & Lehman, L. R. (1998). Teacher, student, and school attributes as predictors of teachers' response to inclusion. *Journal of Special Education, 31,* 480–498.
Purpose	The purpose of the RIS is to measure the responses of general educators to inclusion of students with disabilities in their classrooms.
Description	The RIS (PSIS) is composed of a set of 17 pairs of adjectives, such as Accepting/Opposing and Anxious/Relaxed, rated on a 4-point semantic differential continuum. Before responding to the semantic differential scales, participants read a scenario in which their principal tells them their school is planning to include a student with a disability in their class. Each participant is given one of the five following disability categories: hearing impairment, learning disability, mental retardation, behavior disorder, or a physical handicap requiring the use of a wheelchair. A factor analysis using varimax rotation yielded two independent factors that explained 52.9% of the variance. One factor was labeled Hostility/Receptivity and the other factor was labeled Anxiety/Calmness. Shippen, Crites, Houchins, Ramsey, and Simon (2005) modified the 4-point semantic differential continuum to a 5-point format with descriptions of each point, including a neutral point, for example: Scared, Somewhat Scared, Neutral, Somewhat Relaxed, and Relaxed. A confirmatory factor analysis supported the original factor structure and accounted for 45% of the variance. This modified version was called Preservice Inclusion Survey (PSIS).
Samples	The participants in the original study were 188 students in graduate education classes in the New York metropolitan area, as well as teachers in school settings. Of the total participants, 85.1% were female, 71.3% taught in elementary school, 18.1% in middle school, and 10.6% in high school. The years of experience varied from 1 to 29 ($M = 9.3$, $SD = 8.3$). Participants were 84.6% White American, 6.4% African American, 5.3% Latino/a American, and 2.7% Asian American. A majority of 85.6% taught in public schools. A minority of 35.6% reported having students with special needs in their classes, varying in number from 1 to 12 with a median of 3.
Scoring	The number of items in the subscales of the RIS is as follows: Hostility/Receptivity: 10 items Anxiety/Calmness: 7 items Total RIS: 17 items The scores on each factor are obtained by computing factor scores using weighted sums of responses to each item. Items with greater correlations contributed proportionally more to the factor scores of an individual.

Reliability	The Cronbach's alphas were as follows:
	Hostility/Receptivity: Alpha = .92
	Anxiety/Calmness: Alpha = .87
	Split-half reliabilities were as follows:
	Hostility/Receptivity: $r = .91$
	Anxiety/Calmness: $r = .86$
	Test-retest reliabilities with 42 participants for 2-week interval were as follows:
	Hostility/Receptivity: $r = .87$
	Anxiety/Calmness: $r = .77$
Validity	As expected, type of disability was related to responses to inclusion. Teachers were more hostile toward inclusion of students with mental retardation, learning disabilities, and behavior problems, probably because of the anticipated frustration with teaching such students, suggesting predictive validity.
	Multiple regression analysis showed that teachers with more experience tended to be less receptive toward inclusion of students with disabilities, and teachers with low sense of teaching efficacy and personal efficacy as measured by the Teacher Efficacy Scale (Gibson & Dembo, 1984) tended to be more hostile toward inclusion, suggesting criterion validity. The association of greater class sizes and lack of collaborative support provided further evidence of criterion validity with more anxiety about inclusion of students with disabilities.
	Shippen et al. (2005) showed that scores on anxiety and hostility regarding inclusion of students with disabilities were reduced as a result of participation in a semester-long survey course on exceptionalities—further evidence of predictive validity.
Related References	Shippen, M. E., Crites, S. A., Houchins, D. E., Ramsey, M. L., & Simon, M. (2005). Preservice teachers' perceptions of including students with disabilities. *Teacher Education and Special Education, 28*, 92–99.
Language Versions	English
Contact	Leslie C. Soodak Department of Educational Psychology Rutgers University, Graduate School of Education 10 Seminary Pl. New Brunswick, NJ 08903

10.19 MEASURES OF ATTITUDES TOWARD PERSONS WITH MENTAL ILLNESS

10.19.1 Name of the Measure	Beliefs About Illness BAI
Primary Reference	Norman, R. M. G., Sorrentino, R. M., Windell, D., & Manchanda, R. (2008a). The role of perceived norms in the stigmatization of mental illness. *Social Psychiatry and Psychiatric Epidemiology, 43,* 851–859.
Purpose	The purpose of the BAI is to measure beliefs about mental illness, specifically toward schizophrenia and depression.
Description	The BAI is a 20-item measure rated on a 5-point Likert-type scale ranging from 1 = Strongly Disagree to 5 = Strongly Agree.
	Ten of the items were adapted from the Angermeyer and Matschinger (2004) study of stigma in Germany, and the authors developed another 10 items. A vignette is presented describing a person with either schizophrenia or depression before items on the BAI are rated.
	Principal axis factor analysis with promax rotation was conducted with the anticipation that the factors could be correlated. All items correlated on their respective factors at .40 and greater. Six factors emerged that were similar for each of the two diagnoses presented in the vignette: (1) Personal Responsibility for Illness, (2) Continuity with Normal, (3) Danger, (4) Social Inappropriateness, (5) Talent/Intelligence, and (6) Treatment Outcome. Percentage of explained variances was not reported. BAI items may be found in the primary reference.
Samples	The sample was composed of 200 undergraduate students at the University of Western Ontario in London, Canada: 110 were females and 90 males. The mean age was 21.5 years (*SD* = 5.0).
Scoring	The number of items in the subscales is as follows:
	Personal Responsibility for Illness: 4 items
	Continuity with Normal: 3 items
	Danger: 4 items
	Social Inappropriateness: 3 items
	Talent/Intelligence: 4 items
	Treatment Outcome: 2 items
	Total BAI: 20 items
	Items are rated such that higher scores on the subscales indicate more negative responses to persons with mental illness. Scores on each subscale are obtained by averaging the responses to the relevant items. No total score is computed.
Reliability	Cronbach's alphas to individual subscales were not reported for the first four subscales, but it was noted that they ranged from .74 to .83, and for the last two they were .57 for Talent/Intelligence and .48 for Treatment Outcomes. It was also noted that Angermeyer and Matschinger (2004) also obtained low alphas for the last two subscales.

Validity	Criterion validity was evidenced with men scoring statistically significantly higher than women on the subscale of Personal Responsibility for Illness for both schizophrenia and depression. Responses to the two diagnoses also yielded differences. Individuals diagnosed with schizophrenia compared to individuals diagnosed with depression were rated higher on subscales of Danger and Social Inappropriateness, and lower on Personal Responsibility for Illness and Continuity with Normal.
	The subscales of the BAI were correlated with a social distance measure used by Link, Cullen, Frank, and Wozniak (1987), adapted from the Bogardus Social Distance Scale (Bogardus, 1925), and used in a multiple-regression analysis predicting social distance. For schizophrenia, Social Inappropriateness and Continuity with Normal significantly predicted social distance. For depression, Social Inappropriateness and Continuity with Normal were significant predictors of social distance, suggesting criterion validity.
	Evidence for discriminant validity was provided. None of the six subscales correlated with the Marlowe-Crowne Social Desirability Scale (Crowne & Marlowe, 1960).
Related References	Norman, R. M. G., Sorrentino, R. M., Windell, D., & Manchanda, R. (2008b). Are personal values important in the stigmatization of people with mental illness? *Canadian Journal of Psychiatry, 53,* 848–856.
Language Versions	English
Contact	R. M. M. G. Norman Department of Psychiatry University of Western Ontario Rm. 114A-WMCH 392 South Street London Canada N6A 4G5 Email: rnorman@umo.ca

10.19.2 Name of the Measure	Community Attitudes Toward the Mentally Ill CAMI
Primary Reference	Taylor, S. M., & Dear, M. J. (1981). Scaling community attitudes toward the mentally ill. *Schizophrenia Bulletin, 7,* 225–240.
Purpose	The purpose of CAMI is to measure the attitudes of the general community toward people with mental illness.
Description	The CAMI is a 40-item measure rated on a 5-point Likert-type scale ranging from 1 = Strongly Disagree and 3 = Neutral to 5 = Strongly Agree.
	The pool of 40 items came from three existing measures: (1) Opinion about Mental Illness (OMI; Cohen & Struening, 1962), (2) Community Mental Health Ideology (CMHI; Baker & Schulberg, 1967), and (3) Custodial Mental Illness Ideology (CMI; Gilbert & Levinson, 1956). Seven of the items came from the original OMI and the CMHI; the other items were modified to reflect the community perspective rather than the professional perspective that the three scales were originally intended to reflect.
	The items were organized into four subscales that reflected the labels of subscales found in the original measures: (1) Authoritarianism, (2) Benevolence, (3) Social Restrictiveness, and (4) Community Mental Health Ideology. The items were selected conceptually, and 10 items were placed in each of the subscales. After an initial pilot study with university students and community members, items were revised or replaced if they had low item-total correlations.
	A factor analysis to reproduce a four-factor orthogonal solution explained 42% of the variance. Factor one explained 28.1% of the variance, factor two explained 5.5% of the variance, factor three explained 4.2% of the variance, and factor four explained 3.9% of the variance. Factor one factor-scores correlated .73 with the Authoritarian raw scores, and .72 with the Social Restrictiveness raw scores, suggesting a strong overlap of the subscales. However, they were maintained as separate subscales. Factor two factor-scores correlated .86 with the Community Mental Health Ideology raw scores, and factor three factor-scores correlated .81 with Benevolence raw scores. Factor four factor-scores were moderately correlated with all four raw subscale scores, ranging from −.31 to .51. The raw scores were used in further analysis of reliability and validity.
Samples	The sample was composed of $N = 1,090$ randomly selected residents of metropolitan Toronto, Canada. They were part of a larger study to assess attitudes toward the placement of a mental health treatment facility in the neighborhood. The selection included three levels of socioeconomic status (high, medium, and low), two residential locations (city and suburb), and people from areas with and without existing community mental health facilities.
Scoring	The number of items in each subscale are as follows:
	Authoritarianism: 10 items
	Benevolence: 10 items
	Social Restrictiveness: 10 items
	Community Mental Health Ideology: 10 items
	Total CAMI: 40 items

	Half of the items in each subscale are worded negatively. The scores on each subscale are obtained by summing the ratings on the items after reversing the negatively worded items.

Reliability	The Cronbach's alphas for the subscale scores were as follows:
	
	   Authoritarianism: Alpha = .68
	
	   Benevolence: Alpha = .76
	
	   Social Restrictiveness = .80
	
	   Community Mental Health Ideology: Alpha = .88

Validity	Known-group validity was provided. As expected, older residents reported less sympathetic attitudes toward people with mental illness on all four of the subscales. Also, females were more sympathetic than males on all of the subscales except on Social Restrictiveness, where no differences were obtained. Residents with higher educational levels tended to score higher on the Benevolence and Community Mental Health Ideology scales and lower on Authoritarian and Social Restrictiveness scales. Residents who used or had friends who used mental health services also scored higher on Benevolence and Community Mental Health Ideology scales and lower on Authoritarian and Social Restrictiveness scales. Criterion validity was also evidenced. Residents who considered it desirable being near a community mental health facility were more sympathetic on all four of the subscales than those who did not consider them desirable. The CAMI was not correlated with other similar measures, and social desirability bias was not assessed.
Related References	Addison, S. J., & Thorpe, S. J. (2004). Factors involved in the formation of attitudes toward those who are mentally ill. *Social Psychiatry and Psychiatric Epidemiology, 39,* 228–234. Kingdon, D., Sharma, T., & Hart, D. (2004). What attitudes do psychiatrists hold towards people with mental illness? *Psychiatric Bulletin, 28,* 401–406. Wahl, O. F., & Lefkowits, J. Y. (1989). Impact of television film on attitudes toward mental illness. *American Journal of Community Psychology, 17,* 521–528.
Language Versions	English, Chinese, and Greek
Contact	S. Martin Taylor Department of Geography University of Victoria 3800 Finnerty Road Victoria BC Canada, V8P 5C2 Tel: 250–721–6639 Email: vpr@uvic.ca

10.19.3 Name of the Measure	Opinion About Mental Illness OMI
Primary Reference	Cohen, J. S., & Struening, E. L. (1962). Opinions about mental illness in the personnel of two large mental hospitals. *Journal of Abnormal and Social Psychology, 64,* 439–360.
Purpose	The purpose of OMI is to measure attitudes toward people with mental illness and their personal characteristics, treatment, and origin of mental illness.
Description	The OMI is a 51-item measure rated on a 6-point Likert-type scale ranging from 1 = Strongly Disagree to 6 = Strongly Agree. It is composed of five subscales extracted through factor analysis: (1) Authoritarianism, (2) Benevolence, (3) Mental Hygiene Ideology, (4) Social Restrictiveness, and (5) Interpersonal Etiology. An initial pool of 200 opinion items was prepared from case conferences, casual conversations, paraphrases of ideas current in psychiatric hospitals. The items were reviewed by a group of hospital-experienced research workers and reduced to 55. Additional items were included from other measures (i.e., Gilbert & Levinson, 1956; Nunnally, 1957; Struening, 1957) to bring the total to 70 items. The items were factor analyzed separately for two samples from different psychiatric hospitals using a centroid factor extraction method and quartimax rotation, yielding five comparable factors. Later research verified these factor structures (Cohen & Struening, 1963; Dielman, Stiefel, & Cattel, 1973; Struening & Cohen, 1963) with minor item revisions.
Samples	The participants came from two large Veterans Administration neuropsychiatric hospitals: one from the Northeast ($n = 541$) and the other from the Midwest ($n = 653$). The years of education ranged from less than 8 years to more than 19 years, with 12 years of education being most represented ($n = 144$ and $n = 177$, respectively). The occupations of the participants were clerical, physical medicine, nurse, aide, social work, psychologist, special services, and kitchen workers. Aides were represented by far the most in both hospitals ($n = 245$, and $n = 317$, respectively).
Scoring	The number of items in the five subscales is as follows: Authoritarianism: 11 items Benevolence: 14 items Mental Hygiene Ideology: 9 items Social Restrictiveness: 10 items Interpersonal Etiology: 7 items Total OMI: 51 items No items are reverse scored. The subscale scores are obtained by summing the responses to the items, which are than added or subtracted according to a formula provided in Struening and Cohen (1963, p. 294). No total score is computed.

Reliability	Cohen and Struening (1962) report the following Kuder-Richardson Formula 20 estimates of internal consistency for the two hospitals, respectively:
	
	     Authoritarianism: .82 and .76
	     Benevolence: .49 and .62
	     Mental Hygiene Ideology: .60 and .61
	     Social Restrictiveness: .21 and .23
	     Interpersonal Etiology: .60 and .59
	
	 In a later article, Struening and Cohen (1963) report the following range of internal consistency estimate from three different hospitals:
	
	     Authoritarianism: .77 to .80
	     Benevolence: .70 to .72
	     Mental Hygiene Ideology: .29 to .39
	     Social Restrictiveness: .71 to .76
	     Interpersonal Etiology: .65 to .66

Validity	Repeated confirmations of the five-factor structure of the OMI suggest good factorial validity. Known-group validity was demonstrated as follows: There were predictable significant differences between different occupational groups on the five subscales, with the professional groups reflecting more tolerant and informed opinions. Criterion validity was demonstrated as follows: There was an association between higher levels of education and more tolerant and informed opinions on the subscales. The OMI continues to be used quite extensively in the United States and internationally, adding to the construct validity of the measure.
Related References	Corrigan, P. W., Edwards, A. B., Green, A., Diwan, S. L., & Penn, D. L. (2001). Prejudice, social distance, and familiarity with mental illness. *Schizophrenia Bulletin, 27,* 219–225. Der-Karabetian, A., Kadi, Z., Elmasian, S., & Yetenekian, A. (1975). Attitudes toward mental illness in Lebanon: An initial report. *Lebanese Medical Journal, 28,* 297–318. Knifton, L., Walker, A., & Quinn, N. (2008). Workplace intervention can reduce stigma. *Journal of Public Mental Health, 7,* 40–51. Madianos, M. G., Priami, M., Alevisopoulos, G., Koukia, E., & Rogakou, E. (2005). Nursing students' attitude change toward mental illness and psychiatric case recognition after a clerkship in psychiatry. *Issues in Mental Health Nursing, 26,* 169–183. Nickerson, K. J., Helms, J. E., & Terrell, F. (1994). Cultural mistrust, opinion about mental illness, and Black students' attitudes toward seeking psychological help from white counselors. *Journal of Counseling Psychology, 41,* 378–385.

(Continued)

(Continued)

Language Versions	English
Contact	Elmer L. Struening Mailman School of Public Health Colombia University 100 Haven Ave Tower 2, Suite 31d New York, NY 10032 Phone: 212–928–0631 Fax: 212–928–2219 Email: strueni@pi.cpmc.colombia.edu

10.19.4 Name of the Measure	Participation in Research Attitude Scale PRAS
Primary Reference	McDonald, K. E., Keys, C. B., & Henry, D. B. (2008). Gatekeepers of science: Attitudes toward the research participation of adults with intellectual disability. *American Journal on Mental Retardation, 113,* 466–478.
Purpose	The purpose of the PRAS is to measure the attitudes of intellectual disability researchers and IRB members toward the participation of adults with intellectual disabilities in research.
Description	The PRAS is a 29-item measure rated on a 6-point Likert-type scale ranging from 1 = Disagree Strongly to 6 = Agree Strongly. An initial pool of 46 items was developed. Thirty-one of the items were based on the conceptual underpinnings of the Community Living Attitude Scale (CLAS; Henry, Keys, Jopp, & Balcazar, 1996) that has four subscales (Empowerment, Exclusion, Sheltering, and Similarity). Fifteen of the items were based on the three principals of research of the Belmont Report (1978): Respect for Persons, Beneficence, and Justice. Multiple factor analyses were conducted using principal component analysis with varimax and promax rotations. Three factors and 29 items with structure coefficients greater than .40 were retained that explained 43% of the variance: (1) Opportunity and Choice, explained 19% of the variance, (2) Help in Decision-Making, explained 14% of the variance, and (3) Beneficence, explained 10% of the variance. The items may be found in the primary reference.
Samples	The sample was composed of 260 participants who had published in journals on topics related to intellectual disabilities (*n* = 114), who were members of Institutional Review Boards (IRB) (*n* = 116), and were both researchers and IRB members (*n* = 30): 54% were female; more than 65% were between 30 to 59 years of age; 91% were White American; about three-quarters had doctoral degrees, 11% had medical degrees, and 10% had master's degrees; 8% had some form of disability; 54% had a family member or a friend with some form of disability; 75% had worked or volunteered with people who had intellectual disabilities; and 62% had a colleague with a disability.

Scoring	The number of items in the subscales are as follows:
	
	    Opportunity and Choice: 14 items
	    Help in Decision-Making: 8 items
	    Beneficence: 7 items
	    Total PRAS: 29 items
	
	Five items are reverse scored. The subscale scores are obtained by averaging the ratings of items in each subscale. Higher scores indicate greater endorsement of the attitudes reflected in the subscales. Overall scores are not computed.

(Continued)

(Continued)

Reliability	The Cronbach's alphas of the subscale scores were as follows:
	Opportunity and Choice: Alpha = .86
	Help in Decision-Making: Alpha = .84
	Beneficence: Alpha = .70
Validity	Known-group validity was evidenced as follows: Women scored higher on Opportunity and Choice and Beneficence subscales and lower on Help in Decision-Making. Participants who had closer relationships with people with intellectual disabilities scored lower on Help in Decision-Making; researchers and participants who were both researchers and IRB members scored higher on Opportunity and Choice and lower on Help with Decision-Making.
	Convergent validity was evidenced as follows: The subscales of the PRAS were for the most part correlated moderately in the expected directions with the subscales of the CLAS.
	Discriminant validity was evidenced by showing that none of the subscales of the PRAS were correlated with social desirability as measured by the Impression Management subscale of the Balanced Inventory of Desirable Responding (Paulhus, 2002).
Related References	McDonald, K. E., & Keys, C. B. (2008). How the powerful decide: Access to research participation by those at the margins. *American Journal of Community Psychology, 42,* 79–93.
Language Versions	English
Contact	Kathrine E. McDonald Department of Psychology Portland State University 1721 SW Broadway Portland, OR 9701 Email: kmcdona@pdx.edu

10.19.5 Name of the Measure	Standardized Stigmatization Questionnaire—Version 1 SSQ1
Primary Reference	Haghighat, R. (2005). The development of an instrument to measure stigmatization: Factor analysis and origin of stigmatization. *European Journal of Psychiatry, 19,* 144–154.
Purpose	The purpose of SSQ1 is to measure perceived stigmatization and predisposition to enact stigmatization among the general population toward people with mental illness.
Description	The SSQ1 is a 13-item measure of stigmatization rated on a 4-point Likert-type scale with 1 = No, Not At All, 2 = No, Not So Much, 3 = Yes, A Little, and 4 = Yes, Very Much, or some variant of language depending on the question, such as Definitely No, Perhaps No, etc. A vignette that describes a male patient that receives the diagnosis of schizophrenia precedes the items. The items were put in the form of questions regarding how "most people" would perceive or have a certain opinion about the person in the vignette (Part I). Also, the items were modified to reflect predisposition to enact stigmatization by the respondent by changing the "most people" to "you" (Part II) in the items. An initial pool of 52 items was developed. Twenty-six of the items were based on more than 2,000 comments made by patients, relatives, social workers, and people from different settings such as police stations, hostels, homes, prisons, etc. Another list of 26 items was pooled from Littlewood (1998). Three of the items turned out to be similar to items found in Cohen and Struening (1962) and one found in Cumming and Cumming (1957). Of the 52 initial item pool, 32 items were removed because of redundancy. The remaining 20 items that were rated for perceived stigmatization were analyzed with principal components analysis with varimax as well as oblique rotations. Three factors emerged that retained 13 items and explained 57.55% of the total variance: (1) Social Self-Interest, explained 34.70% of the variance, (2) Evolutionary Self-Interest, explained 7.82% of the variance, and (3) Psychological Self-Interest, explained 15.03%. Although three factors emerged, the author suggests the use of the total scale as a single dimension of stigmatization.
Samples	Patients diagnosed with schizophrenia in remission and their relatives from four inner-city London hospitals of Camden and Islington Community Mental Health NHS Trust. No other demographic information about the sample is provided.
Scoring	The number of items in the three factors were as follows: Social Self-Interest: 4 items Evolutionary Self-Interest: 4 items Psychological Self-Interest: 5 items Total SSQ1: 13 items

(Continued)

(Continued)

	Higher scores reflect more perception of stigmatization. For several (unspecified) items, higher endorsement reflects stigmatization, and for several others, lower endorsement reflects stigmatization. It is not indicated if the scores are summed or averaged.
Reliability	No Cronbach's alphas are reported for individual factors except indicating that they were all above .74. For the total scale, the alphas were as follows: 　Perceived stigmatization (Part I): Alpha = .99 　Enactment of stigmatization (Part II): Alpha = .89
Validity	For divergent validity, the scale was correlated with a 4-item social desirability measure specially developed by the author for the study, with the suggestion that there was some correlation, but no value was specified. Suggestions were made to correlate the SSQ1 in future studies with similar measures to establish criterion validity.
Related References	
Language Versions	English and Italian
Contact	Rahman Haghighat Department of Psychiatry University College London Medical School United Kingdom Email: r.haghaghit@lycos.com

10.20 MEASURES OF ATTITUDES TOWARD PERSONS WHO ARE BLIND AND THOSE WHO ARE DEAF

10.20.1 Name of the Measure	Attitudes Toward Blindness ATB
Primary Reference	Whiteman, M., & Lukoff, I. F. (1964a). A factorial study of sighted people's attitudes toward blindness. *Journal of Social Psychology, 64*, 339–353.
Purpose	The Purpose of the ATB is to measure the attitude of sighted people toward people who are blind.
Description	A pool of 139 items was constructed conceptually under 17 indices that fell into three attitudinal areas: (1) perceived attributes and effectiveness of people who are blind, (2) acceptance or rejection of people who are blind, and (3) attitudes toward the integration of blind persons into sighted people's activities. The items were rated on three different formats: (1) Likert-type Agree-Disagree format, (2) sentence completion form to compare blindness with other physical disabilities, and (3) estimates of the number of people who are blind who have various feelings and attributes, and estimates of the intensity of such feelings. First, corrected split-half reliabilities of the 17 indices were computed to ensure reliability of the indices, and then the scores of the indices were factor analyzed using evening students from Hunter College. The indices were labeled as follows: Emotional Attributes, Individualized Attributes, Intensity Attributes, Competence, Role Adequacy, Activity Adequacy, Conception of Blindness, Evaluations of Blindness, Sentence Completion, Goal Attainment, Personal Interaction, Community Integration, Nonprotectiveness, Pity Avoidance, Generalized Attitude, Contact with Blindness, and Information about Blindness. The 17 indices were subjected to centroid factor analysis and orthogonal rotation. The factor analysis was performed on the Spearman rank-order correlation matrix and the following five factors emerged: (1) Personal Attributes, with the highest correlations on the indices of Intensity Attributes, Emotional Attributes, Competence, and Individualized Attributes; (2) Social Attributes, with the highest correlations on the indices of Personal Interaction, Community Integration, Activity Adequacy, and Role Adequacy; (3) Evaluation of Blindness, with highest correlations on the indices of Evaluation of Blindness, Conception of Blindness, and Emotional Attributes; (4) Nonprotectiveness, with highest correlations on the indices of Nonprotectiveness, Pity-Avoidance, Community Integration, and Sentence Completion; and (5) Interpersonal Acceptance, with highest correlations on the indices of Emotional Attributes, Personal Interaction, and Conception of Blindness. The factor analysis was repeated with students from the New York School of Social Work with an abridged version and some item modifications. Four similar factors emerged, with correlations of indices comparable to the Hunter sample, with variations attributed to the nature of the samples.

(Continued)

(Continued)

Samples	The demographics were comparable in the two samples as detailed in an accompanying article in a previous volume of the *Journal of Social Psychology* (Whiteman & Lukoff, 1964b). The Hunter College participants ($n = 58$) were students in an introductory sociology course; 73% were female; and the median age was 25 years with a range of 17 to 50 years.
	The New York School of Social Work participants ($n = 65$) were first-year students; 75% were female; and the median age was 29 with a range of 25 to 50 years.
Scoring	It is not clear in the primary reference how scores on each factor are obtained; only correlations are reported. In a subsequent publication, Whiteman and Lukoff (1965) use mean scores to report findings. For scoring procedures and for detailed findings of the factor analysis, the authors refer to the following source:
	Document number 8002, ADI Auxiliary Publications Project
	Library of Congress
	101 Independence Ave, SE Washington, DC 20540
Reliability	No reliability information for the factor-based subscales is reported. However, the primary reference provides corrected split-half reliability measures for the 17 indices used in the factor analysis. Subsequent publications also do not provide reliability information for the subscales.
Validity	The finding of comparable factors in two different samples by Whiteman and Lukoff (1964a) suggests factorial validity. Suggesting some known-group validity, Whiteman and Lukoff (1964b) analyzed responses on individual items of the different factors and indices and reported differences between evening students in Hunter College and social work students. Social work students tended to deny unique qualities of people who are blind and tended to be less protective of people who are blind either at the interpersonal or at the public policy level. Whiteman and Lukoff (1965) reported comparable responses to the items when rated for blindness and for general disability by social work students, suggesting the content validity of the items by virtue of their application for disability in general.
	It appears that in the several initial publications by the authors of the ATB, the reliability and validity of the measure were not addressed directly but were more focused on capturing the content and scope of potential attitudes and opinions about people who are blind.
Related References	Whiteman, M., & Lukoff, I. F. (1964b). Attitudes toward blindness in two college groups. *Journal of Social Psychology, 63*, 179–191.
	Whiteman, M., & Lukoff, I. F. (1965). Attitudes toward blindness and other physical handicaps. *Journal of Social Psychology, 66*, 135–145.
Language Versions	English
Contact	Martin Whiteman
	Columbia University
	School of Social Work
	622 West 113th Street
	New York, NY 10027

10.20.2 Name of the Measure	Opinion About Deaf People ODP
Primary Reference	Berkay, P. J., Gardner, J. E., & Smith, P. L. (1995). The development of the Opinion About Deaf People scale: A scale to measure hearing adults' beliefs about the capabilities of deaf adults. *Educational and Psychological Measurement, 55*, 105–114.
Purpose	The purpose of ODP is to measure the beliefs and misconceptions of hearing adults toward the capabilities of adults who are deaf.
Description	The ODP is a 20-item measure rated on a 4-point Likert-type scale ranging from 1 = Strongly Disagree to 4 = Strongly Agree with no neutral point. An initial pool of 35 items was developed from a review of the literature and an interview with six professionals who are deaf regarding anecdotal information about misconceptions. The 35 items were reduced to 20 using a small pilot sample (*n* = 38) of teacher education undergraduate students at a southwestern university. The 20 items were analyzed with a larger sample (*N* = 290) of undergraduates in a general education upper-division sociology class using principal components without iteration and a varimax rotation. Although six factors emerged with eigenvalues greater than 1.00, only one factor was retained that explained 26.9% of the variance. All the items were correlated highly or moderately with this total factor score. The items may be found in the primary reference.
Samples	A total sample was composed of 290 undergraduate students in an upper-division general education sociology class at a southwestern university from a variety of colleges including arts and science, allied health, business administration, and engineering. There were 167 females and 120 males (three did not report gender); the ages ranged from 18 to 50; 42% were college seniors, 34% were juniors, 21% were sophomores, and 3% were freshmen, master's students, or did not report their class standing; 69% were White American and the rest reported an unspecified number of different ethnic groups; 9% reported having a deaf relative; 29% had experiences with deaf classmates, and 13% had experience with deaf coworkers.
Scoring	Ten of the items in the ODP were stated positively and 10 were stated negatively. Agreement or strong agreement with positively stated items is reversed; then the ratings are summed to obtain a single total score ranging from 20 to 80. Higher scores reflect more negative attitudes.
Reliability	The Cronbach's alpha of the ODP scores was .83, and the split-half reliability was .82.
Validity	Evidence for criterion validity was provided. There was a significant correlation between the Attitudes to Deafness scale (ATD) developed by Cowen, Bobrove, Rockway, and Stevenson (1967) and the ODP scores.
Related References	Nikolaraizi, M., & Makri, M. (2004/2005). Deaf and hearing individuals' beliefs about the capabilities of deaf people. *American Annals of the Deaf, 149*, 404–414.

(Continued)

(Continued)

	Vogel, J. J., & Keating, C. F. (2005). Employment of deaf people as influenced by potential employers' perceptions: Pathological compared with sociocultural perspectives. *International Journal of Rehabilitation Research, 28,* 181–183.
Language Versions	English and Greek
Contact	Paul Berkay University of Arkansas Rehabilitation Research and Training Center for Persons who are Deaf or Hard of Hearing 4601 Markham St. Little Rock, AR 72205 Email: pberkay@comp.uark.ed

10.21 MEASURES OF SELF-ACCEPTANCE FOR PERSONS WITH DISABILITIES

10.21.1 Name of the Measure	Acceptance of Disability AD
Primary Reference	Linkowski, D. C. (1971). A scale to measure acceptance of disability. *Rehabilitation Counseling Bulletin, 14*, 236–244.
Purpose	The purpose of AD is to measure the acceptance of disability by people whose disability is primarily neurological or orthopedic in nature.
Description	The AD is a 50-item measure rated on a 6-point Likert-type scale ranging from 1 = Strongly Disagree to 6 = Strongly Agree. The items were developed by the author based on the theory of acceptance of loss of physical ability by Dembo, Leviton, and Wright (1956). The theory conceptualizes acceptance of loss as four value shifts: enlargement of scope of values, subordination to physique, containment of disability effects, and transformation from comparative values to asset values. An original number of items (number unspecified) was independently evaluated by two experts and four graduate students in rehabilitation counseling for clarity and centrality to the theoretical categories. Items were discarded or revised based on their input, ending with 50 items. Principal components analysis was conducted with two small samples: One sample of 46 respondents came from the Woodrow Wilson Rehabilitation Center in Fishersville, Virginia, and the other sample was composed of 55 students with physical disabilities at the University of Illinois, Urbana. The results of the principal components analysis yielded a single factor that explained 48.3% of the variance in the first sample and 68.8% in the second sample.
Samples	The sample from the Woodrow Wilson Rehabilitation was composed of 46 respondents: 27 were males and 19 were females; the ages ranged from 16 to 55, with a mean of 26.3 years. The University of Illinois student sample was composed of 55 respondents: 35 were males and 20 were female. No other demographic information is provided about the samples.
Scoring	An unspecified number of items are negatively stated and are reversed first; then the ratings are summed to obtain a total AD score. Higher scores indicate more acceptance of disability.
Reliability	The Spearman-Brown split-half reliability of the AD for the sample from the Woodrow Wilson Rehabilitation Center was $r = .86$.
Validity	Evidence for known-group validity was provided. The mean scores of the two samples used in the study were compared, and as expected, the student sample scored significantly higher.

(Continued)

(Continued)

	There was evidence of criterion Validity. The Woodrow Wilson Rehabilitation Center sample was administered the Attitudes Toward Disabled Persons Scale Form B (ATDP-B; Yuker, Block, & Campbell, 1962) along with the AD. The ATDP is a measure that was designed to measure the attitudes of people with and without disability toward people with disability. The correlation between the two measures was statistically significant.
	The AD scale has been shown by other researchers to be related to other variables such as perceived social discrimination and multiple disabilities (Li & Moore, 1998), better verbal learning ability by spinal cord injury patients (Schmitt & Elliot, 2004), self-concept (Linkowski & Dunn, 1974), and self-esteem, social support, and health locus of control (Belgrave, 1991), suggesting further evidence of criterion validity.
Related References	Belgrave, F. Z. (1991). Psychosocial predictors of adjustment to disability in African Americans. *Journal of Rehabilitation, 57,* 37–40.
	Li, L., & Moore, D. (1998). Acceptance of Disability and its correlates. *Journal of Social Psychology, 138,* 13–25.
	Linkowski, D. C., & Dunn, M. A. (1974). Self-concept and acceptance of disability. *Rehabilitation Counseling Bulletin, 17,* 28–32.
	Schmitt, M. M., & Elliott, T. R. (2004). Verbal learning ability and adjustment to recent spinal cord injury. *Rehabilitation Psychology, 49,* 288–294.
Language Versions	English, Hebrew, and Swedish
Contact	Author deceased

10.21.2 Name of the Measure	Appearance Management and Social Interaction Scale AMSI
Primary Reference	Kaiser, S. B., Wingate, S. B., & Freeman, C. M. (1987). Acceptance of physical disability and attitudes toward personal appearance. *Rehabilitation Psychology, 32,* 51–58.
Purpose	The purpose of AMSI is to measure the tendency toward management of appearance and attitudes toward acceptance of disability among people with physical disabilities.
Description	The AMSI is a 25-item measure composed of two parts with three subscales in each part rated on a 5-point Likert-type scale, ranging from 1 = Strongly Agree to 5 = Strongly Disagree. The first part deals with the management of appearance and social interactions. The second part deals with acceptance of disability. The pool of items for the first part came from an earlier qualitative study by Kaiser, Freeman, and Wingate (1985) that involved focus group interviews of disabled college students in northern California. Principal components analysis with varimax rotation yielded seven factors, only three of which were retained, that explained 75.7% of the variance: (1) Salience of Dress, explained 47.8% of the variance, (2) Appearance Management/Compensation, explained 15.6% of the variance, and (3) Stigma of Functional Clothing, explained 12.3% of the variance. The nine items for the second part came from a portion of the items in the Acceptance of Disability Scale (Linkowski, 1971). A separate analysis of these items using principal components with varimax rotation yielded three factors and explained 100% of the variance: (1) Self-Satisfaction, explained 66.3% of the variance, (2) De-emphasis on Disability Salience, explained 27.3% of the variance, and (3) Compensatory Behavioral Qualities, explained 6.4% of the variance.
Samples	The participants were composed of 322 nationally sampled university students who were physically disabled who came from all 50 states of the United States. Altogether, 960 surveys were mailed out through the student offices of 72 institutions, with a response rate of 34%: 54% were female, and 46% were male; the average age was 28 years; 34.8% had been born with their disabilities, and 42.2% indicated their disabilities were acquired later in life. About one-half of the sample reported using wheelchairs.

Scoring	The number of items in each subscale is as follows:
	Part I: Appearance Management and Social Interaction
	    Salience of Dress: 8 items
	    Appearance Management/Compensation: 5 items
	    Stigma of Functional Clothing: 3 Items
	Part II: Disability Acceptance
	    Self-Satisfaction: 3 items
	    De-Emphasis on Disability Salience: 3 items
	    Compensatory Behavioral Qualities: 3 items

(Continued)

(Continued)

	Higher ratings on individual items reflect more favorable disposition or acceptance of disability. The scores for each subscale are the factor scores. No summated or average scores are computed.
Reliability	No reliability data was reported.
Validity	Known-group validity was evidenced as follows: As expected, females scored higher on the Salience of Dress subscale. Also, wheelchair users scored lower than the nonusers on the Appearance Management/Compensation factors, reflecting less optimism about the impact of appearance management. Criterion validity was evidenced as follows: As expected, the Appearance Management/Compensation subscale was negatively correlated with De-Emphasis on Disability Salience. Also, De-Emphasis on Disability Salience was correlated negatively with the statement, "People I don't know tend to notice my disability first, and my clothing second." The same statement was also negatively correlated with the Self-Satisfaction subscale.
Related References	
Language Versions	English
Contact	Susan B. Kaiser Women and Gender Studies 2222 Hart Hall One Shield Avenue Davis, CA 95616 Email: sbkaiser@ucdavis.edu Tel: 530–752–4686

10.22 MEASURES OF SELF-STIGMA FOR PERSONS WITH DISABILITIES

10.22.1 Name of the Measure	Depression Self-Stigma Scale DSSS
Primary Reference	Kanter, J. W., Rusch, L. C., & Brondino, M. J. (2008). Depression self-stigma: A new measure and preliminary findings. *Journal of Nervous and Mental Disorders, 196,* 663–670.
Purpose	The purpose of DSSS is to measure negative attitudes about being depressed by people with depression in the general population.
Description	The DSSS is 32-item measure rated on a 7-point Likert-type scale ranging from 1 = Completely Disagree to 7 = Completely Agree with a neutral point of 4 = Neither Agree Nor Disagree.

An initial pool of 59 items was developed based on a search of the literature on stigma and examination of stigma measures. An exploratory factor analysis using maximum likelihood extraction and promax rotation was conducted. Items with structure coefficients of less than .40 were dropped as well as items with secondary correlations of above .30. These item reductions yielded a 32-item scale with five factors: (1) General Self-Stigma, (2) Secrecy, (3) Public Stigma, (4) Treatment Stigma, and (5) Stigmatizing Experiences. The percentage of variances explained by the total and subscale scores were not reported. Scale items may be found in the primary reference. |
| **Samples** | The sample was composed of 391 participants. Of the total sample, 168 were undergraduate students with the following characteristics: The mean age was 20.93 (*SD* = 3.38), ranging from 18 to 42; 75.9% were female. Regarding racial and ethnic background, 77.6% were White American, 9.4% were Asian American, 4.8% were Mexican American, 3.6% were African American, 1.8% were Native American, and 2.8% were of other backgrounds. Of the total sample, 52.8% had no history of depression, 19.6% had a history of only therapy, 1.8% had a history of antidepressant medication, and 25.8% had a history of both therapy and antidepressant medication.

Altogether, 223 of the participants were community members with the following characteristics: The mean age was 38.00 (*SD* = 13.76), ranging from 18 to 79 years; 67.6% were female. Regarding racial and ethnic background, 64.6% were White American, 22.9% were African American, 4.0% were Mexican American, 1.8% were Native American, 1.3% were Asian American, and 5.4% were of other backgrounds. Of the total sample, 25.1% had no history of depression treatment, 13.7% had a history of only therapy, 7.3% had a history of only antidepressant medication, and 53.9% had a history of both therapy and antidepressant medication. |

(Continued)

(Continued)

Scoring	The number of items in each of the subscales is as follows:
	
	    General Self-Stigma: 9 items
	
	    Secrecy: 9 items
	
	    Public Stigma: 4 items
	
	    Treatment Stigma: 4 items
	
	    Stigmatizing Experiences: 6 items
	
	    Total DSSS: 32 items
	
	One item is reverse scored. The subscale scores are computed by summing the ratings of the relevant items. The total DSSS score is similarly computed. Higher scores reflect more negative self-attitudes.

Reliability	The Cronbach's alphas of the subscale and total scores were as follows:
	
	    General Self-Stigma: Alpha = .93
	
	    Secrecy: Alpha = .80
	
	    Public Stigma: Alpha = .86
	
	    Treatment Stigma: Alpha = .79
	
	    Stigmatization Experience: Alpha = .92
	
	    Total DSSS score: Alpha = .95

Validity	Along with the DSSS, four other measures were administered: (1) Center for Epidemiological Studies Depression Scale (CES-D; Radloff, 1977); (2) Depression Attribution Questinnaire-27 (DAQ-27; Corrigan, Markowitz, Watson, Rowan, & Kudiak, 2003); (3) Depression Social Distance Scale (DSDS; Link, 1987); and (4) Cognitive Behavioral Avoidance Scale (CBAS; Ottenbreit & Dobson, 2004). There was evidence of criterion validity. The DSSS total score was correlated significantly in the expected direction with CES-D and with CBAS. The DSSS total score was also correlated, but at a weaker level, with DAQ-27 and with DSDS, suggesting that DSSS is measuring similar but somewhat different constructs than stigma related to severe depression, which these scales were developed to measure. Also, as expected, the Public Stigma subscale was moderately and significantly correlated with the DAQ-27 and DSDS, indicating its similarity but also distinction of measuring stigma associated with a specific disorder from measuring stigma about mental illness in general, which these scales were developed to measure. Known-group validity was demonstrated. Consistent with expectations, women scored significantly higher than men on the total DSSS score and the Public Stigma subscale. Also, as expected, African Americans compared to White Americans scored higher on depression measured by CES-D, as well as higher on the total DSSS score and the subscales of General Stigma and Public Stigma. In a logistic regression analysis with use/no use of depression medication as a predicted variable, Treatment Stigma scores tended to be higher, and Public Stigma tended to be lower for those who had been on medication.

Related References	Manos, R. C., Rusch, L. C., Kanter, J. W., & Clifford, L. M. (2009). Depression self-stigma as a mediator of the relationship between depression severity and avoidance. *Journal of Social and Clinical Psychology, 28,* 1128–1143.
	Rusch, L. C., Kanter, J. W., Manos, R. C., & Weeks, C. E. (2008). Depression stigma in a predominantly low income African American sample with elevated depression symptoms. *Journal of Nervous and Mental Disease, 196,* 919–922.
Language Versions	English
Contact	Jonathan W. Kanter Department of Psychology University of Wisconsin-Milwaukee P. O. Box 413 Milwaukee, WI 53201 Email: jkanter@uwm.edu

10.22.2 Name of the Measure	Internalized Stigma of Mental Illness ISMI
Primary Reference	Ritsher, J. B., Otilingam, P. G., & Grajales, M. (2003). Internalized stigma of mental illness: Psychometric properties of a new measure. *Psychiatry Research, 121*, 31–49.
Purpose	The purpose of ISMI is to measure subjective experience of stigma related to mental illness.
Description	The ISMI is a 29-item measure rated on a 4-point Likert-type scale ranging from 1 = Strongly Disagree to 4 = Strongly Agree. An initial pool of 55 items was developed in consultation with individuals with personal or family history of mental illness and a series of focus groups of consumers from various advocacy and support groups. The research team screened the items, selected 29 items, and placed them in five a priori subscales: (1) Alienation, (2) Stereotype Endorsement, (3) Perceived Discrimination, (4) Social Withdrawal, and (5) Stigma Resistance. The following criterion measures were administered along with the ISMI to the study sample ($N = 127$) of a veterans' hospital's psychiatric outpatients: the Center for Epidemiological Studies-Depression (CES-D; Radloff, 1977), Self-esteem (Rosenberg, 1979), Perceived Devaluation and Discrimination (Link, Struening, Rahav, Phelan, & Nuttbrock, 1997), the Personal Empowerment Scale (Segal, Silverman, & Temkin, 1995), and Recovery Orientation (Harding & Zahniser, 1994). The items of the ISMI were factor analyzed together with the items of each criterion measure separately. Overall, in each case, the items of the ISMI were correlated with a separate factor than the items of the criterion measure. The factor analysis (unspecified) of the ISMI items alone was conducted without the items of the Stigma Resistance subscale because of the inadequacy of the sample size. The four factors that emerged with the remaining 24 items had high structure coefficients that corresponded generally well overall with the items placed in the subscales created by their method (procedures were not specified). No percentages of explained variances by the factors were provided. The subscale items may be found in the primary reference.
Samples	The sample was composed of 127 veterans' hospital outpatients: 117 were male and the mean age was 49.5 ($SD = 8.7$). Regarding racial and ethnic background, 62.1% were White American, 26.4% were African American, and the rest were from other ethnic/racial groups. Of the total sample, 18.4% had college or higher degrees, 44.8% had some college, and 36.8% had a high school diploma or less. Participants had at least one of the following diagnoses: schizophrenia, paranoid psychosis, affective psychosis, depression, PTSD, anxiety disorder, and personality disorder, and 75.6% had substance use diagnosis. The highest diagnostic category was affective psychosis (81.9%).
Scoring	The number of items in the five a priori subscales is as follows: Alienation: 6 items Stereotype Endorsement: 7 items Discrimination Experience: 5 items

	Social Withdrawal: 6 items
	Stigma Resistance: 5 items
	Total ISMI: 29 items
	Items in the Stigma Resistance subscale are reverse scored. Although not specified, it may be inferred that the subscale scores are obtained by averaging the ratings of the items in the relevant subscale. A total ISMI score is computed similarly.

Reliability	The Cronbach's alphas of the subscale scores were as follows:
	     Alienation: Alpha = .79
	     Stereotype Endorsement: Alpha = .72
	     Discrimination Experience: Alpha = .75
	     Social Withdrawal: Alpha = .80
	     Stigma Resistance: Alpha = .58
	     Total 29-item version: Alpha = .90
	     Total 24-item version: Alpha = .91
	 The test-retest reliability of the subscale scores were as follows:
	     Alienation: $r = .68$
	     Stereotype Endorsement: $r = .94$
	     Discrimination Experience: $r = 89$
	     Social Withdrawal: $r = .89$
	     Stigma Resistance: $r = .80$
	     Total 29-item version: $r = .92$
	     Total 24-item version: $r = .73$

Validity	Evidence for criterion validity was provided. As expected, the total score (29 items) of the ISMI was positively and significantly correlated with Devaluation-Discrimination scores and with the CES-D depression scores. The ISMI total scores, also as expected, were negatively and significantly correlated with Self-esteem, Personal Empowerment, and Recovery Orientation. For the 33 African Americans in the group, the Cronbach's alpha of the total ISMI score was .88, and it correlated in the expected direction with all the criterion measures. For the 45 participants with the schizophrenia diagnosis, the Cronbach's alpha for the total ISMI score was .93, and it correlated in the expected direction with all the criterion measures.
Related References	Conner, K. O., Keoske, G., & Brown, C. (2009). Racial differences in attitudes toward professional mental health treatment: The mediating effects of stigma. *Journal of Gerontology Social Work, 52,* 695–712. Ritsher, J., & Phelan, J. (2004). Internalized stigma predicts erosion of morale among psychiatric outpatients. *Psychiatry Research, 129,* 257–265. Werner, P., Aviv, A., & Barak, Y. (2008). Self-stigma, self-esteem and age in persons with schizophrenia. *International Psychogeriatrics, 20,* 174–187.

(Continued)

(Continued)

Language Versions	English, Hebrew, and Turkish
Contact	Jennifer Boyd Ritsher Department of Psychiatry (116A) University of California and San Francisco VA Medical Center 4150 Clement Street San Francisco, CA 94121 Tel: (415) 221–4810 extension 3421 Email: ritsher@itsa.ucsf.edu

10.22.3 Name of the Measure	Perceived Stigma in People With Intellectual Disability PSPID
Primary Reference	Ali, A., Straydom, A., Hassiotis, A., Williams, R., & King, M. (2008). A measure of perceived stigma in people with intellectual disability. *British Journal of Psychiatry, 193,* 410–415.
Purpose	The purpose of PSPID is to measure perceived stigma by people with mild to moderate intellectual disability.
Description	The PSPID is a 10-item measure rated on a dichotomous Yes/No scale. Each item is accompanied by a simple drawing to illustrate the content. A pool of 47 items was developed after examination of the stigma literature. The items were reviewed and evaluated by professionals who provide services to people with intellectual disabilities such as psychiatrists, psychologists, nurses, and occupational therapists, and by six service users for their comprehensibility, relevance, and suitability. The number of items was reduced to 21 based on the feedback received. Item analysis for extreme responses by participants further reduced the number of items to 13. These were subjected to an exploratory factor analysis with varimax rotation. Ten items with structure coefficients of .50 or greater were retained. Two factors emerged that explained 60% of the total variance: (1) Perceived Discrimination and (2) Reaction to Discrimination. One item correlated on both factors but was used in the second factor. The items may be found in the primary reference.
Samples	The participants were 109 people with mild ($n = 94$) or moderate ($n = 15$) intellectual disability: 62 were women and 47 were men; the mean age was 41 years ($SD = 13.6$); 80 were White British and the rest came from 11 different ethnic groups; 12 had physically stigmatizing conditions such as cerebral palsy or mobility problems; 81 were unemployed; and 40 individuals had some form of mental illness such as affective or psychotic disorders.

Scoring	The number of items in the subscales is as follows:
	
	     Perceived Discrimination: 6 items
	
	     Reaction to Discrimination: 4 items
	
	     Total PSPID: 10 items
	
	 The subscale scores are obtained by summing the number of Yes responses. The total score is obtained similarly. No items are reverse scored. Endorsement of items reflects greater stigma.

Reliability	The Cronbach's alphas of the scores were as follows:
	
	     Perceived Discrimination: Alpha = .72
	
	     Reaction to Discrimination: Alpha = .69
	
	     Total PSPID: Alpha = .84

(Continued)

(Continued)

Validity	No differences were obtained on the total stigma score among the different demographic categories of age, ethnicity, level of intellectual disability, presence or absence of physical disability or of mental illness, and employment status.
Related References	
Language Versions	English
Contact	Afia Ali Tower Hamlets Learning Disability Service Beaumont House Mile End Hospital Bancroft Road London E1 4DG UK Email: Afia.ali@thpct.nhs.uk

10.22.4 Name of the Measure	Stigma Questionnaire SQ
Primary Reference	Littlewood, R., Jadhav, S., & Ryder, A. G. (2007). A cross-national study of the stigmatization of severe psychiatric illness: Historical review, methodological considerations and development of the questionnaire. *Transcultural Psychiatry, 44,* 171–202.
Purpose	The purpose of the SQ is to measure stigmatizing attitudes toward people with severe psychiatric illness across multiple national groups.
Description	The SQ is a 14-item single factor measure rated on a 4-point Likert-type scale as follows: 1 = No, Not At All, 2 = No, Not Much, 3 = Yes, A Little, and 4 = Yes, Very Much. The scale was developed to measure stigma toward people with severe mental illness in seven countries: Caribbean Islands, England, Greece, India, Poland, Sri Lanka, and West Africa. An initial item pool of 123 items was composed after reviewing ethnographic and historical accounts of local concepts of mental illness, personal accounts of psychiatric patients, medical professionals, and social workers, and previous studies of attitudes toward mental illness. Collaborators from the targeted countries examined the items for relevance, redundancy, and local meaningfulness, which helped reduce the number to 26. The items were translated using the back-translation method and administered to samples from the seven countries. Items with item-total correlations of less than .20 in each country were eliminated, yielding 14 items. The SQ is preceded by a vignette that describes a young man with schizophrenia, and the items are worded in reference to the person described. These 14 items were then subjected to separate principal component analyses within each sample. Visual inspection of the scree plot supported a single overall component in all seven countries. No percentages of explained variances were provided. The unidimensionality of the composite stigma score was further examined by a confirmatory factor analysis to test the fit of the 14 items. The root mean square error of approximation (RMSEA) and standardized root mean square residuals (SRSR) coefficients were less than .10, suggesting an acceptable unidimensional model. The authors indicate that this does not necessarily support the claim of the unidimensionality of the construct of stigma in these countries but suggests that these 14 items may be used as a composite score of a single scale. The SQ items can be found in the primary reference.
Samples	The sample combined across the seven countries was $N = 1,434$, with numbers ranging from a low of $n = 127$ for Poland to a high $n = 351$ for Greece. The mean ages ranged from a low $M = 24.4$ years for England to a high of $M = 39.6$ years for Poland; the mean years of education ranged from a low $M = 11.0$ years for India to a high $M = 18.2$ years for Sri Lanka; the number of married ranged from a low of $n = 19$ for the Caribbean to a high $n = 104$ for India; and those with family history of mental illness ranged from a low $n = 39$ for Poland to a high $n = 98$ for Greece.

(Continued)

(Continued)

Scoring	The SQ score is obtained by averaging the rating on the 14 items. Eight of the items are reverse-scored.
Reliability	Cronbach's alphas were computed separately for each sample but were not provided separately. The authors report that the alphas were greater than .70 for five of the countries and between .60 and .70 for Sri Lanka and West Africa. They also note that no items with poor reliabilities were obtained.
Validity	No validity data were provided in the primary reference. However, the authors suggest that country-specific comparisons of the various demographic factors would be more meaningful than comparisons across countries.
Related References	Jadhav, S., Littlewood, R., Ryder, A. G., Chakraborty, A., Jain, S., & Barua, M. (2007). Stigmatization of severe mental illness in India: Against the simple industrialization hypothesis. *Indian Journal of Psychiatry, 49,* 189–194. Menon, K. V., & Ranjith, G. (2009). Malayalam cinema and mental health. *International Review of Psychiatry, 21,* 218–223.
Language Versions	All the languages of the countries included in the study: Caribbean, England, Greece, India (local variation), Poland, Sri Lanka, and West Africa.
Contact	Roland Littlewood Centre for Medical Anthropology University College London 48 Riding House Street London, W1N 8AA United Kingdom Email: r.littlewood@ucl.ac.uk

10.22.5 **Name of the Measure**	Stigma Scale SS
Primary Reference	King, M., Dinos, S., Shaw, J., et al. (2007). The Stigma Scale: Development of a standardized measure of the stigma of mental illness. *British Journal of Psychiatry, 190,* 248–254.
Purpose	The purpose of the SS is to measure the stigma experienced by users of mental health services.
Description	The SS is a 28-item measure rated on a 5-point Likert-type scale ranging from 0 = Strongly Disagree to 4 = Strongly Agree. An initial pool of 46 items was developed based on in-depth interviews of 46 mental health service users in the London, England, area. The number of items was reduced to 35 after eliminating items that had test-retest k coefficients of lower than .40. The 35 items were analyzed by means of to a common factor analysis (in contrast to principal components) with promax as well as varimax rotations that yielded similar results. Altogether, 28 items with structure coefficients of .40 and higher were retained. Three factors emerged that explained 72% of the variance: (1) Discrimination, explained 44% of the variance, (2) Disclosure, explained 16% of the variance, and (3) Positive Aspect, explained 12% of the variance. The SS items may be found in the primary reference.
Samples	The sample was composed of 193 mental health service users: 82 were female; the mean age was 42.9 years (*SD* = 12.4), ranging from 19 to 76 years; 76.5% were White British, 5.5% were African British, 3.5% were of Indian or Bangladeshi origin, and 9% were of other ethnic/racial background; the rest did not indicate their ethnic/racial background; 34% were currently employed; 6% were students. Most had received diagnosis of schizophrenia, bipolar affective disorder, depression, or mixed anxiety/depression; about 33% were admitted compulsorily to a psychiatric unit; and 16% reported having had electroconvulsive therapy.
Scoring	The number of items in the SS subscale is as follows: 　Discrimination: 13 items 　Disclosure: 10 items 　Positive Aspects: 5 items 　Total SS: 28 items Nine of the items are reverse scored. The subscale scores are computed by summing the ratings of the relevant items. The total SS score is also computed similarly. Higher scores indicate more negative experiences of stigma.

(Continued)

(Continued)

Reliability	The Cronbach's alphas of the subscale scores were as follows:
	Discrimination: Alpha = .87
	Disclosure: Alpha = .85
	Positive Aspects: Alpha = .64
	Total SS: Alpha = .87
Validity	Criterion validity was evidenced as follows: As predicted, the self-esteem scores measured by the Rosenberg (1979) Self-Esteem Scale were negatively correlated with the total Stigma Scale score, the Discrimination subscale score, the Disclosure subscale score, and Positive Aspects.
Related References	
Language Versions	English
Contact	Michael King Department of Mental Health Sciences Royal Free and University College Medical School Rowland Hill Street London NW3 4QP United Kingdom Tel: +44 (0) 20 7830 Email: m.king@medsch.ucl.ac.uk

Appendix

MENTAL HEALTH CENTER ADULT OUTCOMES

Date:

| | | / | | | / | | | | |

Primary Staff Name (Last, First):   Staff Code:

Race/Ethnicity

Client Name (First & Last):   Client Code:

Race/Ethnicity

PROGRAM CODE: | | | MEDI-CAL: ○ Yes   ○ No

MEASURES   **DATE**   **INITIALS**

Consent Form

ARSMA-II Acculturation Scale (Latino)

MEIM-R Ethnic Identity Scale

[ ][ ]/[ ][ ]/[ ][ ][ ]

Generation

[ ][ ]/[ ][ ]/[ ][ ][ ]

CLEP

[ ][ ]/[ ][ ]/[ ][ ][ ]

BRIEF PSYCHIATRIC RATING SCALE(BPRS)

[ ][ ]/[ ][ ]/[ ][ ][ ]

QUALITY OF LIFE QUESTIONNAIRE (QLSF)

[ ][ ]/[ ][ ]/[ ][ ][ ]

MHSIP

[ ][ ]/[ ][ ]/[ ][ ][ ]

PLEASE CHECK ONE: INTAKE__ANNUAL REVIEW__DISCHARGE__TRANSFER__

IF UNABLE TO COMPLETE PLEASE STATE REASON HERE AND IN PROGRESS NOTE AS WELL:

_____

_____

_____

_____

Client Living Environment Profile (CLEP)

Date:

[ ][ ]/[ ][ ]/[ ][ ][ ]

Client Code:

Client Name (First & Last):

[ ]

SS#:   Date of Birth: Age: Gender:

O Female   O Male

[ ]

Type of Administration: ☐ Intake   ☐ Annual   ☐ Transfer   ☐ Discharge

Instructions:

Circle the number that corresponds to the category that most closely matches the client's PREDOMINANT living situation over the last 12 months. In cases where the client had more than one living situation during the last 12 months, try to choose the environment where he or she spent the longest amount of time.

Next, circle the number that corresponds most closely to the client's CURRENT living environment.

Environment Code		Living Environment Category
Predominant	Current	
1	1	Incarcerated (Prison, County Jail, CYA, Juvenile Hall, etc.)
2	2	Psychiatric Hospital or Residental Treatment Centre (Levels 13–14)
3	3	Group Home (Levels 1–12)
4	4	Foster Care or Therapeutic Foster Care
5	5	Living with Biological or Adoptive Family, Relatives, Friends, or Others in a Home Setting
6	6	Living Independently by Self, with Spouse, Roommate, and/or Dependent Children
7	7	Homeless

Indicate the number of times or days you have experienced each of the following in the past six months; if none write zero "0."

			1. Number of crisis contacts with an outpatient crisis clinic.
			2. Number of days spent in a hospital for mental health.
			3. Number of days in a hospital over-night treatment center for alcohol/drug abuse treatment.
			4. Number of times having problems or run-ins with police.
			5. Number of arrests.
			6. Number of days in jail, or other correctional facility.

Dear Staff,

Please fill out the California Brief Multicultural Competency Scale (CBMCS). This questionniare is a 21-item instrument is specifically designed to measure self-report multicultural competency of the mental health services providers, and it is part of a cultural competence-training curriculum. The scores of your responses will assist the Cultural Competency Unit to provide Behavioral Health's staff with the Cultural Competence training needed.

If you want your score sent to you we will need your name. We want to reassure you that the information obtained will be used only for training purposes and will not be part of your personnel record. Your supervisor will be provided only with the group's overall scores.

Please provide us with the following information:

Employee Number: [   ]   Age: [ ]   Gender: [ ]

DBH Region/Support Svcs [   ]   Program/Clinic [   ]

No. of years with DBH: [ ]   No. of years working in mental health field: [ ]

No. of years working with multicultural clients: [ ]

Race/Ethnicity		Origin/Raised	
1. White American	O	1. Born and raised in the USA	O
2. Latino/a American / Latino	O	2. Born and raised outside of the USA	O
3. African American	O	3. Born in USA and raised outside the USA	O
4. Asian American/Pacific Is.	O	4. Born outside of USA and raised in the USA	O
5. Native American	O	5. Raised in both USA and outside USA	O
6. Other	O		

Job/Position		License Status	
O	1. Psychologist		
O	2. Psychiatrist	1. Licensed	O
O	3. MFT/MSW/LCSW/LPC		
O	4. Nurse		
O	5. Social Worker	2. Pre-licensed	O
O	6. Occupational Therapist		
O	7. Psychiatric Technician		
O	8. Administration/management position	3. Intern	O
O	9. Volunteer (Primary Job Function:_____)		
O	10. Paraprofessional (Primary Job Function:_____)	4. N/A	O
O	11. Clerical/Other non-clinical (Primary Job Function:_____)		
O	12. Other:_____		

Education in the USA		Education outside the USA		
1. PhD	O	1. PhD	O	
2. PsyD	O	2. Master's Degree	O	
3. EdD	O	3. Bachelor Degree	O	
2. Master's Degree	O	4. High School	O	
3. Bachelor Degree	O	5. Other	O	
4. High School	O	6. None	O	
5. Other	O			
6. None	O			

Language

O 1. English only   O 2. Bilingual   What language: _____

MENTAL HEALTH CENTER CHILD OUTCOMES

Primary Staff Name: Staff Code: Date

| | | | | | | | | | | | | | | | | | | | / | | / | | | |

Race/Ethnicity

| | | | | | | | | | | | | | |

Client Name: Client Code:

| | | | | | | | | | | | | | | | | | | | | MEDI-CAL: O Yes   O No

Race/Ethnicity

| | | | | | | | | | | | | | |

PROGRAM CODE: | | |

MEASURES	DATE	INITIALS
Consent Form	| / | / | |	_____
ARSMA-II Acculturation Scale Latino/a	| / | / | |	_____
MEIM Ethnic Identity Scale	| / | / | |	_____
Generation	| / | / | |	_____
(CLESP)	| / | / | |	_____
P.C.I.S. Parent Version	| / | / | |	_____

Y.C.I.S. Child Version (ages 9–18)

Youth Services Survey for Families (YSS-F)

Youth Services Survey (YSS)

PLEASE CHECK ONE: INTAKE_____ ANNUAL REVIEW_____ DISCHARGE_____ TRANSFER_____

Indicate the number of times or days you (the consumer) have experienced each of the following in the past six months; if none write zero "0."

			1. Number of days truant				11. Foster Family Agency
			2. Number of times sent to principal's office for discipline				12. Shelter
			3. Number of days suspended from school				13. Group Home Level 1–11
			4. Number of crisis contacts with an outpatient crisis clinic				14. Group Home Level 12–14
			5. Number of days spent in a hospital for mental health				15. Juvenile Hall
			6. Number of times having problems or run-ins with police				16. Camp/Ranch
			7. Number of arrests				17. CYA
			8. Home				18. Homeless
			9. Kinship				19. Other
			10. Foster Home				

Please check for ☐ English ☐ Spanish

I agree to fill out the attached form(s) to help become better acquainted with my personal background. This information will help us in meeting your personal needs and in our treatment planning goals. I understand that I am filling out this (these) questionnaire(s) of my own free will. I also understand that I can refuse to participate at any point. I further understand that all information obtained is confidential, and that my rights as a client will be fully protected.

Client Name   Client Code   Date

Client's Signature   Date

Parent's Signature if Client is a minor   Date

Forma de Consentimiento

Yo estoy de acuerdo en completer la(s) forma(s) adherida(s) para ayudar a a estar mas familiarizabo com mi historia personal. Esta informacione nos ayudar-a con sus necesidades personales y mejorar el plan de tratamiento. Yo entiendo que estoy llenando este o estos cuestionarios voluntariamente. Tambien entiendo que puedo rehusarme a participar en cualquier momento y que toda la informacion obtenida que puedo rehusarme a participar en cualquier momento y que toda la informacion obtenida es confidencial y que todos mis derechos como paciente estaran completamente protegidos.

Nombre del cliente   Código de cliente Fecha

Firma del cliente   Fecha

Firma del padre si el cliente es menor de edad   Fecha

References

Abedi, J. (2002). Standardized achievement tests and English language learners: Psychometric issues. *Educational Assessment, 8*(3), 231–257.

Achenbach, T. M. (1991). *Manual for the youth self-report and 1991 profile.* Burlington: University of Vermont, Department of Psychiatry.

Acosta, J. (2003). The effects of cultural differences on peer group relationship. *Journal of Prevention and Intervention in the Community, 25,* 13–26.

Adams, G. R., Bennion, L., & Huh, K. (1989). *Objective measure of ego identity development: A reference manual.* Unpublished test manual, University of Guelph, Ontario, CA.

Adams, M., Coltrane, S., & Parke, R. D. (2007). Cross-ethnic applicability of the Gender-Based Attitudes Toward Marriage and Child Rearing scales. *Sex Roles, 56,* 325–339.

Addis, M. E., & Mahalik, J. R. (2003). Men, masculinity, and the contexts of help seeking. *American Psychologist, 58,* 5–14.

Addison, S. J., & Thorpe, S. J. (2004). Factors involved in the formation of attitudes toward those who are mentally ill. *Social Psychiatry and Psychiatric Epidemiology, 39,* 228–234.

Adorno, T. W., Frenkel-Brunswik, E., Levinson, D. J., & Sanford, R. N. (1950). *The authoritarian personality.* New York: Harper.

Adrados, J. L. R. (1993). Acculturation: The broader view. Theoretical framework of the acculturation scales. In M. R. De La Rosa & J. L. R. Adrados (Eds.), *Drug abuse among minority youth: Advances in research and methodology* (pp. 55–77). Rockville, MD: U.S. Department of Health and Human Services, Public Health Service, National Institutes of Health, National Institute on Drug Abuse.

Akutsu, P. D., Tsuru, G. K., & Chu, J. P. (2004). Predictors of nonattendance of intake appointments among five Asian American client groups. *Journal of Consulting and Clinical Psychology, 72*(5), 891–896.

Akutsu, P. D., Tsuru, G. K., & Chu, J. P. (2006). Prioritized assignment to intake appointments for Asian Americans at an ethnic-specific mental health program. *Journal of Consulting and Clinical Psychology, 74*(6), 1108–1115.

Alderete, E., Vega, W. A., Kolody, B., & Aguilar-Gaxiola, S. (1999). Depressive symptomatology: Prevalence and psychological risk factors among Mexican migrant farm workers in California. *Journal of Community Psychology, 27,* 457–471.

Ali, A., Straydom, A., Hassiotis, A., Williams, R., & King, M. (2008). A measure of perceived stigma in people with intellectual disability. *British Journal of Psychiatry, 193,* 410–415.

Allport, G. W. (1954). *The nature of prejudice.* Reading, MA: Addison-Wesley.

Allport, G. W. (1979). *The nature of prejudice.* Cambridge, MA: Presus.

Altschul, I., Oyserman, D., & Bybee, D. (2008). Racial-ethnic self-schemas and segmented assimilation: Identity and the academic achievement of Hispanic youth. *Social Psychology Quarterly, 71,* 302–320.

Altemeyer, B. (1981). *Right-wing authoritarianism.* Winnipeg: University of Manitoba Press.

Altemeyer, B., & Hunsberger, B. E. (1992). Authoritarianism, religious fundamentalism, quest, and prejudice. *International Journal for the Psychology of Religion, 2,* 113–133.

Alvarez, A. N., & Helms, J. (2001). Racial identity and reflected appraisals as influences on Asian Americans' racial adjustment. *Cultural Diversity and Ethnic Minority Psychology, 7,* 217–231.

Alvarez, A. N., Juang, L., & Liang, C. T. H. (2006). Asian Americans and racism: When bad things happen to "model minorities." *Cultural Diversity and Ethnic Minority Psychology, 12,* 477–492.

American Educational Research Association, American Psychological Association, & National Council on Measurement in Education. (1999). *Standards for educational and psychological testing.* Washington, DC: Author. ISBN 0-935302-25-5.

American Psychiatric Association. (2000). *Handbook of psychiatric measures.* Washington, DC: Author.

American Psychological Association. (2000). Guidelines for psychotherapy with lesbian, gay, and bisexual clients. *American Psychologist, 55,* 1440–1452.

American Psychological Association. (2003). Guidelines on multicultural education, training, research, practice, and organizational change for psychologists. *American Psychologist, 58,* 377–402.

Aminidav, C., & Weller, L. (1995). Effects of country of origin, sex, religiosity and social class on breadth of knowledge of retardation. *British Journal of Developmental Disabilities, 41,* 48–55.

Ancis, J. R., Szymanski, D. M., & Ladany, N. (2008). Development and psychometric valuation of the Counseling Women Competencies Scale (CWCS). *The Counseling Psychologist, 36*(5), 719–744.

Anderson, J. (1983). Lix and rix: Variations on a little-known readability index. *Journal of Reading, 26,* 490–496.

Anderson, J., Moeschberger, M., Chen, Jr., M. S., Kunn, P., Wewers, M. E., & Guthrine, R. (1993). An acculturation scale for Southeast Asians. *Social Psychiatry and Psychiatric Epidemiology, 28,* 134–141.

Angermeyer, M. C., & Dietrich, S. (2005). Public beliefs about and attitudes towards people with mental illness: A review of population studies. *Acta Psychiatrica Scandinavica, 113,* 163–197.

Angermeyer, M. C., & Matschinger, H. (2004). The stereotype of schizophrenia and its impact on discrimination against people with schizophrenia: Results of a representative survey in Germany. *Schizophrenia Bulletin, 30,* 1049–1061.

Anthony, W. A. (2000). A recovery-oriented service system: Setting some system-level standards. *Psychiatric Rehabilitation Journal, 24,* 159–168.

Antonak, R. F. (1980). Psychometric analysis of the Attitudes Towards Disabled Persons Scale, Form O. *Rehabilitation Counseling Bulletin, 23,* 169–176.

Antonak, R. F. (1982). Development and psychometric analysis of the Scale of Attitudes Toward Disabled Persons. *Journal of Applied Rehabilitation, 13,* 22–29.

Antonak, R. F. (1985). Societal factors in disablement. *Rehabilitation Counseling Bulletin, 28,* 188–201.

Antonak, R. F. (1990). Psychometric analysis and validation of the Scale of Attitudes toward Persons with Epilepsy. *Journal of Epilepsy, 3,* 11–16.

Antonak, R. F., & Harth, R. (1994). Psychometric analysis and revision of the Mental Retardation Attitude Inventory. *Mental Retardation, 32,* 272–280.

Antonak, R. F., & Larrivee, B. (1995). Psychometric analysis and revision of the Opinion Relative to Mainstreaming Scale. *Exceptional Children, 62,* 139–149.

Antonak, R. F., & Livneh, H. (1988). *The measurement of attitudes toward people with disabilities: Methods, psychometrics and scales.* Springfield, IL: Charles C. Thomas.

Antonak, R. F., & Livneh, H. (1995a). Development, psychometric analysis, and validation of an error-choice test to measure attitude toward persons with epilepsy. *Rehabilitation Psychology, 40,* 25–38.

Antonak, R. R., & Livneh. H. (1995b). Direct and indirect methods to measure attitudes toward persons with disabilities, with an exegesis of the error-choice method. *Rehabilitation Psychology, 40,* 3–24.

Antonak, R. R., & Livneh, H. (2000). Measurement of attitudes toward persons with disabilities. *Disability and Rehabilitation, 22,* 211–224.

Antonak, R. F., & Rankin, P. R. (1982). Measurement and analysis of knowledge and attitudes toward epilepsy and persons with epilepsy. *Social Science and Medicine, 16,* 1591–1593.

Aosved, A. C., & Long, P. J. (2006). Co-occurrence of rape myth acceptance, sexism, racism, homophobia, ageism, classism, and religious intolerance. *Sex Roles, 55,* 481–492.

Aosved, A. C., Long, P. J., & Voller, E. K. (2009). Measuring sexism, racism, sexual prejudice, ageism, classism, and religious intolerance: The Intolerant Schema Measure. *Journal of Applied Social Psychology, 39,* 2321–2354.

Aponte, J. F., & Johnson, L. R. (2000). Impact of culture on the intervention and treatment of ethnic populations. In J. F. Aponte & J. Wohl (Eds.), *Psychological interventions and cultural diversity* (2nd ed., pp. 18–39). Boston, MA: Allyn & Bacon.

Arambula Solomon, T. G., & Gottlieb, N. H. (1999). Measures of American Indian traditionality and its relationship to cervical cancer screening. *Health Care for Women International, 20,* 493–504.

Arbuckle, J. L. (1999). *AMOS 4.0.* Chicago: Small Waters Corporation.

Arbuckle, J. L. (2003). *Amos Graphics Version 5.0.* Chicago: Small Waters Corporation.

Arciniega, G. M., Anderson, T. C., Tovar-Blank, Z. G., & Tracey, T. J. G. (2008). Toward a fuller conception of machismo: Development of a Traditional Machismo and Caballerismo Scale. *Journal of Counseling Psychology, 55,* 19–33.

Arredondo, P., Toporek, R., Brown, S., Jones, J., Locke, D. C., Sanchez, J., & Stadler, H. (1996). *Operationalization of the multicultural counseling competencies*. Alexandria, VA: Association for Multicultural Counseling and Development.

Arredondo, P., Rosen, D. C., Rice, T., Perez, P., & Tovar-Gamero, Z. G. (2005). Multicultural counseling: A 10-year content analysis of the *Journal of Counseling and Development, 83*, 155–161.

Arroyo, C., & Zigler, E. (1995). Racial identity, academic achievement, and the psychological well-being of economically disadvantaged adolescents. *Journal of Personality and Social Psychology, 69*, 903–914.

Arthur, T. E., Reeves, I. G., Cornelius, L. J., Booker, N. C., Morgan, O., Brathwaite, J., Tufano, T., Allen, K., & Donato, I. (2005). A consumer assessment tool for cultural competency within Maryland's public mental health system. *Psychiatric Rehabilitation Journal, 28*(3), 243–250.

Asante, M. K. (1987). *The Afrocentric idea*. Philadelphia: Temple University Press.

Ashmore, R. D., Deaux, K., & McLaughlin-Volpe, T. (2004). An organizing framework for collective identity: Articulation and significance of multidimensionality. *Psychological Bulletin, 130*, 80–114.

Atkinson, D. R., & Hacket, G. (1995). *Counseling diverse populations* (2nd ed.). Boston: McGraw-Hill.

Atkinson, D. R., & Hacket, G. (2004). An introduction to nontraditional interventions and diverse populations. In D. R. Atkinson, & G. Hacket (Eds.), *Counseling diverse populations* (3rd ed., pp. 33–35). Boston: McGraw-Hill.

Atkinson, D. R., Morton, G., & Sue, D. W. (1979). *Counseling American minorities: A cross-cultural perspective*. Dubuque, IA: Brown.

Atkinson, D. R., Morten, G., & Sue, D. W. (Eds.). (1989). *Counseling American minorities: A cross-cultural perspective* (3rd ed.). Dubuque, IA: Brown.

Avramidis, E., Bayliss, P., & Burden, R. (2000). A survey into mainstreaming teachers' attitudes toward the inclusion of children with special education needs in the ordinary school in one local education authority. *Educational Psychology, 20*, 191–211.

Baez, J., Howd, J., & Pepper, R. (2007). *The gay and lesbian guide to college life: A comprehensive resource for lesbian, gay, bisexual, and transgender students and their allies*. New York: Random House.

Bagby, R. M., Parker, J. D. A., & Taylor, G. J. (1994). The twenty-item Toronto Alexithymia Scale-I: Item selection and cross-validation of the factor structure. *Journal of Psychosomatic Research, 38*, 33–40.

Bakan, D. (1966). *The duality of human existence*. Chicago: Rand McNally.

Baker, F., & Schulberg, H. (1967). The development of a community mental health ideology scale. *Community Mental Health Journal, 3*, 216–225.

Baldwin, J. A. (1981). Notes on an Africentric theory of Black personality. *Western Journal of Black Studies, 5*, 172–179.

Baldwin, J. A. (1984). African self-consciousness and the mental health of African-Americans. *Journal of Black Studies, 15*, 177–194.

Baldwin, J. A., & Bell, Y. R. (1985). The African Self-Consciousness Scale: An Africentric personality questionnaire. *Western Journal of Black Studies, 9*, 61–68.

Balsam, K. F., & Szymanski, D. M. (2005). Relationship quality and domestic violence in women's same-sex relationships: The role of minority stress. *Psychology of Women Quarterly, 29*, 258–269.

Bandura, A. (1997a). *Self-efficacy: The exercise of control*. New York: W. H. Freeman.

Bandura, A. (1997b). Self-efficacy: Toward a unifying theory of behavior change. *Psychological Review, 84*, 191–215.

Bardis, P. D. (1959). A familism scale. *Marriage and Family Living, 21*(4), 340–341.

Bargad, A., & Hyde, J. (1991). Women's studies: A study of feminist identity development in women. *Psychology of Women Quarterly, 15*, 181–201.

Barker, F., Wright, B. A., Meyerson, L., & Gonick, M. R. (1953). *Adjustment to physical handicap and illness: A survey of social psychology of physique and disability* (Bulletin 55). New York: Social Science Research Council.

Barona, A., & Miller, J. A. (1994). Short Acculturation Scale for Hispanic Youth (SASH-Y): A preliminary report. *Hispanic Journal of Behavioral Sciences, 16*(2), 155–162.

Barr, S. C., & Neville, H. A. (2008). Examination of the link between parental racial socialization message and racial ideology among Black college students. *Journal of Black Psychology, 34*, 131–155.

Barry, D. T. (2002). An ethnic identity scale for East Asian immigrants. *Journal of Immigrant Health, 4*, 87–94.

Barry, D. T. (2005). Measuring acculturation among male immigrants in the United States: An exploratory study. *Journal of Immigrant Health, 7*, 179–184.

Barry, D. T, Elliott, R., & Evans, E. M. (2000). Foreigner in a strange land: Self-construal and ethnic identity in male Arabic immigrants. *Journal of Immigrant Health, 2*, 133–144.

Barry, D. T., & Grilo, C. M. (2002). Cultural, psychological, and demographic correlates of willingness to use psychological services among East Asian immigrants. *Journal of Nervous and Mental Disease, 190*, 32–39.

Bartky, S. L. (1990). *Femininity and domination: Studies in the phenomenology of oppression*. New York: Routledge.

Bartlett, C. J., Quay, L. C., & Wrightsman, L. S., Jr. (1960). A comparison of two methods of attitude measurement: Likert-type and forced choice. *Educational and Psychological Measurement, 20,* 699–704.

Bastos, J. L., Celeste, R. K., Faerstein, E., & Barros, A. J. D. (2010). Racial discrimination and health: A systematic review of scales with a focus on their psychometric properties. *Social Science & Medicine, 70,* 1091–1099.

Bauman, S. (2005). The reliability and validity of the Brief Acculturation Rating Scale for Mexican Americans-II for children and adolescents. *Hispanic Journal of Behavioral Sciences, 27*(4), 426–441.

Beck, A. T., Ward, C. H., Mendelson, M., Mock, J., & Erbaugh, J. (1961). An inventory for measuring depression. *Archives of General Psychiatry, 4,* 561–571.

Behrens, J. T. (1997). Does the White Racial Identity Attitude Scale measure racial identity? *Journal of Counseling Psychology, 44,* 3–12.

Bekker, M. H. J., & Boselie, K. A. H. M. (2002). Gender and stress: Is gender role stress? A re-examination of the relationship between feminine gender role stress and eating disorders. *Stress and Health, 18,* 141–149.

Belgrave, F. Z. (1991). Psychosocial predictors of adjustment to disability in African Americans. *Journal of Rehabilitation, 57,* 37–40.

Bell, T. J., & Tracey, T. J. G. (2006). The relation of cultural mistrust and psychological health. *Journal of Multicultural Counseling and Development, 34,* 2–14.

Belmont Report: Ethical Principles and Guidelines for the Protection of Human Subjects of Research (1978). Washington, DC: U.S. Government Printing Office, DHEW Pub. No. (OS) 78–0012.

Bem, S. L. (1974). The measurement of psychological androgyny. *Journal of Consulting and Clinical Psychology, 42,* 155–162.

Bem, S. L. (1981). *A manual for the Bem Sex Role Inventory.* Stanford, CA: Consulting Psychologists.

Benet-Martinez, V., & Haritatos, J. (2005). Bicultural identity integration (BII): Components and psychological antecedents. *Journal of Personality, 73,* 1015–1050.

Bennett, A. D., Jr. (2006). Culture and context: A study of neighborhood effects on racial socialization and ethnic identity content in a sample of African American adolescents. *Journal of Black Psychology, 32,* 479–500.

Bennett, M. J. (1993). Towards ethnorelativism: A developmental model of intercultural sensitivity. In R. M. Paige (Ed.), *Education for the intercultural experience* (pp. 21–71). Yarmouth, ME: Intercultural Press.

Berger, J. M. Levant, R. F., McMillan, K. K., Kelleher, W., & Sellers, A. (2005). Impact of gender role conflict, traditional masculinity ideology, alexithymia, and age on men's attitudes toward psychological help seeking. *Psychology of Men and Masculinity, 6,* 73–78.

Berkay, P. J., Gardner, J. E., & Smith, P. L. (1995). The development of the Opinion About Deaf People scale: A scale to measure hearing adults' beliefs about the capabilities of deaf adults. *Educational and Psychological Measurement, 55,* 105–114.

Berrol, C. F. (1984). Training attitudes toward disabled persons: Effect of a special physical education program. *Archives of Physical Medicine and Rehabilitation, 65,* 760–765.

Berry, J. W. (1980). Acculturation as varieties of adaptation. In A. Padilla (Ed.), *Acculturation: Theory, models, and findings* (pp. 9–25). Boulder, CO: Westview.

Berry, J. W. (1990a). Acculturation and adaptation: A general framework. In W. H. Holtzman & T. H. Bornemann (Eds.), *Mental health of immigrants and refugees* (pp. 90–102). Austin, TX: Hogg Foundation for Mental Health.

Berry, J. W. (1990b). Psychology of acculturation. In J. Berman (Ed.), *Cross-cultural perspectives: Nebraska symposium on motivation* (pp. 201–234). Lincoln: University of Nebraska Press.

Berry, J. W. (1997). Immigration, acculturation, and adaptation. *Applied Psychology An International Review, 46,* 5–33.

Berry, J. W. (2003). Conceptual approaches to acculturation. In K. M. Chun, P. B. Organista, & G. Marin (Eds.), *Acculturation: Advances in theory, measurement, and applied research* (pp. 17–37). Washington, DC: American Psychological Association.

Berry, J. W., & Kim, U. (1988). Acculturation in mental health. In P. R. Dagen, J. W. Berry, & N. Sartorius (Eds.), *Health and cross-cultural psychology: Toward applications* (pp. 207–236). Newbury Park, CA: Sage.

Berry, J. W., & Sam, D. (1997). Acculturation and adaptation. In J. W. Berry, M. H. Segall, & I. Kagitcibasi (Eds.), *Handbook of cross-cultural psychology: Vol. 3. Social behavior and applications* (pp. 291–326). Boston: Allyn & Bacon.

Berryman, J. D. (1989). Attitudes of the public toward educational mainstreaming. *Remedial and Special Education, 10,* 44–49.

Berryman, J. D., & Neal, R. Q., Jr. (1980). The cross validation of the Attitude Toward Mainstreaming Scale

(ATMS). *Educational and Psychological Measurement, 40*, 469–474.

Berryman, J. D., Neal, W. R., Jr., & Robinson, J. E. (1980). The validation of a scale to measure attitudes toward the classroom integration of disabled students. *Journal of Educational Research, 73*, 199–203.

Bidell, M. P. (2005). The Sexual Orientation Counselor Competency Scale: Assessing attitudes, skills, and knowledge of counselors working with lesbian, gay, and bisexual clients. *Counselor Education and Supervision, 44*(4), 267–279.

Binning, K. R., Unzueta, M. M., Huo, Y. J., & Molina, L. E. (2009). The interpretation of multiracial status and its relations to social engagement and psychological well-being. *Journal of Social Issues, 65*, 35–50.

Bishop, M., & Boag, E. M. (2006). Teachers' knowledge about epilepsy and attitudes toward students with epilepsy: Results of a national survey. *Epilepsy and Behavior, 8*, 397–405.

Bishop, M., & Slevin, B. (2004). Teachers' attitudes toward students with epilepsy: Results of a survey of elementary and middle schoolteachers. *Epilepsy & Behavior, 5*, 308–315.

Blanck, P. (1995). Assessing five years of employment integration and economic opportunity under the Americans with Disabilities Act. *Mental and Physical Disability Law Reports, 19*, 384–392.

Blankenship, C. J., & Glover-Graf, N. M. (2006). *A study of Mexican and Mexican Americans' beliefs about God in relation to disability*. Unpublished Manuscript.

Blazina, C., Pisecco, S., & O'Neil, J. M. (2005). An adaptation of the Gender Role Conflict Scale for Adolescents: Psychometric issues and correlates with psychological distress. *Psychology of Men and Masculinity, 6*, 39–45.

Bogardus, E. S. (1925). Social distance and its origins. *Journal of Applied Sociology, 9*, 216–226.

Bordin, E. S. (1979). The generalizability of the psychoanalytic concept of the working alliance. *Psychotherapy: Theory, Research and Practice, 16*, 252–260.

Bordin, E. S. (1994). Theory and research on the therapeutic working alliance: New directions. In A. O. Horvath & L. S. Greenberg (Eds.), *The working alliance: Theory, research, and practice* (pp. 13–37). New York: John Wiley.

Bornstein, K. (1998). *My gender workbook*. New York: Routledge.

Bowe, F. G. (1978). *Handicapping America: Barriers to disabled people*. New York: Harper & Row.

Boyce, W. T., & Boyce, J. C. (1983). Acculturation and changes in health among Navaho boarding school students. *Social Science Medicine, 17*, 219–226.

Bozkaya, I. O., Arhan, E., Sedaroglu, A., Soysal, A. S., Ozkan, S., & Gucuyener, K. (2009). Knowledge of, perception of, and attitude toward epilepsy of schoolchildren in Ankara and the effect of an educational program. *Epilepsy & Behavior, 17*, 56–63.

Bracey, J. R., Bamaca, M. Y., & Umana-Taylor, A.J. (2004). Examining ethnic identity and self-esteem among biracial and monoracial adolescents. *Journal of Youth and Adolescence, 33*, 123–132.

Brady, S., & Busse, W. J. (1994). The Gay Identity Questionnaire: A brief measure of homosexual identity formation. *Journal of Homosexuality, 26*, 1–22.

Braginsky, D. D. (1992). Psychology: Handmaiden to society. In S. Koch & D. E. Leary (Eds.), *A century of psychology as a science* (pp. 880–891). Washington, DC: American Psychological Association.

Brannon, R. (1976). The male sex role: Our culture's blueprint of manhood and what it's done for us lately. In D. S. David & R. Brannon (Eds.), *The forty-nine percent majority: The male sex role* (pp. 1–45). Reading, MA: Addison-Wesley.

Brannon, R., & Juni, S. (1984). A scale for measuring attitudes toward masculinity. *JSAS Catalog of Selected Documents in Psychology, 14*, 6 (Ms. 2012).

Breton, R., Isajiew, W. W., Kalbach, W. E., & Reitz, J. G. (1990). *Ethnic identity and equality*. Toronto, Canada: University of Toronto Press.

Brigham, J. C. (1993). College students' racial attitudes. *Journal of Applied and Social Psychology, 23*, 1933–1967.

Brislin, R.W. (1986). The wording and translation of research instruments. In W. J. Lonnier & J. W. Berry (Eds.), *Field methods in cross-cultural research* (pp. 137–164). Beverly Hills, CA: Sage.

Brohan, D., Slade, M., Clement, S., & Thornicroft, G. (2010). Experiences of mental illness stigma, prejudice and discrimination: A review of measures. *BMC Health Services Research, 10*, 1–11.

Brondolo, E., Gallo, L. C., & Myers, H. F. (2009). Race, racism and health: Disparities, mechanisms, and interventions. *Journal of Behavioral Medicine, 32*, 1–8.

Brondolo, E., Kelly, K. P., Coakley, V., Gordon, T., Thompson, S., Levy, E., Cassells, A., Tobin, J. N., Sweeney, M., & Contrada, R. J. (2005). The Perceived Ethnic Discrimination Questionnaire: Development and preliminary validation of a community version. *Journal of Applied Social Psychology, 35*, 335–365.

Brondolo, E., ver Halen, N. B., Pencille, M., Beatty, D., & Contrada, R. J. (2009). Coping with racism: A selective review of the literature and a theoretical and methodological critique. *Journal of Behavioral Medicine, 32,* 64–88.

Brooks, L. J., Haskins, D. G., & Kehe, J. V. (2004). Counseling and psychotherapy with African American clients. In T. B. Smith (Ed.), *Practicing multiculturalism: Affirming diversity in counseling and psychology* (pp. 145–166). Needham Heights, MA: Allyn & Bacon.

Brown, L. M., & Gilligan, C. (1992). *Meeting at the crossroads: Women's psychology and girls' development.* Cambridge, MA: Harvard University Press.

Brown, T., Mu, K., Peyton, C. G., Rodger, S., Stagnitti, K., Hutton, E., Casey, J., Watson, C., Hong, C. S., Huang, Y-H., & Wu, C-Y. (2009). Occupational therapy students' attitudes towards individuals with disabilities: A comparison between Australia, Taiwan, the United Kingdom, and the United States. *Research in Developmental Disabilities: A Multidisciplinary Journal, 30,* 1541–1555.

Brown, W. (1910). Some experimental results in the correlation of mental abilities. *British Journal of Psychology, 3,* 296–322.

Brunk, M. (2002, October). *Youth services surveys.* Paper presented at the meeting of the Mental Health Data Infrastructure Grant Annual Meeting, Washington, DC.

Brunk, M., Innes, K., & Koch, R. (2002). Caregiver perception of services and children's mental health outcomes: Are they related? In C. Newman, C. Liberton, K. Kutash, & R. M. Friedman (Eds.), *The 15th Annual Research Conference Proceedings, A System of Care for Children's Mental Health: Expanding the Research Base* (pp. 145–152). Tampa, FL: University of South Florida, The Louis de la Parte Florida Mental Health Institute, Research and Training Center for Children's Mental Health.

Bryson, S. (1998). Relationship between race and attitudes toward Black men. *Journal of Multicultural Counseling and Development, 26,* 282–293.

Burk, L. R., Burkhart, B. R., & Sikorski, J. F. (2004). Construction and preliminary validation of the Auburn Differential Masculinity Inventory. *Psychology of Men & Masculinity, 5,* 4–17.

Burkard, A. W., & Ponterotto, J. G. (2008). Cultural identity, racial identity, and the multicultural personality. In L. A. Suzuki, & J. G. Ponterotto (Eds.), *Handbook of multicultural assessment: Clinical, psychological, and educational application* (3rd ed., pp. 52–90). San Francisco, CA: Jossey-Bass.

Burkard, A. W., Pruitt, N. T., Medler, B. R., & Stark-Booth, A. M. (2009). Validity and reliability of the Lesbian, Gay, Bisexual Working Alliance Self-Efficacy Scales. *Training and Education in Professional Psychology, 3*(1), 37–46.

Burn, S. M., & Ward, Z. (2005). Men's conformity to traditional masculinity and relationship satisfaction. *Psychology of Men & Masculinity, 6,* 254–263.

Burnam, M. A., Hough, R. L., Karno, M., Escobar, J. I., & Telles, C. A. (1987). Acculturation and lifetime prevalence of psychiatric disorders among Mexican Americans. *Journal of Health and Social Behavior, 28,* 89–102.

Burnam, M. A., Telles, C. A., Karno, M., Hough, R. L., & Escobar, J. I. (1987). Measurement of acculturation in a community population of Mexican Americans. *Hispanic Journal of Behavioral Sciences, 9*(2), 105–130.

Burt, M. R. (1980). Cultural myths and support for rape. *Journal of Personality and Social Psychology, 38,* 217–230.

Buss, A. H., & Perry, M. (1992). The aggression questionnaire. *Journal of Personality and Social Psychology, 63,* 452–459.

Butler, J. (1990). *Gender trouble.* New York: Routledge.

Butler, R., & Parr, H. (Eds.). (1999). *Mind and body spaces: Geographies of illness, impairment and disability.* London: Routledge.

Bynum, E., Burton, T., & Best, C. (2007). Racism experiences and psychological functioning in African American college freshman: Is racial socialization a buffer? *Cultural Diversity and Ethnic Minority Psychology, 13,* 64–71.

Cabassa, L. J. (2003). Measuring acculturation: Where we are and where we need to go. *Hispanic Journal of Behavioral Sciences, 25,* 127–146.

Cacioppo, J. T., Petty, R. E., & Kao, C. F. (1984). The efficient assessment of need for cognition. *Journal of Personality Assessment, 48,* 306–307.

Campbell, D. T. (1971). *White attitudes toward Black people.* Ann Arbor, MI: Institute for Social Research.

Campbell, J., Gilmore, L., & Cuskelly, M. (2003). Changing student teachers' attitudes towards disability and inclusion. *Journal of Intellectual & Developmental Disability, 28,* 369–374.

Campbell, T., Gillaspy, Jr., J. A., & Thompson, B. (1997). The factor structure of the Bem Sex-Role Inventory (BSRI): Confirmatory factor analysis of long and short forms. *Educational and Psychological Measurement, 57,* 118–124.

Campenha-Bacote, J. (1994). *The process of cultural competence in health care: A culturally competent model of care* (2nd ed.). Cincinnati, OH: Transcultural C.A.R.E. Associates.

Cardenas, M., & Barrientos, J. (2008). The Attitudes Toward Lesbians and Gay Men Scale (ATLG): Adaptation and testing the reliability and validity in Chile. *Journal of Sex Research, 45,* 140–149.

Carney, C. G., & Kahn, K. B. (1984). Building competencies for effective cross-cultural counseling: A developmental view. *The Counseling Psychologist, 12*(1), 111–199.

Carter, R. T. (2007). Racism and psychological and emotional injury: Recognizing and assessing race-based traumatic stress. *The Counseling Psychologist, 35,* 13–105.

Carter, R. T., Yeh, C. J., & Mazzula, S. L. (2008). Cultural values and racial identity statuses among Latino students: An exploratory investigation. *Hispanic Journal of Behavioral Sciences, 30,* 5–23.

Cartwright, B. Y., Daniels, J., & Zhang, S. (2008). Assessing multicultural competence: Perceived versus demonstrated performance. *Journal of Counseling & Development, 86*(3), 318–322.

Carver, P. R., Egan, S. K., & Perry, D. G. (2004). Children who question their heterosexuality. *Developmental Psychology, 40,* 43–53.

Casas, J. M., Vasquez, M. J. T., & Ruiz de Esparza, C. A. (2002). Counseling the Latina/o: A guiding framework for a diverse population. In P. B. Pedersen, J. G. Draguns, W. J. Lonner, & J. E. Trimble (Eds.), *Counseling across cultures* (5th ed., pp. 233–158). Thousand Oaks, CA: Sage.

Cass, V. C. (1979). Homosexual identity formation: A theoretical model. *Journal of Homosexuality, 4,* 219–235.

Cassidy, C., O'Conner, R. C., Howe, E., & Warden, D. (2004). Perceived discrimination and psychological distress: The role of personal and ethnic self-esteem. *Journal of Counseling Psychology, 51,* 329–339.

Castillo, L. G., Conoley, C. W., Brossart, D. F., & Quiros, A. E. (2007). Construction and validation of the Intragroup Marginalization Inventory. *Cultural Diversity and Ethnic Minority Psychology, 13*(3), 232–240.

Castro, F. G. (1998). Cultural competence training in clinical psychology: Assessment, clinical intervention, and research. In C. D. Belar (Ed.), *Comprehensive clinical psychology Vol. 10: Sociocultural individual differences* (pp. 127–140). Oxford, UK: Pergamon/Elsevier Science.

Cavazos-Rehg, P. A., Zayas, L. H., Walker, M. S., & Fisher, E. B. (2006). Evaluating an abbreviated version of the Hispanic Stress Inventory for Immigrants. *Hispanic Journal of Behavioral Sciences, 28,* 498–515.

Cervantes, R. C., Padilla, A., & de Snyder, N. S. (1991). The Hispanic Stress Inventory: A culturally relevant approach to psychological assessment. *Psychological Assessment, 3,* 438–447.

Chan, F., Hua, M.-S., Ju, J. J., & Lam, C. S. (1984). Factorial structure of the Chinese Scale of Attitudes Towards Disabled Persons: A cross-cultural validation. *International Journal of Rehabilitation Research, 7,* 317–319.

Chan, K. S., & Hune, S. (1995). Racialization and pan ethnicity: From Asians in America to Asian Americans. In W. D. Hawley & J. W. Anthony (Eds.), *Toward a common destiny: Improving race relationships in America* (pp. 205–233). San Francisco, CA: Jossey-Bass Inc.

Charlton, J. (2000). *Nothing about us without us: Disability oppression and empowerment.* Los Angeles: University of California Press.

Chavez, D. V., Moran, V. R., Reid, S. L., & Lopez, M. (1997). Acculturative stress in children: A modification of the SAFE Scale. *Hispanic Journal of Behavioral Sciences, 19,* 34–45.

Chavous, T. M., Rivas-Drake, D., Smalls, C., Griffin, T., & Cogburn, C. (2008). Gender matters too: The influence of school racial discrimination and racial identity on academic engagement outcomes among African American adolescents. *Developmental Psychology, 44,* 637–654.

Chen, G. A., LePhuoc, P., Guzmán, M. R., Rude, S., & Dodd, B. G. (2006). Exploring Asian American racial identity. *Cultural Diversity and Ethnic Minority Psychology, 12,* 461–476.

Cheng, C.-Y. (2005). *Bicultural identities: Determinants, processes, and effects.* Unpublished doctoral dissertation. Ann Arbor: University of Michigan.

Cheng, C.-Y., & Lee, F. (2009). Multiracial identity integration: Perceptions of conflict and distance among multiracial individuals. *Journal of Social Issues, 65,* 51–68.

Cheng, C.-Y., Sanchez-Burks, J., & Lee, F. (2008). Connecting the dots within: Creative performance and identity integration. *Psychological Science, 19,* 1177–1183.

Chenoweth, L., Pryor, J., Jeon, Y.-H., & Hall-Pullin, L. (2004). Disability-specific preparation programme plays an important role in shaping students' attitudes towards disablement and patients with disabilities. *Learning in Health and Social Care, 3,* 83–91.

Cheryan, S., & Tsai, J. L. (2007). Ethnic identity. In F. T. L. Leong, A. Inman, A. Ebreo, L. Yang, L. Kinoshita, & M. Fu (Eds.), *Handbook of Asian American psychology* (2nd ed., pp. 125–139). Thousand Oaks, CA: Sage.

Chesler, M. A. (1965). Ethnocentrism and attitudes toward the physically disabled. *Journal of Personality and Social Psychology, 2,* 877–882.

Choi, N., & Fuqua, D. R. (2003). The structure of the Bem Sex Role Inventory: A summary report of 23 validation studies. *Educational and Psychological Measurement, 63,* 872–887.

Choi, N., Fuqua, D. R., & Newman, J. L. (2009). Exploratory and confirmatory studies of the structure of the Bem Sex Role Inventory Short Form with two divergent samples. *Educational and Psychological Measurement, 69,* 696–705.

Choi, S.-C., & Kim, K. (2003). A conceptual exploration of the Korean self in comparison with the western self. In K.-K. Hwang, P. B. Pedersen, & I. Daibu (Eds.), *Progress in Asian social psychology: Conceptual and empirical contributions* (pp. 29–42). Westport, CT: Praeger.

Choi-Misailidis, S. (2009). Multiracial-heritage awareness and personal affiliation (M-HAPA): Understanding identity in people of mixed-race descent. In J. G. Ponterotto, J. M. Casas, L. A. Suzuki, & C. M. Alexander (Eds.), *Handbook of multicultural counseling* (3rd ed., pp. 301–311). Thousand Oaks, CA: Sage.

Choney, S., & Behrens, J. (1996). Development of the Oklahoma Racial Attitude Scale-Preliminary Form (ORAS-P). In G. R. Sodowsky & L. Impara (Eds.), *Multicultural assessment in counseling and clinical psychology* (pp. 225–240). Lincoln, NE: Buros Institute of Mental Measurements.

Choney, S. K., Berryhill-Paapke, E., & Robbins, R. R. (1995). The acculturation of American Indians: Developing frameworks, for research and practice. In J. G. Ponterotto, J. M. Casas, L. A. Suzuki, & C. M. Alexander (Eds.), *Handbook of multicultural counseling* (pp. 73–92). Thousand Oaks, CA: Sage.

Chrisler, J. C. (2008). 2007 Presidential Address: Fear of losing control: Power, perfectionism, and the psychology of women. *Psychology of Women Quarterly, 32,* 1–12.

Chu, J. Y., Porche, M. V., & Tolman, D. L. (2005). The Adolescent Masculinity Ideology in Relationships Scale: Development and validation of a new measure for boys. *Men and Masculinities, 8,* 93–115.

Chun, K. M., & Akutsu, P. D. (2003). Acculturation among ethnic minority families. In K. M. Chun, P. B. Balls Organista, & G. Marin (Eds.), *Acculturation: Advances in theory, measurement, and applied research* (pp. 17–37). Washington, DC: American Psychological Association.

Chun, K. M., Balls Organista, P., & Marin, G. (Eds.). (2003). *Acculturation: Advances in theory, measurement, and applied research.* Washington, DC: American Psychological Association.

Chung, R. H. G. (2001). Gender, ethnicity, and acculturation in intergenerational conflict of Asian American college students. *Cultural Diversity and Ethnic Minority Psychology, 7,* 376–386.

Chung, R. H. G., Kim, B. S. K., & Abreu, J. M. (2004). Asian American Multidimensional Acculturation Scale: Development, factor analysis, reliability, and validity. *Cultural Diversity and Ethnic Minority Psychology, 10*(1), 66–80.

Cicchelli, T., & Cho, S.-J. (2007). Teacher multicultural attitudes. *Educational and Urban Society, 39*(3), 370–381.

Cislo, A. M. (2008). Ethnic identity and self-esteem: Contrasting Cuban and Nicaraguan young adults. *Hispanic Journal of Behavioral Sciences, 30,* 230–250.

Claney, D., & Parker, W. M. (1989). Assessing White racial consciousness and perceived comfort with Black individuals: A preliminary study. *Journal of Counseling & Development, 67,* 449–445.

Clark, K. B., & Clark, M. P. (1939). The development of consciousness of self and the emergence of racial identification of Negro pre-school children. *Journal of Social Psychology, 10,* 591–599.

Clark, R., Coleman, A. P., & Novak, J. D. (2004). Brief report: Initial psychometric properties of the everyday discrimination scale in Black adolescents. *Journal of Adolescence, 28,* 363–368.

Clarke, I., III. (2000). Extreme response style in multicultural research: An empirical investigation. *Journal of Social Behavior and Personality, 15,* 291–311.

Cohen, J. (1977). *Statistical power analysis for the social sciences* (rev. ed.). New York: Academic Press.

Cohen, J. S., & Struening, E. L. (1962). Opinions about mental illness in the personnel of two large mental hospitals. *Journal of Abnormal and Social Psychology, 64,* 439–360.

Cohen, J. S., & Struening, E. L. (1963). Opinions about mental illness: Mental hospital occupational profiles and profile clusters. *Psychological Reports, 12,* 111–124.

Cohen, S., Kamarck, T., & Mermelstein, R. (1983, December). A global measure of perceived stress. *Journal of Health and Social Behavior, 24,* 385–396.

Cohen-Kettenis, P. T., Wallien, M., Johnson, L. L., Owen-Anderson, A. F. H., Bradley, S. J., & Zucker, K. J. (2006). A Parent-report Gender Identity Questionnaire for Children: A cross-national, cross-clinic comparative analysis. *Clinical Child Psychology and Psychiatry, 11,* 397–405.

Cohn, A. M., Seibert, L. A., & Zeichner, A. (2009). The role of restrictive emotionality, trait anger, and masculinity threat in men's perpetration of physical aggression. *Psychology of Men & Masculinity, 10,* 218–224.

Cokley, K. O. (2005). Racial(ized) identity, ethnic identity, and Afrocentric values: Conceptual and methodological challenges in understanding African American identity. *Journal of Counseling Psychology, 52,* 517–526.

Cokley, K., Caldwell, L., Miller, K., & Muhammad, G. (2001). Content analysis of the *Journal of Black Psychology* (1985–1999). *Journal of Black Psychology, 27,* 424–438.

Cokley, K. O., & Helm, K. (2001). Testing the construct validity of scores on the Multidimensional Inventory of Black Identity. *Measurement and Evaluation in Counseling and Development, 34,* 80–95.

Cole, E. R., & Jacob Arriola, K. R. (2007). Black students on White campuses: Toward a two-dimensional model of Black acculturation. *Journal of Black Psychology, 33*(4), 379–403.

Cole, E. R., & Yip, T. (2008). Using outgroup comfort to predict Black students' college experiences. *Cultural Diversity and Ethnic Minority Psychology, 14*(1), 57–66.

Comas-Diaz, L. (1997). Mental health needs of Latinos with professional status. In J. G. Garcia & M. C. Zea (Eds.), *Psychological interventions and research with Latino populations* (pp. 142–165). Boston, MA: Allyn and Bacon.

Comas-Diaz, L. (2006). Latino healing: The integration of ethnic psychology into psychotherapy. *Psychotherapy: Theory, Research, Practice, Training, 43,* 436–453.

Committee on Lesbian and Gay Concerns. (1991). Avoiding heterosexual bias in language. *American Psychologist, 46,* 973–974.

Conner, K. O., Keoske, G., & Brown, C. (2009). Racial differences in attitudes toward professional mental health treatment: The mediating effects of stigma. *Journal of Gerontology Social Work, 52,* 695–712.

Connor, J. W. (1997). *Tradition and change in three generations of Japanese-Americans.* Chicago: Nelson-Hall.

Constantine, M. G. (2002). The relationship between general counseling self-efficacy and self-perceived multicultural counseling competence in supervisees. *The Clinical Supervisor, 20*(2), 81–90.

Constantine, M. G., Donnelly, P. C., & Myers, L. J. (2002). Collective self-esteem and Africultural coping styles in African American adolescents. *Journal of Black Studies, 32*(6), 698–710.

Constantine, M. G., Gloria, A. M., & Ladany, N. (2002). The factor structure underlying three self-report multicultural counseling competence scales. *Cultural Diversity and Ethnic Minority Psychology, 8,* 334–345.

Contrada, R. J., Ashmore, R. D., Gary, M. L., Coups, E., Egeth, J. D., Sewell, A., Ewell, K., Goyal, T. M., & Chasse, V. (2001). Measures of ethnicity-related stress: Psychometric properties, ethnic group differences, and associations with well-being. *Journal of Applied Social Psychology, 31,* 1775–1820.

Conway, M., Alfonsi, G., Pushkar, D., & Giannopoulos, C. (2008). Rumination on sadness and dimensions of communality and agency: Comparing White American and visible minority individuals in a Canadian context. *Sex Roles, 58,* 738–749.

Cook, D. A., & Wiley, C. Y. (2000). Psychotherapy with members of African American churches and spiritual traditions. In P. S. Richards & A. E. Bergin (Eds.), *Handbook of psychotherapy and religious diversity* (pp. 369–396). Washington, DC: American Psychological Association.

Coopersmith, S. (1967). *The antecedents of self-esteem.* San Francisco: Freeman.

Corby, B. C., Hodges, E. V. E., & Perry, D. G. (2007). Gender identity and adjustment in Black, Hispanic, and White American preadolescents. *Developmental Psychology, 43,* 261–266.

Corker, M., & French, S. (Eds.). (1999). *Disability discourse.* Philadelphia, PA: Open University Press.

Cormier, L. S., & Hackney, H. (2008). *The professional counselor: A process guide to helping* (6th ed.). Boston: Pearson/Allyn & Bacon.

Cornelius, L. J., Booker, N. C., Arthur, T. E., Reeves, I. G., & Morgan, O. (2004). The validity and reliability testing of a consumer-based cultural competency inventory. *Research on Social Work Practice, 14*(3), 201–209.

Corning, A. F. (2000). Assessing perceived social inequity: A relative deprivation framework. *Journal of Personality and Social Psychology, 78,* 463–477.

Corning, A. F. (2002). Self-esteem as a moderator between perceived discrimination and psychological distress among women. *Journal of Counseling Psychology, 49,* 117–126.

Corrigan, P. W., Edwards, A. B., Green, A., Diwan, S. L., & Penn, D. L. (2001). Prejudice, social distance, and familiarity with mental illness. *Schizophrenia Bulletin, 27,* 219–225.

Corrigan, P. W., Markowitz, F. E., Watson, A. C. Rowan, D., & Kubiak, M. A. (2003). An attribution model of public discrimination towards persons with mental illness. *Journal of Health Social Behavior, 44,* 162–179.

Cortes, D. E., Rogler, L. H., & Malgady, R. G. (1994). Biculturality among Puerto Rican adults in the United States. *American Journal of Community Psychology, 22*(5), 707–721.

Cortes, D. E., Deren, S., Andia, J., Colon, H., Robles, R., & Kang, S. Y. (2003). The use of the Puerto Rican Biculturality Scale with Puerto Rican drug users in New York and Puerto Rico. *Journal of Psychoactive Drugs, 35*(2), 197–207.

Costantino, G., Dana, R. H., & Malgady, R. G. (2008). TEMAS (Tell-Me-A-Story) assessment in multicultural societies. In G. C. Gamst, A. Der-Karabetian, & R. H. Dana (Eds.), *CBMCS Multicultural Reader* (pp. 59–75). Thousand Oaks, CA: Sage.

Cowan, G., Heiple, B., Marquez, C., Khatchadourian, D., & McNevin, M. (2005). Heterosexuals' attitudes toward hate crimes and hate speech against gays and lesbians: Old-fashioned and modern heterosexism. *Journal of Homosexuality, 49,* 67–82.

Cowen, E. L., Bobrove, P. H., Rockway, A. M., & Stevenson, J. (1967). Development and evaluation of Attitudes to Deafness Scale. *Journal of Personality and Social Psychology, 6,* 183–191.

Cowen, E. L., Underberg, R. P., & Verrillo, R. T. (1958). The development and testing of an attitudes to blindness scale. *Journal of Social Psychology, 48,* 297–304.

Crandall, C. S., Preisler, J. J., & Aussprung, J. (1992). Measuring life event stress in the lives of college students: The Undergraduate Stress Questionnaire (USQ). *Journal of Behavioral Medicine, 15,* 627–662.

Crick, N. R. (1996). The role of relational aggression, overt aggression, and prosocial behavior in the prediction of children's future social adjustment. *Child Development, 67,* 2317–2327.

Crisp, C. (2006). The Gay Affirmative Practice scale (GAP): A new measure for assessing cultural competence with gay and lesbian clients. *Social Work, 51*(1), 115–126.

Crisp, C., Wayland, S., & Gordon, T. (2008). Older gay, lesbian, and bisexual adults: Tools for age-competent and gay affirmative practice. *Journal of Gay and Lesbian Social Services, 20*(1/2), 5–29.

Crocker, J., Luhtanen, R., Blaine, B., & Broadnax, S. (1994). Collective self-esteem and psychological well-being among White, Black and Asian college students. *Personality and Social Psychology Bulletin, 20,* 503–513.

Crocker, J., & Major, B. (1989). Social stigma and self-esteem: The self-protective properties of stigma. *Psychological Review, 96,* 608–630.

Cronbach, L. J. (1951). Coefficient alpha and the internal structure of tests. *Psychometrika, 16,* 297–334.

Cronbach, L. J., & Shavelson, R. J. (2004). My current thoughts on coefficient alpha and successor procedures. *Educational and Psychological Measurement, 64*(3), 391–418.

Cross, T. (1988, Fall). Services to minority populations: Cultural competency continuum. *Focal Point,* p. 3.

Cross, T. L., Bazron, B. J., Dennis, K. W., & Isaacs, M. R. (1989). *Towards a culturally competent system of care*

(Vol. 1). Washington, DC: Georgetown University Child Development Center.

Cross, W. E. (1971, July). The Negro-to-Black conversion experience: Toward a psychology of Black liberation. *Black World, 20,* 13–27.

Cross, W. E. (1991). *Shades of Black: Diversity in African American identity.* Philadelphia, PA: Temple University Press.

Cross, W. E., Jr. (1978). The Thomas and Cross models of psychology nigrescence: A review. *Journal of Black Psychology, 51,* 13–31.

Cross, W. E., Jr. (1995). The psychology of Nigrescence: Revising the Cross model. In J. G. Ponterotto, J. M. Casas, L. A. Suzuki, & C. M. Alexander (Eds.), *Handbook of multicultural counseling* (pp. 93–122). Thousand Oaks, CA: Sage.

Cross, W. E., & Fhagen-Smith, P. (1996). Nigrescence and ego identity development: Accounting for differential Black identity patterns. In P. B. Pederson, J. G. Draguns, W. J. Lonner, & J. E. Trimble (Eds.), *Counseling across cultures* (4th ed., pp. 108–123). Thousand Oaks, CA: Sage.

Cross, W. E., Jr., & Vandiver, B. J. (2001). Nigrescence theory and measurement: Introducing the Cross Racial Identity Scale (CRIS). In J. G. Ponterotto, J. M. Casas, L. A. Suzuki, & C. M. Alexander (Eds.), *Handbook of Multicultural Counseling* (2nd ed., pp. 371–393). Thousand Oaks, CA: Sage.

Croteau, J. M., Anderson, M. Z., DiStefano, T. M., & Chung, Y. B. (1998). *Sexual identity management and discrimination: Research toward promoting career success.* Paper presented at the annual convention of the American College Personnel Association, St. Louis, MO.

Croteau, J. M., Bieschke, K. J., Fassinger, R. E., & Manning, J. L. (2008). Counseling psychology and sexual orientation: History, selective trends, and future directions. In S. D. Brown & R. W. Lent (Eds.), *Handbook of counseling psychology* (4th ed., pp. 194–211). Hoboken, NJ: Wiley and Sons.

Crowne, D. P., & Marlowe, D. (1960). A new scale of social desirability independent of psychopathology, *Journal of Counseling Psychology, 24,* 349–354.

Crowne, D. P., & Marlowe, D. (1964). *The approval motive: Studies in evaluative dependence.* New York: Wiley.

Cuéllar, I. (2000). Acculturation and mental health: Ecological transactional relations of adjustment. In I. Cuéllar & F. A. Paniagua (Eds.), *Handbook of multicultural mental health: Assessment and treatment of diverse populations* (pp. 45–62). San Diego, CA: Academic Press.

Cuéllar, I., Arnold, B., & Gonzalez, G. (1995). Cognitive reference of acculturation: Assessment of cultural constructs in Mexican Americans. *Journal of Community Psychology, 23*(4), 399–356.

Cuéllar, I., Arnold, B., & Maldonado, R. (1995). Acculturation Rating Scale for Mexican Americans-II: A revision of the original ARSMA scale. *Hispanic Journal of Behavioral Sciences, 17,* 275–304.

Cuéllar, I., Harris, L., & Jasso, R. (1980). An acculturation scale for Mexican American normal and clinical populations. *Hispanic Journal of Behavioral Science, 2,* 199–217.

Cuéllar, I., Siles, R. I., & Baracamontes, E. (2004). Acculturation: A psychological construct of continuing relevance for Chicana/o psychology. In R. S. Velasquez, L. M. Arellano, & B. W. McNeill (Eds.), *The handbook of Chicana/o psychology and mental health* (pp. 23–42). Mahwah, NJ: Erlbaum.

Cumming, E., & Cumming, J. (1957). *Closed ranks—An experiment in mental health education.* Cambridge, MA: Harvard University Press.

Cumming-McCann, A., & Accordino, M. P. (2005). An investigation of rehabilitation counselor characteristics, White racial attitudes, and self-reported multicultural counseling competencies. *Rehabilitation Counseling Bulletin, 48,* 167–176.

Currie, M. R., Cunningham, E. G., & Findlay, B. M. (2004). The Short Internalized Homonegativity Scale: Examination of the factorial structure of a new measure of internalized homophobia. *Educational and Psychological Measurement, 64,* 1053–1067.

Cuskelly, M., & Bryde, R. (2004). Attitudes towards the sexuality of adults with an intellectual disability: Parents, support staff, and community sample. *Journal of Intellectual & Developmental Disability, 29,* 255–264.

Cuskelly, M., & Gilmore, L. (2007). Attitudes to Sexuality Questionnaire (Individuals with an Intellectual Disability): Scale development and community norms. *Journal of Intellectual & Developmental Disability, 32,* 214–221.

D'Andrea, M., Daniels, J., & Heck, R. (1991). Evaluating the impact of multicultural counseling training. *Journal of Counseling & Development, 70,* 143–150.

D'Andrea, M., Daniels, J., & Noonan, M. J. (1994). *The Multicultural Awareness, Knowledge, and Skills Survey-Teachers Form (MAKSS-Form T).* Honolulu: University of Hawaii, College of Education.

D'Andrea, M., Daniels, J., & Noonan, M. J. (2003). New developments in the assessment of multicultural competence: The Multicultural Awareness-Knowledge-Skills Survey-Teachers Form. In D. B. Pope-Davis,

H. L. K. Coleman, W. M. Liu, & R. L. Toporek (Eds.), *Handbook of multicultural competencies in counseling & psychology* (pp. 154–167). Thousand Oaks, CA: Sage.

Dai, Y. T. (1995). *The effects of family support expectations of filial piety and stress on health consequences of older adults with diabetes mellitus.* Unpublished doctoral dissertation, University of Washington, Seattle, WA.

Dana, R. H. (1993). *Multicultural assessment perspectives for professional psychology.* Needham Heights, MA: Allyn & Bacon.

Dana, R. H. (1996). Assessment of acculturation in Hispanic populations. *Hispanic Journal of Behavioral Sciences, 18,* 317–328.

Dana, R. H. (1998). *Understanding cultural identity in intervention and assessment.* Thousand Oaks, CA: Sage.

Dana, R. H. (2002). Mental health services for African Americans: A cultural/racial perspective. *Cultural Diversity and Ethnic Minority Psychology, 8,* 3–18.

Dana, R. H. (2005). *Multicultural assessment principles, applications, and examples.* Mahwah, NJ: Erlbaum.

Dana, R. H. (Ed.). (2000). *Handbook of cross-cultural and multicultural personality assessment.* Mahwah, NJ: Erlbaum.

Dana, R. H., & Allen, J. (Eds.). (2008). *Cultural competency training in a global society.* New York: Springer.

Dana, R. H., Behn, J. D., & Gonwa, T. (1992). A checklist for the examination of cultural competence in social agencies. *Research in Social Work Practice, 2,* 220–233.

Dana, R. H., Gamst, G., & Der-Karabetian, A. (2008). *CBMCS multicultural training program.* Thousand Oaks, CA: Sage.

Danzinger, K. (1980). On the threshold of the new psychology: Situating Wundt and James. In W. G. Bringmann & R. D. Tweney (Eds.), *Wundt studies: A centennial collection.* Toronto: Hogrefe.

Daugherty, C. G., & Dambrot, F. H. (1986). Reliability of the Attitudes Toward Women Scale. *Educational and Psychological Measurement, 46,* 449–453.

David, E. J. R., & Okazki, S. (2006). The Colonial Mentality Scale (CMS) for Filipino Americans: Scale construction and psychological implications. *Journal of Counseling Psychology, 53,* 241–252.

Davidson, T. M., & Cardemil, E. V. (2009). Parent–child communication and parental involvement in Latino adolescents. *Journal of Early Adolescence, 29*(1), 99–121.

Davis, J. A. (1959). A formal interpretation of the theory of relative deprivation. *Sociometry, 22,* 280–296.

Davis, L. (Ed.). (2006). *The disability reader.* New York: Routledge.

Davis, M. H. (1983). Measuring individual differences in empathy: Evidence for a multidimensional approach. *Journal of Personality and Social Psychology, 44,* 113–126.

Dawis, R. V. (1987). Scale construction. *Journal of Counseling Psychology, 34,* 481–489.

de la Cruz, F. A., Padilla, G. V., & Agustin, E. O. (2000). Adapting a measure of acculturation for cross-cultural research. *Journal of Transcultural Nursing, 11*(3), 191–198.

de la Cruz, F.A., Padilla, G. V., & Butts, E. (1998). Search and research: Validating a Short Acculturation Scale for Filipino-Americans. *Journal of the American Academy of Nurse Practitioners, 10*(10), 453–460.

de Leon, B., & Mendez, S. (1996). Factorial structure of a measure of acculturation in a Puerto Rican population. *Educational and Psychological Measurement, 56*(1), 155–165.

Dean, D. (1961). Alienation: In measurement and meaning. *American Sociological Review, 26,* 753–758.

DeBlaere, C., & Moradi, B. (2008). Structures of the Schedules of Racist and Sexist Events: Confirmatory factor analyses of African American women's responses. *Psychology of Women Quarterly, 32,* 83–94.

Dembo, T., Leviton, L., & Wright, B. A. (1956). Adjustment to misfortune—a problem of social-psychological rehabilitation. *Artificial Limbs, 3,* 4–63.

Deogracias, J. J., Johnson, L. L., Meyer-Bahlburg, H. F. L., Kessler, S. J., Schober, J. M., & Zucker, K. J. (2007). The Gender Identity/Gender Dysphoria Questionnaire for Adolescents and Adults. *Journal of Sex Research, 44,* 370–379.

Department of Mental Health. (2005). *Preliminary discussion of the performance measurement design for the California Mental Health Services Act.* Sacramento, CA: Department of Mental Health.

Depoy, E., & Gilson, S. R. (2010). *Studying disability: Multiple theories and responses.* Thousand Oaks, CA: Sage.

Der-Karabetian, A. (1980). Relation of two cultural identities of Armenian-Americans. *Psychological Reports, 47,* 123–128.

Der-Karabetian, A., & Balian, N. (1995). Ingroup, outgroup, and global-human identity of Turkish Armenians. *Journal of Social Psychology, 132,* 497–504.

Der-Karabetian, A., Dana, R. H., & Gamst, G. (2008). *CBMCS multicultural training program: Participant workbook.* Thousand Oaks, CA: Sage.

Der-Karabetian, A., Kadi, Z., Elmasian, S., & Yetenekian, A. (1975). Attitudes toward mental illness in Lebanon: An initial report. *Lebanese Medical Journal, 28,* 297–318.

Der-Karabetian, A., & Ruiz, Y. (1997). Affective bicultural and global-human identity scales for Mexican-American adolescents. *Psychological Reports, 80,* 1027–1039.

Derogatis, L. R. (1977). *SCL–90 (Revised) version manual-I.* Baltimore: Johns Hopkins University School of Medicine.

Derogatis, L. R. (1993). *Brief Symptom Inventory: Administration, scoring and procedures manual—II.* Minneapolis, MN: National Computing Systems.

Derogatis, L. R., Lipman, R. S., Rickels, K., Uhlenhuth, E. H., & Cori, L. (1974). The Hopkins Symptom Checklist (HSCL): A self-report symptom inventory. *Behavioral Science, 19,* 1–15.

Derogatis, L. R., Rickels, K., & Rock, A. F. (1976). The SCL-90 and the MMPI: A step in the validation of a new self-report scale. *British Journal of Psychiatry, 128,* 280–289.

Dielman, T. E., Steifel, G., & Cattell, R. B. (1973). A check on the factor structure of the Opinions of [sic] Mental Illness Scale. *Journal of Clinical Psychology, 29,* 92–95.

Diener, E., Emmons, R. A., Larsen, R. J., & Griffin, S. (1985). The Satisfaction With Life Scale, *Journal of Personality Assessment, 49,* 71–75.

Digman, J. M. (1990). Personality structure: Emergence of the five-factor model. *Annual Review of Psychology, 41,* 417–440.

Dillon, F. R., Felix-Ortiz, M., Rice, C., De La Rosa, M., Rojas, P., & Duan, R. (2009). Validating the multidimensional measure of Cultural Identity Scale for Latinos among Latina Mothers and Daughters. *Cultural Diversity and Ethnic Minority Psychology, 15,* 191–201.

Dillon, F. R., & Worthington, R. L. (2003). The Lesbian, Gay, and Bisexual Affirmative Counseling Self-Efficacy Inventory (LGB-CSI): Development, validation, and training implications. *Journal of Counseling Psychology, 50*(2), 235–251.

DiIorio, C. A., Kobau, R., Holden, E. W., Berkowitz, J. M., Kamin, S. L., Antonak, R. F., Austin, J. K., Baker, G. A., Bauman, L. J., Giliam, F., Thurman, D. J., & Price, P. H. (2004). Developing a measure to assess attitudes toward epilepsy in the U.S. population. *Epilepsy & Behavior, 5,* 965–975.

Dohrenwend, B. S., Krasnoff, L., Askenasy, A., & Dohrenwend, B. (1978). Exemplification of a method for scaling life events: The PERI Life Events Scale. *Journal of Health and Social Behavior, 19,* 205–229.

Doorenbos, A. Z., Schim, S. M., Benkert, R., & Borse, N. N. (2005). Psychometric evaluation of the Cultural Competence Assessment Instrument among health care providers. *Nursing Research, 54*(5), 324–331.

Doss, B. D., & Hopkins, J. R. (1998). The Multicultural Masculinity Ideology Scale: Validation from three cultural perspectives. *Sex Roles, 38,* 719–741.

Doughty, J., Baker, G. A., Jacoby, A., & Lavaud, V. (2003). Cross-cultural differences in levels of knowledge about epilepsy. *Epilepsia, 44,* 115–123.

Dovidio, J. F. (2001). On the nature of contemporary prejudice: The third wave. *Journal of Social Issues, 57,* 829–849.

Downing, N., & Roush, K. (1984). From passive acceptance to active commitment: A model of feminist identity development for women. *The Counseling Psychologist, 13,* 695–709.

Downs, A. C., & Engleson, S. A. (1982). The Attitudes Toward Men Scale (AMS): An analysis of the role and status of men and masculinity. *JSAS Catalog of Selected Documents in Psychology, 12*(4), 45 (Ms #2503).

Duckitt, J. (1992). Psychology and prejudice: A historical analysis and integrative framework. *American Psychologist, 47,* 1182–1193.

Dunn, T. W., Smith, T. B., & Montoya, J. A. (2006). Multicultural competency instrumentation: A review and analysis of reliability generalization. *Journal of Counseling & Development, 84*(4), 471–482.

Dunton, B. C., & Fazio, R. H. (1997). An individual difference measure of motivation to control prejudiced reactions. *Personality and Social Psychology Bulletin, 23,* 316–326.

Dupoux, E., Wolman, C., & Estrada, E. (2005). Teachers' attitudes toward integration of students with disabilities in Haiti and the United States. *International Journal of Disability, Development and Education, 52,* 43–58.

Duran, E., & Duran, B. (1995). *Native American postcolonial psychology.* Albany, NY: State University of New York.

Edwards, L. M., & Pedrotti, J. T. (2008). A content and methodological review of counseling articles concerning biracial/multiracial issues. *Journal of Counseling Psychology, 55,* 411–418.

Efron, R. R., & Efron, H. Y. (1967). Measurement of attitudes toward the retarded and an application with educators. *American Journal of Mental Deficiency, 72,* 100–106.

Egan, S. K., & Perry, D. G. (2001). Gender identity: A multidimensional analysis with implications for psychosocial adjustment. *Developmental Psychology, 37,* 451–463.

Eiserman, W. D., Shisler, L., & Healey, S. (1995). A community assessment of preschool providers' attitudes toward inclusion. *Journal of Early Intervention, 19,* 149–167.

Eisler, R. M., & Skidmore, J. R. (1987). Masculine gender role stress: Scale development and component factors in the appraisal of stressful situations. *Behavior Modification, 11,* 123–136.

Elizabeth, P. H., & Green, R. (1984). Childhood sex-role behaviors: Similarities and differences in twins. *Acta Geneticae Medicae et Gemellologiae: Twin Research, 33,* 173–179.

Elsberry, N. L. (1975). Comparison of two scales measuring attitudes toward persons with physical disabilities. *Psychological Reports, 36,* 473–474.

English, R. W. (1971). The application of personality theory to explain psychological reactions to physical disability. *Rehabilitation Research and Practice Review, 3,* 35–47.

Enright, M. S., Conyers, L., & Szymanski, E. M. (1996). Career and career-related educational concerns for college students with disabilities: An overview of legislation, theory, and research. *Journal of Counseling and Development, 75,* 103–114.

Equal Employment Opportunity Commission and the U.S. Department of Justice. (1991). *Americans with disability handbook.* Washington, DC: Government Printing Office. Available at http://www.eeoc.gov/laws/statues/ada.cfm

Erikson, E. H. (1968). *Identity: Youth and crisis.* New York, NY: Norton.

Esparza, P., & Sanchez, B. (2008). The role of attitudinal familism in academic outcomes: A study of urban, Latino high school seniors. *Cultural Diversity and Ethnic Minority Psychology, 14,* 193–200.

Espelage, D. L., & Holt, M. L. (2001). Bullying and victimization during early adolescence: Peer influences in psychosocial correlates. *Journal of Emotional Abuse, 2,* 123–142.

Ethier, K. A., & Deaux, K. (1994). Negotiating social identity in a changing context: Maintaining identification and responding to threat. *Journal of Personality and Social Psychology, 67,* 243–251.

Everett, J. E. (1983). Factor comparability as a means of determining the number of factors and their rotations. *Multivariate Behavioral Research, 18,* 197–218.

Eysenck, H. J., & Eysenck, S. B. G. (1975). Manual of the Eysenck Personality Questionnaire. San Diego, CA: EDITS.

Fang, C. Y., & Myers, H. F. (2001). The effects of racial stressors and hostility on cardiovascular reactivity in African American and Caucasian men. *Health Psychology, 20,* 64–70.

Fassinger, R. E. (1997). *Gay Identity Scale.* Unpublished measure, University of Maryland, College Park.

Fassinger, R. E., & Arseneau, J. R. (2007). "I'd rather get wet than be under that umbrella": Differentiating the experiences and identities of lesbian, gay, bisexual, and transgender people. In K. J. Bieschke, R. M. Perez, & K. A. DeBord (Eds.), *Handbook of counseling and psychotherapy with lesbian, gay, bisexual, and transgender clients* (2nd ed., pp. 19–49). Washington, DC: American Psychological Association.

Fassinger, R. E., & McCarn, S. R. (1997). *Lesbian Identity Scale.* Unpublished measure, University of Maryland, College Park.

Fassinger, R. E., & Miller, B. A. (1996). Validation of an inclusive model of sexual minority identity formation on a sample of gay men. *Journal of Homosexuality, 32,* 53–78.

Felix-Ortiz, M., Newcomb, M. D., & Myers, H. (1994). A multidimensional measure of cultural identity for Latino and Latina adolescents. *Hispanic Journal of Behavioral Sciences, 16,* 99–115.

Fenigstein, A., Scheier, M. F., & Buss, A. H. (1975). Public and private self-consciousness: Assessment and theory. *Journal of Consulting and Clinical Psychology, 43,* 522–527.

Fenigstein, A., & Vanable, P. A. (1992). Paranoia and self-consciousness. *Journal of Personality and Social Psychology, 62,* 129–138.

Ferdman, B. M., & Gallegos, P. I. (2001). Latinos and racial identity development. In C. L. Wijeyesinghe & B. W. Jackson III (Eds.), *New perspectives on racial identity development: A theoretical and practical anthology* (pp. 32–66). New York: New York University Press.

Ferrari, A. M. (2002). The impact of culture upon child rearing practices and definitions of maltreatment. *Child Abuse & Neglect, 26*(8), 793–813.

Fichten, C. S., & Amsel, R. (1988). Thoughts concerning interaction between college students who have a physical disability and their nondisabled peers. *Rehabilitation Counseling Bulletin, 32,* 22–40.

Finch, B. K., Kolody, B., & Vega, W. A. (2000). Perceived discrimination and depression among Mexican-origin adults in California. *Journal of Health and Social Behavior, 41,* 295–313.

Findler, L., Vilchinsky, N., & Werner, S. (2007). The Multidimensional Attitude Scale Toward Persons With Disabilities (MAS): Construction and validation. *Rehabilitation Counseling Bulletin, 50,* 166–167.

Fischer, E. H., & Farina, A. (1995). Attitudes toward seeking professional psychological help: A shortened form and considerations for research. *Journal of College Student Development, 36,* 368–373.

Fischer, A. R., & Shaw, C. M. (1999). African Americans' mental health and perceptions of racist discrimination: The moderating effects of racial socialization experiences and self-esteem. *Journal of Counseling Psychology, 46,* 395–407.

Fischer, A. R., Tokar, D. M., Good, G. E., & Snell, A. F. (1998). More on the structure of male role norms: Exploratory and multiple sample confirmatory analyses. *Psychology of Women Quarterly, 22,* 135–155.

Fischer, A. R., Tokar, D. M., & Serna, G. S. (1998). Validity and construct contamination of the Racial Identity Attitude Scale–Long Form. *Journal of Counseling Psychology, 45,* 212–224.

Fischer, A. R., Tokar, R. M., Mergl, M. M., Good, G. E., Hill, M. S., & Blum, S. A. (2000). Assessing women's feminist identity development: Studies of convergent, discriminant, and structural validity. *Psychology of Women Quarterly, 24,* 15–29.

Fischer, E. H., & Turner, J. L. (1970). Orientation to seeking professional psychological help: Development and research utility of an attitude scale. *Journal of Consulting and Clinical Psychology, 45,* 994–1001.

Fisher, C. B., Wallace, S. A., & Fenton, R. E. (2000). Discrimination distress during adolescence. *Journal of Youth and Adolescence, 29,* 679–695.

Fisher, D. G., & Fick, C. (1993). Measuring social desirability: Short forms of the Marlowe-Crowne Social Desirability Scale. *Educational and Psychological Measurement, 53,* 417–424.

Fisher, T., Davis, C. M., Yarber, W. L., & Davis, S. L. (2010). *Handbook of sexuality related measures* (3rd ed.). New York: Taylor & Francis.

Fitzgerald, L., Gelfand, M., & Drasgow, F. (1995). Measuring sexual harassment: Theoretical and psychometric advances. *Basic and Applied Social Psychology, 17,* 425–445.

Flannery, W. P., Reise, S. P., & Yu, J. (2001). An empirical comparison of acculturation models. *Personality and Social Psychology Bulletin, 27*(8), 1035–1045.

Flores, L. Y., Carrubba, M. D., & Good, G. E. (2006). Feminism and Mexican American women: Examining the psychometric properties of two measures. *Hispanic Journal of Behavioral Sciences, 28,* 48–64.

Florian, V., Weisel, A., Kravetz, S., & Shurka-Zernitsky, E. (1989). Attitudes in the kibbutz and city toward persons with disabilities: A multifactorial comparison. *Rehabilitation Counseling Bulletin, 32,* 210–218.

Folkman, S., & Lazarus, R. S. (1988). *Ways of Coping Questionnaire sampler set manual, test booklet, scoring key.* Palo Alto, CA: Mind Garden.

Forbes, G. B., Collinsworth, L. L., Jobe, R. L., Braun, K. D., & Wise, L. M. (2007). Sexism, hostility toward women, and endorsement of beauty ideals and practices: Are beauty ideals associated with oppressive beliefs? *Sex Roles, 56,* 265–273.

Forlin, C., Fogarty, G., & Carroll, A. (1999). Validation of the factor structure of the Interactions with Disabled Persons scale. *Australian Journal of Psychology, 51,* 50–55.

Forman, T. A., Williams, D. R., & Jackson, J. S. (1997). Race, place, and discrimination. *Perspectives on Social Problems, 9,* 231–261.

Fosados, R., McClain, A., Ritt-Olson, A., Sussama, S., Soto, D., Baezconde-Garbanati, L., & Unger, J. B. (2007). The influence of acculturation on drug and alcohol use in a sample of adolescents. *Addictive Behaviors, 32,* 2990–3004.

Fowers, B. J., & Richardson, F. C. (1996). Why is multiculturalism good? *American Psychologist, 51,* 609–621.

Frabroni, M., Saltstone, R., & Hughes, S. (1990). The Frabroni Scale of Ageism (FSA): An attempt at a more precise measure of ageism. *Canadian Journal on Aging, 9,* 56–66.

Franco, J. N. (1983). An acculturation scale for Mexican-American children. *Journal of General Psychology, 108,* 175–181.

Frisby, C. L. (2008). Academic achievement testing for culturally diverse groups. In L. A. Suzuki & J. G. Ponterotto (Eds.), *Handbook of multicultural assessment: Clinical, psychological, and educational applications* (3rd ed., pp. 520–541). San Francisco, CA: John Wiley & Sons.

Fuertes, J. N., Miville, M. L., Mohr, J. J., Sedlacek, W. E., & Gretchen, D. (2000). Factor structure and short form of the Miville-Guzman Universality-Diversity Scale. *Measurement and Evaluation in Counseling and Development, 33,* 157–169.

Fuertes, J. N., & Westbrook, F. D. (1996). Using the Social, Attitudinal, Familial, and Environmental (S.A.F.E.) Acculturation Stress Scale to assess the adjustment needs of Hispanic college students. *Measurement and Evaluation in Counseling and Development, 29,* 67–76.

Fujioka, Y. (2005). Black media images as a perceived threat to African American ethnic identity: Coping responses, perceived public perception, and attitudes towards affirmative action. *Journal of Broadcasting & Electronic Media, 49,* 450–467.

Fuligini, A. J., Tseng, V., & Lam, M. (1999). Attitudes toward family obligations among American adolescents with Asian, Latin American, and European backgrounds. *Child Development, 70,* 1030–1044.

Furnham, A., & Procter, E. (1989). Belief in a just world: Review and critique of the individual difference literature. *British Journal of Social Psychology, 28*(4), 365–384.

Gaertner, S. L., & Dovidio, J. F. (1986). The aversive form of racism. In S. L. Gaertner & J. F. Dovidio (Eds.), *Prejudice, discrimination and racism* (pp. 1–34). Orlando, FL: Academic.

Gaines, Jr., S. O., Marelich, W. D., Bledsoe, K. L., Steers, W. N., Henderson, M. C., Granrose, C. S., Barájas, L., Hicks, D., Lyde, M., Takahashi, Y., Yum, N., Rios, D. I., Garcia, B. F., Farris, K. R., & Page, M. S. (1997). Links between race/ethnicity and cultural values as mediated by race/ethnic identity and moderated by gender. *Journal of Personality and Social Psychology, 72*(6), 1460–1476.

Galambos, N. L., Peterson, A. C., Richards, M., & Gitelson, I. B. (1985). The Attitudes Towards Women Scale for Adolescents (AWSA): A study of reliability and validity. *Sex Roles, 13,* 343–356.

Gamst, F. C., & Norbeck E. (Eds.). (1976). *Ideas of culture: Sources and uses.* New York: Holt, Rinehart, & Winston.

Gamst, G. (2008, March). *An overview of the Multicultural Assessment Intervention Process (MAIP) model.* Paper presented at the Culturally Informed Evidence Based Practices: Translating Research and Policy for the Real World Conference, Bethesda, MD.

Gamst, G., Aguilar-Kitibutr, A., Herdina, A., Hibbs, S., Krishtal, E., Lee, R., Roberg, R., Ryan, E., Stephens, H., & Martenson, L. (2003). Effects of racial match on Asian American mental health consumer satisfaction. *Mental Health Services Research, 5,* 197–208.

Gamst, G., & Dana, R. H. (2005) *Testing the MAIP model: A proposed method for assessing culturally sensitive mental health service delivery for adults and children.* Unpublished manuscript. University of La Verne, La Verne, CA.

Gamst, G., Dana, R. H., & Der-Karabetian, A. (2000). Ethnic match and client ethnicity effects on global assessment and visitation. *Journal of Community Psychology, 28,* 547–564.

Gamst, G., Dana, R. H., Der-Karabetian, A., Aragon, M., Arellano, L. M., & Kramer, T. (2002). Effects of Latino acculturation and ethnic identity on mental health outcomes. *Hispanic Journal of Behavioral Sciences, 24*(4), 479–504.

Gamst, G., Dana, R. H., Der-Karabetian, A., Aragon, M., Arellano, L., Morrow, G., & Martenson, L. (2004). Cultural competency revised: The California Brief Multicultural Competence Scale. *Measurement and Evaluation in Counseling and Development, 37*(3), 163–183.

Gamst, G., Dana, R. H., Der-Karabetian, A., & Kramer, T. (2001). Asian American mental health clients: Effects of ethnic match and age on global assessment and visitation. *Journal of Mental Health Counseling, 23,* 57–71.

Gamst, G., Dana, R. H., Der-Karabetian, A., & Kramer, T. (2004). Ethnic match and treatment outcomes for child and adolescent mental health center clients. *Journal of Counseling & Development, 82,* 457–465.

Gamst, G., Dana, R. H., Meyers, L. S., Der-Karabetian, A., & Guarino, A. J. (2009). An analysis of the Multicultural Assessment Intervention Process model. *International Journal of Culture and Mental Health, 2*(1), 51–64.

Gamst, G., Der-Karabetian, A., & Dana, R. H. (2008). *CBMCS multicultural reader.* Thousand Oaks, CA: Sage.

Gamst, G., Herdina, A., Mondragon, E., Munguia, F., Pleitez, A., Stephens, H., Vo, D., & Cuéllar, I. (2006). Relationship among respondent identity, acculturation, and homeless status on a homeless population's functional status. *Journal of Clinical Psychology, 62*(12), 1485–1501.

Gamst, G., Meyers, L. S., & Guarino, A. J. (2008). *Analysis of variance designs: A conceptual and computational approach with SPSS and SAS.* London: Cambridge University Press.

Gamst, G., Rogers, R., Der-Karabetian, A., & Dana, R. H. (2006). Addressing mental health disparities: A preliminary test of the Multicultural Assessment Intervention Process (MAIP) model. In E. V. Metrosa (Ed.), *Racial and ethnic disparities in health and healthcare.* Hauppauge, NY: Nova Science Publishers.

Garcia, J. (1982). Ethnicity and Chicanos: Measurement of ethnic identification, identity, and consciousness. *Hispanic Journal of Behavioral Sciences, 4,* 295–314.

Garcia, M., & Lega, L. I. (1979). Development of a Cuban ethnic identity questionnaire. *Hispanic Journal of Behavioral Sciences, 1,* 247–261.

Gardner-Kitt, D. L., & Worrell, F. C. (2007). Measuring Nigrescence attitudes in school-aged adolescents. *Journal of Adolescence, 30,* 187–202.

Garner, D. M. (1991). *Eating Disorder Inventory—2 manual.* Odessa, FL: Psychological Assessment Resources.

Garrett, M. T., & Pichette, E. F. (2000). Red as an apple: Native American acculturation and counseling with or without reservation. *Journal of Counseling & Development, 78,* 3–13.

Garvar-Pinhas, A., & Schmelkin, L. P. (1989). Administrators' and teachers' attitudes toward mainstreaming. *Remedial and Special Education, 10,* 38–43.

Gee, G. C., Delva, J., & Takeuchi, D. T. (2006). Relationships between self-reported unfair treatment and prescription medication use, illicit drug use, and alcohol dependence among Filipino Americans. *American Journal of Public Health, 96,* 1–8.

Gerstmann, E. A., & Kramer, D. A. (1997). Feminist identity development: Psychometric analyses of two feminist identity scales. *Sex Roles, 36,* 327–348.

Geisinger, K. F. (1994). Cross-cultural normative assessment: Translation and adaptation issues influencing the normative interpretation of assessment instruments. *Psychological Assessment, 6,* 304–312.

Gething, L. (1991). *The Interaction with Disabled Persons Scale: Manual and kit.* Sydney, Australia: University of Sydney.

Gething, L. (1994). The Interaction with Disabled Persons Scale. *Journal of Social Behavior and Personality, 9,* 23–42.

Gibson, S., & Dembo, M. H. (1984). Teacher efficacy: A construct validation. *Journal of Educational Psychology, 76,* 569–582.

Gil, A. G., Wagner, E. F., & Vega, W. A. (2000). Acculturation, familism and alcohol use among Latino adolescent males: Longitudinal relations. *Journal of Community Psychology, 28*(4), 443–458.

Gilbert, D. C., & Levinson, D. J. (1956). Ideology, personality and institutional policy in the mental hospital. *Journal of Abnormal and Social Psychology, 53,* 263–271.

Gillespie, B. L., & Eisler, R. M. (1992). Development of the Feminine Gender Role Stress Scale: A cognitive-behavioral measure of stress, appraisal, and coping for women. *Behavior Modification, 16,* 426–438.

Gilmore, L., & Chambers, B. (2010). Intellectual disability and sexuality: Attitudes of disability support staff and leisure industry employees. *Journal of Intellectual & Developmental Disability, 35,* 22–28.

Giorgi, A. (1985). Sketch of a psychological phenomenological method. In A. Giorgi (Ed.), *Phenomenology and psychological research* (pp. 12–28). Pittsburgh, PA: Duquesne University Press.

Glaser, J., & Knowles, E. D. (2008). Implicit motivation to control prejudice. *Journal of Experimental Social Psychology, 44,* 164–172.

Glass, G. V., McGaw, B., & Smith, M. L. (1981). *Meta-analysis in social research.* Beverly Hills, CA: Sage.

Glick, P., & Fiske, S. T. (1996). The Ambivalent Sexism Inventory: Differentiating hostile and benevolent sexism. *Journal of Personality and Social Psychology, 70*(3), 491–512.

Glick, P., & Fiske, S. T. (1997). Hostile and benevolent sexism: Measuring ambivalent sexist attitudes toward women. *Psychology of Women Quarterly, 21,* 119–135.

Glick, P., & Fiske, S. T. (1999). The Ambivalence Toward Men Inventory. *Psychology of Women Quarterly, 23,* 519–536.

Glick, P., Lameiras, M., Fiske, S. T., Eckes, T., Masser, B., Volpato, C., Manganelli, A. M., Pek, J. C. X., Huang, L., Sakalli-Ugurlu, N., Castro, Y. R., D'Avila Pereira, M. L., Willemsen, T. M., Brunner, A., Six-Materna, I., & Wells, R. (2004). Bad but bold: Ambivalent attitudes toward men predict gender inequality in 16 nations. *Journal of Personality and Social Psychology, 86,* 713–728.

Gloria, A. M., Ruiz, E. L., & Castillo, E. M. (2004). Counseling and psychotherapy with Latino and Latina clients. In T. B. Smith (Ed.), *Practicing multiculturalism: Affirming diversity in counseling and psychology* (pp. 67–189). Boston, MA: Allyn and Bacon.

Godfrey, S., Richman, C. L., & Withers, T. N. (2000). Reliability and validity of a new scale to measure prejudice: The GRISMS. *Current Psychology, 19,* 3–20.

Goff, P. A., Steele, C. M., & Davies, P. G. (2008). The space between us: Stereotype threat and distance in interracial contexts. *Journal of Personality and Social Psychology, 94,* 91–107.

Goffman, E. (1963). *Stigma: Notes on the management of spoiled identity.* Englewood Cliffs, NJ: Prentice Hall.

Goldman, G. F., & Gelso, C. J. (1997). Kohut's theory of narcissism and adolescent drug abuse treatment. *Journal of Psychoanalytic Psychology, 14,* 81–94.

Gone, J. P. (2007). "We never was happy living like a Whiteman": Mental health disparities and the postcolonial predicament in American Indian communities. *American Journal of Community Psychology, 40,* 290–300.

Gonzalez, G. M., Carter, C., & Blanes, E. (2007). Bilingual computerized speech recognition screening for depression symptoms. *Hispanic Journal of Behavioral Sciences, 29*(2), 156–180.

Goodkind, J. R., Gonzales, M., Malcoe, L. H., & Espinosa, J. (2008). The Hispanic Women's Social Stressor Scale: Understanding the multiple social stressors of U.S.- and Mexico-born Hispanic women. *Hispanic Journal of Behavioral Sciences, 30,* 200–229.

Gordon, E. D., Minnes, P. M., & Holden, R. R. (1990). The structure of attitudes toward persons with disability, when specific disability and context are considered. *Rehabilitation Psychology, 35,* 79–90.

Gordon, M. M. (1964). *Assimilation in American life: The role of race, religion, and national origin.* New York: Oxford University Press.

Gordon, M. M. (1978). *Human nature, class, and ethnicity.* New York: Oxford University Press.

Gore, J. P. (2009). Psychotherapy and traditional healing for American Indians: Exploring the prospects for therapeutic integration. *The Counseling Psychologist, 38 (2),* 166–235.

Gough, H. G. (1987). *California Psychological Inventory: Administrator's Guide.* Palo Alto, CA: Consulting Psychologist Press.

Grace, C. A. (1984). *The relationship between racial identity attitudes and choice of typical and atypical occupations among Black college students.* Unpublished doctoral dissertation, Columbia University Teachers College, New York.

Grady, K. E. (1981). Sex bias in research design. *Psychology of Women Quarterly, 5,* 628–636.

Graf, N. M., Blankenship, C. J., Sanchez, G., & Carlson, R. (2007). Living on the line: Mexican and Mexican American attitudes toward disability. *Rehabilitation Counseling Bulletin, 50,* 153–165.

Grand, S. A., Bernier, J. E., & Strohmer, D. C. (1982). Attitudes toward disabled persons as a function of social context and specific disability. *Rehabilitation Psychology, 27,* 165–173.

Graves, T. (1967). Acculturation, access, and alcohol in a tri-ethnic community. *American Anthropologist, 69,* 396–421.

Green, D. E., Walkey, F. H., McCormick, I. A., & Taylor, A. J. W. (1988). Development and evaluation of the Hopkins Symptom Checklist with New Zealand and United States respondents. *Australian Journal of Psychology, 40,* 6–70.

Green, E. G. T., Staerklé, C., & Sears, D. O. (2006). Symbolic racism and Whites' attitudes toward punitive and preventive crime policies. *Law and Human Behavior, 30,* 435–454.

Green, K., & Harvey, D. (1983). Cross-validation of the Attitude Toward Mainstreaming Scale. *Educational and Psychological Measurement, 43,* 1255–1261.

Green, N. L. (1995). Development of the Perceptions of Racism Scale. *Journal of Nursing Scholarship, 27,* 141–146.

Green, R. G., Kiernan-Stern, M., Bailey, K., Chambers, Claridge, R., Jones, G., Kitson, G., Leek, S., Leisey, M., Vadas, K., & Walker, K. (2005). The Multicultural Counseling Inventory: A measure for evaluating social work student and practitioner self-perceptions of their multicultural competencies. *Journal of Social Work Education, 41*(2), 191–208.

Green, R. G., Kiernan-Stern, M., & Baskind, F. R. (2005). White social workers' attitudes about people of color. *Journal of Ethnic & Cultural Diversity in Social Work, 14,* 47–68.

Grieger, I. (2008). A cultural assessment framework and interview protocol. In L. A. Suzuki & J. G. Ponterotto (Eds.), *Handbook of multicultural assessment: Clinical, psychological, and educational applications* (pp. 132–161). San Francisco: Jossey-Bass.

Grieger, I., & Ponterotto, J. G. (1995). A framework for assessment in multicultural counseling. In J. G. Ponterotto, J. M. Casas, L. A. Suzuki, & C. M. Alexander (Eds.), *Handbook of multicultural counseling* (pp. 357–374). Thousand Oaks, CA: Sage.

Grills, C., & Longshore, D. (1996). Africentrism: Psychometric analyses of a self-report measure. *Journal of Black Psychology, 22*(1), 86–106.

Griner, D., & Smith, T. B. (2006). Culturally adapted mental health interventions: A meta-analytic review. *Psychotherapy: Theory, Research, Practice, & Training, 43,* 531–548.

Grotevant, H. D., & Adams, G. R. (1984). Development of an objective measure to assess ego identity in adolescence: Validation and replication. *Journal of Youth and Adolescence, 13,* 419–438.

Groth-Marnet, G. (2009). *Handbook of psychological assessment* (5th ed.). Hoboken, NJ: John Wiley & Sons.

Gulliksen, H. (1987). *Theory of mental tests.* Hillsdale, NJ: Lawrence Erlbaum Associates. (Original work published in 1950)

Gynther, M. D., Burkhart, B. R., & Hovanitz, C. (1979). Do face-valid items have more predictive validity than subtle items? The case of the MMPI Pd Scale. *Journal of Consulting and Clinical Psychology, 47,* 295–300.

Hafer, M., Wright, W. R., & Godley, S. H. (1983). Dimensionality of the Attitudes Toward Disabled Persons Scale. *Educational and Psychological Measurement, 43,* 459–463.

Haghighat, R. (2005). The development of an instrument to measure stigmatization: Factor analysis and origin of stigmatization. *European Journal of Psychiatry, 19,* 144–154.

Hall, G. C. N. (2001). Psychotherapy research with ethnic minorities: Empirical, ethical, and conceptual issues. *Journal of Counseling and Clinical Psychology, 69,* 502–510.

Hall, G. C. N. & Eap, S. (2007). Empirically supported therapies for Asian Americans. In F. T. L. Leong, A. G. Inman, A. Ebreo, L. H. Yang, L. Kinoshita, & M. Fu (Eds.), *Handbook of Asian American psychology* (2nd ed., pp. 449–468). Thousand Oaks, CA: SAGE Publications.

Hamilton, D. (1981). *Cognitive processes in stereotyping and intergroup behavior.* Hillsdale, NJ: Erlbaum.

Hampton, N. Z., & Xiao, F. (2007). Psychometric properties of the Mental Retardation Inventory-Revised in Chinese college students. *Journal of Intellectual Disability Research, 52,* 299–308.

Hansen, G. L. (1982). Measuring prejudice against homosexuality (homosexism) among college students: A new scale. *Journal of Social Psychology, 117,* 233–236.

Harding, C. M., & Zahniser, J. H. (1994). Empirical correction of seven myths about schizophrenia with implications for treatment. *Acta Psychiatrica Scandinavica Supplement, 384,* 140–146.

Harley, D., Nowak, T., Gassaway, L., & Savage, T. (2002). Lesbian, gay, bisexual, and transgender college students with disabilities: A look at multiple cultural minorities. *Psychology in the Schools, 39,* 525–538.

Harrell, S. P. (1994). *The Racism and Life Experience Scale—Revised.* Unpublished Manuscript.

Harrell, S. P. (2000). A multidimensional conceptualization of racism-related stress: Implications for the well-being of people of color. *American Journal of Orthopsychiatry, 70,* 42–57.

Harter, S. (1998). *The Self-Perception Profile for Children: Revision of the Perceived Competence Scale for Children (Manual).* Denver, CO: University of Denver.

Harth, R. (1971). Attitudes towards minority groups as a construct in assessing attitudes towards the mentally retarded. *Education and Training of the Mentally Retarded, 6,* 142–147.

Hatton, C., & Emerson, E. (1995). The development of a shortened "Ways of Coping" questionnaire for use with direct care staff in learning disability services. *Mental Handicap Research, 8,* 237–251.

Hays, D. G. (2008). Assessing multicultural competence in counselor trainees: A review of instrumentation and future directions. *Journal of Counseling & Development, 86*(1), 95–101.

Hays, D. G., Chang, C. Y., & Decker, S. L. (2007). Initial development and psychometric data for the Privilege and Oppression Inventory. *Measurement and Evaluation in Counseling and Development, 40,* 66–79.

Hazuda, H. P., Haffner, S. M., Stern, M. P., & Eifler, C. W. (1988). Effects of acculturation and socioeconomic status on obesity and diabetes in Mexican Americans. *American Journal of Epidemiology, 128*(6), 1289–1301.

Hazuda, H. P., Stern, M. P., & Haffner, S. M. (1988). Acculturation and assimilation among Mexican Americans: Scales and population-based data. *Social Science Quarterly, 69,* 687–706.

Hegarty, P. (2002). "It's not a choice, it's the way we're built": Symbolic beliefs about sexual orientation in the U.S. and Britain. *Journal of Community & Applied Social Psychology, 12,* 153–166.

Helmreich, R. L., & Spence, J. T. (1978). Work and family orientation questionnaire: An objective instrument to assess components of achievement motivation and attitudes toward family and career. *Catalog of Selected Documents in Psychology, 8,* 35.

Helmreich, R. L., Spence, J. T., & Wilhelm, J. A. (1981). A psychometric analysis of the Personal Attributes Questionnaire. *Sex Roles, 7,* 1097–1108.

Helmreich, R. L., & Stapp, J. (1974). Short forms of the Texas Social Behavior Inventory: An objective of self-esteem. *Bulletin of the Psychonomic Society, 4,* 473–475.

Helms, J. E. (1984). Toward a theoretical model for explaining the effects of race on counseling: A Black and White model. *The Counseling Psychologist, 12,* 153–165.

Helms, J. E. (Ed.). (1990a). *Black and White racial identity: Theory, research, and practice.* Westport, CT: Greenwood.

Helms, J. E. (1990b). Toward a model of White racial identity development. In J. E. Helms (Ed.), *Black and White racial identity: Theory, research, and practice* (pp. 49–66). Westport, CT: Greenwood.

Helms, J. E. (1990c). *"Womanist" identity attitudes: An alternative to feminism in counseling theory and research.* Unpublished Paper. University of Maryland, College Park, MD.

Helms, J. E. (1995). An update of Helms' White and people of color racial identity models. In J. G. Ponterotto, J. M. Casas, L. A. Suzuki, & C. M. Alexander (Eds.), *Handbook of multicultural counseling* (pp. 181–198). Thousand Oaks, CA: Sage.

Helms, J. E. (1996). Toward a methodology for measuring and assessing racial identity as distinguished from ethnic identity. In G. Sodowsky & J. Impara (Eds.), *Multicultural assessment in counseling and clinical Psychology* (pp. 143–192). Lincoln, NE: Buros Institute of Mental Measurement.

Helms, J. E. (2002). A remedy for the Black-White test-score disparity. *American Psychologist, 57,* 303–304.

Helms, J. E. (2007). Some better practices for measuring racial and ethnic identity constructs. *Journal of Counseling Psychology, 54,* 235–246.

Helms, J. E., & Carter, R. T. (1990). Development of the White racial identity inventory. In J. E. Helms (Ed.), *Black and White racial identity: Theory, research, and practice* (pp. 67–80). Westport, CT: Greenwood Press.

Helms, J. E., & Cook, D. A. (1999). *Using race and culture in counseling and psychotherapy: Theory and process.* Boston, MA: Allyn and Bacon.

Helms, J. E., & Parham, T. A. (1996). The Racial Identity Attitude Scale. In R. L. Jones (Ed.), *Handbook of tests and measurements for Black populations* (pp. 167–172). Oakland, CA: Cobb & Henry.

Helms, J. E., & Talleyrand, R. M. (1997). Race is not ethnicity. *American Psychologist, 52,* 1246–1247.

Henley, N. M., Meng, K., O'Brien, D., McCarthy, W. J., & Sockloskie, R. J. (1998). Developing a scale to measure the diversity of feminist attitudes. *Psychology of Women Quarterly, 22,* 317–348.

Henry, D., Keys, C., Jopp, D., & Balcazar, F. (1996). The Community Living Attitudes Scale, Mental Retardation Form: Development and psychometric properties. *Mental Retardation, 34,* 149–158.

Henry, D. B., Duvdevany, I., Keys, C. B., Balcazar, F. E., & Walsh, K. (2004). Attitudes of American and Israeli staff toward people with intellectual disabilities. *Mental Retardation, 42,* 26–36.

Henry, P. J., & Sears, D. O. (2002). The Symbolic Racism 2000 Scale. *Political Psychology, 23,* 253–283.

Herek, G. M. (1984). Attitudes toward lesbians and gay men: A factor analytic study. *Journal of Homosexuality, 10,* 39–51.

Herek, G. M. (1987). Can functions be measured? A new perspective on the functional approach to attitudes. *Social Psychology Quarterly, 50,* 285–303.

Herek, G. M. (1988). Heterosexual attitudes toward lesbians and gay men: Correlates and gender differences. *Journal of Sex Research, 25,* 451–477.

Herek, G. M. (1994). Assessing heterosexuals' attitudes toward lesbians and gay men. In B. Greene & G. M. Herek (Eds.), *Lesbian and gay psychology: Theory, research and clinical applications* (pp. 206–228). Thousand Oaks, CA: Sage Publications.

Herek, G. M. (2004). Beyond "homophobia": Thinking about sexual prejudice and stigma in the twenty-first century. *Sexuality Research & Social Policy, 1,* 6–24.

Herek, G. M. (2009). Hate crimes and stigma-related experiences among sexual minority adults in the United States: Prevalence estimates from a national probability sample. *Journal of Interpersonal Violence, 24,* 54–74.

Herek, G. M., & Capitanio, J. P. (1995). Black heterosexuals' attitudes toward lesbians and gay men in the United States. *Journal of Sex Research, 32,* 95–105.

Herek, G. M., Cogan, J. C., & Gillis, J. R. (2002). Victim experiences in hate crimes based on sexual orientation. *Journal of Social Issues, 58,* 319–339.

Herek, G. M., Gillis, J. R., & Cogan, J. C. (2009). Internalized stigma among sexual minority adults: Insights from a social psychological perspective. *Journal of Counseling Psychology, 56,* 32–43.

Herek, G. M., & Gonzalez-Rivera, M. (2006). Attitudes toward homosexuality among U.S. residents of Mexican descent. *Journal of Sex Research, 43,* 122–135.

Herek, G. M., Kimmel, D. C., Amaro, H., & Melton, G. B. (1991). Avoiding heterosexual bias in psychological research. *American Psychologist, 46,* 973–974.

Herek, G. M., & McLemore, K. A. (2010). The Attitudes toward Lesbians and Gay Men (ATLG) scale. In T. Fisher, C. M. Davis, W. L. Yarber, & S. L. Davis (Eds.), *Handbook of sexuality-related measures* (3rd ed.). New York: Taylor & Francis.

Hergenrather, K., & Rhodes, S. (2007). Exploring undergraduate student attitudes toward persons with disabilities: Application of the Disability Social Relationship Scale. *Rehabilitation Counseling Bulletin, 50,* 66–75.

Hernandez, A. G., & La Fromboise, T. D. (1985, August). *The development of the Cross-Cultural Counseling Inventory.* Paper presented at the meeting of the American Psychological Association, Los Angeles.

Hesbacher, P. T., Rickels, K., Morris, R. J., Newman, H., & Rosenfeld, H. (1980). Psychiatric illness in family practice. *Journal of Clinical Psychiatry, 41,* 6–10.

Hightower, A. D., Work, W. C., Cowen, E. L., Lotyczewski, B. S., Spinell, A. P., Guare, J. C., & Rohrbeck, C.A. (1986). The Teacher–Child Rating Scale: A brief objective measure of elementary children's social problem behaviors and competencies. *School Psychology Review, 15,* 393–409.

Hill, D. B., & Willoughby, B. L. B. (2005). The development and validation of the Genderism and Transphobia Scale. *Sex Roles, 53,* 531–544.

Hill, J. S., Pace, T. M., & Robbins, R. R. (2010). Decolonizing personality assessment and honoring indigenous voices: A critical examination of the MMPI–2. *Cultural Diversity and Ethnic Minority Psychology, 16*(1), 16–25.

Hochschild, A. R. (1989). *The second shift: Working parents and the revolution at home.* New York: Viking.

Hoffman, L. W., & Kloska, D. D. (1995). Parents' gender-based attitudes toward marital roles and child rearing: Development and validation of new measures. *Sex Roles, 32,* 273–295.

Hoffmann, M. L., Powlishta, K. K., & White, K. J. (2004). An examination of gender differences in adolescent adjustment: The effect of competence on gender role differences in symptoms of psychopathology. *Sex Roles, 50,* 795–810.

Hoffmann, T., Dana, R. H., & Bolton, B. (1985). Measured acculturation and MMPI-168 performance of Native American adults. *Journal of Cross-Cultural Psychology, 16*(2), 243–256.

Hohenshil, T. H., & Humes, C. W. (1979). Roles of counseling in ensuring the rights of the handicapped. *Personnel and Guidance Journal, 58,* 221–227.

Holcomb-McCoy, C. C. (2000). Multicultural counseling competencies: An exploratory factor analysis. *Journal of Multicultural Counseling and Development, 28*(2), 83–97.

Holcomb-McCoy, C. C., & Day-Vines, N. (2004). Exploring school counselor multicultural competence: A multidimensional concept. *Measurement and Evaluation in Counseling and Development, 37*(3), 154–162.

Holcomb-McCoy, C., Harris, P., Hines, E. M., & Johnston, G. (2008). School counselors' multicultural self-efficacy: A preliminary investigation. *Professional School Counseling, 11*(3), 166–178.

Holcomb-McCoy, C., & Myers, J. E. (1999). Multicultural competence and counselor training: A national survey. *Journal of Counseling & Development, 77,* 294–302.

Hong, S., Kim, B. S. K., & Wolfe, M. M. (2005). A psychometric revision of the European American Values Scale for Asian Americans using the Rausch model. *Measurement and Evaluation in Counseling and Development, 37,* 194–207.

Hood, R. W., Jr. (1973). Dogmatism and opinion about mental illness. *Psychological Reports, 32,* 1283–1290.

Hooker, E. (1957). The adjustment of the male homosexual. *Journal of Projective Techniques, 21,* 18–31.

Horse, P. G. (2001). Reflections on American Indian identity. In C. L. Wijeyesinghe & B. W. Jackson III (Eds.), *New perspectives on racial identity development: A theoretical and practical anthology* (pp. 91–107). New York: New York University Press.

Hsu, J. (1983). Asian family interaction patterns and their therapeutic implications. *International Journal of Family Psychiatry, 4,* 307–320.

Huang, Y., Brewster, M. E., Moradi, B., Goodman, M. B., Wiseman, M. C., & Martin, A. (2010). Content analysis of literature about LGB people of color: 1998–2007. *The Counseling Psychologist, 38,* 363–396.

Hudson, W. W., Murphy, G. J., & Nurius, P. S. (1983). A short-form scale to measure liberal vs. conservative orientations toward human sexual expression. *Journal of Sex Research, 19,* 258–272.

Hudson, W. W., & Ricketts, W. A. (1980). A strategy for the measurement of homophobia. *Journal of Homosexuality, 5,* 357–372.

Hui, C. H. (1988). Measurement of individualism-collectivism. *Journal of Research in Personality, 22,* 17–36.

Hunt, C. S., & Hunt, B. (2004). Changing attitudes toward people with disabilities: Experimenting with an educational intervention. *Journal of Managerial Issues, 16,* 266–280.

Hunt, L. M., Schneider, S., & Comer, B. (2004). Should "acculturation" be a variable in health research? A critical review of research on U.S. Hispanics. *Social Science and Medicine, 59,* 973–986.

Hunter, J. E., & Schmidt, F. L. (1990). *Methods of meta-analysis: Correcting error and bias in research findings.* Newbury Park, CA: Sage.

Hurt, M. M., Nelson, J. A., Turner, D. L., Haines, M. E., Ramsey, L. R., Erchull, M. J., & Liss, M. (2007). Feminism: What is it good for? Feminine norms and objectification as the link between feminist identity and clinically relevant outcomes. *Sex Roles, 57,* 355–363.

Huynh, Q-L., Howell, R. T., & Benet-Martinez, V. (2009). Reliability of bidimensional acculturation scores. *Journal of Cross-Cultural Psychology, 40*(2), 256–274.

Hwang, W. (2007). Acculturative family distancing: Theory, research and clinical practice. *Psychotherapy Theory, Research, Practice, Training, 43,* 397–409.

Hwang, W., & Goto, S. (2008). The impact of perceived racial discrimination on the mental health of Asian American college students. *Cultural Diversity and Ethnic Minority Psychology, 14,* 326–335.

Hyde, J. S. (2007). New directions in the study of gender similarities and differences. *Current Directions in Psychological Science, 16,* 259–263.

Iacono, T., Tracy, J., Keating, J., & Brown, T. (2009). The Interaction with Disabled Persons scale: Revisiting its internal consistency and factor structure, and examining item-level properties. *Research in Developmental Disabilities, 30,* 1490–1501.

Iazzo, A. N. (1983). The construction and validation of Attitudes Toward Men Scale. *Psychological Record, 33,* 371–378.

Inglehart, R., Basanez, M., & Moreno, A. (1993). *Human values and beliefs: A cross-cultural sourcebook: Political, religious, sexual and economic norms in 43 countries from the 1990–1993 World Values Survey.* Ann Arbor: University of Michigan Press.

Inman, A. G. (2006). South Asian women: Identities and conflict. *Cultural Diversity and Ethnic Minority Psychology, 12*(2), 306–319.

Inman, A. G., Ladany, N., Constantine, M. G., & Morano, C. K. (2001). Development and preliminary validation of the Cultural Values Conflict Scale for South Asian women. *Journal of Counseling Psychology, 48*(1), 17–27.

Iwamoto, D. K., & Liu, W. M. (2010). The impact of racial identity, ethnic identity, Asian values, and race-related stress on Asian Americans and Asian international college students' psychological well-being. *Journal of Counseling Psychology, 57,* 79–91.

Izard, C. E. (1977). *Human emotion.* New York: Plenum.

Izard, C. E. (2004). *The psychology of emotions.* New York: Springer.

Jackson, A. P., & Turner, S. (2004). Counseling and psychotherapy with Native American clients. In T. B. Smith (Ed.), *Practicing multiculturalism: Affirming diversity in counseling and psychology* (pp. 215–233). Boston, MA: Allyn and Bacon.

Jackson, D. N. (1984). *Personality Research Form manual* (3rd ed.). Port Huron, MI: Research Psychologists Press.

Jackson, D. N. (1974). *Personality Research Form—Form E.* Goshen, NY: Research Psychological Press.

Jackson, D. N. A. (1970). A sequential system for personality scale development. *Current Topics in Clinical and Community Psychology, 2,* 61–96.

Jackson, S., & Collingswood, H. (1988). A nation divided on Black progress. *Business Week/Harris Poll,* 1–4.

Jacobson, C. (1985). Resistance to affirmative action: Self-interest or racism? *Journal of Conflict Resolution, 29,* 306–329.

Jadhav, S., Littlewood, R., Ryder, A. G., Chakraborty, A., Jain, S., & Barua, M. (2007). Stigmatization of severe mental illness in India: Against the simple industrialization hypothesis. *Indian Journal of Psychiatry, 49,* 189–194.

Jagose, A. (1996). *Queer theory: An introduction.* New York: New York University Press.

Jakupcak, M., Lisak, D., & Roemer, L. (2002). The role of masculine ideology and masculine gender role stress in men's perpetration of relationship violence. *Psychology of Men and Masculinity, 3,* 97–106.

Jane, D. M., Hunter, G. L., & Lozzi, B. M. (1999). Do Cuban American women suffer from eating disorders: Effects of media exposure and acculturation. *Hispanic Journal of Behavioral Sciences, 21,* 212–218.

Janey, B. A., Janey, N. V., Goncherova, N., & Savchenko, V. (2006). Masculinity ideology in Russian society: Factor structure and validity of the Multicultural Masculinity Ideology Scale. *Journal of Men's Studies, 14,* 93–108.

Janis, I. L., & Field, P. B. (1959). A behavioral assessment of persuasibility: Consistency of individual differences. In C. Hovland & I. L. Janis (Eds.), *Personality and persuasibility* (pp. 29–54). New Haven, CT: Yale University Press.

Jarvis, W. B. G., & Petty, R. E. (1996). The need to evaluate. *Journal of Personality and Social Psychology, 70,* 172–194.

Jenkins, C. D., Kreger, B. E., Rose, R. M., & Hurst, M. (1980). Use of a monthly health review to ascertain illness and injuries. *Public Health Reviews, 70,* 82–84.

Jenkins, P. (2004). *Dream catchers: How mainstream America discovered Native spirituality.* Oxford, UK: Oxford University Press.

Jerrell, J. M. (1995). The effects of client–counselor match on service use and costs. *Administration and Policy in Mental Health, 23,* 119–126.

Jerrell, J. M. (1998). Effect of ethnic matching of young clients and mental health staff. *Cultural Diversity and Mental Health, 4,* 297–302.

Jerrell, J. M. (2006). Psychometrics of the MHSIP adult consumer survey. *Journal of Behavioral Health Services & Research, 33*(4), 483–488.

Johnson, C., & Darrow, A.-A. (Winter, 2003). Attitudes of junior high school music students from Italy and the USA toward individuals with disability. *Bulletin of the Council for Research in Music Education, 155,* 33–43.

Johnson, H., Bloomberg, K., & Iacono, T. (2008). Student and professional attitudes and interests in working with people with complex communication needs. *International Journal of Speech-Language Pathology, 10,* 286–296.

Johnson, L. L., Bradley, S. J., Birkenfeld-Adams, A. S., Kuksis, M. A. R., Maing, D. M., Mitchell, J. N., & Zucker, K. J. (2004). A parent-report Gender Identity Questionnaire for children. *Archives of Sexual Behavior, 33,* 105–116.

Jones, E., & Kay, M. (1992). Instrumentation in cross-cultural research. *Nursing Research, 41*(3), 186–188.

Jones, E. E., Farina, A., Hastorf, A. H., Marcus, H., Miller, D. T., & Scott, R. A. (1984). *Social stigma: The psychology of marked relationships.* New York: Freeman.

Jones, J. M. (1991). Psychological models of race: What have they been and what should they be? In J. Goodchilds (Ed.), *Psychological perspective on human diversity in America* (pp. 7–46). Washington, DC: American Psychological Association.

Jöreskog, K. G., & Sörbom, D. (1989). *LISREL VII: User's reference guide.* Mooresville, IN: Scientific Software.

Jöreskog, K. G., & Sörbom, D. (1993). *LISREL 8* [Computer software]. Chicago, IL: Scientific Software International, Inc.

Jöreskog, K. G., & Sörbom, D. (2006). *LISREL 8.8 for Windows* [Computer software]. Lincolnwood, IL: Scientific Software International, Inc.

Joseph, M., Struckman-Johnson, C., Quevillon, R., & Banka, S. R. (2008). Heterosexual men's attitudes toward gay men: A hierarchical model including masculinity, openness, and theoretical explanations. *Psychology of Men & Masculinity, 9,* 154–166.

Judy, R. W., & D'Amico, C. (1997). *Workforce 2020: Work and workers in the 21st century.* Indianapolis, IN: Hudson Institute.

Kaiser, S. B., Freeman, C. M., & Wingate, S. B. (1985). Stigmata and negotiated outcomes: The management of appearance by persons with physical disabilities. *Deviant Behavior, 6,* 205–224.

Kaiser, S. B., Wingate, S. B., & Freeman, C. M. (1987). Acceptance of physical disability and attitudes toward personal appearance. *Rehabilitation Psychology, 32,* 51–58.

Kanner, A. D., Coyne, J. C., Schaeffer, C., & Lazarus, R. S. (1981). Comparison of two modes of stress measurement: Daily hassles and uplifts versus major life events. *Journal of Behavioral Medicine, 4,* 1–39.

Kanter, J. W., Rusch, L. C., & Brondino, M. J. (2008). Depression self-stigma: A new measure and preliminary findings. *Journal of Nervous and Mental Disorders, 196,* 663–670.

Kao, H.-F. S., & Travis, S. (2005a). Effects of acculturation and social exchange on the expectations of filial piety among Hispanic/Latino parents of adult children. *Nursing and Health Sciences, 7*(4), 226–234.

Kao, H.-F. S., & Travis, S. S. (2005b). Development of the Expectations of Filial Piety Scale-Spanish version. *Journal of Advanced Nursing, 52*(6), 682–688.

Katz, I., & Hass, R. G. (1988). Racial ambivalence and American value conflict: Correlational and priming studies of dual cognitive structures. *Journal of Personality and Social Psychology, 55,* 893–905.

Katz, I., Hass, R. G., & Bailey, J. (1988). Attitudinal ambivalence and behavior toward people with disabilities. In H. E. Yuker (Ed.), *Attitudes toward persons with disabilities.* New York: Springer.

Kazarian, S. S., & Boyadjian, M. D. (2008). Validation of the Multigroup Ethnic Identity Measure among ethnic Armenian adolescents in Lebanon. *Identity: An International Journal of Theory and Research, 8,* 335–347.

Keane, T. M., Caddell, J. M., & Taylor, K. L. (1988). Mississippi Scale for Combat-Related Post-Traumatic Stress Disorder: Three studies in reliability and validity. *Journal of Consulting and Clinical Psychology, 56,* 85–90.

Khalid, R., & Frieze, I. H. (2004). Measuring perceptions of gender roles: The IAWS for Pakistanis and U.S. immigrant populations. *Sex Roles, 51,* 293–300.

Khawaja, N. G., Gomez, I., & Turner, G. (2009). Development of the Multicultural Mental Health Awareness Scale. *Australian Psychologist, 44*(2), 67–77.

Kilmartin, C. (2009). *The masculine self* (4th ed.). Cornwall-on-Hudson, NY: Sloan Publishing.

Kim, B. S. K. (2009). Acculturation and enculturation of Asian Americans: A primer. In N. Tewari & A. N. Alvarez (Eds.), *Asian American psychology: Current perspectives* (pp. 97–112). Mahwah, NJ: Lawrence Erlbaum Associates, Inc.

Kim, B. S. K., & Abreu, J. M. (2001). Acculturation measurement: Theory, current instruments, and future directions. In J. G. Ponterotto, J. M. Casas, L. A. Suzuki, & C. M. Alexander (Eds.), *Handbook of multicultural counseling* (2nd ed., pp. 394–424). Thousand Oaks, CA: Sage.

Kim, B. S. K., Ahn, A. J., & Lam, A. (2009). Theories and research on acculturation and enculturation experiences among Asian American families. In N.-H. Trinh, Y. C. Rho, F. G. Lu, & K. M. Sanders (Eds.), *Handbook of mental health and acculturation in African American families* (pp. 25–43). New York: Human Press.

Kim, B. S. K., Atkinson, D. R., & Yang, P. H. (1999). The Asian Values Scale: Development, factor analysis, validation, and reliability. *Journal of Counseling Psychology, 46*, 342–352.

Kim, B. S. K., Cartwright, B. Y., Asay, P. A., & D'Andrea, M. J. (2003). A revision of the Multicultural Awareness, Knowledge, and Skills Survey-Counselor Edition. *Measurement and Evaluation in Counseling and Development, 36*, 161–180.

Kim, B. S. K., & Hong, S. (2004). A psychometric revision of the Asian Values Scale using the Rasch model. *Measurement and Evaluation in Counseling and Development, 37*, 15–27.

Kim, B. S. K., Li, L. C., & Liang, C. T. H. (2002). Effects of Asian American client adherence to Asian cultural values, session goal, and counselor emphasis of client expression on career counseling process. *Journal of Counseling Psychology, 49*, 342–354.

Kim, B. S. K., Li, L. C., & Ng, G. F. (2005). The Asian American Values Scale-Multidimensional: Development, reliability and validity. *Cultural Diversity and Ethnic Minority Psychology, 11*, 187–201.

Kim, B. S. K., Soliz, A., Orellana, B., & Alamilla, S. G. (2009). Latino/a Values Scale: Development, reliability, and validity. *Measurement and Evaluation in Counseling and Development, 42*(2), 71–91.

Kim, B. S. K., Yang, P. H., Atkinson, D. R., Wolfe, M. M., & Hong, S. (2001). Cultural values similarities and differences among Asian American ethnic groups. *Cultural Diversity and Ethnic Minority Psychology, 7*, 343–361.

Kim, C., Laroche, M., & Tomiuk, M. A. (2001). A measure of acculturation for Italian Canadians: Scale development and construct validity. *International Journal of Intercultural relations, 25*, 607–637.

Kim, J. (2001). Asian American identity development theory. In C. L. Wijeyesinghe & B. W. Jackson III (Eds.), *New perspectives on racial identity development: A theoretical and practical anthology* (pp. 67–90). New York: New York University Press.

Kinder, D. R., & Sears, D. O. (1981). Prejudice and politics: Symbolic racism versus racial threats to the good life. *Journal of Personality and Social Psychology, 40*, 414–431.

King, M., Dinos, S., Shaw, J., Watson, R., Stevens, S., Passetti, F., Weich, S., & Serfaty, M. (2007). The Stigma Scale: Development of a standardized measure of the stigma of mental illness. *British Journal of Psychiatry, 190*, 248–254.

King, P. M., & Howard-Hamilton, P. (2003). Assessment of multicultural competence. *NASPA Journal, 40*(2), 119–133.

Kingdon, D., Sharma, T., & Hart, D. (2004). What attitudes do psychiatrists hold towards people with mental illness? *Psychiatric Bulletin, 28*, 401–406.

Kirkwood, A. D., & Stamm, B. H. (2006). A social marketing approach to challenging stigma. *Professional Psychology: Research and Practice, 5*, 472–476.

Kite, M. E., & Deaux, K. (1986). Attitudes toward homosexuality: Assessment and behavioral consequences. *Basic and Applied Social Psychology, 7*(2), 137–162.

Kitzinger, C. (1987). *The social construction of lesbianism.* Beverly Hills, CA: Sage.

Kline, T. J. B. (2005). *Psychological testing: A practical approach to design and evaluation.* Thousand Oaks, CA: Sage.

Klineberg, O. (1935). *Race differences.* New York: Harper & Brothers.

Klonoff, E. A., & Landrine, H. (1995). The Schedule of Sexist Events: A measure of lifetime and recent sexist discrimination in women's lives. *Psychology of Women Quarterly, 19*, 439–472.

Klonoff, E. A., & Landrine H. (1999). Cross-validation of the Schedule of Racist Events. *Journal of Black Psychology, 25*, 231–254.

Klonoff, E. A., & Landrine, H. (2000). Revising and improving the African American Acculturation Scale. *Journal of Black Psychology, 26*(2), 235–261.

Knifton, L., Walker, A., & Quinn, N. (2008). Workplace intervention can reduce stigma. *Journal of Public Mental Health, 7*, 40–51.

Knight, G. P., Bernal, M. E., Cota, M. K., Garza, C. A., & Ocampo, K. A. (1993). In M. E. Bernal & G. P. Knight (Eds.), *Ethnic identity: Formation and transmission among Hispanic and other minorities*. Albany: State University of New York.

Kobau, R., DiIorio, C. A., Anderson, L. A., & Price, P. (2006). Further validation and reliability testing of the Attitudes and Beliefs about Living with Epilepsy (ABLE) components of the CDC epilepsy program instrument on stigma. *Epilepsy & Behavior, 8*, 552–559.

Kobau, R., DiIorio C., Chapman D., Delvecchio P., & SAMHSA/CDC Mental Illness Stigma Panel Members. (2009). Attitudes about mental illness and its treatment: Validation of a generic scale for public health surveillance of mental illness associated stigma. *Community Mental Health Journal, 46*, 164–176.

Kocarek, C. E., Talbot, D. M., Batka, J. C., & Anderson, M. Z. (2001). Reliability and validity of three measures of multicultural competency. *Journal of Counseling & Development, 79*(4), 486–496.

Kohatsu, E. L. (2005). Acculturation: Current and future directions. In R. J. Carter (Vol. Ed.), *Handbook of racial-cultural psychology and counseling, Vol 1: Theory and research* (pp. 207–231). Hoboken, NJ: Wiley.

Kohatsu, E. L., Concepcion, W. R., & Perez, P. (2010). Incorporating levels of acculturation in counseling practice. In J. G. Ponterotto, J. M. Casas, L. A. Suzuki, & C. M. Alexander (Eds.), *Handbook of multicultural counseling* (3rd ed., pp. 343–356). Thousand Oaks, CA: Sage.

Komiya, N. (2000). Development of the Emotional Openness Scale. *Dissertation Abstracts International, 60*, 6417 (UMI No. AAI9953873).

Koneru, V. K., Weisman de Mamani, A. G., Flynn, P. M., & Betancourt, H. (2007). Acculturation and mental health: Current findings and recommendations for future research. *Applied and Preventive Psychology, 12*(2), 76–96.

Kopplin, D. A., Greenfield, T. K., & Wong, H. Z. (1977). Changing patterns of substance use on campus: A four-year follow-up study. *International Journal of the Addictions, 12*, 73–94.

Korman, M. (1974). National conference on levels and patterns of professional training in psychology: Major themes. *American Psychologist, 29*, 301–313.

Koss, M., & Oros, C. J. (1982). Sexual Experiences Survey: A research instrument investigating sexual aggression and victimization. *Journal of Consulting and Clinical Psychology, 53*, 455–457.

Kovacs, M. (1992). Children's Depression Inventory (CDI) manual. North Tonawanda, NY: Multi-Health Systems.

Kramer, D. A., Kahlbaugh, P. E., & Goldston, R. B. (1992). A measure of paradigm beliefs about the social world. *Journal of Gerontology, 47*, 180–189.

Kressin, N. R., Raymond, K. L., & Manze, M. (2008). Perceptions of race/ethnicity-based discrimination: A review of measures and evaluation of their usefulness for the health care setting. *Journal of Health Care for the Poor and Underserved, 19*, 697–730.

Krieger, N. (1990). Racial and gender discrimination: Risk factors for high blood pressure? *Social Science and Medicine, 30*, 1273–1281.

Krieger, N., Smith, K., Naishadham, D., Hartman, C., & Barbeau, E. M. (2005). Experiences of discrimination: Validity and reliability of a self-report measure for population health research on racism and health. *Social Science & Medicine, 61*, 1576–1596.

Kuder, G. F., & Richardson, M. W. (1937). The theory of the estimation of reliability. *Psychometrika, 2*, 151–160.

Kuder, G. F., & Richardson, M. W. (1939). The calculation of test reliability coefficients based on the method of rational equivalence. *Journal of Educational Psychology, 30*(9), 681–687.

Kumas-Tan, Z., Beagan, B., Loppie, C., MacLeod, A., & Frank, B. (2007). Measures of cultural competence: Examining hidden assumptions. *Academic Medicine, 82*(6), 548–557.

Kurpius, S. E., & Stafford, M. E. (2006). *Testing and measurement: A user-friendly guide*. Thousand Oaks, CA: Sage.

Kwan, K.-L. K. (2000). The Internal-External Identity Measure: Factor analytic structures based on a sample of Chinese Americans. *Educational and Psychological Measurement, 60*, 142–152.

Kwan, K.-L. K., Gong, Y., & Maestas, M. (2010). Language, translation, and validity in the adaptation of psychological tests for multicultural counseling. In J. G. Ponterotto, J. M. Casas, L. A. Suzuki, & C. M. Alexander (Eds.), *Handbook of multicultural counseling* (3rd ed., pp. 397–412). Thousand Oaks, CA: Sage.

Kwan, K.-L. K., & Sodowsky, G. R. (1997). Internal and external ethnic identity and their correlations: A study of Chinese American immigrants. *Journal of Multicultural Counseling and Development, 25*, 51–67.

Kwate, N. O. A. (2003). Cross-validation of the Africentrism Scale. *Journal of Black Psychology, 29*, 308–324.

LaFleur, N. K., Leach, M. M., & Rowe, W. (2002). *Manual: Oklahoma Racial Attitudes Scale*. Unpublished Manual.

LaFromboise, T. D., Coleman, H. L. K., & Hernandez, A. (1991). Development and factor structure of the Cross-Cultural Counseling Inventory-Revised. *Professional Psychology: Research and Practice, 22*(5), 380–388.

LaFromboise, T. D., & Jackson, M. (1996). MCT theory and Native-American populations. In D. W. Sue, A. E. Ivey,

& P. B. Pedersen (Eds.), *A theory of multicultural counseling and therapy* (pp. 192–203). Pacific Grove, CA: Brooks/Cole.

Lam, A. G., & Sue, S. (2001). Client diversity. *Psychotherapy: Theory, Research, Practice, and Training, 38*, 479–486.

Lam, B. T. (2008). The function of acculturation and collective self-esteem on prejudicial attitudes among Vietnamese American young adults. *Journal of Human Behavior in the Social Environment, 18*, 350–363.

Lam, T. C. M. (1995). A review of conceptualization and measurement of acculturation. In *Multicultural education: The state of the art* (Vol. 2, pp. 129–143). Toronto, ON: Multicultural Education Society of Canada.

Landrine, H., & Klonoff, E. A. (1994). The African American Acculturation Scale: Development, reliability, and validity. *Journal of Black Psychology, 20*(2), 104–127.

Landrine, H., & Klonoff, E. A. (1995). The African American Acculturation Scale II: Cross-validation and short form. *Journal of Black Psychology, 21*(2), 124–152.

Landrine, H., & Klonoff, E. A. (1996). *African American acculturation: Deconstructing race and reviving culture.* Thousand Oaks, CA: Sage.

Landrine, H., & Klonoff, E. A. (1996). The Schedule of Racist Events: A measure of racial discrimination and a study of its negative physical and mental health consequences. *Journal of Black Psychology, 22*, 144–168.

Landrine, H., Klonoff, E. A., Corral, I., Fernandez, S., & Roesch, S. (2006). Conceptualizing and measuring ethnic discrimination in health research. *Journal of Behavioral Medicine, 29*, 79–94.

Lara, M., Gamboa, C., Kahramanian, M. I., Morales, L. S., & Hayes Bautista, D. E. (2005). Acculturation and Latino health in the United States: A review of the literature and its sociopolitical context. *Annual Review of Public Health, 26*, 367–97.

Lara-Cantú, M. A. (1989). A sex role inventory with scales for "machismo" and "self-sacrificing woman." *Journal of Cross-Cultural Psychology, 20*, 386–398.

Laroche, M., Kim, C., & Tomiuk, M. A. (1998). Italian ethnic identity and its relative impact on the consumption of convenient and traditional foods. *Journal of Consumer Marketing, 15*, 125–151.

Laroche, M., Kim, C., Tomiuk, M. A., & Belisle, D. (2005). Similarities in Italian and Greek multidimensional ethnic identity: Some implications for food consumption. *Canadian Journal of Administrative Science, 21*, 143–167.

Larrivee, B., & Cook, L. (1979). Mainstreaming: A study of the variables affecting teacher attitude. *Journal of Special Education, 13*, 315–324.

Larsen, K. S., Reed, M., & Hoffman, S. (1980). Attitudes of heterosexuals toward homosexuality: A Likert-type scale and construct validity. *Journal of Sex Research, 16*(3), 245–257.

Larson, K. S., Reed, M., & Hoffman, S. (1980). Attitudes of heterosexuals toward homosexuality: A Likert-type scale and construct validity. *Journal of Sex Research, 16*, 245–257.

Larson, L. M., Suzuki, L. A., Gillespie, K. N., Potenza, M. T., Bechtel, M. A., & Toulouse, A. L. (1992). Development and validation of the Counseling Self-Estimate Inventory. *Journal of Counseling Psychology, 1*, 105–120.

Lazarus, R. S., & Folkman, S. (1984). *Stress, appraisal and coping.* New York: Springer.

Leaper, C., & Van, S. R. (2008). Masculinity ideology, covert sexism, and perceived gender typicality in relation to young men's academic motivation and choices in college. *Psychology of Men & Masculinity, 9*, 139–153.

Leary, M. R. (1983). A brief version of the Fear of Negative Evaluation Scale. *Personality and Social Psychology Bulletin, 9*, 371–375.

Lee, M., Puig, A., Pasquarella-Delay, L., Denney, G., Rai, A. A., Dallape, A., & Parker, W. M. (2007). Revising the White Racial Consciousness Development Scale. *Measurement and Evaluation in Counseling and Development, 39*, 194–208.

Lee, R. M. (2003). Do ethnic identity and other-group orientation protect against discrimination for Asian Americans? *Journal of Counseling Psychology, 50*, 133–141.

Lee, R. M. (2005). Resilience against discrimination: Ethnic identity and other-group orientation as protective factors for Korean Americans. *Journal of Counseling Psychology, 52*, 36–45.

Lee, R. M., Cho, J., Kim, G., & Ngo, V. (2000). Construction of the Asian American Family Conflicts Scale. *Journal of Counseling Psychology, 47*, 211–222.

Lee, R. M., Jung, K. R., Su, J. C., Tran, A. G. T. T., & Bahrassa, N. F. (2009). The family life and adjustment of Hmong American sons and daughters. *Sex Roles, 60*(7–8), 549–558.

Lehman, A. F. (1988). A Quality of Life Interview for the chronically mentally ill. *Evaluation and Program Planning, 11*, 51–62.

Lehman, A. F. (1998). *Quality of Life Interview: Self-Administered Short Form (TL-305 Version) Manual.* Center for Mental Health Services Research, Department of Psychiatry, University of Maryland, Baltimore.

Lehman, P. (2000). *A validity study of the Femininity Ideology Scale.* Master's thesis, Florida Institute of Technology.

Lent, R. W., Hill, C. E., & Hoffman, M. A. (2003). Development and validation of the Counselor Activity Self-Efficacy Scale. *Journal of Counseling Psychology, 50,* 97–108.

Leone, L., Van der Zee, K. I., van Oudenhoven, J. P., Perugini, M., & Ercolani, A. P. (2005). The cross-cultural generalizability and validity of the Multicultural Personality Questionnaire. *Personality and Individual Differences, 38,* 1449–1462.

Leong, C. H. (2007). Predictive validity of the Multicultural Personality Questionnaire: A longitudinal study on the socio-psychological adaptation of Asian undergraduates who took part in a study-abroad program. *International Journal of Intercultural Relations, 31,* 545–559.

Leung, P. (2003). Multicultural competencies and rehabilitation counseling/psychology. In D. B. Pope-Davis, H. L. K. Coleman, W. M. Liu, & Toporek (Eds.), *Handbook of multicultural competencies in counseling and psychology* (pp. 439–455). Thousand Oaks, CA: Sage.

Levant, R. F., Good, G. E., Cook, S. W., O'Neil, J. M., Smalley, K. B., Owen, K., & Richmond, K. (2006). The Normative Male Alexithymia Scale: Measurement of a gender-linked syndrome. *Psychology of Men & Masculinity, 7,* 212–224.

Levant, R. F., Halter, M. J., Hayden, E. W., & Williams, C. M. (2009). The efficacy of alexithymia reduction treatment: A pilot study. *Journal of Men's Studies, 17,* 75–84.

Levant, R. F., Hirsch, L. S., Celentano, E., Cozza, T. M., Hill, S., MacEarchern, M., Marty, N., & Schnedeker, J. (1992). The male role: An investigation of contemporary norms. *Journal of Mental Health Counseling, 14,* 325–337.

Levant, R. F., & Philpot, C. L. (2002). Conceptualizing gender in marital and family therapy research: The gender role strain paradigm. In H. A. Liddle, D. A. Santisteban, R. F. Levant, & J. H. Bray (Eds.), *Family psychology: Science-based interventions* (pp. 301–329). Washington, DC: American Psychological Association.

Levant, R. F., Rankin, T. J., Williams, C. M., Hasan, N. T., & Smalley, K. B. (2010). Evaluation of the factor structure and construct validity of scores on the Male Role Norms Inventory—Revised (MRNI-R). *Psychology of Men & Masculinity, 11,* 25–37.

Levant, R., Richmond, K., Cook, S., House, A. T., & Aupont, M. (2007). The Femininity Ideology Scale: Factor, structure, reliability, convergent, and discriminant validity, and social contextual variation. *Sex Roles, 57,* 373–383.

Levant, R. F., Smalley, K. B., Aupont, M., House, A. T., Richmond, K., & Noronha, D. (2007). Initial validation of the Male Role Norms Inventory—Revised (MRNI-R). *Journal of Men's Studies, 15,* 83–100.

Levinson, D. J., & Huffman, P. E. (1955). Traditional family ideology and its relation to personality. *Journal of Personality, 23,* 251–273.

Levitt, E. E., & Klassen, A. D. (1974). Public attitudes toward homosexuality: Part of the 1970 national survey by the Institute for Sex Research. *Journal of Homosexuality, 1,* 29–43.

Leyser, Y., & Kirk, R. (2004). Evaluating inclusion: An examination of parent views and factors influencing their perspectives. *International Journal of Disability, Development and Education, 51,* 271–285.

Li, L., & Moore, D. (1998). Acceptance of disability and its correlates. *Journal of Social Psychology, 138,* 13–25.

Liang, C. T. H., Alvarez, A. N., Juang, L., & Liang, M. (2007). The role of coping in the relationship between perceived racism and racism-related stress for Asian Americans: Gender differences. *Journal of Counseling Psychology, 54,* 132–142.

Liang, C. T. H., & Fassinger, R. E. (2008). Collective self-esteem in the relationship between racism-related stress and psychological adjustment: A test of moderator and mediator hypotheses. *Cultural Diversity and Ethnic Minority Psychology, 14,* 19–28.

Liang, C. T. H., Li, L. C., & Kim, B. K. S. (2004). The Asian American Racism-Related Stress Inventory: Development, factor analysis, reliability, and validity. *Journal of Counseling Psychology, 51,* 103–114.

Liang, C. T. H., Salcedo, J., Rivera, A. L. Y., & Lopez, M. J. (2009). A content and methodological analysis of 35 years of Latino/a-focus research. *The Counseling Psychologist, 37,* 1116–1146.

Liddle, B. J., Luzzo, D. A., Hauenstein, A. L., & Schuck, K. (2004). Construction and validation of the Lesbian, Gay, Bisexual, and Transgendered Climate Inventory. *Journal of Career Assessment, 12,* 33–50.

Liebkind, K. (1992). Ethnic identity—challenging the boundaries of social psychology. In G. M. Breakwell (Ed.), *The social psychology of identity and the self-concept* (pp. 147–185). London, UK: Academic Press.

Liebkind, K. (2006). Ethnic identity and acculturation. In D. L. Sam & J. W. Berry (Eds.), *The Cambridge handbook of acculturation psychology* (pp. 78–96). Cambridge, MA: Cambridge University Press.

Likert, R. (1932). A technique for the measurement of attitudes. *Archives of Psychology, 140,* 5–53.

Lim, K. V., Heiby, E., Brislin, R., & Griffin, B. (2002). The development of the Khmer Acculturation Scale. *International Journal of Intercultural Relations, 26,* 653–678.

Lin, M. H., Kwan, V. S. Y., Cheung, A., & Fiske, S. T. (2005). Stereotype content model explains prejudice for an envied outgroup: Scale of Anti-Asian American stereotypes. *Personality and Social Psychology Bulletin, 31,* 34–47.

Link, B. G. (1987). Understanding labeling effects in the area of the mental disorders: An empirical assessment of the effects of expectations of rejection. *American Sociological Review, 52,* 96–112.

Link, B. G., Cullen, F. T., Frank, J., & Wozniak, J. F. (1987). The social rejection of former mental patients: Understanding why labels matter. *American Journal of Sociology, 92,* 1461–1500.

Link, B. G., & Phelan, J. C. (2001). Conceptualizing stigma. *Annual Review of Sociology, 27,* 363–385.

Link, B. G., Struening, E. L., Rahav, M., Phelan, J. C., & Nuttbrock, L. (1997). On stigma and its consequences: Evidence from a longitudinal study of men with dual diagnoses of mental illness and substance abuse. *Journal of Health and Social Behavior, 38,* 177–190.

Link, B. G., Yang, L. H., Phelan, J. C., & Collins, P. Y. (2004). Measuring mental illness stigma. *Schizophrenia Bulletin, 30,* 511–540.

Linkowski, D. C. (1971). A scale to measure acceptance of disability. *Rehabilitation Counseling Bulletin, 14,* 236–244.

Linkowski, D. C., & Dunn, M. A. (1974). Self-concept and acceptance of disability. *Rehabilitation Counseling Bulletin, 17,* 28–32.

Lipkus, I. (1991). The construction and preliminary validation of a Global Belief in a Just World Scale and the exploratory analysis of the Multidimensional Belief in a Just World Scale. *Personality and Individual Differences, 12*(11), 1171–1178.

Littlewood, R. (1998). Cultural variation in the stigmatization of mental illness. *Lancet, 352,* 1056–1057.

Littlewood, R., Jadhav, S., & Ryder, A. G. (2007). A cross-national study of the stigmatization of severe psychiatric illness: Historical review, methodological considerations and development of the questionnaire. *Transcultural Psychiatry, 44,* 171–202.

Liu, W. M. (2002). Exploring the lives of Asian American men: Racial identity, male role norms, gender role conflict, and prejudicial attitudes. *Psychology of Men & Masculinity, 3,* 107–118.

Liu, W. M., Pope-Davis, D. B., Nevitt, J., & Toporek, R. L. (1999). Understanding the function of acculturation and prejudicial attitudes among Asian Americans. *Cultural Diversity and Ethnic Minority Psychology, 5,* 317–328.

Livingston, J. (2006). Understanding the psychological development of African American children: The impact of race, class, and social inequality. In K. Freeark & W. S. Davidson II (Eds.), *The crisis in youth mental health: Issues for families, schools, and communities* (Vol. 3, pp. 99–120). Westport, CT: Praeger.

Livneh, H. (1982). Factor analysis of the Attitudes Toward Disabled Persons Scale—Form A. *Rehabilitation Psychology, 27,* 235–243.

Livneh, H. (1985). Factor structure of attitudes toward individuals with disabilities: A replication. *Rehabilitation Counseling Bulletin, 29,* 53–58.

Loewen, J. W. (2005). *Sundown towns: A hidden dimension of American racism.* New York: The New Press.

Loo, C. M., Fairbank, J. A., Scurfield, R. M., Ruch, L. O., King, D. W., Adams, L. J., & Chemtob, C. M. (2001). Measuring exposure to racism: Development and validation of a Race-Related Stressor Scale (RRSS) for Asian American Vietnam Veterans. *Psychological Assessment, 13,* 503–520.

Loo, R. (2001). A psychometric re-analysis of the Interaction with Disabled Persons scale. *Canadian Journal of Behavioral Science, 33,* 245–250.

Lopez, E. C., & Rogers, M. R. (2007). Multicultural competencies and training in school psychology: Issues, approaches, and future directions. In G. B. Esquivel, E. C. Lopez, & S. Nahari (Eds.), *Multicultural handbook of school psychology: An interdisciplinary perspective* (pp. 47–68). New York: Routledge.

Lopez, F. A. (2009). Developmental considerations and acculturation of children. *Hispanic Journal of Behavioral Sciences, 31*(1), 57–72.

Lopez, S. R. (1997). Cultural competence in psychotherapy: A guide for clinicians and their supervisors. In C. E. Watkins Jr. (Ed.), *Handbook of psychotherapy supervision* (pp. 570–588). New York: John Wiley.

Lowery, B., Unzueta, M., Knowles, E., & Geoff, P. (2006). Concern for the in–group and opposition to affirmative action. *Journal of Personality and Social Psychology, 90,* 961–974.

Luhtanen, R., & Crocker, J. (1992). A collective self-esteem scale: Self-evaluation of one's social identity. *Personality and Social Psychology Bulletin, 18,* 302–318.

Lun, J., Sinclair, S., Whitchurch, E. R., & Glenn, C. (2007). (Why) Do I think what you think? Epistemic social tuning and implicit prejudice. *Journal of Personality and Social Psychology, 93,* 957–972.

Lutterman, K. G., & Middleton, R. (1970). Authoritarianism, anomia, and prejudice. *Social Forces, 48,* 485–492.

MacDonald, A. P., Jr., Huggins, J., Young, S., & Swanson, R. A. (1973). Attitudes toward homosexuality: Preservation of sex morality or the double standard? *Journal of Consulting and Clinical Psychology, 40,* 161.

MacLean, D., & Gannon, P. M. (1995). Measuring attitudes toward disability: The Interaction with Disabled Persons Scale revisited. *Journal of Social Behavior and Personality, 4,* 791–806.

Madianos, M. G., Priami, M., Alevisopoulos, G., Koukia, E., & Rogakou, E. (2005). Nursing students' attitude change toward mental illness and psychiatric case recognition after a clerkship in psychiatry. *Issues in Mental Health Nursing, 26,* 169–183.

Magnet de Saissy, C. K. (2009). Acculturation, self-efficacy and social support among Chinese immigrants in Northern Ireland. *International Journal of Intercultural Relations,* 1–10.

Magovcevic, M., & Addis, M. E. (2008). The Masculine Depression Scale: Development and psychometric evaluation. *Psychology of Men and Masculinity, 9,* 117–132.

Mahalik, J. R., Locke, B. D., Ludlow, L. H., Diemer, M. A., Scott, R. P. J., Gottfried, M., & Freitas, G. (2003). Development of the Conformity to Masculine Norms Inventory. *Psychology of Men & Masculinity, 4,* 3–25.

Mahalik, J. R., Morray, E. B., Coonerty-Femiano, A., Ludlow, L. H., Slattery, S. M., & Smiler, A. (2005). Development of the Conformity to Feminine Norms Inventory. *Sex Roles, 52,* 417–435.

Mahalik, J. R., Talmadge, W. T., Locke, B. D., & Scott, R. P. J. (2005). Using the Conformity to Masculine Norms Inventory to work with men in a clinical setting. *Journal of Clinical Psychology, 61,* 661–674.

Mahat, M. (2008). The development of a psychometrically sound instrument to measure teachers' multidimensional attitudes toward inclusive education. *International Journal of Special Education, 23,* 82–92.

Major, B., & O'Brien, L. T. (2005). The social psychology of stigma. *Annual Review of Psychology, 56,* 393–421.

Malcarne, V. L., Chavira, D. A., Fernandez, S., & Liu, P.-J. (2006). The Scale of Ethnic Experience: Development and psychometric properties. *Journal of Personality Assessment, 86*(2), 150–161.

Malcarne, V. L., Fernandez, S., & Flores, L. (2005). Factorial validity of the multidimensional health locus of control scales for three American ethnic groups. *Journal of Health Psychology, 10*(5), 657–667.

Mandara, J., Gaylord-Harden, N. K., Richards, M. H., & Ragsdale, B. L. (2009). The effects of changes in racial identity and self-esteem on changes in African American adolescents' mental health. *Child Development, 80,* 1660–1675.

Manos, R. C., Rusch, L. C., Kanter, J. W., & Clifford, L. M. (2009). Depression self-stigma as a mediator of the relationship between depression severity and avoidance. *Journal of Social and Clinical Psychology, 28,* 1128–1143.

Mansfield, A. K., Addis, M. E., & Courtenay, W. (2005). Measurement of men's help seeking: Development and evaluation of the Barriers to Help Seeking Scale. *Psychology of Men & Masculinity, 6,* 95–108.

Maramba, G. G., & Hall, G. C. N. (2002). Meta-analyses of ethnic match as a predictor of dropout, utilization, and level of functioning. *Cultural Diversity and Ethnic Minority Psychology, 8,* 290–297.

Marcia, J. (1980). Identity in adolescence. In J. Adelson (Ed.), *Handbook of adolescent psychology* (pp. 159–187). New York, NY: Wiley.

Marcia, J. E. (1966). Development and validation of ego identity status. *Journal of Personality and Social Psychology, 5,* 551–558.

Marin, G., & Gamba, R. J. (1996). A new measurement of acculturation for Hispanics: The Bidimensional Acculturation Scale for Hispanics (BAS). *Hispanic Journal of Behavioral Sciences, 8,* 297–316.

Marin, G., & Gamba, R. J. (2003). Acculturation and changes in cultural values. In K. M. Chun, P. B. Balls Organista, & G. Marin (Eds.), *Acculturation: Advances in theory, measurement, and applied research* (pp. 83–93). Washington, DC: American Psychological Association.

Marin, G., Perez-Stable, E. J., & VanOss Marin, B. (1989). Cigarette smoking among San Francisco Hispanics: The role of acculturation and gender. *American Journal of Public Health, 79*(2), 196–198.

Marin, G., Sabogal, F. B., Otero-Sabogal, R., & Perez-Stable, E. J. (1987). Development of a short acculturation scale for Hispanics. *Hispanic Journal of Behavioral Sciences, 9,* 183–205.

Markus, H. R., & Kityama, S. (1991). Culture and the self: Implications for cognition, emotion, and motivation. *Psychological Review, 98*(2), 224–253.

Marshall, P. L. (1996). Multicultural teaching concerns: New dimensions in the area of teacher concerns research. *Journal of Educational Research, 89*(6), 371–379.

Marshall, W. L., & Moulden, H. (2001). Hostility toward women and victim empathy in rapists. *Sexual Abuse: A Journal of Research and Treatment, 13,* 249–255.

Martiniuk, A. L. C., Speechley, K., Secco, M., & Campbell, M. K. (2007). Development and psychometric properties of the Thinking about Epilepsy Questionnaire assessing children's knowledge and attitudes about epilepsy. *Epilepsy & Behavior, 10,* 595–603.

Martiniuk, A. L. C., Speechley, K. N., Secco, M., Campbell, M. K., & Donner, A. (2007). Evaluation of an epilepsy education program for Grade 5 students: A cluster randomized trial. *Epilepsy & Behavior, 10,* 604–610.

Maslach, C., Stapp, J., & Santee, R. T. (1985). Individuation: Conceptual analysis and assessment. *Journal of Personality and Social Psychology, 49,* 729–738.

Massey, S. G. (2009). Polymorphous prejudice: Liberating the measurement of heterosexuals' attitudes toward lesbians and gay men. *Journal of Homosexuality, 56,* 147–172.

Matsudaria, T. (2006). Measures of psychological acculturation: A review. *Transcultural Psychiatry, 43*(3), 462–487.

Matteson, A. V., & Moradi, B. (2005). Examining the structure of the Schedule of Sexist Events: Replication and extension. *Psychology of Women Quarterly, 29,* 47–57.

Mayfield, W. (2001). The development of an Internalized Homonegativity Inventory for Gay Men. *Journal of Homosexuality, 41,* 53–75.

McAdoo, H. P. (1981). *Black families.* Beverly Hills, CA: Sage.

McCarn, S. R., & Fassinger, R. E. (1996). Revisioning sexual minority identity formation: A new model of lesbian identity and its implications for counseling and research. *Counseling Psychologist, 24,* 508–534.

McConahay, J. B. (1982). Self-interest versus racial attitudes as correlates of anti-busing in Louisville. *Journal of Politics, 44,* 692–720.

McConahay, J. B. (1986). Modern racism, ambivalence, and the Modern Racism Scale. In J. F. Dovidio & S. L. Gaertner (Eds.), *Prejudice, discrimination, and racism* (pp. 91–125). San Diego, CA: Academic Press.

McConahay, J. B., Hardee, B. B., & Batts, V. (1981). Has racism declined in America? It depends on who is asking and what is asked. *Journal of Conflict Resolution, 25,* 563–579.

McConahay, J. B., & Hough, J. C. (1976). Symbolic racism. *Journal of Social Issues, 32,* 23–45.

McCreary, D. R., & Sasse, D. K. (2000). An exploration of the drive for muscularity in adolescent boys and girls. *Journal of American College Health, 48,* 297–304.

McDermott, M., & Samson, F. L. (2005). White racial and ethnic identity in the United States. *Annual Review of Sociology, 31,* 245–261.

McDonald, K. E., & Keys, C. B. (2008). How the powerful decide: Access to research participation by those at the

margins. *American Journal of Community Psychology, 42,* 79–93.

McDonald, K. E., Keys, C. B., & Henry, D. B. (2008). Gatekeepers of science: Attitudes toward the research participation of adults with intellectual disability. *American Journal on Mental Retardation, 113,* 466–478.

McIntire, S. A., & Miller, L. A. (2007). *Foundations of psychological testing: A practical approach* (2nd ed.). Thousand Oaks, CA: Sage.

McNeilly, M. D., Anderson, N. B., Armstead, C. A., Clark, R., Corbett, M., Robinson, E. L., Pieper, C. F., & Lepisto, E. M. (1996). The Perceived Racism Scale: A multidimensional assessment of the experience of White racism among African Americans. *Ethnicity & Disease, 6,* 154–166.

Mednick, M. T., & Urbanski, L. L. (1991). The origins and activities of APA's Division of the Psychology of Women. *Psychology of Women Quarterly, 15,* 651–663.

Mena, F. J., Padilla, A. M., & Maldonado, M. (1987). Acculturative stress and specific coping strategies among immigrants and later-generation college students. *Hispanic Journal of Behavioral Sciences, 9*(2), 207–225.

Mendoza, R. H. (1989). An empirical scale to measure type and degree of acculturation in Mexican-American adolescents and adults. *Journal of Cross-Cultural Psychology, 20*(4), 372–385.

Mendoza, R. H. (2006). *Cultural Life Styles Inventory for Mexican-American Adolescents and Adults* (Version 3.0). Unpublished manuscript, California School of Professional Psychology at Alliant International University, Los Angeles, Alhambra, CA.

Menon, K. V., & Ranjith, G. (2009). Malayalam cinema and mental health. *International Review of Psychiatry, 21,* 218–223.

Mercer, S. H., & Cunningham, M. (2003). Racial identity in White American college students: Issues of conceptualization and measurement. *Journal of College Student Development, 44,* 217–229.

Meredith, G. (1967). Ethnic Identity Scale: A study of transgenerational communication patterns. *Pacific Speech Quarterly, 2,* 57–67.

Meredith, L. S., Wenger, N., Liu, H., Harada, N., & Kahn, K. (2000). Development of a brief scale to measure acculturation among Japanese Americans. *Journal of Community Psychology 28*(1), 103–113.

Meyer, I. H. (2003). Prejudice, social stress, and mental health in lesbian, gay, and bisexual populations: Conceptual issues and research evidence. *Psychological Bulletin, 129,* 674–697.

Meyer-Bahlburg, H. F. L., Dolezal, C., Zucker, K. J., Kessler, S. J., Schober, J. M., & New, M. I. (2006). The Recalled Childhood Gender Questionnaire—Revised: A psychometric analysis in a sample of women with congenital adrenal hyperplasia. *Journal of Sex Research, 43*, 364–367.

Meyers, L. S. (2006). *The meaning of validity.* Unpublished manuscript, Department of Psychology, California State University, Sacramento, CA.

Meyers, L. S. (2009). *Reliability, error, and attenuation.* Unpublished manuscript, Department of Psychology, California State University, Sacramento, Sacramento, CA.

Meyers, L. S., Gamst, G., & Guarino, A. J. (2006). *Applied multivariate research: Design and interpretation.* Thousand Oaks, CA: Sage.

Meyers, L. S., Gamst, G., & Guarino, A. J. (2009). *Data analysis using SAS Enterprise Guide.* London: Cambridge University Press.

Mezzich, J. E., Ruiperez, M. A., Yoon, G., Liu, J., & Zapata-Vega, M. I. (2009). Measuring cultural identity: Validation of a modified Cortes, Rogler, and Malgady Bicultural Scale in three ethnic groups in New York. *Culture, Medicine, and Psychiatry, 33*(3), 451–472.

Michailakis, D. (2003). The systems theory concept of disability: One is not born a disabled person, one is observed to be one. *Disability & Society, 18*, 209–229.

Michalko, R. (2002). *The difference disability makes.* Philadelphia, PA: Temple University Press.

Milar, K. S. (2000). The first generation of women psychologists and the psychology of women. *American Psychologist, 55*, 616–619.

Miller, M. J., & Kerlow-Myers, A. E. (2009). A content analysis of acculturation research in career development literature. *Journal of Career Development, 35*, 352–384.

Miller, S. M. (1975). Effects of maternal employment on sex role perception, interests, and self-esteem in kindergarten girls. *Developmental Psychology, 11*, 405–406.

Milliones, J. C. (1980). Construction of a Black consciousness measure: Psychotherapeutic implications. *Psychotherapy: Theory, Research & Practice, 17*, 175–182.

Mio, J. S. (2003). On teaching multiculturalism: History, models, and content. In G. Bernal, J. E. Trimble, A. K. Burlew, & F. T. L. Leong (Eds.), *Handbook of racial & ethnic minority psychology* (pp. 119–146). Thousand Oaks, CA: Sage.

Mirandé, A. (1997). *Hombres y machos: Masculinity and Latino culture.* Boulder, CO: Westview Press.

Miville, M. L., Gelso, C. J., Pannu, R., Liu, W., Touradji, P., Holloway, P., & Fuertes, J. (1999). Appreciating similarities and valuing differences: The Miville-Guzman Universality-Diversity Scale. *Journal of Counseling Psychology, 46*, 291–307.

Mohatt, G. V., & Thomas, L. R. (2006). "I wonder, why would you do it that way?" Ethical dilemmas in doing participatory research with Alaska native communities. In J. Trimble & C. Fisher (Eds.), *The handbook of ethical research with ethnocultural populations and communities* (pp. 93–115). Thousand Oaks, CA: Sage.

Mohr, J., & Fassinger, R. (2000). Measuring dimensions of lesbian and gay male experience. *Measurement and Evaluation in Counseling and Development, 33*, 66–90.

Mohr, J. J. (2002). Heterosexual identity and the heterosexual therapist: An identity perspective on sexual orientation dynamics in psychotherapy. *Counseling Psychologist, 30*, 532–566.

Mohr, J. J., & Fassinger, R. E. (2003). Self-acceptance and self-disclosure of sexual orientation in lesbian, gay and bisexual adults: An attachment perspective. *Journal of Counseling Psychology, 50*, 482–495.

Mohr, J. J., & Rochlen, A. B. (1999). Measuring attitudes regarding bisexuality in lesbian, gay male, and heterosexual populations. *Journal of Counseling Psychology, 46*, 353–369.

Mollen, D., Ridley, C. R., & Hill, C. L. (2003). Models of multicultural counseling competence. In D. B. Pope-Davis, H. L. K. Coleman, W. M. Liu, & R. L. Toporek (Eds.), *Handbook of multicultural competencies in counseling & psychology* (pp. 21–37). Thousand Oaks, CA: Sage.

Monsen, J. J., & Frederickson, N. (2004). Teachers' attitudes towards mainstreaming and their pupils' perceptions of their classroom learning environment. *Learning Environment Research, 7*, 129–142.

Montgomery, D. E., Fine, M. A., & Myers, L. J. (1990). The development and validation of an instrument to assess an optimal Afrocentric worldview. *Journal of Black Psychology, 17*, 37–54.

Montgomery, G. T. (1992a). Acculturation, stressors, somatization patterns among students from extreme South Texas. *Hispanic Journal of Behavioral Sciences, 14*(4), 434–454.

Montgomery, G. T. (1992b). Comfort with acculturation status among students from South Texas. *Hispanic Journal of Behavioral Sciences, 14*(2), 201–223.

Moody-Ayers, S. Y., Stewart, A. L., Covinsky, K. E., & Inouye, S. K. (2005). Prevalence and correlates of perceived societal racism in older African-American adults with Type 2 diabetes mellitus. *Journal of the American Geriatrics Society, 53*, 2202–2208.

Moradi, B., & Hasan, N. T. (2004). Arab American persons' reported experiences of discrimination and mental health: The mediating role of personal control. *Journal of Counseling Psychology, 51,* 418–428.

Moradi, B., & Risco, C. (2006). Perceived discrimination experiences and mental health of Latina/o American persons. *Journal of Counseling Psychology, 53,* 411–421.

Moradi, B., & Subich, L. M. (2002). Feminist identity development measures: Comparing the psychometrics of three instruments. *The Counseling Psychologist, 30,* 66–86.

Moradi, B., & Subich, L. M. (2003). A concomitant examination of the relations of perceived racist and sexist events on psychological distress for African American women. *The Counseling Psychologist, 31,* 451–469.

Moradi, B., Yoder, J. D., & Berendsen, L. L. (2004). An evaluation of the psychometric properties of the Womanist Identity Attitudes Scale. *Sex Roles, 50,* 253–266.

Morris, E. F. (2001). Clinical practice with African Americans: Juxtaposition of standard clinical practices and Africentricism. *Professional Psychology: Research and Practice, 32,* 563–572.

Morrison, M. A., & Morrison, T. G. (2002). Development and validation of a scale measuring modern prejudice toward gay men and lesbian women. *Journal of Homosexuality, 43,* 15–126.

Morrison, M. A., Morrison, T. G., & Franklin, R. (2009). Modern and old-fashioned homonegativity among samples of Canadian and American university students. *Journal of Cross-Cultural Psychology, 40,* 523–542.

Morrison, T. G., & Bearden, A. G. (2007). The construction and validation of the Homopositivity Scale: An instrument measuring endorsement of positive stereotypes about gay men. *Journal of Homosexuality, 52,* 63–89.

Morrison, T. G., Parriag, A. V., & Morrison, M. A. (1999). The psychometric properties of the Homonegativity Scale. *Journal of Homosexuality, 37,* 111–126.

Mosher, D. L., & Sirkin, M. (1984). Measuring a macho personality constellation. *Journal of Research in Personality, 18,* 150–163.

Munley, P. H., Lidderdale, M. A., Thiagarajan, M., & Null, U. (2004). Identity development and multicultural competency. *Journal of Multicultural Counseling and Development, 32,* 283–295.

Muraven, M. (2008). Prejudice as self-control failure. *Journal of Applied Social Psychology, 38,* 314–333.

Mussen, P. H., & Barker, R. G. (1944). Attitudes toward cripples. *Journal of Abnormal and Social Psychology, 39,* 351–355.

Myers, L. J. (1987). The deep structure of culture: Relevance of traditional African culture to contemporary life. *Journal of Black Studies, 18*(1), 72–85.

Myers, H. F. (2009). Ethnicity- and socio-economic status-related stresses in context: An integrative review and conceptual model. *Journal of Behavioral Medicine, 32,* 9–19.

Myers, L. J., Speight, S. L., Highlen, P. S., Cox, C. I., Reynolds, A. L., Adams, E. M., & Hanley, C. P. (1991). Identity development and worldview: Toward an optimal conceptualization. *Journal of Counseling and Development, 70,* 54–63.

Myers, M., & Thompson, V. L. (1994). Africentricity: An analysis of two culture-specific instruments. *Western Journal of Black Studies, 18,* 179–184.

Nagoshi, J. L., Adams, K. A., Terrell, H. K., Hill, E. D., Brzuzy, S., & Nagoshi, C. T. (2008). Gender differences in correlates of homophobia and transphobia. *Sex Roles, 59,* 521–531.

National Institute on Disability and Rehabilitation Research, Office of Special Education and Rehabilitation Service. (1993). *Disability statistics. Rehab brief: Bringing research into effective focus (14/8)*. Available at http://codi.buffolo.edu/graph_based/.demographic/.disstats

Navas, M., Garcia, M. C., Sanchez, J., Rojas, A. J., Pumares, P., & Fernandez, J. S. (2005). Relative Acculturation Extended Model (RAEM): New contributions with regard to the study of acculturation. *International Journal of Intercultural Relations, 29,* 21–37.

Neblett, E. W., Jr., Hammond, W. P., Seaton, E. K., & Townsend, T. G. (2010). Underlying mechanisms in the relationship between Africentric worldview and depressive symptoms. *Journal of Counseling Psychology, 57,* 105–113.

Nelson, T. D. (2009). *Handbook of prejudice, stereotyping, and discrimination.* New York: Taylor and Francis Group.

Neville, H. A., Lilly, R. L., Duran, G., Lee, R. M., & Browne, L. (2000). Construction and initial validation of the Color-Blind Racial Attitudes Scale (CoBRAS). *Journal of Counseling Psychology, 47,* 59–70.

Nguyen, H. H., & von Eye, A. (2002). The Acculturation Scale for Vietnamese Adolescents (ASVA): A bidimensional perspective. *International Journal of Behavioral Development, 26*(3), 202–213.

Nickerson, K. J., Helms, J. E., & Terrell, F. (1994). Cultural mistrust, opinion about mental illness, and Black students' attitudes toward seeking psychological help from White counselors. *Journal of Counseling Psychology, 41,* 378–385.

Nikolaraizi, M., & Makri, M. (2004/2005). Deaf and hearing individuals' beliefs about the capabilities of deaf people. *American Annals of the Deaf, 149,* 404–414.

Nobles, W. W. (1980). African foundations for Black psychology. In R. E. Jones (Ed.), *Black psychology* (2nd ed., pp. 23–36). New York: Harper & Row.

Noh, S., & Kaspar, V. (2003). Perceived discrimination and depression: Moderating effects of coping, acculturation, and ethnic support. *American Journal of Public Health, 93,* 232–238.

Nollen, N., Ahluwalia, J. S., Mayo, M. S., Richter, K., Choi, W. S., Okuyemi, K.S., & Resnicow, K. (2007). A randomized trial of targeted educational materials for smoking cessation in African Americans using transdermal nicotine. *Health Education and Behavior, 34,* 911–927.

Norman, R. M. G., Sorrentino, R. M., Windell, D., & Manchanda, R. (2008a). The role of perceived norms in the stigmatization of mental illness. *Social Psychiatry and Psychiatric Epidemiology, 43,* 851–859.

Norman, R. M. G., Sorrentino, R. M., Windell, D., & Manchanda, R. (2008b). Are personal values important in the stigmatization of people with mental illness? *Canadian Journal of Psychiatry, 53,* 848–856.

Nungesser, L. G. (1983). *Homosexual acts, actors, and identities.* New York: Praeger.

Nunnally, J. C. (1957). The communication of mental health information: A comparison of experts and the public with mass media presentations. *Behavioral Science, 2,* 222–230.

Nunnally, J. C., & Bernstein, I. H. (1994). *Psychometric theory* (3rd ed.). New York: McGraw-Hill.

O'Malley, A. S., Kerner, J., Johnson, A. E., & Mandleblatt, J. (1999). Acculturation and breast cancer screening among Hispanic women in New York City. *American Journal of Public Health, 89*(2), 219–227.

O'Neil, J. M. (1982). Gender role conflict and strain in men's lives: Implications for psychiatrists, psychologists, and other human service providers. In K. Solomon & N. B. Levy (Eds.), *Men in transition: Changing male roles, theory, and therapy* (pp. 5–44). New York: Plenum Press.

O'Neil, J. M. (2008). Summarizing 25 years of research on men's gender role conflict using the Gender Role Conflict Scale: New research paradigms and clinical implications. *The Counseling Psychologist, 36,* 358–445.

O'Neil, J. M., Good, G. E., & Holmes, S. (1995). Fifteen years of theory and research on men's gender role conflict: New paradigms for empirical research. In R. F. Levant & W. S. Pollack (Eds.), *A new psychology of men* (pp. 164–206). New York: Basic Books.

O'Neil, J. M., Helms, B., Gable, R., David, L., & Wrightsman, L. (1986). Gender role conflict scale: College men's fear of femininity. *Sex Roles, 14,* 335–350.

Oetting, E. R., & Beauvais, F. (1990–1991). Orthogonal cultural identification theory: The cultural identification of minority adolescents. *International Journal of the Addictions, 25,* 655–685.

Oetting, E. R., Swaim, R. C., & Chiarella, M. C. (1998). Factor structure and invariance of the Orthogonal Identification Scale among American Indian and Mexican American youth. *Hispanic Journal of Behavioral Sciences, 20*(2), 131–154.

Ojeda, L., Rosales, R., & Good, G. E. (2008). Socioeconomic status and cultural predictors of male role attitudes among Mexican American men: Son más machos? *Psychology of Men & Masculinity, 9,* 133–138.

Olkin, R. (1999). *What psychotherapists should know about disability?* New York: Guilford.

Olkin, R. (2002). Could you hold the door for me? Including disability in diversity. *Cultural Diversity and Ethnic Minority Psychology, 8,* 130–137.

Olmedo, E. L. (1979). Acculturation: A psychometric perspective. *American Psychologist, 34*(11), 1061–1070.

Olmedo, E. L., Martinez, J. L., & Martinez, S. R. (1978). Measure of acculturation for Chicano adolescents. *Psychological Reports, 42,* 159–170.

Omizo, M. M., Kim, B. S. K., & Abel, N. R. (2008). Asian and European American cultural values, bicultural competence, and attitudes toward seeking professional psychological help among Asian American adolescents. *Journal of Multicultural Counseling and Development, 36,* 15–28.

Ossana, S. M., Helms, J. E., & Leonard, M. M. (2001). Do "Womanist" identity attitudes influence college women's self-esteem and perceptions of environmental bias? *Journal of Counseling and Development, 70,* 402–408.

Ottenbreit, N., & Dobson, K. (2004). Avoidance and depression: The construction of the Cognitive-Behavioral Avoidance Scale. *Behavior Research and Therapy, 42,* 293–313.

Overall, J. E., & Gorham, D. R. (1988). The Brief Psychiatric Rating Scale (BPRS): Recent developments in ascertainment and scaling. *Psychopharmacological Bulletin, 24,* 97–99.

Overback, D. (1971). Attitude sampling of institutional charge attendant personnel: Cues for intervention. *Mental Retardation 9,* 8–10.

Owen Blakemore, J. E., & Hill, C. A. (2008). The Child Gender Socialization Scale: A measure to compare traditional and feminist parents. *Sex Roles, 58,* 192–207.

Padilla, A. M. (1980). The role of cultural awareness and ethnic loyalty in acculturation. In A. M. Padilla (Ed.),

Acculturation: Theory, models, and some new findings (pp. 47–84). Boulder, CO: Westview.

Padilla, A. M., Alvarez, M., & Lindholm, K. J. (1986). Generational status and personality factors as predictors of stress in students. *Hispanic Journal of Behavioral Sciences, 8*, 275–288.

Padilla, A. M., & Perez, W. (2003). Acculturation, social identity, and social cognition: A new perspective. *Hispanic Journal of Behavioral Sciences, 25*(1), 35–55.

Padilla, A. M., & Ruiz, R. A. (1974). *Latino mental health.* Washington, DC: Department of Health, Education and Welfare.

Padilla, A. M., Wagatsuma, Y., & Lindholm, K. J. (1985). Acculturation and personality as predictors of stress in Japanese and Japanese-Americans. *Journal of Social Psychology, 125*, 295–305.

Panel on Mental Retardation. (1962). *Report to the president: A proposed program for national action to combat mental retardation.* Washington, DC: U.S. Government Printing Office.

Parham, T. A. (1989). Cycles of psychological nigrescence. *The Counseling Psychologist, 17*, 187–226.

Parham, T. A., & Helms, J. E. (1981). The influence of Black students' racial identity attitudes on preference for counselor's race. *Journal of Counseling Psychology, 28*, 250–257.

Park, Y. S., & Kim, B. S. K. (2008). Asian and European American cultural values and communication styles among Asian American and European American college students. *Cultural Diversity and Ethnic Minority Psychology, 14*, 47–56.

Parker, R., Schaller, J., & Hansman, S. (2003). Catastrophe, chaos, and complexity models and psychosocial adjustment to disability. *Rehabilitation Counseling Bulletin, 46*, 234–241.

Parker, W. M., Moore, M. A., & Neimeyer, G. J. (1998). Altering White racial identity and interracial comfort through multicultural training. *Journal of Counseling and Development, 76*, 302–310.

Parks, J. B., & Robertson, M. A. (2004). Attitudes toward women mediate the gender effect on attitudes toward sexist language. *Psychology of Women Quarterly, 28*, 233–239.

Park-Taylor, J., Ventura, A. B., & Ng, V. (2010). Multicultural counseling and assessment with children. In J. G. Ponterotto, J. M. Casas, L. A. Suzuki, & C. M. Alexander (Eds.), *Handbook of multicultural counseling* (3rd ed., pp. 621–635). Thousand Oaks, CA: Sage.

Parrott, D. J. (2009). Aggression toward gay men as gender role enforcement: Effects of male role norms, sexual prejudice, and masculine gender role stress. *Journal of Personality, 77*, 1137–1166.

Parrott, D. J., Peterson, J. L., Vincent, W., & Bakeman, R. (2008). Correlates of anger in response to gay men: Effects of male gender role beliefs, sexual prejudice, and masculine gender role stress. *Psychology of Men & Masculinity, 9*, 167–178.

Parrott, D. J., & Zeichner, A. (2005). Effects of sexual prejudice and anger on physical aggression toward gay and heterosexual men. *Psychology of Men & Masculinity, 6*, 3–17.

Patel, S. G., Salahuddin, N. M., & O'Brien, K. M. (2008). Career decision-making self-efficacy of Vietnamese adolescents: The role of acculturation, social support, socioeconomic status, and racism. *Journal of Career Development, 34*, 218–240.

Paulhus, D. (1984). Two-component model of socially desirable responding. *Journal of Personality and Social Psychology, 46*, 598–609.

Paulhus, D. (2002). Socially desirable responding: The evolution of a construct. In H. Braum, D. Jackson, & D. Wiley (Eds.), *The role of constructs in psychological and educational measurement.* (pp. 49–69). Mahwah, NJ: Erlbaum.

Paulhus, D. L. (1988). *Assessing self-deception and impression management in self-reports: The Balanced Inventory of Desirable Responding.* University of British Columbia, Vancouver, British Columbia, Canada.

Paulhus, D. L. (1991). Measurement and control of response bias. In J. P. Robinson, P. R. Shaver, & L. S. Wrightsman (Eds.). *Measures of personality and social psychological attitudes* (pp. 17–59). San Diego, CA: Academic Press.

Paulhus, D. L., & Martin, C. L. (1987). The structure of personality capabilities. *Journal of Personality and Social Psychology, 52*, 354–365.

Paulhus, D. L., & Reid, D. B. (1991). Enhancement and denial in socially desirable responding. *Journal of Personality and Social Psychology, 60*, 307–317.

Pearl, M. L., & Galupo, M. P. (2007). Development and validation of the Attitudes toward Same-Sex Marriage Scale. *Journal of Homosexuality, 53*, 117–134.

Pedersen, P. (1999). *Multiculturalism as a fourth force.* Philadelphia: Brunner/Mazel.

Perez, R. M., Debord, K. A., & Bieschke, K. J. (2000). *Handbook of counseling and psychotherapy with lesbian, gay and bisexual clients.* Washington, DC: American Psychological Association.

Perry, J. C., Vance, K. S., & Helms, J. E. (2009). Using the People of Color Racial Identity Attitude Scale among Asian American college students: An exploratory factor analysis. *American Journal of Orthopsychiatry, 79*, 252–260.

Perry, T. L., Ivy, M., Conners, A., & Shelar, D. (2008). Recreation student attitudes towards persons with disabilities: Considerations for future service delivery. *Journal of Hospitality, Leisure, Sport and Tourism, 7,* 4–14.

Perry, W. G. (1970). Forms of intellectual and ethical development in the college years. New York: Holt, Rinehart & Winston.

Pettigrew, T., & Meertens, R. (1995). Subtle and blatant prejudice in western Europe. *European Journal of Social Psychology, 25,* 57–75.

Phillips, J. C., Ingram, K. M., Smith, N. G., & Mindes, E. J. (2003). Methodological and content review of lesbian-, gay-, and bisexual-related articles in counseling journals: 1990–1999. *The Counseling Psychologist, 31,* 25–62.

Phinney, J. S. (1989). Stages of ethnic identity development in minority group adolescents. *Journal of Early Adolescence, 9,* 34–49.

Phinney, J. S. (1990). Ethnic identity in adolescents and adults: Review of research. *Psychological Bulletin, 108,* 499–514.

Phinney, J. S. (1992). The Multigroup Ethnic Identity Measure: A new scale for use with diverse ethnic groups. *Journal of Adolescent Research, 7,* 156–176.

Phinney, J. S. (2003). Ethnic identity and acculturation. In K. M. Chun, P. Balls-Organista, & G. Marin (Eds.), *Acculturation: Advances in theory, measurement, and applied research* (pp. 63–82). Washington, DC: American Psychological Association.

Phinney, J. S. Horenczyk, G., Liebkind, K., & Vedder, P. (2001). Ethnic identity, immigration, and well-being: An interactional perspective. *Journal of Social Issues, 57,* 493–510.

Phinney, J. S., & Ong, A. D. (2007). Conceptualization and measurement of ethnic identity: Current status and future directions. *Journal of Counseling Psychology, 54,* 271–281.

Pierre, M. R., & Mahalik, J. R. (2005). Examining African self-consciousness and Black racial identities as predictors of Black men's psychological well-being. *Cultural Diversity and Ethnic Minority Psychology, 11,* 28–40.

Pieterse, A. L., & Miller, M. J. (2010). Current considerations in the assessment of adults: A review and extension of culturally inclusive models. In J. G. Ponterotto, J. M. Casas, L. A. Suzuki, & C. M. Alexander (Eds.), *Handbook of multicultural counseling* (3rd ed., pp. 649–666). Thousand Oaks, CA: Sage.

Pinteritis, E. J., Poteat, V. P., & Spanierman, L. B. (2009). The White Privilege Attitudes Scale: Development and initial validation. *Journal of Counseling Psychology, 56,* 417–429.

Plant, E. A., & Devine, P. G. (1998). Internal and external motivation to respond without prejudice. *Journal of Personality and Social Psychology, 75,* 811–832.

Plant, E. A., & Devine, P. G. (2009). The active control of prejudice: Unpacking the intentions guiding control efforts. *Journal of Personality and Social Psychology, 96,* 640–652.

Pleck, J. H. (1981). *The myth of masculinity.* Cambridge, MA: MIT Press.

Pleck, J. H. (1995). The gender role strain paradigm: An update. In R. F. Levant & W. S. Pollack (Eds.), *A new psychology of men* (pp. 11–32). New York: Basic Books.

Pleck, J. H., Sonenstein, F. L., & Ku, L. C. (1993). Attitudes toward male roles among adolescent males: A discriminant validity analysis. *Sex Roles, 30,* 481–501.

Pollack, W. S., & Levant, R. F. (1998). *New psychotherapy for men.* New York: Wiley.

Ponterotto, J. G. (1998). Charting a course for research in multicultural counseling training. *Counseling Psychologist, 26,* 43–68.

Ponterotto, J. G. (2008). Theoretical and empirical advances in multicultural counseling and psychology. In S. D. Brown & R. W. Lent (Eds.), *Handbook of counseling psychology* (4th ed., pp. 141–158). Hoboken, NJ: John Wiley & Sons.

Ponterotto, J. G. (2010). Multicultural personality: An evolving theory of optimal functioning in culturally heterogeneous societies. *The Counseling Psychologist, 38*(5), 714–758.

Ponterotto, J. G., & Alexander, C. M. (1996). Assessing the multicultural competence of counselors and clinicians. In L. A. Suzuki, P. Meller, & J. G. Ponterotto (Eds.), *Handbook of multicultural assessment* (pp. 651–672). San Francisco: Jossey-Bass.

Ponterotto, J. G., Baluch, S., & Carielli, D. (1998). The Suinn-Lew Asian Self-Identity Acculturation Scale (SL-ASIA): Critique and research recommendations. *Measurement and Evaluation in Counseling and Development, 31,* 109–124.

Ponterotto, J. G., Baluch, S., Grieg, T., & Rivera, L. (1998). Development and initial score validation of the Teacher Multicultural Attitude Survey. *Educational and Psychological Measurement, 58*(6), 1002–1016.

Ponterotto, J. G., Burkard, A., Rieger, B. P., Grieger, I., D'Onofrio, A., Dubuisson, A., Hoenehan, M., Millstein, B., Parisi, M. J. F., & Sax, G. (1995). Development and initial validation of the Quick Discrimination Index (QDI). *Educational and Psychological Measurement, 55,* 1016–1031.

Ponterotto, J. G., Costa, C., & Werner-Lin, A. (2002). *Counseling across cultures.* Thousand Oaks, CA: Sage.

Ponterotto, J. G., Gretchen, D., & Chauhan, R. V. (2001). Cultural identity and multicultural assessment: Quantitative and qualitative tools for the clinicians. In L. A. Suzuki, J. G. Ponterotto, & P. J. Meller (Eds.), *Handbook of multicultural assessment: Clinical, psychological, and educational applications* (2nd ed., pp. 67–100). San Francisco, CA: Jossey-Bass.

Ponterotto, J. G., Gretchen, D., Utsey, S. O., Reiger, B. P., & Austin, R. (2002). A revision of the Multicultural Counseling Knowledge and Awareness Scale. *Journal of Multicultural Counseling and Development, 30,* 153–180.

Ponterotto, J. G., & Mallinckrodt, B. (2007). Introduction to the special section on racial and ethnic identity in counseling psychology: Conceptual and methodological challenges and proposed solutions. *Journal of Counseling Psychology, 54,* 219–223.

Ponterotto, J. G., & Park-Taylor, J. (2007). Racial and ethnic identity theory, measurement, and research in counseling psychology: Present status and future directions. *Journal of Counseling Psychology, 54,* 282–294.

Ponterotto, J. G., & Potere, J. C. (2003). The Multicultural Counseling Knowledge and Awareness Scale (MCKAS): Validity, reliability and user guidelines. In D. B. Pope-Davis, H. L. K Coleman, W. M. Liu, & R. L. Toporek (Eds.), *Handbook of multicultural competencies in counseling & psychology* (pp. 137–153). Thousand Oaks, CA: Sage.

Ponterotto, J. G., Potere, J. C., & Johansen, S. A. (2002). The Quick Discrimination Index: Normative data and user guidelines for counseling researchers. *Journal of Multicultural Counseling and Development, 30,* 192–206.

Ponterotto, J. G., Rieger, B. P., Barrett, A., & Sparks, R. (1994). Assessing multicultural counseling competence: A review of instrumentation. *Journal of Counseling and Development, 72,* 316–322.

Ponterotto, J. G., & Ruckdeschel, D. E. (2007). An overview of coefficient alpha and reliability matrix for estimating adequacy of internal consistency coefficient with psychological research measures. *Perceptual and Motor Skills, 105*(3, pt1), 997–1014.

Ponterotto, J. G., Utsey, S. O., & Pedersen, P. B. (2006). *Preventing prejudice: A guide for counselors, educators, and parents* (2nd ed.). Thousand Oaks, CA: Sage.

Ponterotto, J. G., & Wise, S. L. (1987). Construct validity study of the Racial Identity Attitude Scale. *Journal of Counseling Psychology, 34,* 218–223.

Pope, R. L., & Mueller, J. A. (2000). Development and initial validation of the Multicultural Competence in Student Affairs-Preliminary 2 Scale. *Journal of College Student Development, 41*(6), 599–608.

Pope-Davis, D. B., Coleman, H. L. K., Liu, W. M., & Toporek, R. L. (2003). *Handbook of multicultural competencies in counseling & psychology.* Thousand Oaks, CA: Sage.

Pope-Davis, D. B., & Dings, J. G. (1995). The assessment of multicultural counseling competencies. In J. G. Ponterotto, J. M. Casas, L. A. Suzuki, & C. M. Alexander (Eds.), *Handbook of multicultural counseling* (pp. 287–311). Thousand Oaks, CA: Sage.

Pope-Davis, D. B., Ligiero, D. P., Liang, C., & Codrington, J. (2001). Fifteen years of the *Journal of Multicultural Counseling and Development*: A content analysis. *Journal of Multicultural Counseling and Development, 29,* 226–238.

Pope-Davis, D. B., & Liu, W. M. (1997). *The Multicultural Environment Inventory.* Unpublished Manuscript.

Pope-Davis, D. B., Liu, W. M., & Toporek, R. L. (2000). The development and initial validation of the Multicultural Environmental Inventory: A preliminary investigation. *Cultural Diversity and Ethnic Minority Psychology, 6*(1), 57–64.

Pope-Davis, D. B., Liu, W. M., Toporek, R. L., & Brittan-Powell, C. S. (2001). What's missing from multicultural competency research: Review, introspection and recommendation. *Cultural Diversity and Ethnic Minority Psychology, 7,* 121–138.

Pope-Davis, D. B., Toporek, R. L., & Ortega, L. (1999, March). *The Multicultural Supervision Scale.* College Park, MD: Author.

Pope-Davis, D. B., Toporek, R. L., Ortega, L., Bashur, M., Liu, W.M., Brittan-Powell, C. S., Liang, C. T. H., & Codrington, J. (2000, August). *Supervisee and supervisor experiences of multicultural supervision.* Symposium presented at the annual meeting of the American Psychological Association, Washington, DC.

Pope-Davis, D. B., Toporek, R. L., & Ortega-Villalobos, L. (2003). Assessing supervisors' and supervisees' perceptions of multicultural competence in supervision using the Multicultural Supervision Inventory. In D. B. Pope-Davis, H. L. K. Coleman, W. M. Liu, & R. L. Toporek (Eds.), *Handbook of multicultural competencies in counseling & psychology* (pp. 211–224). Thousand Oaks, CA: Sage.

Pope-Davis, D. B., Vandiver, B. J., & Stone, L. G. (1999). White racial identity attitude development: A psychometric examination of two instruments. *Journal of Counseling Psychology, 46,* 70–79.

Poteat, V. P. (2007). Peer group socialization of homophobic attitudes and behavior during adolescence. *Child Development, 78,* 1830–1842.

Poteat, V. P., & Espelage, D. L. (2005). Exploring the relation between bullying and homophobic verbal content: The Homophobic Content Agent Target (HCAT) scale. *Violence and Victims, 20,* 513–528.

Poteat, V. P., & Spanierman, L. B. (2008). Further validation of the Psychosocial Costs of Racism to Whites Scale among employed adults. *Journal of Counseling Psychology, 36,* 871–894.

Pothier, D., & Devlin, R. (Eds.). (2006). *Critical disability theory: Essays in philosophy, politics, policy and law.* Vancouver, CA: University British Colombia Press.

Pratto, F., Sidanius, J., Stallworth, L. M., & Malle, B. F. (1994). Social dominance orientation: A personality variable predicting social and political attitudes. *Journal of Personality and Social Psychology, 67,* 741–763.

Pruett, S. R., & Chan, F. (2006). The development and psychometric validation of the Disability Attitude Implicit Association Test. *Rehabilitation Psychology, 51,* 202–213.

Pruett, S. R., Lee, E.-J., Chan, F., Wang, M. H., & Lane, F. J. (2008). Dimensionality of the Contact with Disabled Persons Scale: Results from exploratory and confirmatory factor analyses. *Rehabilitation Counseling Bulletin.*

Quay, L. C., Bartlett, G. J., Wrightsman, L. S., Jr., & Catron, D. (1961). Attitude change in attendant employees. *Journal of Social Psychology, 55,* 27–31.

Quintana, S. M., Troyano, N., & Taylor, G. (2001). Cultural validity and inherent challenges in quantitative methods for multicultural research. In J. G. Ponterotto, J. M. Casas, L. A. Suzuki, & C. M. Alexander (Eds.), *Handbook of multicultural counseling* (2nd ed., pp. 604–630). Thousand Oaks, CA: Sage.

Rader, J., & Gilbert, L. A. (2005). The egalitarian relationship in feminist therapy. *Psychology of Women Quarterly, 29,* 427–435.

Radloff, L. S. (1977). The CES-D scale: A self-report depression scale for research in the general population. *Applied Psychological Measurement, 1,* 385–401.

Raja, S., & Stokes, J. P. (1998). Assessing attitudes toward lesbians and gay men: The Modern Homophobia Scale. *Journal of Gay, Lesbian, and Bisexual Identity, 3,* 113–134.

Ramanathan, V. (2010). *Bodies and language: Health, ailments, disabilities.* Tonawanda, NY: Multilingual Matters.

Ramos-Sanchez, L., & Atkinson, D. R. (2009). The relationships between Mexican American acculturation, cultural values, gender, and help-seeking intentions. *Journal of Counseling and Development, 87*(1), 62–71.

Rasch, G. (1960). *Probabilistic models for some intelligence and attainment tests.* Chicago: MESA Press.

Redfield, R., Linton, R., & Herskovits, M. (1936). Memorandum on the study of acculturation. *American Anthropologist, 38,* 149–152.

Reid, R., Brown, T., Peterson, N., Snowden, L., & Hines, A. (2009). Testing the factor structure of a scale to assess African American acculturation: A confirmatory factor analysis. *Journal of Community Psychology, 37,* 1–13.

Renn, K. A. (2004). *Mixed race students in college: The ecology of race, identity, and community on campus.* New York: State University of New York Press.

Resnicow, K., & Ross-Gaddy, D. (1997). Development of a racial identity scale for low-income African Americans. *Journal of Black Studies, 28,* 239–254.

Resnicow, K., Soler, R., Braithwaite, R. L., Ahluwalia, J. S., & Butler, J. C. (2000). Cultural sensitivity in substance use prevention. *Journal of Community Psychology, 28,* 271–290.

Reynolds, A. L. (2001). Multidimensional cultural competencies: Providing tools for transforming psychology. *The Counseling Psychologist, 29,* 833–841.

Reynolds, C. R., & Richmond, B. O. (1978). What I think and feel: A revised measure of children's manifest anxiety. *Journal of Abnormal Child Psychology, 6,* 271–280.

Reynolds, W. M. (1982). Development of reliable and valid short forms of the Marlowe-Crowne social desirability scale. *Journal of Clinical Psychology, 38,* 119–125.

Rice, G. J. (2009). Attitudes of undergraduate students toward people with intellectual disabilities: Considerations for future policy makers. *College Student Journal, 43,* 207–215.

Rickard, K. M. (1989). The relationship of self-monitored dating behaviors to level of feminist identity on the Feminist Identity Scale. *Sex Roles, 20,* 213–226.

Ridley, C. R. (1985). Imperatives for ethnic and cultural relevance in psychology training programs. *Professional Psychology, Research and Practice, 16*(5), 611–622.

Ridley, C. R. (1995). *Overcoming unintentional racism in counseling and therapy: A practitioner's guide to intentional intervention.* Thousand Oaks, CA: Sage.

Ridley, C. R., Hill, C., & Li, L. (1998). Revisiting and refining the multicultural assessment procedure. *The Counseling Psychologist, 6,* 939–947.

Ridley, C. R., Li, L. C., & Hill, C. L. (1998) Multicultural assessment: Reexamination, reconceptualization, and practice application. *Counseling Psychologist, 26,* 827–910.

Ridley, C. R., Tracey, M. L., Pruitt-Stephens, L., Wimsatt, M. K., & Beard, J. (2008). Multicultural assessment validity: The preeminent ethics issues in psychological assessment. In L. A. Suzuki & J. G. Ponterotto (Eds.), *Handbook of multicultural assessment: Clinical, psychological, and educational applications* (pp. 22–33). San Francisco: Jossey-Bass.

Riggle, E. D. B., Whitman, J. S., Olson, A., Rostosky, S. S., & Strong, S. (2008). The positive aspects of being a lesbian or gay man. *Professional Psychology: Research and Practice, 39,* 210–217.

Rimmerman, A., Hosmi, B., & Duvdevany, I. (2000). Contact and attitudes toward individuals with disabilities among students tutoring children with developmental disabilities. *Journal of Intellectual & Developmental Disability, 25,* 13–19.

Rippy, A. E., & Newman, E. (2008). Adaptation of a scale of race-related stress for use with Muslim Americans. *Journal of Muslim Mental Health, 3,* 53–68.

Ritsher, J., & Phelan, J. (2004). Internalized stigma predicts erosion of morale among psychiatric outpatients. *Psychiatry Research, 129,* 257–265.

Ritsher, J. B., Otilingam, P. G., & Grajales, M. (2003). Internalized stigma of mental illness: Psychometric properties of a new measure. *Psychiatry Research, 121,* 31–49.

Rivera, L. M. (2008). Acculturation and multicultural assessment: Issues, trends, and practice. In L. A. Suzuki & J. G. Ponterotto (Eds.), *Handbook of multicultural assessment: Clinical, psychological, and educational application* (pp. 73–91). San Francisco: John Wiley & Sons.

Roberts, R. E., Phinney, J. S., Masse, L. C., Chin, Y. R., Roberts, C. R., & Romero, A. (1999). The structure of ethnic identity of young adolescents from diverse ethnocultural groups. *Journal of Early Adolescence, 19,* 301–322.

Roccas, S., & Brewer, M. B. (2002). Social identity complexity. *Personality and Social Psychology Review, 6,* 88–106.

Rockquemore, K. A., & Brunsma, D. L. (2008). *Beyond Black* (2nd ed.). Lanham, MD: Rowman & Littlefield.

Rodriguez, N., Bingham Mira, C., Paez, N. D., & Myers, H. F. (2007). Exploring the complexities of familism and acculturation: Central constructs for people of Mexican origin. *American Journal of Community Psychology, 39,* 61–77.

Rodriguez, N., Myers, H. F., Bingham Mira, C., Flores, T., & Garcia-Hernandez, L. (2002). Development of the Multidimensional Acculturative Stress Inventory for Adults of Mexican Origin. *Psychological Assessment, 14,* 451–461.

Rogers, M. R., & Ponterotto, J. G. (1997). Development of the Multicultural School Psychology Counseling Competency Scale. *Psychology in the Schools, 34*(3), 211–217.

Rogler, L. H. (1999). Methodological sources of cultural insensitivity in mental health research. *American Psychologist, 54,* 424–433.

Rogler, L. H., Cortes, D. E., & Malgady, R. G. (1991). Acculturation and mental health status among Hispanics: Convergence and new directions for research. *American Psychologist, 46,* 585–597.

Rombough, S., & Ventimiglia, J. C. (1981). Sexism: A tridimensional phenomenon. *Sex Roles, 7,* 747–755.

Romero, A. J., Cuéllar, I., & Roberts, R. E. (2000). Ethnocultural variables and attitudes toward cultural socialization of children. *Journal of Community Psychology, 28*(1), 79–89.

Rosario, M., Schrimshaw, E. W., & Hunter, J. (2004). Ethnic/racial differences in the coming-out process of lesbian, gay, and bisexual youths: A comparison of sexual identity development over time. *Cultural Diversity and Ethnic Minority Psychology, 10,* 215–228.

Rosario, M., Schrimshaw, E. W., & Hunter, J. (2008). Predicting different patterns of sexual identity development over time among lesbian, gay, and bisexual youths: A cluster analytic approach. *American Journal of Community Psychology, 42,* 266–282.

Rosenberg, M. (1965). *Society and the adolescent self-image.* Princeton, NJ: Princeton University Press.

Rosenberg, M. (1979). *Conceiving the self.* New York: Basic Books.

Rosenberg, M. (1986). *Conceiving the self.* Melbourne, FL: Krieger.

Rosenberg, M. (1989). *Society and the adolescent self-image* (rev. ed.). Middleton, CT: Wesleyan University Press.

Rosenthal, R., & Rosnow, D. B. (1979). Comparing significance levels of independent studies. *Psychological Bulletin, 92,* 500–504.

Rosenthal, R., & Rosnow, R. L. (2008). *Essentials of behavioral research* (3rd ed.). Boston: McGraw-Hill.

Rosenthal, R., & Rubin, D. B. (1982). Comparing effect sizes of independent studies. *Psychological Bulletin, 86,* 1165–1168.

Ross, M. W., & Rosser, B. R. S. (1996). Measurement and correlates of internalized homophobia: A factor analytic study. *Journal of Clinical Psychology, 52,* 15–21.

Ross, M. W., Smolenski, D. J., Kajubi, P., Mandel, J. S., McFarland, W., & Raymond, F. H. (2010). Measurement of internalized homonegativity in gay and bisexual men in Uganda: Cross cultural properties of the internalized homonegativity scale. *Psychology, Health & Medicine, 15*(2), 159–165.

Rothblum, E. D. (2000). "Somewhere in Des Moines or San Antonio": Historical perspectives on lesbian, gay, and bisexual health. In R. M. Perez, K. A. DeBord, & K. J. Bieschke (Eds.), *Handbook of counseling and psychotherapy with lesbian, gay, and bisexual clients* (pp. 57–80). Washington, DC: American Psychological Association.

Roush, S., & Klockars, A. J. (1988). Construct validation of two scales measuring attitudes toward persons with disabilities. *Journal of Rehabilitation, 54,* 25–30.

Rowe, W., Bennett, S. K., & Atkinson, D. R. (1994). White racial identity models: A critique and alternative proposal. *The Counseling Psychologist, 19,* 76–102.

Rowlinson, R. T., & Felner, R. D. (1988). Major life events, hassles, and adaptation in adolescence: Confounding in the conceptualization and measurement of life stress and adjustment revisited. *Journal of Personality and Social Psychology, 55,* 432–444.

Roysircar, G. (2006). Research in multicultural counseling: Client needs and counselor competencies. In C. C. Lee (Ed.), *Multicultural issues in counseling* (pp. 369–387). Alexandria, VA: American Counseling Association.

Roysircar-Sodowsky, G., & Kuo, P. Y. (2001). Determining cultural validity of personality assessment: Some guidelines. In D. Pope-Davis & H. L. K. Coleman (Eds.), *The intersection of race, class, & gender: Implications for multicultural counseling* (pp. 213–239). Thousand Oaks, CA: Sage.

Roysircar-Sodowsky, G., & Maestas, M. V. (2000). Acculturation, ethnic identity, and acculturative stress: Evidence and measurement. In R. H. Dana (Ed.), *Handbook of cross-cultural and multicultural personality assessment* (pp. 131–172). Mahwah, NJ: Earlbaum.

Rubin, Z., & Peplau, L. A. (1975). Who believes in a just world? *Journal of Social Issues, 29,* 73–93.

Rudmin, F. W. (2003). Critical history of the acculturation psychology of assimilation, separation, integration, and marginalization. *Review of General Psychology, 7*(1), 3–37.

Rudmin, F. W. (2009). Constructs, measurements and models of acculturation and acculturative stress. *International Journal of Intercultural Relations, 33*(2), 106–123.

Rudmin, F. W., & Ahmadzadeh, V. (2001). Psychometric critique of acculturation psychology: The case of Iranian migrants in Norway. *Scandinavian Journal of Psychology, 42,* 41–56.

Ruehlman, L., & Karoly, P. (1991). With a little flak from my friends: Development and preliminary validation of the Test of Negative Social Exchange (TENSE). *Psychological Assessment, 3,* 97–104.

Rusch, L. C., Kanter, J. W., Manos, R. C., & Weeks, C. E. (2008). Depression stigma in a predominantly low income African American sample with elevated depression symptoms. *Journal of Nervous and Mental Disease, 196,* 919–922.

Russell, G. L., Fujino, D. C., Sue, S., Cheung, M.-K., & Snowden, L. R. (1996). The effects of counselor–client ethnic match on assessment of mental health functioning. *Journal of Cross-Cultural Psychology, 27,* 598–615.

Russell, J. A., & Barrett, L. F. (1999). Core affect, prototypical emotional episodes, and other things called emotions: Dissecting the elephant. *Journal of Personality and Social Psychology, 76,* 805–819.

Russo, N. F., & Dumont, B. A. (1997). A history of Division 35 (Psychology of Women): Origins, issues, activities, future. In D. A. Dewsbury (Ed.), *Unification through division: Histories of the divisions of the American Psychological Association* (Vol. 2, pp. 211–238). Washington, DC: American Psychological Association.

Ryder, A. G., Alden, L. E., & Paulhus, D. L. (2000). Is acculturation unidimensional or bidimensional? A head-to-head comparison in the prediction of personality, self-identity, and adjustment. *Journal of Personality and Social Psychology, 79,* 49–65.

Sabnani, H., & Ponterotto, J. (1992). Racial/ethnic minority-specific instrumentation in counseling research: A review, critique, and recommendations. *Measurement and Evaluation in Counseling and Development, 24,* 161–187.

Sabnani, H. B., Ponterotto, J. G., & Borodovsky, L. G. (1991). White racial identity development and cross-cultural counselor training: A stage model. *The Counseling Psychologist, 19,* 76–102.

Saez, P. A., Casado, A., & Wade, J. C. (2009). Factors influencing masculinity ideology among Latino men. *Journal of Men's Studies, 17,* 116–128.

Salant, T., & Lauderdale, D.S. (2003). Measuring culture: A critical review of acculturation and health in Asian immigrant populations. *Social Science & Medicine, 57*(1), 71–90.

Sam, D. L., & Berry, J. W. (Eds.). (2006). *The Cambridge handbook of acculturation psychology.* Cambridge, MA: Cambridge University Press.

Sandhu, D. S., & Asrabadi, B. R. (1994). Development of an Acculturative Stress Scale for International Students: Preliminary findings. *Psychological Reports, 75,* 435–448.

Sandhu, D. S., & Asrabadi, B. R. (1998). An Acculturative Stress Scale for International Students: A practical approach to stress management. In C. P. Zalaquette & R. J. Wood (Eds.), *Evaluating stress: A book of resources* (Vol. 2, pp. 1–33). Lanham, MD & London: The Scarecrow Press.

Sarangi, S., & Roberts, C. (Eds.). (1998). *Talk, work and institutional order: Discourse in medical, mediation, and management settings.* New York: Mouton de Gruyter.

Saucier, G. (1994). Mini-markers: A brief version of Goldberg's unipolar big-five markers. *Journal of Personality Assessment, 63,* 506–516.

Schick, V. R., Zucker, A. N., & Bay-Cheng, L. Y. (2008). Safer, better sex through feminism: The role of feminist ideology in women's sexual well-being. *Psychology of Women Quarterly, 32,* 225–232.

Schmelkin, L. P. (1981). Teachers' and nonteachers' attitudes toward mainstreaming. *Exceptional Children, 48,* 42–47.

Schmitt, M. M., & Elliott, T. R. (2004). Verbal learning ability and adjustment to recent spinal cord injury. *Rehabilitation Psychology, 49,* 288–294.

Schneider, D. J. (2004). *The psychology of stereotyping.* New York: Guilford Press.

Schulz, S. (2009). Psychological theories of disability and sexuality: A literature review. *Journal of Human Behavior in the Social Environment, 19,* 58–69.

Schwartz, C., & Armony-Sivan, R. (2001). Students' attitudes to the inclusion of people with disabilities in the community. *Disability and Society, 16,* 403–413.

Schwartz, S., Montgomery, M. J., & Briones, E. (2006). The role of identity in acculturation among immigrant people: Theoretical propositions, empirical questions, and applied recommendations. *Human Development, 49,* 1–30.

Schwartz, S. J. (2007). The applicability of familism to diverse ethnic groups: A preliminary study. *Journal of Social Psychology, 147*(2), 101–118.

Schwartz, S. J., Unger, J. B., Zamboanga, B. L., & Szapocznik, J. (2010). Rethinking the concept of acculturation: Implications for theory and research. *American Psychologist, 65*(4), 237–251.

Scissions, E. H. (1993). *Counseling for results: Principles and practices of helping.* Pacific Grove, CA: Brooks/Cole.

Scotch, R. K. (2001). *From good will to civil rights* (2nd ed.). Philadelphia: Temple University Press.

Scottham, K. M., Sellers, R. M., & Nguyen, H. X. (2008). A measure of racial identity in African American adolescents: The development of the Multidimensional Inventory of Black Identity-Teen. *Cultural Diversity and Ethnic Minority Psychology, 14,* 297–306.

Sears, D. O. (1988). Symbolic racism. In P. A. Katz & D. A. Taylor (Eds.), *Eliminating racism: Profiles in controversy* (pp. 53–84). New York: Plenum.

Seaton, E. K. (2003). An examination of the factor structure of the Index of Race-Related Stress among a sample of African American adolescents. *Journal of Black Psychology, 29,* 292–307.

Seaton, E. K. (2006). Examination of a measure of racial discrimination among African American adolescents. *Journal of Applied Social Psychology, 36,* 1414–1429.

Seaton, E. L. (2009). Perceived racial discrimination and racial identity profiles among African American adolescents. *Cultural Diversity and Ethnic Minority Psychology, 15,* 137–144.

Segal, S. P., Silverman, C., & Temkin, T. (1995). Measuring empowerment in client-run self-help agencies. *Community Mental Health Journal, 31,* 215–227.

Sellers, R. M., Rowley, S. A., Chavous, T. M., Shelton, J. N., & Smith, M. A. (1997). Multidimensional Inventory of Black Identity: A preliminary investigation of reliability and construct validity. *Journal of Personality and Social Psychology, 73,* 805–815.

Sellers, R. M., Shelton, J. N., Cooke, D. Y., Chavous, T. M., Rowley, F. A. J., & Smith, M. A. (1998). A multidimensional model of racial identity: Assumptions, findings, and future directions. In R. L. Jones (Ed.), *African American Identity Development* (pp. 275–302). Hampton, VA: Cobb & Henry.

Sellers, R. M., Smith, M. A., Shelton, J. N., Rowley, S. A. J., & Chavous, T. M. (1998). Multicultural Model of Racial Identity: A re-conceptualization of African American racial identity. *Personality and Social Psychology Review, 2,* 18–39.

Seo, W., & Chen, R. K. (2009). Attitudes of college students toward people with disabilities. *Journal of Applied Rehabilitation Counseling, 40,* 3–8.

Serrano, E., & Anderson, J. (2003). Assessment of a refined short acculturation scale for Latino preteens in rural Colorado. *Hispanic Journal of Behavioral Sciences, 25*(2), 240–253.

Sevig, T. D., Highlen, P. S., & Adams, E. M. (2000). Development and validation of the Self-Identity Inventory (SII): A multicultural identity development instrument. *Cultural Diversity and Ethnic Minority Psychology, 6,* 168–182.

Shelley, D., Fahs, M., Scheinmann, R., Swain, S., Qu, J., & Burton, D. (2004). Acculturation and tobacco use among Chinese Americans. *American Journal of Public Health, 94*(2), 300–307.

Shelton, J. N., & Sellers, R. M. (2000). Situational stability and variability in African American racial identity. *Journal of Black Psychology, 26,* 27–50.

Sherry, A. (2007). Internalized homophobia and adult attachment: Implications for clinical practice. *Psychotherapy: Theory, Research, Practice, Training, 44,* 219–225.

Sheu, H.-B., & Lent, R. W. (2007). Development and initial validation of the Multicultural Counseling Self-Efficacy Scale-Racial Diversity Form. *Psychotherapy, Theory, Research, Practice, & Training, 44*(1), 30–45.

Shih, M., & Sanchez, D. T. (2005). Perspectives and research on the positive and negative implications of having multiple racial identities. *Psychology Bulletin, 131,* 569–591.

Shih, M., & Sanchez, D. T. (2009). When race becomes even more complex: Towards understanding multiracial identity and experiences. *Journal of Social Issues, 65,* 1–11.

Shin, S.-M., Chow, C., Camacho-Gonsalves, T., Levy, R. J., Allen, I. E., & Leff, B. S. (2005). A meta-analytic review of racial-ethnic matching for African American and Caucasian American clients and clinicians. *Journal of Counseling Psychology, 52,* 45–56.

Shippen, M. E., Crites, S. A., Houchins, D. E., Ramsey, M. L., & Simon, M. (2005). Preservice teachers' perceptions of including students with disabilities. *Teacher Education and Special Education, 28,* 92–99.

Siatkowski, A. A. (2007). Hispanic acculturation: A concept analysis. *Journal of Transcultural Nursing, 18*(4), 316–323.

Sidanius, J., & Pratto, F. (1999). *Social dominance: An intergroup theory of social hierarchy and oppression.* New York: Cambridge University Press.

Siebers, T. (2008). *Disability theory.* Ann Arbor: University of Michigan Press.

Siegal, C., Haugland, G., & Chambers, E. D. (2003). Performance measures and their benchmarks for assessing organizational cultural competency in behavioral health care service delivery. *Administration and Policy in Mental Health, 31*(2), 141–170.

Siegel, J. N. (1986). The Multidimensional Anger Inventory. *Journal of Personality and Social Psychology, 51,* 191–200.

Signorella, M. L., & Liben, L. S. (1985). Assessing children's gender-stereotyped attitudes. *Psychological Documents, 15,* 7.

Siller, J. (1969). *The general form of the Disability Factors Scales series (DFS-G).* Unpublished manuscript. New York University School of Education, New York.

Siller, J., & Chipman, A. (1964). Factorial structure and correlates of the Attitudes Toward Disabled Persons Scale. *Educational and Psychological Measurement, 24,* 831–839.

Siller, J., Chipman, A., & Ferguson, L. T., & Vann, D. H. (1967). *Attitudes of the non-disabled toward the physically disabled: Studies in reactions to disability XI.* New York: New York University School of Education.

Simmons, C., Worrell, F. C., & Berry, J. M. (2008). Psychometric properties of scores on three Black racial identity scales. *Assessment, 15,* 259–276.

Simpson, J. A., & Gangestad, S. W. (1991). Individual differences in sociosexuality: Evidence for convergent and discriminant validity. *Journal of Personality and Social Psychology, 60,* 870–883.

Singelis, T. M. (1994). The measurement of independent and interdependent self-construal. *Social Psychology Bulletin, 20,* 224–253.

Siwatu, K. O. (2007). Pre-service teachers' culturally responsive teaching self-efficacy and outcome expectancy beliefs. *Teaching and Teacher Education, 23,* 1086–1101.

Skinner, J. H. (2001). Acculturation: Measures of ethnic accommodation to the dominant American culture. *Journal of Mental Health and Aging, 7*(1), 41–52.

Smedley, B. D., Myers, H. F., & Harrell, S. P. (1993). Minority-status stresses and the college adjustment of ethnic minority freshmen. *Journal of Higher Education, 64,* 434–452.

Smiler, A. P. (2006). Conforming to masculine norms: Evidence for validity among adult men and women. *Sex Roles, 54,* 767–775.

Smiler, A. P., & Epstein, M. (2010). Issues in the measurement of gender. In J. Chrisler & D. R. McCreary (Eds.), *Handbook of gender research in psychology.* New York: Springer.

Smiler, A. P., & Gelman, S. A. (2008). Determinants of gender essentialism in college students. *Sex Roles, 58,* 864–874.

Smith, E. R., Ferree, M. M., & Miller, F. E. (1975). A scale of attitudes toward feminism. *Representative Research in Social Psychology, 6,* 51–56.

Smith, K. T. (1971). Homophobia: A tentative personality profile. *Psychological Reports, 29,* 1091–1094.

Smith, T. B. (2004). *Practicing multiculturalism: Affirming diversity in counseling and psychology.* Boston, MA: Allyn and Bacon.

Smith, T. B. (2010). Culturally congruent practices in counseling and psychotherapy. In J. G. Ponterotto, J. M. Casas, L. A. Suzuki, & C. M. Alexander (Eds.), *Handbook of multicultural counseling* (3rd ed., pp. 439–450). Thousand Oaks, CA: Sage.

Snell, W. E., Jr. (1989). Development and validation of the Masculine Behavior Scale: A measure of behaviors stereotypically attributed to males vs. females. *Sex Roles, 21,* 749–767.

Snell, W. E., Fisher, T. D., & Miller, R. S. (1991). Development of the Sexual Awareness Questionnaire: Components, reliability, and validity. *Annals of Sex Research, 4,* 65–92.

Snipp, C. M. (1989). *American Indians: The first of the land.* New York: Russell Sage.

Snowden, L. R., & Hines, A. M. (1999). A scale to assess African American acculturation. *Journal of Black Psychology, 25*(1), 36–47.

Snyder, C. R., & Fromkin, H. L. (1977). Abnormality as a positive characteristic: The development and validation of a scale measuring need for uniqueness. *Journal of Abnormal Psychology, 86*, 518–527.

Snyder, M., & Gangestad, S. (1986). On the nature of self-monitoring: Matters of assessment, matters of validity. *Journal of Personality and Social Psychology, 51*, 125–139.

Sodowsky, G. R. (1996). The Multicultural Counseling Inventory: Validity and applications in training. In G. R. Sodowsky & J. Impara (Eds.), *Multicultural assessment in counseling and clinical psychology* (pp. 283–324). Lincoln, NE: Buros Institute of Mental Measurement.

Sodowsky, G. R., Kuo-Jackson, P. Y., Richardson, M. F., & Corey, A. T. (1998). Correlates of self-reported multicultural competencies: Counselor multicultural social desirability, race social inadequacy, locus of control, racial ideology, and multicultural training. *Journal of Counseling Psychology, 45*, 256–264.

Sodowsky, G. R., & Lai, E. W. M. (1997). Asian immigrant variables and structural models of cross-cultural distress. In A. Booth, A. C. Crouter, & N. Landale (Eds.), *Immigration and the family: Research and policy on U.S. immigrants* (pp. 211–234). Mahwah, NJ: Lawrence Erlbaum Associates.

Sodowsky, G. R., Lai, E. W. M., & Plake, B. S. (1991). Moderating effects of sociocultural variables on acculturation attitudes of Hispanics and Asian Americans. *Journal of Counseling and Development, 70*(1), 194–204.

Sodowsky, G. R., & Plake, B. S. (1991). Psychometric properties of the American-International Relations Scale. *Educational and Psychological Measurement, 51*(1), 207–216.

Sodowsky, G. R., & Plake, B. S. (1992). A study of acculturation differences among international people and suggestions for sensitivity to within-group differences. *Journal of Counseling & Development, 71*, 53–59.

Sodowsky, G. R., Taffe, R. C., Gutkin, T. B., & Wise, S. L. (1994). Development of the Multicultural Counseling Inventory: A self-report measure of multicultural competencies. *Journal of Counseling Psychology, 41*(2), 137–148.

Solomon, S. E., Rothblum, E. D., & Balsam, K. F. (2004). Pioneers in partnership: Lesbian and gay male couples in civil unions compared with those not in civil unions and married heterosexual siblings. *Journal of Family Psychology, 18*, 275–286.

Sommers-Flanagan, J., & Sommers-Flanagan, R. (2004). *Counseling and psychotherapy theories in context and practice: skills, strategies, and techniques.* Hoboken, NJ: John Wiley & Sons.

Sommers-Flanagan, J., & Sommers-Flanagan, R. (2009). *Clinical interviewing* (4th ed.). Hoboken, NJ: John Wiley & Sons.

Soodak, L. C., Podell, D. M., & Lehman, L. R. (1998). Teacher, student, and school attributes as predictors of teachers' response to inclusion. *Journal of Special Education, 31*, 480–498.

Spanierman, L. B., & Heppner, M. J. (2004). Psychosocial Costs of Racism to Whites Scale (PCRW): Construction and initial validation. *Journal of Counseling Psychology, 51*, 249–262.

Spanierman, L. B., Poteat, V. P., Beer, A. M., & Armstrong, P. I. (2006). Psychosocial costs of racism to Whites: Exploring patterns through cluster analysis. *Journal of Counseling Psychology, 53*, 434–441.

Spanierman, L. B., Todd, N. R., & Anderson, C. J. (2009). Psychosocial costs of racism to Whites: Understanding patterns among university students. *Journal of Counseling Psychology, 56*, 239–252.

Spearman, C. (1910). Correlation calculated with faulty data. *British Journal of Psychology, 3*, 271–295.

Spence, J. T., & Helmreich, R. (1972). The Attitudes Toward Women Scale. *JSAS Catalog of Selected Documents in Psychology, 2*, Ms. #153.

Spence, J. T., & Helmreich, R. L. (1978). *Masculinity and femininity: Their psychological dimensions, correlates, and antecedents.* Austin: University of Texas Press.

Spence, J. T., Helmreich, R. L., & Holahan, C. K. (1979). Negative and positive components of psychological masculinity and femininity and their relationships to self-reports of neurotic and acting out behaviors. *Journal of Personality and Social Psychology, 37*, 1673–1682.

Spence, J. T., Helmreich, R., & Stapp, J. (1973). A short version of the Attitudes toward Women Scale (AWS). *Bulletin of the Psychonomic Society, 2*, 219–220.

Spence, J. T., Helmreich, R. L., & Stapp, J. (1974). The Personal Attributes Questionnaire: A measure of sex role stereotypes and masculinity-femininity. *JSAS Catalog of Selected Documents in Psychology, 4*, 43.

Spence, J. T., Helmreich, R. L., & Stapp, J. (1975). Ratings of self and peers on sex-role attributes and their relations to self-esteem and conceptions of masculinity and femininity. *Journal of Personality and Social Psychology, 30*, 526–537.

Spielberger, C. D., Gorsuch, R. L., Lushene, R., Vagg, P. R., & Jacobs, G. A. (1983). *Manual for the State-Trait*

Anxiety Inventory (Form Y). Palo Alto, CA: Consulting Psychologist Press.

Spradley, J. P. (1979). *The enthographic interview*. New York: Holt, Rinehart & Watson.

Stampp, K. M. (1956). *The peculiar institution: Slavery in the ante-bellum south*. New York: Vintage Books.

Stangor, C. (2009). The study of stereotyping, prejudice, and discrimination within social psychology: A quick history of theory and research. In T. D. Nelson (Ed.), *Handbook of prejudice, stereotyping, and discrimination* (pp. 1–22). New York: Taylor and Francis Group.

Steele, C. M., & Aronson, J. (1995). Stereotype threat and the intellectual test performance of African Americans. *Journal of Personality and Social Psychology, 69*, 797–811.

Stefan, S. (2001). *Unequal rights: Discrimination against people with mental disabilities and the Americans with Disabilities Act*. Washington, DC: American Psychological Association.

Steidel, A. G. L., & Contreras, J. M. (2003). A new familism scale for use with Latino populations. *Hispanic Journal of Behavioral Sciences, 25*(3), 312–330.

Stephenson, M. (2000). Development and validation of the Stephenson Multigroup Acculturation Scale (SMAS). *Psychological Assessment, 12*(1), 77–88.

Stevens, G. W. J. M., Pels, T. V. M., Vollebergh, W. A. M., & Crijnen, A. A. M. (2004). Patterns of psychological acculturation in adult and adolescent Moroccan immigrants living in the Netherlands. *Journal of Cross-Cultural Psychology, 35*(6), 689–704.

Stevens, S. S. (1946). On the theory of scales of measurement. *Science, 103*, 677–680.

Stevens, S. S. (1951). Mathematics, measurement, and psychophysics. In S.S. Stevens (Ed.), *Handbook of experimental psychology* (pp. 1–49). New York: John Wiley.

Stevenson, H. C. (1994). Validation of the Scale of Racial Socialization for African American adolescents: Steps toward multidimensionality. *Journal of Black Psychology, 20*, 445–468.

Stevenson, H. C. (1996). Development of the scale of racial socialization for African American adolescents. In R. Jones (Ed.), *Handbook of tests and measures for Black populations* (Vol. 1, pp. 309–326). Hampton, VA: Cobb & Henry.

Stevenson Jr., H. C., Cameron, R., Herrero-Taylor, T., & Davis, G. Y. (2002). Development of the Teenager Experience of Racial Socialization Scale: Correlates of race-related socialization frequency from the perspective of Black youth. *Journal of Black Psychology, 28*, 84–106.

Stevenson, M. R., & Medler, B. R. (1995). Is homophobia a weapon of sexism? *Journal of Men's Studies, 4*, 1–8.

Stoever, C. J., & Morera, O. F. (2007). A confirmatory factor analysis of the Attitudes toward Lesbians and Gay Men (ATLG) measure. *Journal of Homosexuality, 52*, 189–209.

Stokes, J. E., Murray, C. B., Peacock, M., J., & Kaiser, R. T. (1994). Assessing the reliability, factor structure, and validity of the African Self-Consciousness Scale in a general population of African Americans. *Journal of Black Psychology, 20*, 62–74.

Stone, J. H. (2005). *Culture and disability: Providing culturally competent services*. Thousand Oaks, CA: Sage.

Strong, W. F., McQuillen, J. S., & Hughey, J. D. (1994). En el laberinto de machismo: A comparative analysis of macho attitudes among Hispanic and Anglo college students. *Howard Journal of Communications, 5*, 18–35.

Struening, E. I. (1957). *The dimensions, distribution, and correlates of authoritarianism in a Midwestern university faculty population*. Unpublished doctoral dissertation, Purdue University.

Struening, E. I., & Cohen, J. (1963). Factorial invariance and other psychometric characteristics of five Opinions about Mental Illness factors. *Educational and Psychological Measurement, 23*, 289–298.

Su, J., Lee, R. M., & Vang, S. (2005). Intergenerational family conflict and coping among Hmong American college students. *Journal of Counseling Psychology, 52*(4), 482–489.

Suarez, L., & Pulley, L. (1995). Comparing acculturation scales and their relationship to cancer screening among older Mexican-American women. *Journal of the National Cancer Institute Monographs, 18*, 41–47.

Suarez-Morales, L., Dillon, F., & Szapocznik, J. (2007). Validation of the Acculturative Stress Inventory for Children. *Cultural Diversity and Ethnic Minority Psychology, 13*(3), 213–224.

Sue, D. S., Fujino, D. C., Hu, L., Takeuchi, D. T., & Zane, N. W. S. (1991). Community mental health services for ethnic minority groups: A test of the cultural responsiveness hypothesis. *Journal of Consulting and Clinical Psychology, 59*, 533–540.

Sue, D. W. (1981). *Cross-cultural counseling and psychotherapy*. New York: Pergamon.

Sue, D. W. (2001). Multidimensional facets of cultural competence. *The Counseling Psychologist, 29*(6), 790–821.

Sue, D. W., Arrendondo, P., & McDavis, R. J. (1992). Multicultural counseling competencies and standards: A call to the profession. *Journal of Counseling and Development, 70*, 477–486.

Sue, D. W., Bernier, J. E., Durran, A., Feinberg, L., Pedersen, P., Smith, E. J., & Vasquez-Nuttal, E. (1982). Position paper: Cross-cultural counseling competencies. *The Counseling Psychologist 10*, 45–52.

Sue, D. W., Bingham, R. P., Porche-Burke, L., & Vasquez, M. (1999). The diversification of psychology: A multicultural revolution. *American Psychologist, 54*, 1061–1069.

Sue, D. W., Carter, R. T., Casas, J. M., Fouad, N. A., Ivey, A. E., Jensen, M., LaFromboise, T., Manese, J. E., Ponterotto, J. G., & Vasquez-Nuttall, E. (1998). *Multicultural counseling competencies: individual and organizational development.* Thousand Oaks, CA: Sage.

Sue, D. W., & Sue, D. (1977a). Barriers to effective cross-cultural counseling. *Journal of Counseling Psychology, 24*, 420–429.

Sue, D. W., & Sue, D. (1977b). Ethnic minorities: Failures and responsibilities of the social sciences. *Journal of Non-White Concerns in Personnel and Guidance, 5*, 99–106.

Sue, D. W., & Sue, S. (1972). Ethnic minorities: Resistance to being researched. *Professional Psychology, 2*, 11–17.

Sue, S. (1998). In search of cultural competence in psychotherapy and counseling. *American Psychologist, 53*, 440–448.

Sue, S. (1999). Science, ethnicity, and bias: Where have we gone wrong? *American Psychologist, 54*, 1070–1077.

Sue, S., Allen, D. B., & Conaway, L. (1978). The responsiveness and equality of mental health care to Chicanos and Native Americans. *American Journal of Community Psychology, 6*, 137–146.

Sue, S., & Mckinney, H. (1974). Asian Americans in the community mental health care system. *American Journal of Orthopsychiatry, 45*, 111–118.

Sue, S., Mckinney, H., Allen, D., & Hall, J. (1974). Delivery of community mental health services to Black and White clients. *Journal of Consulting and Clinical Psychology, 42*, 794–801.

Sue, S., Zane, N., Hall, G. C. N., & Berger, L. K. (2009). The case for cultural competency in psychotherapeutic interventions. *Annual Review of Psychology, 60*, 525–548.

Suinn, R. M. (2009). Acculturation: Measurements and review of findings. In N.-H. Trinh, Y.C. Rho, F. G. Lu, & K. M. Sanders (Eds.), *Handbook of mental health and acculturation in Asian American families.* Totowa, NJ: Humana Press.

Suinn, R. M., Ahuna, C., & Khoo, G. (1992). The Suinn-Lew Asian Self-Identity Acculturation Scale: Concurrent and factorial validation. *Educational and Psychological Measurement, 52*, 1041–1046.

Suinn, R. M., Khoo, G., & Ahuna, C. (1995). The Suinn-Lew Asian Self-Identity Acculturation Scale: Cross-cultural information. *Journal of Multicultural Counseling and Development, 23*, 139–148.

Suinn, R. M., Rickard-Figueroa, K., Lew, S., & Vigil, P. (1987). The Suinn-Lew Asian Self-Identification Scale: An initial report. *Educational and Psychology Measurement, 47*, 401–407.

Sundberg, N. D., & Tyler, L. E. (1962). *Clinical psychology.* New York: Appleton Century-Crofts.

Suzuki, L. A., Kugler, J. F., & Aguilar, L. J. (2005). Assessment practices in racial-cultural psychology. In R. T. Carter (Ed.), *Handbook of racial-cultural psychology and counseling* (Vol. 2, pp. 297–315). Hoboken, NJ: Wiley.

Swanson, J. L., Tokar, D. M., & Davis, L. E. (1994). Content and construct validity of the White Racial Identity Attitude Scale. *Journal of Vocational Behavior, 44*, 198–217.

Swim, J. K., Aiken, K. J., Hall, W. S., & Hunter, B. A. (1995). Sexism and racism: Old-fashioned and modern prejudices. *Journal of Personality and Social Psychology, 68*, 199–214.

Swim, J. K., & Cohen, L. L. (1997). Overt, covert, and subtle sexism: A comparison between the Attitudes Toward Woman and Modern Sexism Scales. *Psychology of Women Quarterly, 21*, 103–118.

Szapocznik, J., Scopetta, M. A., Kurtines, W., & Aranalde, M. A. (1978). Theory and measurement of acculturation. *Interamerican Journal of Psychology, 12*, 113–130.

Szymanski, D. M. (2006). Does internalized heterosexism moderate the link between heterosexist events and lesbians' psychological distress? *Sex Roles, 54*, 227–234.

Szymanski, D. M., & Gupta, A. (2009). Examining the relationship between multiple oppressions and Asian American sexual minority persons' psychological distress. *Journal of Gay and Lesbian Social Services, 21*, 267–281.

Szymanski, D. M., Kashubeck-West, S., & Meyer, J. (2008). Internalized heterosexism: A historical and theoretical overview. *Counseling Psychologist, 36*, 510–524.

Tajfel, H. (1981). *Human groups and social categories.* England, UK: Cambridge University Press.

Tajfel, H., & Turner, J. (1986). The social identity theory of intergroup behavior. In S. Worchel & W. G. Austin (Eds.), *The psychology of intergroup relations* (pp. 7–24). Chicago: Nelson-Hall.

Taylor, J. M., Gilligan, C., & Sullivan, A. M. (1995). *Between voice and silence: Women and girls, race and relationship.* Cambridge, MA: Harvard University Press.

Taylor, S. M., & Dear, M. J. (1981). Scaling community attitudes toward the mentally ill. *Schizophrenia Bulletin, 7,* 225–240.

Teague, G. B., Hornik, J., Ganju, V., Johnson, J. R., & McKinney, J. (1997). The MHSIP Mental Health Report Card: A consumer-oriented approach to monitoring the quality of health plans. *Evaluation Review, 21*(3), 330–341.

Terrell, F., & Miller, F. S. (1988). *The development of an Inventory to Measure Experience With Racialistic Incidents Among African Americans.* Unpublished manuscript, University of North Texas.

Terrell, F., & Terrell, S. (1981). An inventory to measure cultural mistrust among Blacks. *Western Journal of Black Studies, 5,* 180–185.

Thomas, A., Palmer, J. K., Coker-Juneau, C. J., & Williams, D. J. (2003). Factor structure and construct validity of the Interaction with Disabled Persons Scale. *Educational and Psychological Measurement, 63,* 465–483.

Thomas, A. J., Witherspoon, K. M., & Speight, S. L. (2008). Gendered racism, psychological distress, and coping styles of African American women. *Cultural Diversity and Ethnic Minority Psychology, 14,* 307–314.

Thomas, C. (1971). *Boys no more.* Beverly Hills, CA: Glencoe Press.

Thompson, B. (1989). Meta-analysis of factor structure studies: A case study example with Bem's androgyny measure. *Journal of Experimental Education, 50,* 585–589.

Thompson, E. H., Jr., & Pleck, J. H. (1986). The structure of male role norms. *American Behavioral Scientist, 29,* 531–534.

Thompson, E. R. (2007). Development and validation of an internationally reliable short-form of the positive and negative affect schedule (PANAS). *Journal of Cross-Cultural Psychology, 38*(2), 227–242.

Thomson, A., Bryson, M., & de Castell, S. (2001). Prospects for identity formation for lesbian, gay, or bisexual persons with developmental disabilities. *International Journal of Disability, Development and Education, 48,* 53–65.

Todosijevic, J., Rothblum, E. D., & Solomon, S. E. (2005). Relationship satisfaction, affectivity, and gay-specific stressors in same-sex couples joined in civil unions. *Psychology of Women Quarterly, 29,* 158–166.

Tokar, D. M., & Fischer, A. R. (1998). Psychometric analysis of Racial Identity Attitude Scale–Long Form. *Measurement and Evaluation in Counseling and Development, 31,* 138–149.

Tolman, D. L., & Debold, E. (1993). Conflicts of body and image: Female adolescents, desire, and the no-body

body. In P. Fallon, M. Katzman, & S. Wooley (Eds.), *Feminist perspectives on eating disorders* (pp. 301–317). New York: Guilford.

Tolman, D. L., Impett, E. A., Tracy, A. J., & Michael, A. (2006). Looking good, sounding good: Femininity ideology and adolescent girls' mental health. *Psychology of Women Quarterly, 30,* 85–95.

Tolman, D. L., & Porche, M. V. (2000). The Adolescent Femininity Ideology Scale: Development and validation of a new measure for girls. *Psychology of Women Quarterly, 24,* 365–376.

Toporek, R. L., Liu, W. M., & Pope-Davis, D. P. (2003). Assessing multicultural competence of the training environment: Further validation for the psychometric properties of the Multicultural Environment Inventory-Revised. In D. B. Pope-Davis, H. L. K. Coleman, W. M. Liu, & R. L. Toporek (Eds.), *Handbook of multicultural competencies in counseling & psychology* (pp. 183–190). Thousand Oaks, CA: Sage.

Toporek, R. L., & Reza, J. V. (2001). Context as a critical dimension of multicultural counseling: Articulating personal, professional, and institutional competence. *Journal of Multicultural Counseling and Development, 29,* 13–30.

Tougas, F., Brown, R., Beaton, A. M., & Joly, S. (1995). Neosexism: Plus ça change, plus c'est pariel. *Personality and Social Psychology Bulletin, 21,* 842–849.

Tracy, J., & Iacono, T. (2008). People with developmental disabilities teaching medical students—Does it make a difference? *Journal of Intellectual and Developmental Disabilities, 33,* 345–348.

Triandis, H. C. (1989). The self and social behavior in differing cultural contexts. *Psychological Review, 96*(3), 506–520.

Trimble, J. E. (2007). Prolegomena of the connotation of construct use in the measurement of ethnic and racial identity. *Journal of Counseling Psychology, 54,* 247–258.

Trimble, J. E., & Fisher, C. (2006). *Handbook of ethical considerations in conducting research with ethnocultural populations and communities.* Thousand Oaks, CA: Sage.

Trimble, J. E., Helms, J. E., & Root, M. P. P. (2002). Social and psychological perspectives on ethnic and racial identity. In G. Bernal, J. E. Trimble, A. K. Burlew, & F. T. L. Leong (Eds.), *Handbook of racial and ethnic minority psychology* (pp. 239–275). Thousand Oaks, CA: Sage.

Trimble, J. E., Helms, J. E., & Root, M. P. P. (2003). Social and psychological perspectives on ethnic and racial identity. In G. Bernal, J. E. Trimble, A. K. Burlew, & F. T. L. Leong (Eds.), *Handbook of racial & ethnic minority psychology* (pp. 239–275). Thousand Oaks, CA: Sage.

Trimble, J. E., & Thurman, P. J. (2004). Ethnocultural considerations and strategies for providing counseling services to Native American Indians. In P. B. Pedersen, J. G. Draguns, W. J. Lonner, & J. E. Trimble (Eds.), *Counseling across cultures* (5th ed., pp. 53–90). Thousand Oaks, CA: Sage.

Troldahl, V. C., & Powell, F. A. (1965). A short-form dogmatism scale for use in field studies. *Social Forces, 44,* 211–214.

Tropp, L. R., Erkut, S., García-Coll, C. G., Alarcón, O., & Vásquez-García, H. A. (1999). Psychological acculturation: Development of a new measure for Puerto Ricans on the U.S. mainland. *Educational and Psychological Measurement, 59*(2), 351–367.

Tsai, G., & Curbow, B. (2001). The development and validation of the Taiwanese Ethnic Identity Scale (TSAI): A "derived etic" approach. *Journal of Immigrant Health, 3,* 199–212.

Tsai, G., Curbow, B., & Heinberg, L. (2003). Sociocultural and developmental influences on body dissatisfaction and disordered eating attitudes and behaviors of Asian women. *Journal of Nervous and Mental Disease, 191,* 309–318.

Tsai, J. L., Mortensen, H., Wong, Y., & Hess, D. (2002). What does "being American" mean? A comparison of Asian American and European American young adults. *Cultural Diversity and Ethnic Minority Psychology, 8*(3), 257–273.

Tsai, J. L., Ying, Y.-W., & Lee, P. A. (2000). The meaning of "being Chinese" and "being American": Variation among Chinese American young adults. *Journal of Cross-Cultural Psychology, 31*(3), 302–332.

Tsai, J. L., Ying, Y.-W., & Lee, P. A. (2001). Cultural predictors of self-esteem: A study of Chinese American female and male young adults. *Cultural Diversity and Ethnic Minority Psychology, 7*(3), 284–297.

Tucker, C. M., Daly, K. D., & Herman, K. C. (2010). Customized multicultural health counseling: Bridging the gap between mental and physical health for racial and ethnic minorities. In J. G. Ponterotto, J. M. Casas, L. A. Suzuki, & C. M. Alexander (Eds.), *Handbook of multicultural counseling* (3rd ed., pp. 505–516). Thousand Oaks, CA: Sage.

Turner, R. J., Taylor, J., & Van Gundy, K. (2004). Personal resources and depression in the transition to adulthood: Ethnic comparisons. *Journal of Health and Social Behavior, 45,* 34–52.

Twenge, J. M. (1997). Attitudes toward women, 1970–1995: A meta-analysis. *Psychology of Women Quarterly, 21,* 35–51.

U.S. Census Bureau. (2000). *Census 2000 demographic profile highlights.* Retrieved January 10, 2008, from http://factfinder.census.gov

U.S. Census Bureau. (2005). Americans with disabilities: 2005 (P70–117). Available at: www.census.gov/hhes/www/disability/sipp/disable05.html

U.S. Census Bureau. (2009). Census brief. The Hispanic population: 2000. Retrieved July 25, 2009, from http:www.census.gov/population/www/cen2000/briefs/phc-t1/tables/tab03.pdf

U.S. Department of Health and Human Services. (2001). *Mental health: Culture, race and ethnicity—A supplement to Mental Health: A report of the Surgeon General.* Rockville, MD: U.S. Department of Health and Human Services, Substance Abuse and Mental Health Services Administration, Center for Mental Health Services, National Institute of Mental Health.

Umana-Taylor, A. J. (2001). *Ethnic identity development among Mexican-origin Latino adolescents living in the U.S.* Unpublished Doctoral Dissertation, University of Missouri, Columbia.

Umana-Taylor, A. J. (2005). Ethnic Identity Scale. In K. A. Anderson Moore & L. H. Lippman, *What do children need to flourish?* (pp. 75–91). New York: Springer.

Umana-Taylor, A. J., & Shin, N. (2007). An examination of ethnic identity and self-esteem with diverse populations: Exploring variation by ethnicity and geography. *Cultural Diversity and Ethnic Minority Psychology, 13,* 178–186.

Umana-Taylor, A. J., & Updegraff, K. A. (2007). Latino adolescents' mental health: Exploring the interrelationships among discrimination, ethnic identity, cultural orientation, self-esteem, and depressive symptoms. *Journal of Adolescence, 30,* 549–567.

Umana-Taylor, A. J., Yazedjian, A., & Bamaca-Gomez, M. (2004). Developing the Ethnic Identity Scale using Eriksonian and social identity perspectives. *Identity: An International Journal of Theory and Research, 4,* 9–38.

Unger, J. B., Gallaher, P., Shakib, S., Ritt-Olson, A., Palmer, P. H., & Anderson Johnson, C. (2002). The AHIMSA acculturation scale: A new measure of acculturation for adolescents in a multicultural society. *Journal of Early Adolescence, 22*(3), 225–251.

Usala, P. D., & Hertzog, C. (1989). Measurement of affective states in adults: Evaluation of an adjective rating scale instrument. *Research on Aging, 11,* 403–426.

Utsey, S. O. (1999). Development and validation of a short version of the Index of Race-Related Stress (IRRS—Brief Version). *Measurement and Evaluation in Counseling and Development, 32,* 149–167.

Utsey, S. O., Adams, E. P., & Bolden, M. (2000). Development and initial validation of the Africultural Coping Systems Inventory. *Journal of Black Psychology, 26*(2), 194–215.

Utsey, S. O., Bolden, M. A., Williams, O., III, Lee, A., Lanier, Y., & Newsome, C. (2007). Spiritual well-being as a mediator of the relation between culture-specific coping and quality of life in a community sample of African Americans. *Journal of Cross-Cultural Psychology, 38*(2), 123–136.

Utsey, S. O., & Hook, J. N. (2007). Heart rate variability as a physiological moderator of the relationship between race-related stress and psychological distress. *Cultural Diversity and Ethnic Minority Psychology, 13*, 250–253.

Utsey, S. O., & Ponterotto, J. G. (1996). Development and validation of the Index of Race-Related Stress (IRRS). *Journal of Counseling Psychology, 43*, 490–501.

Utsey, S. O., & Ponterotto, J. G. (1999). Further factorial validity assessment of scores on the Quick Discrimination Index (QDI). *Educational and Psychological Measurement, 59*, 325–335.

Utsey, S. O., Ponterotto, J. G., Reynolds, A. L., & Cancelli, A. A. (2000). Racial discrimination, coping, life satisfaction, and self-esteem among African Americans. *Journal of Counseling and Development, 78*, 72–80.

Valencia, E. Y., & Johnson, V. (2008). Acculturation among Latino youth and the risk for substance use: Issues of definition and measurement. *Journal of Drug Issues,* Winter, 37–68.

Van Brakel, W. H. (2006). Measuring health-related stigma—A literature review. *Psychology, Health & Medicine, 11*, 307–334.

Van de Vijver, F. J. R., & Phalet, K. (2004). Assessment in multicultural groups: The role of acculturation. *Applied Psychology: An International Review, 53*(2), 215–236.

Van der Zee, K. I., & Brinkmann, U. (2004). Construct validity evidence for the intercultural readiness check against the Multicultural Personality Questionnaire. *International Journal of Selection and Assessment, 12*(3), 285–290.

Van der Zee, K. I., & Van Oudenhoven, J. P. (2000). The Multicultural Personality Questionnaire: A multidimensional instrument of multicultural effectiveness. *European Journal of Personality, 14*, 291–309.

Van der Zee, K. I., & Van Oudenhoven, J. P. (2001). The Multicultural Personality Questionnaire: Reliability and validity of self- and other ratings of multicultural effectiveness. *Journal of Research in Personality, 35*, 278–288.

Van der Zee, K. I., Zaal, J. N., & Piekstra, J. (2003). Validation of the Multicultural Personality Questionnaire in the context of personnel selection. *European Journal of Personality, 17*, S77–S100.

van Well, S., Kolk, A. M., & Arrindell, W. A. (2005). Cross-cultural validity of the Masculine and Feminine Gender Role Stress Scales. *Journal of Personality Assessment, 84*, 271–278.

Vandiver, B. J., Cross, W. E., Jr., Worrell, F. C., & Fhagen-Smith, P. E. (2002). Validating the Cross Racial Identity Scale. *Journal of Counseling Psychology, 49*, 71–85.

Vandiver, B. J., Fhagen-Smith, P. E., Cokley, K. O., Cross, W. E., Jr., & Worrell, F. C. (2001). Cross Nigrescence model: From theory to scale to theory. *Journal of Multicultural Counseling and Development, 29*, 174–200.

Vasgird, D. (2007). Making research trustworthy for Native Americans. *Journal of Empirical Research on Human Research Ethics, 2*(1), 84–85.

Vignes, C., Coley, N., Grandjean, H., Godeau, E., & Arnaud, C. (2008). Measuring children's attitudes towards peers with disabilities: A review of instruments. *Developmental Medicine and Child Neurology, 50*, 182–189.

Villarreal, R., Blozis, S. A., & Widaman, K. F. (2005). Factorial invariance of a Pan-Hispanic Familism Scale. *Hispanic Journal of Behavioral Sciences, 27*(4), 409–425.

Villarreal, R., & Peterson, R. A. (2009). The concept and marketing implications of Hispanicness. *Journal of Marketing Theory and Practice, 17*(4), 303–316.

Vogel, J. J., & Keating, C. F. (2005). Employment of deaf people as influenced by potential employers' perceptions: Pathological compared with sociocultural perspectives. *International Journal of Rehabilitation Research, 28*, 181–183.

Wade, J. C. (1998) Male reference group identity dependence: A theory of male identity. *The Counseling Psychologist, 26*, 349–383.

Wade, J. C. (2008). Masculinity ideology, male reference group identity dependence, and African American men's health-related attitudes and behaviors. *Psychology of Men & Masculinity, 9*, 5–16.

Wade, J. C., & Gelso, C. J. (1998). Reference Group Identity Dependence Scale: A measure of male identity. *The Counseling Psychologist, 26*, 384–412.

Wagner, J. A., III, & Moch, M. K. (1986). Individualism-collectivism: Concept and measure. *Group and Organization Studies, 11*, 280–304.

Wahl, O. F., & Lefkowits, J. Y. (1989). Impact of television film on attitudes toward mental illness. *American Journal of Community Psychology, 17*, 521–528.

Wallace, P. M., Pomery, E. A., Latimer, A. E., Martinez, J. L., & Salovey, P. (2009). A review of acculturation measures and their utility in studies promoting Latin health. *Hispanic Journal of Behavioral Sciences, 20*(10), 1–18.

Wallymahmed, A., McKay-Moffat, S., & Cunningham, C. C. (2007). The Interaction with Disabled Persons scale: A validation with UK midwives. *Social Behavior and Personality: An International Journal, 35,* 1049–1060.

Watson, D., Clark, L. A., & Tellegen, A. (1988). Development and validation of brief measures of positive and negative affect: The PANAS scales. *Journal of Personality and Social Psychology, 54,* 1063–1070.

Watson, D., & Friend, R. (1969). Measurement of social-evaluative anxiety. *Journal of Consulting and Clinical Psychology, 33,* 448–457.

Weaver, H. N. (2005). *Explorations in cultural competence. Journeys to the four directions.* Belmont, CA: Thomson/Brooks Cole.

Weaver, H. N., & Yellow Horse Brave Heart, M. (1999). Examining two facets of American Indian identity: Exposure to other cultures and the influence of historical trauma. *Journal of Human Behavior in the Social Environment, 2*(1–2), 19–33.

Webster, D. M., & Kruglanski, A. W. (1994). Individual differences in need for cognitive closure. *Journal of Personality and Social Psychology, 67,* 1049–1062.

Wegner, D. M., & Shelton, J. N. (1995). *Interracial Contact Scale.* Unpublished manuscript, University of Virginia, Charlottesville.

Weinberg, G. (1972). *Society and the healthy homosexual.* New York: St. Martin's.

Weinrich, J. D., & Klein, F. (2003). Bi-gay, bi-straight, and bi-bi: Three bisexual subgroups identify using cluster analysis of the Klein Sexual Orientation Grid. *Journal of Bisexuality, 2,* 111–139.

Weisel, A., & Florian, V. (1990). Same- and cross-gender attitudes toward persons with physical disabilities. *Rehabilitation Psychology, 35,* 229–238.

Weisel, A., Kravetz, S., Florian, V., & Shurka-Zernitsky, E. (1988). The structure of attitudes toward persons with disabilities: An Israeli validation of Siller's Disability Factor Scales—General (DFS-G). *Rehabilitation Psychology, 33,* 227–238.

Weiss, D. J., Dawis, R. V., England, G. W., & Lofquist, L. H. (1977). *Manual for the Minnesota Satisfaction Questionnaire.* Minneapolis: University of Minnesota.

Werner, P., Aviv, A., & Barak, Y. (2008). Self-stigma, self-esteem and age in persons with schizophrenia. *International Psychogeriatrics, 20,* 174–187.

Wester, K. L., & Trepal, H. C. (2008). Gender. In G. McAuliffe and Associates (Eds.), *Culturally alert counseling: A comprehensive introduction* (pp. 429–460). Thousand Oaks, CA: Sage.

Wester, S. R. (2008). Thinking complexly about men, gender role conflict and counseling psychology. *The Counseling Psychologist, 36,* 462–468.

Westermeyer, J., & Janca, A. (1997). Language, culture and psychopathology: Conceptual and methodological issues. *Transcultural Psychiatry, 34,* 137–152.

Whaley, A. L. (2002). Psychometric analysis of the Cultural Mistrust Inventory with a Black psychiatric inpatient sample. *Journal of Clinical Psychology, 58,* 383–396.

Whaley, A. L., & Davis, K. E. (2007). Cultural competence and evidence-based practice in mental health services. *American Psychologist, 62*(6), 563–574.

Whatley, P. R., Allen, J., & Dana, R. H. (2003). Racial identity and the MMPI in African American male college students. *Cultural Diversity and Ethnic Minority Psychology, 9,* 345–353.

White, C., & Burke, P. (1987). Ethnic role identity among Black and White college students: An interactionist approach. *Sociological Perspectives, 30,* 310–331.

White, J. L. (1984). *The psychology of Blacks: An Afro-American perspective.* Englewood Cliffs, NJ: Prentice-Hall.

Whiteman, M., & Lukoff, I. F. (1964a). A factorial study of sighted people's attitudes toward blindness. *Journal of Social Psychology, 64,* 339–353.

Whiteman, M., & Lukoff, I. F. (1964b). Attitudes toward blindness in two college groups. *Journal of Social Psychology, 63,* 179–191.

Whiteman, M., & Lukoff, I. F. (1965). Attitudes toward blindness and other physical handicaps. *Journal of Social Psychology, 66,* 135–145.

Wijeyesinghe, C. L., Griffin, P., & Love, B. (1997). Racism curriculum design. In M. Adams, L. A. Bell, & P. Griffin (Eds.), *Teaching for diversity and social justice* (pp. 82–110). New York: Routledge.

Williams, D. R., & Mohammed, S. A. (2009). Discrimination and racial disparities in health: Evidence and needed research. *Journal of Behavioral Medicine, 32*(1), 20–47.

Williams, D. R., Neighbors, H. W., & Jackson, J. S. (2003). Racial/ethnic discrimination and health: Findings from community studies. *American Journal of Public Health, 93,* 200–208.

Wilson, D., Foster, J., Anderson, S., & Mance, G. (2009). Racial socialization's moderating effect between poverty stress and psychological symptoms for African American youth. *Journal of Black Psychology, 35,* 102–124.

Wolfe, M. M., Yang, P. H., Wong, E. C., & Atkinson, D. R. (2001). Design and development of the European American Values Scale for Asian Americans. *Cultural Diversity and Ethnic Minority Psychology, 7*(3), 274–283.

Wong, D. K. P. (2008). Do contacts make a difference? The effects of mainstreaming on student attitudes toward people with disabilities. *Research in Developmental Disabilities, 29,* 70–82.

Woo, J. S. T., & Brotto, L. A. (2008). Age of first sexual intercourse and acculturation: Effects on adult sexual responding. *Journal of Sexual Medicine, 5*(3), 571–582.

Woodmansee, J. J., & Cook, S. W. (1967). Dimensions of verbal racial attitudes: Their identification and measurement. *Journal of Personality and Social Psychology, 39,* 848–860.

World Health Organization (WHO). (2001). *International classification of functioning, disability, and health.* Geneva, Switzerland: Author.

World Health Organization (WHO). (2007). *International classification of functioning, disability, and health for children and youth.* Geneva, Switzerland: Author.

Worrell, F. C., Cross, W. E., Jr., & Vandiver, B. J. (2001). Nigrescence theory: Current status and challenges of the future. *Journal of Multicultural Counseling and Development, 29,* 201–210.

Worrell, F. C., Vandiver, B. J., Cross, W. E., Jr., & Fhagen-Smith, P. E. (2004). Reliability and structural validity of Cross Racial Identity Scale scores in a sample of African American adults. *Journal of Black Psychology, 30,* 489–505.

Worthington, R. L., Dillon, F. R., & Becker-Schutte, A. M. (2005). Development, reliability, and validity of the Lesbian, Gay, and Bisexual Knowledge and Attitudes Scale for Heterosexuals (LGB-KASH). *Journal of Counseling Psychology, 52,* 104–118.

Worthington, R. L., Navarro, R. L., Loewy, M., & Hart, J. (2008). Color-blind racial attitudes, social dominance orientation, racial ethnic group membership and college students' perceptions of campus climate. *Journal of Diversity in Higher Education, 1,* 8–19.

Worthington, R. L., Navarro, R. L., Savoy, H. B., & Hampton, D. (2008). Development, reliability, and validity of the Measure of Sexual Identity Exploration and Commitment (MoSIEC). *Journal of Counseling Psychology, 44,* 22–33.

Worthington, R. L., & Reynolds, A. L. (2009). Within-group differences in sexual orientation and identity. *Journal of Counseling Psychology, 56,* 44–55.

Worthington, R. L., Savoy, H. B., Dillon, F. R., & Vernaglia, E. R. (2002). Heterosexual identity development: A multidimensional model of individual and group identity. *The Counseling Psychologist, 30,* 496–531.

Worthington, R. L., Savoy, H. B., & Navarro, R. (2002). *The Measure of Sexual Identity Exploration and Commitment (MoSIEC): Development, reliability, and validity.* Unpublished Manuscript.

Worthington, R. L., Soth-McNett, A. M., & Moreno, M.V. (2007). Multicultural counseling competencies research: A 20-year content analysis. *Journal of Counseling Psychology, 54*(4), 351–361.

Wright, B. A. (1975). Sensitizing outsiders to the position of the insider. *Rehabilitation Psychology, 22,* 129–135.

Wright, Jr., L. W., Adams, H. E., & Bernat, J. (1999). Development and validation of the Homophobia Scale. *Journal of Psychopathology and Behavioral Assessment, 21,* 337–347.

Yamada, A. M., Marsella, A. J., & Yamada, S. Y. (1998). The development of the Ethnocultural Identity Behavioral Index: Psychometric properties and validation with Asian Americans and Pacific Islanders. *Asian American and Pacific Islander Journal of Health, 6,* 36–45.

Yanico, B. Y., Swanson, J. L., & Tokar, D. M. (1994). A psychometric investigation of the Black Racial Identity Scale—Form B. *Journal of Vocational Behavior, 44,* 218–234.

Yaralian, T., Der-Karabetian, A., & Martinez, T. (2009). Acculturation, ethnic identity, and psychological functioning among Armenian-American young adults. *Journal of Society for Armenian Studies, 18,* 157–179.

Yeh, C. J. (2003). Age, acculturation, cultural adjustment, and mental health symptoms of Chinese, Korean, and Japanese immigrant youths. *Cultural Diversity and Ethnic Minority Psychology, 9*(1), 34–48.

Yeh, C. J., & Huang, K. (1996). The collectivist nature of ethnic identity development among Asian-American college students. *Adolescence, 31,* 645–661.

Yeh, C. J., & Inose, M. (2003). International students' reported English fluency, social support satisfaction, and social connectedness as predictors of acculturation stress. *Counselling Psychology Quarterly, 16*(1), 15–28.

Yeh, C. J., & Kwan, K.-L. K. (2010) Advances in multicultural assessment and counseling with adolescents: An ecological perspective. In J. G. Ponterotto, J. M. Casas, L. A. Suzuki, & C. M. Alexander (Eds.), *Handbook of multicultural counseling* (3rd ed., pp. 637–648). Thousand Oaks, CA: Sage.

Yeh, M., McCabe, K., Hough, R. L., Dupuis, S., & Hazen, A. (2003). Racial/ethnic differences in parental endorsement of barriers to mental health services for youth. *Mental Health Services Research, 5,* 65–77.

Yip, T. (2005). Sources of situational variation in ethnic identity and psychological well-being: A palm pilot study of Chinese American students. *Personality and Social Psychology Bulletin, 31,* 1603–1616.

Yoder, J. D. (2009). *Women and gender: Making a difference* (3rd ed.). Cornwall-on-Hudson, NY: Sloan Publishing.

Yoo, H. C., Burrola, K. S., & Steger, M. F. (2010). A preliminary report on a new measure: Internalization of the Model Minority Myth Measure (IM-4) and its psychological correlates among Asian American college students. *Journal of Counseling Psychology, 57*(1), 114–127.

Yoo, H. C., & Lee, R. M. (2005). Ethnic identity and approach-type coping as moderators of the racial discrimination/well-being relation in Asian Americans. *Journal of Counseling Psychology, 52,* 497–506.

Young, R. M., & Meyer, I. H. (2005). The trouble with "MSM" and "WSW": Erasure of the sexual-minority person in public health discourse. *American Journal of Public Health, 95,* 1144–1149.

Yuen, M., & Westwood, P. (2002). Teachers' attitude toward integration: Validation of a Chinese version of the Attitude Toward Mainstreaming Scale (ATMS). *Psychologia, 45,* 1–11.

Yuker, H., Block, J., & Campbell, W. (1962). *A Scale to Measure Attitudes Toward Disabled Persons: Forms A and B.* Albertson. NY: Human Resources Center.

Yuker, H. E. (1965). Attitudes as determinants of behavior. *Journal of Rehabilitation, 31,* 15–16.

Yuker, H. E., & Block, J. R. (1986). *Research with the Attitude Towards Disabled Persons Scales (ATDP) 1960–1985.* Hempstead, NY: Center for the Study of Attitudes Toward Persons with Disabilities, Hofstra University.

Yuker, H. E., Block, J. R., & Cambell, W. J. (1960). *A scale to measure attitudes toward disabled persons* (Human Resources Study No. 5). Albertson, NY: Human Resources Center.

Yuker, H. E., Block, J. R., & Young, J. H. (1966). *The measurement of attitudes toward disabled persons* (Human Resources Study No.7). Albertsons, NY: Human Resources Center.

Yuker, H. E., & Hurley, M. K. (1987). Contact with and attitudes toward people with disabilities: The measurement of intergroup contact. *Rehabilitation Psychology, 32,* 145–154.

Yunger, J. L., Carver, P. R., & Perry, D. G. (2004). Does gender identity influence children's psychological well-being? *Developmental Psychology, 40,* 572–582.

Zak, I. (1973). Dimensions of Jewish-American identity. *Psychological Reports, 33,* 891–900.

Zak, I. (1976). Structure of ethnic identity of Arab-Israeli students. *Psychological Reports, 38,* 239–246.

Zane, N., & Mak, W. (2003). Major approaches to the measurement of acculturation among ethnic minority populations: A content analysis and an alternative empirical strategy. In K. M. Chun, P. B. Balls Organista, & G. Marin (Eds.), *Acculturation: Advances in theory, measurement, and applied research* (pp. 39–60). Washington, DC: American Psychological Association.

Zane, N., Morton, T., Chu, J., & Lin, N. (2004). Counseling and psychotherapy with Asian American clients. In T. B. Smith (Ed.), *Practicing multiculturalism: Affirming diversity in counseling and psychology* (pp. 190–214). Boston, MA: Allyn and Bacon.

Zane, N., Sue, S., Chang, J., Huang, L., Huang, J., Lowe, S., Srinivasan, S., Chun, K., Kurasaki, K., & Lee, E. (2005). Beyond ethnic match: Effects of client–therapist cognitive match in problem perception, coping orientation, and theory goals on treatment outcomes. *Journal of Community Psychology, 33*(5), 569–585.

Zea, M. C., Asner-Self, K. K., Birman, D., & Buki, L. P. (2003). The Abbreviated Multidimensional Acculturation Scale: Empirical validation with two Latino/Latina samples. *Cultural Diversity and Ethnic Minority Psychology, 9*(2), 107–126.

Zeichner, A., & Reidy, D. E. (2009). Are homophobic men attracted to or repulsed by homosexual men? Effects of gay male erotica on anger, fear, happiness, and disgust. *Psychology of Men & Masculinity, 10,* 231–236.

Zemore, S. E. (2007). Acculturation and alcohol among Latino adults in the United States: A comprehensive review. *Alcoholism: Clinical and Experimental Research, 31*(12), 1968–1990.

Zimmerman, M. A., Ramirez-Valles, J., Washienko, K. M., Walter, B., & Dyer, S. (1996). The development of a measure of enculturation for Native American youth. *American Journal of Community Psychology, 24,* 295–310.

Zucker, K. J., Mitchell, J. N., Bradley, S. J., Tkachuk, J., Cantor, J. M., & Allin, S. M. (2006). The Recalled Childhood Gender Identity/Gender Role Questionnaire: Psychometric properties. *Sex Roles, 54,* 469–483.

Zuckerman, M. (1976). *Preliminary manual with scoring keys and norms for Form V of the Sensation Seeking Scale.* Newark: University of Delaware.

Author Index

Subject Index

About the Authors

Glenn C. Gamst, Ph.D., is Professor and Chair of the Psychology Department at the University of La Verne, where he teaches the doctoral advanced statistics sequence. He received his doctorate from the University of Arkansas in experimental psychology. His research interests include the effects of multicultural variables, such as client–provider ethnic match, client acculturation status and ethnic/racial identity, and provider self-perceived cultural competence on clinical outcomes. Additional research interests focus on conversation memory and discourse processing. Gamst has recently coauthored the *CBMCS Multicultural Training Program* and three statistics texts dealing with multivariate statistics, analysis of variance, and statistical analysis using SAS Enterprise Guide.

Christopher T. H. Liang, Ph.D., earned his doctorate in counseling psychology from the University of Maryland, College Park. He currently is an associate professor of psychology at the University of La Verne, where he teaches community psychology to clinical psychology doctoral students and multicultural counseling to master's-level counseling students. He has published articles and chapters addressing a range of multicultural issues including multicultural counseling, impact of multicultural experiences of college students on their diversity attitudes, intersections of gender and race, and racism experiences of Asian Americans. The primary focus of his research program now addresses racism and gender experiences of racialized men and women.

Aghop Der-Karabetian, Ph.D., is a professor of psychology and Associate Vice President for University Assessment at the University of La Verne, where he has taught for the last 30 years. His Ph.D. is in social psychology from the University of Kansas, 1978. He was a Fulbright Scholar (1974–1978) and received the Sears Excellence in Teaching Award (1989) at the University of La Verne. He has conducted research on multicultural issues, ethnic and multiethnic identity, seeking psychological help, sex roles, world-mindedness, and environmental activism. He has authored or coauthored more than 50 refereed publications. He is also a coauthor of the CBMCS Multicultural Training Program for mental health practitioners published by SAGE in 2008. He was one of the cofounders in 2007 of the Armenian American Mental Health Association based in southern California.

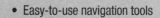